Examination Guide for
Architecture: Drafting and Design, Fourth Edition

Architecture: Drafting and Design is designed for a student's first course in architectural drafting. Take a look at the features found in the new edition of this best selling text.

- Current topics are found in new units entitled Energy Planning which deals with passive solar systems, Climate Control Plans, which deals with active solar systems, and Legal Documents.

- A new continuing problem is found throughout the text within the problems at the end of the units. By assigning this problem to your students they will eventually complete a full set of plans for one structure. Look for the special symbol at the end of each unit.

- More color than ever before. This edition has 128 pages of useful four color illustrating the design section.

- The sections on Electrical Plans and Plumbing Diagrams have been rewritten and reorganized for this edition making them easy to read and clearer to understand.

Donald E. Hepler
Paul I. Wallach

FOURTH EDITION

ARCHITECTURE
DRAFTING AND DESIGN

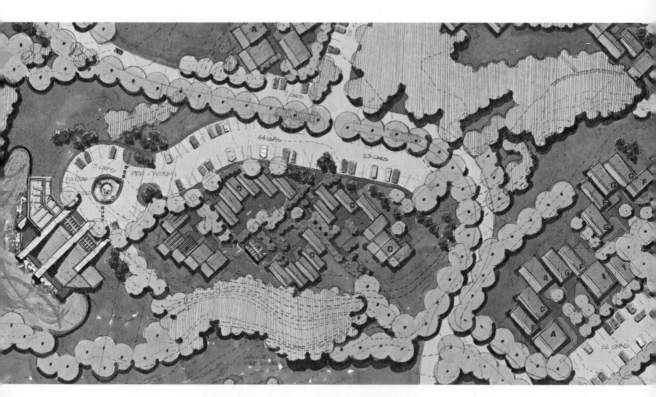

MCGRAW-HILL BOOK COMPANY

NEW YORK   ST. LOUIS   SAN FRANCISCO   DALLAS   AUCKLAND   BOGOTÁ
DUSSELDORF   JOHANNESBURG   LONDON   MADRID   MEXICO   MONTREAL   NEW DELHI
PANAMA   PARIS   SÃO PAULO   SINGAPORE   SYDNEY   TOKYO   TORONTO

Editor: Hal Lindquist
Coordinating Editor: Patricia McCormick
Design Supervisor: Jim Darby
Production Supervisor: Karen Romano

This book was set in 10 point Aster by York Graphic Services, Inc.

Library of Congress Cataloging in Publication Data

Hepler, Donald E.
  Architecture: drafting and design.

  Includes index.
  1. Architectural drawing.   2. Architectural design.
I. Wallach, Paul I.   II. Title.
NA2700.H4 1982   720'.28'4   81-1198
ISBN 0-07-028301-X   AACR2

  5 6 7 8 9 10 DODO 90 89 88 87 86 85 84 83 82

CONTENTS

PART FOUR
Technical Architectural Plans

PART FIVE
Architectural Support Services

PART SIX
Appendix

ABOUT THE AUTHORS

DONALD E. HEPLER completed his undergraduate work at California State College, California, Pennsylvania, and his graduate work at the University of Pittsburgh. He joined Admiral Homes, Inc., as an architectural draftsman and later joined the architectural staffs of Rust Engineering; Patterson, Emerson, and Comstock, Engineers; and Union Switch and Signal Company. After serving as an officer with the United States Army Corps of Engineers, he became head of the Industrial Arts Department, Avonworth High School, Pittsburgh, Pennsylvania. He later joined the faculty of California State College as Associate Professor of Industrial Arts. Working for the McGraw-Hill Book Company since 1961, he is presently Executive Editor for Occupational Trade and Technical Publishing in the Gregg Division.

PAUL I. WALLACH received his undergraduate education at the University of California at Santa Barbara and did his graduate work at Los Angeles State College. He has acquired extensive experience in the drafting, designing, and construction phases of architecture. He has traveled extensively in Europe and the Far East and has studied and taught for several years in Europe. He taught architecture and drafting for 30 years in California at both the secondary school and community college levels. He is presently teaching at the Fashion Institute of Design and Merchandising in San Francisco.

Preface

ARCHITECTURE: DRAFTING AND DESIGN is designed to be used in a first course in architectural drafting. Since a study of mechanical drawing normally precedes a course in architecture, only the principles and practices that are essentially related to architectural drafting are presented in this book.

This fourth edition is divided into six parts: Part One, The Design Process; Part Two, Area Planning; Part Three, Basic Architectural Plans; Part Four, Technical Architectural Plans; Part Five, Architectural Support Services; Part Six, Appendix.

Part One, The Design Process, exposes the student to the elements and principles of architectural design. It also covers the preliminary design considerations necessary for effective planning such as solar orientation, and density and ecological planning.

Part Two, Area Planning, covers the basic elements of planning areas of a structure and the functional techniques used to combine these areas into a composite, effective plan.

Part Three, Basic Architectural Plans, includes the basic techniques and procedures used in preparing architectural floor plans, elevations, and pictorial drawings. Information about scales (including metric) and computer-aided graphics is also covered in this part.

Part Four, Technical Architectural Plans, shows the student how to prepare the many technical architectural plans that are necessary for a complete and detailed description of a basic design.

Part Five, Architectural Support Services, covers the activities in which an architectural drafter may participate but which are not directly related to the drafting function. This includes the preparation of models, schedules and specifications as well as an introduction to the related legal and financial aspects of architectural planning.

Part Six, Appendix, includes reference material on architectural terms, related mathematics, and career information.

ARCHITECTURE: DRAFTING AND DESIGN is organized to be presented consecutively from Part One through Part Six. However, other sequences of study may be more suitable for classes with different emphasis. When the basic emphasis is placed on developing fundamental architectural drafting skills and techniques, Part Three may be studied first. Classes that are specifically oriented to the construction phase of architecture may find Part Four a logical point of departure.

All the illustrations have been selected and/or prepared to reinforce and amplify the principles and procedures described in the text. Whenever possible, each principle and practice has been reduced to its most elementary form and, for easy comprehension, has been directly related to the student's own environment. Reinforcement is continuous throughout the text through the constant repetition of views. The plan, elevation and pictorial interpretation of components is included at every opportunity.

Progression within each section and unit is from the simple to the complex, from the familiar to the abstract. The problems that appear at the end of each unit are organized to provide the maximum amount of flexibility. Most units include problems that range from the simplest, which can be completed in a few minutes, to the complex, which require considerable research and application of the principles of architectural drafting and design. Exercises in this edition that require original design work are marked with a special symbol (⌂⎯⎯⎯⎯). Completion of these exercises will result in the creation of a complete set of related architectural plans.

Since communication in the field of architectural drafting and design depends largely on understanding the vocabulary of architecture, new terms, abbreviations and symbols are defined when they first appear and are reinforced throughout the remainder of the text.

The practice of architecture functions through a utilization of the basic principles of mathematics and science. The correlation of basic scientific and mathematical concepts with architectural principles has been presented whenever appropriate.

In addition to expanding and updating existing units, this edition adds a complete new unit on energy-planning factors with emphasis on passive solar considerations and orientation.

The authors express sincere thanks to Wendy Talcott for the design contributions of Home Planners, Inc., Farmington Hills, Michigan; to Howard Hull for his critical technical review; to Michael Robbins for his preparation of the electrical chapter; to Kathern Saunders for the basic research on solar applicators; to Dana Hepler for the units on orientation, density planning, ecological planning, landscape rendering, plot survey and landscape plans; and to Diane Hepler and Diane Navarro for illustration layout and general artwork for this edition. Appreciation is also extended to Kathleen O'Leary for rewrite services and to Jeri Spiro for manuscript typing and editing.

INTRODUCTION

HISTORY

Fig 1 Early Egyptians used architectural plans.

Celotex Corp.

Fig 2 Early use of bearing-wall construction.

Celotex Corp.

Architecture had its beginning when early humans first fashioned caves or lean-to shelters for their families. Architectural drafting and design began when these people first drew the outline of a shelter in the sand or dirt and planned the use of existing materials. As structures became more complex, the need for more complete drawings became necessary. Figure 1 shows the use of architectural plans by the early Egyptians. But these architectural plans are far below today's standards. Their drawings are crude, and their measurements are not accurate.

An architect uses the knowledge gained from past centuries when designing a building today. The history of architectural design is directly related to progress in other areas of learning. For example, architecture has relied heavily upon the advancements of science and mathematics. From these advancements came new building materials and building methods. New engineering developments and new building materials have brought about more changes in architectural design in the last 30 years than had occurred in all the earlier history of architecture. Yet, many of the basic principles of modern architecture, such as bearing-wall construction and skeleton-frame construction, have been known for centuries. Even today, architectural structures are divided into two basic types, the bearing-wall and the skeleton-frame.

BEARING-WALL CONSTRUCTION

Bearing walls are solid and support themselves and the roof of a structure. Most early architecture, as shown in Fig. 2, used the bearing wall for support. In fact, one of the first major problems in architectural drafting and

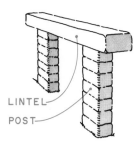

Fig 3 Post-and-lintel construction.

design involved the bearing wall. The problem was how to provide openings in a supporting wall without sacrificing the needed support. One of the first solutions to this problem was the development of the *post-and-lintel* (Fig. 3). In this type of construction, posts large enough to support the lintel (upper horizontal beam), wall, and roof above are used.

The ancient Greeks used *post-and-lintel* construction to erect many of their beautiful buildings (Fig. 4). Most ancient people used stone as their primary building material. The great weight of the stone limited the application of post-and-lintel construction. Furthermore, stone post-and-lintel construction could not support wide openings. Therefore, many posts (columns) were placed close together, as shown in Fig. 5, to provide the needed support. The Greeks and Romans developed many styles of columns and gave names to them. The various styles of column designs were known as *orders*. The orders of architecture developed by the Greeks are known as the *Doric*, the *Ionic*, and the *Corinthian*, as shown in Fig. 6. Later, the Romans developed the *Composite* and the *Tuscan* orders.

Since the Greek climate was well suited to open-air construction, the Greeks used the post-and-lintel technique to great advantage. The Parthenon is a classic example of Greek use of the post-and-lintel.

Oriental architects also made effective use of the post-and-lintel (Fig. 7). They were able to construct buildings with larger openings under the lintel because they used lighter materials, such as wood. The use of lighter materials resulted in the development of a style of architecture that was very light and

Fig 4 Early Greek use of post-and-lintel construction.

Celotex Corp.

Fig 5 Early use of columns.

Celotex Corp.

1

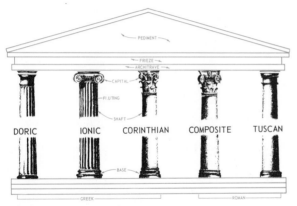

Fig 6 Basic orders of architecture.

Fig 7 Oriental applications of post-and-lintel construction.

Celotex Corp.

graceful. The Oriental post-and-lintel designs were also used extensively for gates and entrances.

THE ARCH

The Romans began a new trend in the design of wall openings when they developed the arch. The *arch* is different from the post-and-lintel because it can *span* (extend over) greater areas without support. It is easier to erect because it is made from many smaller, lighter pieces of stone. The principle of the arch is that each stone is supported by leaning on the *keystone* in the center. The keystone is shaped like a wedge and locks the other stones in place.

THE VAULT

The simple arch led to the development of the vault (Fig. 8). The *vault* is simply a series of arches that forms a continuous covering. This development allowed the use of the arch as a passageway rather than as just an opening in a wall. The cross vault is the intersection of two barrel vaults. The *barrel vault* and the *cross vault* were popular Roman construction devices.

THE DOME

The dome (Fig. 9), is a further refinement of the arch. The *dome* is made of arches so arranged that the bases make a circle and the tops meet in the middle of the ceiling. The Romans felt that the dome gave a feeling of

Fig 8 The barrel vault is a series of arches.

Fig 9 Ancient Siamese use of the dome. Celotex Corp.

Fig 10 Use of the flying buttress.

Fig 11 Contemporary use of new building materials.

power. Therefore, they used domes often in religious and governmental structures.

THE GOTHIC ARCH

Gothic architecture originated in France. It spread throughout western Europe between 1160 and 1530. Another variation of the arch, the pointed arch, was developed in Gothic architecture. The *pointed arch* (Gothic arch) became very popular in Gothic cathedrals because it created a sense of reaching and aspiring by its emphasis on vertical lines. Construction of the pointed arch posed the same problem as did conventional arches, that of spreading at the bottom.

To support the arch at the bottom, a new device known as a *buttress* was developed. Buttresses were gradually moved up the walls and resulted in the development of the *flying buttress*, shown in Fig. 10.

THE PRESENT

TECHNOLOGICAL ADVANCES

Bearing-wall construction is still much used in modern architecture. New building materials, such as reinforced and prestressed concrete, enable the architect to span greater areas. This allows a greater flexibility in design, and therefore greater variety. The development of new materials and new building methods has meant greatly improved structures. Modern buildings are larger, lighter, and safer than ever before. They are also more functional because they serve more uses.

NEW MATERIALS

Advancements in architecture throughout history have depended on the building materials at hand. As recently as American colonial times, builders had only wood, stone, and ceramic materials with which to work. Early American architecture reflects the use of these materials. But a great change came with the development of steel, aluminum, structural glass, prestressed concrete, wood laminates and plastics. Now, buildings can be designed in sizes and shapes never before possible, as shown in Fig. 11.

Many new materials are really old materials used in new ways or in new forms. Sometimes, they are old materials manufactured in a different way. For example, glass is not a new material. But the development of structural glass, glass blocks, corrugated glass, thermal glass, and plate glass in larger sizes has given the architect much greater freedom in the use of this material (Fig. 12).

Wood is also one of the oldest materials used in construction. Yet, the development of

3

Fig 14 Use of structural steel. Bethlehem Steel Corp.

Fig 12 Glass provides great freedom in design. Glaverbel

Fig 13 Use of plastics as a major building material. Rohm and Haars

new structural wood forms, plywoods, and laminates has revolutionized the use of wood in building. The manufacture of stressed-skin panels, boxed beams, curved panels, folded roof plates, and laminated beams has given builders new ways to use wood.

Among the truly new architectural materials is plastic (Fig. 13). The development of vinyl and laminated plastic has provided the architect with a wide range of new materials.

But the material that has contributed most to architectural change is steel. Without the use of steel, construction of most of our large high-rise buildings would be impossible. Even smaller structures can now be built on locations and in shapes that were impossible without the structural stability of steel, as shown in Fig. 14.

The manufacture of aluminum into lightweight, durable sheets and structural shapes has also given greater variety to design. But an old material, concrete, actually changed the basic nature of structural design. New uses of concrete are found in factory-made reinforced and prestressed structural shapes. These shapes are used for floors, roofs, and walls. They have provided the architect with still other tools for structural design.

Today's architects have the opportunity to design the framework of a building of steel, but use a variety of other materials as well. They can use large glass sheets for walls, prestressed concrete for floors, aluminum for casements, plastics for skylights, and wood for cabinets. A wide variety of still other material makes possible different combinations.

NEW CONSTRUCTION METHODS

The development of new materials is usually not possible without the development of new construction methods. For example, large glass panels could not have been used in the eighteenth century even if they had been available, because no large-span lintel-support system had been developed. Only when both new materials and new methods exist is the architect free to design with complete flexibility.

Present-day structures are usually a combination of old and new. In a modern building, examples of the old post-and-lintel method may be used together with skeleton-frame, curtain-wall, or cantilevered construction.

SKELETON FRAME

One of the first methods developed to employ modern materials makes use of the *skeleton frame*. This kind of construction has an open frame to which a wall covering is attached. The frame provides the primary support, and the covering provides the needed shelter. The skeleton frame became popular with the development of framing materials and wall coverings that are light, strong, and usable in a variety of ways. The skeleton frame is now commonly used in family dwellings, as shown in Fig. 15, and in commercial buildings. When steel is used for the skeleton, the skeleton frame is known as *steel-cage* construction.

The use of the skeleton frame, as opposed to bearing-wall construction, has given architects new opportunities. They can now design a structure without direct vertical-line outside base support. In this new type of construction, called *cantilever*, the loads are supported at only one end. Steel is well suited to cantilever construction because loaded steel beams, supported at only one end, can be extended farther without sagging than can any other material (Fig. 16).

Since loads in steel-cage construction are not supported by the outside wall, curtain walls are possible. In this type of building, known as *curtain-wall construction*, a steel

Fig 15 Skeleton-frame construction. Kaufman and Broad

Fig 16 Cantilevered construction. Hedrich-Blessing

Fig 17 Cantilevered and curtain-wall construction. PPG Industries, Inc.

cage is erected, forming the shape of the building. The curtain wall, or skin, is added last. This curtain has no structural relationship to the stability of the building; it acts only as a protection from the weather. Therefore, the curtain wall can be made of materials with little or no structural value, such as glass (Fig. 17), sheet metal, or plastic.

SHAPES

For centuries, architectural development has been restricted by the use and overuse of the square and the cube (right angles) as the basis for most structures. Architects are now using other shapes such as the triangle (Fig. 18), octagon, pyramid, pentagon, *circle* (Fig. 19), and sphere. This has come about with the development of materials that are stronger, lighter, and have a variety of uses. New construction methods also enable architects to design buildings that are completely *functional* (able to fulfill all needs) without reference to any basic geometric form. Many forms are now possible, and even the basic shapes of floor plans can be drawn to meet a variety of needs, as shown in Fig. 19.

Fig 18 Contemporary use of triangular shape.

Bethlehem
Steel Corp.

Fig 19 Use of unconventional shapes.

Home Planners, Inc.

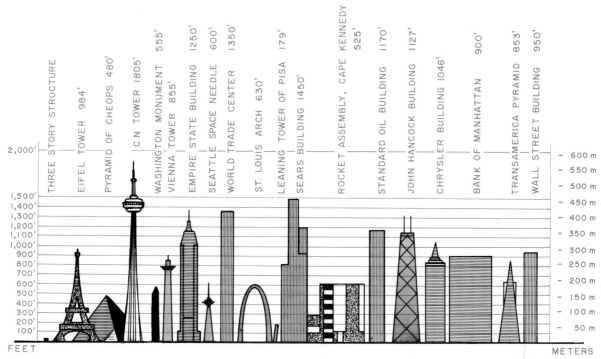

THREE STORY STRUCTURE
EIFEL TOWER 984'
PYRAMID OF CHEOPS 480'
C N TOWER 1805'
WASHINGTON MONUMENT 555'
VIENNA TOWER 855'
EMPIRE STATE BUILDING 1250'
SEATTLE SPACE NEEDLE 600'
WORLD TRADE CENTER 1350'
ST. LOUIS ARCH 630'
LEANING TOWER OF PISA 179'
SEARS BUILDING 1450'
ROCKET ASSEMBLY, CAPE KENNEDY 525'
STANDARD OIL BUILDING 1170'
JOHN HANCOCK BUILDING 1127'
CHRYSLER BUILDING 1046'
BANK OF MANHATTAN 900'
TRANSAMERICA PYRAMID 853'
WALL STREET BUILDING 950'

FEET: 2,000' 1,500' 1,400' 1,300' 1,200' 1,100' 1,000' 900' 800' 700' 600' 500' 400' 300' 200' 100'

METERS: 600 m, 550 m, 500 m, 450 m, 400 m, 350 m, 300 m, 250 m, 200 m, 150 m, 100 m, 50 m

Fig 20 Comparison of the world's tallest structures.

SIZES

New technology uses knowledge gained from advances in science. One of the most striking results has been the use of new materials and new methods to design and build structures of size greater than ever before (Fig. 20). The Sears Tower in Chicago is now the tallest building in the world. But as technology develops even more, buildings can increase to sizes previously thought impossible. Frank Lloyd Wright once proposed a mile-high skyscraper. Ten such structures would house the working office staff of all New York City. Six would suffice for Chicago. The proposed skyscraper would tower far above the largest structures of today.

Who can say what will be possible? The idea of building a geodesic dome over central Manhattan, in New York City, as shown in Fig. 21, certainly seems impossible at the moment. But remember that landing humans on the moon, and flights to and landings on distant planets, also seemed impossible not many years ago.

LOCATION

Today, architects not only design buildings of enormous size but can also choose locations for buildings that were unthought of years ago (Fig. 22). Further advances in transportation and architectural engineering will make even more difficult locations not only possible but workable.

Fig 21 Buckminster Fuller's proposed Manhattan geodesic dome.

with much on-the-job construction work. Typical components include preassembled windows, trusses, and molded bathrooms.

As more components are developed, construction changes from *on site*, piece by piece building, to assembly of component parts on the site. The development of component systems does not necessarily change the nature of design, but it does change the way architects may design (Fig. 23).

Designing with the use of components means the designer must adhere strictly to certain sizes in creating an architectural plan. Sizes of the components are standard, or uniform, just as an automobile is designed with many different, interchangeable parts.

THE FUTURE

The future of architecture will certainly be related to the development of new materials, new construction methods, and sociological changes dealing with the way people live in a given society. With the development of new materials and methods of construction, the architect is freed from the restrictions of traditional materials and methods. The architect becomes a coordinator of the activities of the structural engineer, electrical engineer, acoustical engineer, sociologist, interior designer, and so forth. The architect's plan is in a sense a blend of all such activities.

Designing a structure that will last is a great challenge. The architect, the designer, and the builder must keep abreast of technological changes and advancements in architectural engineering and building design. This is true whether they are designing and building a residence, designing a large building, redeveloping a neighborhood or city, or planning a completely different kind of structure. In any case, anyone working in the field of architectural design must understand people, their habits, their needs, and their activities. Such a person must also be capable of working with shapes, materials, colors, and proportions in order to design aesthetically pleasing and structurally sound buildings.

Fig 22 A previously unbuildable site. Red Cedar Shingle & Shake Bureau

Fig 23 Assembly of architectural components. Simpson Lumber Co.

COMPONENTS

One of the most significant advancements of the past several years is the design and construction of architectural components. *Components* are preconstructed parts of a building; they are parts or sections made in advance. Using components allows the builder to construct parts away from the site, or location, of the building. This does away

PART ONE

PRELIMINARY DESIGN AND PLANNING

This part covers activities and considerations that must be undertaken prior to the formulation of any architectural design. Included here is a coverage of architectural styles, aesthetic design factors, solar orientation, passive energy, and ecological and density planning. A basic understanding of the principles and practices relating to these areas is an essential step before specific architectural design and drafting activities.

FUNDAMENTALS OF DESIGNING AND PLANNING

This section provides background information on architectural styles and types. It also covers the aesthetic factors of design that must be considered prior to the development of an architectural plan.

UNIT 1
ARCHITECTURAL STYLES

SPECIFIC ARCHITECTURAL STYLES

Our architectural heritage is largely derived from European and early American architecture. Nevertheless, specific architectural styles have developed through the years as a result of technological advances and demands of our culture. Styles of the past reflect the culture of the past. Styles of the present reflect our current living habits and needs. Styles of the future will be largely determined by advancements in technology and changes in our living styles and patterns.

EUROPEAN STYLES

The English, French, Italians, and Spanish have provided the most significant influence on our architecture.

Fig 1-1 Tudor style. Masonite Corp.

ENGLISH ARCHITECTURE The *Tudor* style of architecture originated in England during the fifteenth century. Tudor homes feature high-pitched gable roofs, small windows, shallow dormers, Norman towers, and tall

10

Fig 1-2 French chateau style.

chimneys that usually extend high above the roof line.

The *Elizabethan,* or half-timbered, style is an adaptation of the Tudor style. It is characterized by the use of mortar set between timbers. Figure 1-1 shows a modern adaptation of the Elizabethan style of architecture from which many of our modern styles are derived.

FRENCH ARCHITECTURE French provincial architecture was brought to this continent when the French settled Quebec. French provincial architecture can be identified by the *mansard roof.* This roof design was developed by the French architect François Mansard (or, in French, Mansart). On the French provincial home, this roof is high-pitched, with steep slopes and rounded dormer windows projecting from the sides. Figure 1-2 shows an example of French architecture of the *château* style.

SOUTHERN EUROPEAN ARCHITECTURE Spanish architecture was brought to this country by Spanish colonials who settled the Southwest. Spanish architecture is characterized by low-pitched roofs of ceramic tile and by stucco exterior walls. A distinguishing feature of almost every Spanish home is a courtyard patio. Two-story Spanish homes contain open balconies enclosed in grillwork. One-story Spanish homes were the forerunners of the present ranch-style homes that first developed in southern California.

Italian architecture is very similar to Spanish architecture. Distinguishing features

are the use of columns and arches at a loggia entrance, and windows or balconies opening onto a loggia roof. A *loggia* is an open passage covered by a roof. The use of classical moldings around first-floor windows also helps to distinguish the Italian style from the Spanish.

EARLY AMERICAN

Early colonists came to the New World from many different cultures and were familiar with many different styles of architecture.

NEW ENGLAND COLONIAL The colonists who settled the New England coastal areas were influenced largely by English styles of architecture. Lack of materials, time, and equipment greatly simplified their adaptation of these styles. One of the most popular of the New England styles was the *Cape Cod.* This is a one-and-one-half-story gabled-roof house with dormers. It has a central front entrance, a large central chimney, and exterior walls of clapboard or bevel siding. Double-hung windows are fixed with shutters, and the floor plan is generally symmetrical. Cold New England winters also influenced the development of many design features such as shutters, small window areas, and enclosed breezeways. Figure 1-3 shows an example of a New England colonial-style home.

DUTCH COLONIAL Gambrel roofs characterized many small farm buildings in Germany. A *gambrel roof* is a double-pitched roof with projecting overhangs. Many of the Ger-

Fig 1-3 New England colonial style.

Home Planners, Inc.

mans who later settled New York and Pennsylvania made the gambrel roof a part of the Dutch colonial style of architecture.

MID-ATLANTIC COLONIAL The availability of brick, a seasonal climate, and the influence of the architecture of Thomas Jefferson led to the development of the Mid-Atlantic style of architecture illustrated in Fig. 1-4. The style was formal, massive, and ornate. In colonial days, buildings from Virginia to New Jersey were designed in this manner. It was an adaptation of many urban English designs.

SOUTHERN COLONIAL When the early settlers migrated to the South, warmer climates and outdoor living activities led them to develop the Southern colonial style of architecture. As the house became the center of plantation living, the size was increased, and a second story was added. Two-story columns

were used to support the front-roof overhang and the symmetrical gable roof (Fig. 1-5).

RANCH STYLE

As settlers moved West, they adapted architectural styles to meet their needs. The availability of space at ground level eliminated the need for second floors. The amount of space was spread horizontally rather than vertically, which resulted in a rambling plan (Fig. 1-6A). The Spanish and Mexican influence also led to the popularization of the Western *ranch*, which used a U-shaped plan with a patio in the center, as shown in Fig. 1-6B.

VICTORIAN

The Industrial Revolution in this country provided architects and builders with ma-

Fig 1-4 Mid-Atlantic colonial style. Walt Disney Productions

Fig 1-5 Southern colonial style. Home Planners, Inc.

Fig 1-6A Western ranch style.

Fig 1-6B Spanish-Western ranch style.

chinery and equipment for constructing very intricate millwork items. Since living habits had changed little, this new-found technology was used to add decoration to a building. Intricate finials, lintels, parapets, balconies, and cornices were added. Ornate aspects of Victorian architecture (gingerbread) were designed into homes until recent years.

CONTEMPORARY

The development of lighter, stronger building materials combined with the need to produce inexpensive structures in less time led to the evolution of simple functional designs, as shown in Fig. 1-7.

Fig 1-7 Contemporary style.

STYLE SETTERS

Louis Sullivan wrote, "Our architecture reflects us as truly as a mirror." Modern architecture is now reflecting our freedom, our functionalism, and our technological advances. Modern architects are working to achieve even more functionalism, freedom, relationships, and technological refinements in the art and science of architecture.

FUNCTIONALISM

Functionalism is the quality of being useful, of serving a purpose other than adding beauty, or aesthetic value. Louis Sullivan's *"form follows function"* idea has now been accepted by most modern architects. Few items can find their way into an architectural design without performing some specific function, or job. Most modernists feel this is the line of distinction between architecture and sculpture. Architecture performs a function; a piece of sculpture does not. Sculpture may exist and be admired for its aesthetic qualities alone.

Functionalism in architecture has led to extreme applications of simplicity in design. Simplicity and functionalism complement each other. Together, they produce a desired result.

Frank Lloyd Wright is considered the greatest American architect by most. He believed that architecture should be *organic* — that the materials, function, form, and surroundings in nature should be completely coordinated. All of these things should be in agreement, or harmony. The designs of his buildings are X-, L-, and T-shaped, with open areas throughout the living areas. The elevations are low and horizontal.

Wright showed his genius by continually developing new styles and trends in architecture. He believed that even the basic shapes of floor plans should be more diversified with the development of new and more flexible building materials. Wright's *Falling Waters*, (Fig. 16) designed and built over 40 years ago, still maintains a functional, contemporary look. Today, more and more diversified shapes are finding their way into the architectural scene.

FREEDOM

Freedom of expression, freedom in the use of space, and structural freedom in design characterize modern architecture.

Charles Le Corbusier was one of the leading architects who stood for freedom in architectural design. He felt that we must no longer challenge nature with our architecture but rather work with nature. The house, he said, should be looked upon as a machine for living in, or as a tool as serviceable as a typewriter.

Eduardo Torroja used great imaginative powers in working with reinforced and prestressed concrete. Using the forms of folded, undulating, or warped shapes, he designed structures having fluid continuity, beauty, and freedom. He said that complete freedom of expression can be achieved by using flexible materials that allow the architect to express ideas with freedom and independence.

RELATIONSHIPS

Relating the areas of the structure to each other and to its environment has become a well-established principle of modern architecture.

Eero Saarinen proved that functional form need not be rigid and boxlike. His designs have the appearance of gigantic pieces of sculpture. They are gracefully molded, with rhythmically curving and flowing lines. His concrete shell structures show the influence of the style known as expressionism. They also show a perfect understanding and use of space. These designs are a dramatic departure from the regularity of conventional styles.

Oscar Niemeyer, the designer of Brasilia, believes that architectural freedom should be expressed through a conquest of space. Brasilia is a classic example of relating large areas to one another. The capital of Brazil is the only city in the world that was designed to be built at one time. As a result, space could be controlled as it cannot otherwise be in cities whose structures are designed at different times in history.

TECHNOLOGY

Technological advances now allow architects to build large structures of light materials (Fig. 1-8), to erect buildings quickly, and to design the utmost in structural safety into buildings.

Ludwig Mies van der Rohe, the architect of steel, believed that when technology reaches its full development in any culture, it immediately transcends into architecture. His plans are characterized by cubic simplicity. They are masterpieces of precise engineering. These plans depend on proportion, fitness and beauty of material, and mechanical precision of finish.

Walter Gropius believed that in the design of structures, experts from various fields must be consulted. He believed that the work of designers, engineers, sociologists, and builders should be coordinated by the architect. He thought that the design of a structure was so complex that no one person could be aware of all the aspects of the final design.

Many designs reflect the attitude of Minoru Yamasaki that architecture should provide serenity and quiet. Yamasaki's building style involves the covering of walls with a textile-like fabric that hides the structural members (Fig. 1-9). His designs also feature umbrella walls of textured building blocks, axial planes, high natural lighting, and beautiful gardens and pools.

Richard Buckminster Fuller has been acclaimed for his *geodesic domes*. The domes are a product of much research and mathematical calculation. They are based on triangular sections called *tetrahedrons*. The domes are strong, yet lightweight. They can be constructed in a comparatively short time from almost any building materials. One of Fuller's largest domes, at Baton Rouge, Louisiana, has a diameter of 384 feet (Fig. 1-10).

THE ROMANTICISTS

Many architects favor the attempt to bring back to architecture some of the traditional elements of ornament that are a part of the great classic monuments of the past.

Edward D. Stone designed the United States Embassy Building in New Delhi in a

Fig 1-8 Large structures are now built with lighter materials.

Dover Corp. Elevator Div.

Fig 1-9 Extreme simplicity characterizes the World Trade Center.

The Port Authority of New York and New Jersey

Fig 1-10 Buckminster Fuller's geodesic dome.

Fig 1-11 Example of Edward Stone's romantic style.

Fig 1-12 A contemporary interior.

romantic style. He promoted the international style of functional architecture with his design of the Museum of Modern Art in New York City. Stone changed his original style of pure functionalism to become one of the leaders of romanticism. An example of his ornamental elements is the use of the patterned screen wall, called a *grille*. He designs his grilles from bricks, metal screens, and tiles, as shown in Fig. 1-11.

INTERIOR DESIGN

The total architectural style of a structure must be one of the first considerations in developing the interior design style. To be truly authentic, periods should be matched internally and externally. That is, the internal construction and furnishing should be as authentic as the exterior architecture. This means that the elements of design, both inside and outside, must be matched to get a desired consistent style. An Elizabethan-style home should be furnished only with English heritage furniture such as Queen Anne. A French

Fig 1-13 A contemporary exterior.

Potlatch Corp.

Fig 1-14 Period style interior.
Harris
Manufacturing Co.

provincial-style home should be furnished with Louis XIV furniture, and so forth. Most designers do match all European styles, early-American styles, or modern styles of architecture with like, or corresponding, interiors. For example, the interior shown in Fig. 1-12 is consistent in style with the exterior shown in Fig. 1-13. The interior shown in Fig. 1-14 is consistent with the exterior shown in Fig. 1-4.

The role of the architect as a coordinator in these activities will increase. The relationship between art and technology will be refined to enable all types of buildings to be technically appropriate and aesthetically acceptable.

UNIT 2
DESIGN FACTORS

Design activities may be formal or informal. *Informal design* occurs when a product is made by the designer without the use of a plan. *Formal design* involves the complete preparation of a set of working drawings. The working drawings are then used in constructing the product. Buildings are designed formally. A complete set of working drawings

must be prepared before the actual construction begins. Therefore, the major design activity in architectural work occurs during the preparation of sketches, plans, and detailed drawings.

Ideas in the creative stage may be recorded by sketching basic images. These sketches are then revised until the ideas are crystallized—given final form. First sketches rarely produce a finished design. Usually, many revisions are necessary.

A basic idea, regardless of how creative and imaginative, is useless unless the design can be built successfully. Designing involves

Fig 2-1 Curved lines dominate this design.

Georgia Pacific

Fig 2-2 Vertical straight emphasis.

California
Redwood Assoc.

the transfer of basic sketches into architectural working drawings. Every useful building must perform a specific function. Every part of the structure should also be designed to perform a specific function. But today's buildings must be not only functional but aesthetically designed as well.

ELEMENTS OF DESIGN

The *elements of design* are the tools of the designer. They are the ingredients of every successful design. These basic elements are: line, form, color, space, light, and material.

LINE

The element of *line* is used to produce a sense of movement within an object or to produce a greater sense of length or height. Lines enclose space and provide the outline or contour of forms. *Straight lines* are either vertical, horizontal, or diagonal. *Curved lines* have an infinite number of directional variations; they are not limited in the direction they can take. Curved lines dominate the design shown in Fig. 2-1. The straight lines found in Fig. 2-2 create a vertical emphasis.

A vertical line creates the illusion of an increase in height because the eye moves upward to follow the line. A horizontal line creates the illusion of an increase in width as the eye moves horizontally.

In duplicating the various positions of the human body, straight vertical lines create a feeling of strength, simplicity, and alertness. Horizontal lines suggest relaxation and repose. Diagonal lines create a feeling of restlessness or transition. Curved lines indicate soft, graceful, and flowing movements.

As in any art form, the combination of straight and curved lines in patterns is related to the other elements of design to create the most pleasing total design configuration.

FORM

Lines joined together produce *form,* and create the shape of an area. Straight lines joined together produce rectangles, squares, and other geometric shapes. Curved lines form circles, ovals, and ellipses. The proportion of these forms or shapes is an important factor in design. Circles and ovals convey a feeling of completeness. Squares and rectangles produce a feeling of mathematical precision, and should be used accordingly. The form of an object may be closed and solid or closed and volume-containing. It may also be

Fig 2-3 Open form.

Cabin Crafts Carpets
Western Wood Products Assoc.

Fig 2-4 Pale colors recede.

open, as shown in Fig. 2-3. The form of the structure, however, should always be determined by its function.

COLOR

Color is either an integral part of an architectural material or color must be added to create the desired effect. Color in architecture serves to distinguish items, strengthen interest, or reduce eye contact. Color combinations are therefore varied, depending on the purpose being served.

Color *harmonies* are groups of colors used in combination to create pleasing visual images. Color *hue* distinguishes one color from another. Color hue is the name of the color, such as red, yellow, and blue. The *value* of a color is the degree of darkness or lightness within the hue. A *tint* is a color on the lighter portion of the hue. A *shade* represents the darker portion of the hue. *Intensity,* or the saturation of color, refers to the degree of brightness or purity of the color.

Red is associated with warmth (Fig. 2-3) and action. Yellow, which is nearest the sun, is related to cheer and exuberance. Yellow is the greatest attention-creating color. Orange is associated with light and heat. Violet, the color of shadows, creates a feeling of mystery. Green depicts coolness and restraint. For that reason, green is used in industrial building to lessen tension. Blue is associated with coolness, repose, and formality. It is associated with the sky, the ocean, and ice. Blue has been used throughout the ages as the symbol of truth, royalty, and purity.

Color is also used to change the apparent visual dimensions of a building. It is used to make rooms appear higher or longer, lower or shorter. Bold colors, such as red, create the illusion of advancement, while pale colors (pastels) tend to recede. Notice how the pale walls in Fig. 2-4 tend to recede. Color also affects the feeling of temperature in a room. Thus, a blue room will seem colder than a red room at the same temperature.

LIGHT AND SHADOW

Light reflects from the surfaces of forms. *Shadows* appear in the area that light cannot reach. Light and shadow both give a sense of depth to any structure. The effective designer plans the relationship of light and dark areas accordingly (Fig. 2-5). The designer must, therefore, consider which surfaces reflect light instead of absorbing light, and which surfaces refract (bend) light as it passes through the material. The designer must also remember that with continued exposure to light, visual sensitivity decreases. Thus we become adapted to degrees of darkness, or lightness, after extended exposure.

SPACE

Space surrounds form and is contained within it. The design can create a feeling of

19

Fig 2-5 Continuous ceiling creates a feeling of expanded space. Armstrong Cork Co.

Fig 2-6 Relationship of light and dark areas. Armstrong Cork Co.

space. The continuous ceiling shown in Fig. 2-6 creates a feeling of expanded space. Architectural design is the art of defining space and space relationships in a manner that makes use of all other elements of design in a functional and aesthetic manner.

MATERIALS

Materials are the raw substances with which designers create. Materials possess their own color, form, dimension, degree of hardness, and texture. The hardness of the material cannot be altered. However, to some degree, the color, form, and dimension of materials can be altered. Texture is the unique and most significant factor in the selection of appropriate materials. *Texture* refers to the surface finish of an object—its roughness, smoothness, coarseness, or fineness. Surfaces of materials such as concrete, stone, and brick are rough and dull, and suggest strength and informality. Smoother surfaces, such as those of glass, aluminum, and plastics, create a feeling of luxury and formality. The designer must be careful not to include too many different textures of a similar nature. For this reason, masonries (brick and stone, for example) are not usually combined in areas close together. Textures, such as the wood texture shown in Fig. 2-7, are more pleasing when combined with contrasting surfaces.

Rough surfaces reduce the apparent height of a ceiling or distance of a wall and make colors appear darker. Smooth surfaces increase the apparent height of a ceiling or wall and reflect more light, thus making colors appear brighter.

PRINCIPLES OF DESIGN

The basic *principles of design* are the guidelines for using the elements of design to create aesthetically functional buildings. The basic principles of design are: balance, variety, emphasis, unity, opposition, proportion, rhythm, subordination, transition, and repetition.

BALANCE

Balance is the achievement of equilibrium in design. Buildings are *formally balanced* if they are symmetrical. They are *informally balanced* if there is variety, yet harmonious relationship in the distribution of space, form, line, color, light, and shade. The

Fig 2-7 Natural wood texture.

Fig 2-8 An informally balanced (asymmetrical) building.

building shown in Fig. 2-8 is informally (asymmetrically) balanced. The building shown in Fig. 2-9 is formally (symmetrically) balanced.

RHYTHM

When lines, planes, and surface treatments are repeated in a regular sequence (order or arrangement), a sense of rhythm is achieved. The wall divisions in Fig. 2-10 give a sense of rhythm to the design. Rhythm is used to create motion and carry the viewer's eyes to various parts of the space. This is accomplished by the repetition of lines, colors, and patterns.

EMPHASIS

The principle of *emphasis* (domination) is used by the designer to draw attention to an area or subject. Emphasis is achieved through the use of color, form, texture, or line. The window wall, in Fig. 2-11, creates a point of emphasis for that structure.

In architectural design, some emphasis or focal point should be designed into each elevation and interior space. Directing attention to the *point of emphasis* (focal point) is accomplished by the arrangement of features, the use of contrasting colors, line direction, light variations, space relationships, or material changes.

Fig 2-9 Formally balanced (symmetrical) building.

Fig 2-10 Wall divisions provide a sense of rhythm.

Fig 2-11 The window wall creates the point of emphasis for this structure.

Scholz Homes

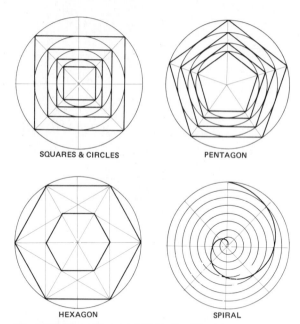

SQUARES & CIRCLES

PENTAGON

HEXAGON

SPIRAL

Fig 2-12 Two-dimensional proportional systems.

Fig 2-13 The same area divided different ways.

PROPORTION

The proportional dimensions (scale) of a building are important. The early Greeks found that rectangular proportions in the ratio of 2 to 3, 3 to 5, and 5 to 8 were more pleasing than others. For example a room 10′ × 15′ and a rug 9′ × 15′ have the proportions 2 to 3 and 3 to 5.

The scale between interior space, furniture, and accessories should be harmonious. Bulky components in small rooms should be avoided. Small components in large rooms should not be used. Figure 2-12 shows several proportional systems used in two-dimensional design. Areas will appear completely different depending on the division of space within the area, as shown in Fig. 2-13.

UNITY

Unity is the expression of the sense of wholeness in the design. Every structure should appear complete. No parts should appear as appendages or afterthoughts. In the building shown in Fig. 2-14, the designer has achieved unity through the use of consistent line and color, even though the building is composed of many different parts. Unity, or harmony, as the name implies, is the joining together of the basic elements of good design to form one harmonious, unified whole.

Unity (or harmony) is achieved through the utilization of any or all of the elements of design, for there is potential for unity within each.

VARIETY

Without variety, any area can become dull and tiresome to the eye of the observer. Too much rhythm, too much repetition, too much unity ruin a sense of variety or contrast. Likewise, too little of any of the elements of design will also result in a lack of variety. Light, shadow, and color are used extensively to achieve variety.

REPETITION

Unity is often achieved through *repetition*. Vertical lines, spaces, and textures are repeated throughout the design to tie the struc-

Fig 2-14 Unity achieved through consistent line and color.

PPG Industries, Inc.

CREATIVITY

Creativity in architecture involves the ability to create mental images of arrangements and forms not yet visible. Creative imagination is the ability to present new patterns, use new objects, and invent new configurations. Thus, creativity and imagination are almost the same in meaning. Both relate to the forces that cause isolated and unrelated factors to come together into arrangements of cohesive unity and beauty.

FUNCTIONAL DESIGN

Any basic idea, no matter how creative or imaginative, is useless unless the design can be implemented successfully and function as planned. Architectural design involves not only how a structure appears but how it functions. Thus, architectural design begins with an assessment of human needs. Remember that *form follows function*. However, functional success alone does not guarantee that the design is aesthetically pleasing. The task of the competent designer is to combine functional efficiency and aesthetics in a unified design. The designer must manipulate the elements of design successfully through the effective application of the principles of design.

No design can exist in isolation. It must always be related to all situations that influence it. Thus, creating a successful design involves manipulating the entire environment.

DESIGN PROCESS

Proceeding logically from a basic idea to a final design is often a long process. Rough ideas are recorded. Sketches are refined and changed many times before the final form is established. Elements of line, texture, color, light, and shadow are combined in the most appropriate relationships. The effects of unity, repetition, rhythm, variety, emphasis, and balance must be achieved without sacrificing the functional or technical aspects of the design.

ture together aesthetically and to achieve unity.

OPPOSITION

Opposites in design add interest. *Opposition* involves contrasting elements such as short and long, thick and thin, straight and curved, black and white. Opposite forms, colors, and lines in a design, when used effectively with the other principles of design, achieve balance, emphasis, and variety.

SUBORDINATION

When emphasis is achieved through some design feature, other features naturally become subordinate—lesser in emphasis or importance. Subordination can be related in design to lines, shapes, or color.

TRANSITION

The change from one color to another, or from a curved to a straight line, if done while maintaining the unity of the design, is known as *transition*. Transition may involve the intersection of molding from one wall to another in the same room, or may apply to a change from one floor surface to another in adjoining rooms. The designer's task in achieving successful transition in all aspects of the design contributes to harmony of different elements of design without sacrificing unity.

Ideas in the creative stage may be recorded by sketching basic images. These sketches are then revised until the basic form is finally crystallized. First sketches rarely produce a finished design. Usually, many revisions are necessary, as shown in Fig. 2-15. Many designers make a habit of never discarding a sketch. They continue to resketch the problem because the fifth sketch may reveal the solution to a problem in the tenth sketch. Ideas may not be combined in a functional design until perhaps 20 or 30 sketches have been made.

CHANGING PATTERNS AND TASTES

Not only must the architectural designer blend the basic elements of design to create a good functional plan, but this must be done as styles and tastes change. There are periods when people prefer open planning. At other times, complete privacy is of primary concern. Individual and public tastes constantly change; but the designer must not be caught in a "fad trap." An effective, creative, designer will recognize the difference between trends and fads. But the designer must be constantly on the alert, always looking for the link between present and future. The contemporary designer must recall past experiences and apply old ideas to new situations in combinations of endless variety.

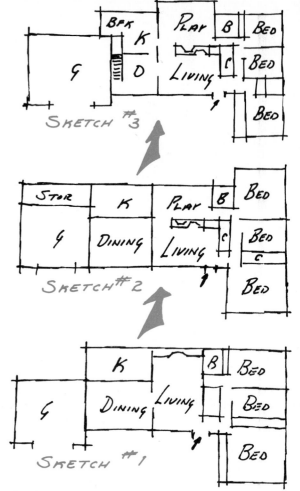

Fig 2-15 Many sketches are used to revise and alter a plan.

PROBLEMS

1 Sketch the front elevation of the house shown in Fig. 2-8. Convert the front-elevation design to a formally balanced elevation.
2 Sketch the house shown in Fig. 2-11 to provide more emphasis on one phase of the design.
3 Sketch the wall shown in Fig. 2-4 to improve the patterns of light and shadow and to provide more unity of texture and line in the design.
4 List the major color you would use to decorate each room in your home. List two supporting colors you would use for contrast or variety.

5 List each element of design and describe your preference for applying each to a residence of your own design.
6 Define these terms: technical design, creative design, aesthetic, informal design, formal design, function, form, space, light, shadow, texture, line, color, beauty, repetition, variety, emphasis, informal balance, formal balance.

ENVIRONMENTAL FACTORS IN DESIGN

UNIT 3
ENERGY PLANNING AND ORIENTATION

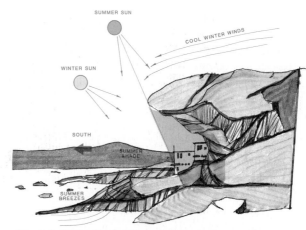

Fig 3-1 Early Native Americans used natural resources for heating and cooling.

Throughout history, the environment has been used in conjunction with the need for shelter. Local resources and climatic conditions have affected heating, cooling, and lighting needs. For example, Native Americans built adobe houses under overhanging cliffs (Fig. 3-1). The cliffs provided shade and protection from the sun's rays during the day. At night, the material used in these houses released the heat accumulated during the day and warmed the building. Even later, when other heat sources were developed, people made a point of conserving fuel, whether it was wood, dung, twisted grass, or blubber. This all changed when fossil fuel became popular.

Inexpensive fossil fuel appeared to be an endless energy source. People used fuel with no thought of saving it. That practice affected the design and construction of buildings. Consequently, architectural designs and materi-

als that previously had been chosen to gain heating and cooling benefits from natural sources soon became *obsolete*, a thing of the past.

By relying on fossil fuel for energy, architects and builders controlled the inside environments of many buildings artificially. There was no regard for energy efficiency, for taking advantage of nature. Buildings were located on hills exposed to strong winds or in sweltering valleys. Windows (of any size and in any quantity) were placed on any side of a

25

building. No longer was there a need to rely on opening windows or pulling shades to cool or warm the structure. Great glass office buildings and towers became a common sight. Their acres of windows could not open to take advantage of natural air movement and temperature changes. Buildings were erected without regard for orientation or energy efficiency. But now, after years of unchecked use and misuse of energy and at considerable cost to the environment, the end of cheap fossil fuels can be seen. Today, considering the finite supply of fossil fuels, there is a need to return to the energy-efficient principles used in earlier days.

PASSIVE SOLAR SYSTEMS

A rapidly growing number of architects, home owners, and builders are rediscovering the natural cooling, heating, and lighting potentials of different climates. This reborn sensitivity has combined with space-age technology to bring about effective alternative directions in architectural design and construction.

We need not sacrifice quality or comfort in order to design buildings that place less demand on energy resources. Natural systems can be used to regulate heating and cooling as effectively as artificially controlled environments. But certain architectural design techniques must be adhered to in order to achieve maximum natural energy efficiency.

PASSIVE SOLAR PRINCIPLES

Passive solar planning makes use of environmental elements only, without additional technical assistance from devices such as solar panels and heat pumps. Passive solar energy systems include: 1. *solar collectors*, 2. *storage facilities*, 3. *distribution channels*, and 4. *control devices*. Figure 3-2 shows the application of these four factors in drawing heat out of a structure in the summer and bringing heat into it during the winter.

Effective passive solar energy systems require the maximum absorption of heat from sunlight and accumulation of that heat in floors, walls, or tanks of water. Absorption of heat in solar collectors is the first phase in any solar energy system.

Fig 3-2 Examples of passive solar planning.

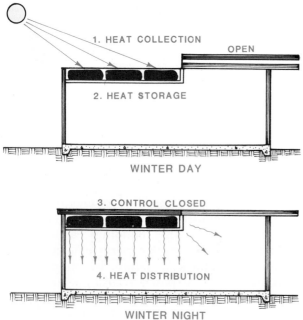

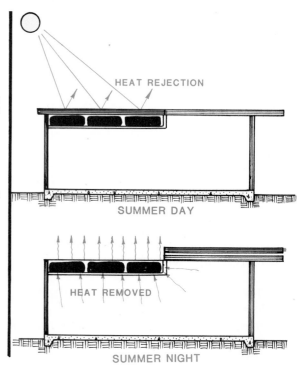

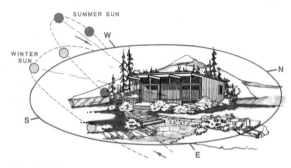

Fig 3-3 Winter and summer sun angles.

Use of the sun's heat in the winter must be maximized. A large southern exposure and south-facing windows collect the largest amounts of heat from sunlight. A car parked in direct sunlight, with windows closed, illustrates this principle. The interior of the car becomes hot because sunlight enters through the windows. The heat is absorbed by the interior surfaces of the car and trapped inside the

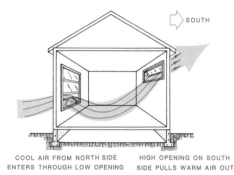

COOL AIR FROM NORTH SIDE
ENTERS THROUGH LOW OPENING

HIGH OPENING ON SOUTH
SIDE PULLS WARM AIR OUT

Fig 3-4 Convection currents draw out warm air.

car as stored heat. This is known as the *greenhouse effect.*

Once the winter sun enters a building through windows, it should be stored in a thermal mass, so that the heat can be used later when the sun's heat is not available. *Thermal mass* is any material that will absorb heat from the sun and later radiate the heat back. The seats in a car act as a thermal mass. Walls, floors, fireplaces, and water drums all work in this manner in a building. In passive solar systems, a thermal mass is the storage and distribution system.

In the summer, it is unnecessary to collect the sun's heat. Rather, protection against the sun's heat may be needed. Fortunately, the sun's angle changes conveniently from summer to winter. Thus it is fairly easy to design buildings that bar summer sun and collect winter sun (Fig. 3-3). To aid in this process, vents and windows should be located to provide optimum natural air convection and ventilation to circulate the warm air as shown in Fig. 3-4. Heavy adobe brick or concrete walls will delay entry of daytime heat into the house. Using fans in the evening to flush out hot air will also keep the house cooler during summer months. Figures 3-5 and 3-6 show examples of the ways passive solar planning can be used in summer and winter.

OVERHANG PROTECTION

The angle of the sun differs in summer and in winter. Therefore, roof overhangs must

Fig 3-5 Use of a passive solar system for cooling and heating.

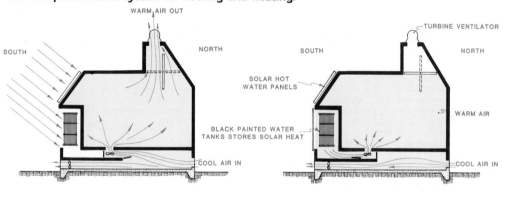

WARM DAYS

COOL NIGHTS

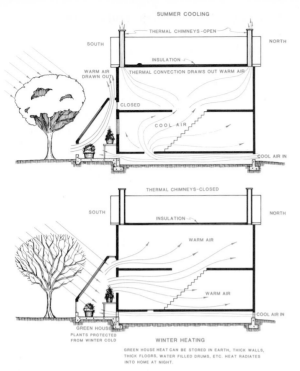

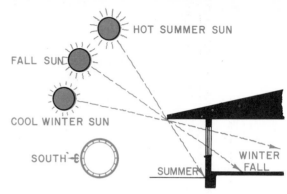

Fig 3-7 Use of overhang to control summer and winter sun heat.

Fig 3-6 Use of greenhouse to store daytime heat and radiate heat at night.

SUMMER   WINTER

Fig 3-8 Use of deciduous trees to control sun and shade.

be designed with a length and angle that will shade the window in summer and allow the sun to enter during the winter (Fig. 3-7). Where no overhang exists, baffles can be used effectively.

VEGETATION

Deciduous trees, which lose their leaves in winter, maximize summer cooling and winter heating by providing shade in the summer and permitting the sun's warmth to penetrate the building in the winter (Fig. 3-8).

Because of their dense structure, evergreens are effective in blocking north or northwest storm winds, thus further insulating a building or redirecting winds during all seasons.

BUILDING MATERIALS

Building materials greatly affect the energy planning of a structure. Some surface materials, such as the adobe used by the Native Americans, effectively collect the sun's

heat during the day and radiate that heat during the night.

Collecting the heat, however, is quite useless if the heat is allowed to escape through the attic, windows, doors, vents, and crannies. Insulating attics, floors, and walls, plugging crannies with insulation or weather stripping, weather-stripping doors, and double-glazing windows prevents such unnecessary heat loss. Figure 3-9 shows common methods of insulation to prevent heat loss. Heat is lost twice as fast through glass as through a wall. Double-glazing creates a buffer zone of dead air space to reduce heat loss through windows (Fig. 3-10).

A bead wall can collect heat and then insulate a home against loss of that heat. The bead wall functions as a window when there is sunshine, collecting heat in the structure. When the weather is cloudy or dark, the space between the panes, filled with small styrofoam balls, keeps the heat inside the house.

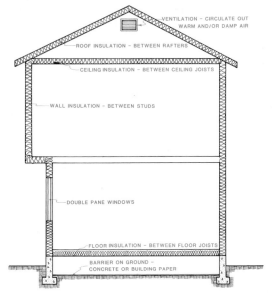

Fig 3-9 Common methods of insulation to prevent heat loss.

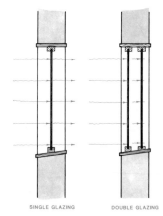

SINGLE GLAZING   DOUBLE GLAZING

Fig 3-10 Use of double-glazing to prevent heat loss.

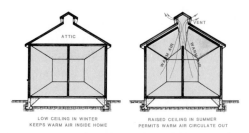

LOW CEILING IN WINTER
KEEPS WARM AIR INSIDE HOME

RAISED CEILING IN SUMMER
PERMITS WARM AIR CIRCULATE OUT

Fig 3-11 Adjustable ceilings keep warm air in winter and expel summer warm air.

Open interiors and higher ceilings encourage ventilation and cooler temperatures. Low ceilings and closed floor plans increase temperatures. However, it is possible to build an adjustable ceiling (Fig. 3-11) to circulate warm air in the summer and hold heat in the winter.

Construction devices and features that contribute to better energy efficiency include: attic exhaust fans and vents; insulation on pipes and ducts, and in walls and floors; energy-saving windows, attics, and foundations; sun controls for windows; weather stripping; caulking—foam and mastics; flue heat-recovery devices; energy-saving thermostats; home fuel-saving devices; heat-absorbing materials; and overhang protection. Figure 3-12 summarizes wall insulation devices and features.

WIND CONTROL

Strong, cold winds can force cold air through wall openings and/or increase the heat loss through exterior walls. Protection can be provided by locating buildings in sheltered valleys or opposite the windward side of hills (Fig. 3-13). Deflecting prevailing winds with baffles, such as attached fences or separate fences (Fig. 3-14), vegetation, or other buildings is also effective. Proper positioning of the structure, as shown in Fig. 3-15, can redirect winds around the structure with a

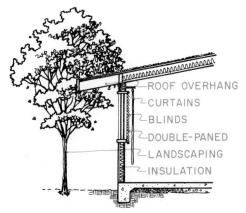

ROOF OVERHANG
CURTAINS
BLINDS
DOUBLE-PANED
LANDSCAPING
INSULATION

Fig 3-12 Common deterrents to heat transfer through walls.

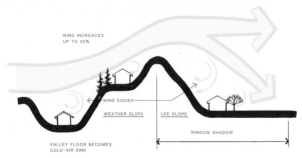

Fig 3-13 Wind control through terrain planning.

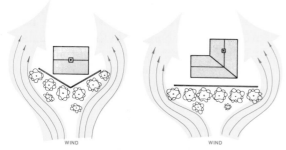

Fig 3-14 Use of detached fences to deflect wind.

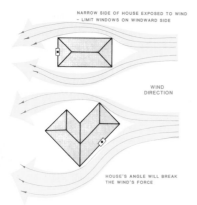

Fig 3-15 Positioning the building to reduce wind effect.

minimum of right-angle contact with large exterior walls. Low roof angles in combination with earth berms can also deflect prevailing wind upward and over the building.

Wind effect can also be reduced by minimizing building openings on the prevailing wind side and by positioning the structure so that winds are not trapped in offsets, courtyards, or patios.

If wind velocities are not excessive (gentle breezes), they may be desirable, especially for summer cooling. Positioning structures near large bodies of water will result in a consistent source of gentle breezes, since cool air will move in to replace rising warm air as shown in Fig. 3-16.

EARTH-SHELTERED HOMES

The earth's characteristic moderate temperature is maximized in the design of earth-sheltered buildings (Fig. 3-17). Regardless of the high or low temperatures, the soil just a short distance below the surface remains at a comfortable and constant temperature.

The thought of living partially underground may seem oppressive. However, with effective planning and proper orientation, adequate natural light can be achieved. The underground location avoids the problems of wind resistance, extreme temperature conditions, and winter storm winds. Underground structures are most effective with solar collectors placed above ground to supply energy.

Construction costs for earth-sheltered homes can be less than those for conventional types of construction if experienced builders are employed. The major care in construction must be waterproofing, which can be accomplished with paint, sealants, membrane blankets, and proper drainage.

Underground structures have the following advantages: low maintenance, low utility costs, safety from fire and wind, security from vandalism, lower insurance rates, long-life construction, smaller heating units, and less air conditioning.

But there are some disadvantages to underground structures, such as: geographical restrictions, humidity-control concerns, view control, the risk of builders not being familiar with needed construction techniques, and difficulty in borrowing money for construction.

ACTIVE SOLAR PLANNING

Planning for active solar systems requires knowledge of both mechanical systems and thermal principles. *Active* solar systems use mechanical devices to drive the components

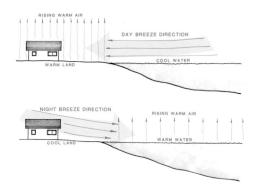

Fig 3-16 Cool air over large bodies of water moves in toward the land to replace rising warm air.

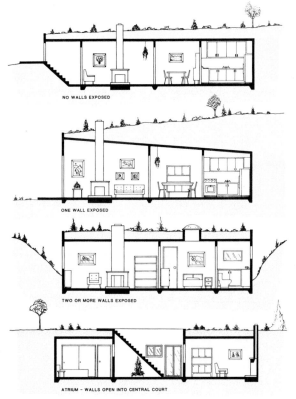

NO WALLS EXPOSED

ONE WALL EXPOSED

TWO OR MORE WALLS EXPOSED

ATRIUM – WALLS OPEN INTO CENTRAL COURT

Fig 3-17 Earth-sheltered homes.

Fig 3-18 Sun's rays should be perpendicular to solar panels.

needed for solar collection, storage, distribution, and control.

Active solar systems must have south-facing solar collectors set at an angle perpendicular to the sun, and roughly equal to the location's latitude. The angle can vary somewhat in either direction without a significant loss of efficiency. But for maximum efficiency, the sun's southern rays should strike the solar panels as perpendicularly as possible, as shown in Fig. 3-18. Step location design increases the amount of area of the sun's exposure. The collectors should have full access to the sun from at least 10 A.M. to 2 P.M. since most solar heat is emitted in the middle hours of the day.

Each solar collector panel acts as a small greenhouse. Sunlight enters through the glass and warms water or air circulating in pipes. The heat is trapped by the water and pumped into storage (Fig. 3-19). Even on a very cold day, with bright or filtered sunlight these panels can be heated to 200°F. Most solar systems have design features that combine both active and passive systems, as shown in Fig. 3-20.

ORIENTATION

The *orientation* of a building is the relationship of the building to its environment. The building site determines much of a structure's orientation (Fig. 3-21). The regional climate of the site must also be considered. Planning to utilize or compensate for air temperature, type and amount of precipitation, humidity, wind speed, wind direction, and available sunlight can mean the difference between fighting the elements or using them to make a structure comfortable.

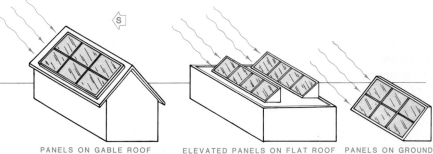

PANELS ON GABLE ROOF   ELEVATED PANELS ON FLAT ROOF   PANELS ON GROUND

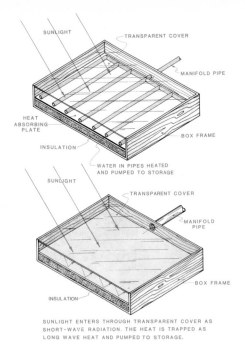

SUNLIGHT ENTERS THROUGH TRANSPARENT COVER AS SHORT-WAVE RADIATION. THE HEAT IS TRAPPED AS LONG WAVE HEAT AND PUMPED TO STORAGE.

Fig 3-19 Sun's heat trapped by water or air in pipes then pumped into storage.

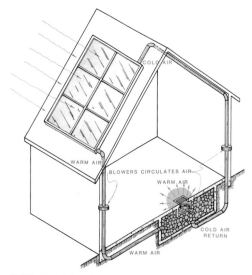

Fig 3-20 Combination active and passive solar systems.

Fig 3-21 Site conditions determine orientation of structures.

In addition to regional climatic factors, the designer must consider the specific physical characteristics of the location. Hills, fences, buildings, and trees affect the wind patterns, temperature, and shading of the site. Slopes, valleys, and large bodies of water also affect air temperature and air movement. Surrounding pavement areas and buildings raise local temperatures because concrete and asphalt collect and store the sun's heat.

Once the characteristics of the site are known, the designer can begin orienting and designing a structure to utilize the site's benefits and minimize its disadvantages. A well-oriented structure is designed to take full advantage of the following existing environmental factors (Fig. 3-22): the sun's heat and light, existing vegetation, desirable and undesirable views, objectionable noise, unpleasant sounds, velocity and direction of prevailing winds or breezes, landform shapes, and relation of site to the neighborhood.

A structure should be oriented to provide maximum control and use of the rays of the sun. In the Northern Hemisphere, the south and west sides of a structure are warmer than the east and north sides. The north side is always cooler because it is consistently shaded. The south side of the building has almost constant exposure to the sun; therefore, it is the warmest side. Ideally, the building should be oriented to absorb as much winter heat as possible and to repel excessive summer heat.

Some states have laws about sun rights. Such laws do not allow any new construction that blocks the sun from another's existing solar panel system or solar exposure (Fig. 3-23).

ROOM LOCATIONS

Rooms should be located so as to absorb the heat of the sun through glass or to be baffled (walled) from the heat of the sun, depending on the functions of the room, season, and time of day. The location of each room should also make maximum use of light from the sun.

Generally, sunshine should be available in the kitchen during early morning and should reach the living areas by afternoon. To accomplish this, kitchen and dining areas

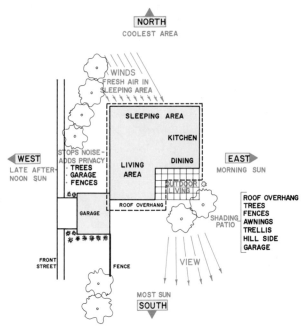

Fig 3-22 Environmental factors affecting orientation.

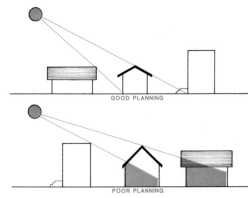

Fig 3-23 Zoning laws prohibit blocking another structure's sun exposure.

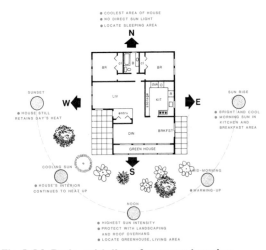

Fig 3-24 Basic guidelines for room location.

should be placed on the south or east side of the house. Living areas placed on the south or west side are desirable because they receive the late-day rays of the sun. The north side is the most appropriate side for placing sleeping areas, since it provides the greatest darkness in the morning and evening and is also the coolest side. North light is also consistent, diffused, and has little glare. Figure 3-24 summarizes the basic guidelines for room placement. The separate entry hall on any side can also cut heat loss considerably because the main house is never in direct contact with the outdoor temperature (Fig. 3-25).

THE LOT

The size of the lot affects the flexibility of choice in locating the house. *Building codes* restrict the placement of houses on lots. Some building codes require that the house be placed no closer than 10 feet (3 meters) to the property line. Others require a distance of 50 feet (15 meters) or more. A line drawn at such a specified distance, within and parallel to the

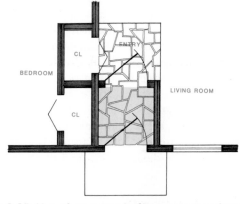

Fig 3-25 Use of an entry baffle to prevent heat loss.

33

property line on all sides, represents the *building line*. The area within the building line is the area in which the building can be located (Fig. 3-26). Building codes also restrict the distance from the house to the street (Fig. 3-27). On small lots, there is often little flexibility in orienting a home. Larger lots offer the greatest opportunity to use a variety of positions for orienting the house.

Lots may be divided into three areas according to function: the private area, the public area, and the service area (Fig. 3-28). The *private area* includes the house and outdoor living space. A southern exposure is usually desirable for the outdoor living area.

The *public area* is the area of the lot that can be viewed by the public. This area is usually located at the front of the house and should provide off-street parking and access to the main entrance.

The *service area* of the lot should be adjacent to the service area of the house. The placement of the house on the lot determines the relative size and relationship of these areas.

INTEGRATION OF STRUCTURE WITH LANDFORM

A site may be hilly and rugged, or it may be smooth and level. Regardless of the shape of the terrain, the house should be designed as an integral part of the site. It should not appear as an appendage to the land but as a functional part of the site.

Frank Lloyd Wright probably did more than any other architect to popularize the integration of the structure and the site. He called this *organic architecture*. One of the most profound examples of organic architecture is *Falling Waters*, at Bear Run, Pennsylvania (Fig. 16). Notice how the bold use of the site, with cantilevered decks extending over a waterfall, integrates the structure with the landform. To achieve complete integration of indoor and outdoor living areas, the house and lot must be designed as part of the same plan.

A house may be compatible with one lot and site and yet appear out of place in another

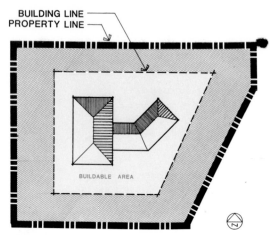

Fig 3-26 Structures cannot be built outside the building line.

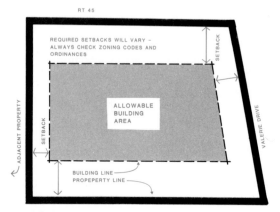

Fig 3-27 Building codes restrict the placement of a structure on a lot.

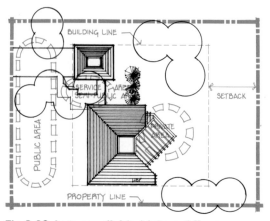

Fig 3-28 Lots are divided into public areas, private areas, and service areas.

location. Split-level homes, for example, are designed for sloping lots where an entrance can be provided on each level. Each level is used functionally to its maximum. The placement of a split-level home on a flat lot does not use the structure or the lot effectively.

PROBLEMS

1 Sketch a 75' × 110' property. Sketch the floor plan shown in Fig. 3-24 to the same scale and place it on the property in the most desirable location.
2 Sketch the lot layout shown in Fig. 3-29.

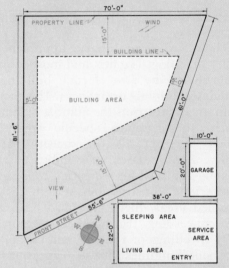

Fig 3-29 Place this house and garage on the lot shown.

Sketch a floor plan of a house and garage on this lot in the most desirable position. Also sketch the position of driveways, walks, and other landscape features. Sketch adjacent lots and show their key landscape features.

3 Using the plan shown in Fig. 3-26, sketch and label passive solar features.
4 Sketch an active solar system for the house shown in Fig. 3-3. Label and sketch the position of collectors, storage facilities, distribution channels, and control devices.

5 List the passive and/or active solar features you would include in a residence of your own design.
6 Define the following terms: solar orientation, site, lot, overhang, wind baffle, building line, public area, private area, service area, organic architecture, earth-sheltered home, active solar planning, passive solar planning, solar collector, hybrid, natural convection, thermal mass, southern exposure, double-glazing, bead wall, deciduous tree.

UNIT 4
DENSITY PLANNING

People have always tended to cluster into communities for protection and to share common facilities (Fig. 4-1). However, the size and population distribution of various communities offer different advantages and disadvantages. Nowadays, the development of transportation has enabled people to live in semi-isolation without sacrificing conveniences or safety (Fig. 4-2). Yet most people work with others and prefer to live in close proximity to others while striving for maximum privacy in their homes. This desire to live close to others, maintain and enjoy com-

35

Fig 4-1 Early Americans practiced density planning.

Celotex Corp.

mon conveniences, and yet have a high degree of privacy makes density planning extremely difficult and complex.

Density, in architectural terms, is the relationship of the number of residential structures and people to a given amount of space. The density of an area is the number of people or families per acre or square mile. For example, a town may have a density of 10 families per acre (hectare) or 50 families per square mile (square kilometer).

AVERAGE DENSITY

The *average density* of an area is the ratio of inhabitants to a geographic area. In large geographic areas such as counties or cities, the density patterns may vary greatly among different parts of the area. For that reason, the average density of a larger geographic area is not as significant as the average density of

Fig 4-2 Semi-isolation is now possible because of good transportation.

Potlatch Corp.

smaller areas. The average density of the area shown in Figure 4-3 at A is the same as the average density of the area shown in Fig. 4-3 at B. However, the *density patterns* of the two areas are significantly different. The number of people living in a large geographic area cannot always be controlled, but planning the most effective density patterns can provide the best possible use of the available land. Density patterns must always be planned for the maximum number of people who may eventually use the area.

PLANNING PHILOSOPHIES

There are several basic approaches to density planning. The first and most common is to restrict the size of each building lot through local *zoning* ordinances. This method automatically restricts the number of families allowed to occupy a specific area. This method also spreads the density pattern equally. Zoning laws also indicate which areas may be used for *industrial*, *commercial*, or *residential* construction. Within residential-zoned areas, there may also be restrictions concerning the number of multiple-family dwellings or the size and capacity of apartment buildings. These restrictions are primarily designed to avoid overcrowding of local school, transportation, and recreational facilities.

The second approach involves clustering residents into fewer structures, such as high-rise apartments or row houses (Fig. 4-4). Transportation, shopping centers, schools, theaters, golf courses, swimming pools, tennis courts, and other support facilities are then planned adjacent to housing units.

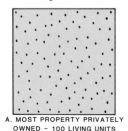 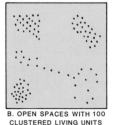

A. MOST PROPERTY PRIVATELY OWNED – 100 LIVING UNITS   B. OPEN SPACES WITH 100 CLUSTERED LIVING UNITS

Fig 4-3 The average density of A is the same as the average density of B.

The third approach is actually a combination of plans. It involves zoning part of the area for single-family residences, specifying other areas for row houses, and reserving some areas for high-rise apartments. The amount of space planned for each type of structure depends on the average density desired.

REDEVELOPMENT

Often, undesirable density patterns develop as a result of population growth or shifts. This occurs especially in older communities. When undesirable density patterns develop, the most appropriate corrective action usually is *redevelopment*. Redevelopment can be either short-term or long-range. *Short-term redevelopment* involves the complete razing of buildings and substituting new housing units, parks, and shopping centers in their place. *Long-range redevelopment* is the changing of the density pattern of an area over a long period of time, according to a predetermined, phased, building plan and time schedule.

NEIGHBORHOOD PLANNING

The smallest residential unit involving density planning is the *neighborhood*. The next largest unit, the *community*, is a combination of neighborhoods. *Regions* are a combination of interrelated communities, neighborhoods, and cities.

A *neighborhood* is a series of homes, whether arranged vertically, as in a high-rise apartment; connected, as in row houses; located on several acres, as in some rural areas; or on small lots, as in most cities. In planning neighborhoods, the designer must consider the following characteristics of people who will live there: their typical age, marital status, numbers of children, lifestyle, and economic level. The following features of the neighborhood must be matched to the needs of these residents: availability of parks and playgrounds, consistency of home design, nearness of shopping areas, and preservation of the natural landscape (Fig. 4-5). The architect must therefore be certain that the needs

Simpson Lumber Co.

Fig 4-4 Row houses or town houses provide individual housing units in dense housing areas.

of the homeowners are consistent with the characteristics of the neighborhood. But keep in mind that a residence isolated from a neighborhood must be planned to include its own facilities for transportation, recreation, security, and maintenance.

RELATIONSHIP OF NEIGHBORHOOD TO COMMUNITY

Not only must a house be related to the site and the site related to the neighborhood, but the neighborhood must be related to the

Fig 4-5 Features of a well-planned neighborhood.

NATURAL BEAUTY   CAREFULLY PLANNED STREETS   CONVENIENT SHOPPING

STREET PLANTING   WELL-DESIGNED HOMES   MINOR PARK AREAS   PLANNED FOOT TRAFFIC

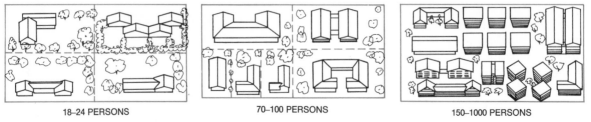

18–24 PERSONS   70–100 PERSONS   150–1000 PERSONS

Fig 4-6 Alternatives in neighborhood planning.

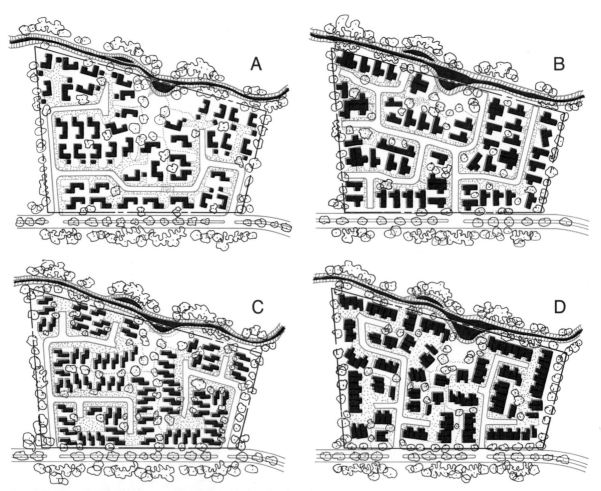

A

B

C

D

Fig 4-7 Use of the same area for different density levels.
A 4 houses per acre   B 6 houses per acre   C 8 houses per acre   D 16 houses per acre

community. Features of the community that must be considered include the availability and quality of: schools, theaters, playgrounds, houses of worship, parking facilities, shopping centers, highway access, automobile service, police and fire protection, and traffic patterns.

CLUSTER PLANNING

Figure 4-6 shows alternatives in planning a 1-acre neighborhood. Figure 4-7 shows how the same area can be planned for 4, 6, 8, and 16 houses per acre. The houses used in each of these plans must be designed carefully to relate to adjacent property.

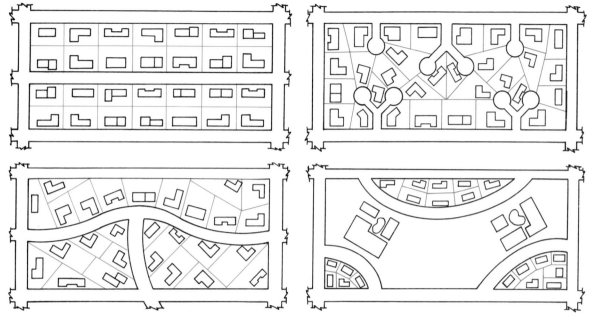

Fig 4-8 Layout of traffic patterns must be changed for different density levels.

Designing areas with heavy population concentrations is more difficult than designing areas that are thinly populated. However, by using the best combination of plans, by effective orientation, and by designing traffic patterns as shown in Fig. 4-8, the designer can achieve maximum expanse.

COMMUNITY PLANNING

Most cities and towns were not planned; they developed without a plan. Thus, most architectural activity in community planning relates to redevelopment (Fig. 4-9) and/or efforts to control and direct future growth according to a long-range master plan. City plans are defined according to the geometric form produced on a map of the area. Each form has its distinct advantages and disadvantages, depending on the terrain, density, and future growth patterns of the area, as forecast by the area's cultural and economic needs (Fig. 4-10).

Architectural plans of the future must make full use of technological advances in construction and transportation. The plans also must take into account the expected rate of growth of cities and towns, and the effect of such growth.

Fig 4-9 Redevelopment of Pittsburgh's Gold Triangle.

Newman Schmidt & John R. Shrader Photo

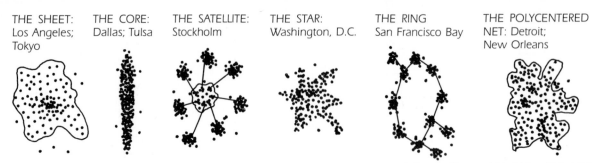

THE SHEET: Los Angeles; Tokyo THE CORE: Dallas; Tulsa THE SATELLITE: Stockholm THE STAR: Washington, D.C. THE RING San Francisco Bay THE POLYCENTERED NET: Detroit; New Orleans

Fig 4-10 Urban landform types.

Architecture of Towns and Cities (McGraw-Hill Book Co.)

PROBLEMS

1 What are the local zoning ordinances in your community? How can they be improved?

2 List the advantages and disadvantages of different types of communities.

3 Redesign a square-mile (square-kilometer) area around your home to provide better density balance.

4 What is the city form of your city, or the city nearest you?

5 Describe the density pattern you prefer for an area in which you wish to locate a residence of your own design.

6 Define these terms: density, average density, density patterns, zoning.

UNIT 5
ECOLOGICAL PLANNING

There are now twice as many people on the earth (4¼ billion) as there were less than a century ago. This population increase, combined with the shift from an *agrarian* (farming) society to an industrial one over the last century, has led to the creation of environmental problems previously unknown. The ever-increasing material needs of our technological economy have created enormous pollution problems that must be solved if humanity is to survive. Designers must plan in a way that eliminates or reduces pollutants.

Fig 5-1 Results of removing trees and foliage from building tracts.

The preservation of natural ecological balances must be a prime requirement in the creation of every design. Architectural creations must be designed to preserve our supply of clean air, pure water, and fertile land. At the same time, sound levels must be controlled

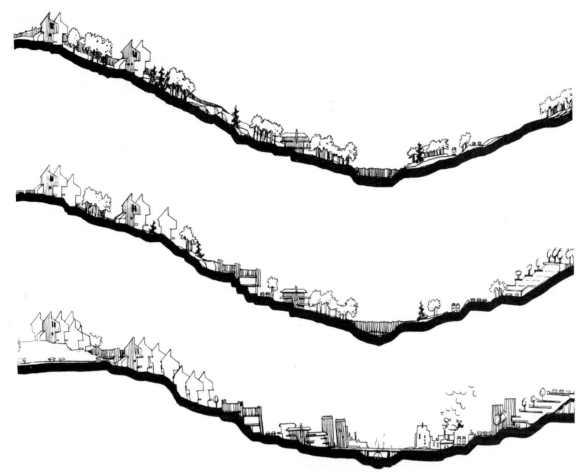

Fig 5-2 Stages and types of site development and destruction.

without sacrificing the aesthetic qualities of good design.

In short, modern buildings must be both functional and aesthetically pleasing, and something more. The contemporary architect or designer must be sure that structures do not interfere with or create problems relating to the environment. That is what is meant by *ecological planning.*

LAND POLLUTION

Land is polluted by the discharge of solid and liquid wastes on land surfaces or by the removal of topsoil, vegetation, or trees from large tracts of land (Fig. 5-1). Figure 5-2 shows several site developments as they relate to their topography. Land pollutants originate from industrial, agricultural, and residential waste and garbage. When pollutants exist in excessive quantities, they create health hazards, contribute to soil erosion, cause unpleasant odors, and overwork sewage-treatment plants.

Architecturally related ways of reducing land pollution include recycling waste material, *compacting* (condensing) waste material to reduce volume, providing for sanitary landfills, and providing for minimum removal of vegetation, especially trees.

Landfill practice involves placing solid waste material in low-lying areas, compacting it into layers (about 10′ thick), and covering it with clean soil. This is called *sanitary landfill.* Thorough landfill projects also include the planting of ground cover—trees and shrubs—on the filled area. Such practice restores the land to its original (or better) condition, both ecologically and aesthetically.

AIR POLLUTION

Air is polluted by the discharge of industrial wastes. Some pollutants are nontoxic and are not suspended in the air for long periods of time. They present an annoyance but usually do not endanger life. Other materials, such as sulfur oxides and organic gases composed of hydrocarbons, nitrous oxides, and carbon monoxide, are extremely dangerous to both animal and plant life. These pollutants are emitted primarily as by-products of manufacturing plants, heating devices, and exhaust systems of vehicles.

To avoid ecological problems, designers must reduce pollution by planning heavy traffic patterns away from heavily populated areas. Designers must also plan or specify electronic air filters or other solid-waste removal systems to eliminate particles before they become airborne. Designs must include features that promote energy conservation. Conserving energy not only diminishes pollution by decreasing fuel consumption but also helps reduce operating costs of buildings.

WATER POLLUTION

Water is polluted by sewage, industrial chemicals, and agricultural wastes dumped into bodies of water. These wastes include pathogens (such as disease-causing bacteria), unstable organic solids, mineral compounds, plant nutrients, and agricultural insecticides. Water pollution results in the destruction of marine life. It presents very serious potential health hazards to animal and human life.

Effective architectural planning can help reduce water pollution through the design of sewage-treatment systems in conjunction with each new construction. Proper density planning, to levels low enough that water sources are not overused for fresh water or

waste disposal, also helps reduce water pollution. Plans must also provide for the removal of industrial wastes without sending them in raw form into waterways. Plans must also eliminate excessive runoff of topsoil into rivers and streams.

VISUAL POLLUTION

Many air, water, and land pollutants, such as unsanitary garbage dumps and smog-producing agents, are not only unhealthy but also visually undesirable. Other sources of pollution, such as junkyards, exposed utility lines, public litter, barren land, and large billboards, may not create health or safety hazards. They are aesthetically objectionable, however, and must be avoided in the architectural design process. The best safeguards against visual pollution consist of following closely the basic principles of design, not only for structures but for the entire landscape, and enacting and enforcing stringent zoning regulations.

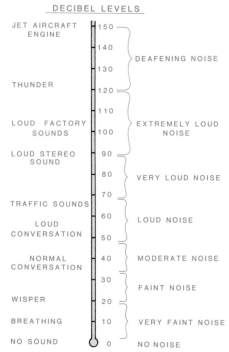

Fig 5-3 Decibel levels of common sounds.

SOUND POLLUTION

Sound levels are measured in decibels, as shown in Figure 5-3. Exposure to excessive decibel levels, over 80, or to even moderate levels, over 60, for long periods creates stress, and can result in neurosis, irritability, and hearing loss in many people. Excessive noise can also create hazardous environments by eliminating people's ability to identify and discriminate between sounds, especially those that warn of danger.

The architect has a number of ways to reduce noise to acceptable levels. Among them are effective floor planning, orientation, landscaping to provide ample noise-buffer space, using acoustical wall panels, making maximum use of buffer foliage, and taking care to control patterns of vehicular traffic. Insulation also helps reduce excessive noise from the outside. But rooms requiring quiet, such as bedrooms, should be located on the side away from the major source of noise. Fabrics such as carpets, drapes, and upholstery also reduce noise by absorbing sound within a room.

PROBLEMS

1 Find buildings in your area that are designed to control pollution.
2 Find buildings in your area that emit pollutants into the air or water or on the land. List ways of correcting these conditions.
3 List diseases caused by air, water, and land pollution.
4 List the ecological factors to be considered in planning a residence of your own design.
5 Define these terms: air pollution, solar energy, electronic filter, water pollution, sanitary landfill, erosion, industrial waste.

PART TWO

AREA PLANNING

Before a set of architectural plans can be prepared, the building must be thought out and a rough design decided upon. In creating the design, the designer must progress logically, step by step through the design process. The first step in this process is to divide plans into various areas according to their specific function. The designer must become familiar with the activities that will occur in each area. A school would be divided into such areas as administrative, classroom, service, and physical-activity areas. In the same way, a house is divided into three major areas for planning purposes: the living area, the service area, and the sleeping area.

Areas constitute the main divisions of a structure. Areas are broken into subdivisions called rooms. These subdivisions are related to the basic function of the area. Part One provides the principles, practices, information, and specific steps necessary to arrange rooms and areas to create the basic elements of an architectural plan.

LIVING AREA

Your first impression of a home is probably the image you retain of the living area. In fact, this is the only area of the home that most strangers observe. The living area is just what the name states, the area where most of the living occurs. It is here the family entertains, relaxes, dines, listens to music, watches television, enjoys hobbies, and participates in other recreational activities.

The total living area is divided into smaller areas (rooms) which are designed to perform specific living functions. The subdivisions of most living areas may include the living room, dining room, recreation or game room, family room, patio, entrance foyer, den or study, and guest lavatories. Other specialized rooms, such as the library, music room, or sewing room, are often included as part of the living area of large houses that have the space to devote to such specialized functions. In smaller homes, many of the standard rooms combine two or more rooms. For example, the living room and dining room are often combined. In extremely small homes, the living room constitutes the entire living area and provides all the facilities normally assigned to other rooms in the living area. Although the subdivisions of the living area are called rooms, they are not always separated by a partition or a wall. Nevertheless, they perform the function of a room, whether there is a complete separation, a partial separation, or no separation.

When rooms are completely separated by partitions and doors, the plan is known as a closed plan. When partitions do not divide the rooms of an area, the arrangement is called an open plan.

In most two-story dwellings, the living area is normally located on the first floor. However, in split-level homes or one-story homes with functional basements, part of the living area may be located on the lower level.

UNIT 6
LIVING ROOMS

The *living room* is the center of the living area in most homes. In small homes the living room may represent the entire living area. Hence, the function, location, decor, size, and shape of the living room are extremely important and affect the design, functioning, and appearance of the other living-area rooms.

FUNCTION

The living room is designed to perform many functions. The exact function depends on the living habits of the occupants. In the home, the living room is often the entertainment center, the recreation center, the library, the music room, the TV center, the reception room, the social room, the study, and occasionally the dining center. In small dwellings, the living room often becomes a guest bedroom. If the living room is to perform all or some of these functions, then it should be designed accordingly. The shape, size, location, decor, and facilities of the room should

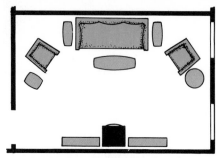

Fig 6-1 A living room specifically planned for television viewing.

be planned to provide for each activity. For example, if the living room is to be used for television viewing, it will be planned differently from a living room without television. Figure 6-1 shows some of the considerations in planning a room for TV viewing.

Many of the facilities normally associated with the living room can be eliminated if a separate, special-purpose room exists for that activity. For example, if television viewing is restricted to a recreation room, then planning for TV in the living room can be eliminated. If a den or study is provided for reading and for storing books, facilities for the use of large numbers of books in the living room can be

eliminated. Regardless of the exact activities anticipated, the living room should always be planned as a functional, integral part of the home. The living room is planned for the comfort and convenience of the family and guests.

LOCATION

The living room should be centrally located. It should be adjacent to the outside entrance, but the entrance should not lead directly into the living room. In smaller residences, the entrance may open into the living room, but whenever possible this arrangement is to be avoided. The living room should not be a traffic access to the sleeping and service area of the house. Since the living room and dining room function together, the living room should be adjacent to the dining room. Figure 6-2 shows the central location of a living room and its proximity to other rooms of the living area.

OPEN PLAN

In an open-plan living area, the living room, dining room, and entrance may be part of one open area, as shown in Fig. 6-3. The liv-

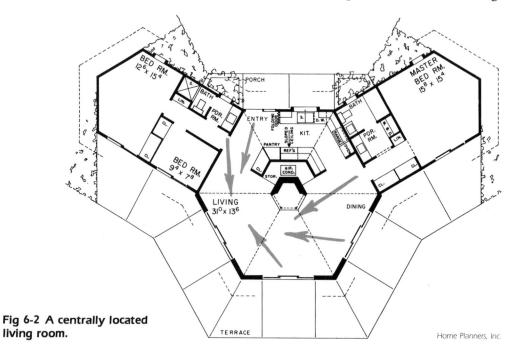

Fig 6-2 A centrally located living room.

Home Planners, Inc.

Fig 6-3 An open-plan
living room.

Bethlehem Steel Corp.

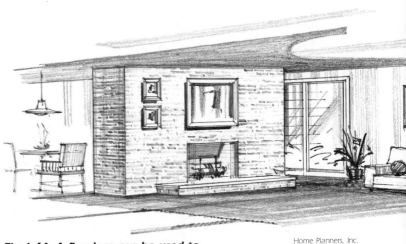

Fig 6-4A A fireplace can be used to
separate the living room from the
dining room without isolation.

Home Planners, Inc.

Fig 6-4B Separation by fireplace and atrium.

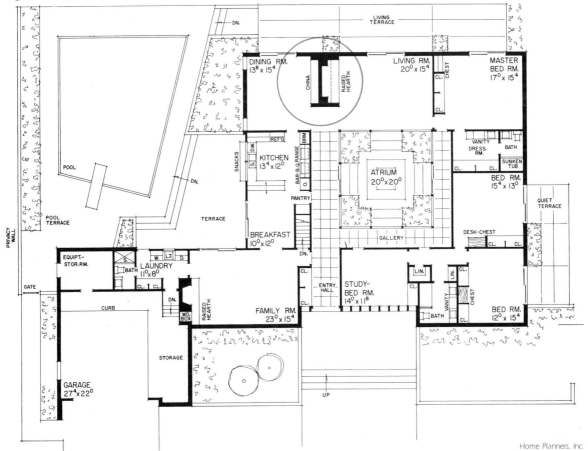

Home Planners, Inc.

Fig 6-5 A living room separated from adjacent rooms by level.

Potlatch Corp.

Separation may also be achieved by the use of area rugs or furniture placement. Of course, these features do not separate the rooms visually, but they do effect a functional separation.

When an open plan is desired and, yet, the designer wants to provide some means of closing off the room completely, sliding doors or folding doors can be used.

CLOSED PLAN

In a closed plan, the living room would be completely closed from the other rooms by means of walls. Access would be through doors, arches, or relatively small openings in partitions (Fig. 6-6).

DECOR

There is no one way to design and decorate a room. The decor depends primarily on the tastes, habits, and personalities of the people who will use the room. If the residents' tastes are modern, the wall, ceiling, and floor treatments should be consistent with the clean, functional lines of modern architecture and modern furniture, as shown in Fig. 6-7. If the residents prefer colonial or period-style

ing room may be separated from other rooms by means of a divider without doors, such as a storage wall. In Fig. 6-4A and B, the living room is separated from the dining room by a fireplace. In Fig. 6-4B, the living room is separated from the rest of the house by an atrium. Often a separation is accomplished by placing the living room on a different level (Fig. 6-5).

Fig 6-6 A closed-plan living room.

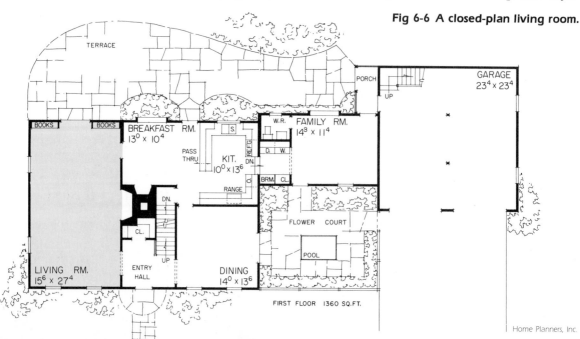

Home Planners, Inc.

Fig 6-7 A contemporary-style living room.

architecture, then this theme should be reflected in the decor of the room.

The living room should appear inviting, comfortable, and spacious. This appearance can be accomplished by an effective use of color and lighting techniques and by the tasteful selection of wall, ceiling, and floor-covering materials. The selection and placement of functional, well-designed furniture also helps the appearance. All these techniques have been combined to create a most desirable total impression in the living room shown in Fig. 6-8. Decorating a room is much like selecting clothing. The color, style, and materials should be selected to minimize faults and to emphasize good points. Figure 6-9 shows that the use of mirrors and floor-to-ceiling drapes along with proper furniture placement can create a spacious effect in a relatively small room.

WALLS

The design and placement of doors, windows, and chimneys along the walls of the living room can change the entire appearance of the room. The kind of wall-covering material used can also affect the appearance. Wall coverings are selected from a variety of materials, including plaster, gypsum wallboard, wood paneling, brick, stone, and glass. Sometimes, furniture is built into the walls. Fireplaces, windows, doors, or openings to other areas should be designed as integral parts of the room. They should not appear as afterthoughts. Notice the difference between the two designs in Fig. 6-10A and B. Figure 6-10A shows a wall, fireplace, and opening designed as a functional part of the room. Figure 6-10B shows the same room with door openings, fireplaces, and wall treatments placed on the wall without reference to other parts of the room.

Fig 6-8 The living room should appear inviting, comfortable, and spacious.

Fig 6-9 Mirrors can help create a spacious effect. PPG Industries, Inc.

Fig 6-12 Translucent glass admits light while it subdues images. PPG Industries, Inc.

Fig 6-10A A functionally designed open-plan living-room wall.

Fig 6-10B A closed-plan living room.

ORIENTATION

The living room should be oriented to take full advantage of the position of the sun and the most attractive view. Since the living room is used primarily in the afternoon and evening, it should be located to take advantage of the afternoon sun.

WINDOWS

When a window is placed in a living-room wall, it should become an integral part of that wall. The view from the window or windows becomes part of the lving-room decor, especially when landscape features are near and are readily observable, as in Fig. 6-11. When planning windows, consider also the various seasonal changes in landscape features.

Although the primary function of a window is twofold, to admit light and to provide a pleasant view of the landscape, there are many conditions under which only the admission of light is desirable. If the view from the

Fig 6-11 The outdoors can become part of the living-room decor. Scholz Homes

window is unpleasant or is restricted by other buildings, translucent glass, which primarily admits light, as shown in Fig. 6-12, can be incorporated into the plan.

Translucent drapes can also be used to admit light while providing a semivisual separation. Window placement in apartment buildings cannot always be altered. However, the location and orientation of the living room must be planned to provide the most desirable furniture arrangement in designing apartment buildings.

FIREPLACE

The primary function of a fireplace is to provide heat, but it is also a permanent decorative feature. The fireplace and accompanying masonry should maintain a clean, simple line consistent with the decor of the room and of the wall where they are placed. In Fig. 6-13, the fireplace and chimney masonry make up the entire wall. Consequently, the fireplace becomes the focal point of the room. The corner fireplace shown in Fig. 6-14 is used as a transition between the living room and the dining room. The fireplace shown in Fig. 6-15 is used as the major separation between the living room and the dining room.

The external appearance of the house must be considered in locating the fireplace, because the location of the fireplace in the room determines the position of the chimney on the roof. This does not mean that the outside of the house should be designed first. But it does mean that the outside appearance must be considered in designing and locating features of the house that appear inside and outside. Examples to be considered are fireplaces, doors, and windows.

FLOORS

The living-room floor should reinforce and blend with the color scheme, textures, and overall style of the living room. Exposed hardwood flooring, room-size carpeting, wall-to-wall carpeting, throw rugs, and sometimes polished flagstone are appropriate for living-room use.

Potlatch Corp.

Fig 6-13 This fireplace design is an integral part of the room.

Home Planners, Inc.

Fig 6-14 A corner fireplace.

Home Planners, Inc.

Fig 6-15 A fireplace used as a divider between the living room and the dining room.

Fig 6-16 An open-beam ceiling.

CEILINGS

Most conventional ceilings are flat surfaces covered with plaster or gypsum board. New building materials, such as laminated beams and arches, and new construction methods now enable architects to design ceilings that conserve building materials and utilize previously wasted space. An open-beam ceiling is shown in Fig. 6-16. Figure 6-17A

Fig 6-17A Cathedral ceilings help make the room look more spacious.

Fig 6-17B A conventional ceiling.

Fig 6-18 Built-in bookshelves conserve floor space.

shows two methods of producing cathedral ceilings in either double-pitch or single-pitch style. The cathedral ceiling makes a room appear more spacious, through the addition of more area. Compare the space provided by the cathedral ceilings shown in Fig. 6-17 at A with the space available in the conventional ceiling shown in Fig. 6-17 at B.

LIGHTING

Living-room lighting is divided into two types, general lighting and local lighting. *General lighting* is designed to illuminate the entire room through the use of ceiling fixtures, wall spots, or cove lighting. *Local lighting* is provided for a specific purpose, such as reading, drawing, or sewing. Local lighting can be supplied by table lamps, wall lamps, pole lamps, or floor lamps.

FURNITURE

Furniture for the living room may or may not reflect the motif and architectural style of the home. Most designers, when working directly with a client, attempt to match the exterior style of the house to the interior furniture style preference of the client. If the client's preference is modern, the lines of the house should be modern. If the preference is colonial, the exterior should have a colonial look.

A special effort should be made to have built-in furniture maintain lines consistent with the remaining wall treatment. Notice

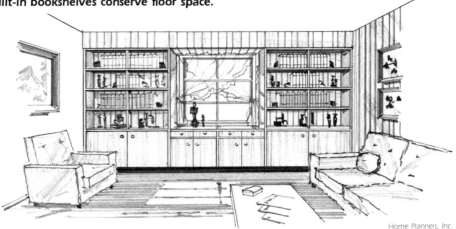

how the built-in book shelves in Fig. 6-18 eliminate the need for other pieces of furniture in that end of the room. The built-in bookshelves and cabinets blends functionally into the total decor of the room. The furniture for the living room is chosen to fit the living needs of the residents. The size, shape, and layout of the room should be designed to accommodate the furniture. Figure 6-19 shows a living room of adequate size which functions well with the necessary furniture. Figure 6-20 shows a room with a size and shape not adequate for the furniture. This latter design is a result of establishing the size and shape of the room without considering the size and number of pieces of furniture to be used.

SIZE AND SHAPE

One of the most difficult aspects of planning the size and shape of a living room, or any other room, is to provide sufficient wall space for the effective placement of furniture. Continuous wall space is needed for the placement of many articles of furniture, especially musical equipment, bookcases, chairs, and couches. The placement of fireplaces, doors,

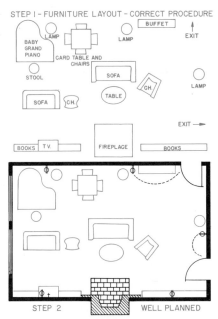

Fig 6-19 A living room planned to accommodate the necessary furniture.

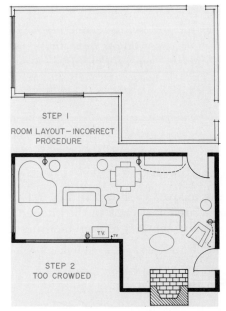

Fig 6-20 A living room of inadequate size for the furniture needed.

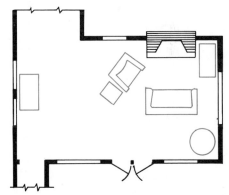

Fig 6-21A A living room with inadequate wall space.

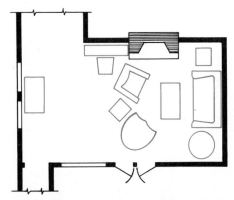

Fig 6-21B A living room with ample wall space for furniture placement.

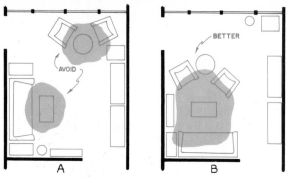

Fig 6-22 Avoid breaking the room into several isolated conversation areas.

furniture placement.

Rectangular rooms are generally easier to plan and to place furniture in than are square rooms. However, the designer must be careful not to establish a proportion that will break the living room into several conversational areas, as shown in Fig. 6-22 at A. This design has actually resulted in the merging of two separate rooms into one. The arrangement shown in Fig. 6-22 at B is much more desirable, since it integrates the total activities of the room without separation.

Living rooms vary greatly in size. A room 12 by 18 feet (12' × 18') (3.7 × 5.5 meters) would be considered a small or minimum-sized living room. A living room of average size would be approximately 16' × 20' (4.9 × 6.1 m), and a very large or optimum-sized living room would be 20' × 26' (6.1 × 7.9 m) or more.

or openings to other rooms should be planned to conserve as much wall space as possible for furniture placement. Figure 6-21A shows a living room with practically no wall space for furniture placement. Figure 6-21B shows the same room with the wall space adjusted so that it provides the space that is necessary for

PROBLEMS

1 Sketch an open-plan living room. Indicate the position of windows, fireplace, foyer, entrance, and dining room.
2 Sketch a closed-plan living room. Show the position of adjacent rooms.
3 Sketch one wall of the living room you designed for Problem 2. Use Fig. 6-10B as a guide.

4 List the furniture you would include in the living room of the house of your design. Cut out samples of this furniture from catalogs or newspapers.
5 Determine the best size for a living room to accommodate these pieces of furniture: a couch, a television set, a stereo, a baby grand piano, a bookcase, a chaise longue, a coffee table, a fireplace, two chairs.
6 Define the following terms: *closed plan, open plan, decor, living area, living room, local lighting, general lighting.*

UNIT 7
DINING ROOMS

The dining facilities designed for a residence depend greatly on the dining habits of the occupants. The dining room may be large and formal, or the dining area may consist of

a dining alcove, as shown in Fig. 7-1. It may also be a breakfast nook in the kitchen. Large homes may contain dining facilities in all these areas.

FUNCTION

The function of a dining area is to provide a place for the family to gather for breakfast,

Fig. 7-1 A dining alcove in the living area.
California Redwood Assoc.

Fig. 7-2 An informal dining area.
Scholz Homes

lunch, or dinner in both casual and formal situations. When possible, a separate dining area potentially capable of seating from eight to twelve persons for dinner should be provided in addition to breakfast or dinette facilities. Contrast the formal dining area shown in Fig. 7-1 with the informal dining facilities shown in the dining area in Fig. 7-2.

LOCATION

Dining facilities may be located in many different areas, depending on the capacity needed and the type of plan. In the closed plan, a separate dining room is usually provided. In an open plan, many different dining locations are possible (Fig. 7-3). Open-area dining facilities are provided in the kitchen shown in Fig. 7-4.

RELATION TO KITCHEN

Regardless of the exact position of the dining area, it must be placed adjacent to the kitchen. The ideal dining location is one that requires few steps from the kitchen to the dining table. However, the preparation of food and other kitchen activities should be baffled from direct view from the dining area.

RELATION TO LIVING ROOM

If dining facilities are not located in the living room, they should be located next to it. Family and guests normally enter the dining room from the living room and use both rooms jointly.

The nearness of the dining room to the kitchen, and to the living room, requires that it be placed between the kitchen and the living area. The dining room in the closed plan shown in Fig. 7-5 is located in this manner.

SEPARATION

Complete separation should be possible between the kitchen and the dining room. The

Fig. 7-3 Plans showing the location of dining facilities in many different areas.

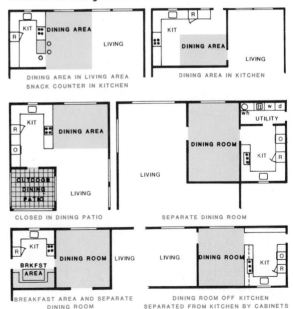

DINING AREA IN LIVING AREA
SNACK COUNTER IN KITCHEN

DINING AREA IN KITCHEN

CLOSED IN DINING PATIO

SEPARATE DINING ROOM

BREAKFAST AREA AND SEPARATE
DINING ROOM

DINING ROOM OFF KITCHEN
SEPARATED FROM KITCHEN BY CABINETS

Fig 7-4 A dining area located in the kitchen.

Fig 7-5 The dining room is located between the living room and the kitchen.

Home Planners, Inc.

64'-0"

GARAGE
15⁴ x 23⁴

BED RM
12⁴ x 15⁴

BATH

FAMILY RM.
15⁰ x 11⁴

KITCHEN
12⁰ x 11⁴

CL.

CL.

LIN. W.R.

CL.

CHINA

DINING RM.
12⁶ x 11⁸

ENTRY CL.

UP

POOL

LIVING RM.
27⁴ x 15⁰

area between the living room and the dining room may be entirely open, partially baffled, or completely closed off. Sometimes, the separation of the dining room and the living room is accomplished by different floor levels or by dividing the rooms with common half walls as shown in Fig. 7-6. Another method of separating the dining area in an open plan is through the use of partial partitions, as shown in Fig. 7-7. Compare these semi-isolated arrangements with the completely open dining areas shown in Figs. 7-8 and 7-9.

OUTSIDE DINING FACILITIES

There is often a need for dining facilities on or adjacent to the patio, as shown in Fig.

Fig 7-6 Separation with half walls.

Home Planners, Inc.

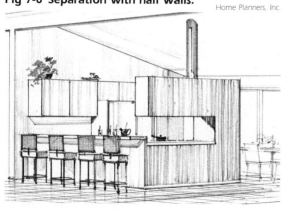

Fig 7-7 A partial wall without a door makes this an open plan.

Home Planners, Inc.

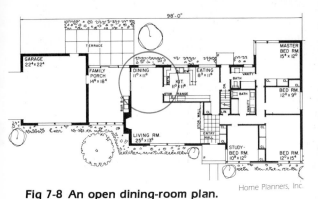

Fig 7-8 An open dining-room plan.

Home Planners, Inc.

Fig 7-9 An open dining area.

Armstrong Cork Company

7-10. The porch or patio should be near the kitchen and directly accessible to it. Locating the patio or dining porch directly outside the dining room or kitchen wall provides maximum use of the facilities. This minimizes the inconvenience of using outside dining facilities (Fig. 7-11).

DECOR

The decor of the dining room should blend with the rest of the house. Floor, wall, and ceiling treatment should be the same in the dining area as in the living area.

If a dining porch or a dining patio is used, its decor must also be considered part of the dining-room decor. This is because the outside dining area is viewed from the inside. Notice how the view of the courtyard in Fig. 7-12 is brought to the inside by the use of window walls directly next to the dining area.

DIVIDERS

If semi-isolation is desired, partial divider walls can be used effectively. These dividers may be planter walls, glass walls, half walls of brick or stone, paneled walls, fireplaces, or grillwork. Figure 7-13 shows the effective use of an atrium to provide semi-isolation for the dining area.

LIGHTING

Controlled lighting can greatly enhance the decor of the dining room. General illumination that can be subdued or intensified can

Fig 7-10 Dining facilities located adjacent to the patio.

Julius Shulman

Fig 7-11 Dining facilities may be moved to a porch in fair weather.

Western Wood Products Association

Fig 7-12 Consider the view when locating the dining area.

American St. Gobain Corp.

Fig 7-14 The use of local lighting over the dining table.

Home Planners, Inc.

provide the right atmosphere for almost any occasion. Lighting is controlled by a rheostat which is commonly known as a *dimmer switch*.

In addition to general illumination, local lighting should be provided for the table either by a direct ceiling spotlight or by a hanging lamp (Fig. 7-14). A hanging lamp can be adjusted down for local dining lighting and up for general illumination when the dining facilities are not in use.

SIZE AND SHAPE

The size and shape of the dining area are determined by the size of the family, the size

Fig 7-13 Use of atrium for separation. Home Planners, Inc.

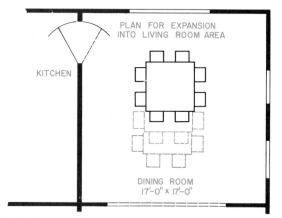

Fig 7-15 A dining area planned for maximum expansion.

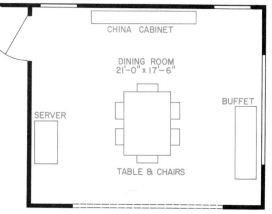

Fig 7-16 Typical furniture placement in a dining room.

and amount of furniture, and the clearances and traffic areas between pieces of furniture.

MAXIMUM PLANNING

The dining area should be planned for the largest group that will dine in it regularly. There is little advantage in having a dining-room table that expands, if the room is not large enough to accommodate the expansion. One advantage of the open plan is that the dining facilities can be expanded in an unlimited manner into the living area, as shown in Fig. 7-15. Thus, the living area temporarily becomes part of the dining area.

FURNITURE

The dining room should be planned to accommodate the furniture. Dining-room furniture may include an expandable table, side chairs, armchairs, buffet, server or serving cart, china closet, and serving bar. In most situations, a rectangular dining room will accommodate the furniture better than a square room. Figure 7-16 shows a typical furniture placement for a dining room.

CLEARANCE

Regardless of the furniture arrangement, a minimum space of 2' (610 millimeters) should be allowed between the chair and the wall or furniture when the chair is pulled to the out position. This allowance will permit serving traffic behind chairs and will permit entrance to and exit from the table without difficulty. A distance of 27 inches (27")

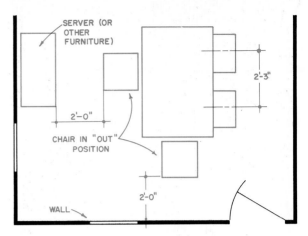

Fig 7-17 Dining-room clearances.

(690 mm) per person should be allowed at the table. This spacing is accomplished by allowing 27" (690 mm) from the center line of one chair to the center line of another, as shown in Fig. 7-17.

RECOMMENDED SIZES

A dining room that would accommodate the minimum amount of furniture—a table, four chairs, and a buffet—would be approximately 10' × 12' (3.0 × 3.7 m). A minimum-sized dining room that would accommodate a dining table, six or eight persons, a buffet, a china closet, and a server would be approximately 12' × 15' (3.7 × 4.6 m). A more nearly optimum-sized dining room would be 14' × 18' (4.3 × 5.5 m) or larger. A room of this size would accommodate a gathering of practically any size.

PROBLEMS

1. Sketch a dining room to include the following furniture: dining table to accommodate six, buffet, china closet. Indicate the relationship to the living room, and provide access to a patio.
2. Sketch a plan for an informal dining area directly adjacent to the kitchen.
3. Sketch an open-plan dining area. Show the relationship of this area to the living room.
4. Sketch a separate dining room. Indicate the position of adjacent rooms.
5. Add a dining porch to the plan shown in Fig. 7-5.
6. Sketch a plan of the dining area shown in Fig. 7-9. Convert this to a closed plan.
7. Redesign the dining area of your own home.

Fig 7-19 Draw a floor plan of this dining area.

Fig 7-18 Draw a floor plan of this dining room.

Armstrong Cork Co.

8 Indicate the position of local lighting and general lighting on one of the plans you have designed.

9 Sketch a dining room to scale, showing the position of all furniture you would like to include in the dining room of a house of your own design.

10 Draw a floor plan of the dining room shown in Fig. 7-18. Show lighting and placement of furniture.

11 Draw a floor plan of the dining area shown in Fig. 7-19.

12 Define the following terms: *buffet, china closet, server, rheostat, dining porch, dining patio, formal dining, casual dining.*

UNIT 8
FAMILY ROOMS

Several years ago the term *family room* did not exist in the architectural vocabulary. The trend toward more informal living because of more leisure time has influenced the popularity of the family room. Today, the majority of homes are designed to include a family room.

FUNCTION

The purpose of the family room is to provide facilities for family-centered activities. It is designed for the entire family, children and adults alike.

Only in extremely large residences is there sufficient space for a separate sewing room, children's playroom, hobby room, or music room. The modern family room often performs the functions of all those rooms. The children's area in the family room in Fig. 8-1 provides facilities for a variety of children's activities. The area of the family room in Fig. 8-2 is designed primarily for watching television and pursuing chess as a hobby.

LOCATION

Activities in the family room often result in the accumulation of hobby materials and clutter. Thus, the family room is often located in an area accessible from, but not visible from, the rest of the living area.

It is quite common to locate the family room adjacent to the kitchen, as shown in Fig. 8-3. This location revives the idea of the old country kitchen in which most family activities were centered.

When the family room is located adjacent to the living room or dining room, it becomes an extension of those rooms for social affairs. In this location, the family room is often separated from the other rooms by folding doors, screens, or sliding doors. The family room shown in Fig. 8-4 is located next to the kitchen and yet is accessible from the living room when the folding door is open.

Another popular location for the family room is between the service area and the living area. The family room shown in Fig. 8-5 is located between the garage, the kitchen, and the entrance. This location is especially appropriate when some service functions, such as home-workshop facilities, are assigned to the family room.

DECOR

The family room is also known as the *activities room* or *multiactivities room*. Decoration of this room should provide a vibrant atmosphere. Ease of maintenance should be one of the chief considerations in decorating the family room.

Fig 8-1 A children's area in the family room.

Lisanti, Inc.

Fig 8-2 A family room designed for television viewing and chess.

Armstrong Cork Company

Fig 8-3 A family room located adjacent to the kitchen.

Home Planners, Inc.

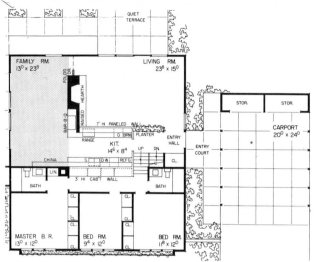

Fig 8-4 A family room accessible from the kitchen and living room.

Home Planners, Inc.

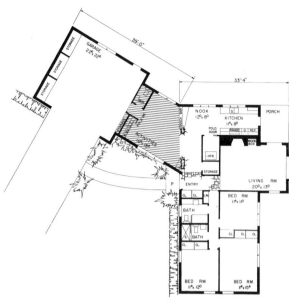

Fig 8-5 A family room located near the service area.

Home Planners, Inc.

FURNITURE

Family-room furniture should be informal and suited to all members of the family. The use of plastics, leather, and wood provides great flexibility in color and style and promotes easy maintenance.

FLOORS

Floors should be resilient—able to keep original shape or condition despite hard use. Linoleum or tile made of asphalt, rubber, or vinyl will best resist the abuse normally given a family-room floor. If rugs are used, they should be the kind that will stand up under

rough treatment. They should also be washable.

WALLS

Soft, easily damaged materials such as wallpaper and plaster should be avoided for the family room. Materials such as tile and paneling are most functional. Chalkboards, bulletin boards, built-in cupboards, and toy-storage cabinets should be used when appropriate. Work areas that fold into the wall when not in use conserve space and may per-

Fig 8-6 Plan for adequate storage in the family room.

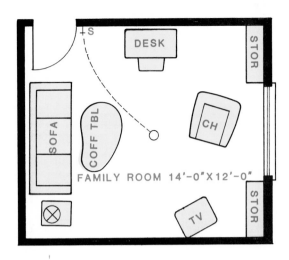

Fig 8-7 A minimum-sized family room.

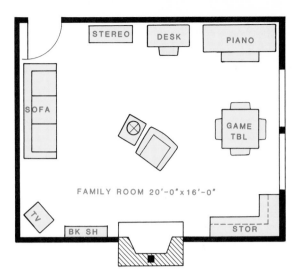

Fig 8-8 An optimum-sized family room.

form a dual function if the cover wall can also be used as a chalkboard or a bulletin board.

STORAGE

Since a variety of hobby and game materials will be used in the family room, sufficient space must be provided for the storage of these materials. Figure 8-6 shows the use of built-in storage facilities, including cabinets, closets, and drawer storage.

CEILINGS

Acoustical ceilings are recommended to keep the noise of the various activities from spreading to other parts of the house. This feature is especially important if the family room is located on a lower level.

SIZE AND SHAPE

The size and shape of the family room depends directly on the equipment needed for the activities the family will pursue in this room. The room may vary from a minimum-sized room, as shown in Fig. 8-7, to the more optimum-sized family room shown in Fig. 8-8. This room contains practically all the equipment almost any family would need in the family room. Included are a piano, a stereo set, a game table, a television set, a studio couch, tables and chairs, bookshelves, a desk, and storage cabinets. Most family-room requirements lie somewhere between the two extremes shown.

PROBLEMS

1 Sketch a family room you would like to include in a home of your own design. Include the location of all furniture and facilities.
2 Determine the size and shape of a family room to accommodate the following activities: television viewing, sewing, knitting, model building, slide viewing, dancing, eating.
3 Design a family room primarily for children's activities.
4 Design a family room that doubles as a guest bedroom.
5 Define the following terms: *sewing room, children's playroom, hobby room, music room, family room, multiactivities, linoleum, asphalt tile, rubber tile, vinyl tile, acoustical ceiling.*

UNIT 9
RECREATION ROOMS

The *recreation room* (game room, playroom) is exactly what the name states. It is a room for play and recreation. It includes facilities for participation in recreational activities.

FUNCTION

The design of the recreation room depends on the number and arrangement of the facilities needed for the various pursuits. Activities for which many recreation rooms are designed include billiards, chess, checkers, table tennis, darts, television watching, eating, and dancing. Designing the recreation room around a music center, as shown in Fig. 9-1, is very practical.

The function of the recreation room often overlaps that of the family room. Overlapping occurs when a multipurpose room is designed to provide for recreational activities such as table tennis and billiards and also includes facilities for more sedentary family activities such as sewing, knitting, model building, and other hobbies.

LOCATION

The recreation room is frequently located in the basement in order to use space that would otherwise be wasted. Basement recreation rooms often provide more space for the use of large equipment, such as table-tennis tables, billiard tables, and shuffleboard. A

Fig 9-1 A recreation room designed around a music center. American Plywood Assoc.

basement recreation room fireplace can be located directly beneath the living-room fireplace on the upper level. The most important reason for locating recreation rooms in the basement of older homes, however, is that the basement is the only available space which can be converted into a recreation room. An example of the conversion of the basement of an older home into a well-planned recreation room is shown in Figs. 9-2A and B.

When the recreation room is located on the ground level, its function can be expanded to the patio or terrace, as shown in Fig. 9-3. Regardless of the level, the recreation room should be located away from the quiet areas of the house.

Fig 9-2A A typical basement before conversion.

Fig 9-2B A basement converted to a recreation room.

Often, the recreation room can actually be separated from the main part of the house. This separation is possible when the recreation room is included as part of the garage or carport design. When a separate location such as this is selected, some sheltered access should be provided from the house to the recreation area.

DECOR

Designers take more liberties in decorating the recreation room than with any other room. They do so primarily because the active, informal atmosphere that characterizes the recreation room lends itself readily to unconventional furniture, fixtures, and color schemes. Bright, warm colors can reflect a party mood. Furnishings and accessories can accent a dramatic central theme. The designer of the recreation room shown in Fig. 9-4 has developed a restful, quietly dignified atmosphere through the use of an Oriental decor. The designer of the recreation room shown in Fig. 9-5 has created a festive yet casual atmosphere using a winter sports theme.

Regardless of the central theme, recreation-room furniture should be comfortable and easy to maintain. The same rules apply to recreation-room walls, floors, and ceilings as

Fig 9-3 Whenever possible, the recreation room should be located adjacent to the patio.

Fig 9-4 A quiet, restful recreation room.

Fig 9-5 A recreation room decorated in a winter sports theme.

Armstrong
Cork Company

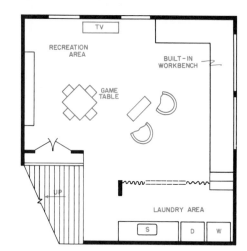

Fig 9-6 A recreation room occupying a large area.

Fig 9-7 A small recreation room.

apply to those of the family room. Floors should be hard-surfaced and easy to maintain. Walls should be paneled or covered with some material that is easily maintained. *Acoustical* (soundproofed) ceilings are recommended if the recreation room is located in the basement or on a lower level.

SIZE AND SHAPE

The size and shape of the recreation room depend on whether the room occupies an area on the main level or whether it occupies basement space. If basement space is used, the only restrictions on the size are the other facilities that will also occupy space in the basement, such as the laundry, the workshop, or the garage. Figure 9-6 shows a recreation room that occupies a rather large basement area that would otherwise be wasted space. Figure 9-7 shows a relatively small recreation room located on the main level of the house. The size of most recreation rooms ranges between these two extremes.

PROBLEMS

1 Sketch a plan of a recreation room you would include in a house of your own design.
2 Sketch a plan for a recreation room, including facilities for billiards, chess, shuffleboard, and television watching.
3 Determine the size and shape of a recreation room to accommodate the following furniture: television set, stereo, chaise longue, studio couch, two lounge chairs, soft-drink bar and stools, bookcase, billiard table.
4 Define the following terms: *game room, playroom, recreation room.*

66

UNIT 10
PORCHES

A *porch* is a covered platform leading into an entrance of a building. Porches are commonly enclosed by glass, screen, or post and railings. A porch is not the same as a patio. The porch is attached structurally to the house, whereas a patio is placed directly on the ground. The porch on the house shown in Fig. 10-1 is connected to a balcony that extends around the perimeter of the house and covers the patio below. Balconies and decks are actually elevated porches.

FUNCTION

Porches serve a variety of functions. Some are used for dining and some for entertaining and relaxing. Others are furnished and function like patios for outdoor living. Still others provide an additional shelter for the entrance to a house or patio. The primary function of a porch depends on the structure and purpose of the building to which it is attached. For example, the porch in Fig. 10-2 provides outdoor living facilities and access to motel

Fig 10-1 This porch extends into a perimeter balcony.
California
Redwood Assoc.

Fig 10-2 A porch used to connect motel units.
Western Wood
Products Assoc.

rooms. The condominium porch shown in Fig. 10-3 is designed as an outdoor private extension to the living room. The porch in Fig. 10-4 is planned to provide maximum appreciation of an ocean view.

VERANDAS

Southern colonial homes such as the one in Fig. 10-5 were designed with large porches, or *verandas*, extending around several sides of the home. Outdoor plantation life centered on the veranda, which was very large.

BALCONIES

A *balcony* is a porch suspended from an upper level of a structure. It usually has no access from the outside. Balconies often provide an extension to the living area or a private extension to a bedroom.

The house shown in Fig. 10-6 is distinguished by several types of balconies. The upper balcony is supported by cantilevered

Fig 10-3 A condominium porch designed for privacy.

Western Wood Products Assoc.

Fig 10-6 The upper balcony provides protection for the porch below.

Western Wood Products Assoc.

Fig 10-4 A porch designed with a view.

Potlatch Corp.

Fig 10-5 A Southern colonial home with a veranda.

Oil by Margaret de Loo

beams and provides an extension that covers the porch below. The porch in turn shelters a patio below it. Hillside lots lend themselves to vertical plans and provide maximum flexibility in using outdoor living facilities.

Spanish- and Italian-style architecture is characterized by numerous balconies. The return of the balcony to popularity has been influenced and accelerated by new developments in building materials. These materials permit large areas to be suspended. The balcony in the house shown in Fig. 10-7A is cantilevered (supported only at one end) on wood joists that extend beyond the exterior wall. The flooring provides lateral support for the joists, as shown in Fig. 10-7B.

The principle of cantileverage, or suspension in space, can also be used to a greater extent with steel construction. An example is shown in the balcony that overhangs the patio in Fig. 10-8.

STOOP

The *stoop* is a projection from a building, similar to a porch. However, a stoop does not provide sufficient space for any activities. It provides only shelter and an access to the entrance of the building.

THE MODERN PORCH

Only in the last several years has the porch been functionally designed and effec-

Fig 10-8 Steel members make large cantilevered distances possible.

Fig 10-7A A cantilevered porch (left).
Fig 10-7B Cantilever supports (right).

Western Wood Products Assoc.

Fig 10-9 This porch is an extension of the living area.

Western Wood Products Assoc.

Fig 10-10 This porch is an integral part of the exterior design.

Rocky Mountain National Park

tively utilized for outdoor living. The classic front porch and back porch that characterized most homes built in this country during the 1920s and 1930s were designed and used merely as places in which to sit. Little effort was made to use the porch for any other activities. A porch for a modern home should be designed for the specific activities anticipated for it. The form of the porch should be determined by its function.

LOCATION

Since the porch is an integral part of the total house design, it must be located where it will function best. The porch in Fig. 10-9 becomes a functional extension of the living area and entry when in use. A porch can be made consistent with the rest of the house by extending the lines of the roof to provide sufficient *overhang,* or projection (Fig. 10-10).

A dining porch should be located adjacent to either the dining room or the kitchen. The dining porch shown in Fig. 10-11 can be approached from the dining room or from the living-area porch.

The porch should be located to provide maximum flexibility. A porch that can function for dining and other living activities is desirable. The primary functions of the porch should be considered when orienting the

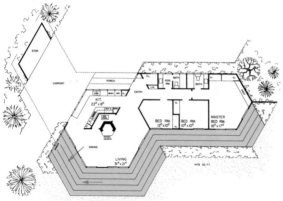

Fig 10-11 Location of a dining porch.

Home Planners, Inc.

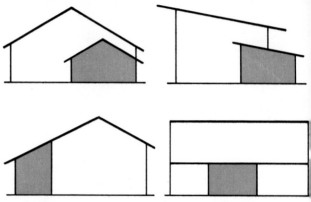

Fig 10-12 The lines of the porch should be consistent with the major lines of the house.

porch with the sun. If much daytime use is anticipated and direct sunlight is desirable, a southern exposure should be planned. If little sun is wanted during the day, a northern exposure would be preferable. If morning sun is desirable, an eastern exposure would be best, and for the afternoon sun, a western exposure.

DECOR

The porch should be designed as an integral and functional part of the total structure. A blending of roof styles and major lines of the porch roof and house roof is especially important (Fig. 10-12). A similar consistency should characterize the vertical columns or support members of the porch. Figure 10-12 shows some relationships that can be established to prevent the tacked-on look and to ensure uniformity in design.

Various materials and methods can be used as deck railing, depending on the degree of privacy or sun and wind protection needed. For example, the sides of the porch shown in Fig. 10-3 provide complete privacy but also block out ventilation. The sides of the porch shown in Fig. 10-13 provide adequate ventilation but also offer semiprivacy and safety. Railings on elevated porches such as this should be designed at a height above 3 feet (915 millimeters) to discourage the use of the top rail as a place to sit.

Porch furniture should withstand deterioration in any kind of weather. Covering mate-

Fig 10-13 The use of vertical strips to provide semiprivacy, safety, and wind baffling.

Western Wood Products Assoc.

rial should be waterproof, stain-resistant, and washable. Protection from wind and rain should be planned. Note how the use of glass on the porch shown in Fig. 10-14 blocks out wind-driven sand and yet allows maximum sun exposure.

SIZE AND SHAPE

Porches range in size from the very large veranda to rather modest-sized stoops, which provide only shelter and a landing surface for the main entrance. Figure 10-15 shows a large

Fig 10-14 Glass windscreens protect this porch from wind and sand.

PPG Industries, Inc.

porch that extends around the entire perimeter of the house. A porch approximately 6′ × 8′ (1.8 × 2.4 m) is considered a minimum size. An 8′ × 12′ (2.4 × 3.7 m) porch is about average. Porches larger than 12′ × 18′ (3.7 × 5.5 m) are considered rather large.

The shape of the porch depends greatly upon how the porch can be integrated into the overall design of the house. Figure 10-16 shows some basic porch shapes that are frequently used.

Fig 10-15 A perimeter porch.

Potlatch Corp.

PROBLEMS

1 Add a porch to the floor-plan sketch shown in Fig. 37-15. Show the exact width and length, and list the materials you recommend for the deck, roof, and enclosure.
2 Add a porch to the sketch shown in Fig. 36-8.

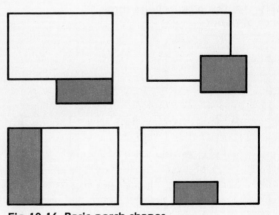

Fig 10-16 Basic porch shapes.

3 Add a porch to a floor plan of your own design.
4 From catalogs, newspapers, and magazines, cut out pictures of porch furniture you would choose for your own porch.
5 Draw or sketch a floor plan of the porch shown in Fig. 10-17. Design and draw access areas to the lake and show which rooms are adjacent to the porch.
6 Define the following terms: *veranda, balcony, cantilever, stoop.*

Stanmar, Inc.

Fig 10-17 Draw a plan of this porch and show access to the lake.

UNIT 11
PATIOS

A *patio* is a covered surface adjacent or directly accessible to the house. The word *patio* comes from the Spanish word for courtyard. Courtyard living was an important aspect of Spanish culture, and courtyard design was an important part of early Spanish architecture.

FUNCTION

The patio at various times may perform outdoors all the functions that the living room, dining room, recreation room, kitchen, and family room perform indoors.

The patio is often referred to by other names, such as *loggia, breezeway,* and *terrace.*

Patios can be divided into three main types according to function: *living patios, play patios,* and *quiet patios.* The home shown in Fig. 11-1A contains all three kinds of patios.

Fig 11-1A This plan includes three kinds of patios.

Home Planners, Inc.

Fig 11-1B Living patio.

California Redwood Assoc

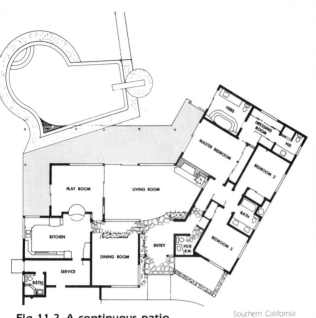

Fig 11-2 A continuous patio.

Southern California
Gas Company

Fig 11-3A A living-area patio viewed from the interior.

PPG Industries, Inc.

Fig 11-3B The living-area patio viewed from the exterior.

PPG Industries, Inc.

LOCATION

Patios should be located adjacent to the area of the home to which they relate. They should also be somewhat secluded from the street or from neighboring residences.

LIVING PATIO Living patios should be located close to the living room or the dining room. When dining is anticipated on the patio, access should be provided from the kitchen or dining room (Fig. 11-1B).

PLAY PATIO It is often advantageous to provide a play patio for use by children and for physical activities not normally associated with the living terrace. The play terrace sometimes doubles as the service terrace and can conveniently be placed adjacent to the service area. Notice the location of the play terrace in Fig. 11-1A. It is related directly to the service area and also to the family room in the living area.

QUIET PATIO The quiet patio can actually become an extension of the bedroom. It can be used for relaxation or even sleeping. The quiet terrace shown in Fig. 11-1A can be entered from the bedrooms or the living area. This type of patio should be secluded from the normal traffic of the home. Often the design of the house will allow these separately functioning patios to be combined in one large, continuous patio. That kind of patio is shown in Fig. 11-2. Here the playroom, living room, master bedroom, and kitchen all have access to the patio.

Fig 11-4 A courtyard patio.

Fig 11-5A A separated patio.

Fig 11-5B Separate covered patio.

PLACEMENT

Patios can be conveniently placed at the end of a building, as the living terrace is placed in Fig. 11-1A. They may be placed between corners of a house as in the play terrace and quiet terrace in Fig. 11-1A and 11-3A and B. Patios may be wrapped around the side of the house, as shown in Fig. 11-2, or they may be placed in the center of a U-shaped house or in a courtyard. The courtyard patio shown in Fig. 11-4 offers complete privacy from all sides.

SEPARATE PATIOS

In addition to the preceding locations, the patio is often located completely apart from the house. When a wooded area, a particular view, or a terrain feature is of interest, the patio can be placed away from the house. When the patio is located in this manner, it should be readily accessible, as shown in Fig. 11-5A and B.

ORIENTATION

When the patio is placed on the north side of the house, the house itself can be used to shade the patio. If sunlight is desired, the patio should be located on the south side of the house. The planner should take full advantage of the most pleasing view and should restrict the view of undesirable sights.

Fig 11-6 A wood-slat patio deck.   *Julius Shulman*

Fig 11-7 A brick-surface patio.   *Olympic Stains*

Fig 11-8 Brick surface surrounds hot tub.

Emerald Pools

DECOR

The materials used in the deck, cover, baffles, and furniture of the patio should be consistent with the lines and materials used in the rest of the home. Patios should not appear to be designed as an afterthought but should appear and function as an integral part of the total design.

PATIO DECK

The *deck* (floor) of the patio should be constructed from materials that are permanent and maintenance-free. Flagstone, redwood, concrete, and brick are among the best materials for use on patio decks. Wood slats such as those shown in Fig. 11-6 provide for drainage between the slats and also create a warm appearance. However, they do require some maintenance.

Brick-surface patio decks are very popular because bricks can be placed in a variety of arrangements to adapt to practically any shape or space. The area between the bricks may be filled with concrete, gravel, sand, or grass (Figs. 11-7 and 11-8).

A concrete deck is effective when a smooth, unbroken surface is desired. Patios where bouncing-ball games are played, or where pool-side cover is desired, can use concrete advantageously.

PATIO COVER

Patios need not be covered if the house is oriented to shade the patio during the times of the day when shade is normally desired. Since a patio is designed to provide outdoor living, too much cover can defeat the purpose of the patio. Coverings can be an extension of the roof structure, as shown in Fig. 11-9. They may be graded or tilted to allow light to enter when the sun is high and to block the sun's rays when the sun is lower. The graded effect can be obtained by placing louvers spaced straight or slanted to admit the high sun and block the low sun, as shown in Fig. 11-10.

Plastic, glass fiber, and other translucent materials used to cover patios admit sunlight and yet provide protection from the direct

Fig 11-9 A roof extension used as a patio cover.

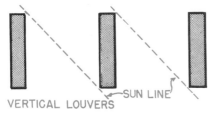

VERTICAL LOUVERS ← SUN LINE

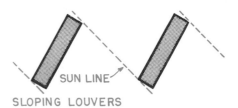

SUN LINE

SLOPING LOUVERS

Fig 11-10 The angle and spacing of louvers is important in sun screening.

Fig 11-11 A combination of baffling devices.

rays of the sun. Translucent covers also provide shelter from rain. When translucent covering is used, it is often desirable to have only part of the patio covered. This arrangement provides sun for part of the patio and shade for other parts. Balconies can also be used effectively to provide shelter for a patio.

WALLS AND BAFFLES

Patios are designed for outdoor living, but outdoor living need not be public living. Some privacy is always desirable. Solid walls can often be used effectively to baffle the patio from a street view, from wind, and from the low rays of the sun. Baffling devices include solid fences, slatted fences, concrete blocks, post and rails, brick or stone walls, and hedges or other shrubbery (Fig. 11-11).

Fig 11-12 A slatted baffle wall provides privacy but admits light and air.

California Redwood Assoc.

Fig 11-13 A baffle wall used to separate the patio from the service entrance.

New Homes Guide

A solid baffle wall is often undesirable because it restricts the view, eliminates the circulation of air, and makes the patio appear smaller. Figure 11-12 shows a baffle wall used to provide privacy for the patio without restricting circulation of air. The baffle wall in Fig. 11-13 is used to separate the patio from the service entrance without restricting the view.

In mild climates, completely enclosing a patio by solid walls can help make the patio function as another room. In such an enclosed patio, some opening should be provided to allow light and air to enter. The grillwork openings on the wall shown in Fig. 11-14 pro-

vide an effective and aesthetically pleasing solution to this problem.

Occasionally, nature provides its own baffle through a rise in the landscape, as shown in Fig. 11-15. This condition is highly desirable and should be taken advantage of, if sufficient drainage away from the house and patio can be maintained.

Fig 11-14 A semi-isolated patio and its plan view.

Home Planners, Inc.

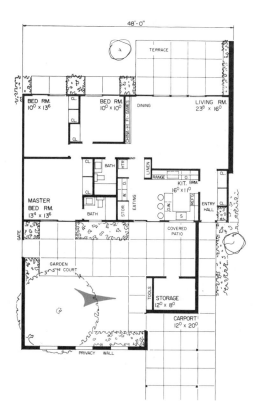

Fig 11-15 A natural patio baffle. Paul J. Peart, Landscape Architect

Fig 11-16 The patio at midday. Julius Shulman

DAY AND NIGHT DECOR

To be totally effective, the patio should be designed for both daytime and nighttime use. Figure 11-16 shows a typical midday use of the patio. Figure 11-17 shows some of the possibilities of nighttime utilization. Correct use of general and local lighting can make the patio useful for many hours each day. If the walls between the inside areas of the house and the patio are designed as in Fig. 11-17, much light from the inside can be utilized on the patio. Figure 11-18 shows some of the specific types of lights and lighting that can be used to illuminate patios at night.

SIZE AND SHAPE

Patios may be as small as the garden terrace shown in Fig. 11-19 or as spacious as the courtyard patio shown in Fig. 11-20. The primary function will largely determine the size. The Japanese garden has no furniture and is designed primarily to provide a baffle and a beautiful view. The courtyard patio is designed for many uses.

Activities should be governed by the amount of space needed for equipment.

Equipment and furnishings normally used on patios include picnic tables and benches, lounge chairs, serving carts, game apparatus, and barbecue pits. The placement of these items and the storage of games, apparatus,

Fig 11-17 The patio should also be designed for nighttime use. Western Wood Products Assoc.

Fig 11-18 Examples of types of patio lighting. Western Wood Products Assoc.

Fig 11-19 A small garden patio. California Redwood Assoc.

and fixtures should determine the size of the patio. Patios vary more in length than in width, since patios may extend over the entire length of the house. A patio 12′ × 12′ (3.7 × 3.7 m) is considered a minimum-sized patio. Patios with dimensions of 20′ × 30′ (6.0 × 9.1 m) or more are not uncommon but are certainly considered large. When a pool is designed for a home, it becomes an integral part of the patio. The poolside and the entire area around the pool function as a patio (Fig. 11-21).

Many pool shapes now available allow the designer to blend the pool into the size and shape of the patio (Fig. 11-22).

When designing and locating a pool, the location of the filter, heater (if used), electrical plumbing, and filter lines must be planned.

Fig 11-20 A spacious courtyard patio. Home Planners, Inc.

Fig 11-21 A pool integrated into the patio design. Libbey-Owens-Ford Company

Fig 11-22 The patio and pool design blended together.

California
Redwood Assoc.

Since the filter runs continuously, it should be located as far from the patio as possible without the use of excessively long plumbing, electrical, and filter supply lines. Figure 11-23 shows the location of this equipment in relationship to the pool and patio.

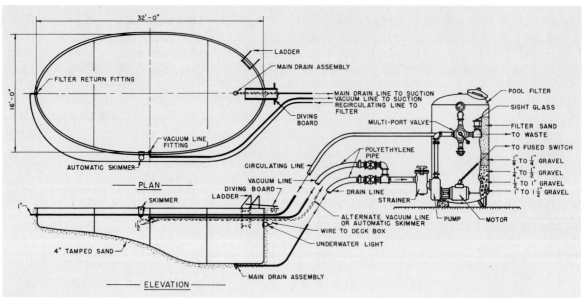

Fig 11-23 Filtering-system equipment must be included in plans.

Lancer Pool Corp.

PROBLEMS

1 Sketch a baffle wall for the exposed patio shown in Fig. 12-6A.
2 What type of covering would you recommend for the patio shown in Fig. 12-6A?
3 Design a covering for the patio shown in Fig. 12-6A. Sketch a top view of your solution.
4 Choose an interesting pool shape and incorporate it in the patio design shown in Fig. 11-20.

Fig 11-24 Add patios to this plan.

Home Planners, Inc.

5 Add a patio design to the floor-plan layout shown in Fig. 11-24.

6 Plan a patio for a house of your own design. Sketch the basic scheme and the facilities.

7 Define the following terms: *patio, loggia, breezeway, terrace, play patio, quiet patio, living patio, flagstone, redwood, concrete, patio deck, patio baffles.*

UNIT 12
LANAIS

Lanai is the Hawaiian word for porch. However, the word lanai is now used to refer to a covered exterior passageway.

FUNCTION

Large lanais are often used as patios, although their main function is to provide shelter for the traffic accesses on the exterior of a building. Lanais are actually exterior hallways (Fig. 12-1A).

Lanais that are located parallel to exterior walls are usually created by extending

Fig 12-1B A lanai created by a roof overhang.

Fig 12-1A Lanais connect living areas.

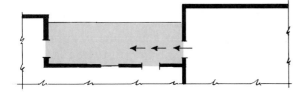

the roof overhang to cover a traffic area, as shown in Fig. 12-1B. Figure 12-2A and B shows a typical lanai plan that eliminates the need for more costly interior halls. Lanais are used extensively in commercial buildings, especially in warmer climates, as shown in Fig. 12-3.

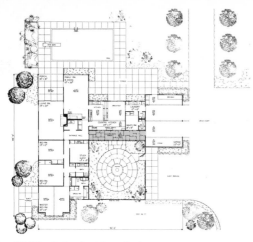

Fig 12-2A A typical lanai plan.

Fig 12-2B View of the lanai shown in Fig 12-2A.

Fig 12-3 Commercial use of a lanai.

Fig 12-4 A lanai used in a U-shaped plan.

Fig 12-5 A patio used as a lanai.

LOCATION

In residence planning, a lanai can be used most effectively to connect opposite areas of a home. Lanais are commonly located between the garage and the kitchen, the patio and the kitchen or the living area, and the living area and the service area. U-shaped houses such as the one shown in Fig. 12-4 are especially suitable for lanais because of the natural connection of the extremes of the U.

When lanais are carefully located, they can also function as sheltered access from inside areas to outside facilities such as patios (Fig. 12-5) or pools (Fig. 12-6A and B) or outdoor cooking areas, as shown in Fig. 12-7. A covered or partially covered patio is also considered a lanai when it doubles as a major access from one area of a structure to another. The patio shown in Fig. 12-8 functions in this manner. A lanai can also be semienclosed, as shown in Fig. 12-9, and provide not only traf-

fic access but also privacy and sun and wind shielding. When lanais are used to connect the building with the street, they actually function as marquees (Fig. 12-10).

DECOR

The lanai should be a consistent, integral part of the design of the structure. The lanai cover may be an extension of the roof overhang, as can be seen in Fig. 12-11, or may be supported by columns, as shown in Fig. 12-12. If glass is placed between the columns, the

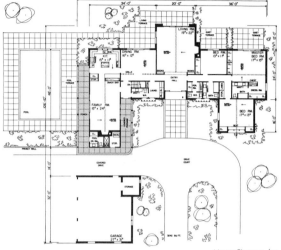

Fig 12-6A A lanai connecting the living areas and the pool.

Home Planners, Inc.

Fig 12-6B Lanais adjacent to courtyard.

Home Planners, Inc.

Fig 12-7 An outdoor cooking area connected by a lanai.

Home Planners, Inc.

Fig 12-8 A large patio and overhang create a lanai.

Home Planners, Inc.

Fig 12-9 A semienclosed lanai.

California Redwood Assoc.

Rendering by George Parenti for the Masonite Corp.

Fig 12-10 A marquee is a type of lanai.

Fig 12-11 A lanai porch created with roof overhang.

Fig 12-13 A large commercial lanai.

Fig 12-12 A lanai supported by columns.

Fig 12-14 A large residential lanai.

Fig 12-15 A long lanai connecting several buildings.

lanai becomes an interior hallway rather than an exterior one. This separation is sometimes the only difference between a lanai and an interior hall.

It is often desirable to design and locate the lanai to provide access from one end of an extremely long building to the other end, as shown in Fig. 12-13. The lines of this kind of lanai strengthen and reinforce the basic lines of the building. The columns supporting the roof overhang in Fig. 12-13 also provide a visual boundary without blocking the view.

If a lanai is to be utilized extensively at night, effective lighting must be provided. Light from within is used when drapes are open, but additional lighting fixtures are used when drapes are closed.

SIZE AND SHAPE

Lanais may extend the full length of a building and may be designed for maximum traffic loads, as shown in Fig. 12-14. They may be as small as the area under a 2' or 3' (610 or 915 mm) roof overhang. However, a lanai at least 4' (1220 mm) wide is desirable. The length and type of cover is limited only by the location of areas to be covered. For example, the lanai shown in Fig. 12-15 extends a very long distance between buildings.

PROBLEMS

1 Draw the outline of a lanai you would plan for a home of your own design.
2 Add a lanai to the plan shown in Fig. 6-4.
3 Add a lanai to the plan shown in Fig. 6-10.
4 Resketch the plan shown in Fig. 6-4. Using dotted lines, sketch the outline of a lanai you would add to this plan.
5 Sketch a floor plan of your own home. Add a lanai to connect two of the areas, such as the sleeping and living areas.
6 Define the following terms: *lanai cover, roof overhang, exterior hallway.*

UNIT 13
TRAFFIC AREAS AND PATTERNS

When an architect plans a commercial structure such as the World Trade Center (Fig. 13-1), both vehicular and pedestrian traffic volume and patterns must be considered. Traffic inside and outside the building must be planned for. Traffic areas for employees, visitors, and deliveries into and out of the building must be allocated using a minimum amount of space. In designing commercial traffic areas as shown in Fig. 3-2, the maximum volume of traffic must be considered.

Planning the traffic areas of a residence is not as complex because of the small number of people involved. Nevertheless, the same basic principle of efficient space allocation prevails. The traffic areas of the home provide passage from one room or area to another.

Fig 13-1 Commercial traffic patterns.   The Port Authority of New York and New Jersey

The main traffic areas of a residence include the halls, entrance foyers, stairs, lanais, and areas of rooms that are part of the traffic pattern.

TRAFFIC PATTERNS

Traffic patterns of a residence should be carefully considered in the design of the room layout. A minimum amount of space should be devoted to traffic areas. Extremely long halls and corridors should be avoided. They are difficult to light and provide no living space. Traffic patterns that require passage through one room to get to another should also be avoided, especially in the sleeping area.

The traffic pattern shown in the plan in Fig. 13-3 is efficient and functional. It contains a minimum amount of wasted hall space without creating a boxed-in appearance. It provides access to each of the areas without passing through other areas. The arrows clearly show that the sleeping area, living area, and service area are accessible from the entrance without passage through other areas. In this plan the service entrance provides access to the kitchen from the carport and other parts of the service area.

One method of determining the effectiveness of the traffic pattern of a house is to imagine yourself moving through the house by placing your pencil on the floor plan and tracing your route through the house as you perform your daily routine. If you trace through a whole day's activities, including those of other members of the household, you will be able to see graphically where the heaviest traffic occurs and whether the traffic areas have been planned effectively. Figure 13-4 shows the difference between a poorly designed traffic pattern and a well-designed traffic pattern.

HALLS

Halls are the highways and streets of the home. They provide a controlled path that connects the various areas of the house. Halls should be planned to eliminate or keep to a minimum the passage of traffic through rooms. Long, dark, tunnel-like halls should be avoided. Halls should be well lighted, light in color and texture, and planned with the decor of the whole house in mind.

One method of channeling hall traffic without the use of solid walls is with the use of dividers. Planters, half-walls, louvered walls, and even furniture can be used as dividers. Figure 13-5 shows the use of furniture components in dividing the living area from the hall.

Fig 13-2 Maximum traffic volume must be planned for in commercial situation.

American Olean Tile Company

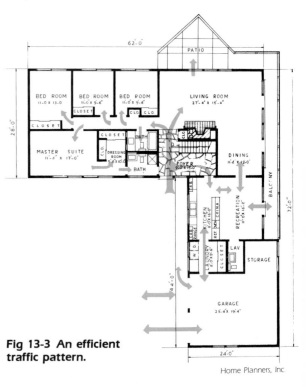

Fig 13-3 An efficient traffic pattern.

Home Planners, Inc.

This arrangement enables both the hall and the living room to share ventilation, light, and heat.

Another method of designing halls and corridors as an integral part of the area design is with the use of movable partitions. The Japanese scheme of placing these partitions between the living area and a hall is shown in Fig. 13-6. In some Japanese homes, this hall actually becomes a lanai when the partition between the living area and the hall is closed

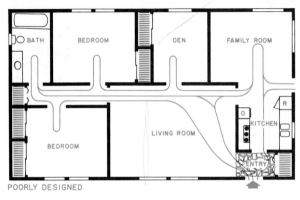

POORLY DESIGNED

WELL DESIGNED

Fig 13-4 The difference between a poorly designed and a well-designed traffic pattern.

Fig 13-5 The use of furniture components in separating traffic areas.

United States
Plywood Corp.

Fig 13-6 The use of movable partitions to separate traffic areas.

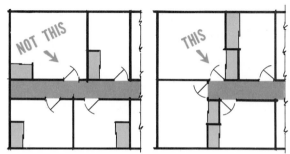

Fig 13-7 Principles of efficient hall design.

and the outside wall is opened. Figure 13-7 shows some of the basic principles of efficient hall design.

STAIRS

Stairs are inclined hallways. They provide access from one level to another. Stairs may lead directly from one area to another without a change of direction, they may turn 90 degrees (90°) by means of a landing, or they may turn 180° by means of landings. Figure 13-8 shows the basic types of stairs.

With the use of newer, stronger building materials and new techniques, there is no longer any reason for enclosing stairs in walls that restrict light and ventilation (Fig. 13-9). Stairs can now be supported by many different devices. The stairs in Fig. 13-10 are center-supported and therefore do not need side walls or other supports. Even when vertical supports are necessary or desirable, completely closing in the wall is not mandatory. Figure 13-11 shows stairs supported by exposed steel rods that maintain the open plan without sacrificing support or safety. These stairs are supported by hanging one side of the tread from steel rods.

Windows should be placed to provide natural light for stairs (Fig. 13-12). Because stairwells should be lighted at all times when in use, natural light is most energy-efficient. If it is difficult to provide natural light, three-way switches should be provided at the top and bottom of the stairwell to control the stair lighting. See Unit 61, "Planning with Electricity."

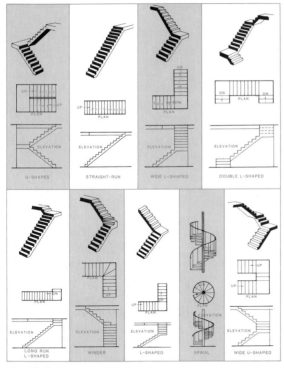

Fig 13-8 Basic types of stairs.

SPACE REQUIREMENTS

There are many variables to consider in designing stairs. The tread width, the riser width, the width of the stair opening, and the headroom all help to determine the total length of the stairwell.

Fig 13-9 An exposed stair system. Armstrong Cork Company

Fig 13-10 Center-supported stairs.

Armstrong Cork Company

Fig 13-11 These stairs are hung from steel rods.

Fig 13-12 When possible, use natural light to illuminate stairwells. California Redwood Assoc.

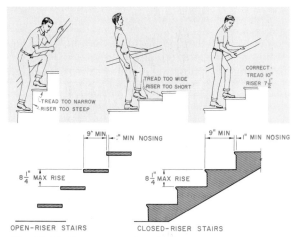

Fig 13-13 Correct tread and riser design is important.

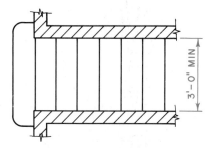

Fig 13-14 Minimum width of stairs.

Fig 13-15 Minimum headroom clearance.

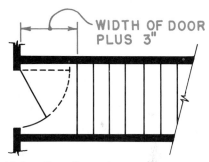

Fig 13-16 Landing dimensions may need allowance for a door.

The *tread* is the horizontal part of the stair, the part upon which you walk. The average width of the tread is 10″ (250 mm). The *riser* is the vertical part of the stair. The average riser height is 7¼″ (185 mm). Figure 13-13 shows the importance of correct tread and riser design.

The overall width of the stairs is the length or distance across the treads. A minimum of 3′ (915 mm) should be allowed for the total stair width. However, a width of 3′—6″ (1070 mm) or even 4′ (1220 mm) is preferred (Fig. 13-14).

Headroom is the vertical distance between the top of each tread and the top of the stairwell ceiling. A minimum headroom distance of 6′—6″ (1.9 m) should be allowed. However, distances of 7′ (2.1 m) are more desirable (Fig. 13-15).

Landing dimensions will probably be determined by the size of the stairs and the space for the stairwell (Fig. 13-8). More clearance must be allowed where a door opens on a landing (Fig. 13-16).

PROBLEMS

1 Sketch the floor plan shown in Fig. 11-14. Redesign the traffic pattern to eliminate passing directly through the living room to get to the sleeping area.

2 Sketch the plan shown in Fig. 11-20. Move the entrance to another location to provide more central access to each of the areas without passing through the others.

3 Resketch the plan shown in Fig. 11-20 in order to shorten the long hall in the bedroom area.

4 Sketch the floor plan of a home of your design. Plan the most efficient traffic pattern by tracing the route of your daily routine.

5 Sketch the floor plan of your own home. Redesign the entrance and halls to make this pattern more efficient.

6 Define the following terms: *traffic pattern, halls, corridors, main traffic areas, movable partitions, minimum stair width, center-supported stairs, tread, riser, headroom, landing.*

UNIT 14
ENTRANCES

Entrances are divided into several different types: the main entrance, the service entrance, and the special-purpose entrance. The entrance is composed of an outside waiting area (porch, marquee, lanai), a separation (door), and an inside waiting area (foyer, entrance hall).

FUNCTION

Entrances provide for and control the flow of traffic into and out of a building. Different types of entrances have somewhat different functions.

MAIN ENTRANCE

The *main entrance* provides access to the house, through which guests are welcomed and from which all major traffic patterns radiate. The main entrance should be readily identifiable by a stranger (Fig. 14-1). It should provide shelter to anyone awaiting entrance. The entrance of the house shown in Fig. 14-1 has two walkways. The one on the right leads to the street; the one on the left leads to the driveway and garage.

Some provision should be made in the main-entrance wall for the viewing of callers

Fig 14-1 A main entrance with a walk leading to the street and to the driveway.
California Redwood Assoc.

from the inside. This can be accomplished through the use of side panels, lights (panes) in the door or windows (Fig. 14-2) which face the side of the entrance.

The main entrance should be planned to create a desirable first impression (Fig. 14-3). A direct view of other areas of the house from the foyer should be baffled but not sealed off. Figure 14-4A, B, and C shows an atrium foyer that channels traffic without creating a closed area. Also, a direct view of exterior parking areas should be baffled from view.

The entrance foyer should include a closet for the storage of outside clothing and bad-weather gear. This foyer closet should have a capacity that will accommodate both family and guests.

Home Planners, Inc.

Fig 14-2 Side windows provide a view of the entrance from the inside.

Fig 14-3 The main entrance must create a desirable first impression.

California
Redwood Assoc.

Fig 14-4A This atrium helps channel traffic without enclosing space.

Scholz Homes

Fig 14-4B View of Fig 14-4A from outside entrance.

Scholz Homes

Fig 14-4C View of living area shown in Fig 14-4A from atrium.

Scholz Homes

MAIN ENTRANCE

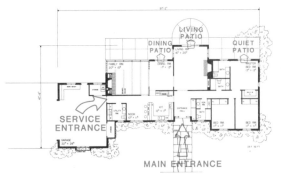

Fig 14-5 The basic types of entrances.

SERVICE ENTRANCE

The *service entrance* provides access to the house through which supplies can be delivered to the service areas without going through other parts of the house. It should also provide access to parts of the service area (garage, laundry, workshop) for which the main entrance is inappropriate and inconvenient.

SPECIAL-PURPOSE ENTRANCES

Special-purpose entrances and exits do not provide for outside traffic. Instead they provide for movement from the inside living area of the house to the outside living areas. A sliding door from the living area to the patio is a special-purpose entrance. It is not an entrance through which street, drive, or sidewalk traffic would have access. Figure 14-5 shows the difference between special-purpose entrances, main entrance, and service entrances.

Fig 14-6 The entrance adjacent to a quiet patio.

PPG Industries, Inc.

LOCATION

The main entrance should be centrally located to provide easy access to each area. It should be conveniently accessible from driveways, sidewalks, or street.

The service entrance should be located close to the drive and garage. It should be placed near the kitchen or food-storage areas.

Special-purpose entrances and exits are often located between the bedroom and the quiet patio, between the living room and the living patio (Fig. 14-6), and between the dining room or kitchen and the dining patio. Figure 14-5 shows the functional placement of all these entrances.

DECOR

The entrance should create a desirable first impression. It should be easily identifiable yet an integral part of the architectural style (Fig. 14-7).

CONSISTENCY OF STYLE

The total design of the entrance should be consistent with the overall design of the house. The design of the door, the side panel, and the deck and cover should be directly related to the lines of the house. The lines of the

Fig 14-7 The entrance must be impressive and keep the architectural style.

Fig 14-8 Left: an entrance with lines related to the lines of the structure. Right: an entrance with lines unrelated to the lines of the structure.

Fig 14-9A A close view of related entrance lines (upper left).
Fig 14-9B Entrance lines related to the remainder of the home (lower left).
Fig 14-9C The foyer of the entrance shown in Figs. 14-9A and 14-9B is consistent in design with the outside (upper right).

Fig 14-10 A maximum-sized open-plan entrance and foyer. American St. Goblain Corp.

Fig 14-11 An elevated entrance. PPG Industries, Inc.

entrances shown at the left in Fig. 14-8 are designed as integral parts of the exterior. The lines of the entrance shown at the right in Fig. 14-8 are unrelated to the major building lines of the structure.

The entrance shown in Fig. 14-9A, B, and C is a good example of entrance design involving all the principles of location, style consistency, lighting utilization, and size and shape effectiveness. Figure 14-9A shows a close view of the entrance. Fig. 14-9B shows the location of the entrance in reference to the entire front of the house, and Fig. 14-9C shows an interior view of the entrance foyer.

OPEN PLANNING

The view from the main entrance to the living area should be baffled without creating a boxed-in appearance. The foyer should not appear as a dead end. The extensive use of glass, effective lighting, and carefully placed baffle walls can create an open and inviting impression. This is accomplished in the entrance shown in Fig. 14-10 by the use of window walls, double doors, roof-overhang extension, and baffle walls that extend the length of the foyer. Open planning between the entrance foyer and the living areas can also be accomplished by the use of louvered walls or planter walls. These provide a break in the

Fig 14-12 Effective use of outside entrance lighting. PPG Industries, Inc.

line of sight but not a complete separation. Sinking or elevating the foyer or entrance approach, as shown in Fig. 14-11, also provides the desired separation without isolation.

FLOORING

The outside portion of the entrance should be weather-resistant stone, brick, or concrete. If a porch is used outside the entrance, a wood deck will suffice. The foyer deck should be easily maintained and be resistant to mud, water, and dirt brought in from the outside. Asphalt, vinyl or rubber tile, stone, flagstone, marble, and terrazzo are most frequently used for the foyer deck. The use of a different material in the foyer area helps to define the area when no other separation exists.

FOYER WALLS

Paneling, masonry, planters, murals, and glass are used extensively for entrance foyer walls. The walls of the exterior portion of the entrance should be consistent with the other materials used on the exterior of the house.

LIGHTING

An entrance must be designed to function day and night. General lighting, spot lighting, and all-night lighting (Fig. 14-12) are effective for this purpose. Lighting can be used to accent distinguishing features or to illuminate the pattern of a wall, which actually provides more light by reflection and helps to identify and accentuate the entrance at night.

Natural lighting, as shown in Fig. 14-13, is also effective in lighting entrance areas during daylight hours.

SIZE AND SHAPE

The size and shape of the areas inside and outside the entrance depend on the budget and the type of plan. Foyers are not bounded by solid walls in the open plan.

THE OUTSIDE

The outside covered portion of the entrance should be large enough to shelter sev-

Fig 14-13 Natural lighting used in a foyer. Western Wood Products Assoc.

eral people at one time. Sufficient space should be allowed on all sides, exclusive of the amount of space needed to open storm doors that open to the outside. Outside shelter areas range in size from the minimum arrangement shown at the right in Fig. 14-14 to the more generous size shown at the left in Fig. 14-14.

THE INSIDE

The inside of the entrance foyer should be sufficiently large to allow several people to enter at the same time, remove their coats, and store them in the closet. A 6' × 6' (1.8 × 1.8 m) foyer, as shown in Fig. 14-15, is considered minimum for this function. A foyer 8' × 10' (2.4 × 3.0 m) is average, but a more desirable size is 8' × 15' (2.4 × 4.6 m), as shown in Fig. 14-16.

Figure 14-16 also shows a foyer arrangement that allows for the swing of the door, something that must be taken into consideration in determining the size of the foyer. If the

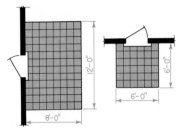

Fig 14-14 The entrance area on the left has optimum dimensions. The entrance on the right has minimum dimensions.

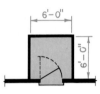

Fig 14-15 A minimum-sized foyer.

foyer is too shallow, passage will be blocked when the door is open, and only one person can enter at a time. Figure 14-9C shows a foyer that is near the optimum size. It is not extremely deep, but it does extend a great distance on either side. This allows sufficient

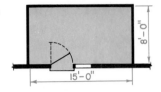

Fig 14-16 An optimum-sized foyer.

traffic to pass. It also allows sufficient movement around the doors when they are opened.

Foyers are normally rectangular because they lead to several areas of the home. They do not need much depth in any one direction. The ideal entry includes:

1 Adequate room to handle traffic flow
2 Access to all three areas of a home
3 A closet
4 Bath access for guests
5 Consistent decor
6 Outside weather protection
7 Effective lighting day and night

PROBLEMS

1 Redesign the entrance shown in Fig. 14-2, adding more shelter space that will be consistent with the main lines of the house.
2 List the characteristics of foyer design in the foyer shown in Fig. 6-2.
  Sketch the foyer layout for the plan shown in Fig. 14-16. Indicate the position of the foyer closet.

3 Redesign and enlarge the foyer for the living area shown in Fig. 8-4. Label the materials you select for the outside deck, overhang, access walk, foyer floor, and foyer walls.

4 Plan a foyer for a house you designed.

Define the following terms: *main entrance, service entrance, foyer, special-purpose entrances, open planning.*

UNIT 15
DENS AND STUDIES

The den or study can be designed for many different purposes, depending on the living habits of its occupants.

FUNCTION

The den may function basically as a reading room, writing room, hobby room, or professional office. For the teacher, writer, or clergyman, the study may be basically a reading and writing room, such as the one shown in Fig. 15-1. For the engineer, architect, drafter, or artist, the den or study may function primarily as a studio and may include such facilities as those shown in the study in Fig. 15-2.

The den or study often doubles as a guest room. Quite often the children's bedroom can provide facilities normally included in a study, such as desk, bookcase, and hobby space.

The den is often considered part of the sleeping area since it may require placement in a quiet part of the house. It also may function primarily in the living area, especially if the study is used as a professional office by a physician or an insurance agent whose clients call at home. Figure 15-3 shows a professional study or office located near the main entrance hall and accessible from the main entrance without passing through any other room or family area.

LOCATION

If a study doubles as an office, it should be located in an accessible area. However, if it is to serve a private use, then it can be located in the basement or attic, using otherwise wasted space.

DECOR AND LIGHTING

The decor of the study should reflect the main activity and should allow for well-diffused general lighting and glareproof local

Fig 15-1 This study is basically a hobby room. Haas Cabinet Company

lighting. Windows positioned above eye level admit the maximum amount of light without exposing distracting eye-level images from the outside.

As in the recreation room, a central theme may be used in the decoration of the study. For people who enjoy reading, the architect

Fig 15-2 This study was planned for drawing and designing activities. Georgia Pacific

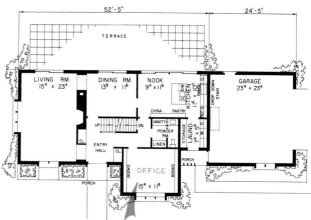

Fig 15-3 A study used as a professional office. Home Planners, Inc.

can create an inviting atmosphere by providing the warmth of a fireplace, adequate bookshelf space, and the natural light from a skylight.

SIZE AND SHAPE

The size and shape of the den, study, or office will vary greatly with its function. Size and shape will depend on whether one or two persons expect to use the room privately or whether it should provide a meeting place for business clients. Studies range in size from just enough space for a desk and chair in a small corner to a large amount of space with a diversity of furnishings, such as the study shown in Fig. 15-4. This illustration shows a study with the maximum number of furnishings, including a desk and chair, lounge chair, studio couch, file cabinets, bookcases, storage space, and coffee table.

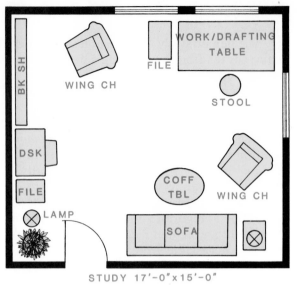

STUDY 17'-0" x 15'-0"

Fig 15-4 A study planned for diversified activities.

PROBLEMS

1 Sketch a plan for a den in a home of your own design.
2 Sketch a plan for a den for your own home.
3 Sketch a plan for a den to accommodate the following facilities: desk, chair, bookcases, drafting table, lounge.

4 Sketch a plan for a den which will double as a guest bedroom.
5 Define the following terms: *den, study, living area, sleeping area, guest room, professional office, central theme.*

SERVICE AREA

The service area includes the kitchen, laundry, garage, workshops, storage centers, and utility room. Since a great number of different activities take place in the service area, it should be designed for the greatest efficiency. The service area includes facilities for the maintenance and servicing of the other areas of the home. The functioning of the living and the sleeping areas is greatly dependent upon the efficiency of the service area.

UNIT 16
KITCHENS

A well-planned kitchen is efficient, attractive, and easy to maintain. To design an efficient kitchen, the designer must consider the function, basic shape, decor, size, and location of equipment.

FUNCTION

The preparation of food is the basic function of the kitchen. However, the kitchen may also be used as a dining area and as a laundry.

DESIGNING FOR EFFICIENCY

The proper placement of appliances, storage cabinets, and furniture is important in planning efficient kitchens. Locating appliances in an efficient pattern eliminates much wasted motion. An efficient *kitchen* is divided into three *areas:* the storage and mixing center, the preparation and cleaning center, and the cooking center (Fig. 16-1).

STORAGE AND MIXING CENTER

The refrigerator is the major appliance in the storage and mixing center. The refrigerator may be free-standing, built-in, or sus-

Fig 16-1 Efficient kitchens are divided into three activity areas.

Tappan Company

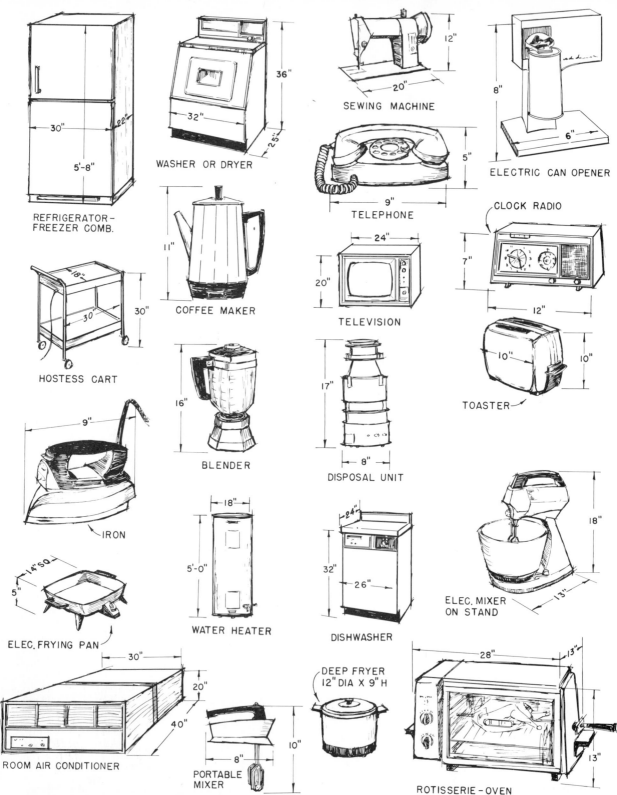

Fig 16-2 Sizes of common appliances.

pended from a wall. The storage and mixing center also includes cabinets for the storage of utensils and ingredients used in cooking and baking, as well as a counter-top work area.

PREPARATION AND CLEANING CENTER

The sink is the major appliance in the preparation and cleaning center. Sinks are available in one- and two-bowl models with a variety of cabinet arrangements and counter-top and drainboard areas. The preparation and cleaning center may also include a waste-disposal unit, an automatic dishwasher, a waste compactor, and cabinets for storing brushes, towels, and cleaning supplies.

COOKING CENTER

The range and oven are the major appliances in the cooking center. The range and oven may be combined into one appliance, or the burners may be installed in the counter top and the oven built into the wall. The cooking center should also include counter-top work space, as well as storage space for minor appliances and cooking utensils that will be used in the area. The cooking center must have an adequate supply of electrical outlets for the many minor appliances used in cooking.

Figure 16-2 shows the size requirements for the storage or installation of many minor appliances that may be located in the various centers.

WORK TRIANGLE

If you draw a line connecting the three centers of the kitchen, a triangle is formed (Fig. 16-3). This is called the *work triangle*. The perimeter of an efficient kitchen work triangle should be between 12' and 22' (3.7 and 6.7 m).

BASIC SHAPES

The position of the three areas on the work triangle may vary greatly. However, the most efficient arrangements usually fall into the following categories.

U-SHAPED KITCHEN The U-shaped kitchen, as shown in Fig. 16-4, is a very efficient arrangement. The sink is located at the bottom of the U, and the range and the refrigerator are at the opposite ends. In this arrangement, traffic passing through the kitchen is completely separated from the work triangle. The open space in the U between the sides may be 4' or 5' (1.2 or 1.5 m). This arrangement produces a very efficient but small kitchen. Figure 16-5 shows various U-shaped-kitchen layouts and the resulting work triangles.

Fig 16-3 The length of the work triangle should be between 12 feet (3.7 meters) and 22 feet (6.7 meters).

Hotpoint Division, General Electric Corp.

Fig 16-4 A U-shaped kitchen.

Hotpoint Division, General Electric Corp.

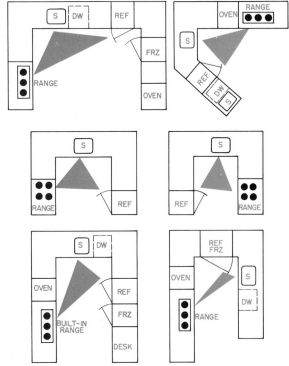

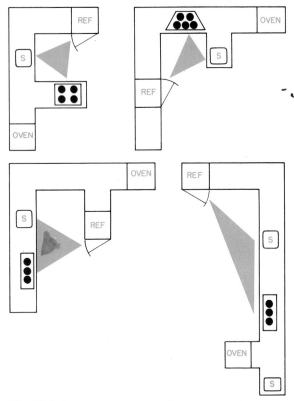

Fig 16-5 Six arrangements for a U-shaped kitchen.

Fig 16-6 Four arrangements for a peninsula kitchen.

Fig 16-7 L-shaped kitchens permit a large area of open floor space.

Tappan Company

PENINSULA KITCHEN The peninsula kitchen is similar to the U kitchen. However, one end of the U is not enclosed with a wall. The cooking center is often located in this peninsula, and the peninsula is often used to join the kitchen to the dining or family rooms. Figure 16-6 shows various arrangements of peninsula kitchens and the resulting work triangles.

L-SHAPED KITCHEN The L-shaped kitchen (Fig. 16-7) has continuous counters and appliances and equipment on two adjoining walls. The work triangle is not in the traffic pattern. The remaining space is often used for other kitchen facilities, such as dining or laundry facilities. If the walls of an L-shaped kitchen are too long, the compact efficiency of the kitchen is destroyed. Figure 16-8 shows several L-shaped kitchens and the work triangles that result from these arrangements.

CORRIDOR KITCHEN The two-wall corridor kitchens shown in Fig. 16-9 are very efficient arrangements for long, narrow rooms. A

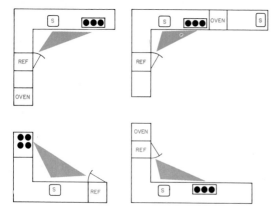

Fig 16-8 Four arrangements for an L-shaped kitchen.

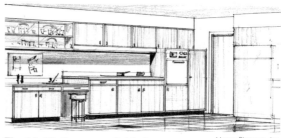

Fig 16-10 A one-wall kitchen.   Home Planners, Inc.

corridor kitchen is unsatisfactory, however, if considerable traffic passes through the work triangle. A corridor kitchen produces one of the most efficient work triangles of all the arrangements.

ONE-WALL KITCHEN A one-wall kitchen is an excellent plan for small apartments, cabins, or houses in which little space is available. The work centers are located in open line and produce a very efficient arrangement (Fig. 16-10). However, in planning the one-wall kitchen, the designer must be careful to avoid having the wall too long and must provide adequate storage facilities. Figure 16-11

shows several one-wall-kitchen arrangements.

ISLAND KITCHEN The island, which serves as a separator for the different parts of the kitchen, usually has a range top or sink, or both, and is accessible on all sides. Other facilities that are sometimes located in the island are the mixing center, work table, buffet counter, extra sink (Fig. 16-12), and snack center. Figure 16-13 shows examples of other island facilities.

FAMILY KITCHEN The family kitchen is an open kitchen using any of the basic plans. Its function is to provide a meeting place for the entire family in addition to providing for the normal kitchen functions. Family kitchens are normally divided into two sections. One section is for food preparation, which includes the three work centers; the other section includes a dining area and family-room facilities, as shown in Fig. 16-14.

Family kitchens must be rather large to accommodate these facilities. An average size

Fig 16-9 Four arrangements for a corridor kitchen.

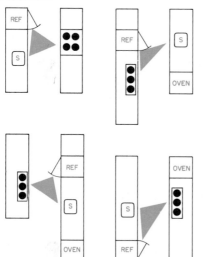

Fig 16-11 Three arrangements for a one-wall kitchen.

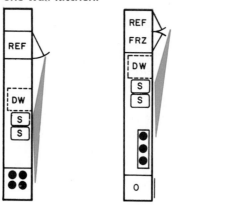

Fig 16-12 A sink island kitchen.

Fig 16-14 This family kitchen is designed for a variety of activities.

Frigidaire Division, General Motors Corp.

for a family kitchen is 15 feet (4.6 m) square. Figure 16-15 shows several possible arrangements for family kitchens.

DECOR

Even though kitchen appliances are of contemporary design, some homemakers prefer to decorate kitchens with a period or colo-

Fig 16-13 Four island-kitchen arrangements.

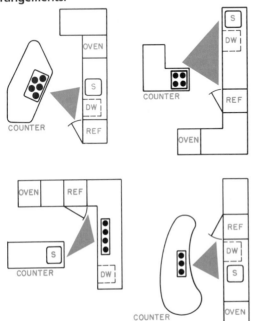

nial motif. The design of the cabinets, floors, walls, and accessory furniture must therefore be accented to give the desired effect. Compare the colonial kitchen shown in Fig. 16-16 with the modern kitchen shown in Fig. 16-17. You will notice that it is somewhat easier to design the lines of the modern kitchen in harmony with the lines of the major appliances. However, front panels can be added to many appliances to make them conform to the style and color scheme of the kitchen. The kitchen shown in Fig. 16-16 is a colonial version of the kitchen shown in Fig. 16-17.

Regardless of the style, kitchen walls, floors, counter tops, and cabinets should require a minimum amount of maintenance. Materials that are relatively maintenance-free include stainless steel, stain-resistant plastic, ceramic tile, washable wall coverings, washable paint, asphalt vinyl tile, and laminated plastic counter tops.

LOCATION

Since the kitchen is the core of the service area, it should be located near the service entrance and near the waste-disposal area. The children's play area should also be visible

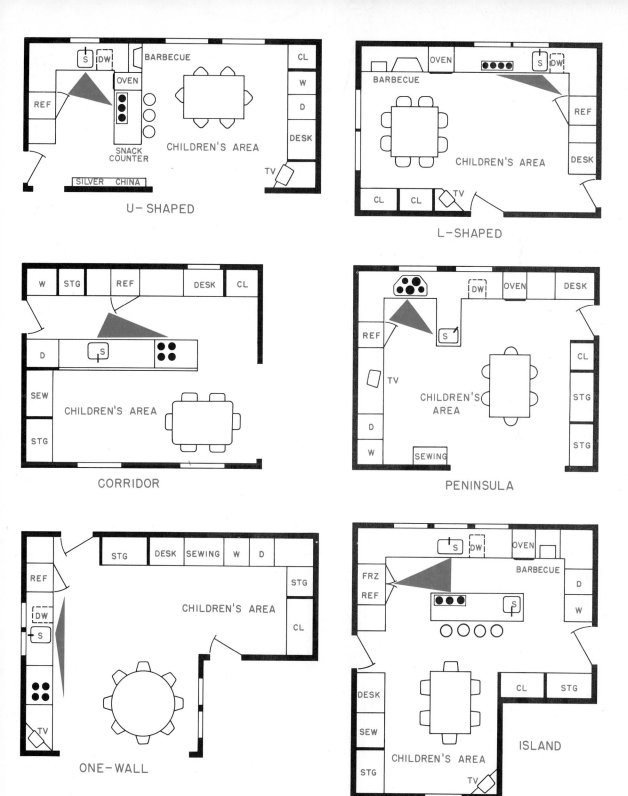

Fig 16-15 Six family-kitchen plans.

Fig 16-16 A colonial kitchen decor.

Consoweld Corp.

Fig 16-17 A modern kitchen decor.

Consoweld Corp.

Fig 16-18 The refrigerator door and major cabinet doors should open into the work triangle.

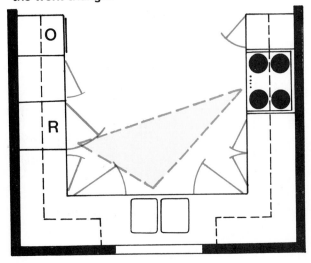

from the kitchen, and the kitchen must be adjacent to the dining area and outdoor eating areas.

KITCHEN PLANNING GUIDES

The following guides for kitchen planning provide a review of the more important factors to consider in designing efficient and functional kitchens:

1. The traffic lane is clear of the work triangle.
2. The work areas include all necessary appliances and facilities.
3. The kitchen is located adjacent to the dining area.
4. The kitchen is located near the children's play area.
5. The view from the kitchen is cheerful and pleasant.
6. The centers include (a) the storage center, (b) the preparation and cleaning center, and (c) the cooking center.
7. The work triangle measures less than 22' (6.7 m).

Fig 16-19 Typical heights of kitchen working surfaces.

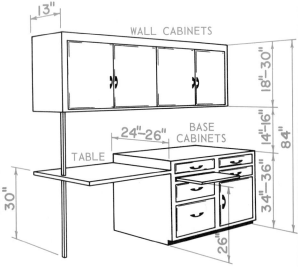

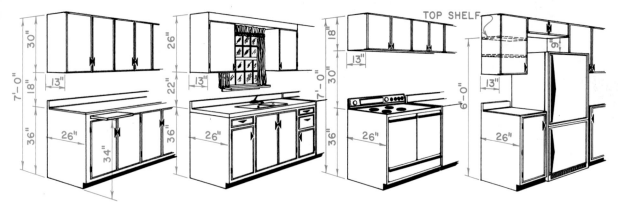

Fig 16-20 Typical heights of kitchen cabinets.

8 Electrical outlets are provided for each work center.
9 Adequate storage facilities are available in each work center.
10 Shadowless and glareless light is provided and is concentrated on each work center.

11 Adequate counter space is provided for meal preparation.
12 Ventilation is adequate.
13 The oven and range are separated from the refrigerator by at least one cabinet.
14 Doors on appliances swing away from the work-counter area (Fig. 16-18).

Fig 16-21 Basic steps in drawing kitchen plans.

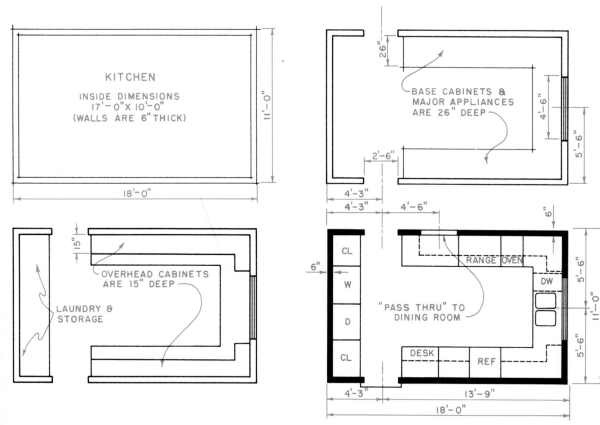

15 Lapboard heights are 26″ (660 mm) (Fig. 16-19).

16 Working heights for counters are 36″ (915 mm) (Fig. 16-20).

17 Working heights for tables are 30″ (760 mm).

18 The combination of base cabinets, wall cabinets, and appliances provides a consistent standard unit without gaps or awkward depressions or extensions.

PROBLEMS

1 Sketch a floor plan of the island kitchen shown in Fig. 16-1, using the scale ¼″ = 1′—0″.

2 Sketch a floor plan of the U-shaped kitchen shown in Fig. 16-4. Show the position of the dining area in relation to this kitchen, using the scale ¼″ = 1′—0″.

3 Sketch a floor plan of the island kitchen shown in Fig. 16-13. Change it to a peninsula kitchen, using the scale ¼″ = 1′—0″.

4 Remodel the kitchen shown in Fig. 16-22. Change door arrangements and dining facilities as needed.

5 Sketch a floor plan of the kitchen in your own home. Prepare a revised sketch to show how you would propose to redesign this kitchen. Make an attempt to reduce the size of the work triangle.

DRAWING KITCHENS

In planning and drawing kitchen floor plans, use template planning techniques and procedures as outlined in Unit 31, "Functional Room Planning." However, once basic dimensions are established or if room dimensions are predetermined, follow the steps outlined in Fig. 16-21 in drawing a kitchen floor plan.

6 Sketch a floor plan of a kitchen you would include in a house of your own design, using the scale ¼″ = 1′—0″.

7 Define the following terms: *work triangle, U-shape, peninsula, L-shape, corridor, island, family kitchen, storage and mixing center, planning and preparation center, cooking center, major appliances, minor appliances, base cabinet, wall cabinet, counter top, service area.*

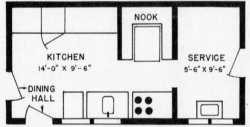

Fig 16-22 Remodel this kitchen.

UNIT 17
UTILITY ROOMS

The *utility room* may include facilities for washing, drying, ironing, sewing, and storing household cleaning equipment. It may contain heating and air-conditioning equipment or even some pantry shelves for storing groceries. Other names for rooms of this type are *service room, all-purpose room,* and *laundry room* (Fig. 17-1).

If the utility room is used for heating and air-conditioning, space must be planned for the furnace, heating and air-conditioning ducts, hot-water heater, and any related equipment such as humidifiers or air purifiers.

SHAPE AND SIZE

The shapes and sizes of utility rooms differ, as shown in Fig. 17-2. The average floor space required for appliances, counter, and storage area is 100 square feet (10 m²). However, this size may vary according to the budget or needs of the household.

STYLE AND DECOR

Style and decor in a utility room depend on the function of the appliances, which are themselves an important factor in the appearance of the room. Simplicity, straight lines, and continuous counter spaces produce an orderly effect and permit work to progress easily. Such features also make the room easy to clean.

An important part of the decor is the color of the paint used for walls and cabinet finishes. Colors should harmonize with the colors used on the appliances. All finishes should be washable. The walls may be lined with sound-absorbing tiles or wood paneling.

The lighting in a utility room should be carefully planned so that it will be 48" (1220 mm) above the equipment used for washing, ironing, and sewing (Fig. 17-3). However, the lighting fixtures placed above the preparation area and laundry sinks can be farther from the work-top area, as shown in Fig. 17-3.

THE LAUNDRY AREA

The laundry area is only one part of the utility room, but it is usually the most important center. To make laundry work as easy as possible, the appliances and working spaces in a laundry area should be located in the order in which they will be used. Such an arrangement will save time and effort. There are four steps in the process of laundering. The equipment needed for each of these steps should be grouped so that the person doing the laundry can proceed from one stage to the next in an orderly and efficient way (Fig. 17-4).

Frigidaire Division, General Motors Corporation

Fig 17-1 Two main functions of a utility room include washing and drying clothes.

Fig 17-2 The size of a utility room varies according to the budget and needs of the family.

VERY SMALL
70 SQUARE FEET

SMALL
90 SQUARE FEET

AVERAGE
100 SQUARE FEET

LARGE
120 SQUARE FEET

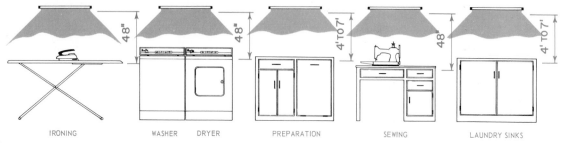

Fig 17-3 The lighting for a utility room must be carefully planned.

Fig 17-4 The appliances and working spaces should be arranged in the order in which they are used.

RECEIVING AND PREPARING LAUNDRY The first step in laundering—receiving and preparing the items—requires hampers or bins, as well as counters on which to collect and sort the articles. Near this equipment there should be storage facilities for laundry products such as detergents, bleaches, and stain removers.

WASHING The next step, the actual washing, takes place in the area containing the washing machine and laundry tubs or sink.

DRYING The equipment needed for this stage of the work includes a dryer, indoor drying lines, and space to store clothespins.

IRONING AND STORAGE For the last part of the process, the required equipment consists of an iron and a board, a counter for folding, a rack on which to hang finished ironing, and facilities for sewing and mending. If a sewing machine is included, it may be portable, or it may fold into a counter or wall.

LOCATION

SEPARATE LAUNDRY AREA The location of the laundry area in a utility room is desirable because all laundry functions, including repairs, are centered in one place. A further advantage of the separate room is that laundering is kept well apart from the preparation of foods (Fig. 17-5).

Space is not always available for a utility room, however, and the laundry appliances and space for washing and drying may need to be located in some other area. Wherever it is placed, the equipment in the laundry unit

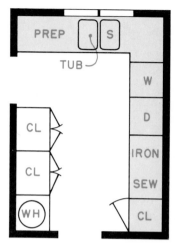

Fig 17-5 Plan of a separate laundry area.

Fig 17-6 Location of laundry in kitchen.

should be arranged in the order in which the work must be done.

THE KITCHEN Placing the laundry unit in the kitchen has some advantages. The unit is in a central location and is near a service entrance. Plumbing facilities are near, and counters may be used for folding (Fig. 17-6).

OTHER LOCATIONS Laundry appliances may be located in a closet (Fig. 17-7), on a service porch, in a basement, or in a garage or carport. The service porch, basement, garage, or carport provides less expensive floor space than other parts of the house.

Fig 17-7 The plan of an alternate laundry location. Having the laundry near the kitchen will minimize plumbing problems.

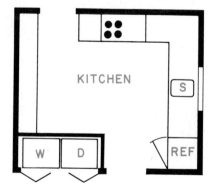

1 Sketch a complete laundry floor plan from that shown in Fig. 17-1. Show positions of appliances and equipment.
2 Design a utility room with a complete laundry within an area of 100 square feet, or 10 m² if working with a metric scale.
3 Design a utility room for the house you are designing.
4 Define the following terms: *utility room, laundry area, hamper, water heater.*

UNIT 18

GARAGES AND CARPORTS

Storage of the automobile occupies a large percentage of the available space of the house or property. Garages and carports must therefore be designed with the greatest care to ensure maximum utilization of space.

GARAGE

A *garage* is a structure designed primarily to shelter an automobile. It may be used for

DETACHED   BREEZEWAY

ATTACHED   UNDER HOUSE   SUBTERRANEAN

Fig 18-1 Possible locations for the garage.

many secondary purposes—as a workshop, for example—or for storage space. A garage may be connected with the house (*integral*) or it may be a separate building (*detached*). Figure 18-1 shows several possible garage locations.

Fig 18-2 A carport provides only overhead protection.

Home Planners, Inc.

Fig 18-3 The garage style must be integrated with the house style.

Scholz Homes

Home Planners, Inc.

Fig 18-4 A breezeway provides protection for a detached garage.

CARPORT

A *carport* is a garage with one or more of the exterior walls removed. It may consist of a freestanding roof completely separate from the house, or it may be built against the existing walls of the house (Fig. 18-2). Carports are most acceptable in mild climates where complete protection from cold weather is not needed. A carport offers protection primarily from sun and precipitation.

The garage and the carport both have distinct advantages. The garage is more secure and provides more shelter. However, carports lend themselves to open-planning techniques and are less expensive to build than garages.

DESIGN

The lines of the garage or carport should be consistent with the major building lines of the house. The style of the garage should be consistent with the style of architecture used in the house (Fig. 18-3).

The garage or carport must never appear as an afterthought. Often a patio, porch, or breezeway is planned between the garage and the house to integrate a detached garage with the house (Fig. 18-4). A covered walkway from the garage or carport to the house should be provided if the garage is detached.

The garage floor must be solid and easily maintained. A concrete slab 3" or 4" (75 or 100 mm) thick provides the best deck for a garage or carport. The garage floor must have adequate drainage either to the outside or

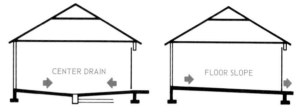

Fig 18-5 Proper drainage is important for the garage.

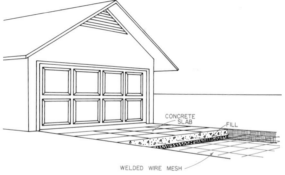

Fig 18-6 Steel-wire mesh in the concrete will help keep the pavement and garage floor from cracking.

through drains located inside the garage (Fig. 18-5). A vapor barrier consisting of waterproof materials under the slab should be provided. The driveway should be of asphalt or concrete construction, preferably with welded-wire fabric to maintain rigidity (Fig. 18-6).

The design of the garage door greatly affects the appearance of the garage. Several types of garage doors are available. These include the two-leaf swinging, overhead, four-leaf swinging, and sectional roll-up doors (Fig. 18-7). Several electronic devices are available for opening the door of the garage from the car.

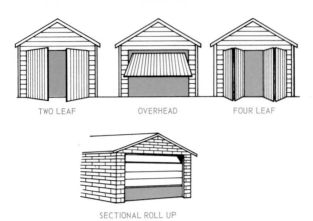

TWO LEAF   OVERHEAD   FOUR LEAF

SECTIONAL ROLL UP

Fig 18-7 Four common types of garage doors.

SIZE

The size and number of automobiles and the additional facilities needed for storage or workshop use should determine the size of the garage (Fig. 18-8).

The dimensions of a single-car garage range between 11' × 19' (3.4 × 5.8 m) and 13' × 25' (4.0 × 7.6 m). A garage that is 16' × 25' (4.9 × 7.6 m) is more desirable if space is needed for benches, mowers, tools, and the storage of children's vehicles. A full double garage is 25' × 25' (7.6 × 7.6 m).

A two-car garage does not cost twice as much as a one-car garage. However, if the second half is added at a later date, the cost will more than double.

STORAGE

Storage is often an additional function of most garages. The storage space over the hood of the car should be utilized effectively (Fig. 18-9). Cabinets should be elevated from the floor several inches to avoid moisture and to facilitate cleaning the garage floor. Garden-tool cabinets can be designed to open from the outside of the garage.

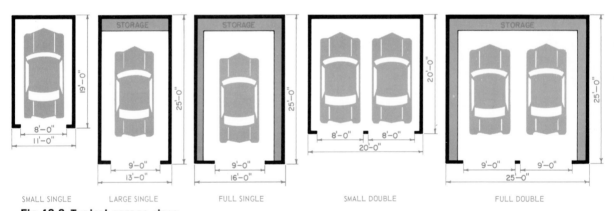

SMALL SINGLE   LARGE SINGLE   FULL SINGLE   SMALL DOUBLE   FULL DOUBLE

Fig 18-8 Typical garage sizes.

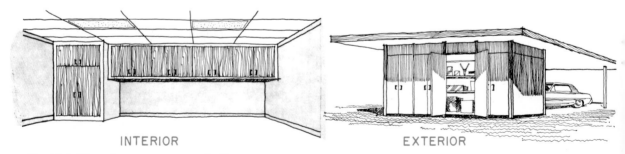

INTERIOR   EXTERIOR

Fig 18-9 Plans for storage space in the garage or carport.

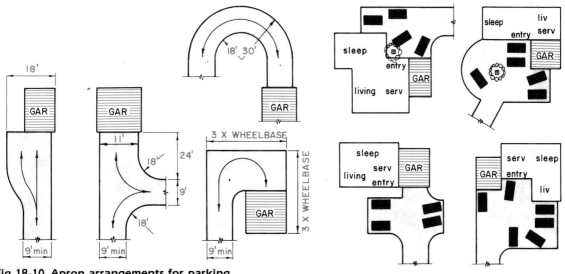

Fig 18-10 Apron arrangements for parking and turning.

DRIVEWAY

A driveway can be planned for purposes other than providing access to the garage and temporary parking space for guests. By adding a wider space to an apron at the door of the garage, an area can be provided for car washing and polishing and for a hard, level surface for children's games. Aprons are often needed to provide space for turning the car in order to eliminate backing out onto a main street (Fig. 18-10).

The driveway should be accessible to all entrances, and the garage should provide easy access to the service area of the home. Suffi-

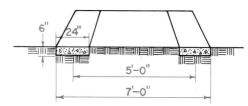

Fig 18-11 A typical driveway width.

cient space in the driveway should be provided for parking of guests' cars.

Driveways should be designed at least several feet wider than the track of the car (approximately 9′ or 2.7 m). However, slightly wider driveways are desirable (Fig. 18-11) for access and pedestrian traffic.

PROBLEMS

1 Sketch the floor plan from Fig. 11-14, and design a garage, apron, and driveway for it.
2 Sketch a front elevation for a small single garage, using the scale ¼″ = 1′—0″.

3 Design a full double garage for the house of your design, and draw in storage, laundry, and workbench.

4 Convert a large double garage to a recreation and entertainment area. Sketch the layout.
5 Sketch a two-car garage plan. Show the following storage facilities: storage wall, outside storage, boat slung from ceiling, laundry area, gardening equipment, storage over the hood of the cars.
6 Define these architectural terms: *garage, carport, breezeway, subterranean, apron, integral garage, detached garage.*

UNIT 19
MAINTENANCE AND WORKSHOP AREA

The home work area is designed for activities ranging from hobbies to home-maintenance work (Fig. 19-1). The home work area may be located in part of the garage, in the basement, in a separate room, or in an adjacent building (Fig. 19-2).

LAYOUT

Power tools, hand tools, workbench space, and storage should be systematically planned. A workbench complete with vise is needed in every home work area. The average workbench is 36″ (915 mm) high. A movable workbench is appropriate when large projects are to be constructed. A *peninsula workbench* provides three working sides and storage compartments on three sides. A dropleaf workbench is excellent for work areas where a minimum amount of space is available.

HAND TOOLS

Some hand tools are basic to all types of hobbies or home-maintenance work. These basic tools include a claw hammer, carpenter's square, files, hand drills, screwdrivers, planes, pliers, chisels, scales, wrenches, saws, a brace and bit, mallets, and clamps.

POWER TOOLS

Although power tools are not absolutely necessary for the performance of most home workshop activities, they do make the performance of many tasks easier and quicker. Some of the more common power tools used in home workshops include electric drills, sabersaws, routers, band saws, circular saws, radial-arm saws, jointers, belt sanders, lathes, and drill presses. Placement of equipment should be planned to provide the maximum

Fig 19-1 The home work area is often used for home maintenance and hobby work.

Lisanti, Inc.

Fig 19-2 The home workshop may be located in the garage, the basement, or a separate building.

SEPARATE SHOP

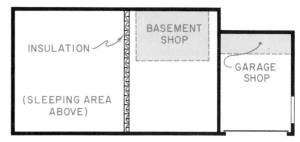

INSULATION

BASEMENT SHOP

GARAGE SHOP

(SLEEPING AREA ABOVE)

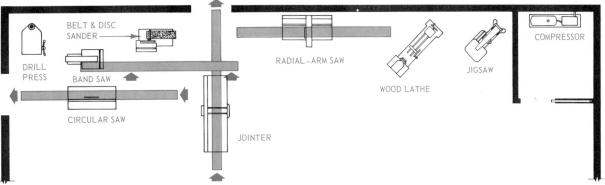

Fig 19-3 Machinery must be spaced for proper clearances.

amount of work space. Figure 19-3 suggests clearances necessary for safe and efficient machine operation.

Multipurpose machines are machines that can perform a variety of operations. Multipurpose equipment is popular for use in the home workshop since the purchase of only one piece of equipment is necessary and the amount of space needed is relatively small, compared with the amount of space needed for a variety of machines.

Tools and equipment needed for working with large materials should be placed where the material can be easily handled. Separate-drive motors can be used to drive more than one piece of power equipment, in order to conserve motors. Separate electrical circuits for lights and power tools should be included in the plans for the home workshop area.

STORAGE FACILITIES

Maximum storage facilities in the home work area are essential. Hand tools may be stored in cabinets that keep them dust-free and safe, or hung on perforated hardboard, as shown in Fig. 19-4. Tools too small to be hung should be kept in special-purpose drawers, and any inflammable finishing material, such as turpentine or oil paint, should be stored in metal cabinets.

SIZE AND SHAPE

The size of the work area depends on the size and number of power tools and equipment, the amount of workbench area, and the

Fig 19-4 Perforated hardboards can be used for hanging tools.

Georgia Pacific

Fig 19-5 A three-stage development of a workshop.

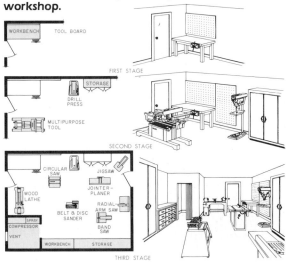

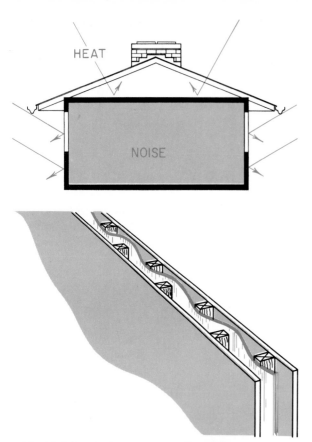

Fig 19-6 Insulation prevents disturbing noises from entering other parts of the house.

added, it will fit appropriately into the basic plan (Fig. 19-5).

The designer must anticipate the type and number of materials for which storage space will be needed and design the storage space accordingly.

DECOR

The work area should be as maintenance-free as possible. Glossy paint or tile retards an accumulation of shop dust on the walls. Exhaust fans eliminate much of the dust and the gasses produced in the shop. The shop floor should be of concrete or linoleum for easy maintenance. Abrasive strips around machines will eliminate the possibility of slipping. Do not locate noisy equipment near the children's sleeping area. Interior walls and ceilings should be soundproofed by offsetting studs and adding adequate insulation to produce a sound barrier (Fig. 19-6).

Light and color are most important factors in designing the work area. Pastel colors, which reduce eye strain, should be used for the general color scheme of the shop. Extremely light colors that produce glare, and extremely dark colors that reduce effective illumination, should be avoided. Adopting one of the major paint manufacturers' color systems for color coding will help to create a pleasant atmosphere in the shop and will also help to provide the most efficient and safest working conditions.

General lighting should be provided in the shop to a level of 100 footcandles (1076 lux) on machines and worktable tops.

amount of tool and material storage facilities provided. The size of the work area should be planned for maximum expansion, even though only a workbench or a few tools may be available when the area is first occupied. Therefore, space for the maximum amount of facilities should be planned and located when the area is designed. As new equipment is

PROBLEMS

1 Design a small work area to fit into a single garage that will also house a car (see Unit 18).
2 Design a work area to fill one side of a double garage (see Unit 18).
3 Design a work area in a double garage for an activity other than woodworking (ceremics, jewelry, metalworking, or au-

tomotive repairs, for example). Show what tools and work areas are necessary.

4 Design a work area for the house of your choice. Use a basement or garage location.
5 Define the following architectural terms: *dehumidifier, workbench, perforated hardboard, flammable, hand tools, power tools, multipurpose tools.*

UNIT 20
STORAGE AREAS

Storage areas should be provided for general storage and for specific storage within each room (Fig. 20-1). Areas that would otherwise be considered wasted space should be used as general storage areas. Parts of the basement, attic, or garage often fall into this category. Effective storage planning is necessary to provide storage facilities within each room that will create the least amount of inconvenience in securing the stored articles. Articles that are used daily or weekly should be stored in or near the room where they will

be used. Articles that are used only seasonally should be placed in more permanent general storage areas.

STORAGE FACILITIES

Storage facilities, equipment, and furniture used for storage within the various rooms of the house are divided into the following categories (Fig. 20-2):

WARDROBE CLOSETS A *wardrobe closet* is a shallow clothes closet built into the wall. The minimum depth for the wardrobe is 24" (610 mm). If this closet is more than 30" (760 mm) deep, you will be unable to reach the back of the closet. Swinging or sliding doors should expose all parts of the closet to your reach. A disadvantage of the wardrobe

Fig 20-1 Locations of storage areas.

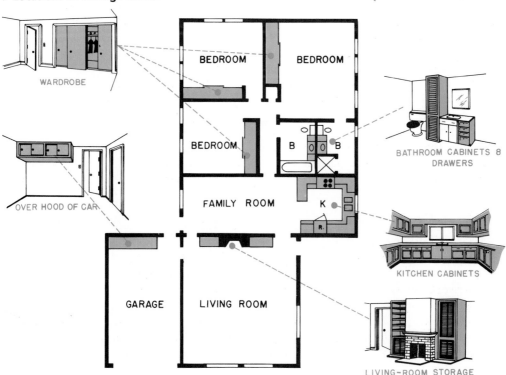

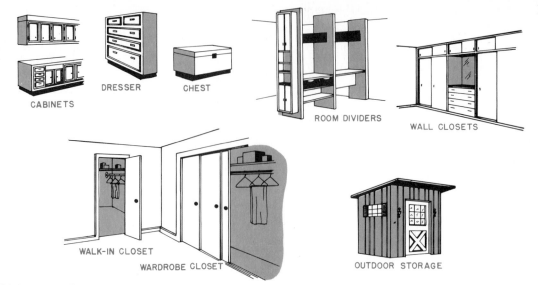

Fig 20-2 **Types of storage facilities.**

closet is the amount of wall space needed for the doors (Fig. 20-3).

WALK-IN CLOSETS Walk-in closets are closets large enough to walk into. The area needed for this type of closet is an area equal to the amount of space needed to hang clothes plus enough space to walk and turn. Although some area is wasted in the passage, the use of the walk-in closet does provide more wall area for furniture placement, since only one door is needed (Fig. 20-4).

WALL CLOSETS A *wall closet* is a shallow closet in the wall holding cupboards, shelves, and drawers. Wall closets are normally 18″ (460 mm) deep, since this size provides access to all stored items without using an excessive amount of floor area (Fig. 20-5). Figure 20-6 is an example of effective wall storage closets.

Protruding closets that create an offset in a room should be avoided. Often by filling the entire wall between two bedrooms with closet

Fig 20-3 **Dimensions for wardrobe closets.**

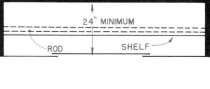

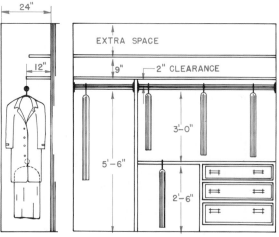

Fig 20-4 **Dimensions for walk-in closets.**

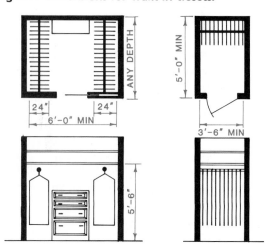

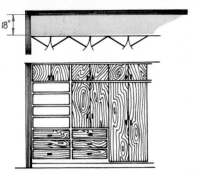

Fig 20-5 Wall storage uses a minimum of floor space.

Fig 20-6 Built-in closets and drawer storage.

Home Planners, Inc.

space, it is possible to design a square or rectangular room without the use of offsets (Fig. 20-7). Doors on closets should be sufficiently wide to allow easy accessibility. Swing-out doors have the advantage of providing extra storage space on the back of the door. However, space must be allowed for the swing. For this reason, sliding doors are usually preferred. All closets, except very shallow linen closets, should be provided with lighting.

CHESTS AND DRESSERS Chests and dressers are free standing pieces of furniture used for storage, generally in the bedroom. They are available in a variety of sizes, usually with shelves and drawers.

ROOM DIVIDERS A room divider often doubles as a storage area, especially when a protruding closet divides several areas. Room dividers often extend from the floor to the ceiling or may only be several feet high. Many room dividers include shelves and drawers that open from both sides (Fig. 20-8).

LOCATION

Different types of storage facilities are necessary for areas of the home, depending on the type of article to be stored. The most appropriate types of storage facilities for each room in the house are as follows:

Living room: room divider, built-in wall cabinets (Fig. 20-9), bookcases, window seats

Dining area: room divider, built-in wall closet

Family room: built-in wall storage, window seats

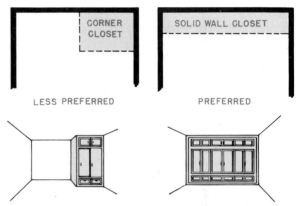

Fig 20-7 Avoid closets that create offsets.

Fig 20-8 Room dividers can be used for storage.

Home Planners, Inc.

121

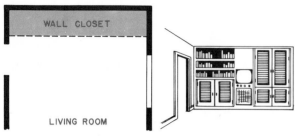

Fig 20-9 Built-in wall cabinets.

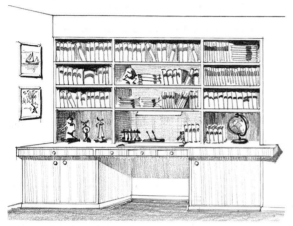

Fig 20-10 Den storage.

Recreation room: built-in wall storage

Porches: under porch stairs, walk-in closet

Patios: sides of barbecue, separate building

Outside: closets built into the side of the house

Halls: solid built-in wall closets, ends of blind halls.

Entrance: room divider, wardrobe, walk-in closet

Den: built-in wall closet, window seats, bookcases (Fig. 20-10).

Kitchen: wall and floor cabinets, room divider, wall closets (Fig. 20-11).

Utility room: cabinets on floor and walls

Garage: cabinets over hood of car, wall closets along sides, added construction on the outside of the garage

Work area: open tool board, wall closets, cabinets

Bedroom: walk-in closet, wardrobe closet, under bed, foot of bed, head of bed, built-in cabinets and shelves, dressers, chests

Bathroom: cabinets on floor and walls, room dividers

Abbott Hall

Fig 20-11 Kitchen cabinet storage.

PROBLEMS

1 Draw the floor plan in Fig. 32-8, using the scale $\frac{1}{4}'' = 1'-0''$. Add all needed storage space.

2 Draw the floor plan in Fig. 13-3, using the scale $\frac{1}{4}'' = 1'-0''$. Add all the needed storage space.

3 Draw the floor plan in Fig. 32-9, using the scale $\frac{1}{4}'' = 1'-0''$. Add all needed storage space.

4 How many square feet of storage area are there in Fig. 20-11? Is this at least 7 percent of the area of the house?

5 Add storage facilities to the first and second floor of the house shown in Fig. 33-19. Sketch your solution and label each storage area.

6 Add storage facilities to the house of your design.

SLEEPING AREA

One-third of our time is spent in sleeping. Because of its importance, the sleeping area should be planned to provide facilities for maximum comfort and relaxation. The sleeping area is usually located in a quiet part of the house and contains bedrooms, baths, dressing areas, and nurseries.

UNIT 21
BEDROOMS

Houses are usually classified by size according to the number of bedrooms; for example, a three-bedroom home, or a four-bedroom home. In a home there are bedrooms, master bedrooms, and nursery rooms, according to the size of the family.

FUNCTION

The primary function of a bedroom is to provide facilities for sleeping. Some bedrooms may also provide facilities for writing, reading, sewing, listening to music, or generally relaxing.

NUMBER OF BEDROOMS

Ideally, each member of the family should have his or her own private bedroom. A family with no children may require only one bedroom. However, two bedrooms are usually desirable, in order to provide one for guest use (Fig. 21-1). Three-bedroom homes are most popular because they provide a minimum of accommodation for a family with one boy and one girl. As a family enlarges,

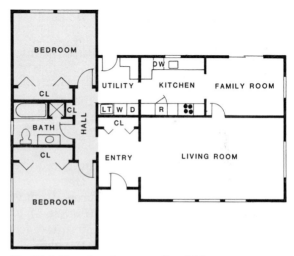

Fig 21-1 The sleeping area should be away from the activity area of the home.

boys can share one bedroom and girls can share the other. With only two bedrooms, that is not possible.

SIZES AND SHAPES

The size and shape of a bedroom depend upon the amount of furniture needed. A minimum-sized bedroom would accommodate a single bed, bedside table, and dresser. In contrast, a complete master bedroom might include a double bed or twin beds, bedside stands, dresser, chest of drawers, lounge chair, dressing area, and adjacent master bath (Fig. 21-2).

123

Fig 21-2 Dressing area adjacent to the master bedroom.

Scholz Homes

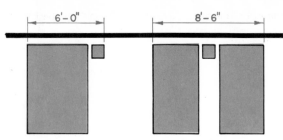

Fig 21-4 Much wall space is needed for bedroom furniture.

Fig 21-5 A small bedroom.

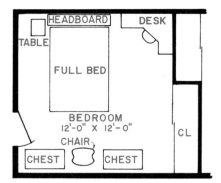

Fig 21-6 An average-sized bedroom.

SPACE REQUIREMENTS

The type and style of furniture included in the bedroom should be chosen before the size of the bedroom is established. The size of the furniture should determine the size of the room, and not the reverse. Average bedroom furniture sizes are shown in Fig. 21-3. The wall space needed for twin beds is 8'—6" (2.6 m). A full bed with a night stand requires 6' (1.8 m) of wall space (Fig. 21-4).

A small bedroom would average from 90 to 100 square feet (8 to 10 m²) (Fig. 21-5), an average bedroom from 100 to 150 square feet (10 to 15 m²) (Fig. 21-6), and a large bedroom over 200 square feet (20 m²) (Fig. 21-7).

Fig 21-3 Typical bedroom furniture sizes.

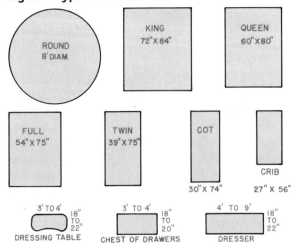

WALL SPACE

Since wall space is critical in the placement of furniture in the bedroom, the designer must plan for maximum wall space. One method of conserving wall space for bedroom furniture placement is to use high windows. High, shallow windows allow furniture to be placed underneath, and they also provide some privacy for the bedroom.

BEDROOM DOORS

Unless it has doors leading to a patio, the bedroom will normally have only one access

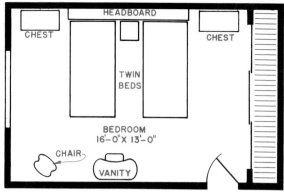

Fig 21-7 A large bedroom.

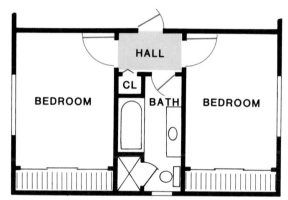

Fig 21-8 Bedroom doors should not open into halls.

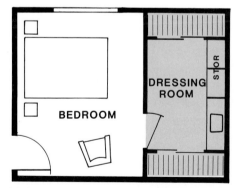

Fig 21-9 A dressing area.

door from the inside. Entrance doors, closet doors, and windows should be grouped to conserve wall space whenever possible. Separating these doors slightly will spread out the amount of unusuable wall space by eliminating long stretches of unused wall space. Slid-

ing doors for closets and for entrance doors help to conserve valuable wall space in bedrooms. If swinging doors are used, the door should always swing into the bedroom and not into the hall (Fig. 21-8).

DRESSING AREAS

Dressing areas are sometimes separate rooms or an alcove or a part of the room separated by a divider (Fig. 21-9).

NOISE CONTROL

Since noise contributes to fatigue, it is important to plan for the elimination of as much noise as possible from the bedroom area (Fig. 21-10). The following guides for noise control will help you design bedrooms that are quiet and restful:

1 The bedroom should be in the quiet part of the house, away from major street noises.
2 Carpeting or soft cork wall panels help to absorb many noises.
3 Rooms above a bedroom should be carpeted.
4 Floor-to-ceiling draperies help to reduce noise.
5 Acoustical tile in the ceiling is effective in reducing noise.
6 Trees and shrubbery outside the bedroom help deaden sounds.
7 The use of insulating glass in windows and sliding doors helps to seal off the bedroom.
8 The windows of an air-conditioned room should be kept closed during hot weather. Air conditioning eliminates much noise and aids in keeping the bedroom free from dust and pollen.
9 Air is a good insulator; therefore, closets provide additional buffers which eliminate much noise coming from other rooms.
10 In extreme cases when complete soundproofing is desired, fibrous materials in

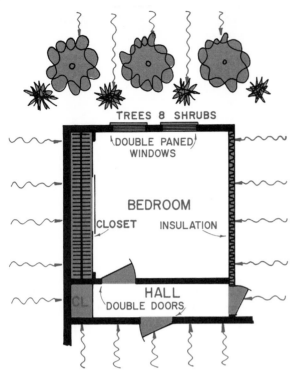

Fig 21-10 Some methods of bedroom noise control.

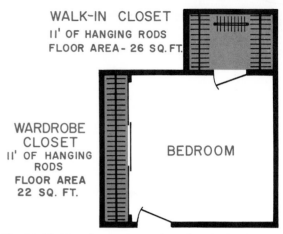

WALK-IN CLOSET
11' OF HANGING RODS
FLOOR AREA- 26 SQ. FT.

WARDROBE CLOSET
11' OF HANGING RODS
FLOOR AREA 22 SQ. FT.

BEDROOM

Fig 21-11 Hanging rods are best for storing clothing.

Home Planners, Inc.

Fig 21-12 Built-in storage helps eliminate offsets.

the walls may be used, and studs may be offset to provide a sound buffer.

11 Placing rubber pads under appliances such as refrigerators, dishwashers, washers, and dryers often eliminates much vibration and noise throughout the house.

STORAGE SPACE

Storage space in the bedroom is needed primarily for clothing and personal accessories. Storage areas should be easy to reach, easy to maintain, and large. Walk-in closets or wardrobe closets should be built in for hanging clothes (Fig. 21-11). Care should be taken to eliminate offset closets. Balancing offset closets from one room to an adjacent bedroom helps solve this problem. Providing built-in storage facilities also helps in overcoming awkward offsets, as shown in Fig. 21-12. Except for the storage space provided in dressers, chests, vanities, and dressing tables, most storage space should be provided in the closet.

Double rooms (Fig. 21-13) allow for maximum storage, yet provide flexibility and privacy as the family expands.

VENTILATION

Proper ventilation is necessary and is conducive to sound rest and sleep. Central air conditioning and humidity control provide constant levels of temperature and humidity and are an efficient method of providing ventilation and air circulation. When air conditioning is available, the windows and doors may remain closed. Without air conditioning, windows and doors must provide the ventilation. Bedrooms should have cross-ventilation.

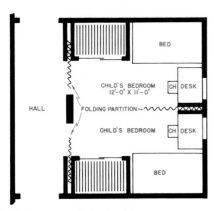

Fig 21-13 A convertible double room.

However, the draft must not pass over the bed (Fig. 21-14). High ribbon windows provide light, privacy, and cross-ventilation without causing a draft on the bed. Jalousie windows are also effective, since they direct air upward.

NURSERIES

Children's bedrooms and nurseries need special facilities. They must be planned to be comfortable, quiet, and sufficiently flexible to change as the child grows and matures (Fig. 21-15). Storage shelves and rods in closets should be adjustable so that they may be raised as the child becomes taller. Light switches should be placed low, with a delay switch which allows the light to stay on for some time after the switch has been thrown.

Chalkboards and bulletin boards help make the child's room usable. Adequate facilities for study and some hobby activities should be provided, such as a desk and worktable as shown in Fig. 21-16. Storage space for books, models, and athletic equipment is also desirable.

DECOR

Bedrooms should be decorated in quiet, restful tones. Matching or contrasting bedspreads, draperies, and carpets help accent the color scheme. Uncluttered furniture with simple lines also helps to develop a restful atmosphere in the bedroom.

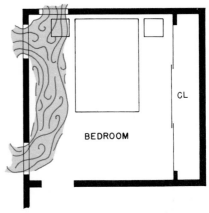

Fig 21-14 Cross-ventilation that does not pass over the bed is desirable.

Fig 21-15 Bedroom furnishings must change as children grow older.

BABY'S BEDROOM

CHILD'S BEDROOM

TEENAGER'S BEDROOM

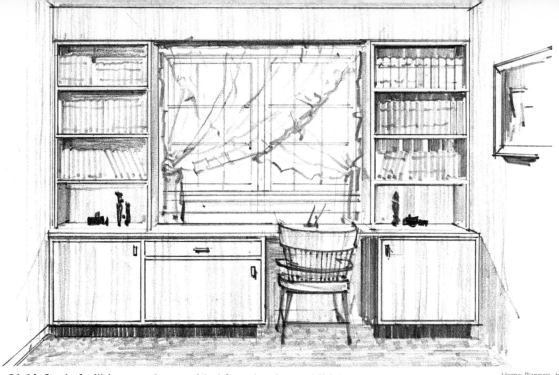

Fig 21-16 Study facilities must be provided for school-age children.

Home Planners, Inc.

PROBLEMS

1 Design a bedroom, 100 square feet (or 10 m²) in size, for a very young child.

2 Design a bedroom, 150 square feet (or 15 m²) in size, for a teenager.

3 Design a master bedroom that is 200 square feet (or 20 m²) in size.

4 List five things that make a bedroom comfortable for you. Draw the furniture and show its placement to illustrate your list.

5 How could you make your own bedroom more comfortable?

6 A family composed of a mother, a father, and a baby bought a home with the bedroom area shown in Fig. 21-17. The family has expanded and now consists of the mother, the father, and two teenagers. Redesign their bedroom area to fit their needs. Additional area may be added to the exterior of the house.

7 The bath shown in Fig. 21-2 adjoins a master bedroom. Sketch or draw a floor plan of a master bedroom suite using this bath.

8 Design the bedroom areas for the home of your choice.

9 Define these architectural terms: *alcove, insulation, acoustical tile, cross-ventilation.*

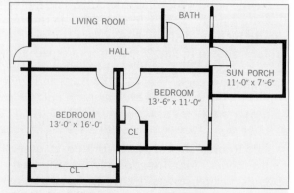

Fig 21-17 Redesign the sleeping area for a family of four.

UNIT 22
BATHS

The design of the bathroom requires careful planning, as does every other room in the house. The bath must be planned to be functional, attractive, and easily maintained (Fig. 22-1).

FUNCTION

In addition to the normal functions of the bath, facilities may also be included for dressing, exercising, sunning, and laundering (Fig. 22-2). Designing the bath involves the appropriate placing of fixtures; providing for adequate ventilation, lighting, and heating; and planning efficient runs for plumbing pipes.

Ideally, it would be advisable to provide a bath for each bedroom, as in Fig. 22-3. Usually, this provision is not possible, and a central bath is designed to meet the needs of the

Fig 22-1 A functional and efficient bath.

entire family (Fig. 22-4). A bath for general use and a bath adjacent to the master bedroom are a desirable compromise (Fig. 22-5). When it is impossible to have a bath with the master bedroom (Fig. 22-6), the general bath should be accessible from all bedrooms in the sleeping area. A bath may also function as a dressing room (Fig. 22-7). In this case, a combina-

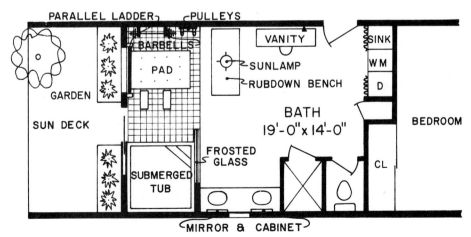

Fig 22-2 A bath may be designed for many functions.

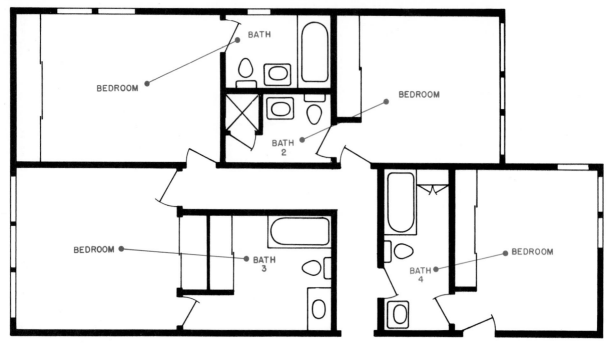

Fig 22-3 A bath for each bedroom would be ideal.

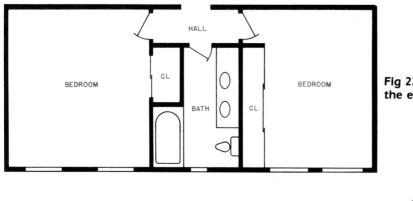

Fig 22-4 A central bath serves the entire family.

Fig 22-5 A bath for the master bedroom and another bath for other bedrooms is a convenient arrangement.

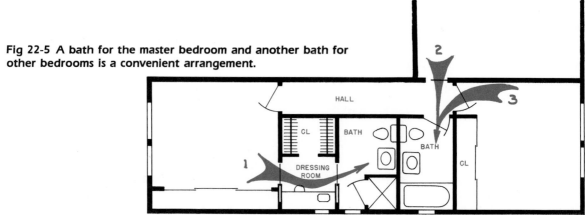

Fig 22-6 A master bedroom bath.

Southern California
Edison Co.

tion bath and dressing room with space for clothing storage can be placed between the bathroom and the bedroom.

FIXTURES

The three *basic fixtures* included in most bathrooms are a *lavatory, water closet,* and *tub or shower.* The efficiency of the bath is greatly dependent upon the effectiveness of the arrangement of these three fixtures. Mirrors should be located a distance from the tub to prevent fogging. Sinks should be well lighted and free from traffic. If sinks are placed 18" (460 mm) from other fixtures, they need no separate plumbing lines. The water closet needs a minimum of 15" (380 mm) from the center to the side wall or other fixtures (Fig. 22-8). Tubs and showers are available in a great variety of sizes and shapes. Square, rectangular, or sunken-pool tubs allow flexibility in fixture arrangement.

VENTILATION

Baths should have either natural ventilation from a window or forced ventilation from an exhaust fan. Care should be taken to place windows in a position where they will not cause a draft on the tub or interfere with privacy.

LIGHTING

Lighting should be relatively shadowless in the area used for grooming (Fig. 22-9). Shadowless general lighting can be achieved

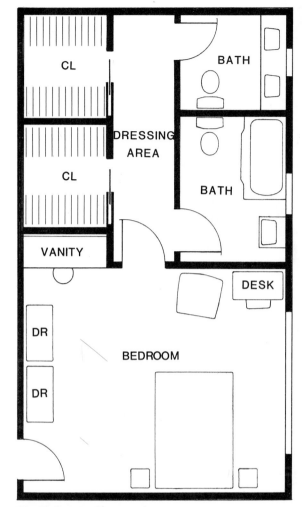

Fig 22-7 A bedroom with a compartment bath and dressing area.

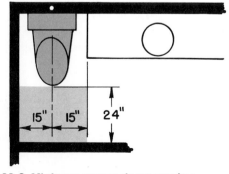

Fig 22-8 Minimum water-closet spacing.

131

Fig 22-9 Shadowless lighting is desirable.

Fig 22-10 Skylights used for bath illumination.

by the use of fluorescent tubes on the ceiling, covered with glass or plastic panels. Skylights, as shown in Fig. 22-10, can also be used for general illumination if the bath is without outside walls.

HEATING

Heating in the bath is most important to prevent chills. In addition to the conventional heating outlets, an electric heater or heat lamp is often used to provide instant heat. It is advisable to have the source of heat under the window to eliminate drafts. All heaters should be properly ventilated.

PLUMBING LINES

The plumbing lines that carry water to and from the fixtures should be concealed and minimized as much as possible. When two bathrooms are placed side by side, placing the fixtures back to back on opposite sides of the plumbing wall results in a reduction of the length of plumbing lines (Fig. 22-11). In multiple-story dwellings, the length of plumbing lines can be reduced and a common plumbing wall used if the baths are placed directly above each other. When a bath is placed on a second floor, a plumbing wall must be provided through the first floor for the soil and water pipes.

LAYOUT

There are two basic types of bathroom layout, the compartment and the open plan. In the *compartment plan, partitions* (sliding doors, glass dividers, louvers, or even plants) are used to divide the bath into several compartments, one housing the water closet, another the lavatory area, and the third the bathing area (Fig. 22-12). In the *open plan,* all bath fixtures are completely visible.

A bath designed for or used by children should include a low or tilt-down mirror, benches for reaching the lavatory, low towel racks, and shelves for bath toys.

SIZE AND SHAPE

The size and shape of the bath are influenced by the spacing of basic fixtures, the

132

Fig 22-11 Fixture arrangements that keep plumbing lines to a minimum.

Fig 22-12 A compartment bath.

Consoweld Corp.

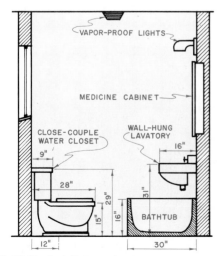

VAPOR-PROOF LIGHTS

MEDICINE CABINET

CLOSE-COUPLE WATER CLOSET

WALL-HUNG LAVATORY

16"

9"

28"

29"

31"

16"

15"

12"

30"

BATHTUB

Fig 22-13 Typical fixture sizes.

number of auxiliary functions requiring additional equipment, the arrangement or compartmentalization of areas, and the relationship to other rooms in the house.

FURNITURE

Typical fixture sizes, as shown in Fig. 22-13, greatly influence the ultimate size of the bath. Figure 22-14 shows minimum-sized baths. Figure 22-15 shows small baths. Figure 22-16 shows average baths, and Fig. 22-17 shows large baths. Regardless of the size, these baths contain the three basic fixtures: lavatory, tub or shower, and water closet.

The sizes given here refer to complete baths and not to *half-baths*, which include only a lavatory and water closet. Half-baths are used in conjunction with the living area and therefore are not designed for bathing.

ACCESSORIES

In addition to the three basic fixtures, the following accessories are often included in a bath designed for optimum use:

exhaust fan
sunlamp
heat lamp
instant wall heater
medicine cabinet
extra mirrors
magnifying mirror
extra counter space
dressing table
whirlpool bath
foot-pedal control for water
single-mixing, one-control faucets
facility for linen storage
clothes hamper
bidet

Figure 22-18 shows a bath with many of these extra features.

DECOR

The bath should be decorated and designed to provide the maximum amount of light and color. Materials used in the bath should be water-resistant, easily maintained, and easily sanitized. Tiles, linoleum, marble,

133

4'-3" x 4'-3"   5'-6" x 4'-3"

Fig 22-14 Minimum-sized baths.

6'-0" x 5'-6"   4'-6" x 5'-6"   8'-6" x 3'-0"

Fig 22-15 Small baths.

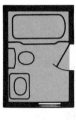

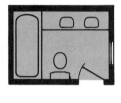

5'-0" x 7'-6"   6'-0" x 8'-0"   8'-0" x 5'-6"

Fig 22-16 Average-sized baths.

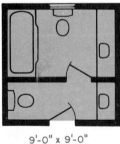
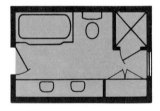

9'-0" x 9'-0"   11'-0" x 7'-0"

Fig 22-17 Large baths.

Fig 22-18 A bath designed with many Armstrong Cork Co.
extra features.

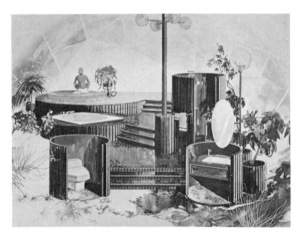

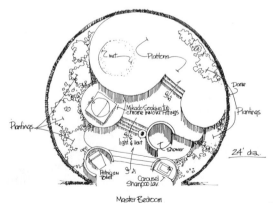

Fig 22-19 Bathrooms can be creatively Kohler Co.
designed.

plastic laminate, and glass are excellent materials for bathroom use. If wallpaper or wood paneling is used, it should be waterproof. If plastered or dry-wall construction is exposed, a gloss or semigloss paint should be used on the surface.

Fixtures and accessories should match in color. Fixtures are now available in a variety

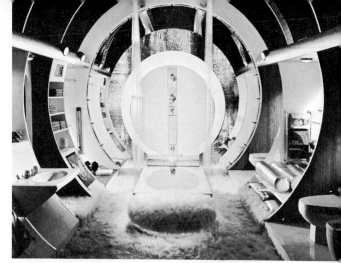

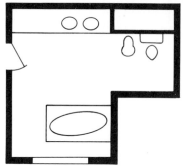

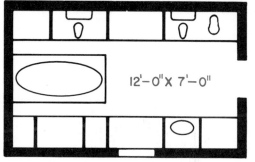

Fig 22-20 Roman decor.

Fig 22-21 Oriental decor.

12'-0" X 7'-0"

Fig 22-22 Bath designed around space-age theme.

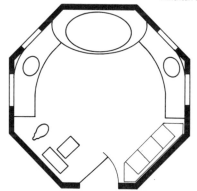

of colors. Matching counter tops and cabinets are also available.

Baths need not be small boxes with plumbing fixtures. With new building materials and products, bathrooms can be designed in an infinite number of arrangements and decors, as shown in Fig. 22-19.

New materials and components are now available which enable the designer to plan bathrooms with modular units that range from one-piece molded showers and tubs to entire bath modules. In these units, plumbing and electrical wiring are connected after the unit is installed.

Today's bathroom need not be strictly functional and sterile in decor. Bathrooms can be planned and furnished in a variety of styles. Figures 22-20 through 22-22 show examples of a variety of bathroom decors and motifs.

PROBLEMS

1 Make a plan for adding fixtures to Fig. 22-23.

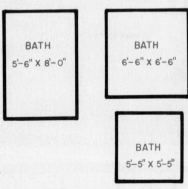

Fig 22-23 Add fixtures to these plans.

2 Draw a plan for remodeling the bath in Fig. 22-24, making the room more efficient.

Fig 22-24 Remodel this bath.

3 Draw a plan for remodeling the bath in Fig. 22-25, making the room more efficient.

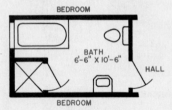

Fig 22-25 Remodel this bath.

4 Design one bedroom and bath in an area of 12' × 17' (or 3.6 × 5.2 m).

5 Sketch or draw a floor plan of the bath shown in Fig. 22-18.

6 Design two bedrooms and a bath in an area 13' × 34' (or 4.0 × 10.4 m).

7 Design two bedrooms and a bath or a master bedroom with bath in an area of 500 square feet (or 50 m²).

8 Redesign the floor plan shown in Fig. 6-2. Add two bedrooms and expand the bath facilities to accommodate these rooms.

9 Draw the plans for the bath areas in the home of your design.

10 Define these architectural terms: *water closet, lavatory, fixture, open bath, sunken tub, shower stall, square tub, rectangular tub.*

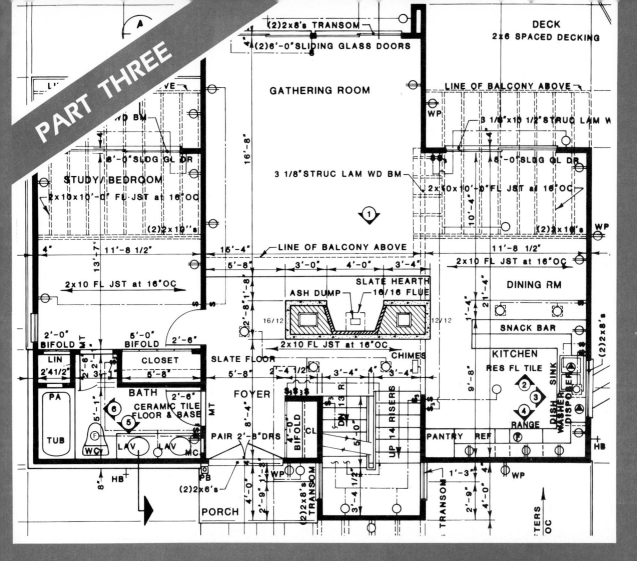

BASIC ARCHITECTURAL PLANS

The general design of a structure is interpreted through several basic architectural plans. These include floor plans, elevations, and pictorial drawings. Floor plans show the arrangement of the internal parts of the design. Elevations graphically describe the exterior design. Pictorial drawings are prepared to show how the structure will appear when complete. In Part Three you will learn how to prepare these basic architectural drawings.

DRAFTING TECHNIQUES

Most of the drafting skills and techniques used in architectural work are similar to those you have learned in mechanical drawing courses. However, there are some drafting procedures that are somewhat different. These involve the use of line techniques, templates, lettering practices, timesaving devices, and dimensioning practices. The differences are primarily due to the large size of most architectural drawings and to the great speed with which architectural plans must be prepared. For those reasons architectural drawings contain many abbreviated techniques.

UNIT 23
ARCHITECTURAL LINE WEIGHTS

Architects use various line weights to emphasize or de-emphasize areas of a drawing. Architectural drafters also use different line weights. Architectural line weights are standardized in order to make possible the consistent interpretation of architectural drawings. Figure 23-1 shows some of the common types of lines and line weights used on architectural drawings. This figure is often called the alphabet of lines. You should learn the name of the line, the number of the pencil used to make the line, and the technique used to draw the line.

USE OF
ALPHABET OF LINES

Hard pencils, as shown in Fig. 23-2, are used for architectural layout work. Medium pencils are used for most final lines, and soft pencils are used for lettering, cutting-plane lines, and shading pictorial drawings. Figure 23-2 shows a comparison of the various types of pencils and the lines they produce. Figure 23-3 shows methods of sharpening pencil points to produce different line weights.

FLOOR-PLAN LINES

Figure 23-4 shows some of the common lines used on architectural floor plans. Those lines are described below:

Object, or *visible, lines* are used to show the main outline of the building, including exterior walls, interior partitions, porches, patios, driveways, and walls. These lines should be the outstanding lines on the drawing.

Dimension lines are thin unbroken lines upon which building dimensions are placed.

Extension lines extend from the visible lines to permit dimensioning. They are drawn very lightly to eliminate confusion with the building outlines.

Hidden lines are used to show areas that

138

NAMES	SYMBOLS	PENCILS

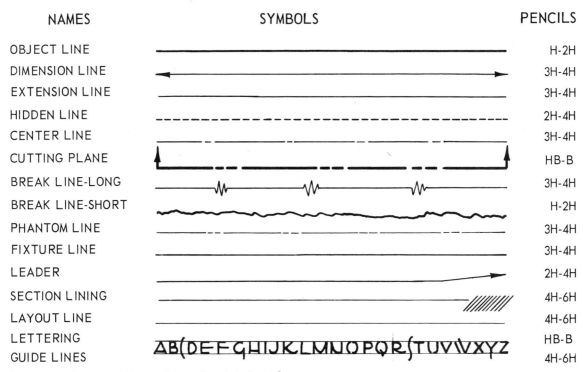

OBJECT LINE		H-2H
DIMENSION LINE		3H-4H
EXTENSION LINE		3H-4H
HIDDEN LINE		2H-4H
CENTER LINE		3H-4H
CUTTING PLANE		HB-B
BREAK LINE-LONG		3H-4H
BREAK LINE-SHORT		H-2H
PHANTOM LINE		3H-4H
FIXTURE LINE		3H-4H
LEADER		2H-4H
SECTION LINING		4H-6H
LAYOUT LINE		4H-6H
LETTERING		HB-B
GUIDE LINES	ABCDEFGHIJKLMNOPQRSTUVWXYZ	4H-6H

Fig 23-1 Architectural line weights; the alphabet of lines.

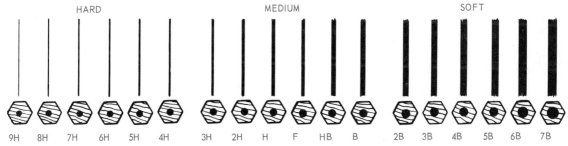

HARD   MEDIUM   SOFT

9H 8H 7H 6H 5H 4H   3H 2H H F HB B   2B 3B 4B 5B 6B 7B

Fig 23-2 Degrees of hardness of lead, cross sections of pencils, and their matching lines used for architectural drawings.

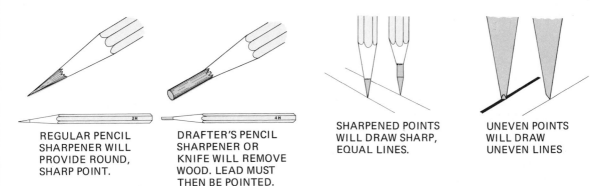

REGULAR PENCIL SHARPENER WILL PROVIDE ROUND, SHARP POINT.

DRAFTER'S PENCIL SHARPENER OR KNIFE WILL REMOVE WOOD. LEAD MUST THEN BE POINTED.

SHARPENED POINTS WILL DRAW SHARP, EQUAL LINES.

UNEVEN POINTS WILL DRAW UNEVEN LINES

Fig 23-3 Results of pencil pointing.

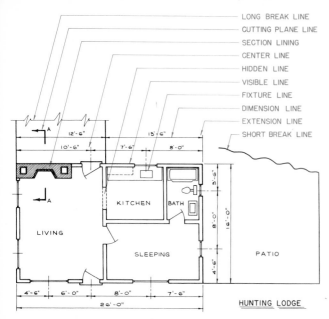

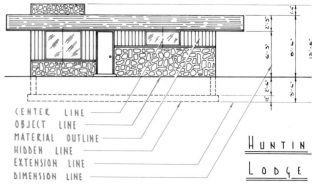

Fig 23-5 Types of lines used on elevation drawings.

Fig 23-4 Types of lines used on floor plans.

are not visible on the surface but which exist behind the plane of projection. Hidden lines are also used in floor plans to show objects *above* the floor section, such as wall cabinets, arches, and beams.

Center lines denote the center of symmetrical objects such as exterior doors and windows. These lines are usually necessary for dimensioning purposes.

Cutting-plane lines are very heavy lines used to denote an area to be sectioned. In this case, the only part of the cutting-plane line drawn is the extreme ends of the line. This is because the cutting-plane line would interfere with other lines on this drawing.

Break lines are used when an area cannot or should not be drawn entirely. A ruled line with freehand breaks is used for long, straight breaks. A wavy, uneven freehand line is used for smaller, irregular breaks.

Phantom lines (not shown but see Fig. 35-21) are used to indicate alternate positions of moving parts, adjacent po-

sitions of related parts, and repeated detail.

Fixture lines outline the shape of kitchen, laundry, and bathroom fixtures, or built-in furniture. These lines are light to eliminate confusion with object lines.

Leaders are used to connect a note or dimension to part of the building. They are drawn lightly and sometimes are curved to eliminate confusion with other lines.

Section lines are used to draw the section lining in sectional drawings. A different material symbol is used for each building material. The section lining is drawn lighter than the object lines.

ELEVATION LINES

Figure 23-5 shows the application of the lines used on architectural elevation drawings. The technique and weight of each of the lines are exactly the same as those for the lines used on floor plans except that they are drawn on a vertical plane.

PAPER

Since the type of paper on which the line is drawn will greatly affect the line weight, different pencils may be necessary. Weather conditions such as temperature and humidity, also greatly affect the line quality. During periods of high humidity, harder pencils must be employed.

PROBLEMS

1 Identify the types of lines indicated by the letters in Fig. 23-6.
2 List the grade of pencil you would use to draw each of the lines shown in Fig. 23-4.
3 Practice drawing each of the lines shown in Fig. 23-1, using your T square and triangle.
4 Draw an object line, a dimension line, and a cutting-plane line on several different surfaces, such as tracing paper, tracing cloth, vellum, bond paper, and illustration board. Compare the results.
5 Define these terms: *line weights, alphabet of lines, hard lead, soft lead, object lines, dimension lines, extension lines, hidden lines, center lines, cutting-plane lines, break lines, phantom lines, fixture lines, leaders, section lines, elevation lines.*

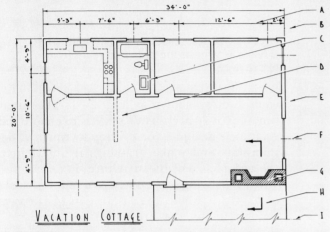

Fig 23-6 Identify the types of lines lettered A through I.

UNIT 24
ARCHITECT'S SCALES

In ancient times, simple structures were built without detailed architectural plans and even without established dimensions. The outline of the structure and the position of each room could be determined experimentally by "pacing off" approximate distances. The builder could then erect the structure, using existing materials, by adjusting sizes and dimensions as necessary during the building process. In this case, the builder played the role of the architect, designer, contractor, carpenter, mason, and, perhaps, the manufacturer of materials and components. Today, design requirements are so demanding, and materials so diverse, that a complete dimensioned set of drawings is absolutely necessary to insure proper execution of the design as conceived by the designer. In the preparation of these drawings, the modern designer must use reduced-size scales. The ability to use architects' scales accurately is required not only in preparing drawings but in checking existing architectural plans and details before estimating an interior design project. The architect's scale is the trademark of the architect, just as the stethoscope is the universal trademark of the physician. The architect's scale is used not only for preparing drawings, but also is used in a variety of related architectural jobs such as bidding, estimating, specification writing, and model building.

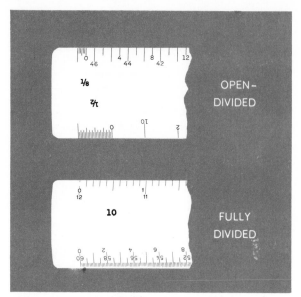

Fig 24-1 Kinds of divisions on architect's scales.

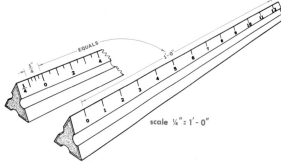

Fig 24-2 On a drawing $\frac{1}{4}"$ may represent 1'—0".

REDUCED SCALE

The architect's scale is used to reduce a structure's sizes so that it can be drawn smaller than actual size on paper. The architect's scale is also used to enlarge a detail for clarity or to dimension it accurately.

DIVISIONS

Architect's scales are either open-divided or fully divided. In *fully divided scales,* each main unit on the scale is fully subdivided into smaller units all along the scale. On *open-divided scales,* only the main units of the scale are *graduated,* (marked off) all along the scale, but there is a fully subdivided extra unit at

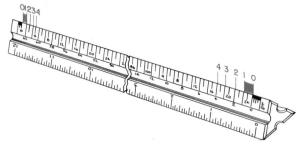

Fig 24-3 The scale that reads from right to left is twice as large as the scale that reads from left to right.

each end, as shown in Fig. 24-1. The main function of an architect's scale is to enable the architect, designer, or drafter to think of dimensions and make drawings in relation to the actual size of the structure. For example, when a drawing is prepared to a reduced scale of $\frac{1}{4}" = 1'$, a line that is drawn $\frac{1}{4}"$ long is thought of by the drafter as 1', not as $\frac{1}{4}"$, (Fig. 24-2).

TYPES

Architect's scales are of either the bevel or the triangular style. You will notice that the triangular scale has 6 sides, which will accommodate 11 different scales. These scales are a full scale of 12" graduated 16 parts to an inch, and 10 other open-divided scales which include ratios of $\frac{3}{32}$, $\frac{1}{8}$, $\frac{3}{16}$, $\frac{1}{4}$, $\frac{3}{8}$, $\frac{1}{2}$, $\frac{3}{4}$, 1, $1\frac{1}{2}$, and 3 to 1. Two scales are located on each face. One scale reads from left to right. The other scale, which is half as large, reads from right to left. For example, the $\frac{1}{4}"$ scale and, half of this, the $\frac{1}{8}"$ scale are placed on the same face. Similarly, the $\frac{3}{4}"$ scale and the $\frac{3}{8}"$ scale are placed on the same face but are read from different directions. Be sure you are reading in the correct direction when using an open-divided scale. Otherwise, your measurement could be wrong, since the second row of numbers read from the opposite side at half scale, or twice the scale, as seen in Fig. 24-3.

The architect's scale can be used to make the divisions of the scale equal 1' or 1". For example, on the $\frac{1}{2}"$ scale shown in Fig. 24-4, $\frac{1}{2}"$ represents 1". The same scale in Fig. 24-5 is

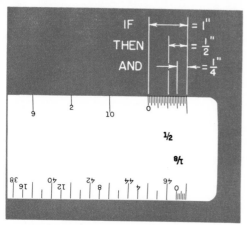

Fig 24-4 If ½" equals 1", then the divisions represent fractions of an inch.

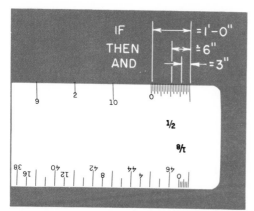

Fig 24-5 If ½" equals 1'—0", then the divisions represent fractions of a foot, or inches.

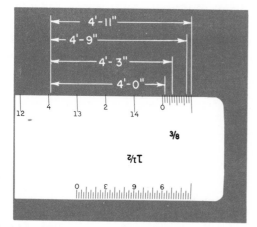

Fig 24-6 Subdivisions at the end of an open-divided scale are used for inch measurement.

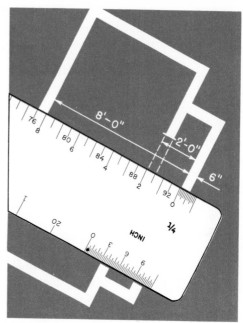

Fig 24-7 Subdivisions of the architect's scale can be used to indicate overall dimensions and subdimensions.

shown representing 1'. Therefore ½" can equal 1" or 1'.

Since buildings are large, most major architectural drawings use a scale that relates the parts of an inch to a foot. Architectural details such as cabinet construction and joints often use the parts of an inch to represent 1". In either case, on open-divided scales the divided section at the end of the scale is not a part of the numerical scale. When measuring with the scale, start with the zero line, not with the fully divided section. Always start with the number of feet you wish to measure and then add the additional inches in the subdivided area. For example, in Fig. 24-6 the distance of 4'—11" is gotten by measuring from the line 4 to 0 for feet. Then measure on the subdivided area, 11" past 0. On this scale, each of the lines in the subdivided parts equals 1". On smaller scales, these lines may equal only 2". On larger scales, they may equal ½". Figure 24-7 shows a further application of this use of the architect's scale. You will notice that the dimensioned distance of 8'—0" extends from the 8 to the 0 on the scale, and the 6" wall is shown as one-half of the subdivided foot on the end. Likewise, you can read the distance of 2'—0" on the ¼" scale shown in this illustration.

SCALE SELECTION

The selection of the proper scale is sometimes difficult. If the structure to be drawn is extremely large, a small scale must be used. Small structures can be drawn to a larger scale, since they will not take up as much space on the drawing sheet. Most floor plans, elevations, and foundation plans of residences are drawn to ¼" scale, whereas construction details pertaining to these drawings are often drawn to ½", ¾", or even 1" = 1'. Remember that as the scale changes, not only does the length of each line increase or decrease but also the width of the various wall thicknesses increases or decreases. The actual appearance of a typical corner wall drawn to $\frac{1}{16}$" = 1'—0", $\frac{1}{8}$" = 1'—0", ¼" = 1'—0" and ½" = 1'—0" is shown in Fig. 24-8. You can see that the wall drawn to the scale of $\frac{1}{16}$" = 1'—0" is small and that a great amount of detail would be impossible. The ½" = 1'—0" wall would probably cover too large an area on the drawing if the building were very large. Therefore, the ¼" and $\frac{1}{8}$" scales are the most popular for this type of work.

USE OF THE SCALE

The architect's scale is only as accurate as its user. In using the scale, do not accumulate distances. That is, always lay out overall dimensions first (Fig. 24-9). The width and the length will be correct and their position will not change if you are slightly off in measuring any of the subdivisions that make up the overall dimension. Furthermore, if your overall dimensions are correct, you will find it easier to check your subdimensions, because if one is off, another will also be incorrect.

Figure 24-10 shows the comparative distances used to measure 1'—9" as it appears on various architect's scales. All these scales represent 1'—9" as a reduced size. This same comparison would exist if we related the

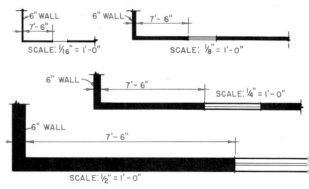

Fig 24-8 Comparison of a similar wall drawn to several different scales.

scales to 1" rather than 1'. In this case, a distance of 1¾" would have the same line length as 1'—9" on the foot representation. The $\frac{3}{32}$", $\frac{3}{16}$", $\frac{1}{8}$", ¼", $\frac{3}{8}$", ½", and ¾" scales represent a distance smaller than full size (1¾"). The 1½" and 3" scales represent a distance 1½ and 3 times as large as the full scale. Figure 24-11 shows the same comparison, using a distance of 5'—6" on the foot-equivalent scale. If an inch-equivalent scale were used, the distance shown would be 5½".

CIVIL ENGINEER'S SCALE

The civil engineer's scale is often used for plot plans, surveys, and landscape plans. Each scale divides the inch into decimal parts. These parts are 10, 20, 30, 40, 50, and 60 parts per inch (Fig. 24-12). Each one of these units can represent any distance, such as an inch, foot, yard, or mile, depending on the final drawing size. The civil engineer's scale can also be used to draw floor plans. The scale ¼" = 1'—0" (1:48 ratio) is the same as 1" = 4' (1:48 ratio) (Fig. 24-13).

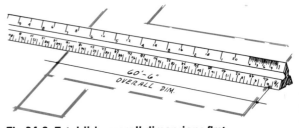

Fig 24-9 Establish overall dimensions first.

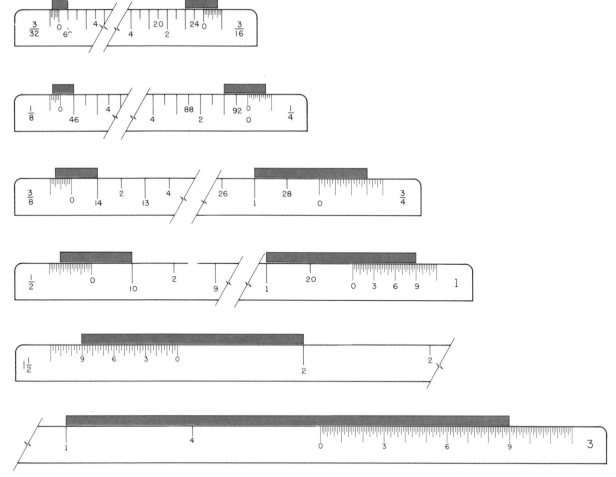

Fig 24-10 The distance 1'—9" as it appears on several architect's scales.

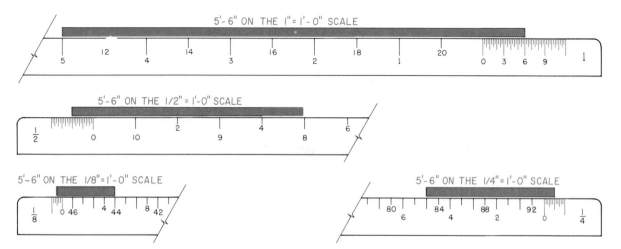

Fig 24-11 The distance 5'—6" shown on several architect's scales.

CIVIL ENGINEER'S SCALE (decimals)

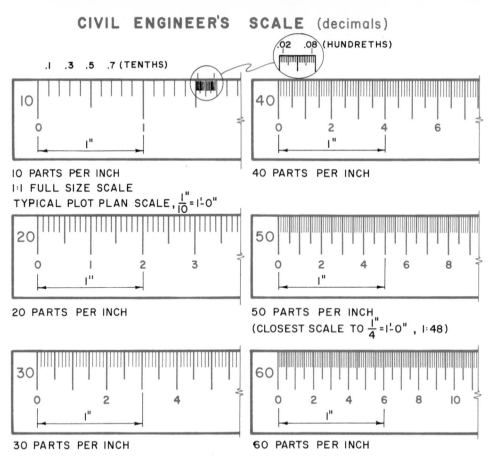

.1 .3 .5 .7 (TENTHS)

.02 .08 (HUNDRETHS)

10 PARTS PER INCH
1:1 FULL SIZE SCALE
TYPICAL PLOT PLAN SCALE, $\frac{1''}{10}$ = 1'-0"

40 PARTS PER INCH

20 PARTS PER INCH

50 PARTS PER INCH
(CLOSEST SCALE TO $\frac{1''}{4}$ = 1'-0" , 1:48)

30 PARTS PER INCH

60 PARTS PER INCH

Fig 24-12 The civil engineer's scale is a decimal scale.

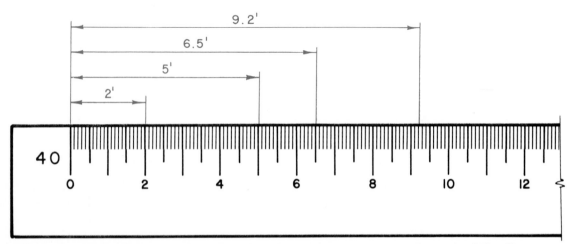

Fig 24-13 Use of civil engineer's decimal dimensions for architectural drawing. The scale of 1" = 4'
is the same as $\frac{1}{4}$" = 1'—0".

146

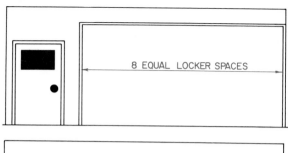

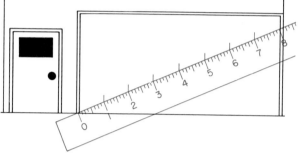

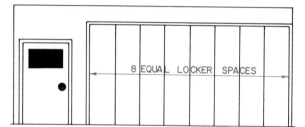

FULL ARCHITECT'S SCALE

The full side of the architect's scale is useful in dividing any area into an equal number of parts by following these steps:

Scale the distance available, as shown in Fig. 24-14. Next, place the zero point of the architect's scale on one side line. Then count off the correct number of spaces, using any convenient unit, such as 1″ or ½″. Place the last unit mark on the line opposite the zero point line. In Fig. 24-14, the 8-inch mark is used since 1-inch divisions are the most convenient. Mark each division and draw the dividing lines. Measure the horizontal distance between the lines to find the actual spacing; then multiply by the number of spaces to check your work.

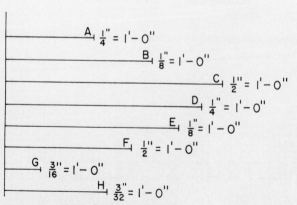

Fig 24-14 **Dividing an area into an equal number of parts.**

PROBLEMS

1 Measure the distances indicated on the horizontal lines, using the scale indicated in Fig. 24-15.

$$A, \frac{1}{4}'' = 1'-0''$$

$$B, \frac{1}{8}'' = 1'-0''$$

$$C, \frac{1}{2}'' = 1'-0''$$

$$D, \frac{1}{4}'' = 1'-0''$$

$$E, \frac{1}{8}'' = 1'-0''$$

$$F, \frac{1}{2}'' = 1'-0''$$

$$G, \frac{3}{16}'' = 1'-0''$$

$$H, \frac{3}{32}'' = 1'-0''$$

Fig 24-15 **Measure these distances.**

2 Measure the distances between the following letters in Fig. 24-16, using the ¼″ = 1′—0″ scale: AB, AL, DE, EJ, KO, ST, FT, CK, EP.

3 Measure the same distances shown in Problem 2, using the ⅛″ = 1″ scale.

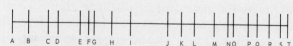

Fig 24-16 **Measure the distances between the letters.**

147

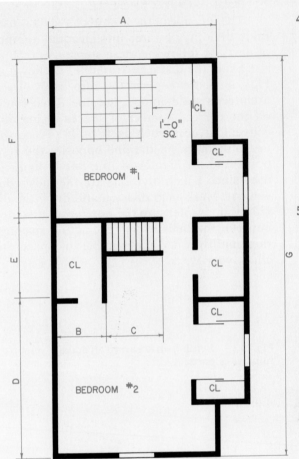

4 Answer the following questions concerning the plan shown in Fig. 24-17:
   a. What is the overall length of the building?
   b. What are the dimensions of bedroom 1, including the closets?
   c. What is the length of the stairwell opening?
   d. What are the dimensions of bedroom 2?
   e. Determine the length of dimensions A through G.
5 Define these terms: *open-divided, fully divided, architect's scale, decimal scale, triangular scale, reduced scale, division, inch-equivalent scale, foot-equivalent scale, full scale.*

Fig 24-17 List the sizes of each room shown in this plan.

UNIT 25
METRIC SCALES

The basic units of measure in the metric system are the *meter* (m) for distance, the *kilogram* (kg) for mass (weight), and the *liter* (L) for volume. Since most measurements used on architectural drawings are distances, multiples or subdivisions of the meter are most commonly used.

PREFIXES

The meter (Fig. 25-1) is a base unit of one. To eliminate the use of many zeros, prefixes are used to change the base (meter) to larger or smaller amounts by units of 10.

Prefixes that represent multiples of meters are deka-, hecto-, and kilo-. A dekameter equals 10 meters. A hectometer equals 100 meters. A kilometer equals 1000 meters. The most useful multiple of the meter is the kilometer.

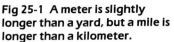

Fig 25-1 A meter is slightly longer than a yard, but a mile is longer than a kilometer.

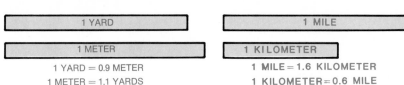

| 1 YARD | 1 MILE |
| 1 METER | 1 KILOMETER |

1 YARD = 0.9 METER   1 MILE = 1.6 KILOMETER
1 METER = 1.1 YARDS   1 KILOMETER = 0.6 MILE

Fig 25-2 A centimeter is one one-hundredth of a meter.

ONE METRE

1 m = 100 cm
1 m = 1000 mm
1 cm = 10 mm

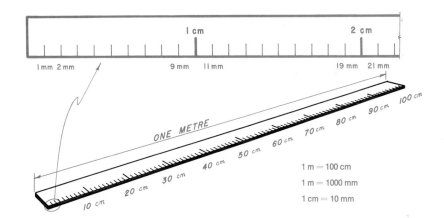

Fig 25-3 A millimeter is one one-thousandth of a meter.

ONE METRE

1 m = 100 cm
1 m = 1000 mm
1 cm = 10 mm

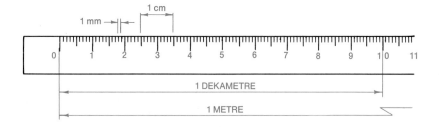

Fig 25-4 A meter scale subdivided into millimeters.

1 DEKAMETRE
1 METRE

Prefixes that represent subdivisions of meters are deci-, centi-, and milli-. A decimeter equals one-tenth (0.1) of a meter. A centimeter equals one one-hundredth (0.01) of a meter (Fig. 25-2). A millimeter equals one one-thousandth (0.001) of a meter (Fig. 25-3). The most useful subdivisions of a meter are the centimeter and the millimeter.

Table 25-1 PREFIXES CHANGE THE BASE UNIT BY INCREMENTS OF 10				
	Prefix	Symbol	+ Meter =	
$1000 = 10^3$	kilo	k	kilometer	km
$100 = 10^2$	hecto	h	hectometer	hm
$10 = 10^1$	deka	da	dekameter	dam
$0.1 = 10^{-1}$	deci	d	decimeter	dm
$0.01 = 10^{-2}$	centi	c	centimeter	cm
$0.001 = 10^{-3}$	milli	m	millimeter	mm

Figure 25-4 shows a portion of a meter scale. The numbers on the scale mark every tenth line and represent centimeters. Each line represents millimeters. Note that there are 10 millimeters between each centimeter.

Table 25-1 gives many of the most useful metric prefixes and shows the relationship of these prefixes to the meter. The prefixes may be applied to all base metric units except mass. This is because the base unit for mass is a multiple unit, the kilogram. The prefixes are applied to the gram for mass units. This consistent use of prefixes for distance, mass, and volume makes the metric system much easier to use than our customary system. The number of metric base units is fewer, making it easier to remember. Table 25-2 compares the number of base units in the metric system with those in the customary system.

There are prefixes which extend the range upward to 10^{12} (tera) and downward to 10^{-18} (atto). These very large and very small units are used primarily for scientific notations in areas such as astronomy and microbiology.

In the United States, there is a disagreement as to how to spell meter. Many people are in favor of an American spelling, **meter,** as is used in this book. Many other people, including those in industries that are using the metric system, prefer to spell it **metre.** All English-speaking countries using the metric system except the United States have adopted the metre spelling. Both spellings are correct, and until one spelling becomes more popular in the United States than the other you should know that meter and metre mean the same thing. This is also true for liter and litre.

METRIC DIMENSIONS

Linear metric sizes used on basic architectural drawings such as floor plans and elevations are expressed in meters and decimal

Table 25-2 THE METRIC SYSTEM USES FEWER BASE UNITS THAN THE CUSTOMARY SYSTEM					
Metric system					
LENGTH	MASS-WEIGHT	CAPACITY	TEMPERATURE	ELECTRIC CURRENT	TIME
Meter	Gram	Liter	Celsius	Ampere	Second
Customary system					
LENGTH	MASS-WEIGHT	CAPACITY	TEMPERATURE	ELECTRIC CURRENT	TIME
Inch	Ounce	Teaspoon	Fahrenheit	Ampere	Second
Foot	Pound	Tablespoon			Minute
Yard	Ton	Fluid ounce			Hour
Fathom	Grain	Cup			
Rod	Dram	Pint			
Furlong		Quart			
Mile		Gallon			
		Barrel			
		Peck			
		Bushel			

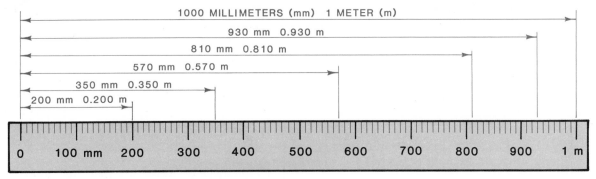

Fig 25-5 Dimensions are read in millimeters or meters (3 decimal places).

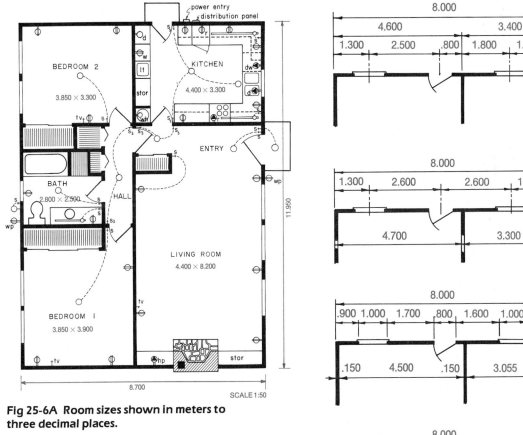

Fig 25-6A Room sizes shown in meters to three decimal places.

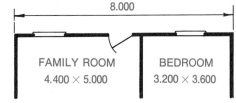

Fig 25-6B Examples of dimensions in meters to three decimal places.

parts of a meter, as shown in Fig. 25-5. Dimensions on these plans are usually carried to three decimal points, as shown in Figs. 25-6A and B. Small detail drawings usually use millimeters, which eliminate the use of decimal points, as shown in Fig. 25-7.

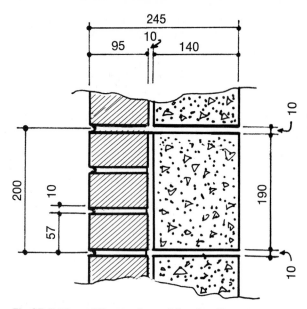

Fig 25-7 The millimeter is used for detail dimensioning.

Table 25-3 ARCHITECTURAL USE OF METRIC RATIOS		
Use	Ratio	Comparison to 1 meter
CITY MAP	1 : 2500	(0.4 mm equals 1 m)
	1 : 1250	(0.8 mm equals 1 m)
PLAT PLANS	1 : 500	(2 mm equals 1 m)
	1 : 200	(5 mm equals 1 m)
PLOT PLANS	1 : 100	(10 mm equals 1 m)
	1 : 80	(12.5 mm equals 1 m)
FLOOR PLANS	1 : 75	(13.3 mm equals 1 m)
	1 : 50	(20 mm equals 1 m)
	1 : 40	(25 mm equals 1 m)
DETAILS	1 : 20	(50 mm equals 1 m)
	1 : 10	(100 mm equals 1 m)
	1 : 5	(200 mm equals 1 m)

METRIC DRAWING RATIOS

Metric scales such as those shown in Figs. 25-8 and 25-9 are used in the same manner as the architect's scale is used to prepare reduced-size drawings. Metric scales, however, use ratios in increments of 10 rather than the fractional ratios of 12 used in architect's scales. Just as with fractional scales, the ratio chosen depends on the size of the drawing compared to the full size of the object. Table 25-3 and Fig. 25-10 show some common metric ratios and the various types of architectural drawings for which they are used. It is important to prepare *all* drawings in a set using metric ratios or to prepare all drawings in a set using the customary fractional system. Do not mix metric and customary units. If approximate conversion from one system to the other is necessary, Table 25-4 can be used.

Fig 25-8 A metric scale showing two ratios.

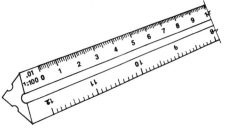

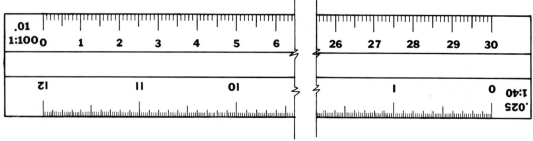

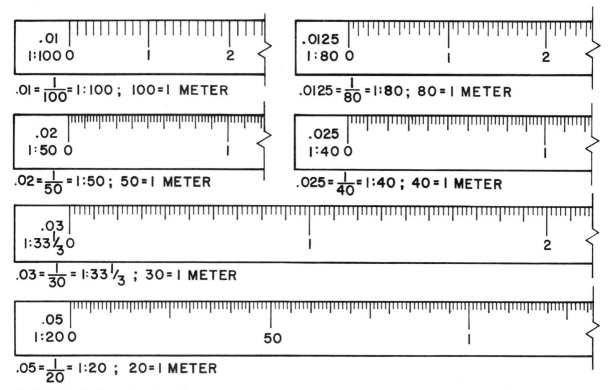

Fig 25-9 Typical metric ratios.

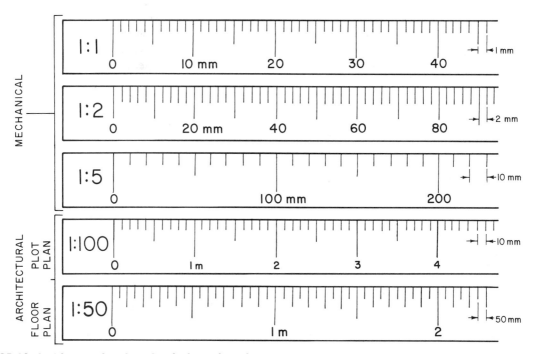

Fig 25-10 Architectural and mechanical metric scales.

Table 25-4 APPROXIMATE METRIC UNITS COMPARED TO SIMILAR CUSTOMARY UNITS

	When you know:	You can find:	If you multiply by:
LENGTH	inches	millimeters	25.4
	feet	centimeters	30.48
	yards	meters	0.9
	miles	kilometers	1.6
	millimeters	inches	0.04
	centimeters	inches	0.4
	meters	yards	1.1
	kilometers	miles	0.6
AREA	square inches	square centimeters	6.5
	square feet	square meters	0.09
	square yards	square meters	0.8
	square miles	square kilometers	2.6
	acres	square hectometers (hectares)	0.4
	square centimeters	square inches	0.16
	square meters	square yards	1.2
	square kilometers	square miles	0.4
MASS	ounces	grams	28.0
	pounds	kilograms	0.45
	short tons	megagrams (metric tons)	0.9
	grams	ounces	0.035
	kilograms	pounds	2.2
	megagrams (metric tons)	short tons	1.1
LIQUID VOLUME	ounces	milliliters	30.0
	pints	liters	0.47
	quarts	liters	0.95
	gallons	liters	3.8
	milliliters	ounces	0.034
	liters	pints	2.1
	liters	quarts	1.06
	liters	gallons	0.26
TEMPERATURE	degrees Fahrenheit	degrees Celsius	$\frac{5}{9}$ (after subtracting 32)
	degrees Celsius	degrees Fahrenheit	$\frac{9}{5}$ (then add 32)

Table 25-5 PROBABLE STANDARD LENGTHS OF CONSTRUCTION LUMBER IN METERS

1.8 m	3.0 m	4.2 m	5.4 m
2.1 m	3.3 m	4.5 m	5.7 m
2.4 m	3.6 m	4.8 m	6.0 m
2.7 m	3.9 m	5.1 m	6.3 m

Table 25-6 PROBABLE STANDARD LUMBER SHEET SIZES IN MILLIMETERS

Size (mm)
1800 × 1200
2400 × 1200
2700 × 1200
3000 × 1200
3600 × 1200
2400 × 900

154

Table 25-7 PROBABLE STANDARD SIZES OF CONSTRUCTION LUMBER IN MILLIMETERS

Thickness, mm	Width, mm								
	75	100	125	150	175	200	225	250	300
16 ×	75	100	125	150					
19 ×	75	100	125	150					
22 ×	75	100	125	150					
25 ×	75	100	125	150	175	200	225	250	300
32 ×	75	100	125	150	175	200	225	250	300
36 ×	75	100	125	150					
38 ×	75	100	125	150	175	200	225		
40 ×	75	100	125	150	175	200	225		
44 ×	75	100	125	150	175	200	225	250	300
50 ×	75	100	125	150	175	200	225	250	300
63 ×		100	125	150	175	200	225		
75 ×		100	125	150	175	200	225	250	300
100 ×		100		150		200		250	300
150 ×				150		200			300
200 ×						200			
250 ×								250	
300 ×									300

When accurate conversion from customary to metric units is necessary, consult a handbook or use METRIC PRACTICE GUIDE, ANSI/ASTM E380-76.

As metrication becomes more widely used in the United States, building materials will be manufactured in metric sizes. Tables 25-5, 25-6, and 25-7 show metric sizes of construction lumber and sheet lumber that will probably become standard.

PROBLEMS

1 Measure common objects, such as your book, desk, and room, using a metric scale. Record your results. Compare your measurements with customary measurements.

2 Measure the lines shown in Fig. 24-16 in metric units.

3 Change the dimensions on Fig. 34-3 to metric units.

4 Draw a complete set of plans using metric units.

5 Define the following terms: *meter, kilogram, liter, millimeter, kilometer, prefix, centimeter, metric system, customary system, ratio.*

UNIT 26
DRAFTING INSTRUMENTS AND EQUIPMENT

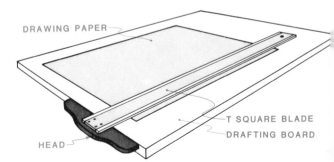

Fig 26-1 A T square placed on a drawing board.

Architectural designers need an assortment of instruments and supplies, including a large, adjustable drawing table or board. An overhead adjustable lamp is required, in addition to general illumination. The variety of pens, pencils, and instruments needed by designers are described in this unit.

A course in mechanical drawing usually precedes a course in architectural drawing. Therefore, only the procedures, practices, and techniques specifically related to the use of instruments for architectural drafting are presented in this unit.

T SQUARE

The *T square* is used primarily as a guide for drawing horizontal lines and for guiding the triangle when drawing vertical and inclined lines. The T square is also the most useful instrument for drawing extremely long lines that deviate from the horizontal plane. Common T square lengths for use in architectural drafting are 18″, 24″, 36″, and 42″.

T squares must be held tightly against the edge of the drawing board, and triangles must be held firmly against the T square to ensure accurate horizontal and vertical lines. Since only one end of the T square is held against the drawing board, considerable sag occurs when extremely long T squares are not held securely.

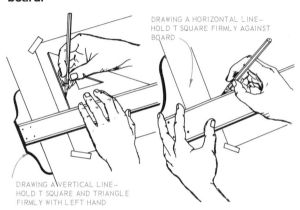

Fig 26-2 Drawing horizontal and vertical lines with a T square and triangle.

HORIZONTAL LINES

Horizontal lines are always drawn with the aid of some instrument such as the T square, parallel slide, or drafting machine. In drawing horizontal lines with the T square, hold the head of the T square firmly against the left working edge of the drawing board (if you are right-handed). This procedure keeps the blade in a horizontal position to draw horizontal lines from left to right. Figure 26-1 shows the T square placed on the drawing board in the correct manner for drawing floor plans and elevations. Figure 26-2 shows the correct method of drawing horizontal lines, using the T square.

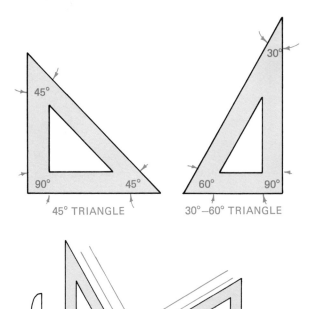

45° TRIANGLE   30°–60° TRIANGLE

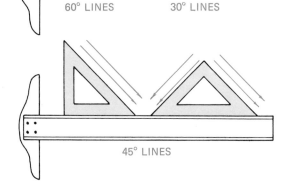

60° LINES   30° LINES

45° LINES

Fig 26-3A Use of a T square and triangles to draw angles.

VERTICAL LINES

Triangles are used with the T square for drawing vertical or inclined lines. The 8″, 45° triangle and the 10″, 30°-60° triangle are preferred for architectural work. Figure 26-2 shows the correct method of drawing vertical lines, using the T square and triangle.

Triangles are used to draw vertical and inclined lines with either a T square or parallel slide. A variety of possible combinations produce numerous angles, as shown in Fig. 26-3A and B. The 45° triangle is frequently employed to draw miter (45°) lines that are used to turn angles of buildings, as shown in Fig. 26-4. Triangles are also used to draw various symbols. Figure 26-4 also shows the use of the 30°-60° triangle in drawing a door symbol.

Triangles (and inverted T squares) are often used to project perspective lines to vanishing points, as shown in Fig. 26-5. The adjustable triangle is used to draw angles that cannot be laid out by combining the 45° and 30°-60° triangles. Figure 26-6 shows an application of the adjustable triangle.

PARALLEL SLIDE

The *parallel slide* performs the same function as the T square. It is used as a guide for drawing horizontal lines and as a base for aligning triangles in drawing vertical lines.

Extremely long lines are common in many architectural drawings such as floor plans and elevations. Since most of these lines should be drawn continuously, the parallel

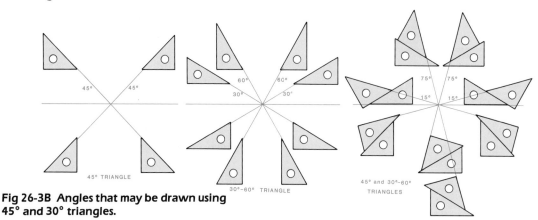

45° TRIANGLE   30°–60° TRIANGLE   45° and 30°–60° TRIANGLES

Fig 26-3B Angles that may be drawn using 45° and 30° triangles.

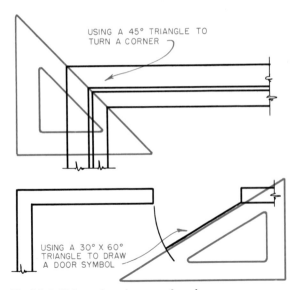

Fig 26-4 Using triangles on a drawing.

USING A 45° TRIANGLE TO TURN A CORNER

USING A 30° X 60° TRIANGLE TO DRAW A DOOR SYMBOL

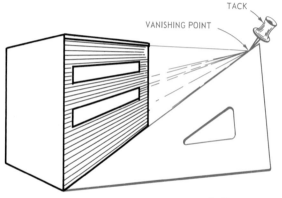

Fig 26-5 Projecting lines to a vanishing point with a triangle.

TACK

VANISHING POINT

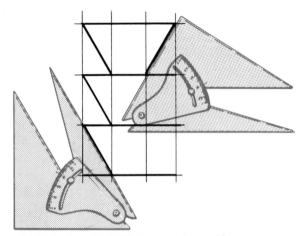

Fig 26-6 An adjustable triangle is used for angles of any number of degrees.

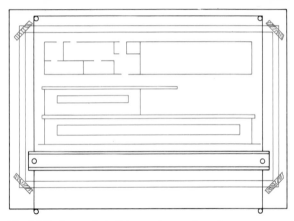

Fig 26-7 A parallel slide used on a drawing board.

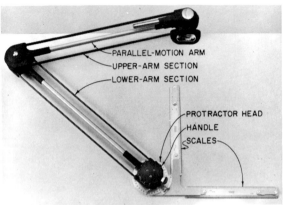

Fig 26-8 A drafting machine.

PARALLEL-MOTION ARM
UPPER-ARM SECTION
LOWER-ARM SECTION

PROTRACTOR HEAD
HANDLE
SCALES

Vemco

slide is used extensively by architectural drafters.

The parallel slide is anchored at both sides of the drawing board, as shown in Fig. 26-7. This attachment eliminates the possibility of sag at one end, which is a common objection to the use of the T square.

In using the parallel slide, the drawing board can be tilted to a very steep angle without causing the slide to fall to the bottom of the board. If the parallel slide is adjusted correctly, it will stay in the exact position in which it is placed.

DRAFTING MACHINE

Using a drafting machine eliminates the need for the architect's scale, triangle, T square, or parallel slide. A *drafting machine* consists of a head to which two scales are at-

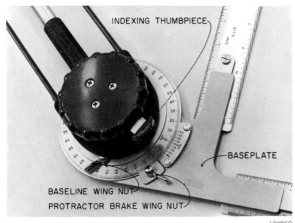

Fig 26-9 Location of the indexing thumbpiece.

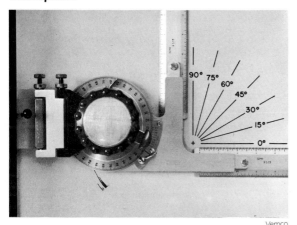

Fig 26-10 Angles at which the scales will lock.

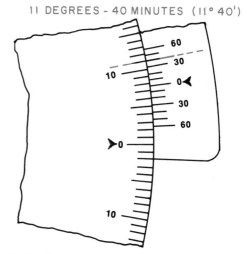

Fig 26-11 Use of the vernier scale.

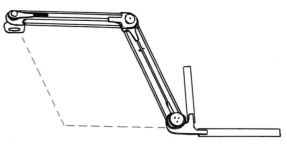

Fig 26-12 Alternative position of the arm.

tached (Fig. 26-8). These *scales* (arms) of the drafting machine are graduated like other architect's scales. They are usually made of aluminum or plastic. The two scales are attached to the head of the drafting machine perpendicular to each other. The horizontal scale performs the function of a T square or parallel slide in drawing horizontal lines. The vertical scale performs the function of a triangle in drawing vertical lines.

The head of the drafting machine can be rotated so that either of the scales can be used to draw lines at any angle. When the indexing thumbpiece, shown in Fig. 26-9, is depressed and then released, the protractor head of the drafting machine will lock into position every 15°. Figure 26-10 shows the intervals at which the scales will index from a horizontal line. If the indexing thumbpiece remains depressed,

the protractor head can be aligned to any degree. The protractor brake-wing nut is used to lock the head in position. If accuracy in minutes is desired, the *vernier scale* (Fig. 26-11) is used to set the protractor head at the desired angle. In this case, the vernier clamp is used to lock the head in the exact position when the desired setting is achieved.

For every position of the head of the drafting machine, there are two possible positions of the elbow. If some position of the lower arm covers the vernier scale, shifting the elbow to the position shown in Fig. 26-12 will avoid this difficulty.

The drafting machine is used to the greatest advantage in architectural work for the preparation of architectural detail drawings. It is sometimes unsatisfactory for large floor plans and elevations that require long horizontal or vertical lines. However, a track

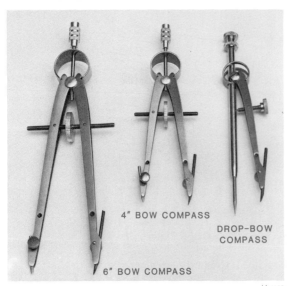

Fig 26-13 Examples of bow compasses

Vemco

4" BOW COMPASS

DROP-BOW COMPASS

6" BOW COMPASS

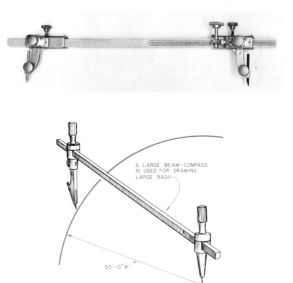

A LARGE BEAM-COMPASS IS USED FOR DRAWING LARGE RADII

50'-0" R

Fig 26-14 The use of a large beam-compass.

drafting machine, with the head mounted on a vertical slide, is very effective for large drawings provided they do not require continuous long lines.

COMPASS

A *compass* is used in architectural work to draw circles, arcs, radii, and parts of many symbols. Small circles are drawn with a bow pencil compass (Fig. 26-13). To use the bow, set it to the desired radius, and hold the stem between the thumb and forefinger. Rotate the compass with a forward clockwise motion and forward inclination.

Large circles on architectural drawings, such as those used to show the radius of driveways, walks, patios, and stage outlines, are drawn with a large *beam-compass*, as shown in Fig. 26-14. Figure 26-15 shows the use of the compass in drawing door symbols.

CURVED LINES

Many architectural drawings contain irregular lines that must be repeated. *Flexible rules,* such as those shown in Fig. 26-16, are used to repeat irregular curves that have no true radius or series of radii and cannot be drawn with a compass. Curved lines that are not part of an arc can also be drawn with a *french* (irregular) *curve* as shown in Fig. 26-17.

DIVIDERS

Dividing an area into an equal number of parts is a common task performed by architectural drafters. In addition to the architect's scale (see Unit 24), the *dividers* are used for this purpose. To divide an area equally by the trial-and-error method, first adjust the dividers until they appear to represent the desired division of the area. Then place one point at the end of the area and step off the distance with the dividers. If the divisions turn out to be too short, increase the opening on the dividers. Repeat the process until the line is equally divided. If the divisions are too long, decrease the setting. Figure 26-18 shows the use of dividers in dividing an area into an equal number of parts.

Dividers are also used frequently to transfer dimensions and to enlarge or reduce the size of a drawing. Figure 26-19 shows the use of dividers to double the size of a floor plan. This work is done by setting the dividers to the distances on the plan and then stepping off the distance twice on the new plan.

CORRECTION EQUIPMENT

The designer employs a variety of erasers. *Basic erasers* are used for general purposes. *Gum erasers* are used for light lines. *Kneaded*

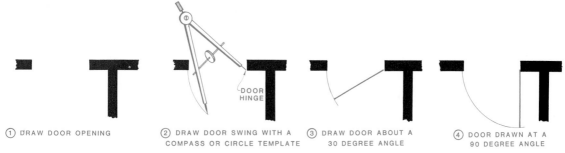

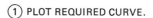

① DRAW DOOR OPENING

② DRAW DOOR SWING WITH A COMPASS OR CIRCLE TEMPLATE

③ DRAW DOOR ABOUT A 30 DEGREE ANGLE

④ DOOR DRAWN AT A 90 DEGREE ANGLE

Fig 26-15 Drawing door symbols.

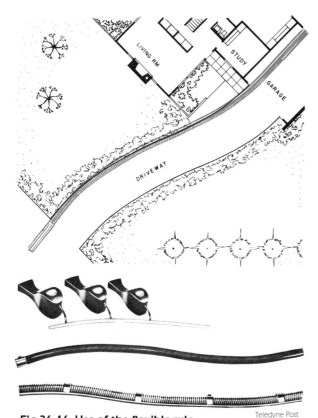

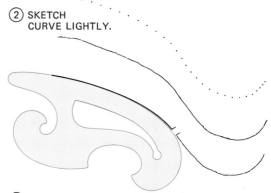

① PLOT REQUIRED CURVE.

② SKETCH CURVE LIGHTLY.

③ FIT IRREGULAR CURVE OVER PART OF THE LINE. DO NOT DRAW THE EXTENT.

④ MOVE IRREGULAR CURVE TO FIT ANOTHER SECTION OF LINE. NOTE THE OVERLAPPING OF CONNECTING LINES. THIS INSURES A SMOOTH LINE. CONTINUE STEPS ③ AND ④ TO COMPLETE ANY IRREGULAR LINE.

Fig 26-16 Use of the flexible rule.

Teledyne Post

Fig 26-17 Use of irregular curve.

erasers pick up loose graphite by dabbing, and dry cleaner bags remove smudges. Powder, sprinkled on the drawing, enables drafting instruments to move freely and also keeps the drawing and instruments clean.

Electric erasers are very fast and do not damage the surface of the drawing paper, since a very light touch can be used to eradicate lines.

A *drafting brush* is used periodically to remove eraser and graphite particles and to

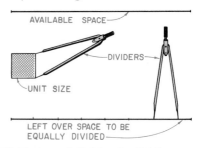

AVAILABLE SPACE

DIVIDERS

UNIT SIZE

LEFT OVER SPACE TO BE EQUALLY DIVIDED

Fig 26-18 The use of dividers in dividing areas.

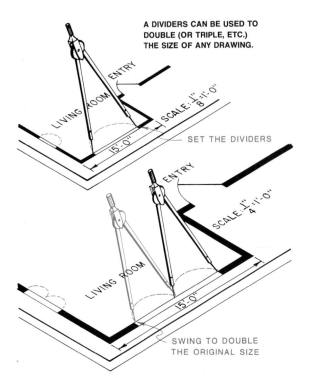

A DIVIDERS CAN BE USED TO DOUBLE (OR TRIPLE, ETC.) THE SIZE OF ANY DRAWING.

LIVING ROOM

ENTRY

SCALE: 1/8" = 1'-0"

15'-0"

SET THE DIVIDERS

ENTRY

SCALE: 1/4" = 1'-0"

LIVING ROOM

15'-0"

SWING TO DOUBLE THE ORIGINAL SIZE

keep them from being redistributed on the paper.

Erasing shields are thin pieces of metal or plastic with a variety of different-shaped openings. A line to be erased is exposed through an appropriate opening without disturbing nearby lines that are to remain on the drawing.

INKING PENS

Architectural drafters use ink drawings for much presentation work. Two basic types of inking pens are used. The *ruling pen* has an adjustable blade for drawing lines of different widths. The *technical fountain pen* has a line of fixed width. As a result, a different technical pen is needed for each width represented on the drawing.

Fig 26-19 The use of dividers to enlarge an area.

PROBLEMS

1 Using a T square and triangle, parallel slide and triangle, or drafting machine, draw the floor plan shown in Fig. 33-12.
2 Using drafting instruments and an architect's scale, draw the elevation shown in Fig. 38-1 to the scale $\frac{1}{4}$" = 1'—0". Add horizontal dimensions.

3 With a flexible rule, lay out the driveway shown in Fig. 32-9 using a scale of $\frac{1}{8}$" = 1'—0".
4 Define the following terms: *T square, 45° triangle, 60° triangle, vertical lines, horizontal lines, parallel slide, drafting machine, flexible rule, dividers, compass.*

UNIT 27
COMPUTERIZED DRAFTING AND DESIGN SYSTEMS

Speed and accuracy are important in producing finished drawings. Through computer-aided drafting methods, finished drawings are produced in a fraction of the time required by traditional methods. The computer performs complicated computations, giving architects and engineers more time for creative design. The use of a computer also allows fast and accurate checking of a design at any time in the design's development. The sequence of producing architectural drawings with a computer-aided system is shown in Fig. 27-1A and B.

With appropriate information fed into the computer, the system can perform the following functions:

mirror reversals of drawings
combine and change symbols
revolve a drawing or part of a drawing
recall any stored information
locate any information anywhere on drawings
change scale sizes
plan with modular building units
plan with orientation factors

INPUT

To graphically record data into the computer memory bank, the designer works with a *digitizer*. The digitizer may have an arm that moves in two directions on the x-axis and the y-axis (Fig. 27-2). The digitizer may also be a cathode-ray tube (CRT) and a light pen (Fig. 27-3). Additional input can be fed into the computer with a free-cursor digitizer which will move in any direction. The input source may be from a keyboard, teletypewriter, premade computer program, or tablet digitizer. The digitizer changes graphic information

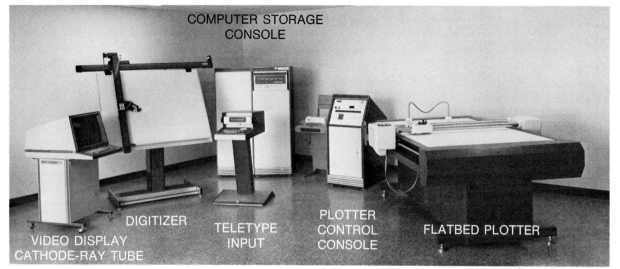

COMPUTER STORAGE CONSOLE

DIGITIZER
VIDEO DISPLAY CATHODE-RAY TUBE
TELETYPE INPUT
PLOTTER CONTROL CONSOLE
FLATBED PLOTTER

Auto-trol Corp.

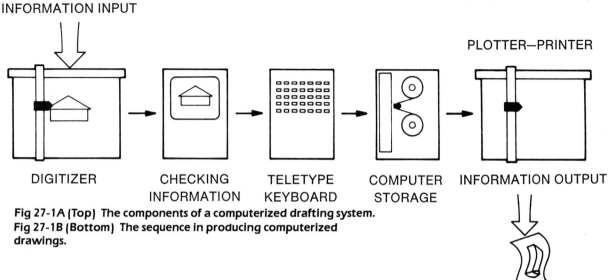

INFORMATION INPUT

PLOTTER—PRINTER

DIGITIZER — CHECKING INFORMATION — TELETYPE KEYBOARD — COMPUTER STORAGE — INFORMATION OUTPUT

Fig 27-1A (Top) The components of a computerized drafting system.
Fig 27-1B (Bottom) The sequence in producing computerized drawings.

163

(lines) into numbered coordinates (digits) which can be stored in the computer. When a designer uses the system in the sequence shown in Fig. 27-4, a table of standard architectural symbols is created by making a rough sketch of each symbol on the digitizer. These symbols are then fed into the computer. The designer then positions the digitizer follower at the location of each symbol on a sketch and records the coordinates with the symbol on the keyboard. The lines on the drawing are then connected, and necessary information and dimensions are added. When the design is thought to be satisfactory, it can be checked and stored in the computer.

Designing is also simplified by use of a large bank of repeated architectural details and data that is entered into the computer memory files and coded for recall. This information consists of architectural symbols such as those for windows, doors, electrical fixtures, walls, standard room sizes, stairs, furniture, roof styles, building and structural materials, and general architectural line work. The information would also contain engineering data.

The digitizer converts rough sketches, drawings, layouts, and artwork into coordinate information that is stored in the computer. This information can be recalled on command (Fig. 27-5). Recalled drawings may also be presented in various positions (Fig. 27-6).

A printout or a video display may be used to verify and check the accuracy of the symbols or design. Input information from paper tapes, magnetic tapes, magnetic discs, magnetic drums, or punch cards is stored in the computer memory banks. This information is stored as temporary or as permanent data. At any time during the development of a design, changes can be made. The graphic display of the input can be edited, added to, deleted, or repositioned. Checking a design is made easier when the design can be rotated and viewed in different positions. The stored library of digitized standard symbols provides for fast layout and for corrections or changes that a designer must make. Different types of pictorial drawings can also be generated from a working drawing (Fig. 27-7).

When designing with a computerized scope (CRT) and light pen (Fig. 27-8), the process is the same as with the digitizer, except that all original sketching is done directly on the CRT with the light pen. All stored symbols can be called up and positioned with the light pen. The design work is all done directly on the scope. When the designer is satisfied with the design and has made all changes and verifications, the design

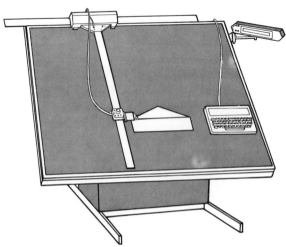

Fig 27-2 A digitizer moves in two directions on an x-y axis.

Fig 27-3 A CRT and light-pen digitizer.

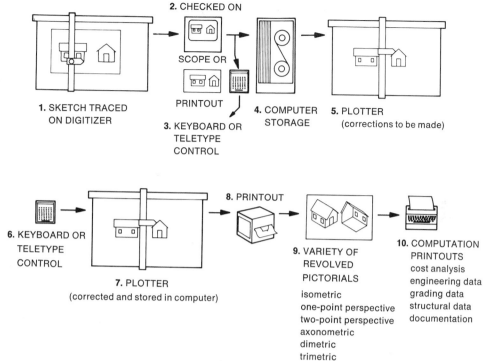

1. SKETCH TRACED ON DIGITIZER

2. CHECKED ON

SCOPE OR

PRINTOUT

3. KEYBOARD OR TELETYPE CONTROL

4. COMPUTER STORAGE

5. PLOTTER (corrections to be made)

6. KEYBOARD OR TELETYPE CONTROL

7. PLOTTER (corrected and stored in computer)

8. PRINTOUT

9. VARIETY OF REVOLVED PICTORIALS

isometric
one-point perspective
two-point perspective
axonometric
dimetric
trimetric

10. COMPUTATION PRINTOUTS
cost analysis
engineering data
grading data
structural data
documentation

Fig 27-4 The sequence of producing a variety of data.

is recorded into the computer memory bank for future recall or changes.

COMPUTER

The computer is called the *graphics control center*. All input information is digitized into the computer. That is, the information is translated into electric pulses and magnetic currents, which is a language the computer understands. The computer has the capability to modify the data on immediate recall. This information provides automated artwork as sketches are translated into commands accepted by the automated drafting machine. All information stored can be called for and generated by the computer controls.

GRAPHICS OUTPUT

The *plotter*, or automatic drafting machine, produces the graphic output. There are

two basic types of plotters, the *flatbed* (Fig. 27-9) and the *drum* plotter. The plotter follows instruction from the computer to produce the artwork, maps, data reductions, changes, or

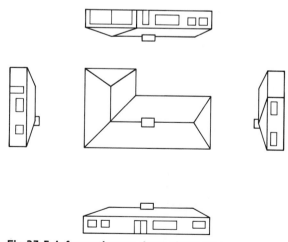

Fig 27-5 Information on these views was stored in the computer in coordinate form. They were drawn (recalled) on command.

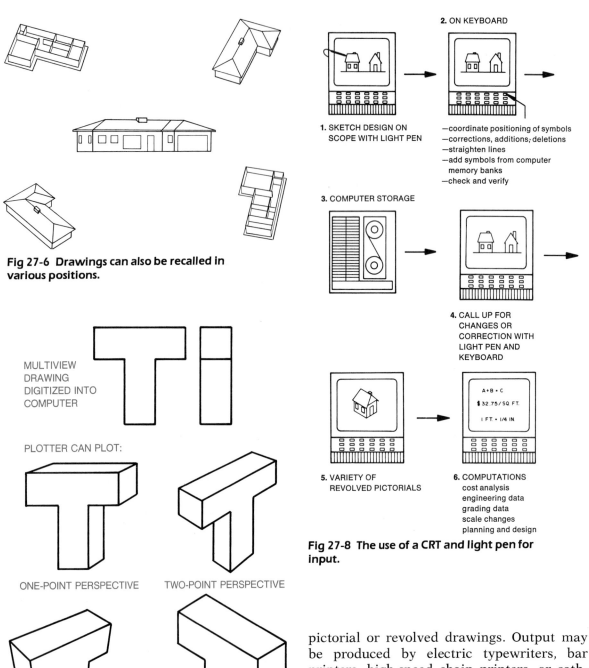

Fig 27-6 Drawings can also be recalled in various positions.

2. ON KEYBOARD

1. SKETCH DESIGN ON SCOPE WITH LIGHT PEN

—coordinate positioning of symbols
—corrections, additions, deletions
—straighten lines
—add symbols from computer memory banks
—check and verify

3. COMPUTER STORAGE

4. CALL UP FOR CHANGES OR CORRECTION WITH LIGHT PEN AND KEYBOARD

A + B = C

$ 32.75 / SQ. FT.

I FT. = 1/4 IN.

5. VARIETY OF REVOLVED PICTORIALS

6. COMPUTATIONS
cost analysis
engineering data
grading data
scale changes
planning and design

Fig 27-8 The use of a CRT and light pen for input.

MULTIVIEW DRAWING DIGITIZED INTO COMPUTER

PLOTTER CAN PLOT:

ONE-POINT PERSPECTIVE

TWO-POINT PERSPECTIVE

THREE-POINT PERSPECTIVE

ISOMETRIC

Fig 27-7 Different types of pictorial drawings can be produced from the same input.

pictorial or revolved drawings. Output may be produced by electric typewriters, bar printers, high-speed chain printers, or cathode-ray tubes.

COMPUTERIZED LAND DRAWINGS

Drawings of land surfaces are of great value to the civil engineer and landscape architect. To produce computerized drawings of land surfaces, the computer operator feeds contour points into the computer. The operator can then receive output information from the computer on cut analysis, fill analysis, contour maps (Fig. 27-10), cross sections, drainage maps, slope maps, grid perspectives, presentation grids, and perspective land maps (Fig. 27-11). In addition, the computer can perform such mathematical computations as volume of earth to be moved or filled and time and cost of earth-moving operations.

OTHER ARCHITECTURAL USES

Computer-aided drafting systems can provide a perspective drawing (Fig. 27-12) of a building from a digitized floor plan and elevation. Such systems can also redraw a plot plan from an original (Fig. 27-13) or record engineering data on a drawing, as shown in Fig. 27-14.

Land properties can also be computerized and used by landscape architects to determine feasibility of specific areas of the terrain for architectural use (Fig. 27-15).

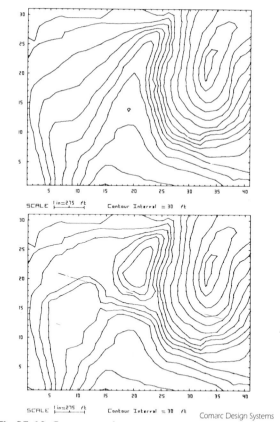

Comarc Design Systems

Fig 27-10 Computer-drawn contour maps.

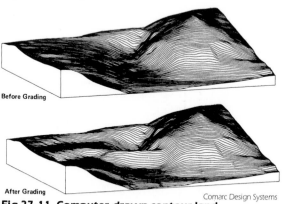

Comarc Design Systems

Fig 27-11 Computer-drawn contour land maps.

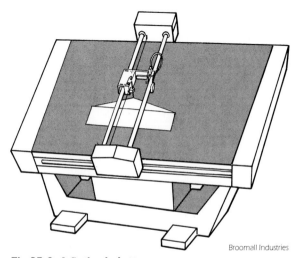

Broomall Industries

Fig 27-9 A flatbed plotter.

Calcomp

Fig 27-12 Perspective view drawn by a computer system.

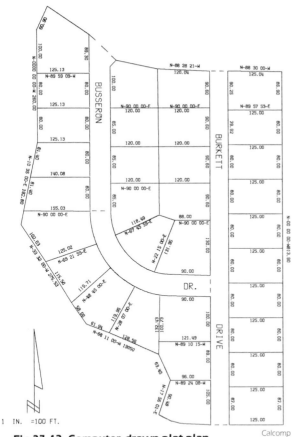

Fig 27-13 Computer-drawn plat plan.

Calcomp

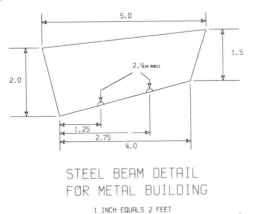

STEEL BEAM DETAIL
FOR METAL BUILDING

1 INCH EQUALS 2 FEET

Complot

Fig 27-14 Computer-generated engineering data.

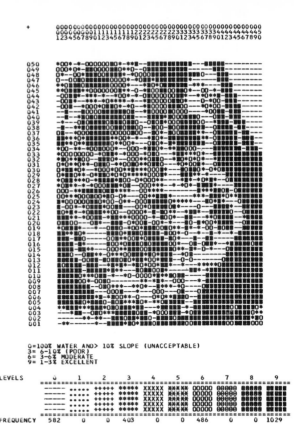

0=100% WATER AND> 10% SLOPE (UNACCEPTABLE)
3= 6-10% (POOR)
6= 3-6% MODERATE
9= 1-3% EXCELLENT

LEVELS	0	1	2	3	4	5	6	7	8	9
FREQUENCY	582	0	0	403	0	0	486	0	0	1029

LITTLE'S CREEK STUDY AREA
MARSHFIELD, MASSACHUSETTS

DEPARTMENT OF LANDSCAPE ARCHITECTURE
THE SCHOOL OF ARCHITECTURE
THE OHIO STATE UNIVERSITY
DATA BASE CREATED BY:
DEPARTMENT OF LANDSCAPE ARCHITECTURE, HARVARD UNIVERSITY

TOPOGRAPHIC SLOPE

Department of Landscape Architecture, Harvard
Department of Landscape Architecture, Ohio State University

Fig 27-15 Computer study of topographic slope.

PROBLEMS

1 List the steps in the development of a computerized drawing from a rough sketch.

2 Define the following terms: *software, hardware, digitizer, plotter, input, printout.*

UNIT 28
TIME-SAVERS

Architectural drawings must frequently be prepared quickly because construction often begins immediately upon completion of the working drawings. Under these conditions, speed in the preparation of drawings is of utmost importance. For this reason, many timesaving devices are employed by architectural drafters. The purpose of these timesaving devices is to eliminate unnecessary time on the drawing board without sacrificing the quality of the drawing.

ARCHITECTURAL TEMPLATES

Templates are pieces of paper, cardboard, metal, or plastic. Openings in the template are shaped to represent the outline of various symbols and fixtures. A symbol or fixture is traced on the drawing by following the outline with a pencil or pen. This procedure eliminates the repetitious task of measuring and laying out the symbol each time it is to be used on the drawing.

GENERAL-PURPOSE TEMPLATES
Templates such as the one shown in Fig. 28-1A have openings that represent many different types of symbols and fixtures. This template is positioned to be used to outline a door symbol as shown in Fig. 28-1B. Four other general-purpose templates are shown in Fig. 28-2.

SPECIAL-PURPOSE TEMPLATES
Many architectural templates are used to draw only one type of symbol. Special tem-

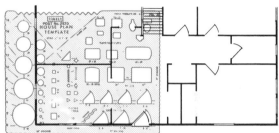

Fig 28-1A Floor-plan symbols.

Timely Products Co.

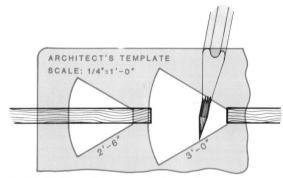

Fig 28-1B Use of door-symbol template.

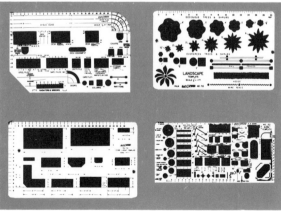

Fig 28-2 General-purpose architectural templates.

Rapidesign, Inc.

plates are available for doors, windows, landscape features, electrical symbols, plumbing symbols, furniture, structural steel, outlines, lettering, and circle and ellipse guides. Figure 28-3 shows how a special landscape template

169

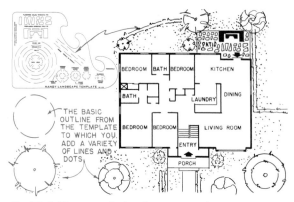

Fig 28-3 The use of a landscape template.

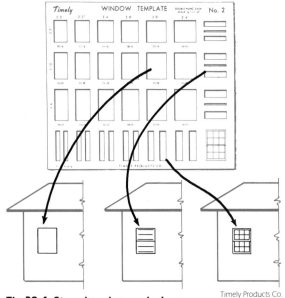

Fig 28-4 Steps in using a window template.

Timely Products Co.

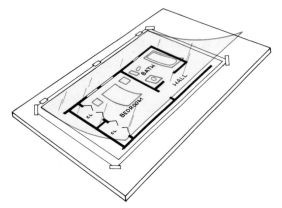

Fig 28-5 The use of an acetate overlay.

Fig 28-6 A permanent overlay.   Chart-Pak, Inc.

is used to draw landscape symbols on a drawing. When symbols contain many intersecting lines, templates often provide only the basic outline. The detailing is completed by freehand methods. The landscape symbols shown in Fig. 28-3 are completed in this manner.

Each part of the symbol is drawn by using a different opening in the template. For example, in using the template shown in Fig. 28-4, the center part of the template is employed to outline the window. The horizontal lines are then added by using the openings at the right of the template as shown. The vertical lines are added by using the opening at the bottom of the template.

When the major axis of a symbol is to be aligned with the lines of the drawing, it is necessary to use a T square, drafting machine, or parallel slide as a guide. This alignment is made by resting one true edge of the template against the blade of the T square, parallel slide, or drafting machine. This procedure is also necessary to ensure the alignment of symbols that are repeated in an aligned pattern.

OVERLAYS

An *overlay* is any sheet that is placed over the original drawing. The information placed on the overlay becomes part of the interpretation of the original drawing.

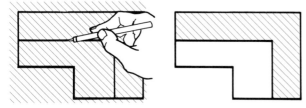

Fig 28-7 A section-lining overlay.

Fig 28-8 Examples of common architectural underlays.

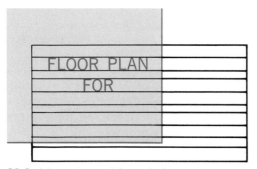

Fig 28-9 A lettering-guide underlay.

Fig 28-10 A title-block underlay.

TEMPORARY OVERLAYS

Most overlays are made by drawing on translucent material such as acetate, tracing cloth, or vellum. Overlays are used in the design process to add to or change features of the original drawing without marking the drawing.

Overlays are also used to add to a drawing features that would normally complicate the original drawing. Lines that would become hidden and many other details can be made clear by preparing this information on an overlay. Figure 28-5 shows the use of an acetate overlay.

PERMANENT OVERLAYS

Overlays that adhere to the surface of the drawing, such as the overlay shown in Fig. 28-6, save much drawing-board time. Attaching a preprinted symbol or fixture by this method is considerably faster than drawing it.

In addition to fixture and symbol overlays, continuous material symbols are often used on architectural drawings. Figure 28-7 shows the use of a section-lining overlay. These overlays are self-adhering and can be cut to any desired size or shape.

UNDERLAYS

Underlays are drawings or parts of drawings that are placed under the original drawing and traced on the original.

SYMBOL UNDERLAYS

Many symbols and features of buildings are drawn more than once. The same style of door or window or the same type of tree or shrubbery may be drawn many times by the architectural drafter in the course of a day. It is a considerable waste of time to measure and lay out these features each time they are to be drawn. Therefore, many drafters prepare a series of underlays of the features repeated most often on their drawings. Figure 28-8 shows several underlays commonly used on architectural drawings. Underlays are commonly prepared for doors, windows, fireplaces, trees, walls, and stairs.

LETTERING UNDERLAYS

Lettering guidelines, as shown in Fig. 28-9, are frequently prepared on underlays. When the guidelines are placed under the drawing, the drafter may trace the line from the original drawing, thus eliminating the measurement of each line. If the underlay remains under the drawing while it is being lettered, the guideline on the drawing can be considerably lighter so that the drafter does not need to erase heavy guidelines. The spacing of other lines, such as crosshatching and brick-symbol lines, is also prepared on underlays.

Drawing paper preprinted with title blocks is a considerable time-saver (Fig. 28-10). However, when printed title blocks are not available, the title-block underlay is often used to save valuable layout time and to ensure the correct spacing of lettering.

USE OF UNDERLAYS

Underlays are master drawings. To be effective, they must be prepared to the correct scale and carefully aligned. The underlay is first positioned under the drawing and aligned with light guidelines (Fig. 28-11); then it is traced on the drawing. The underlay can now be removed or moved to a new location to trace the symbol or feature again if necessary. Architects use master underlays many times.

Underlays do not necessarily replace the use of instruments or scales in original design work. They are most effective when symbols are continually repeated. Figure 28-12 shows a comparison of the use of the scale, dividers, and underlay in laying out wall thicknesses. The use of the underlay in this case is only possible after the original wall dimensions have been established by the use of the scale.

GRIDS

Grid sheets are used under the tracing paper as underlays and are removed after the drawing is finished, or the drawing is prepared on nonreproducible grid paper. Nonreproducible grid paper does not reproduce

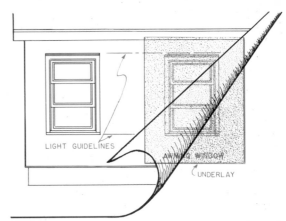

Fig 28-11 The correct positioning of an underlay.

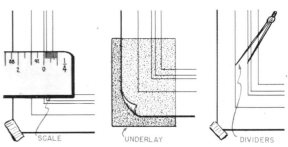

Fig 28-12 The scale, an underlay, or dividers may be used to lay out wall thickness.

when the original drawing is copied through photographic processes. Figure 28-13A and B shows an original drawing complete with nonreproducible grid lines and the print from this drawing without grid lines.

SQUARED PAPER

Squared (graph) paper is available in graduations of 4, 8, 16, and 32 squares per inch. Squared paper is also available in decimal-divided increments of 10, 20, and 30 or more squares per inch. Decimal-divided squared paper is used for the layout of survey and plot plants. Metric graph paper is ruled in millimeters.

PICTORIAL GRIDS

Grids prepared with isometric angles and preplotted to perspective vanishing points are used for pictorial illustrations. *Perspective* and

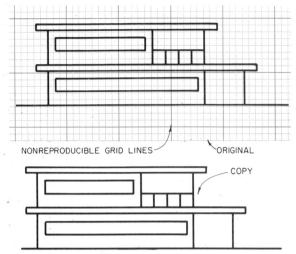

Fig 28-13A An example of the use of nonreproducible grid paper.

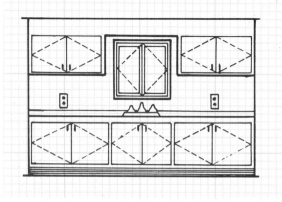

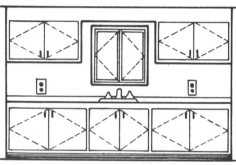

Fig 28-13B Use of nonreproducible grid paper with interior detail.

isometric grid paper are available with many angles of projection.

Perspective grids can be obtained with the vanishing point placed at various intervals from the station point and with the horizon placed in various locations. An example of one perspective grid is shown in Fig. 28-14.

TAPE

Many types of manufactured tape can be substituted for lines and symbols on architectural drawings.

PRESSURE-SENSITIVE TAPE

Tape with printed symbols and special lines is used to produce lines and symbols that otherwise would be difficult and time-consuming to construct. Figure 28-15 shows

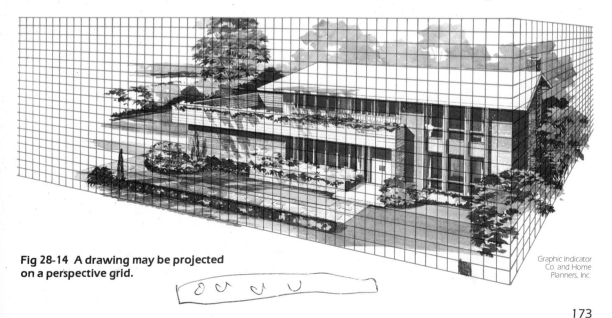

Fig 28-14 A drawing may be projected on a perspective grid.

Graphic Indicator
Co. and Home
Planners, Inc.

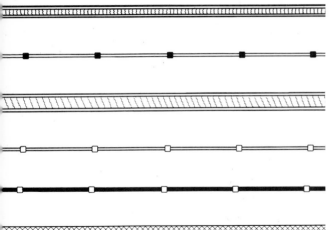

Fig 28-15 Architectural symbol tape.

Chart-Pak, Inc.

Fig 28-17 Pressure-sensitive tape used on a map overlay.

Chart-Pak, Inc.

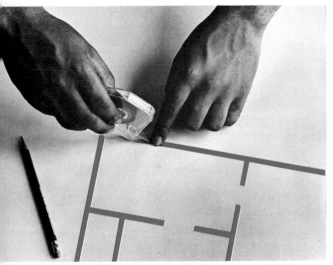

Fig 28-16 Rolling on pressure-sensitive tape.

Bond Ryder Assoc.

Fig 28-18 Reverse uses of pressure-sensitive tape.

some of the various symbols and lines available in this kind of tape. A special roll-on applicator enables the drafter to draw lines by using tape, as shown in Fig. 28-16. This method is used extensively on overlays (Fig. 28-17). Figure 28-18 shows another application of this kind of tape.

MATTE-SURFACE TAPE

Temporary changes can be added to a drawing by drawing the symbol, note, or change on translucent matte-surface tape. If the drawing is changed, the tape can be re-moved and a new symbol added, or the symbol can be made permanent. The proposed closet wall in Fig. 28-19 was prepared on transparent tape. If the arrangement is unsatisfactory, the tape can be removed without destroying the drawing.

MASKING TAPE

Masking tape has other timesaving uses besides its use to attach the drawing to the drawing board. Strips of masking tape help ensure the equal length of lines when ruling many close lines. Strips of tape are placed on

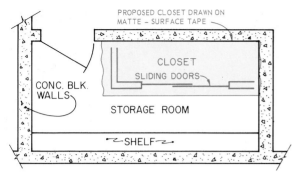

Fig 28-19 A trial layout prepared on a matte-surface tape.

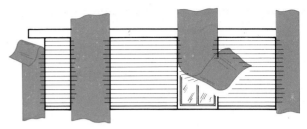

Fig 28-20 The use of masking tape to save time drawing many similar lines.

the drawing to mask the areas not to be lined. The lines are then drawn on the paper and extended on the tape. When the tape is removed, the ends of the lines are even and sharp, as shown in Fig. 28-20. This procedure eliminates the careful starting and stopping of the pencil stroke with each line.

Since masking tape will pull out some graphite, a piece of paper can be placed on drawings to perform the masking function for large areas. If a small area is to remain unlined, sometimes it is easier to line through the surface and erase the small area, using an erasing shield as shown in Fig. 28-21.

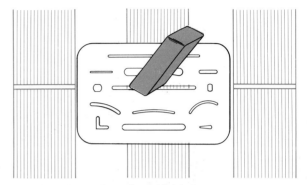

Fig 28-21 Use of erasing shield to remove unwanted lines.

ABBREVIATIONS

Stenographers use shorthand to speed and condense their work. Architects also use shorthand. Architects' shorthand consists of symbols and abbreviations. When a symbol does not describe an object completely, a word or phrase must be used. Words and phrases can occupy much space on a drawing. Abbreviations therefore should be used to minimize this space. Refer to Section 28 for a list of architectural abbreviations.

RUBBER STAMPS

For architectural symbols that are often repeated, the use of rubber stamps is effective and timesaving. Stamps can be used with any color ink, or stamps can be used in faint colors to provide an outline that can then be rendered with pencil or ink. Rubber stamps are

Fig 28-22 Examples of common rubber-stamp symbols.

used most often for symbols that do not require precise positioning on the drawing, such as landscape features, people, and cars. However, stamps may be used for furniture outlines and for labels. Figure 28-22 shows some common symbols used on rubber stamps.

BURNISHING PLATES

Burnishing plates are embossed sheets with raised areas representing an outline of a symbol or texture lines. The plates are placed under a drawing; then a soft pencil is rubbed over the surface of the drawing. This creates lines on the drawing over the raised portions of the plate. The use of burnishing plates al-

lows the drafter to create consistent texture lines throughout a series of drawings with a minimum use of time.

PHOTOGRAPHIC REPRODUCTION

Often a section of a drawing needs to be changed, or a design element needs to be repeated on many drawings. The entire drawing need not be redrawn, nor must the design element be drawn repeatedly on each drawing. The section to be redrawn or repeated can be drawn once, attached to the drawing, and then the entire drawing can be reproduced through photographic processes.

PROBLEMS

1 Prepare an underlay for a fireplace.
2 Prepare a title-strip underlay with the following information: your name, school or company, drawing number, teacher or supervisor, title of drawing series, title of specific drawing.
3 Prepare a lettering-guide underlay for $\frac{1}{8}''$, $\frac{1}{4}''$, and $\frac{3}{16}''$ letters.
4 Identify the following abbreviations: CL, FTG, HB, FL. See Section 28.

5 Redraw and add fixtures to the bathroom layouts shown in Fig. 22-24.
6 Draw and add fixtures to the kitchen shown in Fig. 33-23, using a template.
7 Add doors to the plan shown in Fig. 28-3, using a door template.
8 Add landscape features to the plan shown in Fig. 33-3, using a landscape-plan template.
9 Define the following terms: *template, overlay, underlay, graph paper, perspective grid, matte-surface tape, burnishing plates.*

UNIT 29

ARCHITECTURAL LETTERING AND WRITTEN COMMUNICATION

Architectural lettering differs greatly from lettering used on engineering drawings because most architectural drawings are shown to a client. Architectural drawings not only must be correct and meaningful but must look attractive to the client.

PURPOSE

Figure 29-1 shows a plan without any lettering. This plan does not communicate a complete description of the size and function of the various components. All labels, notes, dimen-

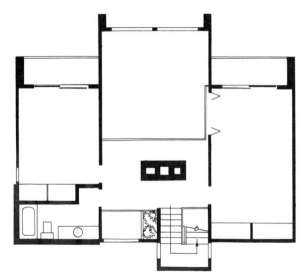

Fig 29-1 A plan without lettering.

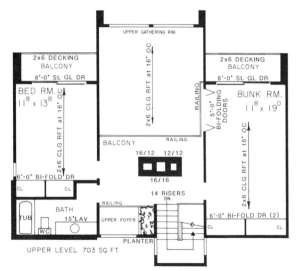

Fig 29-2 The same plan with lettering added.

sions, and descriptions must be legibly lettered on architectural drawings if they are to function as an effective means of graphic communication.

Legible, well-formed letters and numerals do more for a drawing than merely aid in communication. Effective lettering helps give the drawing a finished and professional look. Poor lettering is the mark of an amateur. The plan shown in Fig. 29-2 is more easily interpreted and appears more professional because

lettering was used. In fact, Fig. 29-1 would be almost impossible to understand without the labeling of area functions and minimum dimensions.

STYLES

Because architectural designs are somewhat personalized, many lettering styles have been developed by various architects. Never-

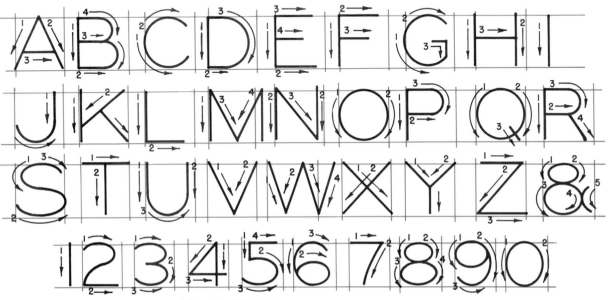

Fig 29-3 The American National Standard Alphabet.

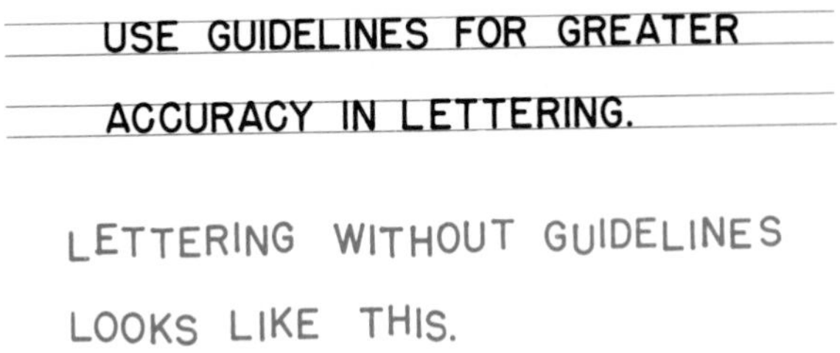

USE GUIDELINES FOR GREATER ACCURACY IN LETTERING.

LETTERING WITHOUT GUIDELINES LOOKS LIKE THIS.

Fig 29-4 Always use guidelines when lettering.

theless, these personalized styles are all based on the *American National Standard Alphabet* shown in Fig. 29-3.

RULES FOR ARCHITECTURAL LETTERING

Much practice is necessary to develop the skills necessary to letter effectively. Although architectural lettering styles may be very different, all professional drafters follow certain basic rules of lettering. If you follow these rules, you will develop accuracy, consistency, and speed in lettering your drawings.

1. Always use guidelines in lettering. Notice what a difference guidelines make in the lettering shown in Fig. 29-4.
2. Choose one style of lettering, and practice the formation of the letters of that style until you master it. Figure 29-5 compares the effect of using a consistent style with that of using an inconsistent style. Each letter in the inconsistent style may be correct, but the effect is undesirable.
3. Make letters bold and distinctive. Avoid a delicate, fine touch.
4. Make each line quickly from the beginning to the end of the stroke. See the difference between letters drawn quickly and those drawn slowly in Fig. 29-6.
5. Practice with larger letters (about ¼", or 6 mm), and gradually reduce the size until you can letter effectively at ¹⁄₁₆", or 2 mm.
6. Practice spacing by lettering words and sentences, not alphabets. Figure 29-7

CONSISTENT STYLE
CONSISTENT STYLE
INCONSISTENT STYLE

Fig 29-5 Always use a consistent lettering style.

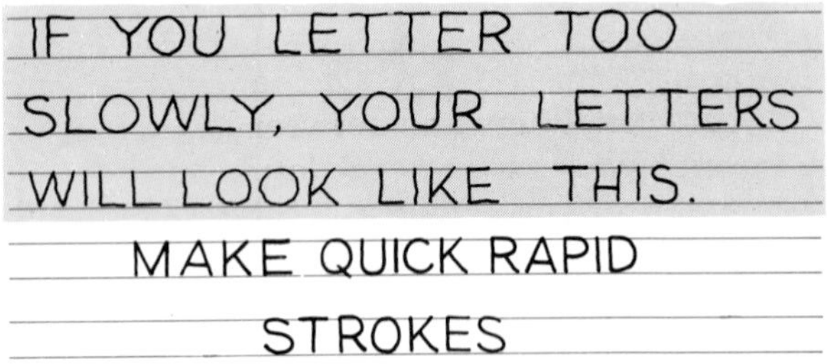

IF YOU LETTER TOO SLOWLY, YOUR LETTERS WILL LOOK LIKE THIS.
MAKE QUICK RAPID STROKES

Fig 29-6 Make each letter stroke quickly.

UNIFORM SPACING
UNEVEN SPACING

Fig 29-7 Uniform spacing of letters is important.

IF YOUR LETTERS SLANT AT TIMES PRACTICE THE FOLLOWING:

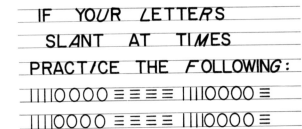

Fig 29-8 Practice making horizontal and vertical lines.

IF YOU CANNOT KEEP A CONSTANT SLANT, USE GUIDE LINES AT 68° OR 75°.

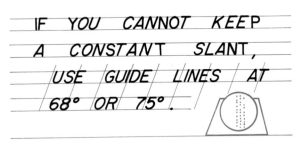

Fig 29-9 Maintain the same degree of slant if slant lettering is used.

shows the effect of uniform and even spacing of letters.

7 Form the habit of lettering whenever possible—as you take notes, address envelopes, or write your name.

8 Practice only the capital alphabet. Lowercase letters are rarely used in architectural work.

9 Do not try to develop speed at first. Make each stroke quickly, but take your time between letters and between strokes until you have mastered each letter. Then gradually increase your speed. You will soon be able to letter almost as fast as you can write script.

10 If your lettering has a tendency to slant in one direction or the other, practice making a series of vertical and horizontal lines, as shown in Fig. 29-8.

11 If slant lettering is desired, practice slanting the horizontal strokes approximately 68°. The problem with most slant lettering, as shown in Fig. 29-9, is that it is difficult to maintain the same degree of slant continually. The tendency is for more and more slant to creep into the style.

12 Letter the drawing last to avoid smudges and overlapping with other areas of the drawing. This procedure will enable you to space out your lettering and to avoid lettering through important details.

13 Use a soft pencil, preferably an HB or F. A soft pencil will glide and is more easily controlled than a hard pencil.

14 Numerals used in architectural drawing should be adapted to the style, just as the alphabet is adapted. Fractions also should be made consistent with the style. Fractions are $1\frac{2}{3}$ times the height of the whole number. The numerator and the denominator of a fraction are each $\frac{2}{3}$ of the height of the whole number, as shown in Fig. 29-10. Notice also that in the expanded style, the fraction is slashed to conserve vertical space. The fraction takes the same amount of space as the whole number. (See rule 5, Fig. 34-3.)

15 The size of the lettering should be related to the importance of the labeling (Fig. 29-11).

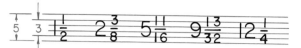

Fig 29-10 Proper fraction proportions.

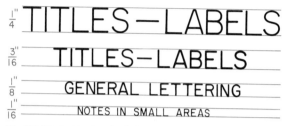

Fig 29-11 Lettering height should relate to the importance of the label size.

Fig 29-12 Lettering used for drawings that are to be microfilmed.

Fig 29-13 A common lettering template. Teledyne Post

16 If drawings are to be microfilmed, use microfont lettering (Fig. 29-12).

17 Specialized lettering templates can also be used (Fig. 29-13).

PAPER

Since the type of paper on which the line is drawn will greatly affect the line weight, different pencils may be necessary. Weather conditions, such as temperature and humidity, also greatly affect the line quality. During periods of high humidity, harder pencils must be employed.

TYPESET LETTERING

Typeset letters, although more consistent in size and style than hand lettering, are much slower to apply. Some typeset letters are applied one letter at a time by the *pressure sensitive method*. This type of application is used primarily for major labels on architectural drawings. Words, sentences, and dimensions can be set in type on opaque paper or transparent tape and positioned in place on the drawing with rubber cement or wax-backed paper. In architectural work, transparent tape labels can be positioned without covering the lines that pass close to or through the label.

UNIT 30
ARCHITECTURAL DRAWING TECHNIQUES

In addition to the precise technical line work used on floor plans and elevations, other line techniques are used to create realism in architectural drawings. Some of the line techniques used are variation in the distance between lines or dots, variation in the width of lines, blending of lines, and use of gray tones or solid black areas (Fig. 30-1). These techniques are used to show materials, texture, contrast between areas, or light and shadow patterns. Some common combinations of line patterns are shown in Fig. 30-2. The use of

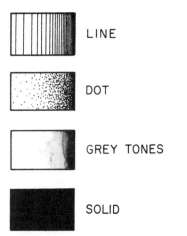

LINE

DOT

GREY TONES

SOLID

Fig 30-1 **Some types of line techniques.**

these techniques to show texture on a perspective drawing is shown in Fig. 30-3.

Varying the interval between lines drawn with pencil or pen can indicate texture, light, and density pattern, as shown in Fig. 30-4. When less precise line identification is de-

PENCIL TECHNIQUES

Fig 30-2 Examples of line-pattern combinations.

Fig 30-3 Methods of illustrating textures.

Fig 30-4 Line-rendering techniques.

Fig 30-5 Wash-drawing technique used Home Planners, Inc.
for landscape rendering.

Fig 30-6 Combination of line and wash Home Planners, Inc.
techniques.

sired, the use of *wash-drawing* (water-color) techniques is effective. The drawing shown in Fig. 30-5 is a wash drawing. The drawing shown in Fig. 30-6 is rendered using a combination of wash techniques over a line drawing.

Floor plans and elevation drawings are prepared primarily for the builder. These drawings must be accurately scaled and dimensioned. However, some floor plans and elevation drawings are rendered to provide the prospective customer with a better idea of the final appearance of the building. Figure

30-7 shows a presentation floor plan and elevation. These plans have no dimensions but include items such as plantings, floor surfaces, and material textures not usually found on floor plans or elevations used for construction purposes. Screens, lines, and patterns (Fig. 30-8) can also be applied by the use of appliqués.

Sketching is a communications medium used constantly by designers. In fact, most designers begin with a rough sketch. Sketches are used to record dimensions and the placement of existing objects and features prior to beginning a design. Sketches are used to show clients alternative possibilities concerning the approach to the design problem.

Sketching on graph paper helps increase speed and accuracy. Sketches also help record ideas off the job and help the designer remember unique features about a structure or site so that the actual design activity can take place in a different location.

In sketching, use a soft pencil. Hold the pencil comfortably. Draw the pencil, do not push it. Position the paper so your hand can move freely, as shown in Fig. 30-9. Sketch in short, rapid strokes. Long, continuous lines tend to bend on the arc line from elbow to fingers. To be effective, a sketch must be readable by another person without additional explanations.

The accuracy, effectiveness, and appearance of the finished drawing depend largely on the selection of the correct pencil and the pointing of that pencil. Fig. 23-2 shows the degrees of hardness of drawing pencils rang-

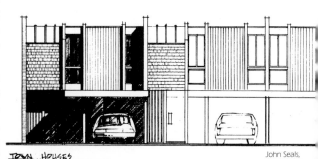

John Seals,
Architect

Fig 30-7 A presentation drawing.

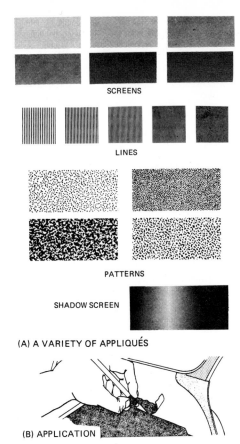

SCREENS

LINES

PATTERNS

SHADOW SCREEN

(A) A VARIETY OF APPLIQUÉS

(B) APPLICATION

Fig 30-8 Use of appliqués.

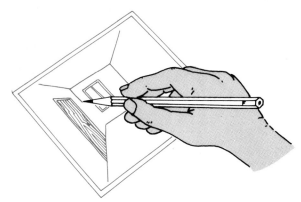

Fig 30-9 Method of holding pencil for sketching.

ing from 9H, extremely hard, to 7B, extremely soft. Pencils in the hard range are used for layout work. Pencils in the soft range are used for sketching and rendering. Floor plans of the type prepared by designers are usually drawn with pencils in a medium range. When the pencil is too soft, it will produce a line that smudges. If the pencil is too hard, a groove will be left in the paper and the line will be very difficult to erase. Since the blackness of the line also depends on the hardness of the lead, it is necessary to select the correct degree of hardness for pencil tracings. Different degrees of hardness react differently, depending on the type of paper used.

Sharpen the drawing pencil by exposing approximately one-half inch of lead. Then form the lead into a sharp conical point on a sanding pad. Slowly rotate the pencil while you rub it over the sanding pad. A smooth single-cut file may also be used. Mechanical pencil ejector sharpeners which eliminate sharpening and lead pointers are also available and convenient for this task.

PROBLEMS

1 Add texture to the surfaces of the elevation shown in Fig. 37-12.
2 Define these terms: *line, tone, wash drawing, presentation drawing.*

3 Sketch the elevation shown in Fig. 30-3.
4 Sketch the floor plan shown in Fig. 33-2.

DRAWING FLOOR PLANS

The most commonly used architectural drawing is the floor plan. The floor plan is a drawing of the outline and partitions of a building as you would see them if the building were cut horizontally about 4' (or for practical purposes 1 m) above the floor line. The floor plan provides more specific information about the design of the building than any other plan. To design a floor plan that will be accurate and functional, the designer must determine what facilities will be included in the various areas of the building. These various areas must be combined into an integrated plan. Only then can a final floor plan be prepared that includes a description and sizes of all the materials and areas contained in the design. The floor plan is used as a base for the projection of other drawings.

UNIT 31
FUNCTIONAL ROOM PLANNING

Not long ago, the outside of most homes was designed before the inside. A basic square, rectangle, or series of rectangles was established to a convenient overall size and then rooms were fitted into these forms.

Today, the inside of most homes is designed before the outside, and the outside design is determined by the size and relationship of the inside areas. This is known as *designing from the inside out.*

BASIC REQUIREMENTS

In designing from the inside out, the architect evolves the plan from basic room requirements. By learning about the living habits and tastes of the occupants, the architect determines what facilities are required for each room. In this way, the furniture, fixtures, and amount of space that will be appropriate for the activities are provided for.

SEQUENCE OF DESIGN

When designing from the inside out, the home planner first determines what furniture and fixtures are needed. Next, the amount and size of furniture must be determined. The style selected will greatly affect the dimensions of the furniture.

After the furniture dimensions are established, furniture templates can be made and arranged in functional patterns. Room sizes can then be established by drawing a perimeter around the furniture placements.

When the room sizes are determined, rooms can be combined into areas, and areas into the total floor plan. Finally, the outside is designed by projecting the elevations from the floor plan. Figure 31-1 shows the importance

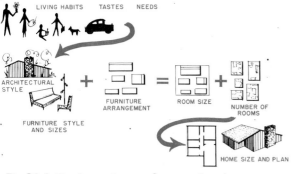

Fig 31-1 The importance of room planning in arriving at the overall design.

of room planning in the overall sequence of planning a home.

FURNITURE

Furniture styles vary greatly in size and proportion. Sizes of furniture therefore cannot be decided on until the style is chosen. The furniture style should be consistent with the style of architecture (Fig. 31-2).

SELECTION

Furniture should be selected according to the needs of the occupants (Fig. 31-3 at A and B). A piano should be provided for someone interested in music. A great amount of bookcase space must be provided for the avid reader. The artist, drafter, or engineer may require drafting equipment in the den or study. A good starting point in room planning is to list the uses to be made of each room. Then, make a list of furniture needed for each of these activities. For example: I want to *watch television*; therefore, I need a *television set* and a *lounge chair*. I want to *read*; therefore, I need a *lounge chair*, a *reading lamp*, and a *bookcase*. I want to *listen to records*; therefore, I need a *stereo*.

From these requirements, a rather comprehensive list of needed furniture can be compiled. When the exact style is determined, the width and length of each piece of furniture can also be added to the list, as shown below.

Living room
1 couch 34″ × 100″ (864 × 2540 mm)
2 armchairs 30″ × 36″ (762 × 914 mm)

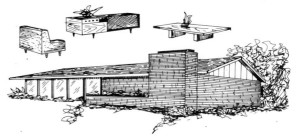

Fig 31-2 Furniture style should be consistent with the architectural style.

1 chaise 28″ × 60″ (711 × 1524 mm)
1 TV 26″ × 24″ (660 × 610 mm)
1 stereo system 24″ × 56″ (610 × 1422 mm)
1 bookcase 15″ × 48″ (381 × 1219 mm)
1 floor lamp 6″ × 14″ (152 × 356 mm)
1 coffee table 18″ × 52″ (457 × 1321 mm)
2 end tables 14″ × 30″ (356 × 762 mm)
1 baby grand piano 60″ × 80″ (1524 × 2032 mm)

Dining room
1 dining table 44″ × 72″ (1118 × 1829 mm)
2 armchairs 28″ × 36″ (711 × 914 mm)
4 chairs 26″ × 36″ (660 × 914 mm)
1 china closet 18″ × 42″ (457 × 1067 mm)
1 buffet 26″ × 56″ (660 × 1422 mm)

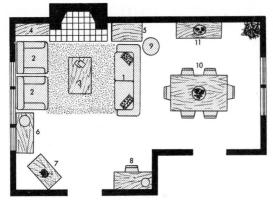

COMBINATION LIVING-DINING ROOM

1 - CHESTERFIELD	7 - TV CONSOLE
2 - LOUNGE CHAIR	8 - DESK
3 - COFFEE TABLE	9 - FLOOR LAMP
4 - BOOKCASE	10 - DINING ROOM TABLE
5 - END TABLE	AND 6 CHAIRS
6 - STEREO	11 - BUFFET

Fig 31-3A Living needs determine the amount of furniture.

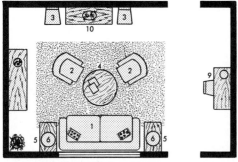

FURNITURE GROUPING AROUND COFFEE TABLE

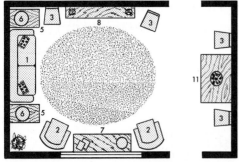

MULTIPURPOSE LIVING ROOM

1 - CHESTERFIELD	7 - STEREO
2 - LOUNGE CHAIR	8 - BUILT-IN CABINET
3 - CHAIR	9 - DESK AND CHAIR
4 - COFFEE TABLE	10 - BUFFET
5 - END TABLE	11 - FOLDING TABLE
6 - LAMP	

Fig 31-3B Life-style determines the furniture arrangement.

Similar lists should be prepared for the kitchen, bedrooms, nursery, bath, and all other rooms where furniture is required. Figure 31-4 shows some typical furniture dimensions that can be included with the furniture lists.

FURNITURE TEMPLATES

Arranging and rearranging furniture in a room is heavy work. It is much easier to arrange furniture by the use of templates (Fig. 31-5). *Furniture templates* are thin pieces of paper, cardboard, plastic, or metal that repre-

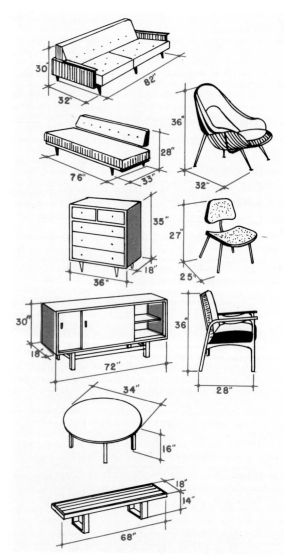

Fig 31-4 Some typical furniture dimensions.

Fig 31-5 Templates represent the width and length of each piece of furniture.

Table 31-1	COMMON FURNITURE SIZES		
Item	Length, in (mm)	Width, in (mm)	Height, in (mm)
COUCH	72(1829)	30(762)	30(762)
	84(2134)	30(762)	30(762)
	96(2438)	30(762)	30(762)
LOUNGE	28(711)	32(813)	29(737)
	34(864)	36(914)	37(940)
COFFEE TABLE	36(914)	20(508)	17(432)
	48(1219)	20(508)	17(432)
	54(1372)	20(508)	17(432)
DESK	50(1270)	21(533)	29(737)
	60(1524)	30(762)	29(737)
	72(1829)	36(914)	29(737)
STEREO CONSOLE	36(914)	16(406)	26(660)
	48(1219)	17(432)	26(660)
	62(1575)	17(432)	27(660)
END TABLE	22(559)	28(711)	21(533)
	26(660)	20(508)	21(533)
	28(711)	28(711)	20(508)
TV CONSOLE	38(965)	17(432)	29(737)
	40(1016)	18(457)	30(762)
	48(1219)	19(483)	30(762)
SHELF MODULES	18(457)	10(254)	60(1524)
	24(610)	10(254)	60(1524)
	36(914)	10(254)	60(1524)
	48(1219)	10(254)	60(1524)
DINING TABLE	48(1219)	30(762)	29(737)
	60(1524)	36(914)	29(737)
	72(1829)	42(1067)	28(711)
BUFFET	36(914)	16(406)	31(787)
	48(1219)	16(406)	31(787)
	52(1321)	18(457)	31(787)
DINING CHAIRS	20(508)	17(432)	36(914)
	22(559)	19(483)	29(737)
	24(610)	21(533)	31(787)
Item	Diameter, in (mm)		Height, in (mm)
DINING TABLE (ROUND)	36(914)		28(711)
	42(1067)		28(711)
	48(1219)		28(711)

sent the width and length of pieces of furniture. They are used to determine exactly how much floor space each piece of furniture will occupy. One template is made for each piece of furniture on the furniture list.

Templates are always prepared to the scale that will be used in the final drawing of the house. The scale most frequently used on floor plans is $\frac{1}{4}'' = 1'—0''$. Scales of $\frac{3}{16}'' = 1'—0''$ and $\frac{1}{8}'' = 1'—0''$ are sometimes used.

Wall-hung furniture, or any projection from furniture, even though it does not touch the floor, should be included as a template because the floor space under this furniture is not usable for any other purpose.

Templates show only the width and length of furniture and the floor space covered (Fig. 31-6A and B). Table 31-1 shows common furniture sizes that can be used as a guide in constructing furniture templates.

ROOM ARRANGEMENTS

Furniture templates are placed in the arrangement that will best fit the living pattern anticipated for the room. Space must be allowed for free flow of traffic and for opening and closing doors, drawers, and windows. Figure 31-7 shows furniture templates placed in different arrangements before the room dimensions are established.

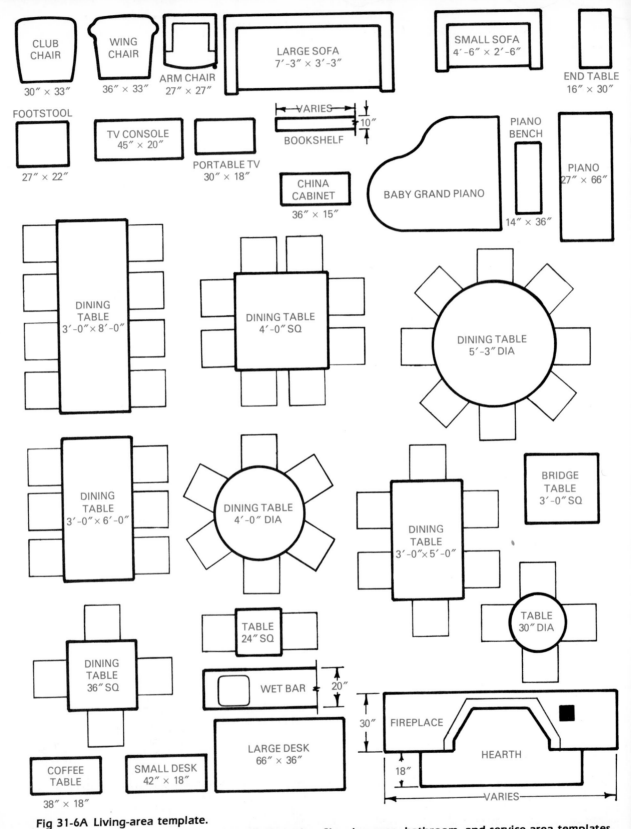

CLUB CHAIR
30″ × 33″

WING CHAIR
36″ × 33″

ARM CHAIR
27″ × 27″

LARGE SOFA
7′-3″ × 3′-3″

SMALL SOFA
4′-6″ × 2′-6″

END TABLE
16″ × 30″

FOOTSTOOL
27″ × 22″

TV CONSOLE
45″ × 20″

PORTABLE TV
30″ × 18″

VARIES
10″
BOOKSHELF

CHINA CABINET
36″ × 15″

BABY GRAND PIANO

PIANO BENCH
14″ × 36″

PIANO
27″ × 66″

DINING TABLE
3′-0″ × 8′-0″

DINING TABLE
4′-0″ SQ.

DINING TABLE
5′-3″ DIA.

DINING TABLE
3′-0″ × 6′-0″

DINING TABLE
4′-0″ DIA.

DINING TABLE
3′-0″ × 5′-0″

BRIDGE TABLE
3′-0″ SQ.

DINING TABLE
36″ SQ.

TABLE
24″ SQ.

TABLE
30″ DIA.

WET BAR
20″

FIREPLACE
30″
HEARTH
18″
VARIES

LARGE DESK
66″ × 36″

COFFEE TABLE
38″ × 18″

SMALL DESK
42″ × 18″

Fig 31-6A Living-area template.

Fig 31-6B Opposite: Sleeping-area, bathroom, and service-area templates.

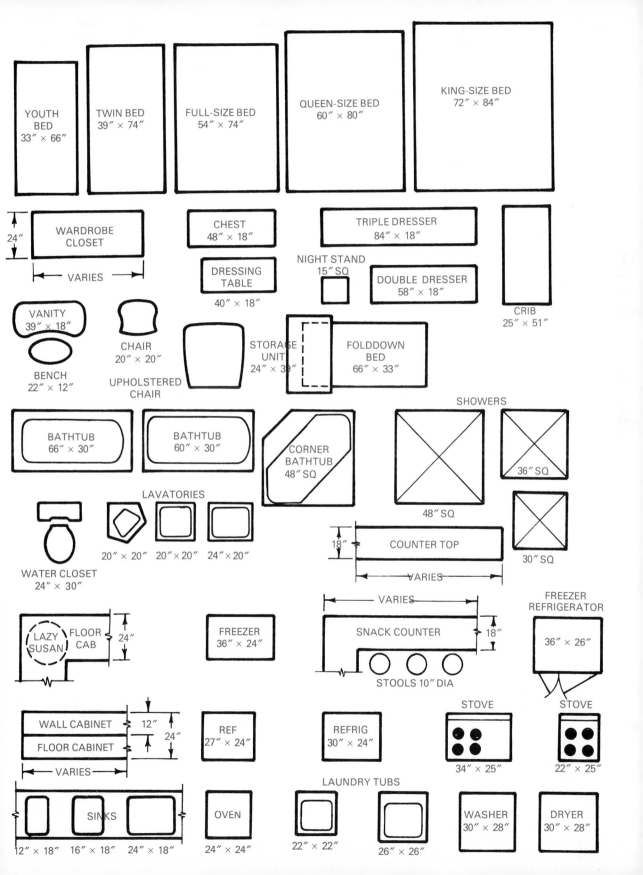

YOUTH BED
33″ × 66″

TWIN BED
39″ × 74″

FULL-SIZE BED
54″ × 74″

QUEEN-SIZE BED
60″ × 80″

KING-SIZE BED
72″ × 84″

24″

WARDROBE CLOSET

VARIES

CHEST
48″ × 18″

TRIPLE DRESSER
84″ × 18″

NIGHT STAND
15″ SQ

DRESSING TABLE
40″ × 18″

DOUBLE DRESSER
58″ × 18″

CRIB
25″ × 51″

VANITY
39″ × 18″

CHAIR
20″ × 20″

STORAGE UNIT
24″ × 39″

FOLDDOWN BED
66″ × 33″

BENCH
22″ × 12″

UPHOLSTERED CHAIR

BATHTUB
66″ × 30″

BATHTUB
60″ × 30″

CORNER BATHTUB
48″ SQ

SHOWERS

36″ SQ

48″ SQ

30″ SQ

LAVATORIES

20″ × 20″   20″ × 20″   24″ × 20″

18″   COUNTER TOP

VARIES

WATER CLOSET
24″ × 30″

VARIES

LAZY SUSAN   FLOOR CAB   24″

FREEZER
36″ × 24″

SNACK COUNTER   18″

STOOLS 10″ DIA

FREEZER REFRIGERATOR
36″ × 26″

WALL CABINET   12″
FLOOR CABINET   24″

VARIES

REF
27″ × 24″

REFRIG
30″ × 24″

STOVE
34″ × 25″

STOVE
22″ × 25″

LAUNDRY TUBS

SINKS

12″ × 18″   16″ × 18″   24″ × 18″

OVEN
24″ × 24″

22″ × 22″

26″ × 26″

WASHER
30″ × 28″

DRYER
30″ × 28″

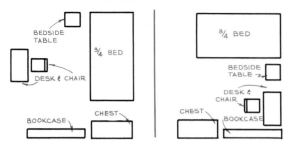

Fig 31-7 Room dimensions should be determined by arrangement and number of pieces of furniture.

DETERMINING ROOM DIMENSIONS

After a suitable furniture arrangement has been established, the room dimensions can be determined by drawing an outline around the furniture, as shown in Fig. 31-8.

Room templates are made by cutting around the outline of the room. Figure 31-9 shows some typical room templates constructed by cutting around furniture template arrangements.

COMMON ROOM SIZES

Determining what room sizes are desirable is only one aspect of room planning. Since the cost of the home is largely determined by the size and number of rooms, room sizes must be adjusted to conform to the acceptable price range. Table 31-2 shows sizes for each room in large, medium, and small dwellings. These dimensions represent only average widths and lengths. Even in large homes where perhaps no financial restriction exists, room sizes are limited by the size of building materials. Furthermore, a room can become too large to be functional for the purpose intended.

CHECKING METHODS

It is sometimes difficult to visualize the exact amount of real space that will be occupied by furniture or that will be occupied by furniture or that should be allowed for traffic through a given room. One device used to give

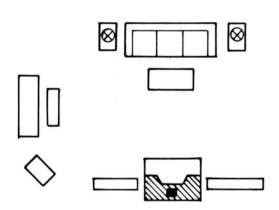

STEP 1   ARRANGE FURNITURE

Fig 31-8 The preferred method of determining room dimensions.

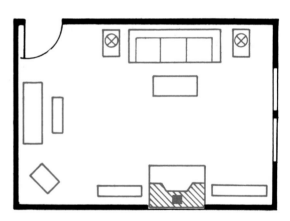

STEP 2   DRAW THE WALLS

Table 31-2 ROOM SIZES FOR SMALL, AVERAGE, AND LARGE HOMES					
	Living room, ft²/m²	Dining room, ft²/m²	Kitchen, ft²/m²	Bedrooms, ft²/m²	Bath, ft²/m²
SMALL HOME	200/18.5	155/14.4	110/10.2	140/13.0	40/3.7
AVERAGE HOME	250/24.2	175/16.2	135/12.5	170/15.7	70/6.5
LARGE HOME	300/27.8	195/18.1	165/15.3	190/17.6	100/9.3

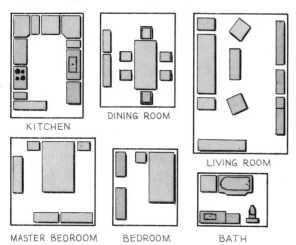

KITCHEN

DINING ROOM

LIVING ROOM

MASTER BEDROOM   BEDROOM   BATH

Fig 31-9 Typical placement of furniture templates.

CLOSET

NITE STAND

BEDROOM
12'-0"x12'-0"

6'-0"

DRESSER

CHAIR

the layman a point of reference is a template of a human figure, as shown in Fig. 31-10. With this template you can imagine yourself moving through the room to check the appropriateness of furniture placement and the adequacy of traffic allowances.

The experienced architect and home planner does not always go through the procedure of cutting out furniture templates and arranging them into patterns to arrive at room sizes. But the architect uses templates frequently to recheck designs. Until you are completely familiar with furniture dimensions and the sizes of building materials, the use of the procedures outlined here is recommended.

Fig 31-10 Comparative size of a room with the size of its inhabitants.

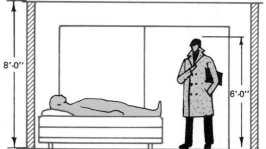

8'-0"

6'-0"

PROBLEMS

1 Rearrange the following steps in their proper order in room planning:
   a. Make list of furniture needed.
   b. Choose furniture style.
   c. Choose home style.
   d. Determine living habits.
   e. Make furniture templates.
   f. Determine room dimensions.
   g. Arrange furniture templates.
   h. Determine sizes of furniture.

2 Choose a style of furniture suitable for use in your home. Visit a furniture store and sketch examples of furniture suitable for a modern, a colonial, and a period house.

3 Define your living needs and activities. List each piece of furniture needed for each room in order to fulfill these needs. Example:

Living Habit	Furniture Needed
Watching TV	TV set
Playing table tennis	Table-tennis table
Writing	Desk, chair

4 Make a list of furniture you would need for a home you might design. The list should include the number of pieces and size (width and length) of each piece of furniture.

5 Make a furniture template ($\frac{1}{4}$" = 1'—0") for each piece of furniture

you would include in a home of your design.

6 Start a scrapbook of furniture styles by selecting examples from current magazines.

7 Define the following terms: *furniture template, furniture dimensions, room dimensions, furniture style.*

UNIT 32
FLOOR-PLAN DESIGN

The architect or designer develops and records ideas through preliminary sketches that are later transformed into final working drawings. These ideas are directly translated into sketches that may approximate the final design. The architect knows through experience how large each room or area must be made to perform its particular function. He or she can mentally manipulate the relationships of areas and record design ideas through the use of sketches. This skill is attained after much experience.

LEARNING DESIGN PROCEDURES

Until you have gained much experience in designing floor plans, you may have difficulty in creating floor plans by the same methods professionals use. In the beginning, you should rely on more tangible methods of designing.

The information in this unit outlines the procedures you should use in developing floor-plan designs. These procedures repre-

sent real activities that relate to the mental activities of a professional designer. Figure 32-1 shows the sequence of these design activities in developing a floor plan. You will notice that the sequence includes the development of room templates through the use of furniture templates, as described in Unit 31. These room templates become the building blocks used in floor-plan designing. The room templates are arranged, rearranged, and moved into various patterns until the most desirable plan is achieved. Think of these room templates as pieces of a jigsaw puzzle that are manipulated to produce the final picture. Figure 32-2 shows a typical set of room templates prepared for use in floor-plan design.

PLANNING WITH ROOM TEMPLATES

A residence or any other building is not a series of separate rooms, but a combination of several activities areas. In the design of floor plans, room templates are first divided into area classifications, as shown in Fig. 32-3. The templates are then arranged in the most desirable plan for each area (Fig. 32-4). Next, the area arrangements are combined in one plan (Fig. 32-5). The position of each room is then sketched and revised to achieve unity.

As you combine areas, you will need to rearrange and readjust the position of individ-

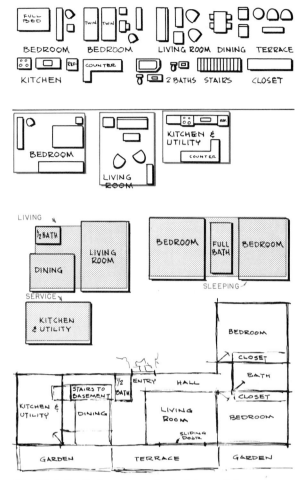

Fig 32-1 Preliminary rough sketches of floor plans are prepared from template layouts of the living, service, and sleeping areas.

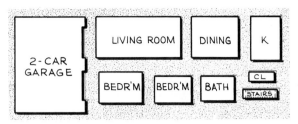

Fig 32-2 Room templates prepared for floor-plan design use.

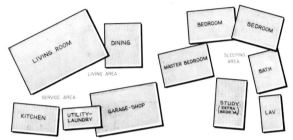

Fig 32-3 Room templates divided into areas.

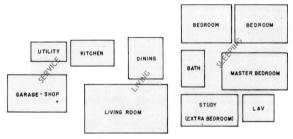

Fig 32-4 Templates arranged into area plans.

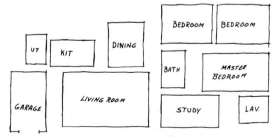

Fig 32-5 Area templates combined into one plan.

ual rooms. At this time, you should consider the traffic pattern, compass direction, street location, and relationship to landscape features. Space must be allowed for stairways and halls. Figure 32-6 shows some common allowances for stairwells on the floor plan. Unless closets have been incorporated in the room template, adequate space must also be provided for storage spaces.

Rooms and facilities such as the recreation room, laundry, workshop, and heating equipment are often placed in the basement. The designer must be sure that the floor plan developed provides sufficient space on the

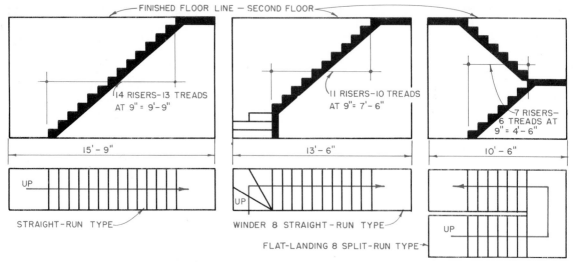

Fig 32-6 Space must be allowed for halls and stairways.

lower level for these facilities. In two-story houses, the sleeping area is usually placed on the level above the ground floor. Templates should also be developed for rooms on that level, but they must be adjusted to conform to the sizes established for the first level.

FLOOR-PLAN SKETCHING

Preparing a layout for a room template is only a preliminary step in designing the floor plan. The template layout shows only the desirable size, proportion, and relationship of each room to the entire plan.

PRELIMINARY SKETCHING

Template layouts such as the one shown in Fig. 32-5 usually contain many irregularities and awkward corners because room dimensions were established before the overall plan was completed. These offsets and indentations can be smoothed out by increasing the dimensions of some rooms and changing slightly the arrangement of others. These alterations are usually made by sketching the template layout. At this time, features such as fireplaces, closets, and divider walls can be added where appropriate.

Think of this first floor-plan sketch as only the beginning. Many sketches are usually

necessary before the designer achieves an acceptable floor plan. In successive sketches the design should be refined further. Costly and unattractive offsets and indentations can be eliminated. Modular sizes can be established that will facilitate the maximum use of standard building materials and furnishings. The exact positions and sizes of doors, windows, closets, and halls can be determined.

Refinement of the design is done by resketching until a satisfactory sketch is reached. Except for very minor changes, it is always better to make a series of sketches than to erase and change the original sketch. Many designers use tracing paper to trace the acceptable parts of the design and then change the poor features on the new sheet. This procedure also provides the designer with a record of the total design process. Early sketches sometimes contain solutions to problems that develop later in the final design. Final sketches can still be improved as shown in Fig. 32-7.

PLAN VARIATIONS

Many different room arrangements are possible within the same amount of space. Figure 32-8 shows two methods of rearranging and redistributing space to overcome poor design features.

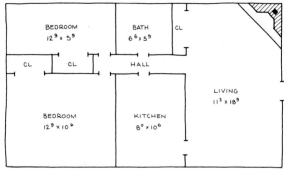

FIRST SKETCH

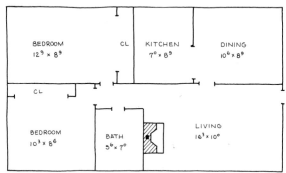

SECOND SKETCH

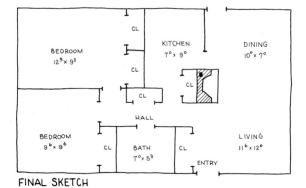

FINAL SKETCH

Fig 32-7 Revisions may be made to final sketches.

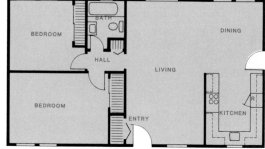

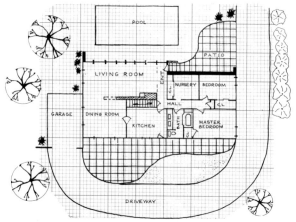

Fig 32-8 Many different room arrangements are possible within the same amount of space.

Fig 32-9 A final sketch prepared on cross-section paper.

FINAL SKETCHING

Single-line sketches are satisfactory for basic planning purposes. However, they are not adequate for establishing final sizes. A final sketch (Fig. 32-9) should be prepared on cross-section paper to provide a better description of wall thicknesses and to include property features. This sketch should include the exact position of doors, windows, and partitions. It should also include the location of shrubbery, trees, patios, walks, driveways, courts, pools, and gardens. Figure 32-10 shows the many plan variations possible by combining basic geometric shapes on different levels. Notice how the areas are arranged to achieve the most convenient plan.

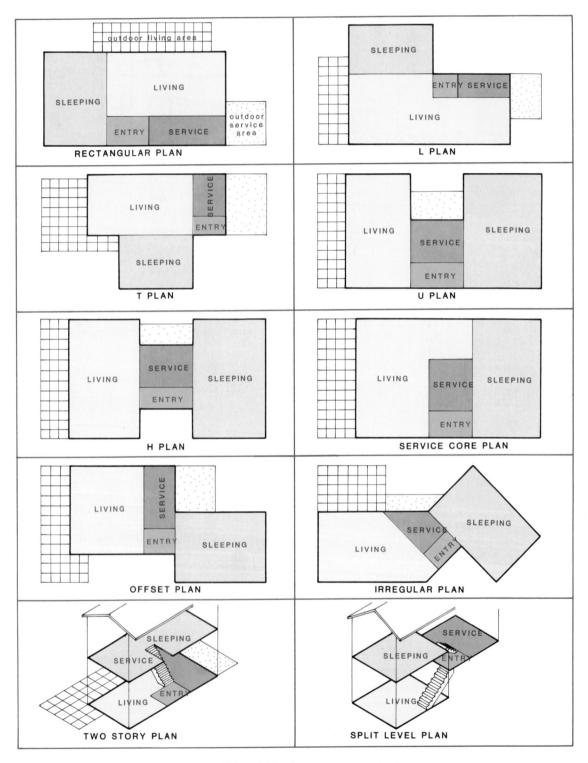

Fig 32-10 Many different plans are possible within the same amount of space.

Fig 32-11 A closed plan.

Home Planners, Inc.

OPEN PLANNING

When the rooms of a plan are divided by solid partitions, doors, or arches, the plan is known as a *closed plan*. A closed plan is shown in Fig. 32-11. If the partitions between the rooms of an area are eliminated, such as in Fig. 32-12, then the plan is known as an *open plan*.

The open plan is used mostly and to best advantage in the living area. Here the walls that separate the entrance foyer, living room, dining room, activities room, and recreation room can be removed or partially eliminated. These open areas are created to provide a sense of spaciousness, to aid lighting efficiency, and to increase the circulation of air through the areas.

Obviously, not all the areas of a residence lend themselves well to open-planning techniques. For example, a closed plan is almost always used in the sleeping area.

The floor plan for an open plan is developed in the same manner as for a closed plan. However, in the open plan the partitions are often replaced by dividers or by variations in level to set apart the various functions.

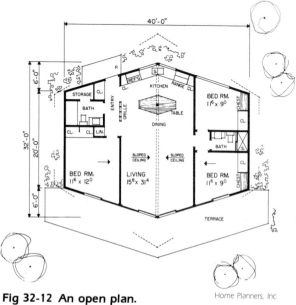

Fig 32-12 An open plan.

Home Planners, Inc.

14' WIDE × 64' LONG, 896 SQUARE FEET

12' WIDE × 64' LONG, 768 SQUARE FEET

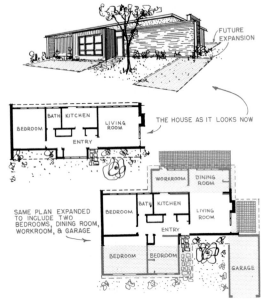

12' WIDE × 58' LONG DOUBLE EXPANDABLE, 815 SQUARE FEET

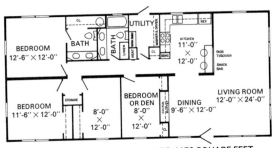

24' WIDE × 49' LONG DOUBLE-WIDE, 1176 SQUARE FEET

Fig 32-13 A mobile-home design must fit within the limits of the overall size.

When designing floor plans for modular units such as apartments or mobile homes (Fig. 32-13), the designer must develop a plan within predetermined dimensional limits.

EXPANDABLE PLANS

Because of limitations of time or money, it is sometimes desirable to construct a house

Fig 32-14 An expandable plan.

over a long period of time. When the complete construction is delayed, the house should be built in several steps. The basic part of the house can be constructed first. Then additional rooms (usually bedrooms) can be added in future years as the need develops.

When future expansion of the plan is anticipated, the complete floor plan should be drawn before the initial construction begins, even though the entire plan may not be complete at that time. If only part of the building is planned and built, and a later addition is made, the addition will invariably look tacked on. This appearance can be avoided by designing the floor plan for expansion, as shown in Fig. 32-14.

PROBLEMS

1 Prepare room templates and use them to make a functional arrangement for the living area, service area, and sleeping area of a house.

2 Arrange templates for a sleeping area, service area, and living area in a total composite plan.

3 Make a floor-plan sketch of the arrangement you completed in Problem 2. Have your instructor criticize this sketch, and then you revise it according to the recommendations.

4 After you have completed a preliminary line sketch, prepare a final sketch complete with wall thicknesses, overall dimensions, driveways, walks, and shrubbery. Use Fig. 32-9 as a guide.

5 Arrange the templates found in Fig. 32-15 in a floor-plan arrangement. Make a sketch of this arrangement, and revise the sketch until you arrive at a suitable plan.

6 Make room templates of each room in your own home. Rearrange these templates according to a remodeling plan, and make a sketch.

7 Convert the floor plan shown in Fig. 32-16 to an open plan. Sketch your solution.

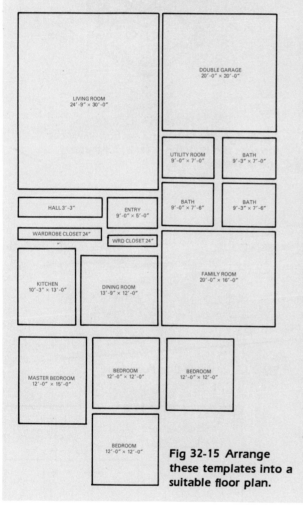

Fig 32-15 Arrange these templates into a suitable floor plan.

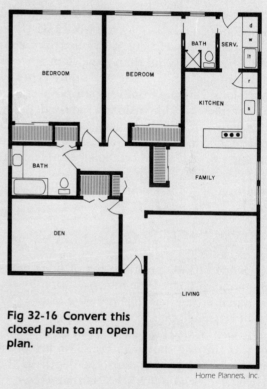

Fig 32-16 Convert this closed plan to an open plan.

Home Planners, Inc.

8 Define the following terms: *room template, floor-plan sketching, sketch, template layout, final sketching, open planning, closed plan, expandable plan.*

UNIT 33
COMPLETE FLOOR PLAN

A *floor plan* is a drawing of the outline and partitions of a building as you would see them if the building were cut (sectioned) horizontally about 4′ (1.2 m) above the floor line, as shown in Fig. 33-1. There are many types of floor plans, ranging from very simple sketches to completely dimensioned and detailed floor-plan working drawings. (See the special floor-plan symbols which are shown in these sections: 8, elevation symbols; 10, location-plan symbols; 14, electrical symbols; 15, air-conditioning symbols; and 16, plumbing symbols.)

TYPES OF FLOOR PLANS

Some of the various types of floor plans commonly prepared for interpretation by the layman are the *single-line drawing* (Fig. 33-2), the *abbreviated plan* (Fig. 33-3), and the *pictorial floor plan* (Fig. 33-4). Bird's-eye views such as the one shown in Fig. 33-5 are often prepared to convey a sense of depth to the viewer. Pictorial plans such as that shown in Fig. 33-6 are often prepared to show the relationship among various areas of the lot.

These plans are satisfactory for general use. However, a completely dimensioned floor plan is necessary to show the amount of detail necessary for construction purposes.

Floor-plan sketches such as those shown in Figs. 33-2 through 33-6 are sufficient for rough layout and preliminary design purposes but are not accurate or complete enough to be used as working drawings. An

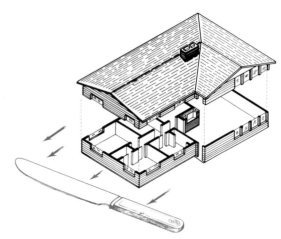

Fig 33-1 A floor plan is a section view cut through the building 4 feet (1.2 meters) above the floor line.

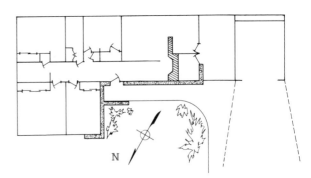

Fig 33-2 A single-line floor plan.

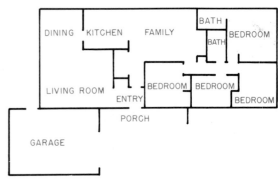

Fig 33-3 An abbreviated floor plan.

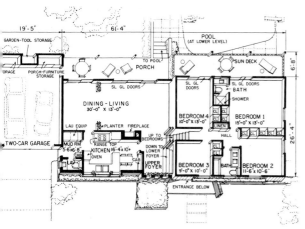

Fig 33-4 A pictorial floor plan.

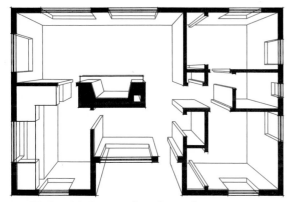

Fig 33-5 A bird's-eye view floor plan.

accurate floor plan, complete with dimensions and material symbols, must be prepared. When a plan of this type is developed, the contractor can interpret the desires of the designer without consultation. The prime

Fig 33-6 A flat-pictorial floor plan.

function of a working-drawing floor plan is to communicate information to the contractor. A complete floor plan eliminates many misunderstandings between the designer and the builder. The builder's judgment must be used to fill in the omitted details if an incomplete floor plan is prepared. The function of the designer is transferred to the builder when that happens.

FLOOR-PLAN SYMBOLS

Architects substitute symbols for materials and fixtures, just as stenographers substitute shorthand for words. It is obviously more convenient and time-saving to draw a symbol of a material than to repeat a description every time that material is used. It would be impossible to describe all construction materials used on floor plans, such as fixtures, doors, windows, stairs, and partitions, without the use of symbols.

Figures 33-7 through 33-11 show common symbols used on floor plans together with the related elevation symbol. These include symbols for doors, windows, appliances, fixtures, sanitation facilities, and building materials. Floor-plan symbols for plumbing, heating, air-conditioning, and electrical components are covered later in those specialized units. Figure 33-12 shows the application of some of these symbols to a floor plan, and Fig. 33-13 shows the relationship of floor-plan symbols to construction features.

Although architectural symbols are standardized, some variations of symbols are used in different parts of the country. Figure 33-14 shows several methods architects use for drawing construction details and the outside walls of frame buildings.

Wall openings indicated on floor plans show the relationship between the wall and ceiling, as shown in Fig. 33-15A.

Since it is impossible to show a complete plan at the normal scale of $\frac{1}{4}'' = 1'-0''$, Fig. 33-15B shows a portion of the plan found in Fig. 69-1 as it would be drawn at $\frac{1}{4}'' = 1'-0''$.

Learning and remembering floor-plan symbols will be easier if you associate each

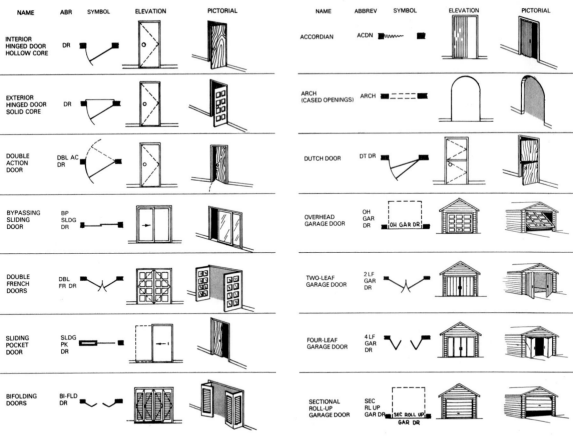

Fig 33-7 Door symbols.

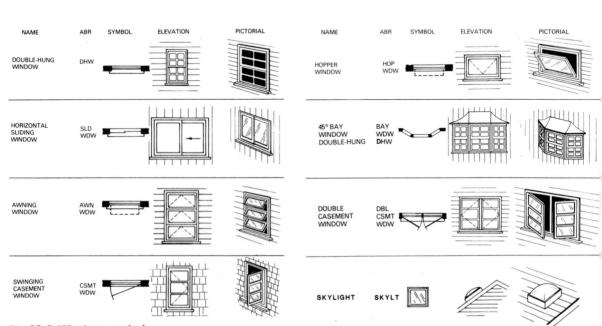

Fig 33-8 Window symbols.

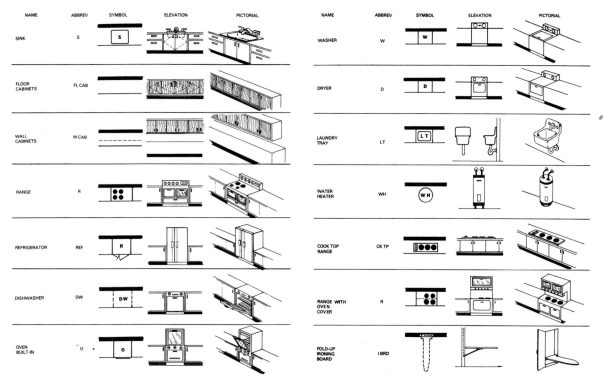

Fig 33-9 Appliance and fixture symbols.

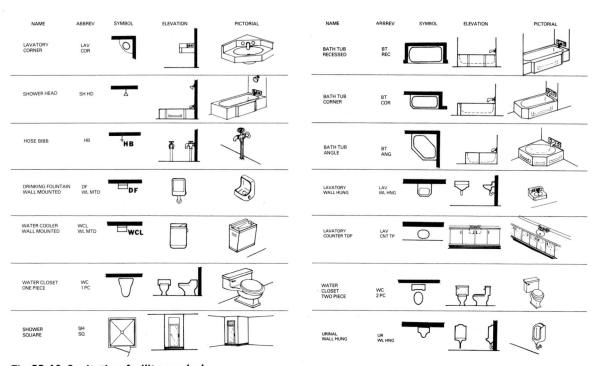

Fig 33-10 Sanitation facility symbols.

NAME	ABBRV	SECTION SYMBOL	ELEVATION	NAME	ABBRV	SECTION SYMBOL	ELEVATION
EARTH	E			CUT STONE, ASHLAR	CT STN ASH		
ROCK	RK			CUT STONE, ROUGH	CT STN RGH		
SAND	SD			MARBLE	MARB		
GRAVEL	GV			FLAGSTONE	FLG ST		
CINDERS	CIN			CUT SLATE	CT SLT		
AGGREGATE	AGR			RANDOM RUBBLE	RND RUB		
CONCRETE	CONC			LIMESTONE	LM ST		
CEMENT	CEM			CERAMIC TILE	CER TL		
TERAZZO CONCRETE	TER CONC			TERRA-COTTA TILE	TC TL		
CONCRETE BLOCK	CONC BLK			STRUCTURAL CLAY TILE	ST CL TL		
CAST BLOCK	CST BLK			TILE SMALL SCALE	TL		
CINDER BLOCK	CIN BLK			GLAZED FACE HOLLOW TILE	GLZ FAC HOL TL		
TERRA-COTTA BLOCK LARGE SCALE	TC BLK			TERRA-COTTA BLOCK SMALL SCALE	TC BLK		

Fig 33-11A Building material symbols.

NAME	ABBRV	SECTION SYMBOL	ELEVATION	NAME	ABBRV	SECTION SYMBOL	ELEVATION
COMMON BRICK	COM BRK			WELDED WIRE MESH	WWM		
FACE BRICK	FC BRK			FABRIC	FAB		
FIREBRICK	FRB			LIQUID	LQD		
GLASS	GL			COMPOSITION SHINGLE	COMP SH		
GLASS BLOCK	GL BLK			RIDGID INSULATION SOLID	RDG INS		
STRUCTURAL GLASS	STRUC GL			LOOSE-FILL INSULATION	LF INS		
FROSTED GLASS	FRST GL			QUILT	QLT		
STEEL	STL			SOUND INSULATION	SND INS		
CAST IRON	CST IR			CORK INSULATION	CRK INS		
BRASS & BRONZE	BRS BRZ			PLASTER WALL	PLST WL		
ALUMINUM	AL			PLASTER BLOCK	PLST BLK		
SHEET METAL (FLASHING)	SHT MTL FLASH			PLASTER WALL AND METAL LATHE	PLST WL & MT LTH		
REINFORCING STEEL BARS	REBAR			PLASTER WALL AND CHANNEL STUDS	PLST WL & CHN STD		

Fig 33-11B Building material symbols.

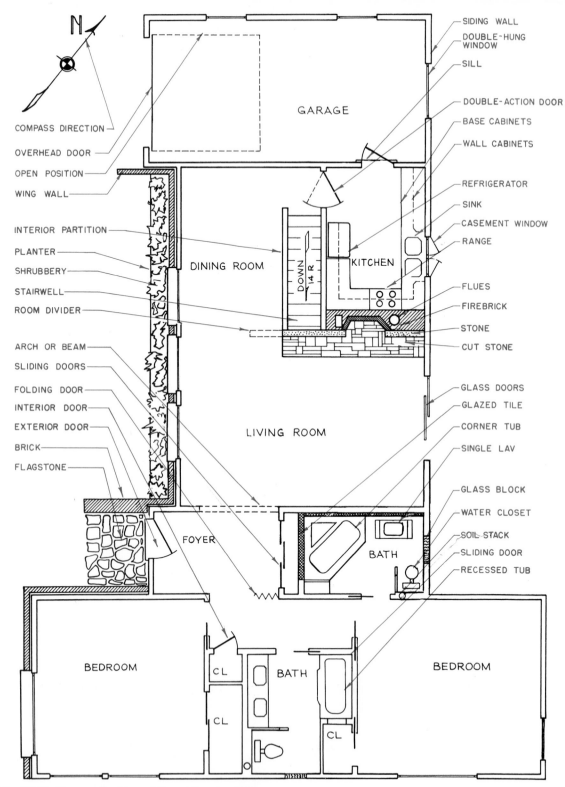

Fig 33-12 The application of floor-plan symbols.

SIDING WALL
DOUBLE-HUNG WINDOW
SILL

DOUBLE-ACTION DOOR
BASE CABINETS
WALL CABINETS

REFRIGERATOR
SINK
CASEMENT WINDOW
RANGE

FLUES
FIREBRICK
STONE
CUT STONE

GLASS DOORS
GLAZED TILE
CORNER TUB
SINGLE LAV

GLASS BLOCK
WATER CLOSET
SOIL STACK
SLIDING DOOR
RECESSED TUB

COMPASS DIRECTION
OVERHEAD DOOR
OPEN POSITION
WING WALL

INTERIOR PARTITION
PLANTER
SHRUBBERY
STAIRWELL
ROOM DIVIDER

ARCH OR BEAM
SLIDING DOORS
FOLDING DOOR
INTERIOR DOOR
EXTERIOR DOOR
BRICK
FLAGSTONE

N

GARAGE

DINING ROOM

KITCHEN

DOWN 14 R

LIVING ROOM

FOYER

BATH

BEDROOM

CL

CL

BATH

CL

BEDROOM

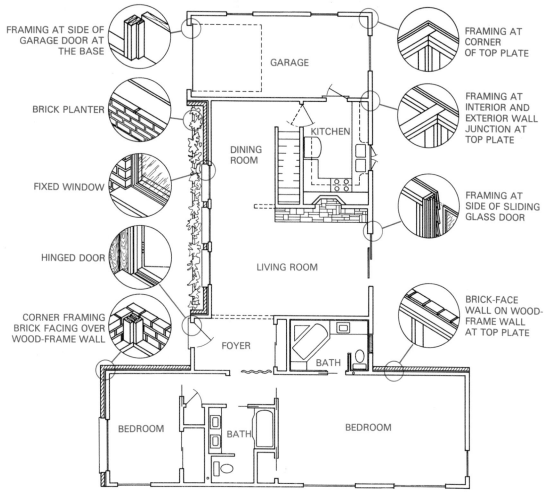

FRAMING AT SIDE OF GARAGE DOOR AT THE BASE

FRAMING AT CORNER OF TOP PLATE

BRICK PLANTER

FRAMING AT INTERIOR AND EXTERIOR WALL JUNCTION AT TOP PLATE

FIXED WINDOW

FRAMING AT SIDE OF SLIDING GLASS DOOR

HINGED DOOR

BRICK-FACE WALL ON WOOD-FRAME WALL AT TOP PLATE

CORNER FRAMING BRICK FACING OVER WOOD-FRAME WALL

GARAGE

DINING ROOM

KITCHEN

LIVING ROOM

FOYER

BATH

BEDROOM

BATH

BEDROOM

Fig 33-13 Methods of showing construction details on a floor plan.

symbol with the actual material or facility it represents. For example, as you learn the telephone-jack symbol, you should associate this symbol with the actual appearance of the telephone jack.

Floor-plan symbols often represent the exact appearance of the floor-plan section as viewed from above, but sometimes this representation is not possible. Many floor-plan

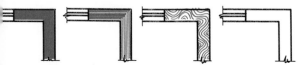

Fig 33-14 Methods of showing wall construction on a floor plan.

symbols are too intricate to be drawn to the scale $\frac{1}{4}'' = 1'—0''$ or $\frac{1}{8}'' = 1'—0''$. Therefore, many details are eliminated on the floor-plan symbols.

STEPS IN DRAWING FLOOR PLANS

For maximum speed, accuracy, and clarity, the following steps, as illustrated in Fig. 33-16, should be observed in laying out and drawing floor plans:

1 Block in the overall dimensions of the house and add the thickness of the outside walls with a hard pencil (4H).

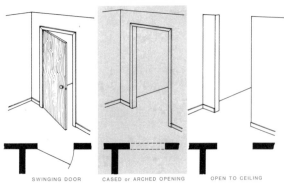

SWINGING DOOR   CASED or ARCHED OPENING   OPEN TO CEILING

Fig 33-15A Floor-plan symbols for wall openings.

5 Add door and window symbols with a 2H pencil.
6 Add symbols for stairwells.
7 Erase extraneous layout lines if they are too heavy. If they are extremely light, they can remain.
8 Draw the outlines of kitchen and bathroom fixtures.
9 Add the symbols and sections for any masonry work, such as fireplaces and planters.
10 Dimension the drawing (see Unit 34).

SECOND-FLOOR PLAN

Bilevel, two-story, one-and-one-half-story, and split-level homes require a separate floor plan for each additional level, as shown in Fig. 33-17. This floor plan is prepared on tracing paper placed directly over the first-

2 Lay out the position of interior partitions with a 6H pencil.
3 Locate the position of doors and windows by center line and by their widths (4H).
4 Darken the object lines with an F pencil.

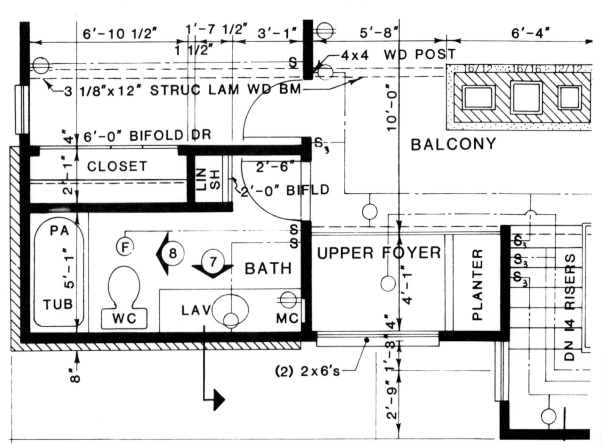

Fig 33-15B Part of a full-size drawing prepared at $\frac{1}{4}'' = 1'—0''$.

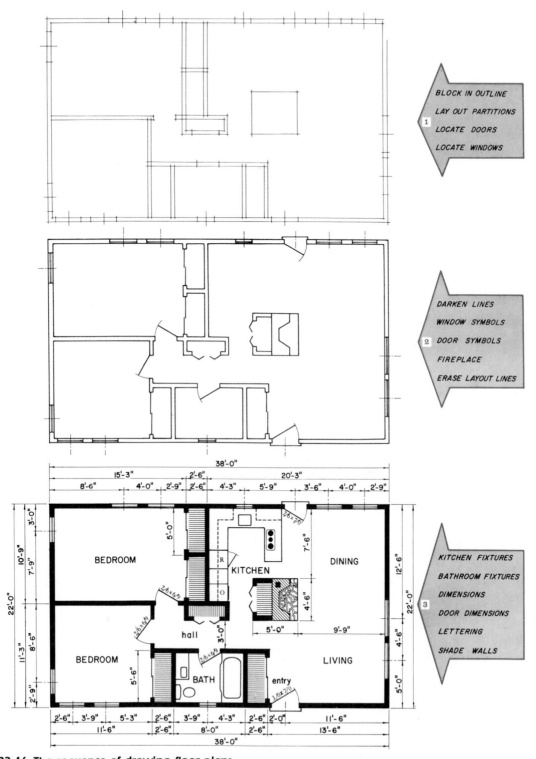

Fig 33-16 The sequence of drawing floor plans.

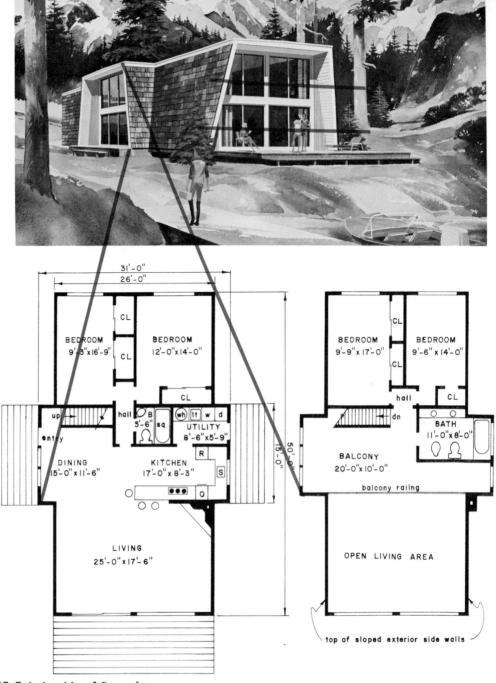

Fig 33-17 Relationship of floor-plan locations to pictorial rendering.

floor plan to ensure alignment of walls and bearing partitions. When the major outline has been traced, the first-floor plan is removed. Figure 33-18 shows a second-floor plan projected from the first-floor plan. Align-ment of features such as stairwell openings (Fig. 33-19), outside walls, plumbing walls, and chimneys is critical in preparing the sec-ond-floor plan. Figure 33-20 shows a typical second-floor plan of a one-and-one-half-story

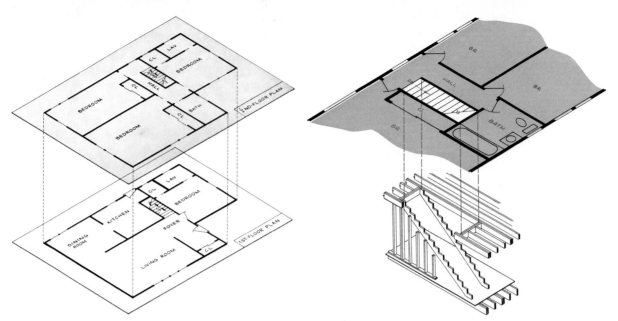

Fig 33-18 Projection of the second-floor plan.

Fig 33-19 Relationship of first- and second-floor openings.

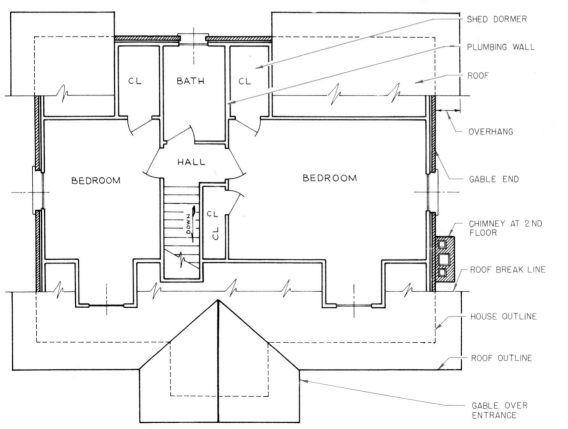

Fig 33-20 A one-and-one-half-story second-floor plan.

SHED DORMER

PLUMBING WALL

ROOF

OVERHANG

GABLE END

CHIMNEY AT 2ND FLOOR

ROOF BREAK LINE

HOUSE OUTLINE

ROOF OUTLINE

GABLE OVER ENTRANCE

CL BATH CL

HALL

BEDROOM

BEDROOM

DOWN

CL

CL

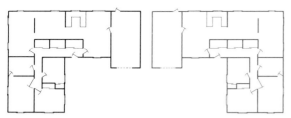

Fig 33-21 A full second-floor plan.

Home Planners, Inc.

Fig 33-22 A reversed plan.

house with the roof line broken. This drawing, in addition to revealing the second-floor plan, shows the outline of the roof. In this plan, dotted lines are used to show the outline of the building under the roof.

Figure 33-21 shows a second-floor plan of a two-story house. In this plan, there is no break, since the first-floor plan is the same size as the second-floor plan. This plan is prepared by tracing over the first-floor outline.

ALTERNATIVE PLANS

A technique frequently used to alter or adapt the appearance of the house and the location of various rooms is the practice of reversing a floor plan. Figure 33-22 shows a floor plan with its reversed counterpart. This reversal is accomplished by turning the floor plan upside down and tracing the mirror image of the floor plan to provide either a right-hand or a left-hand plan.

PROBLEMS

1 Draw a complete floor plan, using a sketch of your own design as a guide, and using the scale $\frac{1}{4}'' = 1'-0''$.

2 Draw a complete floor plan from the sketch shown in Fig. 33-23, using the scale $\frac{1}{4}'' = 1'-0''$.

3 Measure the rooms and draw a complete floor plan of your home. Use the scale $\frac{1}{4}'' = 1'-0''$ or $\frac{1}{8}'' = 1'-0''$.

4 After making a floor-plan sketch of your home, revise this sketch to show how you would propose to remodel your home. Then make a complete floor-plan drawing of the remodeled design, using the scale $\frac{1}{4}'' = 1'-0''$ or $\frac{1}{8}'' = 1'-0''$.

5 Draw the second-floor plan of your own home if it has one, or create one. Use the scale $\frac{1}{4}'' = 1'-0''$.

6 Identify the symbols in Fig. 33-24.

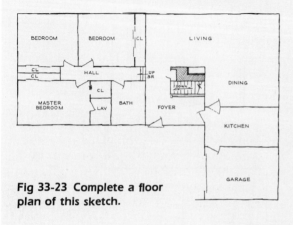

Fig 33-23 Complete a floor plan of this sketch.

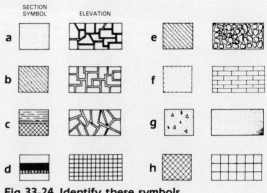

Fig 33-24 Identify these symbols.

7 Draw a complete floor plan, using the sketch shown in Fig. 33-25 as a guide. Make any alterations necessary to adapt the cabin to your own needs, as a hunting cabin or seaside lodge, for example.

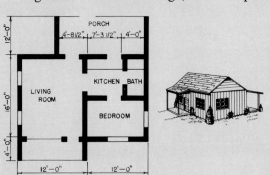

Fig 33-25 Draw a complete floor plan of this cabin.

8 Draw a complete floor plan, using the sketch shown in Fig. 33-26 as a guide.

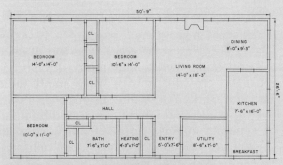

Fig 33-26 Draw a complete floor plan using this layout as a guide.

9 Draw a complete floor plan from the abbreviated plan shown in Fig. 33-27.

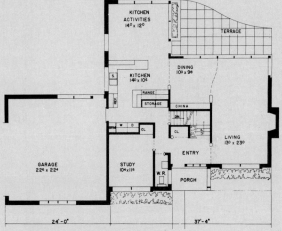

Fig 33-27 Draw a complete floor plan of this abbreviated plan. Home Planners, Inc.

10 Identify the symbols shown in Fig. 33-28.

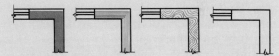

Fig 33-28 Different methods of showing walls on a floor plan.

11 Define these terms: *floor plan, single-line floor plan, pictorial floor plan, bird's-eye view, floor-plan symbols, second-floor plan, alternative plan, plumbing wall, right-hand plan, left-hand plan.*

UNIT 34
FLOOR-PLAN DIMENSIONING

In colonial times, simple cabins could be built without architectural plans and without established dimensions. The outline of the house and the position of each room could be determined experimentally by pacing off approximate distances. The owner could then erect the dwelling, using existing materials and adjusting sizes and dimensions as neces-

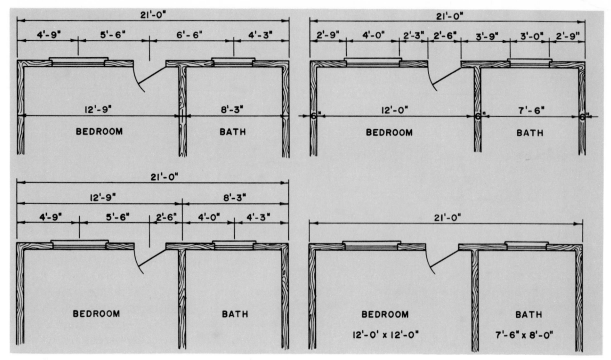

Fig 34-1 Some methods of dimensioning floor plans.

sary. The owner acted in the capacities of architect, designer, contractor, carpenter, and materials manufacturer.

Today, building materials are so varied, construction methods so complex, and design requirements so demanding that a completely dimensioned drawing is necessary to complete any building exactly as designed.

SIZE DESCRIPTION

Dimensions show the builder the width and length of the building. They show the location of doors, windows, stairs, fireplaces, and planters. Just as symbols and notes show exactly what materials are to be used in the building, dimensions show the sizes of materials and exactly where they are to be located.

Dimensioning architectural drawings differs from dimensioning mechanical drawings in many ways and for many reasons. Dimensioning practices often vary among designers. Several common methods of dimensioning floor plans are shown in Fig. 34-1. Because a large building must be drawn on a relatively

small sheet, a very small scale ($\frac{1}{4}'' = 1'-0''$ or $\frac{1}{8}'' = 1'-0''$) must be used. The use of such a small scale means that many dimensions must be crowded into a very small area. Therefore, only major dimensions such as the overall width and length of the building and of separate rooms, closets, halls, and wall thicknesses are shown on the floor plan. Dimensions too small to show directly on the floor plan are described either by a note on the floor plan or by separate, enlarged details. *Enlarged details* are sometimes merely enlargements of some portion of the floor plan. They may also be an allied section indexed to the floor plan. Separate details are usually necessary to interpret adequately the dimensioning of fireplaces, planters, built-in cabinets, door and window details, stair-framing details, or any unusual construction methods.

COMPLETE DIMENSIONS

The number of dimensions included on a floor plan depends largely on how much freedom of interpretation the architect wants to give to the builder. If complete dimensions

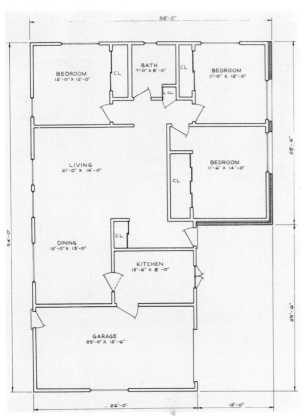

Fig 34-2 A floor plan with minimum amount of dimensions.

are shown on the plan, a builder cannot deviate greatly from the original design. However, if only a few dimensions are shown, then the builder must determine many of the sizes of areas, fixtures, and details. When you rely on a builder to provide dimensions, you place the builder in the position of a designer. A good builder is not expected to be a good designer. Supplying adequate dimensions will eliminate the need for guesswork.

LIMITED DIMENSIONS

A floor plan with only limited dimensions is shown in Fig. 34-2. This type of dimensioning, which shows only the overall building dimensions and the width and length of each room, is sufficient to summarize the relative sizes of the building and its rooms for the prospective owner. These dimensions are not sufficient for building purposes.

A floor plan must be completely dimensioned (Fig. 34-3) to ensure that the house will be constructed precisely as designed. These dimensions convey the exact wishes of the architect and owner to the builder, and little tolerance is allowed the contractor in interpreting the size and position of the various features of this plan. The exact size of each room, closet, door, or window is given.

RULES FOR DIMENSIONING

Many construction mistakes result from errors in architectural drawings. Most errors in architectural drawing result from mistakes in dimensioning. Dimensioning errors are therefore costly in time, efficiency, and money. Familiarization with the following rules for dimensioning floor plans will eliminate much confusion and error. These rules are illustrated by the numbered arrows in Fig. 34-3.

1. Architectural *dimension lines* are unbroken lines with dimensions placed above the line. Arrowheads of several styles are optional (Fig. 34-4).
2. Foot and/or inch marks are used on all architectural dimensions.
3. Dimensions over 1' are expressed in feet and inches.
4. Dimensions less than 1' are shown in inches.
5. A slash is often used with fractional dimensions to conserve vertical space.
6. Dimensions should be placed to read from the right or from the bottom of the drawing.
7. Overall building dimensions are placed outside the other dimensions.
8. Line and arrowhead weights for architectural dimensioning are the same as those used in dimensioning mechanical drawings.
9. Room sizes may be shown by stating width and length.
10. When the area to be dimensioned is too small for the numerals, they are placed outside the extension lines.

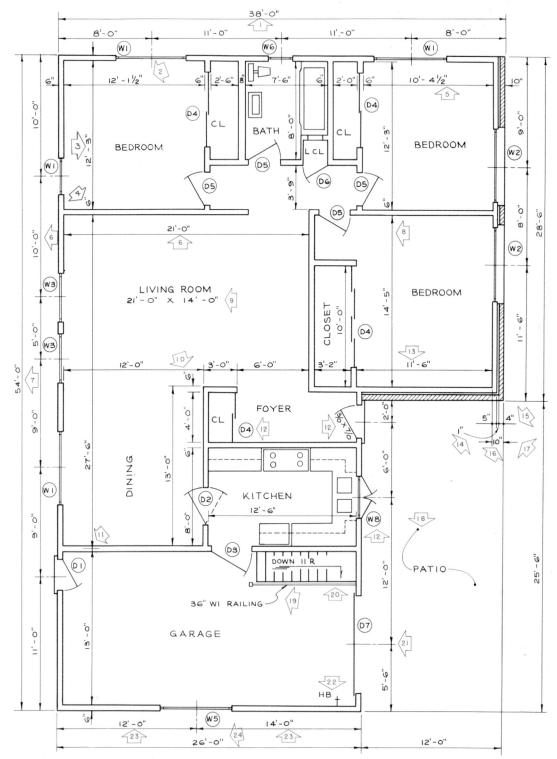

Fig 34-3 Rules for dimensioning architectural floor plans.

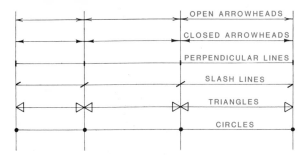

Fig 34-4 Different styles of arrowheads used on dimension lines.

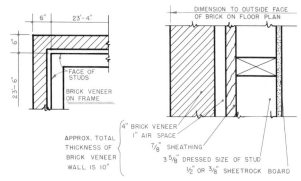

Fig 34-5 Brick or stone dimensions must be added to the framing dimensions.

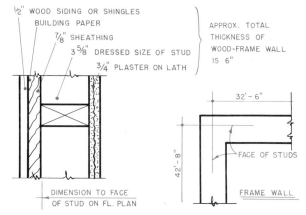

Fig 34-6 When framing dimensions alone are desired, the dimensions should read to the face of the stud.

11 Rooms are sometimes dimensioned from center lines of partitions; however, rule 13 is preferred.

12 Window and door sizes may be shown directly on the door or window symbol or may be indexed to a door or window schedule.

13 Rooms are dimensioned from wall to wall, exclusive of wall thickness.

14 Curved leaders are sometimes used to eliminate confusion with other dimension lines.

15 When areas are too small for arrowheads, dots may be used to indicate dimension limits.

16 The dimensions of brick or stone veneer must be added to the framing dimension (Fig. 34-5).

17 When the space is small, arrowheads may be placed outside the extension lines.

18 A dot with a leader refers to the large area noted.

19 Dimensions that cannot be seen on the floor plan or those too small to place on the object are placed on leaders for easier reading.

20 In dimensioning stairs, the number of risers is placed on a line with an arrow indicating the direction (down or up).

21 Windows, doors, pilasters, beams, and areaways are dimensioned to their center lines.

22 Use abbreviations when symbols do not show clearly what is intended.

23 Subdimensions must add up to overall dimensions $(14'—0'' + 12'—0'' = 26'—0'')$.

24 Architectural dimensions always refer to the actual size of the building regardless of the scale of the drawing. The building in Fig. 34-3 is $38'—0''$ wide.

25 Refer to Fig. 34-6. When framing dimensions are desirable, rooms are dimensioned by distances to the outside face of the studs in the partitions.

26 Since building materials vary somewhat in size, first establish the thickness of each component of the wall and partition, such as furring thickness, panel thickness, plaster thickness, stud thickness, brick and tile thicknesses. Add these thicknesses together to establish the total wall thickness. Common thicknesses of wall and partition materials are shown in Fig. 34-7.

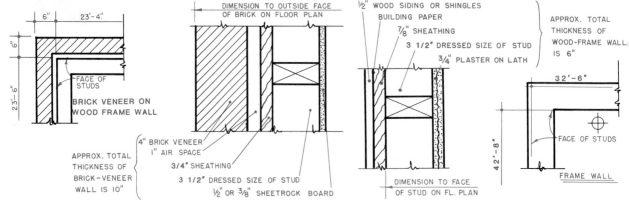

Fig 34-7 Methods of dimensioning various wall and partition thicknesses. partition thicknesses.

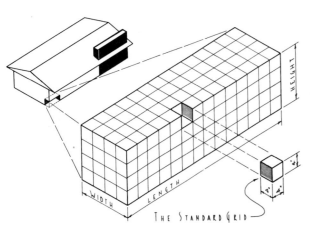

Fig 34-8 A modular grid.

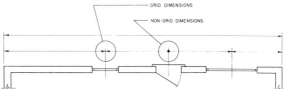

Fig 34-9 Modular dimensioning methods.

All other rules of floor-plan dimensioning adhere to the American National Standard Drafting Manual.

MODULAR CONSTRUCTION

Buildings to be erected with modular components must be designed within modular limits. In dimensioning by the modular system, building dimensions are expressed in standard sizes. This procedure ensures the proper fitting of the various components. Planning rooms to accommodate standard materials also saves considerable labor, time, and material. The modular system of coordinated drawings is based on a standard grid placed on the width, length, and height of a

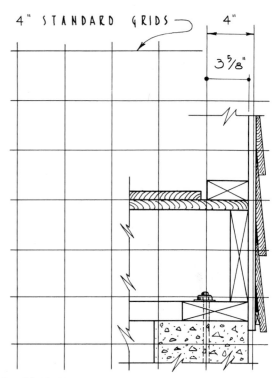

Fig 34-10 Modular dimensions, as applied to detail drawings.

building, as shown in Fig. 34-8.

In modular designing, an effort is made to establish all building dimensions (width, length, and height) to fall on some 4″ module, if the building material can be selected to conform to this module. As new building materials are developed, their sizes are established to conform to modular sizes. However, many building materials do not conform to the 4″ grid, and therefore the dimensioning procedure must be adjusted accordingly. Dimensions that align with the 4″ module are known as *grid dimensions*. Dimensions that do not align with the 4″ module are known as *nongrid dimensions*. Figure 34-9 shows the two methods of indicating grid dimensions and nongrid dimensions. Grid dimensions are shown by conventional arrowheads, and nongrid dimensions are shown by dots instead of arrowheads on the dimension lines.

In many detail drawings, it is possible to eliminate the placement of some dimensions by placing the grid lines directly on the drawing, as shown in the detail given in Fig. 34-10. When the 4″ grid lines coincide exactly with the material lines, no dimensions are needed, since each line represents 4″ and any building material that is an increment of 4″ is reflected by placement on this grid. Other dimensions that do not coincide, such as the 3⅝″ stud dimension shown in Fig. 34-10, must be dimensioned by conventional methods.

PROBLEMS

1. Dimension a floor plan that you have completed for a previous assignment.
2. Sketch or draw and dimension the floor plan shown in Fig. 34-11, using the scale ¼″ = 1′—0″.
3. Dimension the floor plan shown in Fig. 34-11 by the modular method.

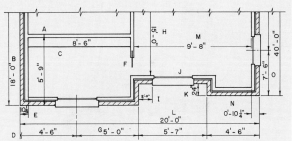

Fig 34-12 **Find the dimensioning errors shown by the letters.**

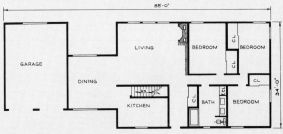

Fig 34-11 **Dimension this floor plan.**

4. Find the dimensioning errors in Fig. 34-12. List the dimensioning rule violated in each case. (Example: L violates rule 7.)
5. Draw and dimension the floor plan of your own home.
6. Sketch or draw the floor plan shown in Fig. 34-13 and completely dimension your plan.

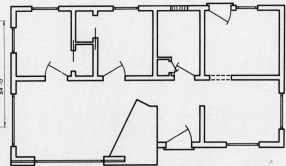

Fig 34-13 **Draw a floor plan of this house, complete with dimensions.**

7. Define the following terms: *dimension line, fractional dimensions, overall dimensions, center lines, extension lines, leader lines, subdimensions, framing dimensions, modular dimensioning, grid dimensions.*

ELEVATION DRAWINGS

The main features of the interior of a building are shown on the floor plan. The main features of the outside of a building are shown on elevation drawings. Elevation drawings are orthographic drawings of the exterior of a building. They are prepared to show the design, materials, dimensions, and final appearance of the exterior of a building.

UNIT 35
ELEVATION DESIGN

Designing the elevation of a structure is only one part of the total design process. However, this is the part of the building that most people see, and it is the part they use to judge the entire structure.

RELATIONSHIP WITH THE FLOOR PLAN

Since a structure is designed from the inside out, the design of the floor plan normally precedes the design of the elevation. The complete design process requires a continual relationship between the elevation and the floor plan through the entire process.

Much flexibility is possible in the design of elevations, even in those designed from the same floor plan. Figure 35-1 shows the development of two different elevations from the same basic floor plan. When the location of doors, windows, and chimneys has been established on the floor plan, the development of an attractive and functional elevation for the structure still depends on the factors of roof style, overhang, grade-line position, and relationship of windows, doors, and chimneys to the building line. Figure 35-1 clearly shows that choosing a desirable elevation design is not an automatic process that follows the floor-plan design, but a development which calls on the imagination.

The designer should keep in mind the fact that only horizontal distances can be established on the floor plan and that the vertical heights, such as heights of windows and doors, must be shown on the elevation. As these vertical heights are established, the appearance of the outside and the functioning of the heights as they affect the internal functioning of the house must be considered, as shown in Fig. 35-2.

FUNDAMENTAL SHAPES

The basic architectural style of a building is more closely identified with the design of

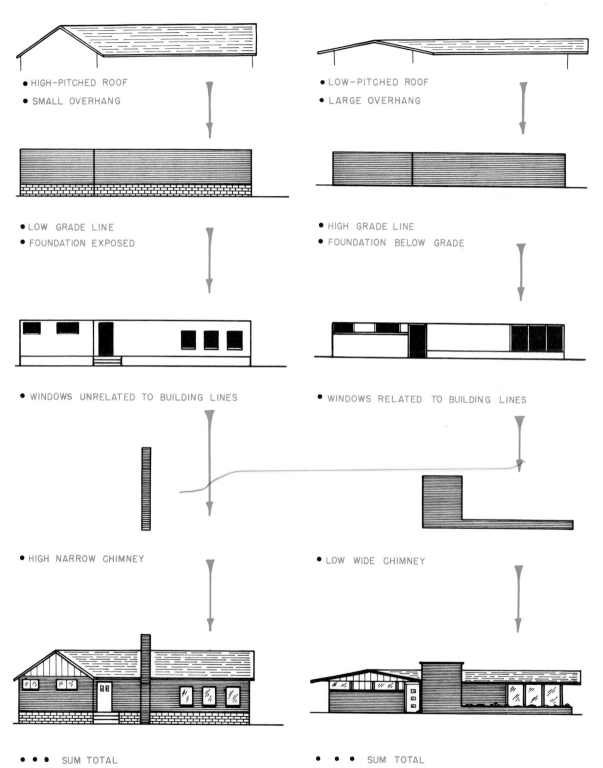

- HIGH-PITCHED ROOF
- SMALL OVERHANG

- LOW-PITCHED ROOF
- LARGE OVERHANG

- LOW GRADE LINE
- FOUNDATION EXPOSED

- HIGH GRADE LINE
- FOUNDATION BELOW GRADE

- WINDOWS UNRELATED TO BUILDING LINES

- WINDOWS RELATED TO BUILDING LINES

- HIGH NARROW CHIMNEY

- LOW WIDE CHIMNEY

• • • SUM TOTAL

• • • SUM TOTAL

Fig 35-1 Many factors affect the total appearance of the elevation.

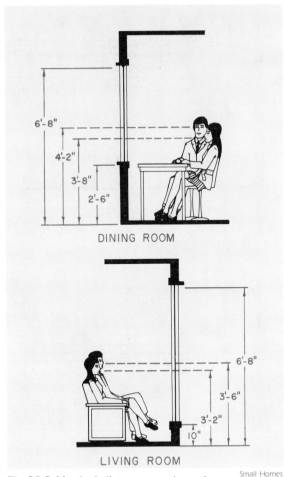

DINING ROOM

LIVING ROOM

Small Homes
Council

Fig 35-2 Vertical distances, such as the heights of windows and doors, can be shown only on an elevation drawing.

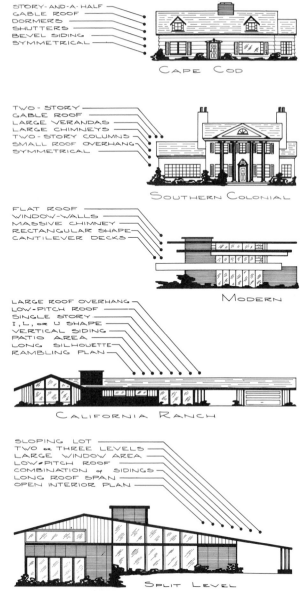

STORY-AND-A-HALF
GABLE ROOF
DORMERS
SHUTTERS
BEVEL SIDING
SYMMETRICAL

CAPE COD

TWO-STORY
GABLE ROOF
LARGE VERANDAS
LARGE CHIMNEYS
TWO-STORY COLUMNS
SMALL ROOF OVERHANG
SYMMETRICAL

SOUTHERN COLONIAL

FLAT ROOF
WINDOW-WALLS
MASSIVE CHIMNEY
RECTANGULAR SHAPE
CANTILEVER DECKS

MODERN

LARGE ROOF OVERHANG
LOW-PITCH ROOF
SINGLE STORY
I, L, or U SHAPE
VERTICAL SIDING
PATIO AREA
LONG SILHOUETTE
RAMBLING PLAN

CALIFORNIA RANCH

SLOPING LOT
TWO or THREE LEVELS
LARGE WINDOW AREA
LOW-PITCH ROOF
COMBINATION of SIDINGS
LONG ROOF SPAN
OPEN INTERIOR PLAN

SPLIT LEVEL

Fig 35-3 The style of architecture will greatly determine the exterior appearance of the building.

the elevation than with any other factor. Consequently the selection of the basic type of structure must be compatible with the architectural style of the elevation. The elevation design can be changed to create the appearance of different architectural styles if the basic building type is consistent with that style (Fig. 35-3).

BASIC TYPES

Within basic styles of architecture there is considerable flexibility in the type of structure.

The basic types of structures include the *one-story* (Fig. 35-4), the *one-and-one-half-story*

(Fig. 35-5), the *two-story* (Fig. 35-6), the *split-level* (Fig. 35-7), and the *bilevel* (Fig. 35-8).

ROOF STYLES

Nothing affects the silhouette of a house more than the roof line. The most common roofs are the gable roof, hip roof, flat roof, and shed roof (Fig. 35-9). A change in the roof style

Fig 35-4 Types of one-story structures.

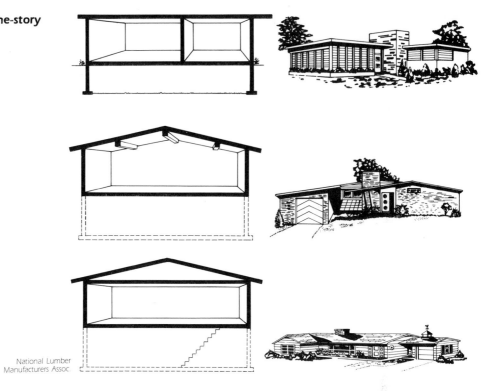

National Lumber
Manufacturers Assoc.

Fig 35-5 A one-and-one-half-story home.

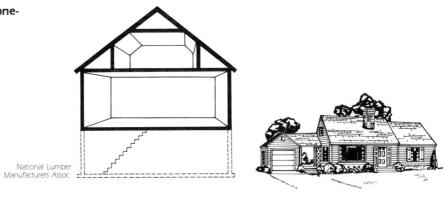

National Lumber
Manufacturers Assoc.

Fig 35-6 A two-story house.

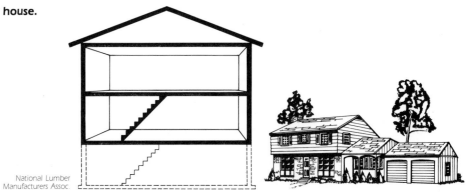

National Lumber
Manufacturers Assoc.

Fig 35-7 A split-level home.

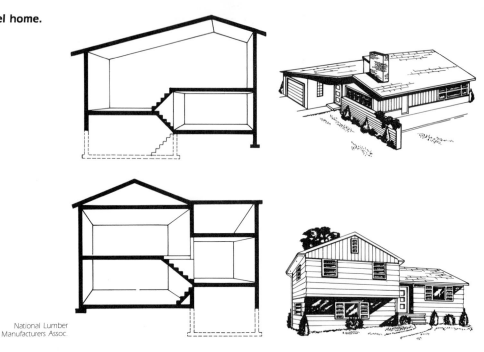

of a structure greatly affects the appearance of the elevation even when all other factors remain constant, as shown in Fig. 35-10.

Gable roofs, as shown in Fig. 35-11, are used extensively on Cape Cod and ranch homes. The *pitch* (angle) of a gable roof varies from the high-pitch roofs found on chalet-style buildings (Fig. 35-12) to the low-pitch roofs found on most ranch homes. Figure 35-13 shows the relationship between the

Fig 35-8 The bilevel house.

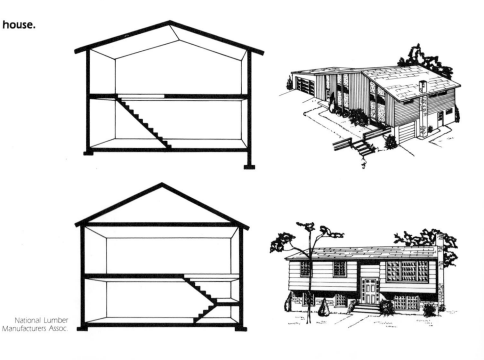

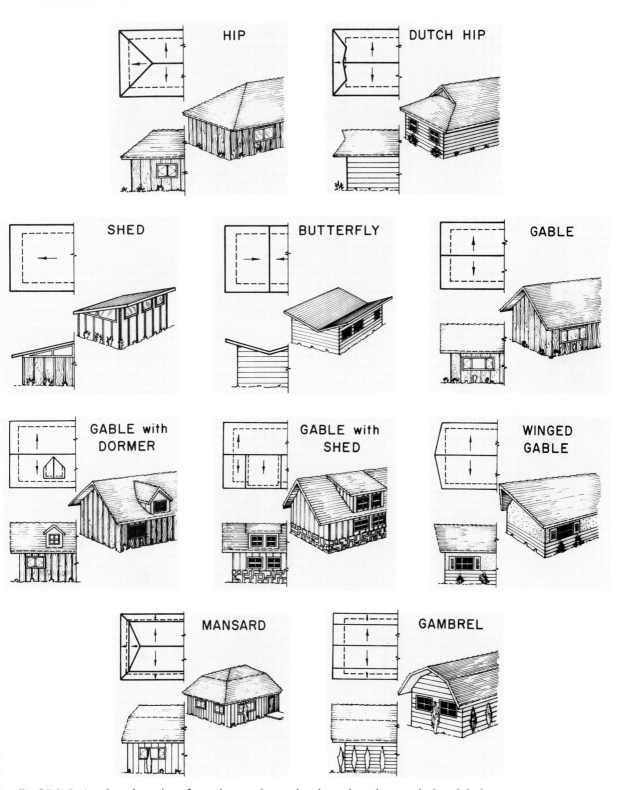

HIP

DUTCH HIP

SHED

BUTTERFLY

GABLE

GABLE with DORMER

GABLE with SHED

WINGED GABLE

MANSARD

GAMBREL

Fig 35-9 Style of roofs and roof overhangs shown in plan, elevation, and pictorial views.

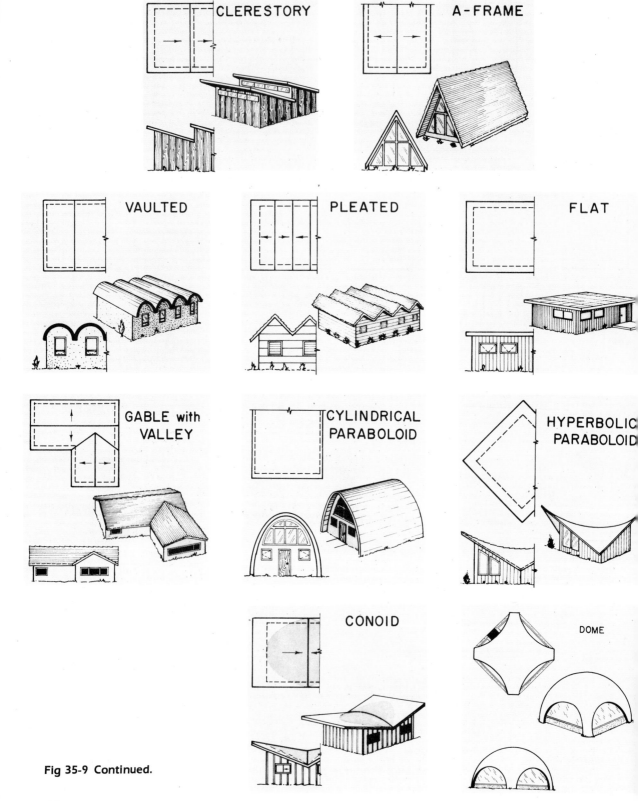

CLERESTORY

A-FRAME

VAULTED

PLEATED

FLAT

GABLE with VALLEY

CYLINDRICAL PARABOLOID

HYPERBOLIC PARABOLOID

CONOID

DOME

Fig 35-9 Continued.

226

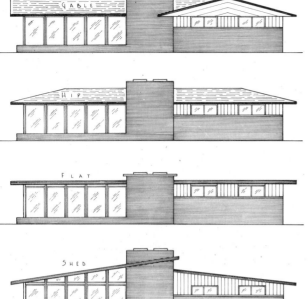

Fig 35-10 The type of roof greatly affects the appearance of the elevation.

Home Planners, Inc.

Fig 35-11 A house with many gable roofs.

Master Plan Services, Inc.

Fig 35-12 A high-pitch gable roof.

actual appearance of a gable roof and the appearance of a gable roof on an elevation drawing.

Hip roofs are used when eave-line protection is desired around the entire perimeter of the building. Notice how the hip-roof overhang shades the windows of the house in Fig. 35-14. For this reason, hip roofs are very popular in warm climates. Figure 35-15 shows the way a hip roof appears on an elevation drawing. Hip roofs are commonly used on Regency and French Provincial homes.

Flat roofs are used to create a low silhouette on many modern homes (Fig. 35-16). Since no support is achieved by the leaning together of rafters, slightly heavier rafters are needed for flat roofs. Built-up asphalt construction is often used on flat roofs. Water may be used as an insulator and solar heater on flat roofs. Figure 35-17 illustrates a flat roof on an elevation drawing.

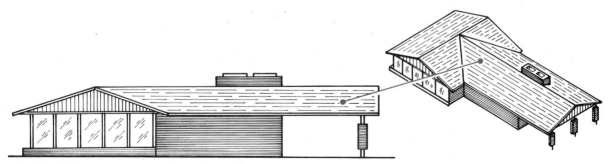

Fig 35-13 The appearance of a gable roof on an elevation drawing.

Fig 35-14 A house with a hip roof.

Home Planners, Inc.

Fig 35-15 The appearance of a hip roof on an elevation drawing.

Shed roofs are flat roofs that are higher at one end than at the other. They may be used effectively when two levels exist and where additional light is needed. The use of *clerestory windows* between the two sheds (Fig. 35-18) provides skylight illumination. The double shed is really very advantageous on hillside split-level structures. Figure 35-19 shows a shed roof on an elevation.

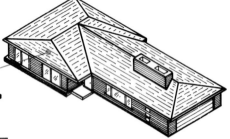

Fig 35-16 A home with a flat roof.

American Plywood Assoc.

Fig 35-17 The appearance of a flat roof on an elevation drawing.

The geodesic dome may constitute the roof (Fig. 35-20) or may extend completely to the ground and be part of the side wall of a structure as well.

OVERHANG

Sufficient roof overhang should be provided to afford protection from the sun, rain, and snow. The length and angle of the overhang will greatly affect its appearance and its functioning in providing protection. Figure 35-21 shows that when the pitch is low, a larger overhang is needed to provide protection. However, with a high-pitch roof, the overhang may block the view from the inside, if extended to equal the protection of the low-pitch overhang.

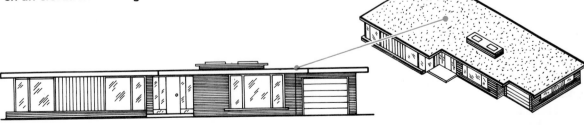

Fig 35-18 A shed roof with clerestory windows.

Fig 35-20 A geodesic dome.

Kaiser Aluminum and Chemical Corp.

Fig 35-19 The appearance of a shed roof on an elevation drawing.

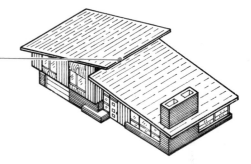

To provide protection and at the same time allow sufficient light to enter the windows, slatted overhangs may be used.

Figure 35-22 shows the effect of a small overhang. Figure 35-23 shows the protection afforded by a large overhang. The edge of the overhang does not always need to be parallel to the sides of the house. This arrangement makes possible very large distances from wall to gutter.

FORM AND SPACE

The total appearance of the elevation depends upon the relationship among the areas of the elevation such as surfaces, doors, windows, and chimneys. The balance of these areas, the emphasis placed on various components of the elevation, the texture, the light, the color, and the shadow patterns all affect greatly the general appearance of the elevation.

RELATED AREAS

The elevation should appear as one integral and functional facade rather than as a surface in which holes have been cut for windows and doors and to which structural components, such as chimneys, have been added without reference to the other areas of the elevation. Figure 35-24 shows a house with well-related lines and areas. Doors, windows, and chimney lines should constitute part of the general pattern of the elevation and should not exist in isolation. Figure 35-25 shows an elevation in which the windows and doors are related to the major lines of the elevation. Figure 35-26 shows the same elevation with unrelated doors and windows.

WINDOWS

When the vertical lines of the windows are extended to the eave line from the ground line or planter line or some division line in the

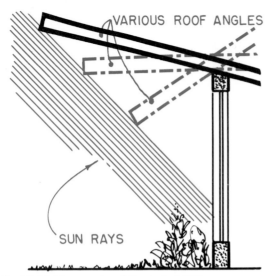

Fig 35-21 The angle of the overhang determines its length.

Fig 35-25 An elevation drawing, showing related lines.

Fig 35-26 Unrelated elevation lines.

Fig 35-22 The effect of a small overhang.

Fig 35-23 The advantage of a large overhang.

Fig 35-24 A house with well-related lines and areas.

Home Planners, Inc.

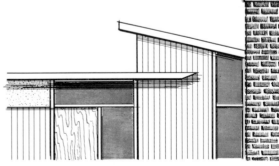

Home Planners, Inc.

Fig 35-27 Effective relationships between roof, windows, siding, and chimney.

separation of materials, the vertical lines become related to the building. Horizontal lines of a window extending from one post to another, or from one vertical separation in the elevation to another, as between a post and a chimney, also help to relate the window to the major lines of the elevation. For example, the windows in Fig. 35-27 were related by being extended to fill the area between posts and between the door and eave line.

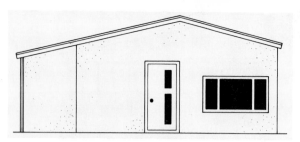

Fig 35-29 Unextended door and window lines.

DOORS

Doors can easily be related to the major lines of the house by extending the area above the door to the *ridge line*, or divider, and making the side panels consistent with the door size, as shown in Fig. 35-28. A comparison between Fig. 35-29 and Fig. 35-30 shows the effect of extending the door lines vertically and horizontally to integrate the door with the window line and the overall surface of the elevation.

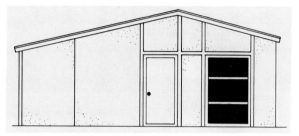

Fig 35-30 Door and window lines extended horizontally and vertically.

SHAPE

Although it is important to relate the lines of the elevation to each other, nevertheless, the overall shape of the elevation should reflect the basic shape of the building. Do not attempt to camouflage the shape of the elevation. An example of such camouflage is the old Western store (Fig. 35-31), whose builder tried to disguise the actual elevation by constructing a false front.

Fig 35-31 Avoid elevation camouflage.

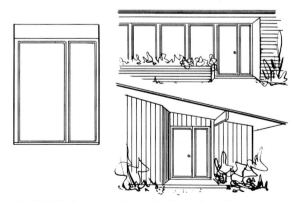

Fig 35-28 A door unit related to the other lines of the elevation.

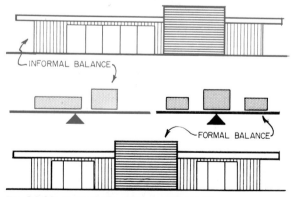

Fig 35-32 A formally and an informally balanced elevation.

Fig 35-33 Every elevation should have some point of emphasis.

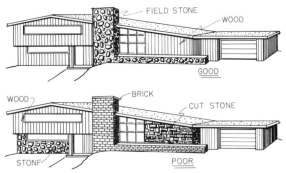

Fig 35-34 The effect of combining too many materials.

Patio walls, fences, or other structures may block the view of the elevation wall. If such blocking occurs, it is advisable to draw the elevation with the wall in position, to show how the elevation will appear when viewed from a distance. It is advisable also to draw the elevation as it will exist inside the wall.

BALANCE

The term *balance* refers to the symmetry of the elevation. An elevation is either *formally* or *informally* balanced (Fig. 35-32). Formal balance is used extensively in colonial and period styles of architecture. Informal balance is more widely used in modern residential architecture. Informally balanced elevations are frequently used in modern designs such as ranch and split-level styles.

EMPHASIS

Elevation emphasis, or *accent*, can be achieved by several different devices. An area may be accented by mass, by color, or by material. Every elevation should have some point of emphasis. Compare the two elevations in Fig. 35-33. Note that in the second example the chimney and the roof have been accented to provide a focal point.

LIGHT AND COLOR

An elevation that is composed of all light areas or all dark areas tends to be uninteresting and neutral. Some balancing of light, shade, and color is desirable in most elevations. This can be achieved through developing shadow patterns by depressing areas, by using overhang, by grading, and by color variation.

TEXTURE

An elevation contains many kinds of materials such as glass, wood, masonry, and ceramics. These must be carefully and tastefully balanced to be effective. An elevation composed of too few materials is ineffective and neutral. Likewise, an elevation that uses too many materials, especially masonry, is equally objectionable.

In choosing the materials for the elevation, the designer should not mix horizontal and vertical siding or different types of masonry. If brick is the primary masonry used, brick should be used throughout. It should not be mixed with stone. Similarly, it is not desirable to mix several types of brick or several types of stone. Figure 35-34 shows the effect of mixing too many materials in an elevation.

LINES

The lines of an elevation are the *ground line*, *eave line*, and *ridge line*. These are horizontal lines. One of these lines should be emphasized. In Fig. 35-35, the horizontal eave line has been accented by being extended over the porch. The lines of an elevation can help to create horizontal or vertical emphasis. If the ground line, ridge line, and eave line are ac-

Fig 35-35 Emphasis placed on the horizontal eave line.

Home Planners, Inc.

Fig 35-36 Horizontal emphasis.

Home Planners, Inc.

cented, the emphasis will be placed on the horizontal, as shown in Fig. 35-36. If the emphasis is placed on vertical lines such as corner posts and columns, the emphasis will be vertical. Figure 35-37 shows a comparison between placing the emphasis on horizontal lines and placing the emphasis on vertical lines. In general, low buildings will usually appear longer and lower if the emphasis is placed on horizontal lines.

Lines should be consistent. The lines of an elevation should appear to flow together as one integrated line pattern. It is usually better to continue a line through an elevation for a long distance than to break the line and start it again. Figure 35-38 shows the difference between a building with consistent lines and a building with inconsistent lines. Rhythm can be developed by the use of lines, and lines can

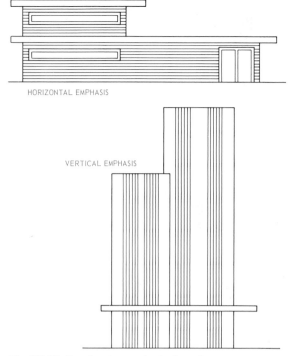

Fig 35-37 Emphasis on vertical and on horizontal lines.

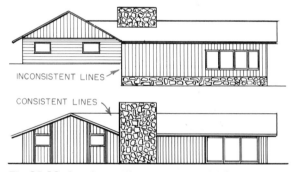

Fig 35-38 Consistent lines are essential for good elevation design.

be repeated in various patterns. When a line is repeated, the basic consistency of the elevation is considerably strengthened.

PROBLEMS

1 Sketch an elevation of your own design. Trace the elevation, adding a flat roof, gable roof, shed roof, and butterfly roof. Choose the one you like best and the one that is most functional for your design.

2 Sketch the front elevation of your home. Vary the roof style, making it consistent with the major lines of the elevation. Redesign the elevation, relating the door and window lines to the major lines of the building.

3 Too many materials are used in the building shown in Fig. 35-39. Sketch an elevation of this house and change the building materials to be consistent with the design.

Fig 35-39 Resketch this elevation to eliminate the inconsistent use of materials.

4 State as many facts as you can about the elevation design of the home in Fig. 35-11.

5 Sketch the elevation shown in Fig. 35-17 with a hip roof, double-shed roof, and gable roof. Resketch this illustration, using different siding materials.

6 Identify the roof shown in Fig. 35-36.

7 Resketch the bottom elevation shown in Fig. 35-33. Place the emphasis on an area of the elevation other than the chimney.

8 Resketch the formally balanced elevation shown in Fig. 35-32. Convert this elevation to an informally balanced elevation.

9 Resketch the elevation shown in Fig. 35-19. Change the roof style and siding materials.

10 Redesign the elevation in Fig. 35-40 with a different roof.

11 Sketch the elevation shown in Fig. 35-15, using a double-shed roof.

12 Define the following terms: *one-story house, one-and-one-half-story house, bi-level, split-level, hip roof, flat roof, gable roof, shed roof, high pitch, low pitch, celestial windows, gambrel roof, mansard roof, butterfly roof, overhang, related lines, unrelated lines, ridge lines, eave lines, ground lines, formal balance, informal balance, texture emphasis.*

Fig 35-40 Redesign this elevation with a different roof.

UNIT 36
ELEVATION PROJECTION

Elevation drawings are projected from the floor plan of an architectural drawing just as the side views are projected from the front view of an orthographic drawing.

To visualize and understand multiview (orthographic) projection, imagine a house surrounded by a transparent box, as shown in Fig. 36-1. If you draw the outline of the structure on the transparent planes that make up the box, you create the orthographic views

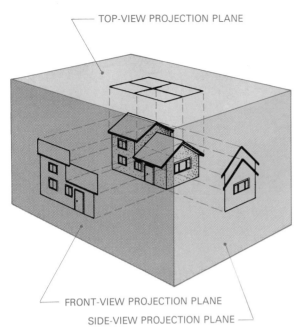

TOP-VIEW PROJECTION PLANE

FRONT-VIEW PROJECTION PLANE

SIDE-VIEW PROJECTION PLANE

Fig 36-1 Projection box shows three planes of a building.

you need. These are the front view on the front plane, the side view on the side plane, and the top view on the top plane. When the planes of the top, bottom, and sides are hinged (swung) out from the front plane, as shown in Fig. 36-2, the six views of the house are shown exactly as they are positioned on an orthographic drawing. Study the position of each view as it relates to the front view. The right side is to the right of the front view, the left side is to the left, the top (roof) view is on the top, the bottom view is on the bottom. The rear view is to the left of the left-side view, since, when this view hinges around to the back, it would fall into this position.

Notice that the length of the front view, top (roof) view, and bottom view are exactly the same as the length of the rear view. Notice also that the heights and alignments of the front view, right side, left side, and rear view are the same. Memorize the position of these views and remember that the lengths of the front, bottom, and top views are *always* the same. Similarly, the heights of the rear, left, front, and right side are *always* the same.

All six views are rarely used to depict architectural structures. Instead, only four elevations (sides) are usually shown, and the top view is usually replaced with a section through the structure called a floor plan. The roof plan and foundation plan are also developed from the top view. The bottom view is never developed in a construction drawing.

ELEVATION PLANES

You may think of the elevation as a drawing placed on a vertical plane. Figure 36-3 shows how the vertical planes are related to the floor-plan projection.

FUNCTIONAL ORIENTATION

Four elevations are normally projected from the floor plan. When these elevations are classified according to their function, they are called the front elevation, the rear elevation, the right elevation, and the left elevation. The front view of the house is known as the *front elevation*. The view projected from the rear of the house is known as the *rear elevation*. The view projected from the right side of the house is known as the *right elevation*, and the view projected from the left side of the house is known as the *left elevation*. When these elevations are all *projected* on the same drawing sheet, the rear elevation appears to be upside down and the right and left elevations appear to rest on their sides. Because of the large size of most elevation drawings, and because of the desirability of drawing elevations as we normally see them, each elevation is usually drawn with the ground line on the bottom and the roof on the top of the sheet (Fig. 36-4).

COMPASS ORIENTATION

The north, east, south, and west compass points are often used by architects to describe and label elevation drawings. This method is preferred when there is no so-called front or rear view to a structure. When this method is used, the north arrow on the floor plan is the key to the designation of the elevation title. For example, in Fig. 36-5 the rear elevation is

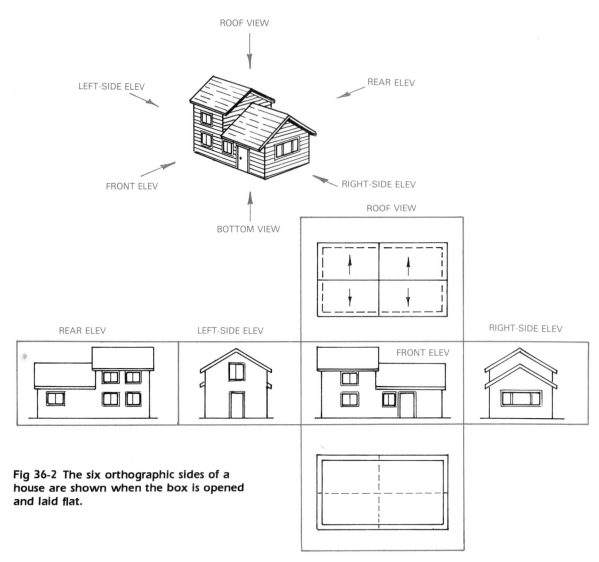

ROOF VIEW

LEFT-SIDE ELEV

REAR ELEV

FRONT ELEV

RIGHT-SIDE ELEV

BOTTOM VIEW

ROOF VIEW

REAR ELEV

LEFT-SIDE ELEV

FRONT ELEV

RIGHT-SIDE ELEV

Fig 36-2 The six orthographic sides of a house are shown when the box is opened and laid flat.

BOTTOM VIEW

Fig 36-3 Elevation planes of projection.

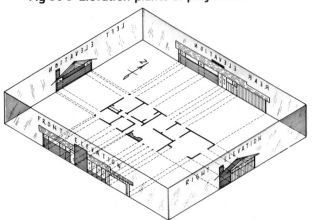

facing north. Therefore, the rear elevation could also be called the north elevation. Here the front elevation is the south elevation, and the left elevation is the west elevation.

AUXILIARY ELEVATIONS

When a floor plan has more than four sides, or sides that deviate from the normal 90° projection, an *auxiliary elevation* view is often necessary. To project an auxiliary elevation, follow the same rules for projecting orthographic auxiliaries. Project the auxiliary elevation perpendicular to the wall of the

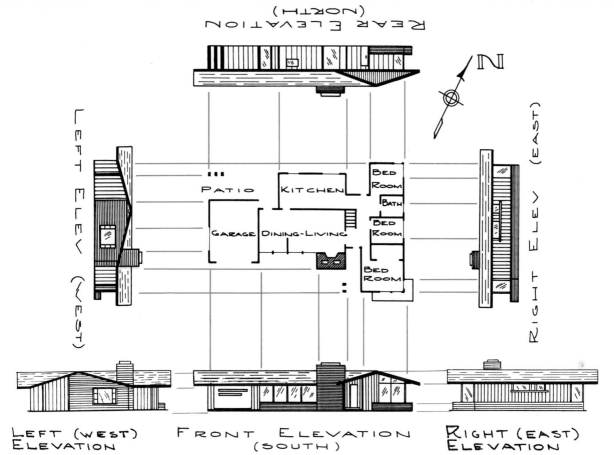

PATIO

KITCHEN

BED ROOM

BATH

BED ROOM

GARAGE | DINING-LIVING

BED ROOM

LEFT (WEST) ELEVATION

FRONT ELEVATION (SOUTH)

RIGHT (EAST) ELEVATION

Fig 36-4 The preferred relationship of side and front elevation views is with the ground line on the bottom of the sheet.

floor plan from which you are projecting, as shown in Fig. 36-6. When an auxiliary elevation is drawn, it is usually prepared in addition to the standard elevations and does not replace them. It merely clarifies the foreshortened lines of the major elevations caused by the receding angles.

STEPS IN PROJECTING ELEVATIONS

The major lines of an elevation are derived by projecting vertical lines from the floor plan and measuring the position of horizontal lines from the ground line.

VERTICAL-LINE PROJECTION

Vertical lines representing the main lines of the building should first be projected as shown in Fig. 36-7. These lines show the overall length and width of the building. They also show the length of the major parts or offsets of the building. The position of the chimney, doors, and windows are also projected from the floor plan.

HORIZONTAL-LINE PROJECTION

Horizontal lines that represent the height of the eave line, ridge line, and chimney line above the ground line are measured, then drawn to intersect with the vertical lines drawn from the floor plan, as shown in Fig. 36-7. The intersection of these lines provides the overall outline of the elevation.

ROOF-LINE PROJECTION

The ridge line and eave line cannot be accurately located until the *roof pitch* (angle)

237

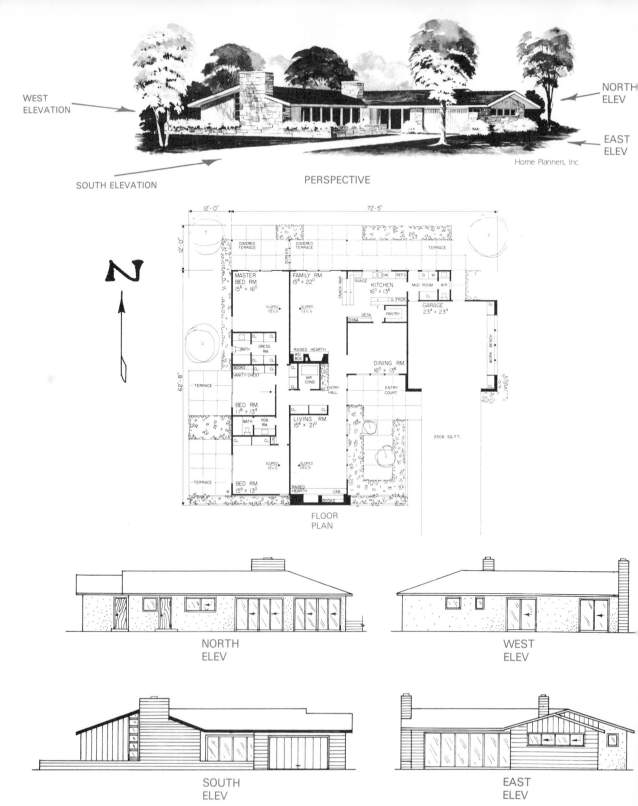

WEST
ELEVATION

NORTH
ELEV

EAST
ELEV

SOUTH ELEVATION

PERSPECTIVE

Home Planners, Inc.

12'-0"

72'-5"

12'-0"

62'-8"

N

COVERED TERRACE

COVERED TERRACE

SCREEN

TERRACE

MASTER BED RM. 15⁶ x 16⁰

FAMILY RM. 15⁶ x 22⁰

SMACK-BAR

S. DW. REFG

D. W.

MUD ROOM

W.R.

SLOPED CEIL'G

SLOPED CEIL G

RANGE

KITCHEN 16⁰ x 13⁶

Q. FRZR.

GARAGE 23⁴ x 23⁴

CL.

BATH

DRESS. RM.

DESK

PANTRY

CHINA

WORK BENCH

CL.

BOOKS

VANITY-CHEST

CL.

RAISED HEARTH

W.D. BOX

CL.

DINING RM. 16⁰ x 13⁶

TERRACE

AIR COND.

CL.

ENTRY HALL

BED RM. 11⁸ x 13⁴

BATH

PDR. RM.

ENTRY COURT

CL.

LIN.

LIVING RM. 15⁶ x 21⁰

2506 SQ. FT.

CL.

CL.

CL.

TERRACE

SLOPED CEIL'G

SLOPED CEIL G

BED RM. 15⁶ x 13⁰

RAISED HEARTH

CAB.

BOOKS

FLOOR PLAN

NORTH ELEV

WEST ELEV

SOUTH ELEV

EAST ELEV

Fig 36-5 Compass direction used to identify elevation.

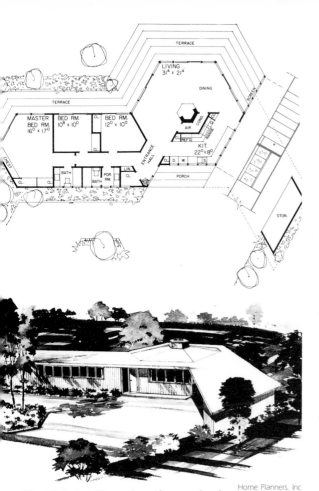

Fig 36-6 Auxiliary elevation projection.

Home Planners, Inc.

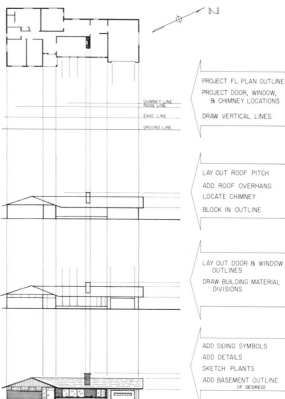

Fig 36-7 The sequence of projecting elevations.

PROJECT FL. PLAN OUTLINE
PROJECT DOOR, WINDOW, & CHIMNEY LOCATIONS
DRAW VERTICAL LINES

LAY OUT ROOF PITCH
ADD ROOF OVERHANG
LOCATE CHIMNEY
BLOCK IN OUTLINE

LAY OUT DOOR & WINDOW OUTLINES
DRAW BUILDING MATERIAL DIVISIONS

ADD SIDING SYMBOLS
ADD DETAILS
SKETCH PLANTS
ADD BASEMENT OUTLINE
(IF DESIRED)

is established. On a high-pitch roof, there is a greater distance between the ridge line and the eave line than on a low-pitch roof. Figure 36-8 shows a high-pitch roof and a low-pitch roof.

Pitch is the angle of the roof and is described in terms of the ratio of the *rise over the run* (rise/run). *Run* is the horizontal distance covered by a roof. *Rise* is the vertical distance. The run is always expressed in units of 12. Therefore, the pitch is the ratio of the rise to 12.

When the roof pitch is established, the rise and the run should be drawn to scale and the roof angle established by connecting the extremities of these lines, as shown in Fig. 36-9. Next, the roof angle can be extended and

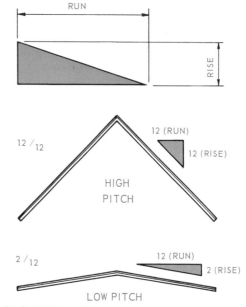

Fig 36-8 A high-pitch and a low-pitch roof.

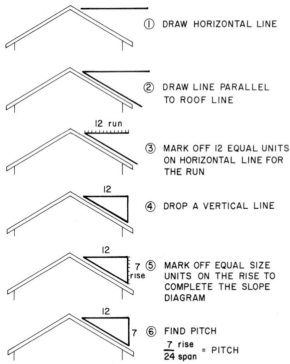

① DRAW HORIZONTAL LINE

② DRAW LINE PARALLEL TO ROOF LINE

12 run

③ MARK OFF 12 EQUAL UNITS ON HORIZONTAL LINE FOR THE RUN

12

④ DROP A VERTICAL LINE

12

7 ⑤ MARK OFF EQUAL SIZE
rise   UNITS ON THE RISE TO COMPLETE THE SLOPE DIAGRAM

12

7 ⑥ FIND PITCH

$$\frac{7 \text{ rise}}{24 \text{ span}} = \text{PITCH}$$

Fig 36-9 The sequence of projecting roof outline.

the overhang measured from the outside wall to the eave. When the center line of the house is established, the exact positions of the ridge line and eave line are established. Then the eave line and ridge line are projected and blocked-in.

BLOCKING-IN THE OUTLINE

After the roof outline has been established, the major lines of the house are drawn. This drawing is made by following the outline developed from the intersection of horizontal and vertical lines. The outlines of materials, doors, windows, chimney, and roof are drawn in their final line weight.

ADDING ELEVATION SYMBOLS

The next step is to add the elevation symbol for each material and feature on the elevation, as shown in Fig. 36-10.

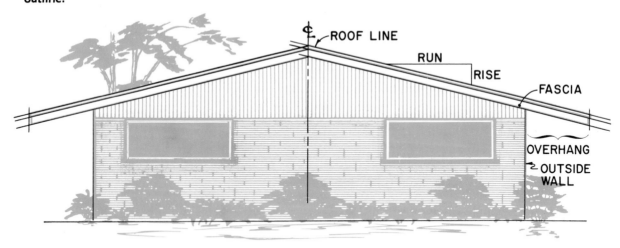

1. Lay out rise and run to establish roof angle.
2. Extend angle to show roof line.
3. Draw parallel line to show fascia.
4. Draw vertical line for outside wall.
5. Measure width of overhang and draw vertical line.
6. Measure distance from top of outside wall to grade line.
7. Draw and extend grade line.
8. Measure from outside wall to center line of roof; draw vertical center line.
9. Draw opposite side of roof showing outside wall and width of overhang.
10. Darken all object lines.
11. Add siding symbols and door or window symbols.
12. Add gutter or cornice details.
13. Dimension if necessary.
14. Add landscaping if desired.

Fig 36-10 Symbols added to elevation.

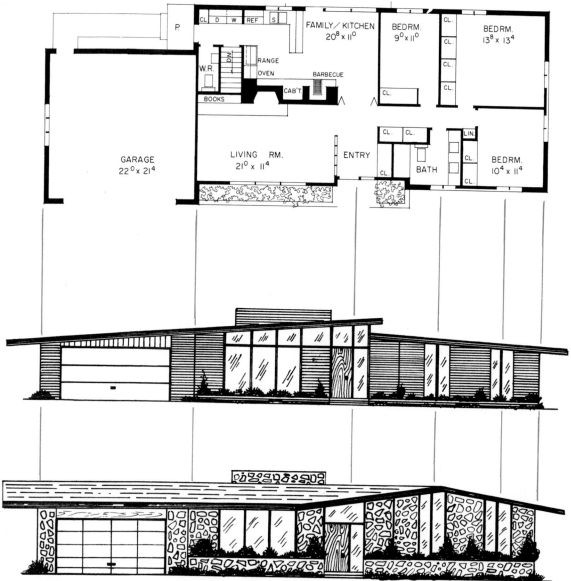

Fig 36-11 Two different elevation styles projected from one floor plan.

Home Planners, Inc.

FLEXIBILITY

It is possible to project many different elevation styles from one floor plan. The pitch, size of overhang, position of the grade line, window position and style, chimney size and style, and the door style and position all can be manipulated to create different effects. Figure 36-11 shows two different elevations projected from the same floor plan. Here the change was accomplished primarily by varying the distances between the major vertical lines of the elevation.

INTERIOR ELEVATIONS

Floor plans show horizontal arrangements of partitions, fixtures, and appliances, but do not show the design of interior walls. *Interior elevations* are necessary to show the

Fig 36-12 Interior wall elevation.

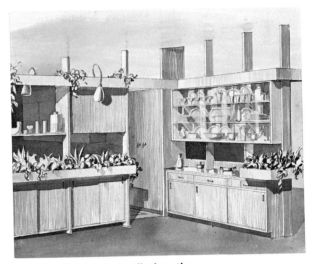

Fig 36-13 Planter wall elevation.

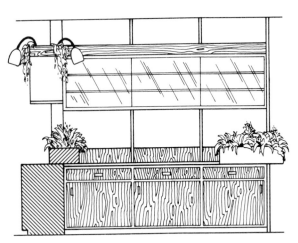

EAST WALL

NORTH WALL

WEST WALL

SOUTH WALL

Fig 36-14 Kitchen wall elevations.

design of interior vertical planes. Figure 36-12 shows a comparison of an interior pictorial drawing and an interior elevation of the same wall area. Similarly, Fig. 36-13 shows an interior elevation of a planter wall accompanied by a pictorial interpretation of the same area.

Because of the need to show cabinet height and counter arrangement detail, interior wall elevations are most often prepared for kitchen and bathroom walls as shown in Fig. 36-14. An interior wall elevation shows the appearance of the wall as viewed from the center of the room.

A coding system is used in place of labels to identify the walls on the floor plans for which interior elevations have been prepared when many are drawn. The code symbol shows the direction of the view, the elevation detail number, and the page in the set where found. If only a few interior elevations are prepared, then the title of the room and the compass location of the wall is the only identification needed. The compass system is shown in Fig. 36-14 and the coding system in Fig. 36-15.

The steps in drawing an interior elevation are outlined in Fig. 36-16.

1 Outline the floor plan as in step 1.
2 Projections are made from the floor-plan outline perpendicular from each corner as in step 2.
3 Then ceiling lines are added to give each wall its specified height as in step 3.
4 Details are then projected directly from the floor plan to each elevation drawing as in step 4.

Projecting the interior elevation in this manner results in an elevation drawn on its side or upside down. Interior elevation drawings, like exterior elevations, are not prepared in the original position as they are projected from the floor plans. Interior elevations are positioned with the floor line on the bottom as normally viewed. Once the features of the

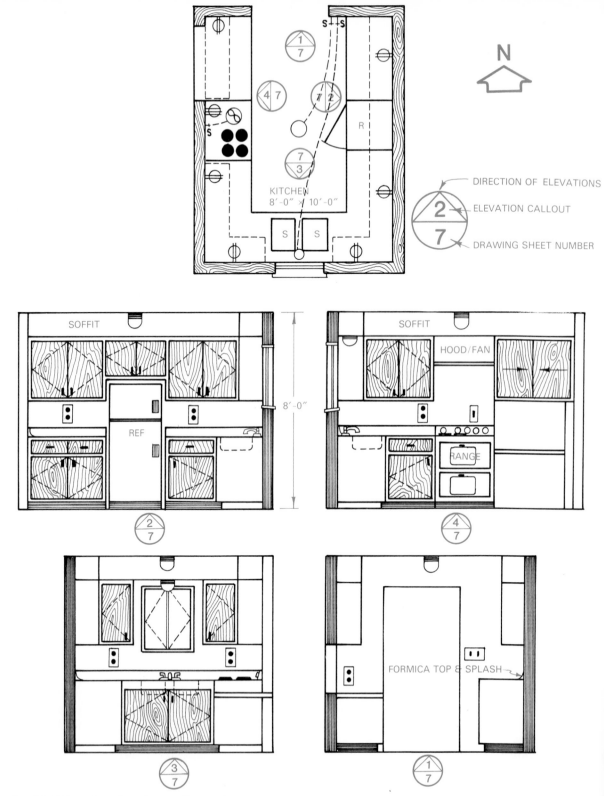

Fig 36-15 Interior elevation coding system.

Fig 36-16 Sequence of drawing interior elevations.

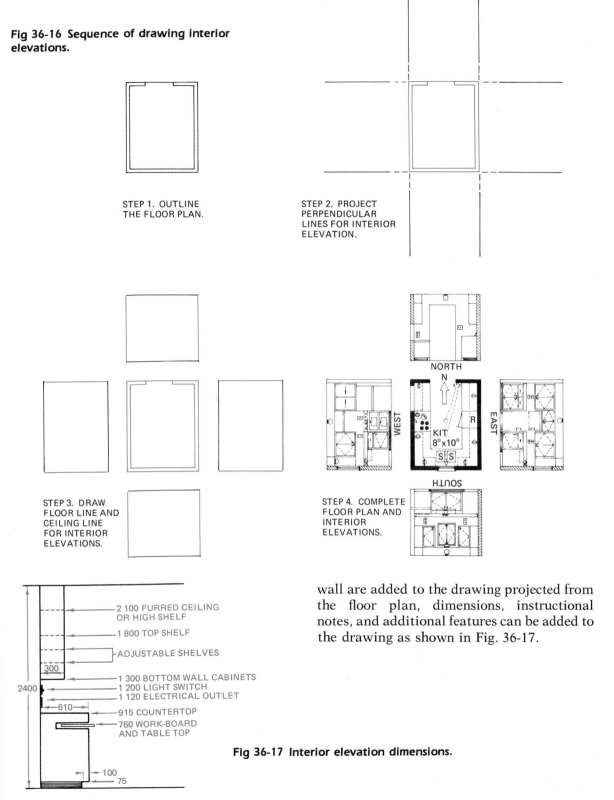

STEP 1. OUTLINE THE FLOOR PLAN.

STEP 2. PROJECT PERPENDICULAR LINES FOR INTERIOR ELEVATION.

STEP 3. DRAW FLOOR LINE AND CEILING LINE FOR INTERIOR ELEVATIONS.

STEP 4. COMPLETE FLOOR PLAN AND INTERIOR ELEVATIONS.

NORTH

N

WEST

EAST

KIT 8'x10'

SOUTH

2 100 FURRED CEILING OR HIGH SHELF

1 800 TOP SHELF

ADJUSTABLE SHELVES

300

1 300 BOTTOM WALL CABINETS

2400

1 200 LIGHT SWITCH

1 120 ELECTRICAL OUTLET

610

915 COUNTERTOP

760 WORK-BOARD AND TABLE TOP

100

75

wall are added to the drawing projected from the floor plan, dimensions, instructional notes, and additional features can be added to the drawing as shown in Fig. 36-17.

Fig 36-17 Interior elevation dimensions.

245

PROBLEMS

1 Project the front, rear, right, and left elevations of a floor plan of your own design.
2 Sketch the front elevation of your home.
3 Project and sketch or draw the front elevation suggested in the pictorial drawing and floor plan in Fig. 14-5.
4 Complete the elevation-projection problem shown in Fig. 36-18 by drawing the elevation on the terrain as shown.
5 Sketch the front and right elevations of the house shown in Fig. 12-6A.
6 Define the following terms: *front elevation, rear elevation, right elevation, left elevation, north elevation, east elevation, south elevation, west elevation, auxiliary elevations, pitch, rise, run.*

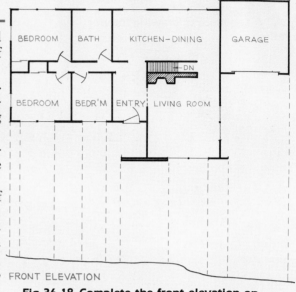

Fig 36-18 Complete the front elevation on the terrain, as shown.

UNIT 37
ELEVATION SYMBOLS

Symbols are needed to clarify and simplify elevation drawings. Symbols help to describe the basic features of the elevation. They show what building materials are used, and they describe the style and position of doors and windows. Symbols also help to make the elevation drawing look realistic. Some of the most common elevation symbols are shown on the elevation drawing in Figs. 37-1 and 37-2.

MATERIAL SYMBOLS

Figure 37-3 shows the relationship between material symbols used on an elevation and the actual material as it is used in construction. Most architectural symbols look very similar to the material they represent. However, in many cases the symbol does not show the exact appearance of the material. For example, the symbol for brick, as shown in Fig. 37-3, does not include all the lines shown in the pictorial drawing. Representing brick on the elevation drawing exactly as it appears is a long, laborious, and unnecessary process. Therefore, like the symbol for brick, many elevation symbols are simplifications of the actual appearance of the material. The symbol often resembles the appearance of the material at a distance. Figure 37-4 shows a

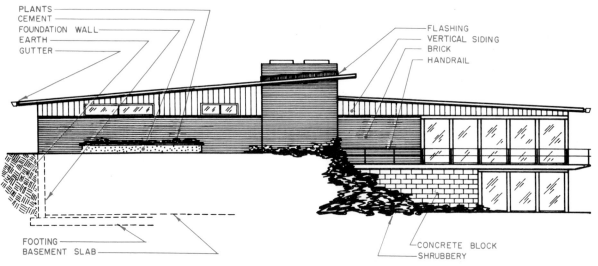

PLANTS
CEMENT
FOUNDATION WALL
EARTH
GUTTER

FLASHING
VERTICAL SIDING
BRICK
HANDRAIL

FOOTING
BASEMENT SLAB

CONCRETE BLOCK
SHRUBBERY

Fig 37-1 Symbols help make the elevation look more realistic.

CONTINUOUS SILL
HORIZONTAL SIDING
PLYWOOD
DOWNSPOUT

FLUES
CUT STONE
SHINGLES
GLASS

Fig 37-2 Some common elevation symbols in use.

full-size portion, at $\frac{1}{4}'' = 1'—0''$ scale, of the plan shown in Fig. 69-5. For a more detailed list of elevation and related plan symbols, refer back to Figs. 33-7 through 33-11.

WINDOW SYMBOLS

The position and style of windows greatly affect the appearance of the elevation. Windows are, therefore, drawn on the elevation with as much detail as the scale of the drawing permits. Parts of windows that should be shown on all elevation drawings include the sill, sash, mullions, and muntins (Fig. 37-5). Figure 37-6 shows the method of illustrating casement, awning, and sliding windows. Figure 37-7 shows the parts of a double-hung window in more detail.

In addition to showing the parts of a window, it is also necessary to show the direction of the hinge for casement and awning windows. Figure 37-8 shows the method of indicating the direction of the hinge on elevation drawings. The direction of the hinge is shown by dotted lines. The point of the dotted line shows the part of the window to which the hinge is attached.

Many different styles of windows are available, as shown in Fig. 33-8. These illustrations also show the normal amount of de-

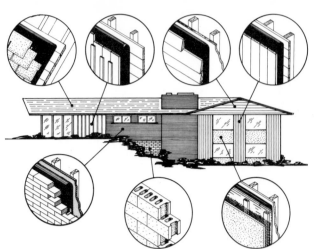

Fig 37-3 The relationship between material symbols and materials used in construction.

tail used in drawing windows on elevations.

Architects often use an alternative method of showing window styles on elevation drawings. In this alternative method, the drafter prepares a window-detail drawing, as shown in Fig. 37-9, to a larger scale. The designer then prepares a separate window drawing in detail for each different style of

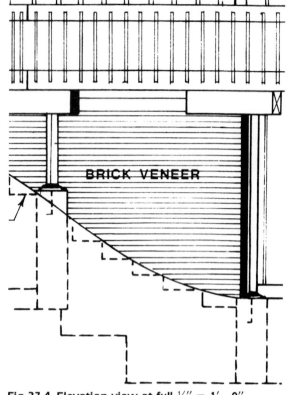

BRICK VENEER

Fig 37-4 Elevation view at full $\frac{1}{4}'' = 1'—0''$.

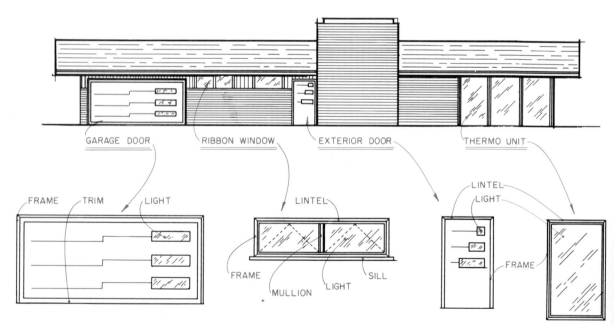

GARAGE DOOR   RIBBON WINDOW   EXTERIOR DOOR   THERMO UNIT

FRAME   TRIM   LIGHT   LINTEL   LINTEL   LIGHT

FRAME   MULLION   LIGHT   SILL   FRAME

Fig 37-5 Window symbols as they appear on elevation drawings.

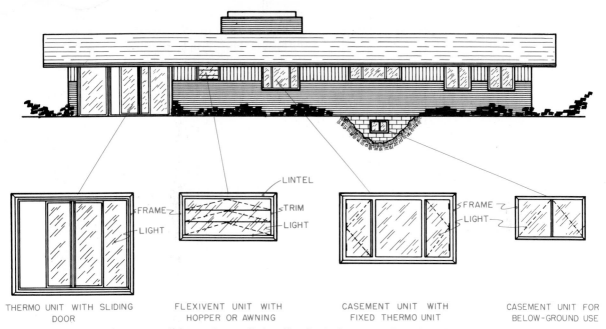

THERMO UNIT WITH SLIDING
DOOR

FLEXIVENT UNIT WITH
HOPPER OR AWNING

CASEMENT UNIT WITH
FIXED THERMO UNIT

CASEMENT UNIT FOR
BELOW-GROUND USE

Fig 37-6 Often it is not possible to show all details of windows on elevation drawings.

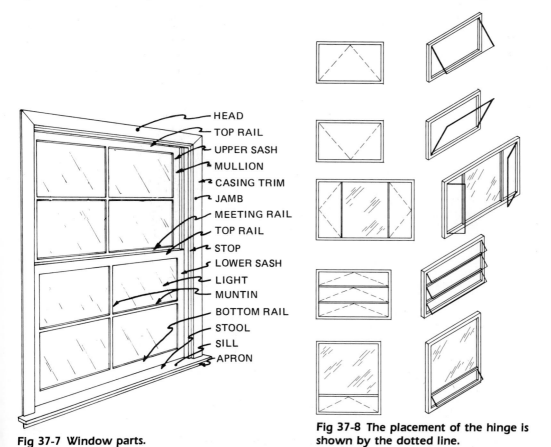

HEAD
TOP RAIL
UPPER SASH
MULLION
CASING TRIM
JAMB
MEETING RAIL
TOP RAIL
STOP
LOWER SASH
LIGHT
MUNTIN
BOTTOM RAIL
STOOL
SILL
APRON

Fig 37-7 Window parts.

Fig 37-8 The placement of the hinge is shown by the dotted line.

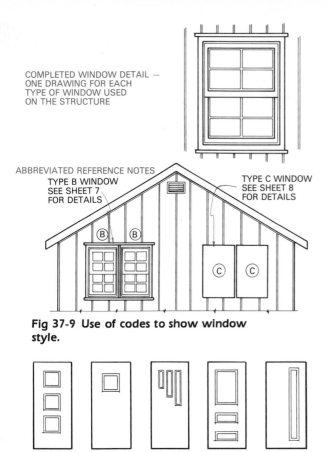

COMPLETED WINDOW DETAIL — ONE DRAWING FOR EACH TYPE OF WINDOW USED ON THE STRUCTURE

ABBREVIATED REFERENCE NOTES

TYPE B WINDOW SEE SHEET 7 FOR DETAILS

TYPE C WINDOW SEE SHEET 8 FOR DETAILS

Fig 37-9 Use of codes to show window style.

Fig 37-10 Examples of exterior-door styles.

window to be used. When the elevation is drawn, only the position of the window is shown. The style of window to be included in this opening is then shown by a letter or number indexed to the letter or number used for the large detail drawing. Sometimes, the window symbol is abbreviated and indexed in the same way to a more complete detail. Unit 70 contains further treatment of door and window schedules.

DOOR SYMBOLS

Doors are shown on elevation drawings by methods similar to those used for illustrating window style and position. They are either drawn completely, if the scale permits, or shown in abbreviated form. Sometimes, the outline is indexed to a door schedule. The complete drawing of the door, whether shown on an elevation or on a separate detail, should show the division of panels and lights, sill, jamb, and head-trim details.

Many exterior door styles are available (Fig. 37-10). The total relationship of the door and trim to the entire elevation cannot be seen unless the door trim is also shown (Fig. 37-11).

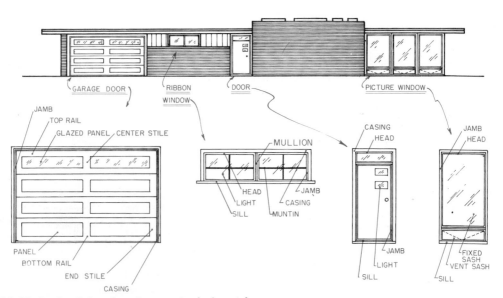

GARAGE DOOR

RIBBON WINDOW

DOOR

PICTURE WINDOW

JAMB
TOP RAIL
GLAZED PANEL   CENTER STILE

PANEL
BOTTOM RAIL
END STILE
CASING

MULLION

HEAD
LIGHT
SILL

JAMB
CASING
MUNTIN

CASING
HEAD

JAMB
LIGHT
SILL

JAMB
HEAD

FIXED SASH
VENT SASH
SILL

Fig 37-11 Methods of drawing door and window trim.

Exterior doors are normally larger than interior doors. Exterior doors must provide access for larger amounts of traffic and be sufficiently large to permit the movement of furniture. They must also be thick enough to provide adequate insulation and sound barriers. Common exterior door sizes include widths of 2'—8", 3'—0", and 3'—6" (0.8, 0.9 and 1.1 m). Common exterior door heights range from 6'—8" to 7'—6" (2.0 to 2.3 m).

PROBLEMS

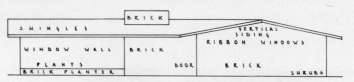

Fig 37-12 Add symbols to this elevation.

1 Draw and add symbols to the elevation outline shown in Fig. 37-12.
2 Redesign the front elevation of your home. Change siding materials and door and window styles.

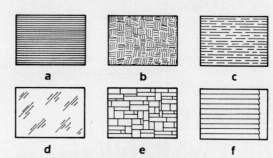

3 Add elevation symbols to an elevation of your own design.
4 Identify the elevation symbols shown in Fig. 37-13.

Fig 37-13 Identify these elevation symbols.

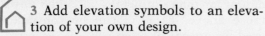

Fig 37-14 Draw the front elevation of this house, complete with symbols.

Home Planners, Inc.

5 Draw the front elevation of the house shown in Fig. 37-14. Show elevation symbols.
6 Redesign and finish the front elevation of the house shown in Fig. 37-15, using brick as the basic siding material.

Fig 37-15 Redesign and finish this elevation.

Home Planners, Inc.

7 Draw the front and left-side elevations of the house shown in Fig. 37-16. Use symbols for the siding materials shown.

8 Draw the front and right-side elevations of the home shown in Fig. 35-36. Use the existing siding materials or redesign the elevation, changing the materials as you wish.

Fig 37-16 Draw a front and left-side elevation of this house.

Boise Cascade

UNIT 38
ELEVATION DIMENSIONING

Horizontal (width and length) dimensions are placed on floor plans. Vertical (height) dimensions are placed on elevation drawings.

Many dimensions on elevation drawings show the vertical distance from a datum line.

The *datum line* is a reference that remains constant. Sea level is commonly used as the datum for many drawings, although any distance above sea level can be conveniently used for a vertical reference.

Dimensions on elevation drawings show the height above the datum of the ground line. They also show the distance from the ground line to the floor, ceiling, and ridge and eave lines, and to the tops of chimneys, doors, and windows. Distances below the ground line are shown by dotted lines.

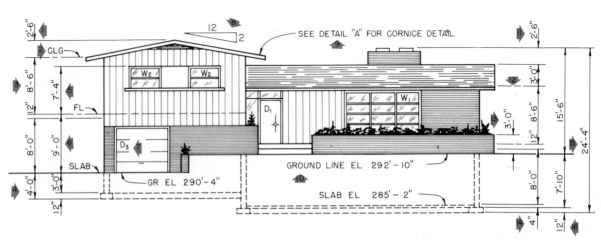

Fig 38-1 Rules for elevation dimensioning.

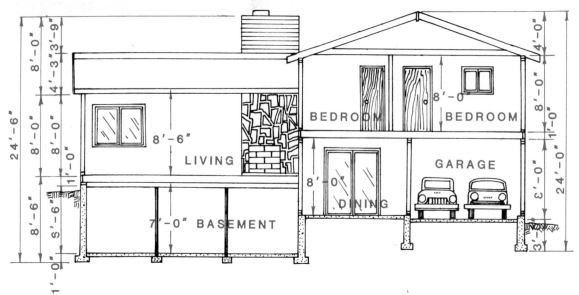

Fig 38-2 Alternate elevation-dimensioning method.

RULES FOR ELEVATION DIMENSIONING

Elevation dimensions must conform to basic standards to ensure consistency of interpretation. The arrows on the elevation drawing in Fig. 38-1 show the application of the following rules for elevation dimensioning:

1 Vertical elevation dimensions should be read from the right of the drawing.
2 Levels to be dimensioned should be labeled with a note, term, or abbreviation.
3 Room heights are shown by dimensioning from the floor line to the ceiling line.
4 The depth of *footers* (footings) is dimensioned from the ground line.
5 Heights of windows and doors are dimensioned from the floor line to the top of the windows or doors.
6 Elevation dimensions show only vertical distances. Horizontal distances are shown on the floor plan.

7 Windows and doors may be indexed to a door or window schedule, or the style of the windows and doors may be shown on the elevation drawing.
8 The roof pitch is shown by indicating the rise over the run.
9 Dimensions for small, complex, or obscure areas should be indexed to a separate detail.
10 Ground-line elevations are expressed as heights above the datum.
11 Heights of chimneys above the ridge line are dimensioned.
12 Floor and ceiling lines are shown by center lines that function as extension lines.
13 Heights of planters and walls are dimensioned from the ground line.
14 Thicknesses of slabs are dimensioned.
15 Overall height dimensions are placed on the outside of subdimensions.
16 Thicknesses of footers are dimensioned.
17 Where space is limited, the alternative method in Fig. 38-2 can be used to show feet and inches.

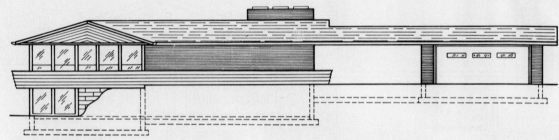

Fig 38-3 Add dimensions to this elevation.

Home Planners, Inc.

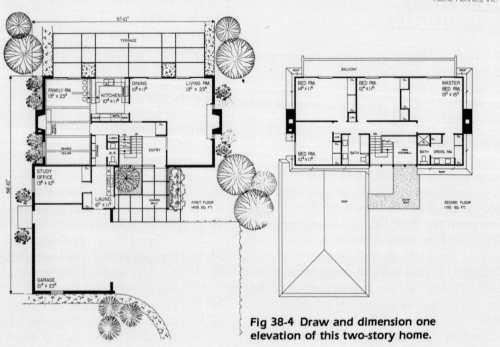

Fig 38-4 Draw and dimension one elevation of this two-story home.

PROBLEMS

1 Add the elevation dimensions to an elevation drawing of your own design.
2 Add dimensions to the elevation drawing shown in Fig. 38-3.
3 Dimension an elevation drawing of your home.
4 Draw an elevation of the home shown in Fig. 38-4. Completely dimension this elevation, following the rules for dimensioning outlined in this unit.
5 Enter the missing dimensions on the elevation shown in Fig. 38-5.

6 Finish and dimension the elevation shown in Fig. 38-6.

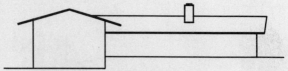

Fig 38-6 Finish and dimension this elevation.

7 Define these terms: *datum line, sea level, vertical dimensions, ground line, ceiling line, ridge line, eave line, chimney line, room height, door schedule, window schedule, slab thickness, footer thickness, overall dimensions, subdimensions.*

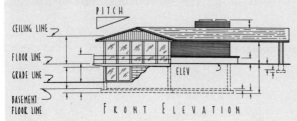

Fig 38-5 Add dimensions to this elevation.

UNIT 39
ELEVATION LANDSCAPE RENDERING

Elevation drawings, although accurate in every detail, do not show exactly how the building will appear when it is complete and landscaped. The reason is that elevation drawings do not show the position of trees, shrubbery, and other landscape features that would be part of the total elevation design. Adding these landscape features to the elevation drawing creates a more realistic drawing of the house.

INTERPRETIVE DRAWING

Figure 39-1 shows some of the advantages of adding landscape features to an elevation drawing. The elevation shown in Fig. 39-1 at A, when dimensioned, would be adequate for construction purposes. However, the illustration shown in Fig. 39-1 at B more closely resembles the final appearance of the house.

Dimensions and hidden lines are omitted when landscape features are added to elevation drawings. Drawings of this kind are prepared only to interpret the final appearance of the house (Fig. 39-2). They are not used for construction purposes.

SEQUENCE

An elevation drawing is converted into a landscape elevation drawing in several basic

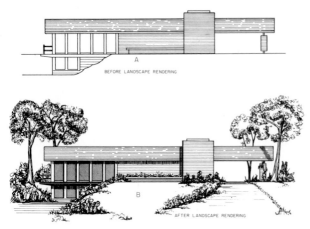

Fig 39-1 An elevation drawing before (A) and after (B) landscape rendering.

steps, as shown in Fig. 39-3. After material symbols are added to the elevation, the positions of trees and shrubs are added. The elevation lines within the outlines of the trees and shrubs are erased, and details are added. Finally, shade lines are added to trees, windows, roof overhangs, chimneys, and other major projections of the house. The addition of landscape features should not hide the basic lines of the house. If many trees or shrubs are placed in front of the house, it is best to draw them in their winter state.

Fig. 39-4A shows several methods of drawing trees and shrubs using single-line techniques on elevation drawings. Figure 39-4B shows the same trees and shrubs ren-

Fig 39-2 Rendered elevations make the house appear complete and desirable.

Karen and Seals
Architects, Inc.

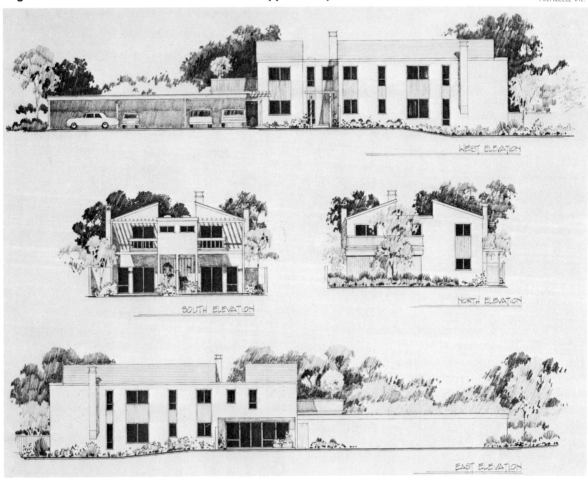

Fig 39-3 The sequence of adding landscape features to an elevation.

Fig 39-4A Examples of sketches for drawing trees and shrubbery on an elevation.

Fig 39-4B The same trees and shrubs rendered with watercolor techniques.

dered with watercolor techniques. The drafter should use the medium that best suits the elevation drawing to be rendered.

LANDSCAPE PLANNING

The importance of effective landscape design is obvious when the property shown in Fig. 39-5 is compared with the property shown in Fig. 39-6. Functional landscape planning not only enhances the appearance of the house but also provides shade from the sun and a baffle from the wind. When carefully planned, landscaping can provide area privacy and traffic control.

Fig 39-5 Landscaping greatly affects the appearance of the elevation.

Julius Shulman

Fig 39-6 A house looks bare without landscaping.

Shakertown Corp.

PROBLEMS

1 Add landscape features to the elevation shown in Fig. 39-7.

2 Add trees, shrubs, plants, and shadows to an elevation of your own design.

3 Add landscape features to an elevation drawing of your home. Improve the present landscape treatment.

4 Draw an elevation of the house shown in Fig. 39-8. Add different landscape features to this drawing.

5 Define these terms: *landscape rendering, interpretive drawings, shade lines.*

Fig 39-7 Add landscape features to this elevation.

Fig 39-8 Add different landscape features to this front elevation.

Home Planners, Inc.

PICTORIAL DRAWINGS

Pictorial drawings, both isometric and perspective, are picturelike drawings. They show several sides of an object in one drawing. Isometric drawings are used extensively in mechanical engineering work. The perspective drawing is more popular as an architectural pictorial drawing. Since the subject of most architectural pictorial drawings is much larger than that of most engineering drawings, perspective techniques are necessary to eliminate distortion of the object.

UNIT 40
EXTERIORS

ISOMETRIC DRAWINGS

Isometric drawings have constant angles (30°) from the horizon. Thus receding lines are parallel. Figure 40-1 shows a comparison of isometric, oblique, and perspective drawings. Because of the size, especially length, of most architectural structures, isometric drawings result in great visual distortion of receding areas. Notice the more realistic appearance of the perspective drawing compared with the isometric and oblique drawings in Fig. 40-1. Figure 40-2 also shows the different distortions by superimposing an isometric outline of a building over a perspective drawing of the same building.

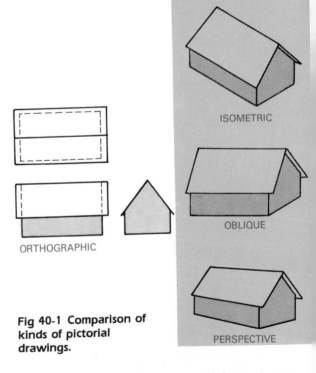

ORTHOGRAPHIC

ISOMETRIC

OBLIQUE

PERSPECTIVE

Fig 40-1 Comparison of kinds of pictorial drawings.

PERSPECTIVE DRAWINGS

In *perspective drawings*, receding lines showing the parts of a building that are furthest from your view appear to be going to meet. They are not drawn parallel. To give an example of a perspective view, as you look down a railroad track, the tracks appear to come together and vanish at a point on the distant horizon. Similarly, the horizontal

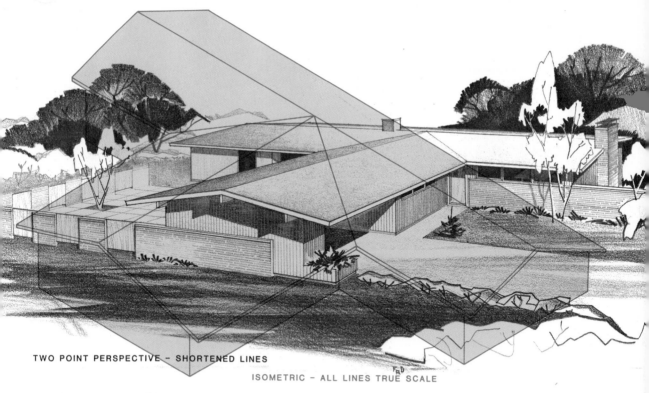

TWO POINT PERSPECTIVE - SHORTENED LINES

ISOMETRIC - ALL LINES TRUE SCALE

Fig 40-2 Comparison of isometric and perspective projections.

lines of the building shown in Fig. 40-3 appear to be coming together. A perspective drawing, more than any other kind of drawing, resembles a photograph.

On a perspective drawing, the receding lines of a building are purposely drawn closer together on one or several sides of the building to create the illusion of depth. The point at which these lines intersect is known as the *vanishing point.* Just as railroad tracks would appear to come together on the horizon, the vanishing points in a perspective drawing are always placed on a horizon line.

In preparing perspective drawings, the *horizon line* is the same as your line of sight. If the horizon line is placed through the building, the building will appear at your eye level. If the horizon line is placed below the building, the building will appear to be above your eye level. If the horizon line is placed above the building, it will appear to be below your line of sight. Figure 40-4 shows the effect of horizon-line placement on, above, and below

the building. Applications of horizon-line placement are shown in Fig. 40-5 (through the building), 40-6 (below the building), and 40-7 (above the building).

Fig 40-3 Long horizontal lines appear to meet.

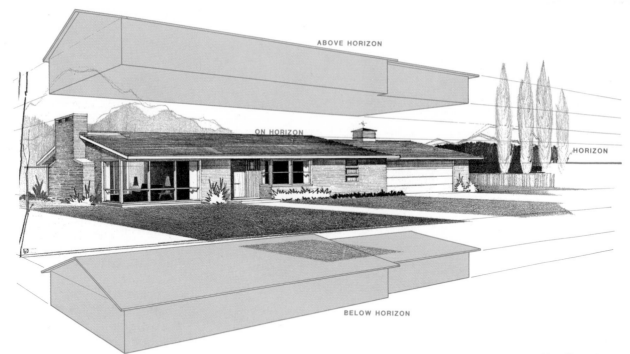

Fig 40-4 The effect of horizon-line placement.

Because perspective drawings do not reveal the true size and shape of the building, perspective drawings are never used as working drawings. To make the drawing appear more realistic, the actual length of the receding sides of the drawing are shortened. Figure 40-8 shows a perspective drawing with shortened sides and an isometric drawing that is

Fig 40-5 The horizon extends through this building.

Fig 40-6 The horizon is below this building.

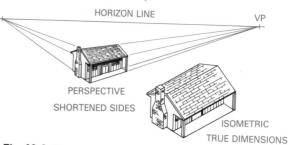

Fig 40-8 The length of receding lines should be shortened on perspective drawings.

prepared to the true dimension of the building. The two sides of the isometric drawing appear distorted because we are accustomed to seeing areas decrease in depth from our point of vision.

ONE-POINT PERSPECTIVE

A *one-point perspective* is a drawing in which the front view is drawn to its true scale and all receding sides are projected to a single vanishing point located on the horizon. If the vanishing point is placed directly behind the object, as can be seen in the center of Fig. 40-9, no sides would show unless they were drawn with hidden lines. If the vanishing point is placed directly to the right or to the left of the object, with the horizon passing through the object, only one side (left or right) will show. If the object is placed above the horizon line and vanishing point, the bottom of the object will show. If the object is placed below the horizon line and vanishing point, the top of the object will show.

The one-point perspective is relatively simple to draw. The front view is drawn to the exact scale of the building. The corners of the front view are then projected to one vanishing point. Follow these steps in drawing or

Fig 40-7 The horizon line placed above a structure.

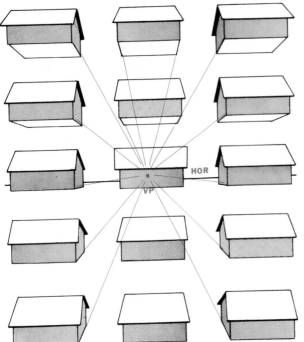

Fig 40-9 A one-point perspective can show any three sides.

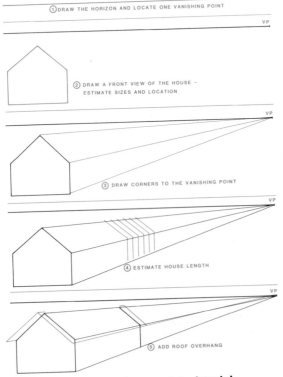

① DRAW THE HORIZON AND LOCATE ONE VANISHING POINT

② DRAW A FRONT VIEW OF THE HOUSE – ESTIMATE SIZES AND LOCATION

③ DRAW CORNERS TO THE VANISHING POINT

④ ESTIMATE HOUSE LENGTH

⑤ ADD ROOF OVERHANG

Fig 40-10 Sequence of one-point pictorial projection.

sketching a one-point perspective as shown in Fig. 40-10.

1 Draw the horizon line and mark the position of the vanishing point. With the vanishing point to the left, you see the left side of the building, to the right you see the right side of the building, and to the rear you see only the front of the building if the line extends through the building.

2 Draw the front view of the building, estimating sizes and location.

3 Project all visible corners of the front view to the vanishing point.

4 Estimate the length of the house. Draw lines parallel with the lines of the front view to indicate the back of the building.

5 Make all object lines heavy, such as roof overhang. Erase the horizon and projection lines leading to the vanishing point.

Remember that vanishing points need not always fall outside the building outline. However, when they are located within, only the frontal plane will show, as in Fig. 40-11. Figure 40-12 shows an easy device for projecting lines to a vanishing point.

TWO-POINT PERSPECTIVE

A *two-point perspective* drawing is one in which the receding sides are projected to two vanishing points, one on each end of the horizon line (Fig. 40-13). In a two-point perspective, no sides are drawn exactly to scale. All sides recede to vanishing points. Therefore, the only true-length line on a two-point perspective is the vertical corner of the building from which the sides are projected.

When the vanishing points are placed close together on the horizon line, considerable distortion results because of the acute receding angles (Fig. 40-14). When the vanishing points are placed farther apart, the drawing looks more realistic. One vanishing point is often placed farther from the building than the other vanishing point. This placement allows one side of the building to recede at a sharp angle while the other recedes less sharply. The vanishing points for the perspective drawing shown in Fig. 40-15 are placed

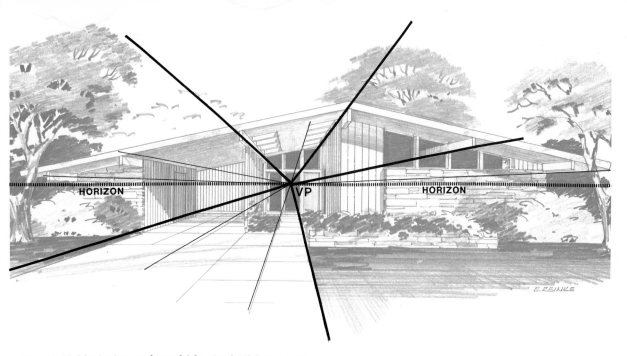

Fig 40-11 Vanishing point within the building outline.

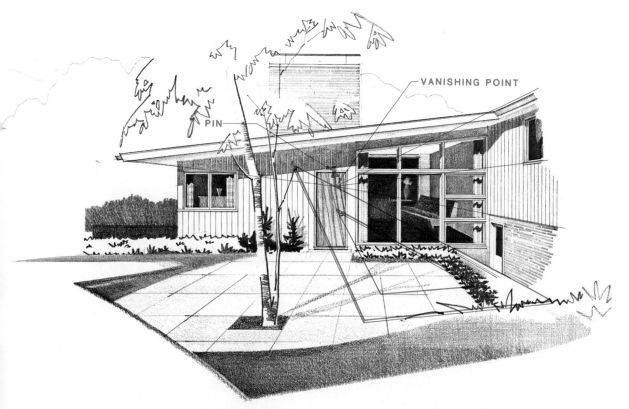

Fig 40-12 Projecting lines to a vanishing point.

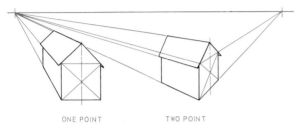

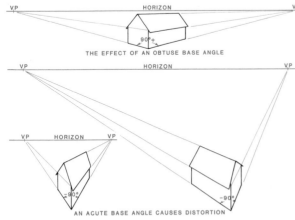

Fig 40-13 The use of two vanishing points on the horizon, compared to one.

THE EFFECT OF AN OBTUSE BASE ANGLE

AN ACUTE BASE ANGLE CAUSES DISTORTION

Fig 40-14 The distance between vanishing points affects the angles of the object.

Fig 40-15 The effect of placing the left vanishing point closer to the building than the right vanishing point.

closer to the left of the building than to the right. Consequently, the angle created by the receding lines on the left is great. The angle created by the lines receding to the right, the front of the house, is small.

VERTICAL PLACEMENT

The distance an object is placed above or below the horizon line also affects the amount of distortion in the drawing. Moving an object a greater distance vertically from the horizon line has the same effect as moving the vanishing points closer together. Objects placed close to the horizon line, either on it, above it, or below it, are less distorted than objects placed a great distance from the horizon (Fig. 40-16).

SEQUENCE

In drawing or sketching a simple two-point perspective, the steps outlined in Fig. 40-17 can be followed. However, in projecting a two-point perspective from an established floor plan and to develop a more accurate per-

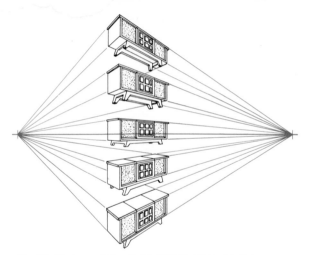

Fig 40-16 Less distortion occurs close to the horizon.

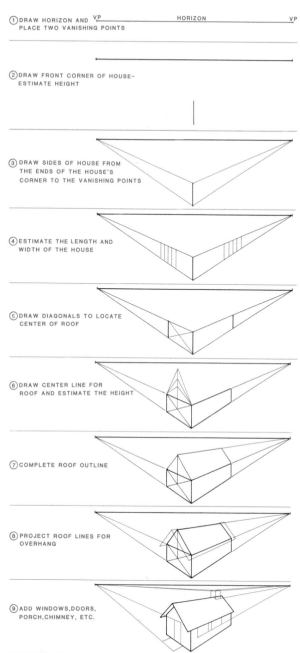

① DRAW HORIZON AND ^{VP} HORIZON VP
PLACE TWO VANISHING POINTS

② DRAW FRONT CORNER OF HOUSE—
ESTIMATE HEIGHT

③ DRAW SIDES OF HOUSE FROM
THE ENDS OF THE HOUSE'S
CORNER TO THE VANISHING POINTS

④ ESTIMATE THE LENGTH AND
WIDTH OF THE HOUSE

⑤ DRAW DIAGONALS TO LOCATE
CENTER OF ROOF

⑥ DRAW CENTER LINE FOR
ROOF AND ESTIMATE THE HEIGHT

⑦ COMPLETE ROOF OUTLINE

⑧ PROJECT ROOF LINES FOR
OVERHANG

⑨ ADD WINDOWS, DOORS,
PORCH, CHIMNEY, ETC.

Fig 40-17 Steps in preparing a two-point perspective.

spective, the steps in Fig. 40-18A through D should be followed:

1 Draw a horizontal picture-plane line (Fig. 40-18A).
2 Position the long side of the floor plan at an angle of 30° with the picture plane.
3 Locate the station point down from the picture plane about twice the width of the floor plan.
4 Project lines from the station point to the picture plane parallel to the front and end of the floor plan.
5 Draw the ground line (Fig. 40-18B).
6 Draw a horizon line about 6 feet or 2 m above the ground, depending on your scale.
7 Project lines down from the picture-plane intersection found in step 4 that intersect the horizon line to establish the vanishing points.
8 Position the front elevation drawing on the ground line (Fig. 40-18C).
9 Extend key elevation lines horizontally.
10 Project key floor-plan lines toward the station point.
11 Where the floor-plan lines of step 10 intersect the picture plane, project lines down vertically.
12 Establish the corners of the building, the doors, and the windows at the points of intersection of the vertical and horizontal lines.
13 Connect intersections to the vanishing points to establish perspective outline.
14 Add the building extensions (Fig. 40-18D).
15 Locate and draw the chimney.

267

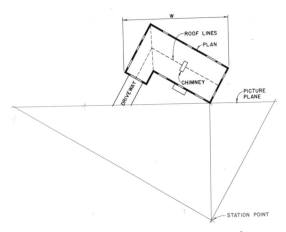

Fig 40-18A Establish the picture plane and station point.

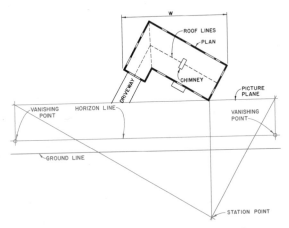

Fig 40-18B Locate the vanishing points and ground line.

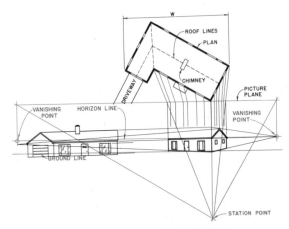

Fig 40-18C Project and intersect similar floor-plan and elevation lines.

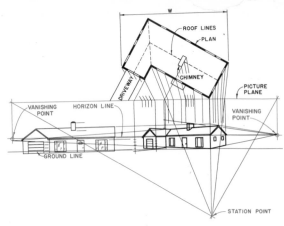

Fig 40-18D Project building extensions from the floor plan and elevation.

THREE-POINT PERSPECTIVE

Three-point-perspective drawings are used to overcome the height distortion of tall buildings. In a one- or two-story building, the vertical lines recede so slightly that, for practical purposes, they are drawn vertically. However, the top or bottom of extremely tall

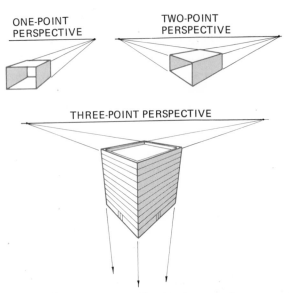

Fig 40-19 Comparison of one-, two-, and three-point perspective drawings.

buildings appears smaller than the area nearest the viewer. A third vanishing point, as shown in Fig. 40-19, may be used to provide the desired recession. The greater the vertical distance between the horizon and the lower vanishing point, the more closely the vertical lines approach a parallel state and the less is the distortion. The farther the third vanishing point is placed away from the object, the more acute the angle and, therefore, the greater is the distortion. If the lower vanishing point is placed so far below or above the horizon that the angles are hardly distinguishable, then the advantage of a three-point perspective is lost, and a two-point perspective with parallel vertical lines should be drawn.

PROBLEMS

1 Draw a two-point perspective of a building of your own design.
2 Project a two-point-perspective drawing from the floor plan and elevation shown in Fig. 36-3.
3 Draw a two-point perspective of the house shown in Fig. 33-27, using the scale $\frac{1}{8}'' = 1'-0''$.
4 Trace the building shown in Fig. 40-20. Find the position of the vanishing point and the horizon.

Fig 40-20 Find the horizon and vanishing points.

5 Project a one- and two-point-perspective drawing of the house shown in Fig. 36-1.
6 Use the layout and floor plan shown in Fig. 40-21 to project a two-point perspective. Sketch a design of the elevation prior to projection.
7 Draw a one-point and a two-point perspective of your own home.

8 Sketch a three-point perspective of the tallest building in your community.
9 Define these terms: *pictorial, one-point perspective, two-point perspective, three-point perspective, isometric, vanishing point, horizontal, vertical, parallel, horizon, station point, base line.*

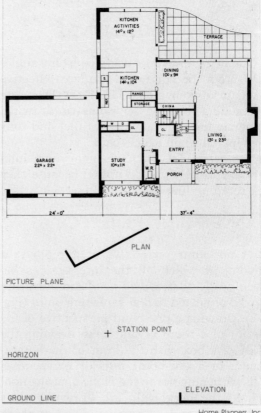

Home Planners, Inc.

Fig 40-21 Design an elevation and project a two-point perspective of this plan.

UNIT 41
INTERIORS

A pictorial drawing of the interior of a building may be an isometric drawing, a one-point-perspective drawing, or a two-point-perspective drawing. Pictorial drawings may be prepared for the entire floor plan. More commonly, however, pictorial drawings are prepared for a single room or living area.

ISOMETRIC DRAWINGS

Isometric drawings using constant angles of 30° from the horizontal are most effective for pictorial floor plans (Fig. 41-1). There are no receding lines on an isometric drawing. Isometric lines are always parallel and may be prepared to an exact scale.

Isometric drawings of single room interiors are usually not desirable, because they lack receding lines.

ONE-POINT PERSPECTIVE

A *one-point perspective* of a room is a drawing in which all the intersections between walls, floors, ceilings, and furniture may be projected to one vanishing point (Fig. 41-2). Drawing a one-point perspective of the interior of a room is similar to drawing the inside of a box with the front of the box removed. In a one-point interior perspective, walls perpendicular to the plane of projection, such as the back wall, are drawn to their proper scale and proportion. The vanishing point on the horizon line is then placed somewhere on this wall (actually behind this wall). The points of intersection where this wall in-

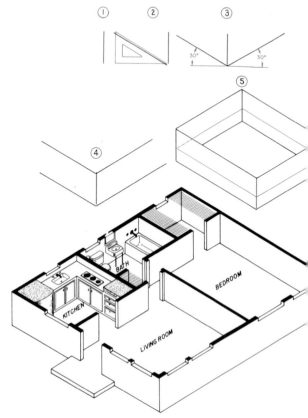

Fig 41-1 An isometric drawing of a floor plan.

tersects the ceiling and floor are then projected from the vanishing point to form the intersection between the side walls and the ceiling and the side walls and the floor.

VERTICAL PLACEMENT

If the vanishing point is placed high, very little of the ceiling will show in the projection, but much of the floor area will be revealed (Fig. 41-3A). If the vanishing point is placed near the center of the back wall, an equal amount of ceiling and floor will show (Fig. 41-3B). If the vanishing point is placed low on the wall, much of the ceiling but very little of

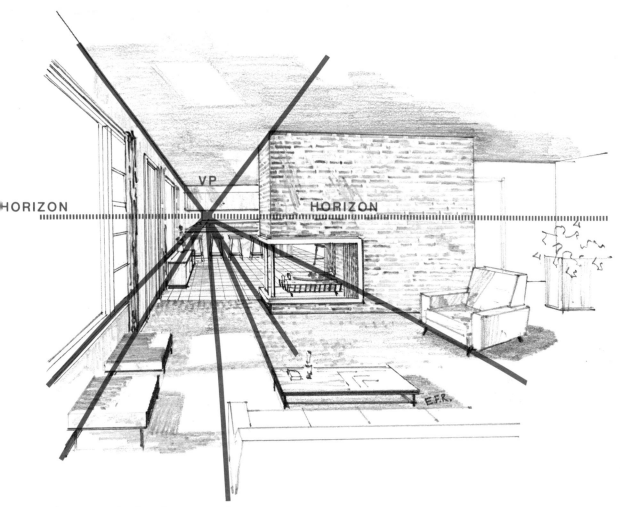

Fig 41-2 A one-point interior perspective.

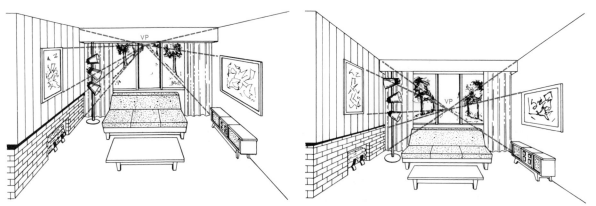

Fig 41-3A The effect of a high central vanishing point.

Fig 41-3B The effect of a centrally located vanishing point.

Fig 41-3C The effect of a low central vanishing point.

Home Planners, Inc.

Fig 41-4A Right-wall emphasis is obtained by placing the vanishing point to the extreme left.

the floor will be shown (Fig. 41-3C). Since the horizon line and the vanishing point are at your eye level, you can see that the position of the vanishing point affects the angle from which you view the object.

HORIZONTAL PLACEMENT

Moving the vanishing point from right to left on the back wall has an effect on the view of the side walls. If the vanishing point is placed toward the left, more of the right wall will be revealed (Fig. 41-4A). Conversely, if the vanishing point is placed near the right side,

more of the left wall will be revealed in the projection (Fig. 41-4B). If the vanishing point is placed in the center, an equal amount of right wall and left wall will be shown. When one wall should dominate, place the vanishing point on the extreme end of the opposite wall.

When projecting wall offsets and furniture, always block-in the overall size of the item to form a perspective view, as shown in Fig. 41-5. The details of furniture or closets or

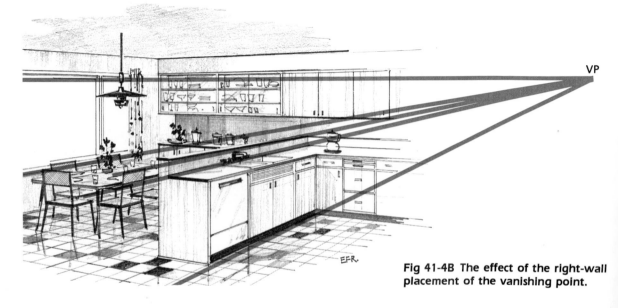

VP

Fig 41-4B The effect of the right-wall placement of the vanishing point.

VP

EFR.

Fig 41-5 Always block-in furniture.

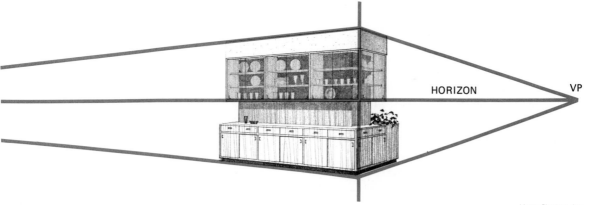

HORIZON   VP

Fig 41-6 A two-point interior perspective.

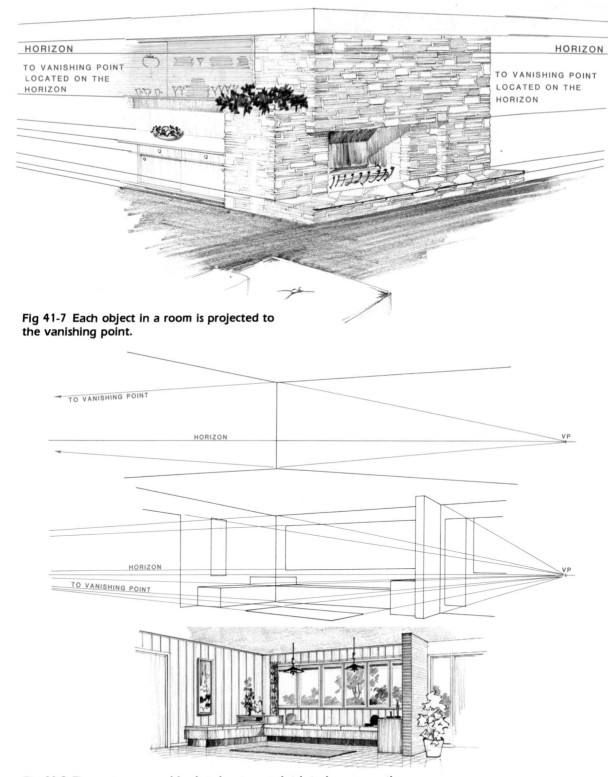

HORIZON

TO VANISHING POINT LOCATED ON THE HORIZON

HORIZON

TO VANISHING POINT LOCATED ON THE HORIZON

Fig 41-7 Each object in a room is projected to the vanishing point.

TO VANISHING POINT

HORIZON

VP

HORIZON

HORIZON

TO VANISHING POINT

VP

Fig 41-8 The sequence used in drawing two-point interior perspectives.

even of persons can then be completed within this blocked-in cube or series of cubes.

TWO-POINT PERSPECTIVE

Two-point perspectives are normally prepared to show the final design and decor of two walls of a room. The base line on an interior two-point perspective is similar to the base line on an exterior two-point perspective. The base line in the drawing shown in Fig. 41-6 is the corner of the cabinet. Two rooms or an L-shaped room can best be shown projected to each vanishing point.

Once the walls are projected to the vanishing points in the two-point perspective, each object in the room can also be projected to the vanishing point as in external two-point perspectives. Projecting the fireplace shown in Fig. 41-7 to the vanishing point is the same as projecting a flat-roof house or building.

The sequence of steps in drawing two-point interior perspectives is shown in Fig. 41-8. Figure 41-9 shows the relationships between working drawings and perspective drawings.

Pictorial grids (Fig. 41-10) are recommended to eliminate the projection of horizon and vanishing points. However, the proper

ONE-POINT PERSPECTIVE

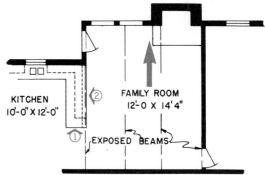

Fig 41-9 A comparison of a plan and a perspective drawing.

grid must be selected to provide the horizon and vanishing-point position necessary to reveal the room at the angle desired.

Fig 41-10 Interior pictorial grid.

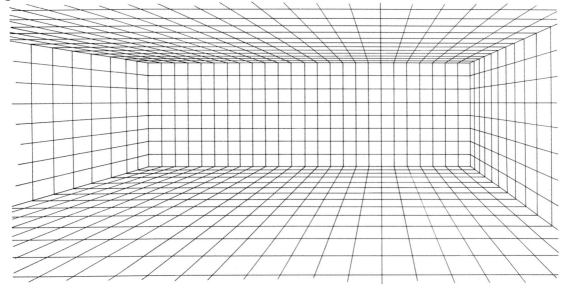

PROBLEMS

1 Trace the drawing shown in Fig. 41-11. With a colored pencil, project the ceiling and floor lines to find the vanishing points and the horizon line.

Fig 41-11 Find the vanishing points and horizon line.

Fig 41-12 Find the vanishing points. Draw in the right wall of the living area.

2 Trace the perspective shown in Fig. 41-12. Find the position of the vanishing point. Extend the drawing to include the right wall of the living area.

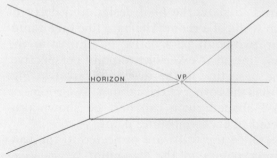

Fig 41-13 Sketch furniture in a room with this perspective.

3 Prepare a one-point interior perspective of your own room.

4 Prepare a one-point perspective of a room of your own design.

5 Draw a one-point interior perspective of a classroom. Prepare one drawing to show much of the ceiling and left wall. Prepare another drawing to show much of the floor and right wall.

6 Trace the lines in Fig. 41-13 and sketch in furniture.

7 Define these terms: *isometric, interior perspective.*

UNIT 42
RENDERING

To *render* a pictorial drawing is to make the drawing appear more realistic. This may be done through the media of pencil, pen and ink, watercolors, pastels, or airbrush. Drawings are rendered by adding realistic texture to the materials and establishing shade and shadow patterns.

MEDIA

Soft pencils are one of the most effective media for rendering architectural drawings because tones can be greatly varied by the weight of the line used. Smudge blending to add tone can be accomplished by rubbing a finger over penciled areas. Figure 42-1A shows

Fig 42-1A Pencil rendering.

Fig 42-1B Pen-and-ink rendering.

pencil techniques used to create an architectural rendering.

Pen-and-ink renderings of architectural drawings vary greatly. Strokes must be placed farther apart to create light effects and closer together to produce darker effects (Fig. 42-1B). Watercolor techniques are also popular in architectural rendering. Fig. 42-1C shows wash techniques added to an exterior line drawing to produce realistic effects. Figure 42-1D shows a wash rendering of an interior perspective drawing.

Fig 42-1C Watercolor rendering.

Fig 42-1D Combination of line and wash techniques.

SHADE

When you *shade* an object, you lighten the part of the object exposed to the sun or other light sources and darken the part of the object not exposed to the sun or light source (Fig. 42-2). Notice how the lower part of Fig. 42-3 is shaded darker, and the top shaded lighter, to show the different exposure to the sun. Likewise, the right portion of Fig. 42-4 is shaded

SHADOWING AND RENDERING

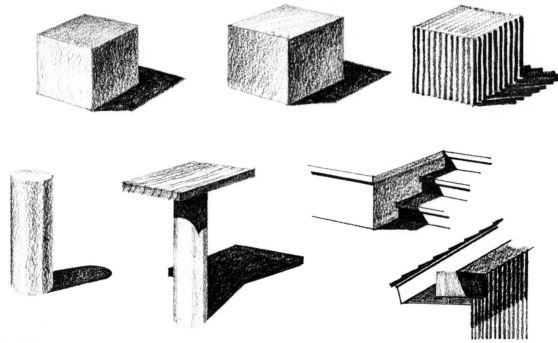

Fig 42-2 The use of shading to show sunlight on high areas.

Fig 42-3 The use of shading to show depth and light angles.

SWISS

Fig 42-4 Methods of shading to show distance.

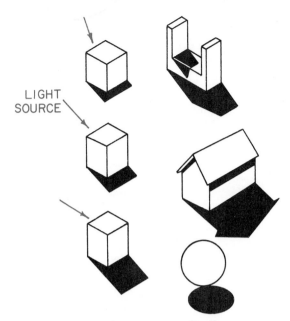

LIGHT SOURCE

Fig 42-5 Shadow the area opposite the light source.

darker to denote distance and lack of direct sunlight. When objects with sharp corners are exposed to strong sunlight, one area may be extremely light and the other side of the object extremely dark. However, when objects and buildings have areas that are round (cylindrical), so that their parts move gradually from dark to light areas, a gradual shading from extremely dark to extremely light must be made.

SHADOW

In order to determine what areas of the building will be drawn darker to indicate *shadowing*, the angle of the sun in the illustration must be established. When the angle of the sun is established (Fig. 42-5), all shading should be consistent with the direction and angle of the shadow. On buildings that are drawn considerably below the horizon line,

Fig 42-6 Shadows reveal hidden outlines.

Home Planners, Inc.

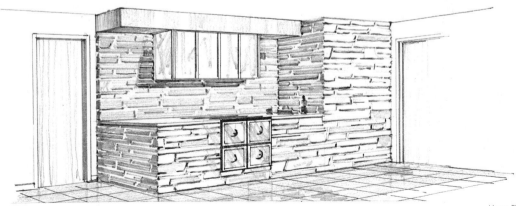

Fig 42-7 Texture rendering.

Home Planners, Inc.

279

Fig 42-8A Block-in the basic outline.

Fig 42-8B Prepare the sketch for rendering.

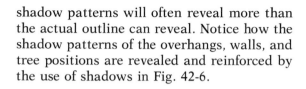

Fig 42-8C Texture is added to building materials.

Fig 42-8D The completed rendering.

shadow patterns will often reveal more than the actual outline can reveal. Notice how the shadow patterns of the overhangs, walls, and tree positions are revealed and reinforced by the use of shadows in Fig. 42-6.

TEXTURE

Giving *texture* to an architectural drawing means making building materials appear as rough or as smooth as they actually are. Smooth surfaces are no problem since they are very reflective and hence are very light. Only a few reflection lines are usually necessary to illustrate smoothness of surfaces such as aluminum, glass, and painted surfaces. On rough surfaces, the thickness or roughness of the material can often be shown by shading. Texture rendering is effective in Fig. 42-7 in showing the texture of the materials used.

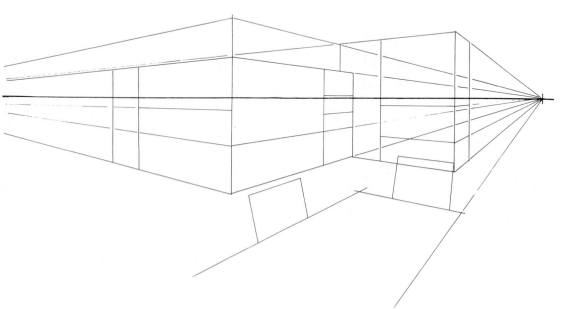

Fig 42-9A Basic layout.

SEQUENCE

In preparing pictorial renderings, proceed in the following sequence, as shown in Fig. 42-8.

1 Block-in with single lines the projection of the perspective (Fig. 42-8A).
2 Sketch the outline of building materials in preparation for rendering (Fig. 42-8B). This work can be done with a soft pencil, a ruling pen, or a crow-quill pen. Establish a semiangle and sketch shadows and shading. Darken windows, door areas, and under-roof overhangs.

3 Add texture to the building materials. For example, show the position of each brick with a chisel-point pencil. Leave the mortar space white and lighten the pressure for the areas that are in direct sunlight (Fig. 42-8C).

Fig 42-9B Added detail.

Fig 42-9C Finished rendering.

Fig 42-10 Methods of rendering trees and shrubs on plan views.

Richard B. Pollman

Fig 42-11 Window-rendering techniques.

4 Complete the rendering by emphasizing light and dark areas and establishing more visible contrasts of light and dark shadow patterns (Fig. 42-8D). Figure 42-9A, B, and C show a similar sequence in the development of an interior rendering.

TECHNIQUES

Figures 42-10 through 42-17 show the application of various rendering techniques to architectural drawings. Figure 42-10 shows some of the techniques used to draw trees and

FENCES AND WALLS

Fig 42-12 Methods of rendering fences and walls.

CHIMNEYS

Fig 42-13 Pencil renderings of chimneys.

PEOPLE

Fig 42-14A Architectural sketches of people.

Fig 42-14B The use of people to show traffic patterns.

shrubs on pictorial drawings. These methods are used to show tree placement without blocking out the view of the buildings. Figure 42-11 shows depth and shadows in rendering windows. Notice that some windows are rendered to show reflected light, and others are drawn to reveal the room behind, as though the window were open. Rendering fences and walls (Fig. 42-12) and rendering chimneys (Fig. 42-13) require a combination of shade, shadow, and texture techniques.

Sketches of people are often necessary to show the relative size of a building and to put the total drawing in proper perspective. Since people should not interfere with the view of the building, architects frequently draw people in outline or in extremely simple form (Fig. 42-14A). People are also used to show traffic patterns and size differences (Fig. 42-14B)

AUTOS

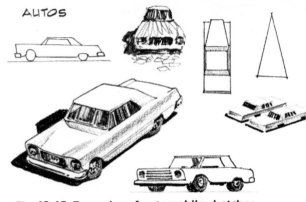

Fig 42-15 Examples of automobile sketches for use on architectural drawings.

SIDING

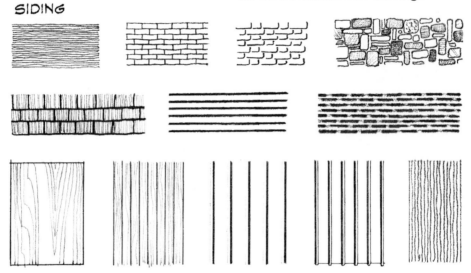

Fig 42-16 Rendering different kinds of siding.

DOORS

Fig 42-17 Methods of rendering doors.

and to provide a feeling of perspective and depth. Automobiles are added to architectural renderings (Fig. 42-15) to provide proper perspective and to give a greater feeling for external traffic patterns.

It is also important to utilize proper rendering techniques to show texture and shadows on flat surfaces, such as siding (Fig. 42-16) and doors (Fig. 42-17). Notice that most of this is done by light shading and also by variation of the pencil-stroke widths.

One popular technique that can be used to convert a perspective line drawing into a rendering is to apply screen tones. The drawings shown in Fig. 42-18 are simple line drawings with various shades of screens added to denote texture and shadow. The use of more realistic pencil technique to show texture and shadows is illustrated in Fig. 42-19.

ABBREVIATED RENDERING

Often it is necessary or desirable to render only one part of a building. In such cases, the other attached parts may be only outlined and the rendering gradually dimin-

PERSPECTIVE COMPOSITION

Fig 42-18 The area-tone method of rendering.

PERSPECTIVE TECHNIQUES

Fig 42-19 A combination of pencil techniques showing shade, shadow, and texture.

Fig 42-20 A partial rendering.

ished, instead of abruptly stopped. Figure 42-20 was prepared to show only the porch of the house. However, the relationship to the remainder of the house is important and, therefore, the house is shown in outline.

PROBLEMS

1 Render a perspective drawing of your own house.

2 Render a perspective drawing of a house of your own design.

3 Render a perspective sketch of your school. Choose your own medium: pencil, pen and ink, watercolors, pastels, or airbrush.

4 Complete the perspective shown in Fig. 42-21 and completely render the drawing in pencil.

5 Define these terms: *render, texture, shade, shadow, chisel-point, crow-quill.*

Fig 42-21 Complete this rendering.

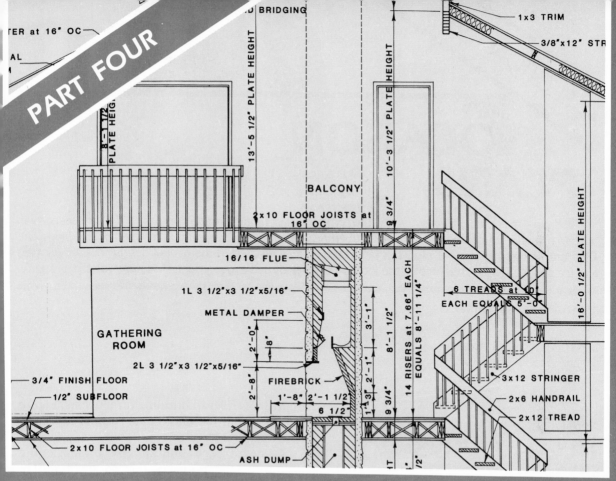

TECHNICAL ARCHITECTURAL PLANS

Basic architectural plans, such as floor plans, elevations, and pictorial drawings, are adequate for describing the general design of a structure. However, to ensure that the building will be completed as specified, a more complete and detailed description of the construction features of the design must be prepared. Technical architectural plans are prepared for this purpose. These include location plans, sectional drawings, foundation plans, framing plans, electrical plans, energy-system plans, plumbing diagrams, and modular-construction plans. In Part Four you will learn the basic practices and procedures in preparing technical architectural plans, and the relationship of a set of architectural plans.

LOCATION PLANS

Location plans are necessary to give the builder essential information about the property. They are of three types: the plot, the landscape, and the survey. The plot plan shows the location of all structures on the property. The landscape plan shows how the various features of the landscape will be used in the overall design. The survey plan shows the geographical features of the property.

UNIT 43
PLOT PLANS

Plot plans are used to show the location and size of all buildings on the lot. Overall building dimensions and lot dimensions are shown on plot plans. The position and size of walks, drives, patios, and courts are also shown. Compass orientation of the lot is given, and contour lines are sometimes shown. Figure 43-1 shows the key figures and the symbols commonly used on plot plans.

GUIDES FOR DRAWING PLOT PLANS

The numbered arrows in Fig. 43-2 illustrate these guides for drawing plot plans:

1 Draw only the outline of the main structure on the lot. Cross-hatching is optional.
2 Draw the outlines of other buildings on the lot.
3 Show overall building dimensions. Figure 43-3 shows dimensional standards recommended for plot plans.
4 Locate each building by dimensioning from the property line to the building (Fig. 43-3). The *property line* shows the legal limits of the lot on all sides.
5 Show the position and size of driveways.
6 Show the location and size of walks.
7 Indicate grade elevation of key surfaces such as patios, driveways, and courts.
8 Outline and show the symbol for surface material used on patios and terraces.
9 Label streets adjacent to the outline.
10 Place overall lot dimensions either on extension lines outside the property line or directly on the property line.
11 Show the size and location of courts.
12 Show the size and location of pools, ponds, or other bodies of water.
13 Indicate the compass orientation of the lot by the use of a north arrow.
14 Use a decimal scale such as $1'' = 10'-0''$, or $1'' = 20'-0''$, or a metric scale for preparing the plot plan.
15 Show the position of utility lines on a plot plan or a survey plan (Fig. 43-4).

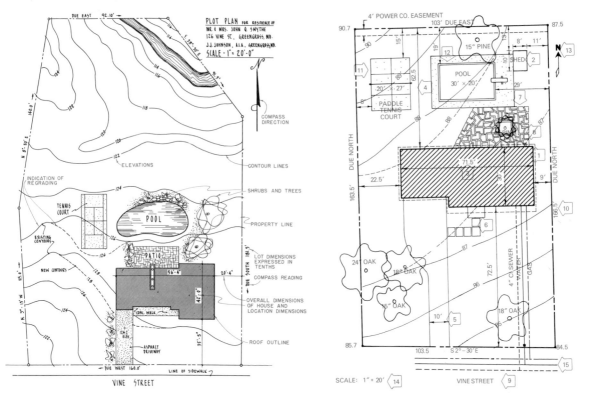

Fig 43-1 Plot-plan symbols.

Fig 43-2 Guides for drawing plot plans.

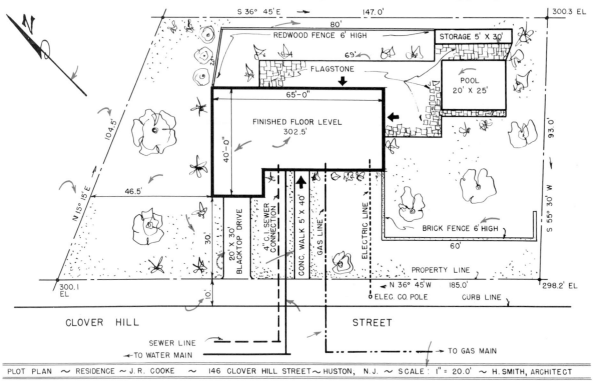

Fig 43-3 Plot-plan dimensions.

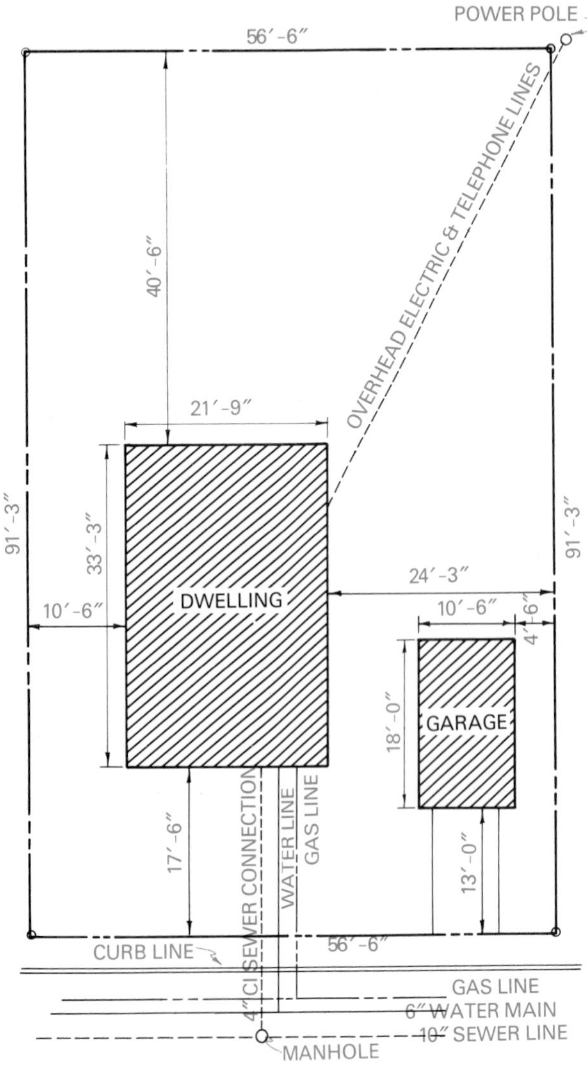
POWER POLE
56′-6″
OVERHEAD ELECTRIC & TELEPHONE LINES
40′-6″
21′-9″
91′-3″
33′-3″
91′-3″
24′-3″
10′-6″
DWELLING
10′-6″
6″
4′
18′-0″
GARAGE
17′-6″
4″ CI SEWER CONNECTION
WATER LINE
GAS LINE
13′-0″
CURB LINE
56′-6″
GAS LINE
6″ WATER MAIN
10″ SEWER LINE
MANHOLE

Fig 43-4 Utility line shown on plot plan.

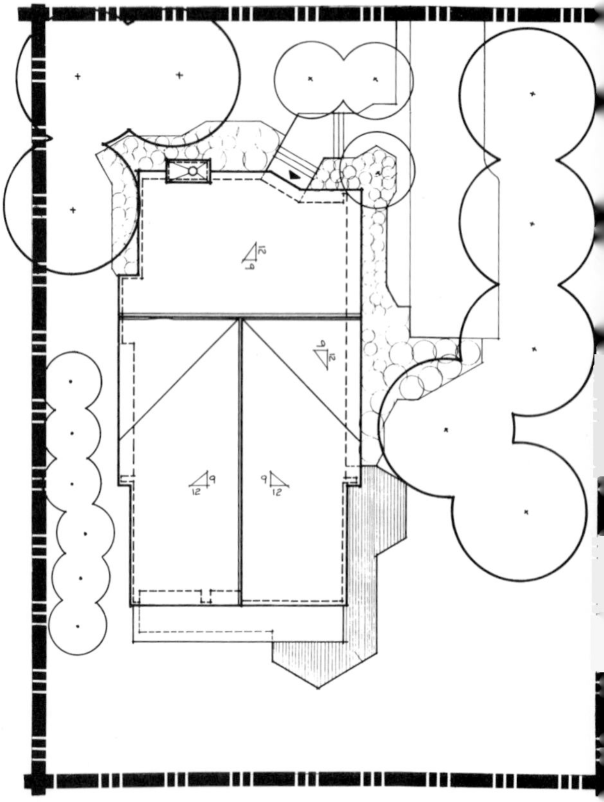

Fig 43-6 The roof outline is often shown on plot plans.

Fig 43-5 Entrance symbols.

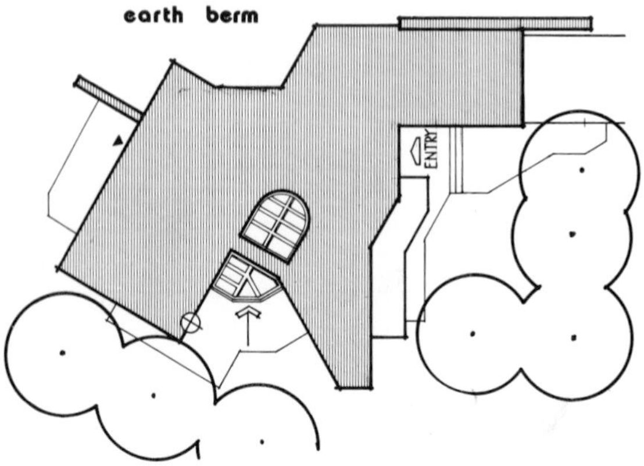
earth berm
ENTRY

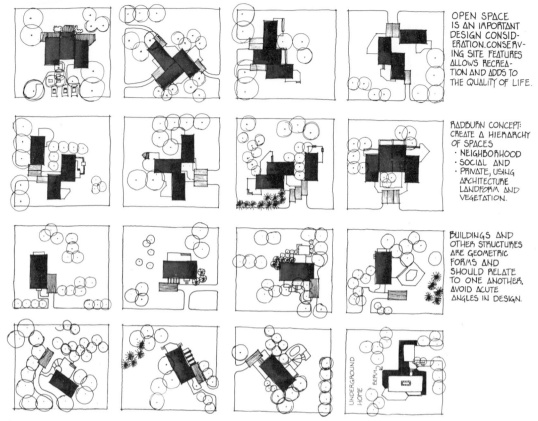

OPEN SPACE IS AN IMPORTANT DESIGN CONSIDERATION. CONSERVING SITE FEATURES ALLOWS RECREATION AND ADDS TO THE QUALITY OF LIFE.

RADBURN CONCEPT: CREATE A HIERARCHY OF SPACES
· NEIGHBORHOOD
· SOCIAL AND
· PRIVATE, USING ARCHITECTURE LANDFORM AND VEGETATION.

BUILDINGS AND OTHER STRUCTURES ARE GEOMETRIC FORMS AND SHOULD RELATE TO ONE ANOTHER. AVOID ACUTE ANGLES IN DESIGN.

UNDERGROUND HOME

BERM

Fig 43-7 Alternative plot plans.

ALTERNATIVE FEATURES

Although plot plans should be prepared according to the standards shown in Fig. 43-2, many optional features also may be included in plot plans. For example, sometimes the interior partitions of the residence are given to show a correspondence between the outside living areas and those inside. Some architects prefer to include only the outline of the building on the plot plan, while others favor cross-hatching or shading the buildings.

The position of entrances to buildings are sometimes noted on plot plans, as shown in Fig. 43-5. This device provides an interpretation of the access to the house from the outside, without requiring a detailed plan of the inside.

Contour lines are another optional feature on plot plans. On lots that deviate greatly in contour, contour lines are necessary.

The plot plan is also often used to show the outline of the roof, as in Fig. 43-6. When this outline is shown, the drawing gives the effect of looking down on the top of the lot.

VARIATION IN PLAN

There are many ways to place buildings on a lot. Sometimes alternative plot plans are developed to determine the best overall arrangement, as shown in Fig. 43-7. Variations are also possible in developing almost any detail of a plot plan. The steps for preparing a plot plan are shown in Fig. 43-8.

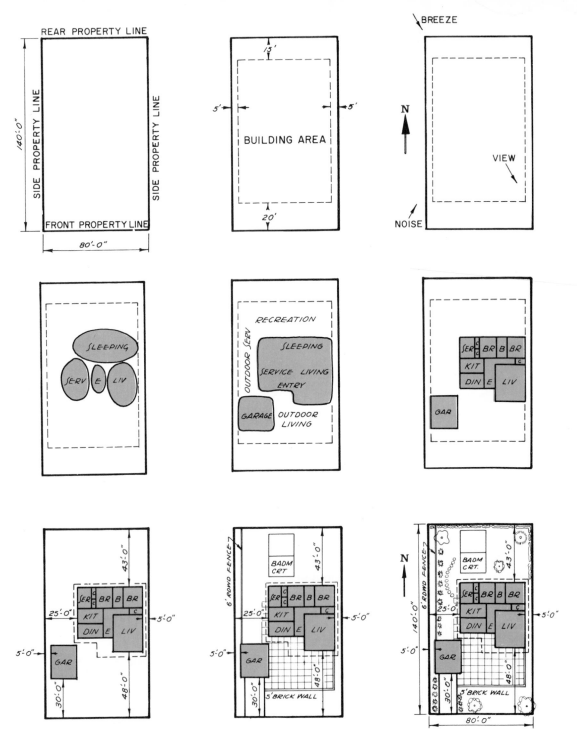

Fig 43-8 Steps in drawing a plot plan.

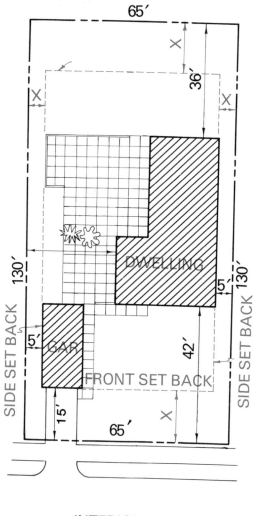

INTERIOR LOT

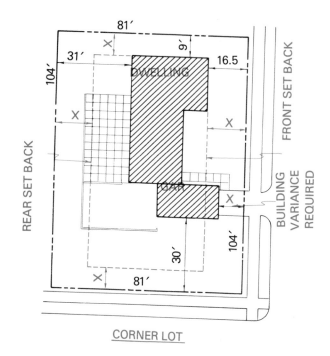

CORNER LOT

Fig 43-9 Property and building lines shown on plot plans.

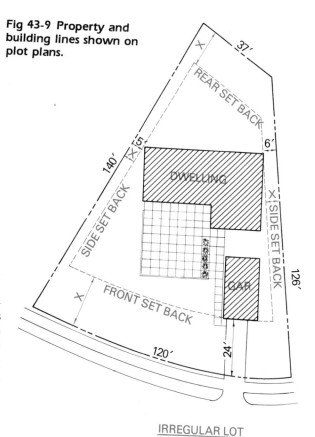

IRREGULAR LOT

SETBACK REQUIREMENTS

Property lines show the legal limits of a lot on all sides. However, most building codes require that buildings be located (set back) specified minimum distances from property lines. Figures 43-9A, B, and C show typical building-line setback requirements for different types of lots. Figure 43-10 shows alternative plans depending on setback requirements.

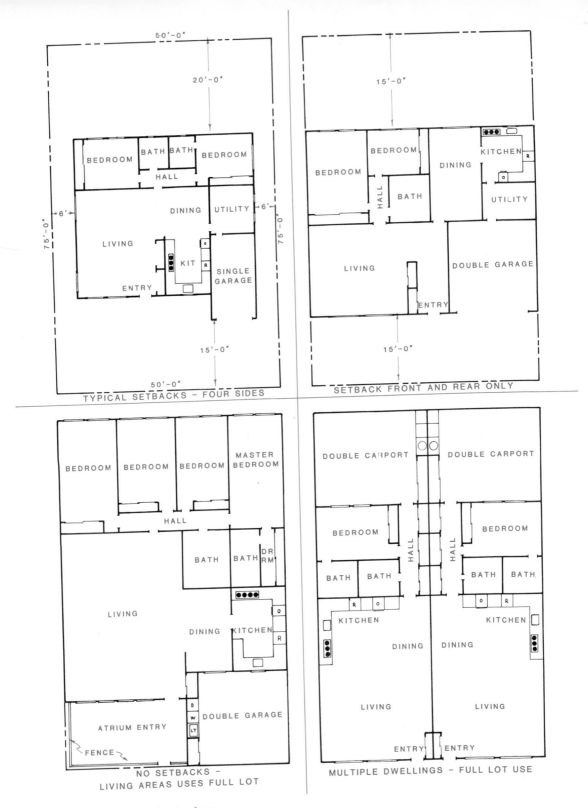

Fig 43-10 Alternative set-back plans.

PROBLEMS

1 Draw a plot plan of your own home.

2 From a survey plan you have developed, complete a plot plan showing the position of the residence you are designing.

3 Place the outline of a residence on the plot plan shown in Fig. 43-11. Include a two-car garage, swimming pool, and tennis court on this plan. Remember to take full advantage of existing landscape features.

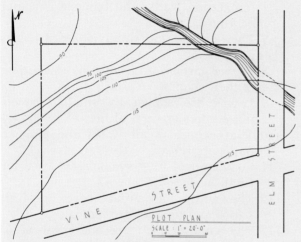

Fig 43-11 Locate a residence on this lot.

4 Draw a plot plan for the house shown in Fig. 43-12. Make the lot 100′ × 150′.

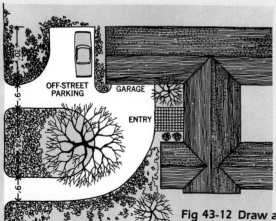

Fig 43-12 Draw a plot plan for this home.

5 Sketch one of the properties shown in Fig. 4-5. Prepare a template of the house to the same scale and place it on the property in the most desirable location.

6 Sketch the lot layout shown in Fig. 43-13. Place templates of the house and garage on this lot in the most desirable position. Also sketch the position of driveways, walks, and other landscape features you would add to this design. Sketch adjacent lots and show their key landscape features.

7 Define these terms: *plot plan, lot, compass orientation, contour lines, property line, grade elevation.*

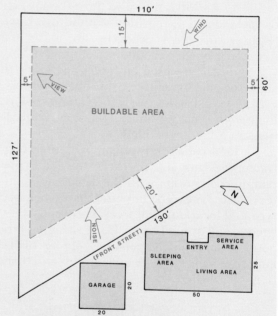

Fig 43-13 Place templates of the house and garage on the best location.

UNIT 44
LANDSCAPE PLANS

The primary function of the *landscape plan* is to show the types and location of vegetation for the lot. It may also show the contour of the land and the position of buildings. Such features are often necessary to make the placement of the vegetation meaningful.

Symbols are used on landscape plans to show the position of trees, shrubbery, flowers, vegetable gardens, hedgerows, and lawns. Figure 44-1 shows some common symbols used on a landscape plan.

A landscape architect or gardening contractor designs and prepares the landscape plan in cooperation with the designing architect. The landscape architect specifies the type and location of all trees, shrubs, flowers, hedges, and ground cover. He or she often proposes changes in the existing contour of the land to enhance the site appearance and function.

GUIDES FOR PREPARING LANDSCAPE PLANS

The following guides in preparing landscape plans are illustrated by the numbered arrows shown in Fig. 44-2:

1 The elevation of all trees is noted to show the datum level.
2 Vegetable gardens are shown by outlining the planting furrows.
3 Orchards are shown by outlining each tree in the pattern.

4 The property line is shown to define the limits of the lot.
5 Trees are located to provide shade and windbreaks and to balance the decor of the site.
6 Shrubbery is used to provide privacy, define boundaries, outline walks, conceal foundation walls, and balance irregular contours.
7 The outlines and subdivisions of courts are shown.
8 Flower gardens are shown by the outline of their shapes.
9 Lawns are shown by small, sparsely placed dots or vertical lines.
10 The outlines of all walks and planned paths are shown.
11 Conventional map symbols are used for small bridges.
12 The outline and surface covering of all patios and terraces are indicated.
13 The name of each tree and shrub is labeled on the symbol.
14 All landscaping should enhance the function and appearance of the site.
15 Flowers should be located to provide maximum beauty and ease of maintenance.
16 Buildings are outlined, crosshatched, or shaded. In some cases, the outline of the floor plan is shown in abbreviated form. This helps to show the relationship of the outside to the inside living areas.
17 Hedges are used as screening devices to provide privacy, to divide areas, to control traffic, or to serve as windbreaks.
18 Each tree or shrub is indexed to a planting schedule, if there are too many to be labeled on the drawing, as suggested in 13.
19 A tree is shown by drawing an outline of the area covered by its branches. This

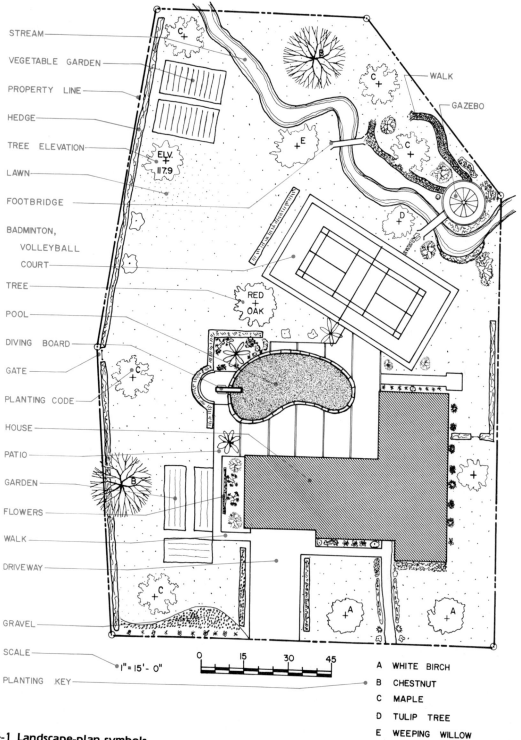

STREAM

VEGETABLE GARDEN

PROPERTY LINE

HEDGE

TREE ELEVATION

LAWN

FOOTBRIDGE

BADMINTON,
VOLLEYBALL
COURT

TREE

POOL

DIVING BOARD

GATE

PLANTING CODE

HOUSE

PATIO

GARDEN

FLOWERS

WALK

DRIVEWAY

GRAVEL

SCALE

PLANTING KEY

WALK

GAZEBO

ELV.
117.9

RED
OAK

1" = 15'- 0"

0   15   30   45

A   WHITE BIRCH
B   CHESTNUT
C   MAPLE
D   TULIP TREE
E   WEEPING WILLOW

Fig 44-1 Landscape-plan symbols.

2

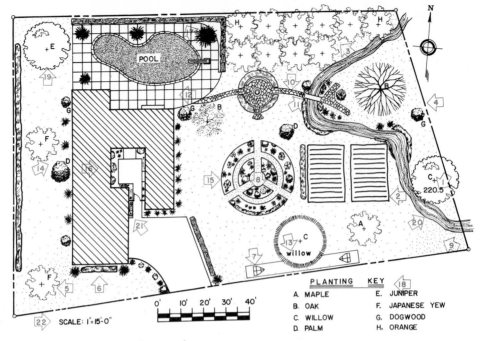

PLANTING KEY

A. MAPLE   E. JUNIPER
B. OAK   F. JAPANESE YEW
C. WILLOW   G. DOGWOOD
D. PALM   H. ORANGE

0' 10' 20' 30' 40'

SCALE: 1"=15'-0"

Fig 44-2 Guides for preparing landscape plans.

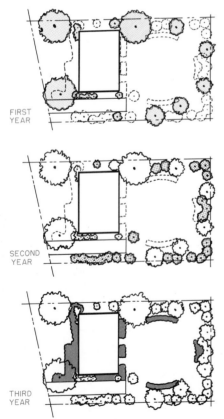

FIRST YEAR

SECOND YEAR

THIRD YEAR

Fig 44-3 A phased landscape plan.

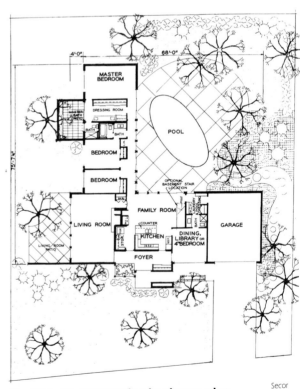

Fig 44-4 An interpretive landscape plan Secor
without detail dimension. Landscape Co.

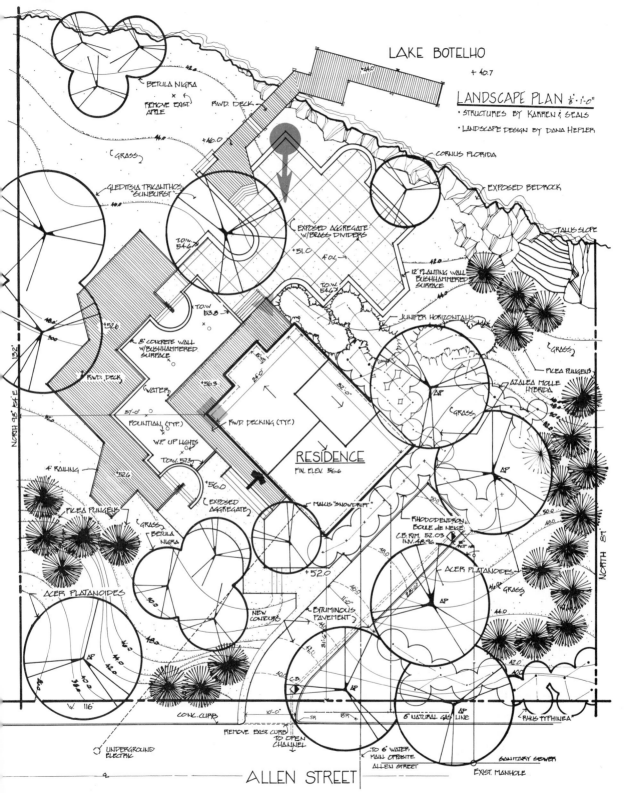

Fig 44-5A A landscape plan with all materials labeled.

Paul J. Peart, AILA

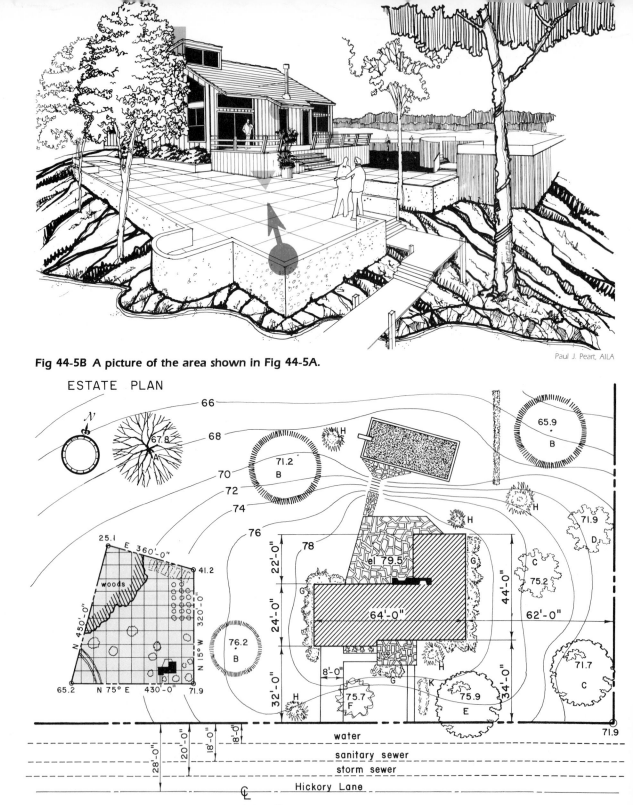

Fig 44-5B A picture of the area shown in Fig 44-5A.

Paul J. Peart, AILA

ESTATE PLAN

Fig 44-6 An estate plan with a partial detail.

symbol varies from a perfect circle to irregular lines representing the appearance of branches. A plus sign (+) indicates the location of the trunk.

20 Water is indicated by irregular parallel lines.

21 Shrubbery in front of the house should be low in order not to interfere with traffic or with window location.

22 An engineer's scale is used to prepare landscape plans. This is the measure surveyors use.

PHASING

The complete landscaping of a lot may be prolonged through several years. This procedure is sometimes followed because of a lack of time to accomplish all the planting necessary, or for financial reasons. Figure 44-3 shows a landscape plan divided into three different phases for completion. When a landscape plan is *phased*, the total plan is drawn, and then different shades or colors are used to designate the items that will be planted in the first year, in the second year, and in the third year. A plan can be phased over many years or several months, depending on the schedule for completion of the landscaping.

VARIATIONS

Many landscape plans, such as the one shown in Fig. 44-4, are strictly interpretive and contain few or no dimensions. The plan shown in Fig. 44-5 is a detailed landscape plan. The view drawn in Fig. 44-5B is located by the arrow in Fig. 44-5A.

COMBINATION PLANS

Often, the lot or estate is too large to be shown accurately on a standard landscape plan. A scale such as $1'' = 20'-0''$ may not show the entire estate; or a scale must be used that is so small that the features cannot be readily identified, labeled, and dimensioned. One solution to such a problem is to prepare a total plan of the large estate to a large scale. This is indexed to a drawing of the immediate area around the house. Figure 44-6 shows the total estate plan as an insert in the drawing showing the lower right-hand corner of the estate developed in more detail.

It is sometimes desirable or necessary to combine all the features of the survey, plot plan, and landscape plan in one plan. In such a combination, all the symbol dimensions are incorporated in one location plan, as shown in Fig. 44-6. This includes contour lines and the exact position of vegetation and buildings.

PROBLEMS

1 Add landscape features to your own plot plan.
2 Sketch the property in Fig. 43-4 and add the landscape symbols where named.

Fig 44-7 Place this house on a 100' × 200' lot. Home Planners, Inc.

3 Place the house shown in Fig. 44-7 on a 100' × 200' lot. Prepare a landscape drawing of the lot according to your own taste.

4 Add landscape symbols as indicated by the labels in Fig. 44-8.

5 Define these terms: *landscape plan, landscape symbol, landscape architect, gardening contractor, datum level, orchards, tree-location symbol, map symbols.*

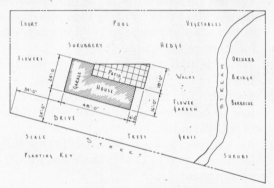

Fig 44-8 Add landscape symbols to this plan.

UNIT 45
SURVEY PLANS

A *survey* is a drawing showing the exact size, shape, and levels of a lot. When prepared by a licensed surveyor, the survey can be used as a legal document. It is filed with the deed to the property. The lot survey includes the length of each boundary, tree locations, corner elevations, contour of the land, and position of streams, river, roads or streets, and utility lines. It also lists the name of the owner of the lot and of the owner or title of adjacent lots.

A survey drawing must be accurate and must communicate a complete description of the features of the lot. Symbols are used extensively to describe the features of the terrain. Figure 45-1 shows the survey symbols most frequently used. Some symbols depict the appearance of a feature. Most survey symbols are *schematic* representations of some feature. Figure 45-2 shows topographic symbols used on survey, plat, and geographical survey plans.

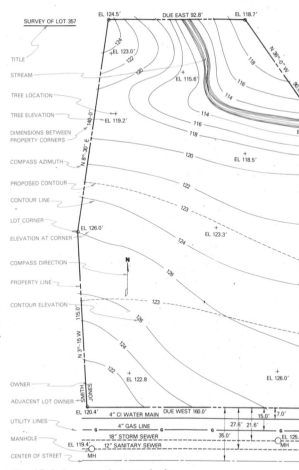

Fig 45-1 Survey-plan symbols.

302

Fig 45-2 Topographic symbols.

NAME	ABBREV	SYMBOL	NAME	ABBREV	SYMBOL
TREES	TR		GRAVEL	GRV	
GROUND COVER	GRD CV		CULTIVATED AREA	CULT	
BUSHES SHRUBS	BSH SH		WATER	WT	
OPEN WOODLAND	OP WDL		WELL	W	
ORCHARD	OR		NORTH-MERIDIAN ARROWS	N MER ARR	
MARSH	MRS		PROPERTY LINE	PR LN	
SUBMERGED MARSH	SUB MRS		SURVEYED CONTOUR LINE	SURV CON LN	
DENSE FOREST	DN FR		ESTIMATED CONTOUR	EST CON	
SPACED TREES	SP TR		FENCE	FN	
TALL GRASS	TL GRS		RAILROAD TRACKS	RR TRK	
LARGE STONES	LRG ST		PAVED ROAD	PV RD	
SAND	SND		UNPAVED ROAD	UNPV RD	
DRY CRACKED CLAY	DRY CRK CLY		POWER LINE	POW LN	

NAME	ABBREV	SYMBOL	NAME	ABBREV	SYMBOL
POWER TRANSMISSION LINE	PW TR LN		BOUNDRY, LAND GRANT	BND LD GR	
GENERAL LINE LABEL TYPE	GN LN	oil line	BOUNDRY, U.S. LAND SURVEY TOWNSHIP	BND US LD SUR TWN	
WELL LABEL TYPE	WL	oil	BOUNDRY, TOWNSHIP APPROXIMATED	BND TWN	
TANK LABEL TYPE	TK	water	BOUNDRY, SECTION LINE U.S. LAND SURVEY	BND SEC LN US LD SUR	
MINING AREA	MIN AR		BOUNDRY, SECTION LINE APPROXIMATED	BND SEC LN	
SHAFT	SHF		BOUNDRY, TOWNSHIP NOT U.S. LAND SURVEY	BND TWN	
TUNNEL ENTRANCE	TUN ENT		INDICATION CORNER SECTION	COR SEC	
BOUNDRY, STATE	BND ST		BOUNDRY MONUMENT	BND MON	
BOUNDRY, COUNTY	BND CNTY		U.S. MINERAL OR LOCATION MONUMENT	U.S. MIN MON	
BOUNDRY, TOWN	BND TWN		DEPRESSION CONTOURS	DEP CONT	
BOUNDRY, CITY INCORPORATED	BND CTY		FILL	FL	
BOUNDRY, NATIONAL OR STATE RESERVATION	BND NAT OR ST RES		CUT	CT	
BOUNDRY, SMALL AREAS: PARKS, AIRPORTS, ETC.	BND		LEVEE	LEV	

NAME	ABBREV	SYMBOL	NAME	ABBREV	SYMBOL
WATER LINE	WT LN		IMPROVED LIGHT DUTY ROAD	IMP LT DTY RD	
GAS LINE	G LN		TRAIL UNIMPROVED DIRT ROAD	TRL UNIM DRT RD	
SANITARY SEWER	SAN SW		ROAD UNDER CONSTRUCTION	RD CONST	
SEWER TILE	SW TL		BRIDGE OVER ROAD	BRG OV RD	
SEPTIC-FIELD LEACH LINE	SP FLD LCH LN		RAILROAD TUNNEL	RR TUN	
PROPERTY CORNER WITH ELEVATION	PROP CR EL	EL 70.5	ROAD OVERPASS	RD OVP	
SPOT ELEVATION	SP EL	+ 78.8	ROAD UNDERPASS	RD UNP	
WATER ELEVATION	WT EL	80	SMALL DAM	SM DA	
BENCH MARKS WITH ELEVATIONS	BM/EL	BM X 84.2 BM △ 84.2	LARGE DAM WITH LOCK	LRG DM LK	
HARD-SURFACE HEAVY DUTY ROAD — FOUR OR MORE LANES	HRD SUR HY DTY RD		BUILDINGS	BLDGS	
HARD-SURFACE HEAVY DUTY ROAD — 2 OR 3 LANES	HRD SUR HY DTY RD		SCHOOL	SCH	
HARD-SURFACE MEDIUM DUTY ROAD — FOUR OR MORE LANES	HRD SUR MED DTY RD		CHURCH	CH	
HARD-SURFACE MEDIUM DUTY ROAD — 2 OR 3 LANES	HRD SUR MED DTY RD		CEMETARY	CEM	† CEM

NAME	ABBREV	SYMBOL	NAME	ABBREV	SYMBOL
LEVEE WITH ROAD	LV RD		LAKE, INTERMITTEN	LK INT	
MINE DUMP	MN DP		LAKE, DRY	LK DRY	
RIVER	RV		REEF	RF	
STREAM PRENNIAL	ST PRE		SOUNDING WATER DEPTH CURVE	SND WT DPT CUR	30
STREAM INTERMITTENT	ST INT		EXPOSED WRECK	EX WRK	
AQUEDUCT ELEVATED	AQ EL		SUNKEN WRECK	SUN WRK	
AQUEDUCT TUNNEL	AQ TUN		EXPOSED ROCK IN WATER	EX RK WK	
STREAM DISAPPEARING	ST DIS		EXPOSED ROCK NAVIGATION DANGER	EX RK NAV DAN	
SMALL RAPIDS	SM RP		SPRING	SP	
SMALL WATER FALL	SM WT FL		PILINGS	PLG	
LARGE RAPIDS	LRG RP		CANAL WITH LOCK	CN LK	
WASH	WSH		SWAMP	SWP	
LARGE WATER FALL	LRG WT FL		SHORELINE	SH LN	

GUIDES FOR DRAWING SURVEYS

The numbered arrows in Fig. 45-3 correspond to the following guides for preparing survey drawings:

1 Record the elevation above the datum of the lot at each corner.
2 Represent the size and location of streams and rivers by wavy lines (blue lines on geographical surveys).
3 Use a cross to show the position of existing trees. The elevation at the base of the trunk is shown.
4 Indicate the compass direction of each property line by degrees, minutes, and seconds. Figure 45-4 shows the relationship of each property-line compass direction to the compass orientation of the lot.
5 Use a north arrow to show compass direction.
6 Break contour lines to insert the height of contour above the datum.
7 Show lot corners by small circles.
8 Draw the property line by using a heavy line with two dashes repeated throughout.
9 Show elevations above the datum or sea level by contour lines (brown lines on geographical survey maps—see Fig. 45-18).
10 Show any proposed change in grade line by dotted contour lines. Figure 45-5 shows how a lot is planned for recontour and how the recontour lines are established to show new heights above the datum.
11 Show lot dimensions directly on the property line. The dimension on each line indicates the distance between corners.
12 Give the names of owners of adjacent lots outside the property line. The name of the owner of the property is shown inside the property line.
13 Dimension the distance from the property line to all utility lines.
14 Show the position of utility lines by dotted lines. Utility lines are labeled according to their function.

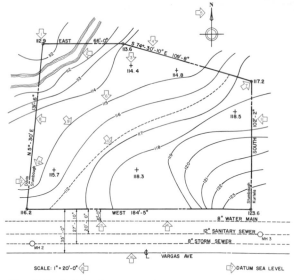

Fig 45-3 Guides for preparing survey plans.

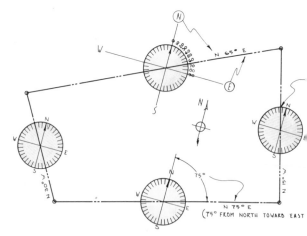

Fig 45-4 An azimuth projection.

15 Draw surveys with an engineer's scale. Common scales for surveys are 1″ = 10′—0″ and 1″ = 20′—0″.
16 Show existing streets and roads either by center lines or by curb or surface outlines.
17 Indicate the datum level used as reference for the survey.

LOT LAYOUT

The size and shape of lots can be determined by several different methods. However,

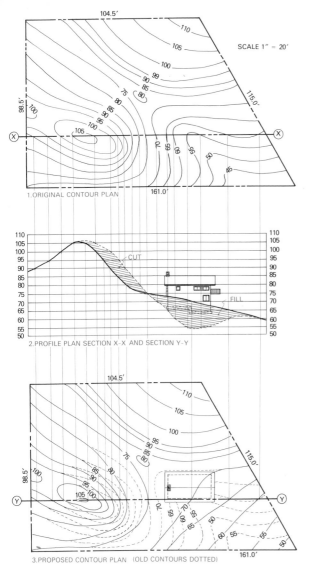

SCALE 1" = 20'

1.ORIGINAL CONTOUR PLAN

CUT

FILL

2.PROFILE PLAN SECTION X-X AND SECTION Y-Y

3.PROPOSED CONTOUR PLAN   (OLD CONTOURS DOTTED)

Fig 45-5 Recontour lines show grade changes.

LOT DIMENSIONS

The exact shape of the lot is shown by the property line. The property line is dimensioned by its length and angle. The angle of each property line from north is known as an *azimuth*. Figure 45-4 shows how the azimuth of each line is determined with a compass or protractor. In Fig. 45-4, on the upper property line, **N** indicates that the bearing of that property line reads from north; 65° means that the property is 65° from north; **E** means that the line is between north and east. Hence, **N 65° E** means 65° from north heading east.

The angle of the property line is established by intersecting the property line with the center of the compass when the compass needle is aligned with north. The degree of the angle of this property line is then read on the circumference of the compass, as shown in Fig. 45-6.

TRANSIT METHOD

Surveyors use a transit to establish the angle (azimuth) of each property line. The *transit* is a telescope that can be set at any desired angle. Once an angle is set, the line may be projected to a rod at any visible distance, as shown in Fig. 45-7. A second line can then be projected by rotating the transit to the desired angle between the property lines. The

Fig 45-6 Property-line angles are read on the circumference of the compass.

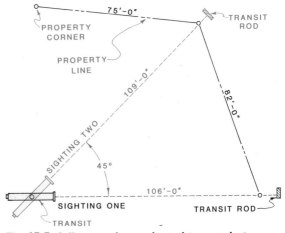

Fig 45-7 A line can be projected to a rod at any visible distance.

the methods of dimensioning lots are the same.

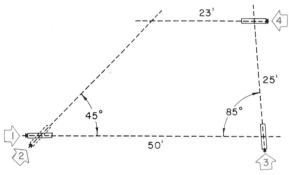

Fig 45-8 The sequence of establishing the angle and length of each property line.

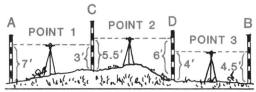

Fig 45-9A Establishing height with a level.

Fig 45-9B Projecting several elevations from one point.

tance. In Fig. 45-9A, position A is ½' higher than position B. Figure 45-9B shows how several elevations can be projected from one known point. For example, if position A is a known value above the datum, a level line can be projected to position C. By measuring any distance up on point C, a level line can be established between C and D, and likewise between D and B. Figure 45-9C shows what the surveyor sees as he or she looks through the level and determines the elevation on a rod.

Fig 45-9C A view of a rod through a level.

rotation and projection are shown in position 2, Fig. 45-7.

In measuring the length of each property line, surveyors use a steel tape or chain. Figure 45-8 shows the sequence of using the transit and chain to establish the angle and the length of each property line. Step 1 shows the projection of a line 50' long. Step 2 shows the rotation of an angle 45° from this line. Step 3 shows a line projected 85° from the other end of the first line at a distance of 25'. Step 4 shows the projection to intersect the line established in step 2. This is called *closing*.

Heights of various parts of the line are established by sighting through a level from a known to an unknown distance. Figure 45-9 shows how a level is used to measure a distance from the known to an unknown dis-

To establish levels with the transit, the surveyor sets up the instrument so that all points can be seen through the telescope. The reading from the rod on the cross hairs is recorded. The rod is then moved to the second position to be established. The rod is raised or lowered until the original reading is located. The bottom of the rod is then on the same level with the original point.

To find the difference in elevation between two points, such as points A and B in Fig. 45-9A, sight on a rod held over point A. Note the reading where the horizontal cross hairs of the telescope cut the graduation on the rod. Then with the rod held at point B, rotate the telescope in a horizontal plane. Again sight on the rod. Note where the horizontal cross hairs cut the graduation on the rod. The difference between reading A (6') and reading B (6½') will give the difference in elevation between the two points. The ground at point B is ½' lower than at point A.

When you cannot find the difference in elevation of two points by keeping the transit in one place, several different points must be used. This was shown in Fig. 45-9B.

PLANE-TABLE METHOD

The plane-table method is an alternative method of plot layout. This method is less accurate than the transit method since it relies on the unaided eye and not on a graduated telescope. Furthermore, this method is generally used to draw a lot that has been established rather than to lay out a lot.

The *plane table* is a drawing board mounted on a tripod. The plane table is placed on a starting point, as shown in step 1, Fig. 45-10. The first line is established by sighting from corner A to corner B. The distance from corner A to corner B is then measured and drawn to scale on the plane table. Next, the line AE is drawn by sighting from the starting point A to corner E.

In step 2, the plane table is moved to a point over corner B. Line AB is kept in the same position. Line BC is then established by sighting from corner B to corner C and measuring this distance. Step 3 establishes line CD by moving the plane table to corner C and sighting to corner D. Step 4 completes the layout by sighting from corner D back to corner E.

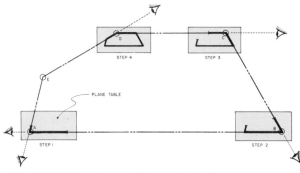

Fig 45-10 The plane-table method of property-line layout.

CONTOUR LINES

Show the various heights of the lot above an established plane known as the *datum*. Sea level is the universal datum line, although many municipalities have established datum points to aid surveyors. The datum is always zero.

Contour lines result from an imaginary cut made through the terrain at regular intervals. Figure 45-11 shows how this cut forms contour lines. The *contour interval*, or the vertical distance between contour lines, can be any convenient distance. It is usually an increment of 5'. Contour intervals of 5', 10', 15', and 20' are common on large surveys. The use of smaller contour intervals gives a more accurate description of the slope and shape of the terrain than does the use of larger intervals.

Land on any part of a contour line has the same altitude, or height, above the datum. Contour lines are therefore always continuous. The area intersected by contour lines may be so vast that the lines may go off the

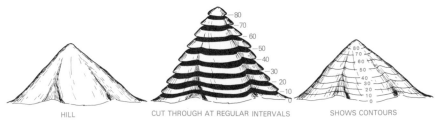

Fig 45-11 Contour lines result from imaginary cuts made through the terrain.

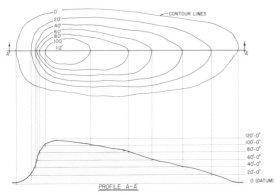

Fig 45-12 The projection of a profile from contour lines.

drawing. However, if a larger geographical area were drawn, the lines would ultimately meet and close. Figure 45-12 shows how contours are projected from a profile through a hill. Contour lines that are very close together indicate a very steep slope. Contour lines that are far apart indicate a more gradual slope.

Surveyors often note elevation heights on a grid, as shown in Fig. 45-13A. This can be done easily in the field. A drafter can then use these grid heights to prepare a contour map, as shown in Fig. 45-13B. For example, the 4200-foot contour line (see Fig. 45-13B) represents the location on the drawing that is at a level 4200 feet above the datum. Follow the 4200-foot intersection points shown in Fig. 45-13A and you will see how the contour map was developed. A profile of part of the contour map is shown in Fig. 45-13C.

GEOGRAPHICAL SURVEYS

Geographical survey maps are similar to surveys except that they cover extremely large areas. The entire world is divided into geographical survey regions. However, not all these regions have been surveyed. When large areas are to be covered, a small scale is used. When smaller areas are to be covered, a larger scale—such as 1 to 25,000—can be used. Figure 45-14 shows a typical portion of a geographical survey map. Geographical survey maps show the general contour of the area,

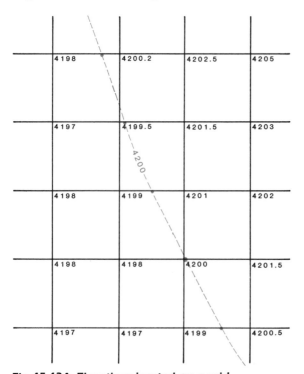

Fig 45-13A Elevations located on a grid.

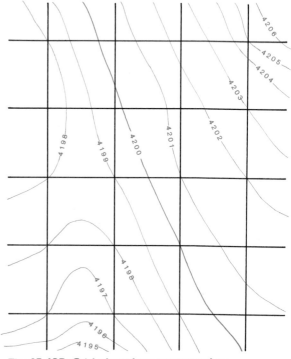

Fig 45-13B Grid elevations converted to contour lines.

natural features of the terrain, and constructed features.

PLAT PLANS

Plat plans are outlines of land subdivisions. They may be of home developments, industrial parks, or urban neighborhoods. They show the size and shape of each parcel of property in the area.

There is a regular pattern of dividing and subdividing each geographical survey region. The survey region is subdivided into township grids that are 24 square miles large. Then each township grid is divided into 16, 6-square-mile, townships. Each township is further divided into 36, 1-square-mile, sections. Figure 45-15 shows the division of township grids into townships. It also shows one township divided into sections.

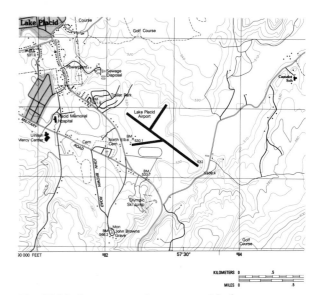

Fig 45-14 A segment of a geographical survey map.

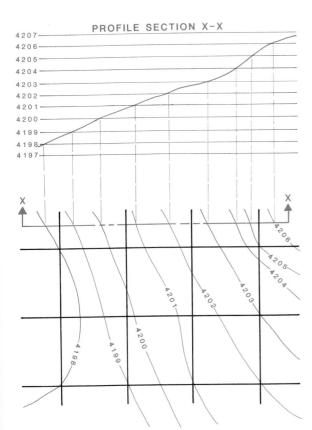

Fig 45-13C A profile section projected from contour lines.

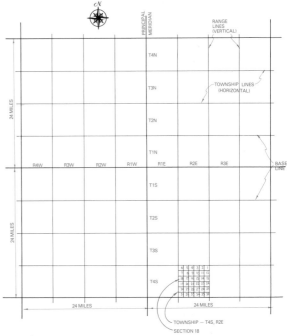

Fig 45-15 Division of township grids.

Plat plans are further subdivisions of township sections and are identified by sections. Plat plans are identified in the following order: name of plat, section, township, county, state.

309

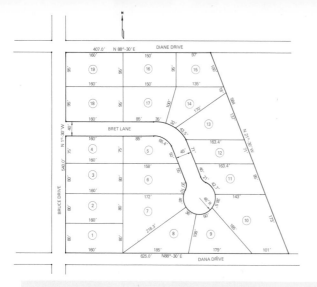

Plat plans are located from a specific corner of a particular section in order to identify the plat in relation to the entire township grid. The dimensions of grid properties within the plat are described in the identical manner in which survey plans describe individual lots (Fig. 45-16).

Fig 45-16 Dimensions of grid properties.

PROBLEMS

1 Make a survey of a lot in your neighborhood, using the plane-table method.
2 Use a compass to find the azimuth of streets that surround your home.
3 Select a lot in your community suitable for a home site and prepare a survey of this property.
4 Find what the established datum for your community is.
5 Determine the azimuth of each property line shown in Fig. 45-17. Use a protractor or compass.

6 What is the contour interval used in Fig. 45-17?
7 Draw a profile for the area shown by the cutting plane line in Fig. 45-18.

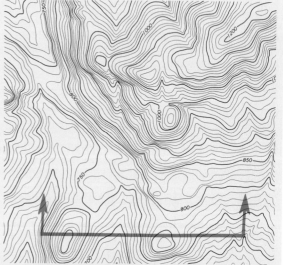

Fig 45-18 Draw a profile of this area.

8 Draw a survey of the ideal property on which you would build the home of your design.
9 Identify the following terms: *survey, contour lines, lot cornice, dotted contour lines, utility lines, azimuth bearing, transit, angle, surveyor, plane table, contour interval, geographical surveys.*

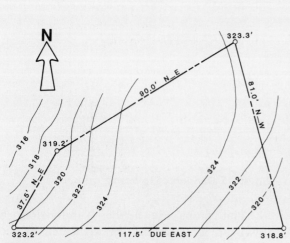

Fig 45-17 Determine the azimuth of each property line.

SECTIONAL DRAWINGS

Sectional drawings reveal the internal construction of an object. Architectural sectional drawings are prepared for the entire structure (full sections), or are prepared for specific parts of the building (detail sections). The size and complexity of the part usually determines the type of section.

UNIT 46
FULL SECTIONS

Architects frequently prepare drawings that show a building cut in half. Their purpose is to show how the building is constructed. These drawings are known as *longitudinal* or *transverse sections*. *Longitudinal* means lengthwise. A longitudinal section is one showing a lengthwise cut through the house. *Transverse* means across. A transverse section is one showing a cut across the building.

Transverse and longitudinal sections have the same outlines as the elevation drawings of the building. Figure 46-1 is a section cut parallel to the short axis of the building. Figure 46-2 is a section cut parallel to the major axis of the building.

THE CUTTING PLANE

The *cutting plane* is an imaginary plane that passes through the building. The position of the cutting plane is shown by the cutting-

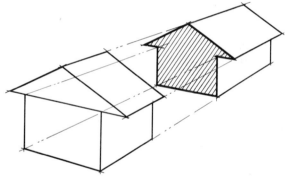

Fig 46-1 A transverse section through the minor axis of the building.

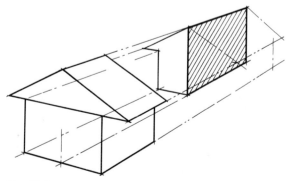

Fig 46-2 A longitudinal section through the major axis of the building.

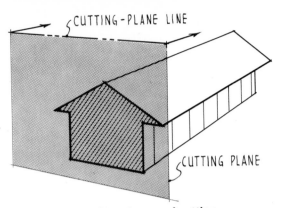

Fig 46-3 The cutting plane and cutting-plane line.

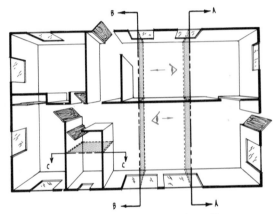

Fig 46-4 Arrows on the cutting-plane line determine the position from which these sections are viewed.

Fig 46-5 The alternative method of drawing cutting-plane lines.

plane line. The cutting-plane line is made up of a long heavy line followed by two dashes. Figure 46-3 shows a cutting-plane line and the cutting plane it represents. The cutting-plane line is placed in the part to be sectioned, and the arrows at its ends show the direction from which the section is to be viewed. For example, in Fig. 46-4, section BB would be viewed from the right; section AA would be viewed from the left.

The cutting-plane line often interferes with dimensions, notes, and details. An alternate method of drawing cutting-plane lines is used to overcome this interference. The alternate method is shown in Fig. 46-5. Notice that only the extremes of the cutting-plane line are used. The cutting-plane line is then *assumed to be a straight line* between these extremes.

When a cutting-plane line must be offset to show a different area, the offsetting corners are drawn as shown in Fig. 46-6. The *offset cutting plane* is often used to show different wall sections on one sectional drawing.

SYMBOLS

Section-lining symbols sometimes represent the way building materials look when they are cut through. Many, however, are purely symbolic in order to conserve time on the drawing board. A floor-plan drawing is actually a horizontal section. Many of the symbols used in floor plans also apply to longitudinal sections. However, there are some materials that are only found in longitudinal sections. Symbols for many building materials are shown in Fig. 46-7.

A building material is only sectioned when the cutting-plane line passes through it. The outline of all other materials visible behind the plane of projection must also be drawn in the proper position and scale.

Figure 46-8 shows various building materials as they appear in a transverse section across the gable end of a residence. Figure 46-9 shows the same building materials as they appear on a longitudinal section.

Because full sections show the construction method used in the entire building, they

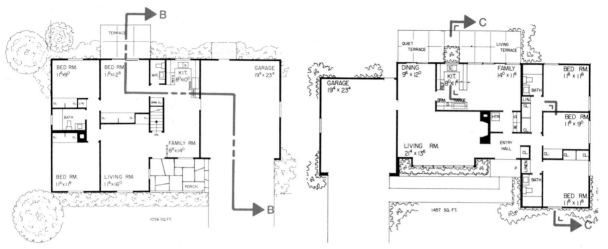

Fig 46-6 The use of an offset cutting-plane line.

must be drawn to a relatively small scale. The use of this small scale often makes the drawing and interpretation of minute details extremely difficult or impossible. Removed detail sections are often used to eliminate this problem as shown in Fig. 46-10.

STEPS IN DRAWING FULL SECTIONS

In drawing full sections, the architect actually constructs the framework of a house on paper. Figure 46-11 shows the progressive

NAME	ABBRV	SECTION SYMBOL	ELEVATION	NAME	ABBRV	SECTION SYMBOL	ELEVATION
EARTH	E			CUT STONE, ASHLAR	CT STN ASH		
ROCK	RK			CUT STONE, ROUGH	CT STN RGH		
SAND	SD			MARBLE	MARB		
GRAVEL	GV			FLAGSTONE	FLG ST		
CINDERS	CIN			CUT SLATE	CT SLT		
AGGREGATE	AGR			RANDOM RUBBLE	RND RUB		
CONCRETE	CONC			LIMESTONE	LM ST		
CEMENT	CEM			CERAMIC TILE	CER TL		
TERAZZO CONCRETE	TER CONC			TERRA-COTTA TILE	TC TL		
CONCRETE BLOCK	CONC BLK			STRUCTURAL CLAY TILE	ST CL TL		
CAST BLOCK	CST BLK			TILE SMALL SCALE	TL		
CINDER BLOCK	CIN BLK			GLAZED FACE HOLLOW TILE	GLZ FAC HOL TL		
TERRA-COTTA BLOCK LARGE SCALE	TC BLK			TERRA-COTTA BLOCK SMALL SCALE	TC BLK		

NAME	ABBRV	SECTION SYMBOL	ELEVATION	NAME	ABBRV	SECTION SYMBOL	ELEVATION
COMMON BRICK	COM BRK			WELDED WIRE MESH	WWM		
FACE BRICK	FC BRK			FABRIC	FAB		
FIREBRICK	FRB			LIQUID	LQD		
GLASS	GL			COMPOSITION SHINGLE	COMP SH		
GLASS BLOCK	GL BLK			RIDGID INSULATION SOLID	RDG INS		
STRUCTURAL GLASS	STRUC GL			LOOSE-FILL INSULATION	LF INS		
FROSTED GLASS	FRST GL			QUILT	QLT		
STEEL	STL			SOUND INSULATION	SND INS		
CAST IRON	CST IR			CORK INSULATION	CRK INS		
BRASS & BRONZE	BRS BRZ			PLASTER WALL	PLST WL		
ALUMINUM	AL			PLASTER BLOCK	PLST BLK		
SHEET METAL (FLASHING)	SHT MTL FLASH			PLASTER WALL AND METAL LATHE	PLST WL & MT LTH		
REINFORCING STEEL BARS	REBAR			PLASTER WALL AND CHANNEL STUDS	PLST WL & CHN STD		

Fig 46-7 Some common sectional symbols.

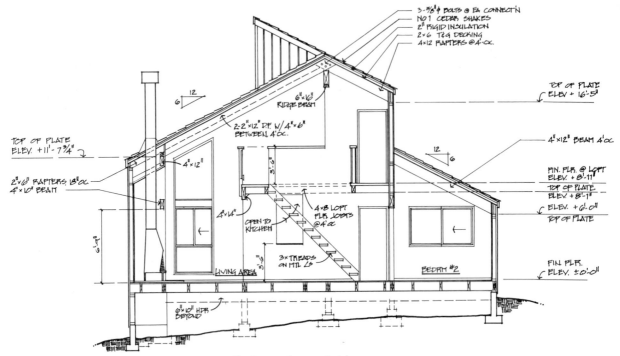

Fig 46-8 A section of a house, perpendicular to the roof ridge.

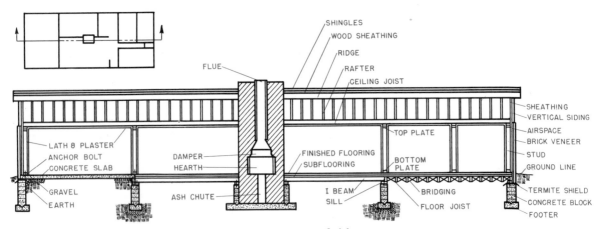

Fig 46-9 A section through a house, parallel with the roof ridge.

steps in the layout and drawing of a gable-end section:

1 Lightly draw the floor line approximately at the middle of the drawing sheet.

2 Measure the thickness of the subfloor and of the joist and draw lines representing these under the floor line.

3 From the floor line, measure up and draw the ceiling line.

4 Measure down from the floor line to establish the top of the basement slab and footer line, and draw in the thickness of the footer.

5 Draw two vertical lines representing the thickness of the foundation and the footer.

6 Construct the sill detail and show the alignment of the stud and top plate.

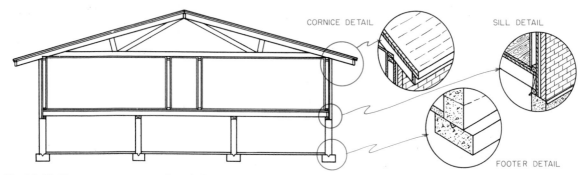

Fig 46-10 Three common sectional details are the cornice, sill, and footer.

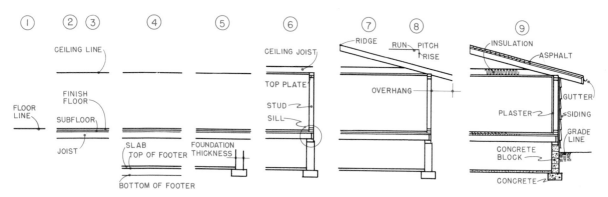

Fig 46-11 The sequence of projecting an elevation section.

7 Measure the overhang from the stud line and draw the roof pitch by projecting from the top plate on the angle that represents the rise over the run.

8 Establish the ridge point by measuring the distance from the outside wall horizontally to the center of the structure.

9 Add details and symbols representing siding and interior finish.

SECTIONAL DIMENSIONING

Since full sections expose the size and shape of building materials and components not revealed on floor plans and elevations, these sections are an excellent place on which to locate many detail dimensions. Full-section dimensions primarily show specific elevations, distances, and the exact size of building materials.

Figure 46-12 shows some of the more important dimensions that can be placed on full sections. The rules for dimensioning elevation

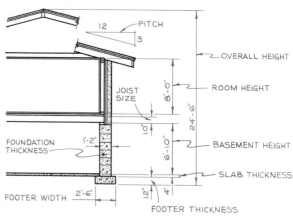

Fig 46-12 Methods of dimensioning elevation sections.

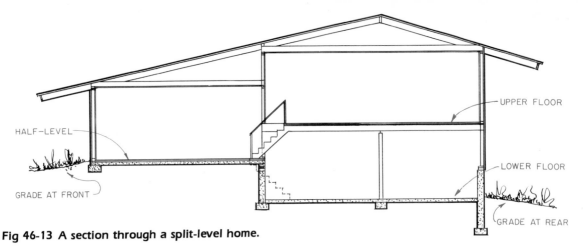

Fig 46-13 A section through a split-level home.

CLERESTORY (VIEW OF SKY, LETS IN LIGHT, CUTS ELECTRICAL COSTS)

SOLAR PANELS (STORAGE IS IN BACK TRIANGLE)

BALCONY (VIEW OF TOTAL LOT)

CONCEALED DRAINAGE AND SPOUT (PERFORATED PIPE W/2% SLOPE)

PATIO; QUARRIED FROM SITE

CONCRETE 1" OVER DECK

METAL DECK; AIR POCKETS REDUCE SOUND
RWF STEEL BEAM (60K) #12

PLANTER

ELEV. 17.5 M

VENTILATION

DRAIN W/CATCH BASIN

DRAIN

4" CONCRETE SLAB

6" DRAIN TILE (TYP.)

Fig 46-14 Full section without structural details.

drawings apply also to full elevation sections (see Unit 38).

MULTILEVEL SECTIONS

Full sections are especially effective and necessary for showing the various methods of constructing multilevel buildings, since footers, grade lines, slabs, and floor lines vary greatly. Figure 46-13 shows a section of a split-level home. It is difficult to show the re-

lationship of the various levels and the construction of each without using this kind of section.

NONTECHNICAL SECTIONS

Full sections without structural details or dimensions, as shown in Fig. 46-14, are used to show size and proportional relationships. Notice how cars and people relate the size of the structure to the various design features.

PROBLEMS

1 Draw a full section of a house you have designed.
2 Draw a full section of your home.
3 Draw a full section of your schoolroom.
4 Draw and dimension a longitudinal section AA of the plan shown in Fig. 46-15.
5 Draw section BB, Fig. 46-15.
6 Identify the symbols found in Fig. 46-16.
7 Define these terms: *longitudinal section, transverse section, cutting plane, offset cutting plane, section lining, full section.*

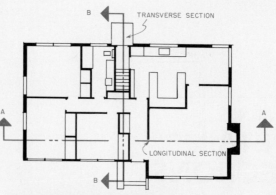

Fig 46-15 Draw and dimension sections AA and BB.

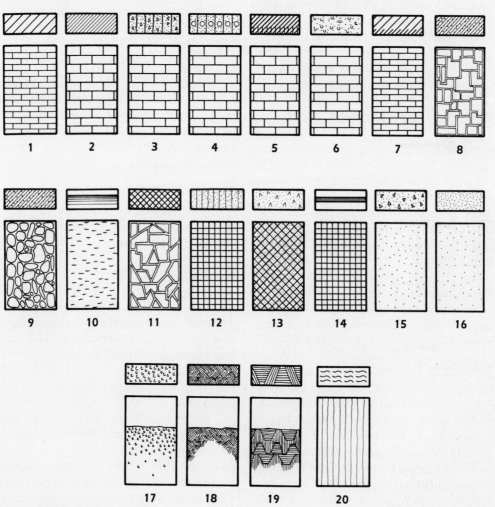

Fig 46-16 Identify these materials.

317

UNIT 47
DETAIL SECTIONS

Because full sections of a floor plan are usually drawn to a small scale ($\frac{1}{8}'' = 1'-0''$ or $\frac{1}{4}'' = 1'-0''$), many parts are difficult to interpret and dimension. In order to reveal the exact position and size of many small members, the drafter needs an enlarged section.

VERTICAL WALL SECTIONS

One method of showing sections larger than is possible in the full section is through the use of *break lines*. Break lines are used to reduce vertical distances on exterior walls. Using break lines allows the drafter to draw the area larger than is possible when the entire distance is included in the drawing. Break lines are placed where the material does not change over a long distance. Figure 47-1 shows the difference between a brick-veneer wall drawn completely to a small scale and the same wall enlarged by the use of break lines. Figure 47-2 shows the use of break lines to enlarge a frame-wall section.

Some sections need to be drawn for interpretation or dimensioning. Sometimes, it is impossible to draw an entire wall section to a large enough scale, even when using break lines. When that is the case, you draw a removed section. A *removed section* is one drawn away from the original location on the same sheet or on another sheet. Removed sections are frequently drawn for the ridge, cornice, sill, footer, and beam areas, as shown in Fig. 47-3.

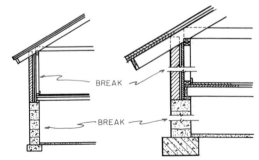

Fig 47-1 Sections can be drawn larger when break lines are used.

CORNICE SECTIONS

Figure 47-4 shows several typical cornice sections and the pictorial interpretation of each. *Cornice sections* are used to show the relationship between the outside wall, top plate, and rafter construction. Some cornice sections show gutter details.

SILL SECTIONS

Sill sections, as shown in Fig. 47-5, show how the foundation supports and intersects with the floor system and the outside wall.

FOOTER SECTIONS

A *footer section* is needed to show the width and length of the footer, the type of material used, and the position of the foundation wall on the footer. Figure 47-6 shows several footer details and the pictorial interpretation of each type.

BEAM DETAILS

Beam details are necessary to show how the joists are supported by beams and how the beams support columns or foundation walls. As in all other sections, the position of the cutting-plane line is extremely important. Figure 47-7 shows two possible positions of the cutting plane. If the cutting-plane line is placed parallel to the beam, you see a cross section of

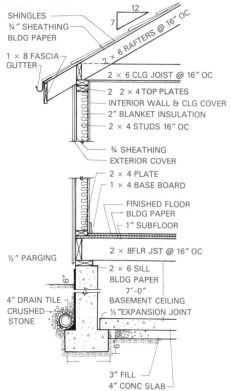

SHINGLES
¾" SHEATHING
BLDG PAPER
12
7
2 × 6 RAFTERS @ 16" OC
1 × 8 FASCIA
GUTTER
2 × 6 CLG JOIST @ 16" OC
2 2 × 4 TOP PLATES
INTERIOR WALL & CLG COVER
2" BLANKET INSULATION
2 × 4 STUDS 16" OC
¾ SHEATHING
EXTERIOR COVER
2 × 4 PLATE
1 × 4 BASE BOARD
FINISHED FLOOR
BLDG PAPER
1" SUBFLOOR
2 × 8FLR JST @ 16" OC
½" PARGING
2 × 6 SILL
BLDG PAPER
7'-0"
BASEMENT CEILING
½"EXPANSION JOINT
4" DRAIN TILE
CRUSHED
STONE
3" FILL
4" CONC SLAB

Fig 47-2 The use of break lines on a frame-wall section.

the joist, as shown at A. If the cutting-plane line is placed perpendicular to the beam, you see a cross section of the beam, as shown at B. Figure 47-8 shows a similar section through a built-up wood girder.

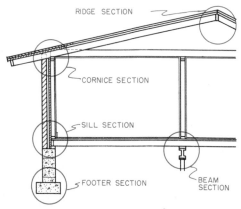

RIDGE SECTION
CORNICE SECTION
SILL SECTION
FOOTER SECTION
BEAM SECTION

Fig 47-3 Removed sections are often drawn of the ridge, cornice, sill, footer, and beam areas.

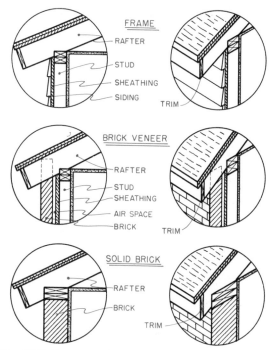

FRAME
RAFTER
STUD
SHEATHING
SIDING
TRIM

BRICK VENEER
RAFTER
STUD
SHEATHING
AIR SPACE
BRICK
TRIM

SOLID BRICK
RAFTER
BRICK
TRIM

Fig 47-4 Compare the pictorial section with the orthographic section.

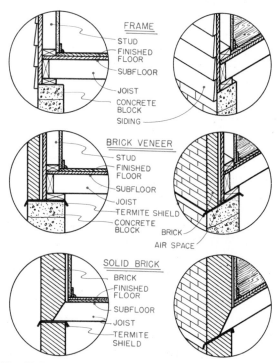

FRAME
STUD
FINISHED FLOOR
SUBFLOOR
JOIST
CONCRETE BLOCK
SIDING

BRICK VENEER
STUD
FINISHED FLOOR
SUBFLOOR
JOIST
TERMITE SHIELD
CONCRETE BLOCK
BRICK
AIR SPACE

SOLID BRICK
BRICK
FINISHED FLOOR
SUBFLOOR
JOIST
TERMITE SHIELD

Fig 47-5 A comparison of sill sections and the sill constructions they represent.

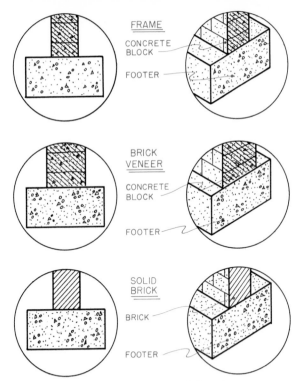

Fig 47-6 A comparison of pictorial and orthographic footer sections.

Sometimes, it is desirable or necessary to show the relationship between the beam detail and a detail of the sill area. This relationship is especially needed when a room is sunken or elevated. In Fig. 47-9, the beam and

sill areas on one sectional drawing are shown by breaking the area between the sill and the beam.

INTERIOR-WALL SECTIONS

To illustrate the methods of constructing inside partitions, sections are often drawn of interior walls at the base and at the ceiling. *Base sections* (Fig. 47-10A) show how the wall-finishing materials are attached to the studs and how the intersection between the floor and wall is constructed. The section at the ceiling, as shown in Fig. 47-10B, is drawn to show the intersection between the ceiling and the wall and to show how the finishing materials of the wall and ceiling are related. Vertical wall sections are also prepared for stair and fireplace details (Fig. 47-11).

HORIZONTAL-WALL SECTIONS

Horizontal-wall sections of interior and exterior walls can be drawn to clarify wall-framing construction.

EXTERIOR WALLS

A floor plan is a horizontal section. However, many details are omitted from the floor plan because of the small scale used. Very few construction details are necessary to interpret

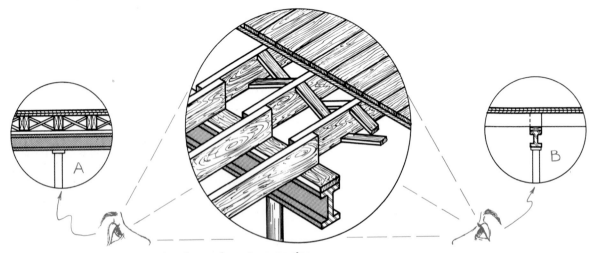

Fig 47-7 Beam sections can be drawn from two angles.

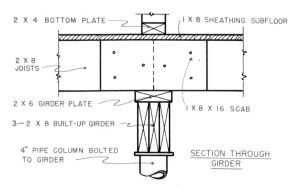

Fig 47-8 A section through a built-up wood girder.

2 X 4 BOTTOM PLATE
1 X 8 SHEATHING SUBFLOOR
2 X 8 JOISTS
2 X 6 GIRDER PLATE
1 X 8 X 16 SCAB
3 — 2 X 8 BUILT-UP GIRDER
SECTION THROUGH GIRDER
4" PIPE COLUMN BOLTED TO GIRDER

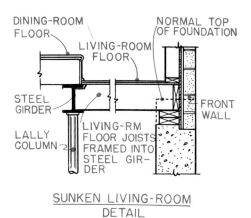

DINING-ROOM FLOOR
NORMAL TOP OF FOUNDATION
LIVING-ROOM FLOOR
STEEL GIRDER
FRONT WALL
LALLY COLUMN
LIVING-RM FLOOR JOISTS FRAMED INTO STEEL GIRDER

SUNKEN LIVING-ROOM DETAIL

Fig 47-9 The beam section and sill section can be shown on the same drawing by use of break lines.

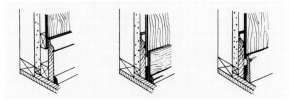

Fig 47-10A Pictorial sections through the base of an interior partition.

Fig 47-10B Pictorial sections at the intersection of interior wall and ceiling.

United States Plywood Corp.

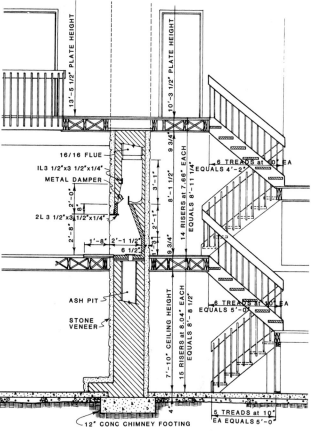

Fig 47-11 Vertical wall section.

adequately the floor plan. If the floor plan is drawn exactly as a true horizontal section, it will appear similar to the sections shown in Fig. 47-12. When more information is needed to describe the exact construction of the outside corners and the intersections between interior partitions and outside walls, horizontal sections of the type shown in Fig. 47-12 are prepared.

INTERIOR-WALL SECTIONS

Typical sections are often drawn of interior-wall intersections. Unusual wall-construction methods are *always* sectioned. For example, a horizontal section is needed to show the inside corner construction of a paneled wall (Fig. 47-13). An outside corner section of paneling construction is shown in Fig. 47-14. Horizontal sections are also used extensively to show how paneled joints and other building joints are constructed (Fig. 47-15).

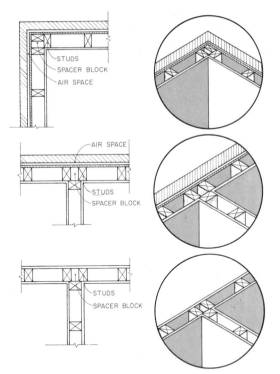

Fig 47-12 Horizontal sections through exterior-wall intersections.

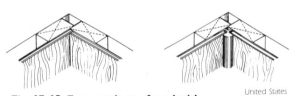

United States
Plywood Corp.

Fig 47-13 Two sections of an inside paneled-wall corner.

United States
Plywood Corp.

Fig 47-14 Two sections of an outside paneled-wall corner.

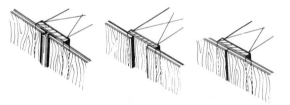

Fig 47-15 Panel-joint details.

Horizontal sections are also very effective in illustrating the various methods of attaching building materials together. For example, the sections shown in Fig. 47-16 illustrate the various methods for attaching furring and paneling to interior walls.

WINDOW SECTIONS

Because much of the actual construction of most windows is hidden, a section is necessary for the correct interpretation of window-construction methods. Figure 47-17 shows the window areas commonly sectioned. These include the head, jamb, and sill construction.

VERTICAL SECTIONS

Sill and head sections are vertical sections that are sometimes prepared in the same drawing. Preparing sill and head sections on the same drawing is possible only when a small scale is used. If a larger scale is needed, the sill and head must be drawn independently, or a break line must be used. Figure 47-18 shows the relationship between the cutting-plane line and the sill and head sections. The circled areas in Fig. 47-19 show the areas that are removed when a separate head and sill section is prepared.

HORIZONTAL SECTIONS

When a cutting-plane line is extended horizontally across the entire window, the resulting sections are known as *jamb sections*. Figure 47-20 shows the method of projecting the jamb details from the window-elevation drawing. Since the construction of both jambs is usually the same, the right jamb drawing is the reverse of the left. Only one jamb detail is normally drawn. The builder interprets the one jamb as the reverse of the other.

COMMERCIAL DETAILS

Many window manufacturers use pictorial sectioning techniques to show the correct installation of windows. The relationship between a manufactured window and the framing methods necessary for correct fitting is shown in Fig. 47-21.

MASONRY WALLS   WOOD FRAME WALLS

WOOD DOWEL
FURRING STRIP,SCREWED, NAILED, OR GLUED
PANELING
ADHESIVE NAIL ANCHOR
FURRING STRIP
PANELING
2×4 STUDS
NAILED GYPSUM BOARD
PANELING
2×4 STUDS
PANELING

Fig 47-16 Methods of attaching paneling shown in section.

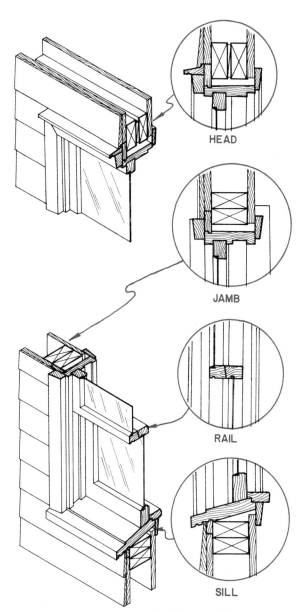

HEAD

JAMB

RAIL

SILL

Fig 47-17 Window head, jamb, and sill sections.

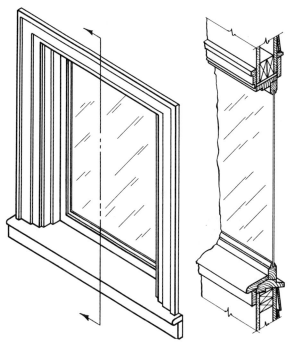

Fig 47-18 Head and sill sections are in the same plane.

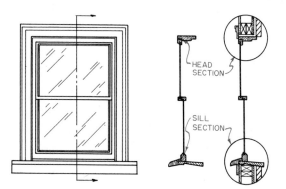

HEAD SECTION

SILL SECTION

Fig 47-19 The projection of the head and sill section.

323

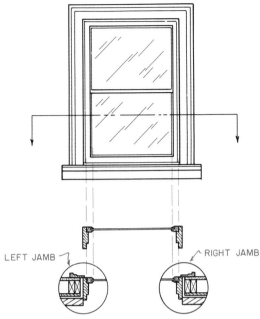

LEFT JAMB   RIGHT JAMB

Fig 47-20 The projection of the left- and right-jamb section.

DOOR SECTIONS

A horizontal section of all doors is shown on a floor plan. However, this section is almost completely symbolic and lacks sufficient detail for installation. An enlarged jamb, head, and sill section, as shown in Fig. 47-22, is necessary to show door-construction methods. When a cutting-plane line is extended vertically through the sill and head, a section similar to the one shown in Fig. 47-23 is revealed. However, these sections are often too small to show the desired degree of detail necessary for construction. A removed section, as shown in Fig. 47-24, is drawn to show the enlarged head and sill sections.

Since doors are normally not as wide as they are high, an adequate jamb detail can be projected, as shown in Fig. 47-25, without the use of break lines or removed sections. Figure 47-26 shows the method of projecting the left and right jamb sections from the door elevation drawing. Occasionally, architectural drafters prepare sectional drawings of the rough framing details of the door head, sill, and jamb, exclusive of the door and door

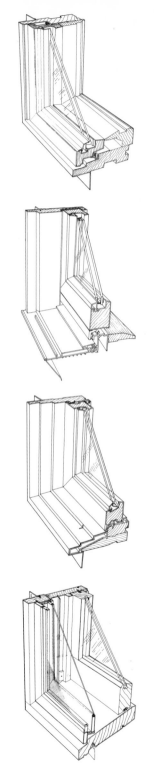

Perma-shield

Fig 47-21 A pictorial section showing sill, jamb, and head details.

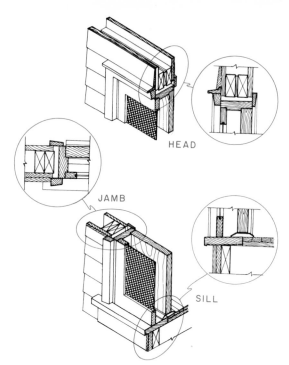

HEAD

JAMB

SILL

Fig 47-22 Head, jamb, and sill details can be removed or drawn pictorially.

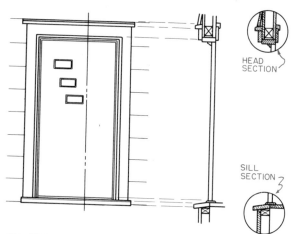

HEAD SECTION

SILL SECTION

Fig 47-24 The projection of the head and sill sections of a door frame.

Fig 47-23 The head and sill sections of a door, in the same plane.

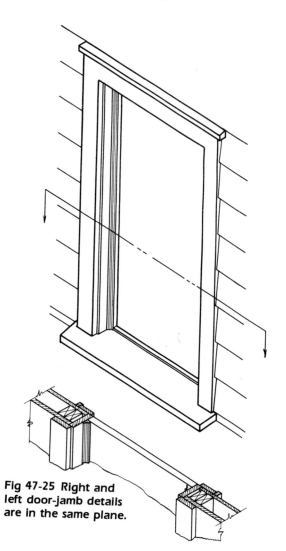

Fig 47-25 Right and left door-jamb details are in the same plane.

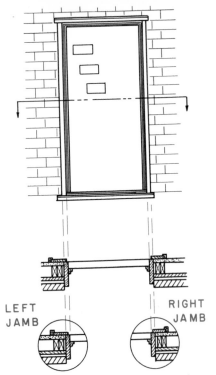

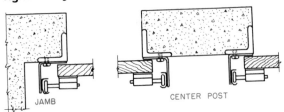

LEFT JAMB   RIGHT JAMB

Fig 47-26 The projection of the left and right door-jamb section.

JAMB   CENTER POST

Fig 47-27 Special brackets and devices often require detailed sectional drawing.

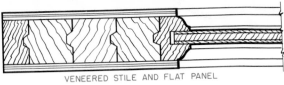

VENEERED STILE AND FLAT PANEL

Fig 47-28 Interior door construction is shown by a sectional drawing.

frame assembly. In such drawings, the drafter draws the framing section with the door frame and door removed. Usually, however, door sections are prepared with the framing trim and door in their proper locations.

Drawings of garage doors and industrial-size doors are usually prepared with sections of the brackets and apparatus necessary to house the door assembly, as shown in Fig. 47-27. This is done even when stock doors are used.

Rarely is the architectural drafter called upon to prepare sectional drawings of internal door-construction details. Most doors are purchased from manufacturers' stock.

Occasionally, doors are supplied by the manufacturer specifically for a building. Only when a special door is to be manufactured is a sectional drawing prepared of the internal detail of the door construction (Fig. 47-28).

PROBLEMS

1 Draw a large cornice, sill, and footer section from the circled sections shown in Fig. 47-3.

2 Draw a section through the girder, as shown in Fig. 47-8, revolving the cutting plane line 90°.

3 Draw a head, jamb, and sill section of a typical window and a typical door of the house you have designed.

4 Draw a sill, cornice, and footer section of the house you have designed.

5 Draw a sill, cornice, and footer section of your home.

6 Prepare an interior-wall section at the ceiling and at the floor line to accompany the section shown in Fig. 47-8.

7 Draw a detail section of the intersection of the inside foundation-support wall, I beam, and interior partition, as shown in Fig. 47-9.

8 Define these terms: *break line, removed section, interior-wall sections, vertical-wall sections, horizontal-wall sections, jamb sections, head sections, sill sections.*

FOUNDATION PLANS

The methods and materials used in constructing foundations vary greatly in different parts of the country and are continually changing. The basic principles of foundation construction are the same, regardless of the application.

Every structure needs a foundation. The function of a foundation is to provide a level and uniformly distributed support for the structure. The foundation must be strong enough to support and distribute the load of the structure, and sufficiently level to prevent the walls from cracking and the doors and windows from sticking. The foundation also helps to prevent cold air and dampness from entering the house. The foundation waterproofs the basement and forms the supporting walls of the basement.

UNIT 48
FOUNDATION MEMBERS

The structural members of the foundation vary according to the design and size of the foundation.

FOOTING

The *footing,* or *footer* (Fig. 48-1), distributes the weight of the house over a large area. Concrete is commonly used for footers because it can be poured to maintain a firm contact with the supporting soil. Concrete is also effective because it can withstand heavy weights and is a relatively decay-proof material. Steel reinforcement is sometimes added to the concrete footer to keep the concrete

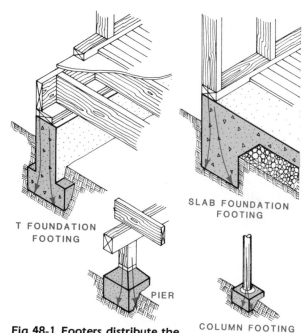

T FOUNDATION FOOTING

SLAB FOUNDATION FOOTING

PIER

COLUMN FOOTING

Fig 48-1 Footers distribute the weight of the building over a wide area.

from cracking and to provide additional support. The footer must be laid on solid ground to support the weight of the building effectively and evenly. In cold climates, the footer must be placed below the frost line.

FOUNDATION WALLS

The function of the *foundation wall* is to support the load of the building above the ground line and to transmit the weight of the house to the footing. Foundation walls are normally made of concrete, stone, brick, or concrete block (Fig. 48-2). When a complete excavation is made for a basement, foundation walls also provide the walls of the basement (Fig. 48-3).

PIERS AND COLUMNS

Piers and *columns* are vertical members, usually made of concrete, brick, steel, or wood. They are used to support the floor systems (Fig. 48-4). Piers or columns may be used as the sole support of the structure. They also may be used in conjunction with the foundation wall and provide only the intermediate support between girders or beams, as shown in Fig. 48-5.

ANCHOR BOLTS

Anchor bolts are embedded in the top of the foundation walls or piers (Fig. 48-6A and B). The exposed part of the bolt is threaded so that the first wood member (the sill) can be bolted onto the top of the foundation wall. Anchor bolts for residential use are ½" (12.7 mm) in diameter and 10" (254 mm) long. They are spaced at approximately 6' (1.8 m) intervals, starting 1' (0.3 m) from each corner.

SILLS

Sills are wood members that are fastened with anchor bolts to the foundation wall (Fig. 48-7). Sills provide the base for attaching the exterior walls to the foundation.

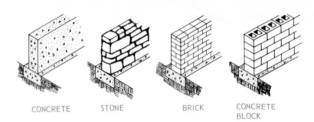

CONCRETE STONE BRICK CONCRETE BLOCK

Fig 48-2 Foundation walls are constructed of concrete, stone, brick, or concrete block.

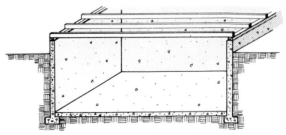

Fig 48-3 A foundation wall can also be a basement wall.

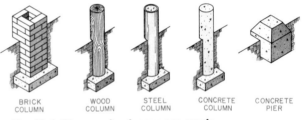

BRICK COLUMN WOOD COLUMN STEEL COLUMN CONCRETE COLUMN CONCRETE PIER

Fig 48-4 Piers and columns are made of concrete, brick, steel, or wood.

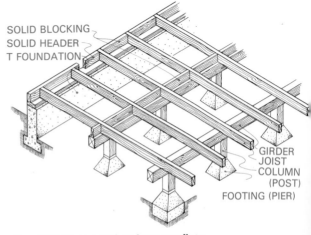

SOLID BLOCKING
SOLID HEADER
T FOUNDATION

GIRDER
JOIST
COLUMN (POST)
FOOTING (PIER)

Fig 48-5 Piers used as intermediate support.

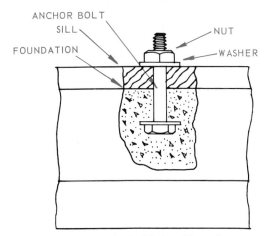

Fig 48-6A Anchor bolts hold the sill to the foundation.

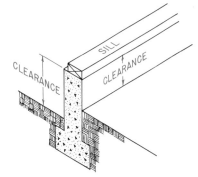

Fig 48-7 The sill is the point of contact between the foundation and the framework of the building.

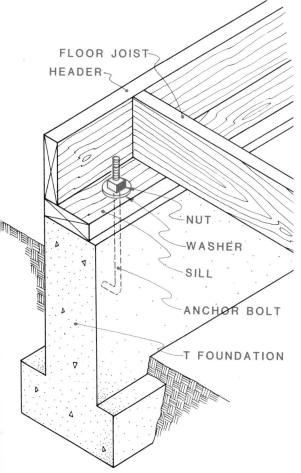

Fig 48-6B Pictorial foundation section showing an anchor bolt.

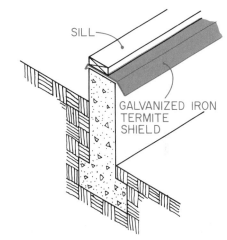

Fig 48-8 Placement of a termite shield between the foundation and the sill protects the wood from termites.

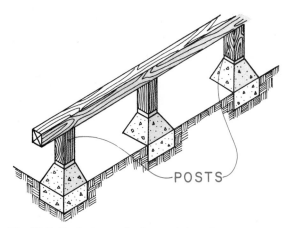

Fig 48-9 Posts transmit the weight of girders and beams to the footings.

329

A galvanized iron sheet is often placed under the sill to check termites (Fig. 48-8), since the sill is normally the lowest wood member used in the construction. Building laws specify the distance required from the bottom of the sill to the grade line inside and outside the foundation.

POSTS

Posts are wood members that support the weight of girders or beams and transmit the weight to the footings (Fig. 48-9).

CRIPPLES

Cripples are used to raise the floor level without the use of a higher foundation wall (Fig. 48-10). Since the load of the structure must be transmitted through the cripples, these are usually heavy members, often four-by-fours (4 × 4's) spaced at close intervals or two-by-fours (2 × 4's) spaced even closer.

GIRDERS

Girders are major horizontal support members upon which the floor system is laid. They are supported by posts and piers and are secured to the foundation wall as shown in Fig. 48-11. Girder sizes are closely regulated by building codes. The allowable span of the girder depends on the size of the girder. A decrease in the size of a girder means that the span must be decreased by adding additional column supports under the girder. Built-up wood girders for residential construction are normally made from 2 × 8's or 2 × 10's spiked together. Figure 48-12 shows a girder intersecting a foundation wall in a girder pocket.

STEEL BEAMS

Steel beams perform the same function as wood girders. However, steel beams can span larger areas than can wood girders of an equivalent size.

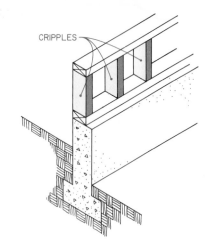

Fig 48-10 Cripples raise the height of a floor without raising the foundation height.

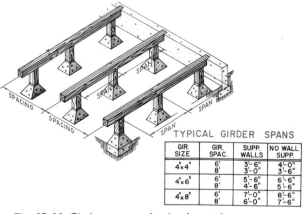

TYPICAL GIRDER SPANS

GIR. SIZE	GIR. SPAC.	SUPP. WALLS	NO WALL SUPP.
4"×4"	6'	3'-6"	4'-0"
	8'	3'-0"	3'-6"
4"×6"	6'	5'-6"	6'-6"
	8'	4'-6"	5'-6"
4"×8"	6'	7'-0"	8'-6"
	8'	6'-0"	7'-6"

Fig 48-11 Girders are major horizontal support members.

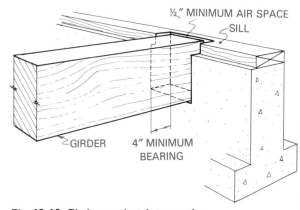

Fig 48-12 Girder pocket intersection.

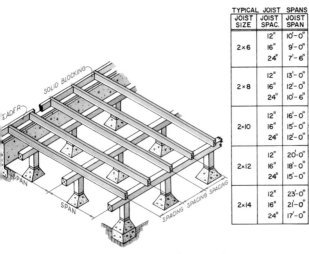

TYPICAL JOIST SPANS		
JOIST SIZE	JOIST SPAC.	JOIST SPAN
2×6	12"	10'-0"
	16"	9'-0"
	24"	7'-6"
2×8	12"	13'-0"
	16"	12'-0"
	24"	10'-6"
2×10	12"	16'-0"
	16"	15'-0"
	24"	12'-0"
2×12	12"	20'-0"
	16"	18'-0"
	24"	15'-0"
2×14	12"	23'-0"
	16"	21'-0"
	24"	17'-0"

Fig 48-13 Joists support the floor and rest on girders.

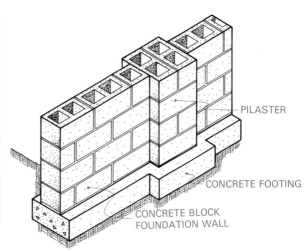

Fig 48-14 Concrete block foundation pilaster.

JOISTS

Joists are the part of the floor system that is placed on the girders. Joists span either from girder to girder or from girder to the foundation wall. The ends of the joists butt against a header or extend to the end of the sill, with blocking placed between them as shown in Fig. 48-13.

PILASTERS

Pilasters are reinforcements in a wall designed to provide more rigidity without increasing the width of the wall over the entire length. Figure 48-14 shows a typical pilaster in a concrete foundation wall. Building codes normally specify the size and spacing of pilasters, depending on the wall width, height, and material.

PROBLEMS

1 Draw a slab-foundation plan to the scale ½" = 1'—0" for the floor plan shown in Fig. 6-2.
2 Draw a T-foundation plan for Fig. 48-15, using the scale ¼" = 1'—0".
3 Draw a slab foundation for Fig. 48-15, using the scale ¼" = 1'—0".
4 Draw the foundation plan for the house you are designing.
5 Know these architectural terms: *foundation, structural members, footing, concrete, foundation wall, pier, column, anchor bolt, sill, post, cripple, girder, span, spacing, joists.*

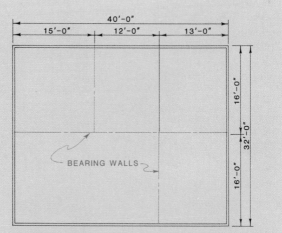

Fig 48-15 Draw a T and/or slab foundation for this plan.

UNIT 49
FOUNDATION TYPES

The type of foundation the architect selects for a structure depends on the nature of the soil, the size and weight of the structure, the climate, building laws, and the relationship of the floor to the grade line (Fig. 49-1). Foundations are divided into three basic types: the T foundation, the slab foundation, and the pier-and-column foundation (Fig. 49-2).

T FOUNDATIONS

The *T foundation* consists of a trench footer upon which is placed a concrete wall or

Fig 49-1 Foundation positions.

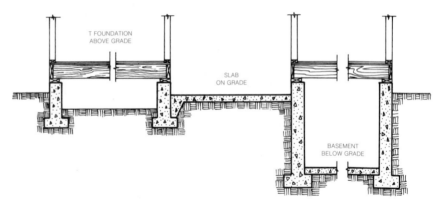

Fig 49-2 Types of foundations.

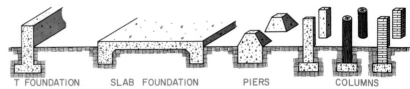

Fig 49-3 T foundation and intermediate supports.

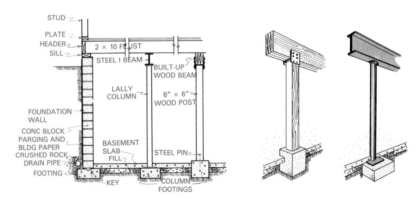

332

Fig 49-4 Elements of a T foundation.

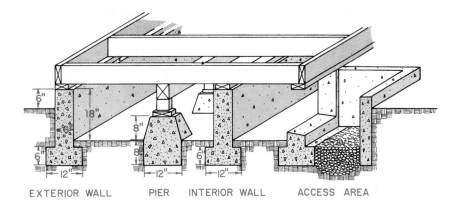

EXTERIOR WALL   PIER   INTERIOR WALL   ACCESS AREA

Fig 49-5 Methods of drawing T-foundation details.

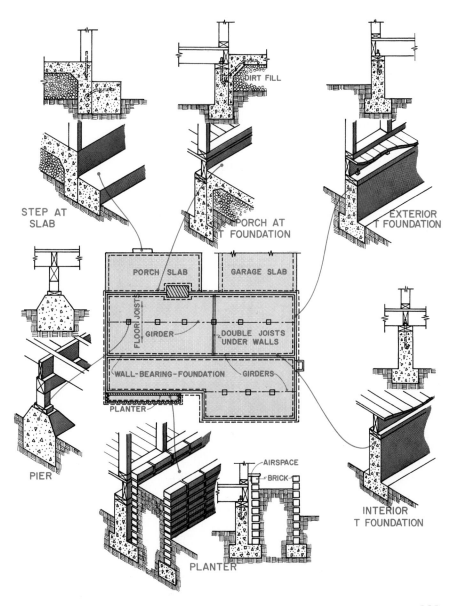

STEP AT SLAB

PORCH AT T FOUNDATION

DIRT FILL

EXTERIOR T FOUNDATION

PIER

PORCH SLAB   GARAGE SLAB

FLOOR JOIST

GIRDER

DOUBLE JOISTS UNDER WALLS

WALL-BEARING-FOUNDATION   GIRDERS

PLANTER

AIRSPACE

BRICK

PLANTER

INTERIOR T FOUNDATION

Fig 49-6 Slab-foundation support methods.

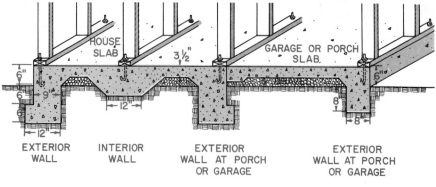

EXTERIOR WALL   INTERIOR WALL   EXTERIOR WALL AT PORCH OR GARAGE   EXTERIOR WALL AT PORCH OR GARAGE

Fig 49-7 Slab-foundation details.

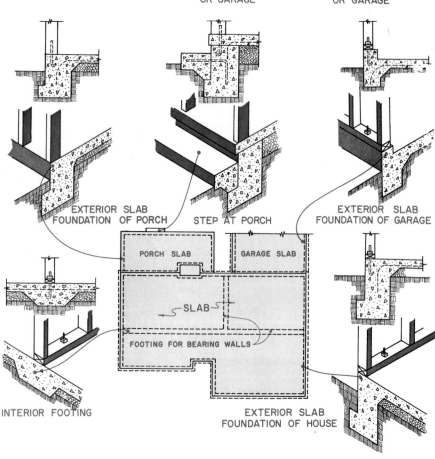

EXTERIOR SLAB FOUNDATION OF PORCH   STEP AT PORCH   EXTERIOR SLAB FOUNDATION OF GARAGE

PORCH SLAB   GARAGE SLAB

SLAB

FOOTING FOR BEARING WALLS

INTERIOR FOOTING

EXTERIOR SLAB FOUNDATION OF HOUSE

a concrete-block wall. The T foundation and intermediate supports is a popular foundation in structures with accessible basements (Fig. 49-3). The combination of the footer and the wall forms an inverted T (Fig. 49-4).

The details of construction relating to the T foundation and the methods of representing this construction on the foundation plan are shown in Fig. 49-5.

SLAB FOUNDATIONS

A *slab foundation* is a poured solid slab of concrete. The slab is poured directly on the ground, with footers placed where extra support is needed (Fig. 49-6). A slab foundation requires considerably less labor to construct than do most other foundation types. Details of the slab foundation and methods of draw-

334

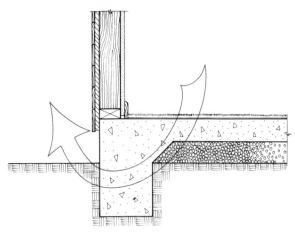

Fig 49-8 Slabs lose heat around the perimeter.

ing slab foundations are shown in Fig. 49-7. Slab foundations lose heat around their perimeter (Fig. 49-8).

PIER-AND-COLUMN FOUNDATIONS

The *pier-and-column foundation* consists of individual footers upon which columns are placed. Fewer materials and less labor are needed for the pier-and-column foundation (Fig. 49-9). The main objection to using pier-and-column foundations for most residence work is that a basement is not possible when this construction is used.

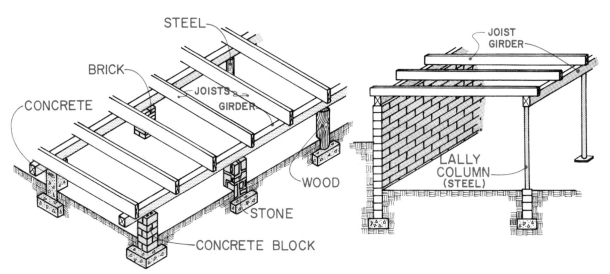

Fig 49-9 Pier and column construction.

PROBLEMS

1 Sketch Fig. 49-10, using the scale $\frac{1}{4}'' = 1'-0''$ for a T foundation.
2 Sketch Fig. 49-10, using the scale $\frac{1}{4}'' = 1'-0''$ for a slab foundation.
3 Sketch Fig. 49-10, using the scale $\frac{1}{4}'' = 1'-0''$ for a pier foundation.
4 Know these architectural terms: *contractor, grade, slab, T foundation, column, frost line.*

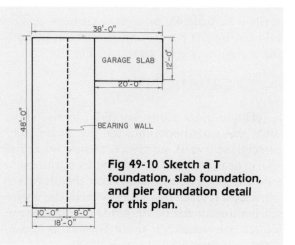

Fig 49-10 Sketch a T foundation, slab foundation, and pier foundation detail for this plan.

UNIT 50
FOUNDATION DRAWINGS

The designer must be familiar with all methods of foundation construction in order to design the most practical and economical foundation. The designer must choose the most appropriate foundation for the type of soil, climate, and structure to be supported (Fig. 50-1). He or she must prepare working drawings that will facilitate the layout, excavation, and construction of the foundation.

LAYOUT

The size and shape of the foundation are normally laid out with a transit and measuring tape. String is then used with batter boards to indicate the exact position of the excavation line, footer line, and foundation-wall line, as shown in Fig. 50-2. The angle of the corners can be set with a transit, as described in Unit 45, or square corners can be laid out by the 8-6-10 unit method of obtaining a right angle, as shown in Fig. 50-3.

EXCAVATIONS

Foundation plans should clearly show what parts of the foundation are to be completely excavated, partly excavated for crawl space, or unexcavated. The depth of the excavation should be shown also on the elevation drawings. If a basement is planned, the entire excavation for the basement is dug before the footers are poured. If there is to be no basement, a trench excavation is made.

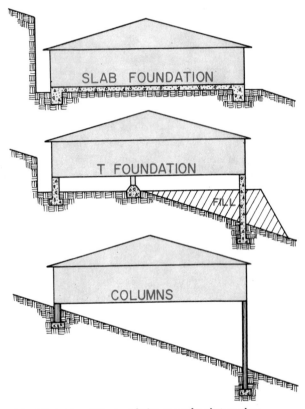

Fig 50-1 Conditions of the terrain determine the type of foundation used.

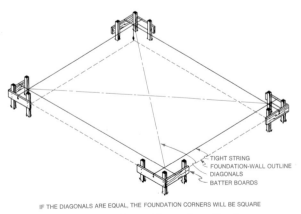

TIGHT STRING
FOUNDATION-WALL OUTLINE
DIAGONALS
BATTER BOARDS

IF THE DIAGONALS ARE EQUAL, THE FOUNDATION CORNERS WILL BE SQUARE

Fig 50-2 The batter-board layout method.

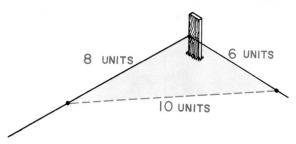

8 UNITS **6 UNITS**

10 UNITS

Fig 50-3 Establishing right angles by the 6-8-10 unit method.

T FOUNDATIONS

The T foundation is prepared by pouring the footer in an excavated trench, leveling the top of the footer, and erecting a concrete block or masonry wall on top of the footer. If concrete foundation walls are to be used, building forms are erected on top of the footer. Concrete is poured into these forms. After the concrete dries, the wood is removed and may be reused for other forms. When a poured foundation wall is to be used, the concrete mix is sand, gravel, water, and cement. After the

forms are filled, the concrete is leveled with a strike board so that it has a rough, nonslip surface. By continuing the depth of the T foundation, a basement area is formed (Fig. 50-4).

SLAB FOUNDATIONS

The excavation for a slab foundation is made for the footings only. Two-by-sixes are used to construct the forms for the slab, as shown in Fig. 50-5. The entire foundation is then poured, and the top of the slab is leveled with a strike board. Slab foundations and basement floors in T foundations should be waterproofed. This can be done by putting a waterproof membrane between the slab and the ground. Slabs are often reinforced with steel-wire mesh placed inside the slab before pouring, as shown in Fig. 50-6.

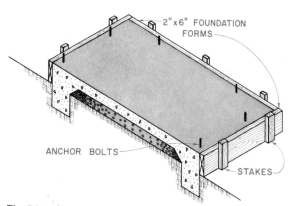

Fig 50-5 Slab-form construction.

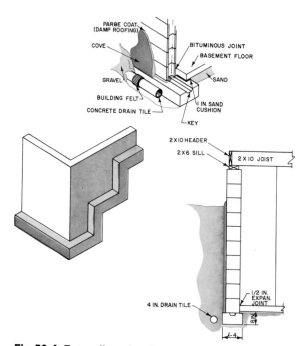

Fig 50-4 Extending the depth of a T foundation forms basement walls.

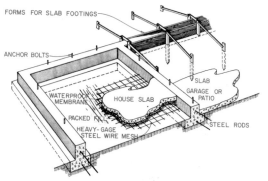

Fig 50-6 A reinforced slab foundation.

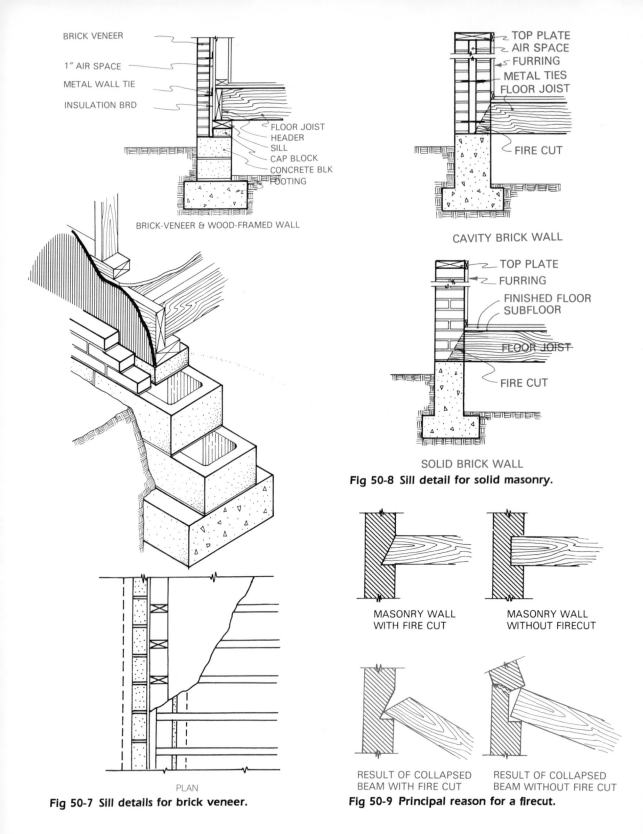

BRICK VENEER

1″ AIR SPACE

METAL WALL TIE

INSULATION BRD

FLOOR JOIST
HEADER
SILL
CAP BLOCK
CONCRETE BLK
FOOTING

BRICK-VENEER & WOOD-FRAMED WALL

TOP PLATE
AIR SPACE
FURRING
METAL TIES
FLOOR JOIST

FIRE CUT

CAVITY BRICK WALL

TOP PLATE
FURRING
FINISHED FLOOR
SUBFLOOR

FLOOR JOIST

FIRE CUT

SOLID BRICK WALL

Fig 50-8 Sill detail for solid masonry.

PLAN

Fig 50-7 Sill details for brick veneer.

MASONRY WALL
WITH FIRE CUT

MASONRY WALL
WITHOUT FIRECUT

RESULT OF COLLAPSED
BEAM WITH FIRE CUT

RESULT OF COLLAPSED
BEAM WITHOUT FIRE CUT

Fig 50-9 Principal reason for a firecut.

338

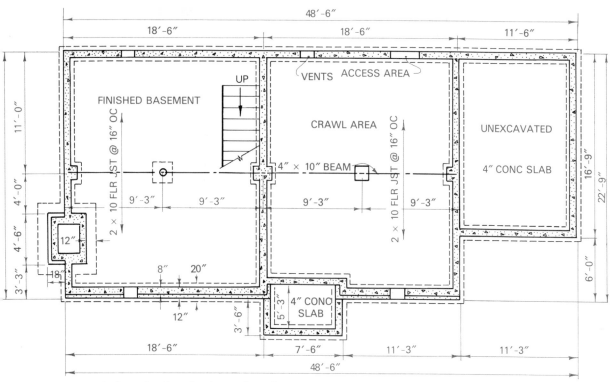

Fig 50-10 Foundation plan in a horizontal section.

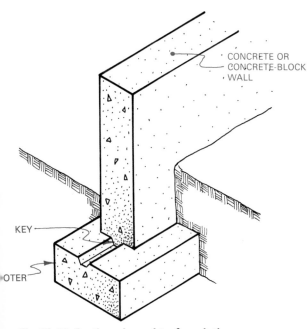

Fig 50-11 Sections keyed to foundation plan.

Types and sizes and mixtures of materials for foundations are rigidly controlled by most building codes. The designer must check the building code for the area.

SILL DETAILS

A drawing showing the intersection between exterior foundation walls and the floor system is known as a *sill detail*. The *sill* is the link between the framework of the structure and the foundation. Sill details are sections through the foundation extending through the floor line. Figure 50-7 shows a sill detail as it would appear for a brick-veneer structure, and Fig. 50-8 shows a sill detail for solid masonry and cavity masonry walls. Notice that in solid masonry or cavity masonry walls, a *fire cut* is included on all wood members that extend into the masonry. This fire cut is made to eliminate destruction of the masonry wall if the beam collapses, as shown in Fig. 50-9.

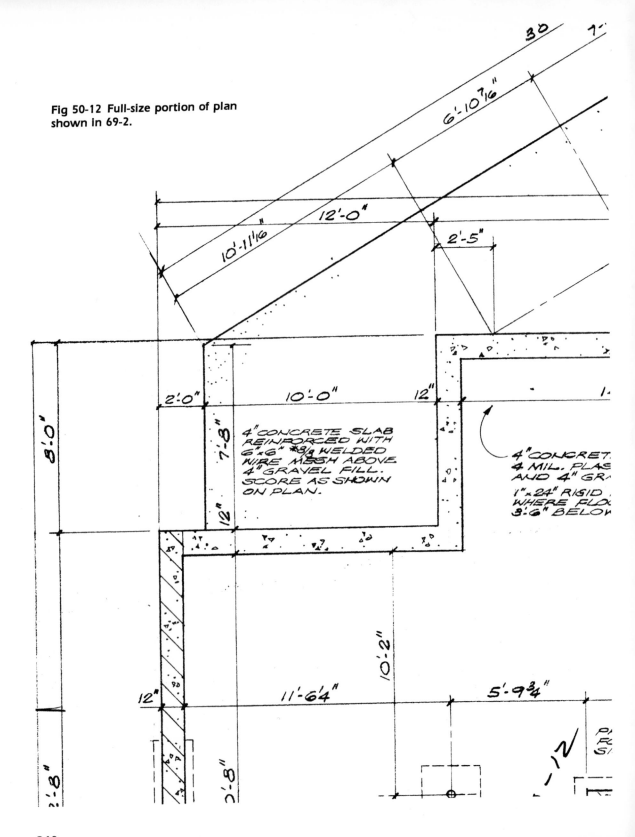

Fig 50-12 Full-size portion of plan shown in 69-2.

30

1'

6'-10 7/16"

12'-0"

10'-11 1/16"

2'-5"

2'-0"

10'-0"

12"

1'

8'-0"

7'-8"

12"

4" CONCRETE SLAB
REINFORCED WITH
6"x6" #8/8 WELDED
WIRE MESH ABOVE
4" GRAVEL FILL.
SCORE AS SHOWN
ON PLAN.

4" CONCRET.
4 MIL. PLAS
AND 4" GR

1"x24" RIGID
WHERE FLO
3'-6" BELOW

10'-2"

12"

11'-6 1/4"

5'-9 3/4"

2'-8"

2'-8"

340

FOUNDATION PLANS

Foundation plan views are similar to other floor plans, except that they represent a section through the foundation just below the top of the foundation, as shown in Fig. 50-10. Other sections (Fig. 50-11) are keyed to the foundation plan through the use of section lines. Figure 50-12 shows a portion of the plan found in Fig. 69-3 at full $\frac{1}{4}'' = 1'-0''$ scale.

PROBLEMS

1 In Fig. 50-13, how many cubic feet of dirt must be excavated? How many cubic yards? How many cubic feet of concrete must be poured for the footing? How many cubic yards for the slab?

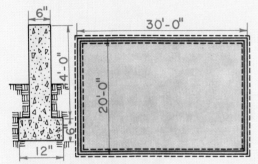

Fig 50-13 Determine the size of the excavation and the amount of concrete needed for this foundation.

2 In Fig. 50-14, how many cubic yards of dirt must be excavated for the footings? How many cubic yards of concrete will be used?

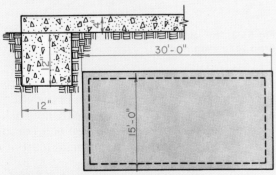

Fig 50-14 Determine the size of the excavation and the amount of concrete needed for this foundation.

3 What is the concrete mix for foundations in your community? Check your building code.

4 List several different types of foundations and materials used in your community.

5 Draw sections A, B, and C of the foundation plan shown in Fig. 50-15.

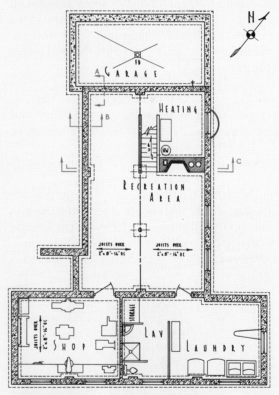

Fig 50-15 Draw sections A, B, and C of this foundation.

6 Define these architectural terms: *excavations, foundation forms, steel-wire mesh, strike board, waterproof membrane.*

UNIT 51
FIREPLACES

Provision must be made in the foundation plans to support the weight of the fireplace and chimney (Fig. 51-1). A solid reinforced concrete footer is used in most plans. This footer is usually 12″ (305 mm) thick and extends at least 12″ (305 mm) past the perimeter of the chimney.

Fireplaces are designed in three types: those constructed totally on the site (Fig. 51-1), those using a manufactured firebox and flue system (Fig. 51-2), and freestanding units.

FIREPLACE

The main part of the fireplace is the *firebox*. The firebox reflects heat and draws smoke up the chimney. Included in the firebox are the sides, back, smoke chamber, flue, throat, and damper (Fig. 51-1). Most fireboxes

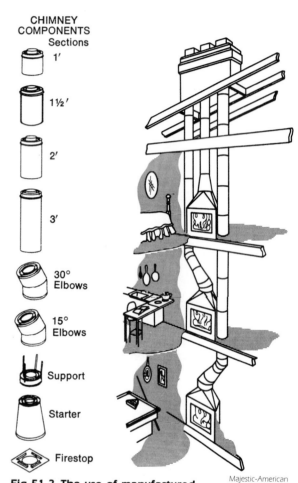

CHIMNEY COMPONENTS

Sections

1′

1½′

2′

3′

30° Elbows

15° Elbows

Support

Starter

Firestop

Fig 51-2 The use of manufactured fireplace components.

Majestic-American Standard

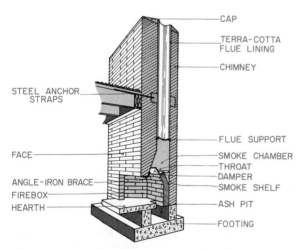

CAP

TERRA-COTTA FLUE LINING

CHIMNEY

STEEL ANCHOR STRAPS

FLUE SUPPORT

SMOKE CHAMBER

THROAT

DAMPER

SMOKE SHELF

FACE

ANGLE-IRON BRACE

FIREBOX

HEARTH

ASH PIT

FOOTING

Fig 51-1 The major components of fireplace and chimney structure.

are constructed in a factory. The mason places the firebox in the proper location in the chimney construction and lines it with firebrick. Figure 51-2 shows the installation of a manufactured unit prior to the addition of masonry covering.

Masonry used in fireplaces and chimneys is usually of brick, stone, or concrete. Firebrick is used to line the firebox. The hearth also should be constructed of fire-resistant material such as brick, tile, marble, or stone.

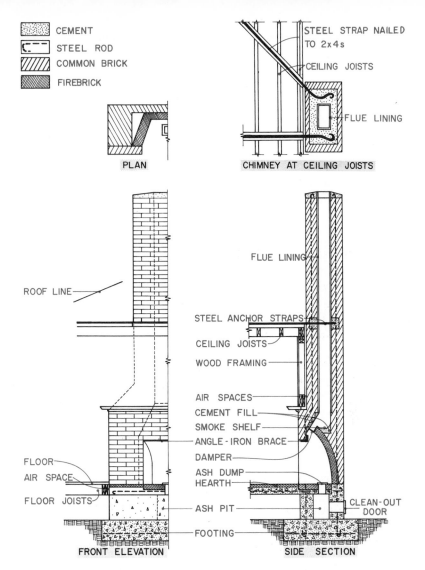

Fig 51-3 A sectional drawing of a fireplace and chimney.

CEMENT
STEEL ROD
COMMON BRICK
FIREBRICK

PLAN

CHIMNEY AT CEILING JOISTS

STEEL STRAP NAILED TO 2x4s

CEILING JOISTS

FLUE LINING

ROOF LINE

FLUE LINING

STEEL ANCHOR STRAPS

CEILING JOISTS

WOOD FRAMING

AIR SPACES

CEMENT FILL

SMOKE SHELF

ANGLE-IRON BRACE

DAMPER

FLOOR

AIR SPACE

FLOOR JOISTS

ASH DUMP

HEARTH

CLEAN-OUT DOOR

ASH PIT

FOOTING

FRONT ELEVATION

SIDE SECTION

The best method of drawing construction details of a fireplace is to prepare a sectional drawing, as shown in Fig. 51-3. This gives the position of the firebox and the size of materials used in the footer, hearth, face, flue, and cap of the chimney. It also shows the relationship of the chimney to the floor and ceiling lines of the structure.

CHIMNEY

A chimney extends from the footer through the roof of the house. The footer must be of sufficient size to support the entire weight of the chimney. The chimney extends above the roof line to provide a better draft for drawing the smoke and to eliminate the possibility of sparks igniting the roof.

The height of the chimney above the roof line varies somewhat, according to local building codes. In most areas the minimum distance is 2' (610 mm).

The chimney is secured to ceiling and floor joists by iron straps embedded in the brickwork. Floor joists and ceiling joists around the chimney and fireplace and hearth should have sufficient clearance to protect them from the heat. Most building codes specify this distance.

The designer must also indicate the type and size of flues to be inserted in the chimney. One flue is necessary for each fireplace or fur-

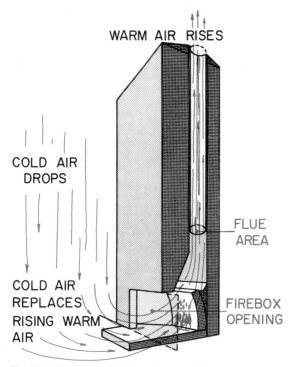

Fig 51-4 The functioning of a fireplace flue.

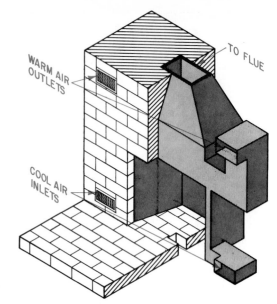

Fig 51-5 The placement of warm-air ducts.

Fireplaces add warmth and atmosphere to a room. However, most of the heat produced by some fireplaces goes up the chimney. To reduce this heat loss and redirect some of this heat, warm-air outlets, balanced by cold-air outlets, can be installed, as shown in Fig. 51-5.

nace leading into the chimney. Note the three flues serving the three fireplaces in Fig. 51-2. The flue from the fireplace or from the furnace in the basement extends directly to the top of the chimney, completely bypassing the first-floor fireplaces. The first-floor fireplace flues completely bypass the second-floor fireplace flues, and so forth. The size of each flue must be at least one-tenth the opening of the fireplace to accommodate the rise of warm air (see Fig. 51-4). Designing for adequate warm-air rise is critical to the effective operation (*draw*) of the fireplace. Inadequate draw, either from using too small a flue or from improper chimney placement, can result in smoke leading into the room rather than being drawn up the chimney.

Many fireplaces are constructed by using some manufactured components and constructing the remainder on the site. The design of the fireplace usually determines the amount of manufactured components that can be used. Unconventional fireplaces usually use few standard components.

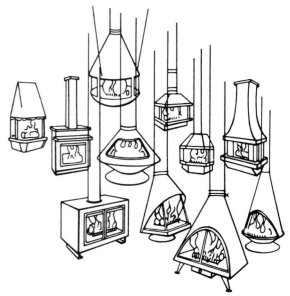

Fig 51-6 Free-standing fireplaces come in a variety of shapes and sizes.

Majestic-American Standard

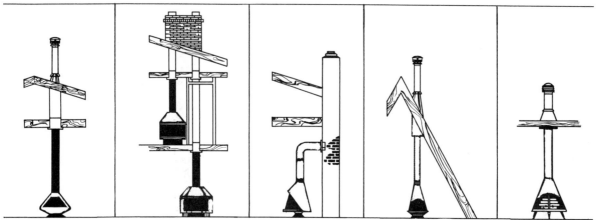

Fig 51-7 Some fireplace exhaust-system design options.

Majestic-American
Standard

PREFABRICATED FIREPLACES

Freestanding metal fireplaces constructed of heavy-gauge steel, as shown in Fig. 51-2, are available in a variety of shapes (Fig. 51-6). They are relatively light wood-burning stoves and therefore need no concrete foundation for support. A stovepipe leading into the chimney provides the exhaust flue. Figure 51-7 shows several methods of designing the exhaust system. Since metal units reflect more heat than masonry, the metal fireplace is much more efficient, especially if centrally located. These fireplaces can be mounted on the walls or on legs, or they can be built into the chimney. Prefabricated fireplaces do not require a foundation to support their weight. They are complete, ready-to-install fireplaces. Nevertheless, a fire-resistant material such as concrete, brick, stone, or tile must be used beneath and around these fireplaces (Fig. 51-2).

PROBLEMS

1 Redraw the fireplace in Fig. 51-1, using the scale ½" = 1'—0".

2 Design a fireplace for the house you are designing.

3 Identify the parts of the fireplace shown in Fig. 51-8.

4 Define these architectural terms: *firebox, chimney, smoke chamber, flue, throat, damper, draft, draw, ceiling joist, firebrick, prefabricated fireplace, chimney sections.*

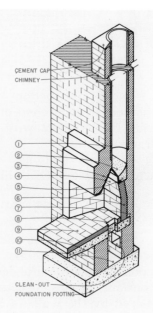

CEMENT CAP
CHIMNEY

① ② ③ ④ ⑤ ⑥ ⑦ ⑧ ⑨ ⑩ ⑪

CLEAN-OUT
FOUNDATION FOOTING

Fig 51-8 Identify the numbered parts.

FRAMING PLANS

Most of the basic engineering principles upon which modern framing methods are based have been known for centuries. However, it has not been until recent years that the development of materials and construction methods has allowed the full use of these principles. Today's architect can choose among many basic materials in the design of the basic structural framework of a building. New and improved methods of erecting structural steel, new developments in laminating and processing preformed wood structural members, developments and refinements in the use of concrete and masonry products such as prestressed concrete slabs, and continual progress in standardization in the design of structural components all provide the architect with the flexibility to design the most appropriate structural system for a building at the lowest possible cost and with the smallest waste of materials and time.

UNIT 52
TYPES OF FRAMING

New construction materials and new methods of using conventional materials provide the architect with much flexibility in framing design.

Stronger buildings can now be erected with lighter and fewer materials.

PRINCIPLES OF FRAMING

Regardless of the materials used and the methods employed, the physical principles upon which structural design is based remain constant. In most structures, the roof is supported by the wall framework and interior partitions or columns. Each exterior wall and bearing partition is supported by the *foun-dation*, which, in turn, is supported by a *footing*. The footing distributes this load over a wide area of load-bearing soil and thus ties the entire structural system to the ground (Fig. 52-1).

EARLY FRAMING METHODS

In earlier centuries, people did not have strong, light framing materials such as structural steel, aluminum, or sized and seasoned lumber. Therefore, extremely heavy material such as stone was used to support the great weight of a building. Foundations were large and footers enormous, to support and spread the heavy load. Walls were frequently constructed larger at the base than at the top, and a very elaborate system of column support was developed.

CURRENT FRAMING METHODS

Today, most buildings are constructed with a basic skeleton framework. A structural tie, such as *sheathing* or *diagonal bracing*, is covered with protective siding. The structural

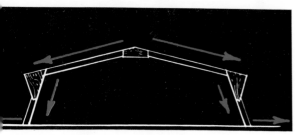

Fig 52-1 Major lines of support.

DEAD LOADS

Dead loads are those loads caused by the weight of the construction materials. The dead loads of the roof (Fig. 52-3) must be supported by the walls or bearing partitions. The dead loads of the walls must be supported by the foundation. Every piece of lumber, plywood, glass, and sheet metal, and every nail and brick adds to the total dead load of the structure.

LIVE LOADS

Live loads are those loads that may vary from structure to structure. Live loads of a floor include furniture and people, as shown in Fig. 52-4. Live loads of a roof include such variables as wind, snow, and even rain when the roof is flat (Fig. 52-5). As you learn more about the construction of roofs, floors, and walls in the succeeding units, you will learn how to design these structurally so that they will withstand normal live and dead loads.

system is somewhat related to the structure of most vertebrates. The framework functions like the skeleton in providing the basic rigid frame. The structural tie, whether it be sheathing on a wooden structure or cross-bracing on a steel framework, acts like the muscles in holding the framework in the desired position. The protective covering, which is similar to the skin, provides the necessary protection from the weather (Fig. 52-2).

LOADS

Loads that must be supported by the structure are divided into two types, live loads and dead loads.

STRENGTH OF MATERIALS

The stability of the building depends on the strength of the material used and the con-

Fig 52-2 The skeleton of a building is similar to the skeleton of a person.

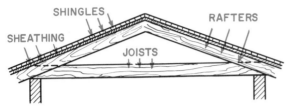

Fig 52-3 Dead loads.

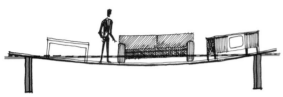

Fig 52-4 Live loads.

Fig 52-5 Live loads acting upon a roof.

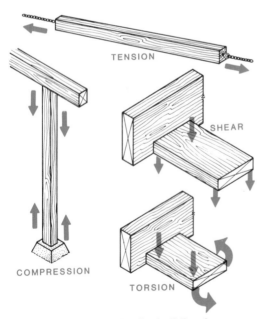

Fig 52-6 The framework of a building is designed to overcome tensions, compression, shear, and torsion.

nection of members to overcome *tension, compression, shear,* and *torsion* (Fig. 52-6). The strength of the building material is irrelevant if the building is not structurally stable. Likewise, the building will be inadequate if the building materials are weak, regardless of the stability of the design (Fig. 52-7).

The strength of the building material is significant only when related to the structure. Most lumber and even steel are relatively flexible until tied into the structure. Grasp a piece of paper between your thumb and forefinger, as shown in Fig. 52-8. The other end of the paper will drop. If you fold this same piece of paper, you will be able to support it from one end easily. This principle is applied to the use of structural members in building design.

Figure 52-9 shows that turning a member on its side will mostly eliminate *vertical deflection* (bending) but *horizontal deflection* is unaffected. Combining the horizontal and vertical members (to make a channel) reduces both the vertical and horizontal deflection. Combining two horizontal members with one vertical member (as in an I beam) provides even more stability.

It would seem that the design of structures is a relatively simple matter. The mate-

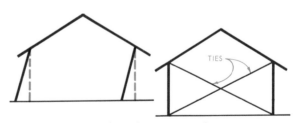

Fig 52-7 The stability of a structure is determined by its design.

Fig 52-8 The strength of a material is related to its shape.

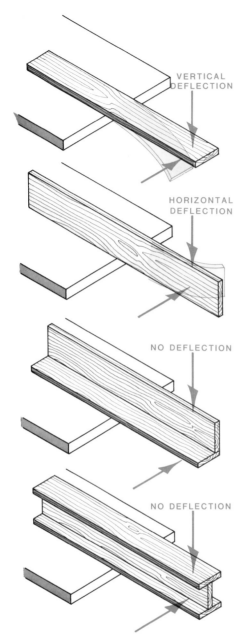

VERTICAL DEFLECTION

HORIZONTAL DEFLECTION

NO DEFLECTION

NO DEFLECTION

Fig 52-9 Deflections can be eliminated by combining members.

rials must be strong enough and the structure rigid enough. But it is not that simple. Care must be taken not to overdesign the structure. A beam that is one size too large will not support the structure any better than will a member of the right size. Overdesigning (except for allowing safety margins) a few items of this kind can cost thousands of dollars on a large job. For example, the member used to support the loads in Fig. 52-10 at A is considerably overdesigned. The support used in Fig. 52-10 at B is satisfactory. The support used in Fig. 52-10 at C is inadequately designed. Achieving the perfect balance, as shown in Fig. 52-10 at B, is the goal of every structural designer.

WOOD FRAMING

Early pioneers used wood as the basic construction material in building log cabins. Wood was used in its raw form to make the entire solid wall.

CONVENTIONAL FRAMING

Skeleton-frame construction was developed and the log cabin passed from the American scene. Skeleton-frame construction came about through the development of machinery able to mass-produce sized and seasoned lumber. However, limits on the sizes of lumber that could be handled effectively on the job led to the use of relatively small structural members placed at close intervals. Figure 52-11 shows the anatomy of a house constructed by this method. The framing methods shown here have been in use practically from the end of the log-cabin period to the present day.

POST-AND-BEAM CONSTRUCTION

The use of post-and-beam construction methods has been increased by the popularity

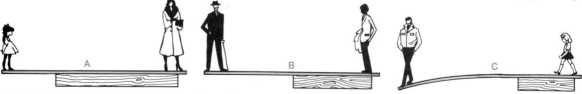

A   B   C

Fig 52-10 Structrual stability depends on the support and the spacing of support members.

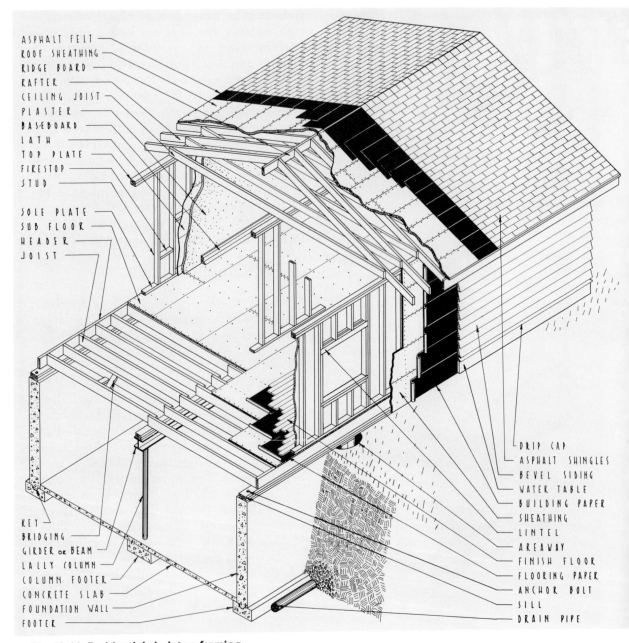

ASPHALT FELT
ROOF SHEATHING
RIDGE BOARD
RAFTER
CEILING JOIST
PLASTER
BASEBOARD
LATH
TOP PLATE
FIRESTOP
STUD

SOLE PLATE
SUB FLOOR
HEADER
JOIST

KEY
BRIDGING
GIRDER or BEAM
LALLY COLUMN
COLUMN FOOTER
CONCRETE SLAB
FOUNDATION WALL
FOOTER

DRIP CAP
ASPHALT SHINGLES
BEVEL SIDING
WATER TABLE
BUILDING PAPER
SHEATHING
LINTEL
AREAWAY
FINISH FLOOR
FLOORING PAPER
ANCHOR BOLT
SILL
DRAIN PIPE

Fig 52-11 Residential skeleton framing.

of indoor-outdoor living. The practicality of manufacturing large heat-resistant windows and window walls and the accessibility of larger wood members have popularized the post-and-beam method of construction. This method is based on the use of larger members spaced at greater intervals. This spacing ac-commodates large windows and sliding doors that unite the indoors and outdoors in a sin-gle-living space.

Figure 52-12 shows a comparison of the post-and-beam method of construction and the conventional method. Figure 52-13 shows some of the basic details of post-and-beam

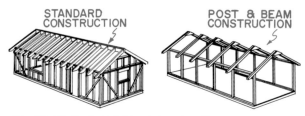

Fig 52-12 Post-and-beam construction compared to conventional construction.

construction. The preparation of the various framing plans using both post-and-beam and conventional wood-framing methods will be presented in succeeding units.

STEEL FRAMING

Steel framing is similar in principle to post-and-beam framing. Figure 52-14 shows a comparison of the use of posts, beams, and planks in post-and-beam wood construction and the use of columns, beams, and slabs in steel construction. Although structural-steel exterior framing walls utilize different materials, the position and location of steel studs on exterior wall panels are shown (Fig. 52-15) in the same manner as on wood skeleton-frame walls.

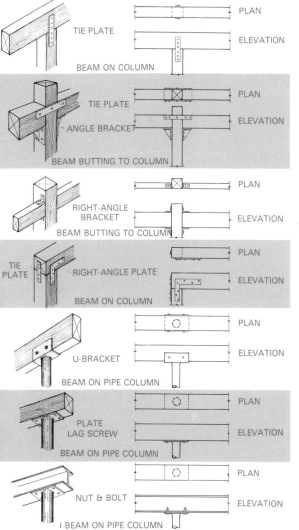

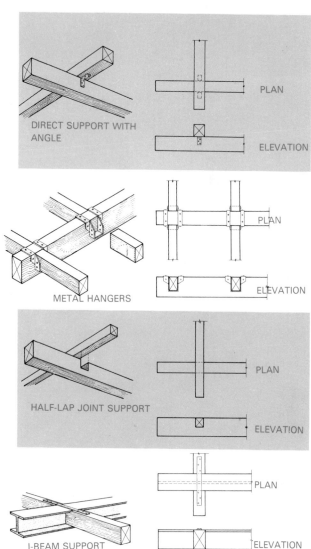

Fig 52-13 Basic details of post-and-beam construction.

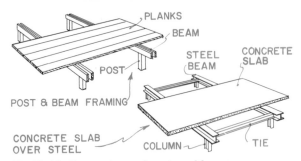

Fig 52-14 Comparison of post-and-beam construction with steel and concrete slab construction.

Steel columns perform the same function as wooden posts in providing the vertical support. Steel beams, like wood girders, support the floor or roof system. Steel framing, however, can support more weight and span longer distances because of the rigidity of structural steel members. For this reason, steel framing is used to erect tall multiple-story buildings. In fact, the greatest utilization of structural-steel framing has been for large commercial and industrial buildings such as schools, churches, and office buildings.

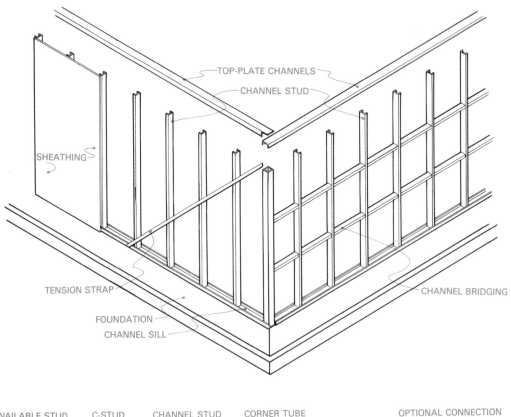

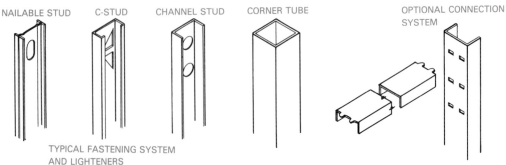

Fig 52-15 Structural-steel framing.

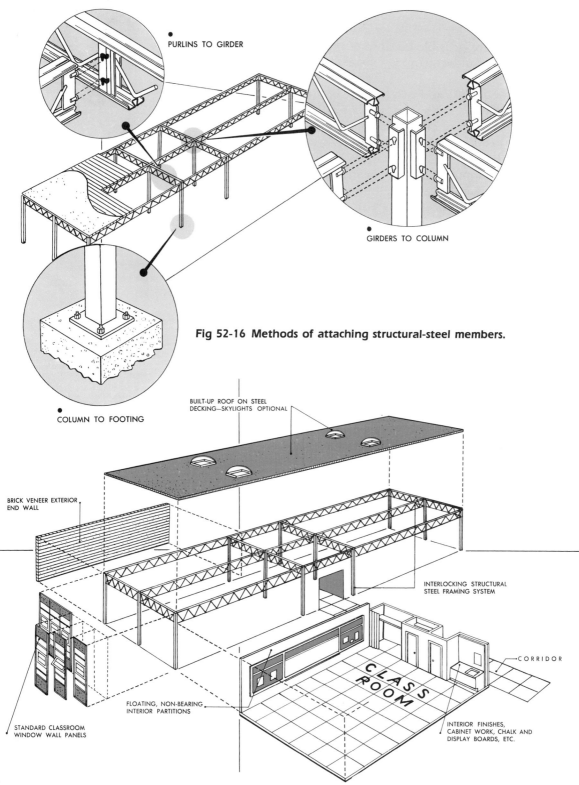

PURLINS TO GIRDER

GIRDERS TO COLUMN

COLUMN TO FOOTING

Fig 52-16 Methods of attaching structural-steel members.

BUILT-UP ROOF ON STEEL
DECKING—SKYLIGHTS OPTIONAL

BRICK VENEER EXTERIOR
END WALL

INTERLOCKING STRUCTURAL
STEEL FRAMING SYSTEM

CLASS ROOM

CORRIDOR

FLOATING, NON-BEARING
INTERIOR PARTITIONS

STANDARD CLASSROOM
WINDOW WALL PANELS

INTERIOR FINISHES,
CABINET WORK, CHALK AND
DISPLAY BOARDS, ETC.

Fig 52-17 Structural-steel framework permits flexibility in design.

Macomber, Inc.

Steel has also gained popularity as a framing material for smaller structures. Cantilever decks are possible because of the long distances that can be spanned by steel beams (see Fig. 10-8).

Because of the rigid attachment of steel members to each other and to footers and walls, a minimum of cross-bracing is needed (Fig. 52-16). Structural-steel framework can be designed to span long distances without intervening support. Longer spans create large unobstructed areas by eliminating the need for columns or bearing partitions. These large clear-span areas provide the designer with considerable flexibility in the design and location of interior partitions. Figure 52-17 shows some of the flexibilities in the interior design and in the exterior-wall treatment in steel construction.

Structural-steel members are available in a variety of shapes and sizes. Figure 52-18 shows some of the standardized shapes used in architectural work. Structural aluminum members are also used for house framing.

PREFABRICATION

From the time of the construction of the Pyramids, prefabricated component parts have been used in building. The word *fabricate* simply means to put together. The combination of *pre* and *fabricate* indicates that the parts of the structure are put together away from the building site.

BEGINNINGS

In its simplest form, prefabrication dates back to the time when primitive people cut and trimmed wood and tanned skins before building a shelter. Hannibal carried prefabricated huts across the Alps in a war with the Romans. Portable buildings were used by the United States army in the 1800s for barracks and small field hospitals. The Union army used these structures for its troops during the Civil War.

Throughout the early twentieth century, from 1900 to about 1940, prefabrication became popular for houses. Its use was a modified do-it-yourself approach to home building.

NAME	SYMBOL	SECTION	PICTORIAL
SQUARE BAR			
ROUND BAR			
PLATE			
ANGLE			
CHANNEL			
BULB ANGLE	BULB∠		
WIDE FLANGE	WF		
I-BEAM	I		
TEE	T		
ZEE	Z		
LALLY COLUMN			

Fig 52-18 Standard structural-steel shapes.

A few companies ventured into prefabrication of a complete house package including ceiling, wall, and floor panels, complete with plumbing and electrical work installed in the walls. At the same time, conventional builders were accepting prefabrication for some parts of a house. They recognized, for example, that a better and less expensive window sash could be produced in a plant than could be hand-made on the job site. As builders became more aware of the time, labor, and materials that could be saved by prefabrication, they began to use preassembled cabinets, prefitted doors,

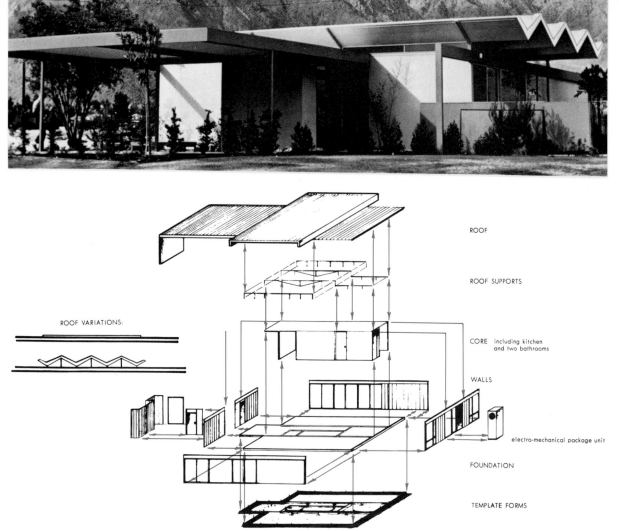

ROOF VARIATIONS:

ROOF

ROOF SUPPORTS

CORE including kitchen and two bathrooms

WALLS

electro-mechanical package unit

FOUNDATION

TEMPLATE FORMS

Fig 52-19 The maximum utilization of factory components.

Steelways Magazine; American Iron and Steel Institute

prefinished sink tops, prefinished floors, and other prefabricated parts.

PREFABRICATION TODAY

Today, the most successful companies producing factory-made homes rely on some use of conventional framing methods. They simply apply the techniques of mass production to their production methods. The goal is to minimize custom-job work without sacrificing the quality of the construction.

The National Association of Home Builders has sponsored the design and construction of an experimental house to determine to what extent factory-finished materials can be applied throughout the house. Figure 52-19 shows some of the basic components of this prefabricated house.

FACTORY-BUILT STRUCTURES

All structures are factory-built to some extent; that is, not all the materials or components are manufactured or put together on the site. Some structures are simply precut. This means that all the materials are cut to specification at the factory, and then assembled on the site by conventional methods.

With the most common type of prefabricated homes, the major components, such as the walls, trusses, decks, and partitions, are assembled at the factory. The utility work, such as installation of electrical, plumbing, and heating systems, is completed on site. The final finishing work, such as installation of floors, roof coverings, and walls, is also done on site.

There are some factory-built homes, however, that are constructed in complete modules at the factory and require only final electrical-outlet, roof-overhang, and assembly-fastening work on site to complete the job.

With the exception of mobile homes, most factory-built homes require some on-site preparation. Designers have been working for years to develop residential designs that would eliminate or greatly curtail the amount of on-site preparation.

MOBILE HOMES

The first completely factory-built homes were trailers, or mobile homes. The mobile-home buyer, unlike the buyer of a conventional factory-built home, has little option to adjust or customize the design of the residence. He or she does have opportunities to select from many different sizes, models, and interior components.

The mobility of our population, the increasing cost of real estate, and rising real-estate taxes have contributed to the growth of the mobile-home industry. One study estimates that approximately 25 percent of all one-family houses in the United States are mobile homes.

Thus, the mobile-home designer must plan homes that can be mass-produced but also provide a variety of options for the prospective buyer. A variety of sizes must also be

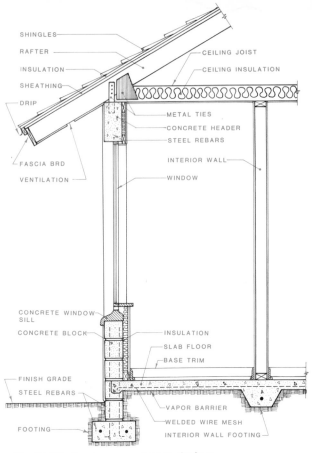

Fig 52-20 Hurricane-resistant design.

designed to span the price range of various consumers.

SPECIAL FRAMING

Extreme climate or environmental conditions require special construction methods. For example, the construction shown in Fig. 52-20 is designed to withstand hurricane winds.

PROBLEMS

Define the following architectural terms: *span, framework, skeleton frame, structural tie, sheathing, live load, dead load, tension, compression, shear, torsion, deflection, equi-* *librium, conventional wood framing, post-and-beam framing, column, beam, post, plank, cantilever, bearing partition, nonbearing partition.*

UNIT 53
FLOOR FRAMING PLANS

Floor framing plans range from those plans that show the structural support for the floor platform, to drawings that show the construction details of the intersections of the floor system with foundation walls, fireplaces, stairwells, and so forth. *Platform-floor systems* are those systems that are suspended from foundation walls and/or beams.

METRICATION FOR UNIT 53

The tables in this unit are concerned with joist spans and safe loads for various members. They all use customary units. As the construction industry converts to the metric system of measure, new lumber sizes will probably become standard. New tables similar to those found in this unit will then become available in metric units for those new standards. To make the metric equivalent of the tables available would not be a practical approach to metrication and would give a false impression of metric standards. For individual assignments, the appropriate data from any of the tables may be converted to metric by using Table 25-4.

TYPES OF PLATFORM-FLOOR SYSTEMS

Platform-floor systems are divided into three types: conventional, plank-and-beam, and panelized floor systems. These types are shown in Fig. 53-1.

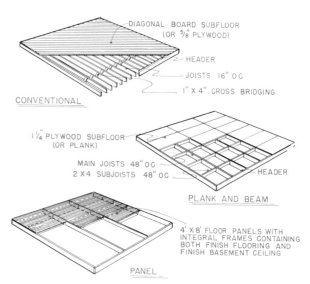

Fig 53-1 Types of platform-floor systems.

CONVENTIONAL SYSTEMS
The conventionally framed platform system provides a most flexible method of floor framing for a wide variety of design conditions. Floor joists are spaced at 12", 16", 24", or 32" intervals and are supported by the side walls of the foundation or by beams.

POST-AND-BEAM SYSTEMS
The *plank-and-beam* (post-and-beam) method of floor framing uses fewer members that are larger than conventional framing members. Because of the size and rigidity of the members, the need for bridging for stability between joists is eliminated.

PANELIZED SYSTEMS
Panelized floor systems are composed of preassembled sandwich panels of a variety of skin and core materials. Core-panel systems are used for long clear spans over basement construction and for shorter spans in non-basement houses.

DESIGN

The design of the floor system depends on load, type of material, size of the members, spacing of the support members, and distance between the major support members (*span*). Figure 53-2 shows that as the load is increased, the span must be decreased to compensate for the increase, or the member must be made larger or of a stronger material. The design of floor systems, therefore, demands very careful calculation in determining the live and dead loads acting on the floor. The most appropriate material for posts, beams or girders, and blocking must be selected. The design also requires determination of the exact size of the posts, beams, and deck materials and joists and establishment of the exact spacing between posts, girders, and joists.

The parts of a floor system that must be selected on the basis of the loads, material, size, and spacing include the deck, joist, girders or beams, and posts or columns.

FLOOR DECKING

Decking is the top surface of a floor system. The floor deck, in addition to bridging, provides lateral support for the joists. Decking usually consists of a subfloor and a finished floor, although in some systems they are combined. Subfloor decking materials consist of diagonal wood members, plywood sheets, prefabricted panels, plank boards, concrete slabs, or corrugated steel sheets. Plywood sheets, as shown in the example in Fig. 53-3, are laid directly over joists, and partitions rest directly on the subfloors.

The functions of the subfloor are as follows:

1 It increases the strength of the floor and provides a surface of the laying of a thin finished floor.
2 It helps to stiffen the position of the floor joist.
3 It serves as a working surface during construction.
4 It helps to deaden sound.

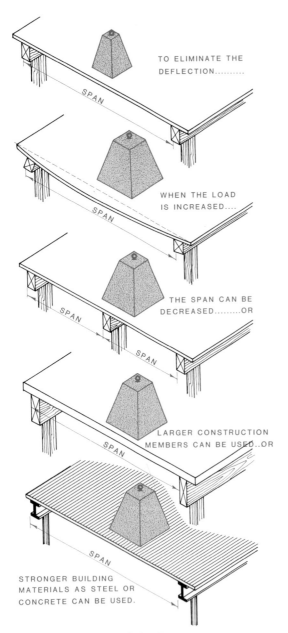

TO ELIMINATE THE DEFLECTION.........

SPAN

WHEN THE LOAD IS INCREASED....

SPAN

THE SPAN CAN BE DECREASED.........OR

SPAN

SPAN

LARGER CONSTRUCTION MEMBERS CAN BE USED..OR

SPAN

SPAN

STRONGER BUILDING MATERIALS AS STEEL OR CONCRETE CAN BE USED.

Fig 53-2 The design of the floor system depends on many factors.

Other experimental methods of core-component design and construction are continually being developed and refined to reduce the on-site construction costs. Research in engineering and wood technology is continually extending the use of components for support systems.

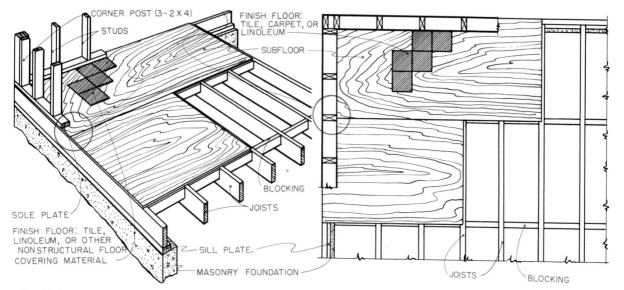

Fig 53-3 A floor-framing plan with blocking shown.

CORNER POST (3- 2 X 4)
STUDS
FINISH FLOOR: TILE, CARPET, OR LINOLEUM
SUBFLOOR
BLOCKING
JOISTS
SOLE PLATE
FINISH FLOOR: TILE, LINOLEUM, OR OTHER NONSTRUCTURAL FLOOR COVERING MATERIAL
SILL PLATE.
MASONRY FOUNDATION
JOISTS
BLOCKING

Fig 53-4 Floor-framing showing solid blocking and cross bridging.

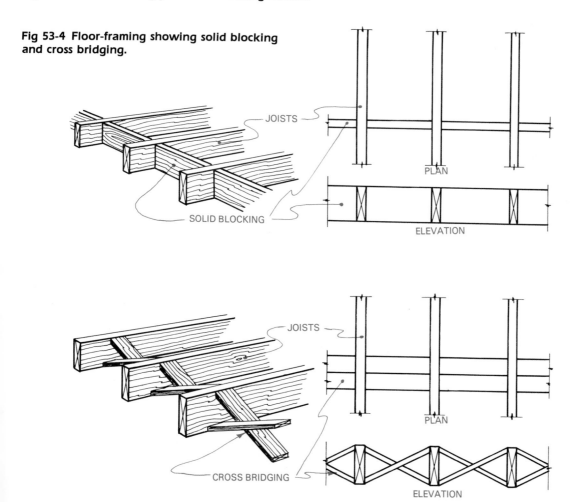

JOISTS
PLAN
SOLID BLOCKING
ELEVATION

JOISTS
PLAN
CROSS BRIDGING
ELEVATION

5 It prevents dust from rising through the floor.

6 It helps to insulate.

Finished flooring is installed over the subfloor and butted against the partition framing members. The finished floor provides a wearing surface over the subfloor, or over the joist if there is no subfloor. Hardwood, such as oak, maple, beech, and birch, is used for finished floors. Tile is often used as a finished floor, as shown in Fig. 53-3.

When steel subfloor decks are used, they are usually constructed of corrugated sheet steel. These subfloors act as platform surfaces during construction and also provide the necessary subfloor surface for a concrete slab floor. When precast-concrete floor systems are used, one of the concrete slab members functions as subflooring.

JOISTS

To determine the proper joists to use, you must consider the load, spacing, and strength of the joist material.

LOADS

Only live loads bear directly on the decking and joists. Therefore, the total live load for the room having the heaviest furniture and the heaviest traffic should be used to compute the total load for the entire floor. To find the live load in pounds per square foot, divide the total room load in pounds by the number of square feet supporting the load. To find the live load for a floor in kilograms per square meter, divide the total room load in kilograms by the number of square meters supporting the load.

Table 53-1   MAXIMUM SPANS FOR JOISTS

Live load—pounds per square foot	Spacing	2 inches wide by depth of—					3 inches wide by depth of—				
		6	8	10	12	14	6	8	10	12	14
10	12	12- 9	16- 9	21- 1	24- 0	—	14- 7	19- 3	24- 0	—	—
	16	11- 8	15- 4	19- 4	23- 4	24- 0	13- 6	17- 9	22- 2	24- 0	—
	24	10- 3	14- 6	17- 3	20- 7	24- 0	11-11	15- 9	19-10	23- 9	24- 0
20	12	11- 6	15- 3	19- 2	23- 0	24- 0	13- 3	17- 6	21- 9	24- 0	—
	16	10- 5	13-11	17- 6	21- 1	24- 0	12- 0	16- 1	20- 2	24- 0	—
	24	9- 2	12- 3	15- 6	18- 7	21- 9	10- 6	14- 2	17-10	21- 6	24- 0
30	12	10- 8	14- 0	17- 9	21- 4	24- 9	12- 4	16- 4	20- 5	24- 5	—
	16	9- 9	12-11	16- 3	19- 6	22- 9	11- 4	14-11	18- 9	22- 7	26- 4
	24	8- 6	11- 4	14- 4	17- 3	20- 2	10- 0	13- 2	16- 8	19-11	23- 4
40	12	10- 0	13- 3	16- 8	20- 1	23- 5	11- 8	15- 4	19- 3	23- 1	26-11
	16	9- 1	12- 1	15- 3	18- 5	21- 5	10- 8	14- 0	17- 8	21- 3	24-10
	24	7-10	10- 4	13- 1	15- 9	18- 5	9- 4	12- 4	15- 7	18- 9	22- 1
50	12	9- 6	12- 7	15-10	19- 1	22- 4	11- 0	14- 7	18- 4	22- 0	25- 8
	16	8- 7	11- 6	14- 7	17- 6	20- 5	10- 0	13- 4	16-10	20- 3	23- 8
	24	7- 3	9- 6	12- 1	14- 7	17- 0	8-10	11- 9	14-10	17-10	20-10
60	12	9- 0	12- 0	15- 2	18- 3	21- 4	10- 6	14- 0	17- 7	21- 1	24- 7
	16	8- 1	10-10	13- 8	16- 6	19- 3	9- 7	12-10	16- 1	19- 4	22- 7
	24	6- 8	8-11	11- 3	13- 7	15-11	8- 5	11- 3	14- 1	17- 0	20- 0
70	12	8- 7	11- 6	14- 6	17- 6	20- 6	10- 1	13- 5	16-11	20- 5	23- 9
	16	7- 8	10- 2	12-10	15- 6	18- 3	9- 3	12- 3	15- 5	18- 7	21-10
	24	6- 5	8- 5	10- 7	12- 9	15- 0	8- 0	10- 7	13- 4	16- 1	18-10

SPACING AND STRENGTH OF MATERIAL

When the live load is determined, the size and spacing of joists can be established by referring to Table 53-1. This table is based on #1 Southern white pine with a fiber stress of 1200 pounds per square inch and a *modulus of elasticity* (ratio of stress and strain) of 1,600,000 pounds per square inch. For other materials, such as redwood or Douglas fir lumber, with different fiber stresses and different moduli of elasticity, a different table should be used.

An example of the use of Table 53-1 is as follows: If the live loads are approximately 40 pounds per square foot and 16″ spaces are desired between joists, you can see that a 2 × 8 is good for a spacing of only 12′—1″. For a span larger than 12′—1″, a joist of larger cross section is necessary. Figure 53-4 shows methods of drawing both plan and elevation views of joists with solid blocking, or wood cross-bridging.

SIZE

You can see, therefore, that as the size, spacing, and load vary, the spans must vary accordingly. Or if the span is changed, the dimensions of the spacing of the joist must

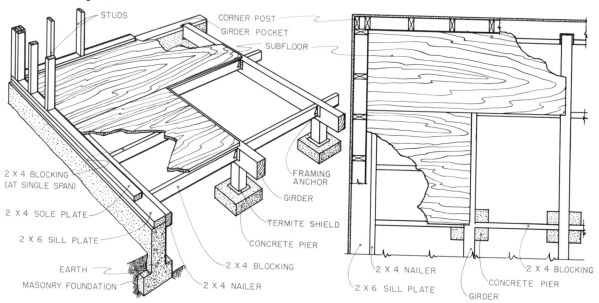

Fig 53-5 A method of drawing floor-framing systems to show joists and deck relationship.

change accordingly. Figure 53-3 indicates the method of drawing part of the floor framing plan that shows the size and position of joists and the blocking between joists. In this particular detail, the relative position of the subfloor, finished floor, sill, and exterior walls is also shown. In Fig. 53-5 there is an alternative floor system showing the relationship be-

Fig 53-6 Girder and blocking substitute for joists.

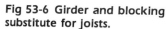

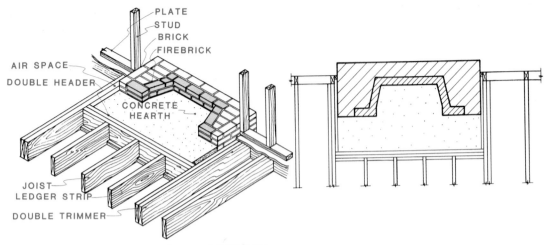

Fig 53-7 Double headers are used around fireplaces.

tween the joists of the floor and the finished
floor and sill.

In some systems, the floor system may
appear to have no joists, as shown in Fig. 53-6.
However, in this system the girder and blocking perform the function of the joist. The girders rest directly on posts, and the subflooring
rests directly on the girders. In this construction, these girders are spaced more closely
than most girders that support joists. The subflooring can be nailed or glued with adhesives
to bond structural members together.

HEADERS

Whenever it is necessary to cut regular
joists to provide an opening for a stairwell or
a hearth, it is necessary to provide auxiliary
joists called *headers*. Headers are placed at
right angles to the regular joists, to carry the
ends of joists that are cut. A header cannot be
of greater depth than any other joist; therefore, headers are usually *doubled* (placed side
by side) to compensate for the additional load.
Figure 53-7 shows the use of the double

Fig 53-8 Headers around chimney openings.

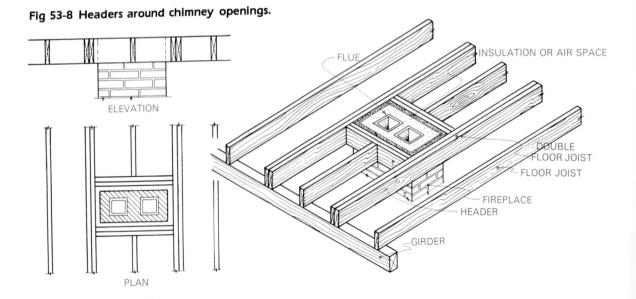

header as compensation for the joists that are cut to provide space for the fireplace. Figure 53-8 shows similar use of headers around chimney openings.

Additional support is also needed under bearing partitions. Figure 53-9 shows the use of double joists under partitions, with and without spacers. If space for pipes or wires is needed, spacers are used.

GIRDERS AND BEAMS

All the weight of the floor system, including the live loads and the dead loads, is transmitted to bearing partitions. These loads are then transmitted either to the foundation wall, to intermediate supports (Fig. 53-10), or to horizontal supports known as *girders* or *beams* (Fig. 53-11).

To determine the exact spacing, size, and type of girder to support the structure, follow these steps:

1 Determine the total load acting on the entire floor system in pounds per square foot. Divide the total live and dead loads by the number of square feet of floor space. For example, if the combined load for the floor system shown in Fig. 53-12 is 48,000 pounds, then there are 50 pounds per square foot of load acting on the floor (48,000 pounds divided by 960 square feet equals 50 pounds per square foot).

2 Lay out the proposed position of all columns and beams. It will also help to sketch the position of the joists to be sure that the joist spans are correct, as shown in Fig. 53-12.

3 Determine the number of square feet supported by the girder (*girder load area*). The girder load area is determined by multiplying the length of a girder from column to column by the girder load width. The *girder load width* is the distance extending on both sides of the center line of the girder, halfway to the nearest support, as shown in Fig. 53-12. The remaining distance from a girder load area to the outside wall is supported by the outside wall.

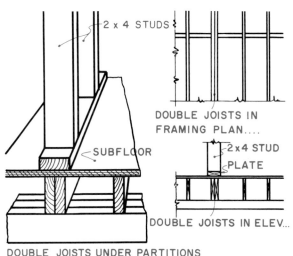

DOUBLE JOISTS IN FRAMING PLAN....

DOUBLE JOISTS IN ELEV...

DOUBLE JOISTS UNDER PARTITIONS

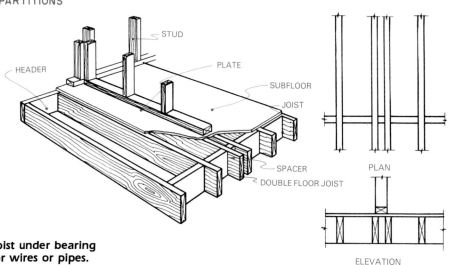

Fig 53-9 Double floor joist under bearing partition with spacer for wires or pipes.

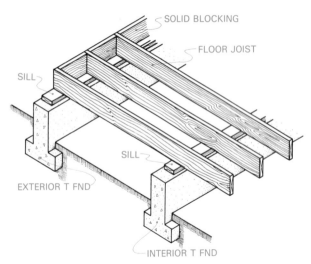

Fig 53-10 **Loads transmitted to intermediate supports.**

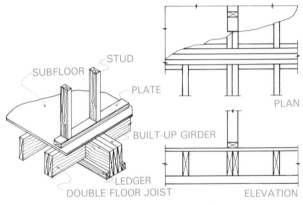

Fig 53-11 **Loads transmitted to girders.**

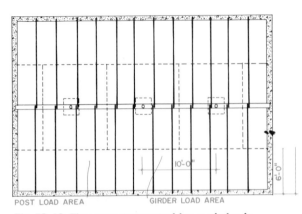

Fig 53-12 **The area supported by a girder is known as the tributary area.**

4 To find the load supported by the girder load area, multiply the girder load area by the load per square foot. For example, the girder load in Fig. 53-12 is 6000 pounds (120 square feet × 50 pounds per square foot).

5 Select the most suitable material to carry the load at the span desired. Built-up wood girders will span a greater length than a standard wood girder. However, I beams will span a greater length without intervening support.

6 Select the exact size and classification of the beam or girder. Use Table 53-2 to select the most appropriate wood girder. For example, to support 6000 pounds over a 10′ span, either an 8 × 8 solid girder or a 6 × 10 built-up girder would suffice. The girder should be strong enough to support the load, but any size larger is a waste of materials. The only alternative to increasing the size of the girder is to decrease the size of the span.

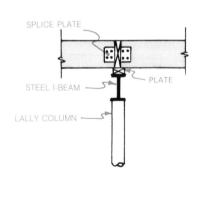

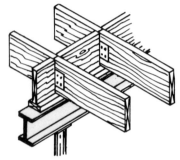

Fig 53-13 **Steel beam supporting wood joists.**

Table 53-2	SAFE LOADS FOR WOOD GIRDERS				
	Safe load in pounds for spans from 6 to 10 feet				
Girder size	6 ft	7 ft	8 ft	9 ft	10 ft
6 × 8 SOLID	8 306	7 118	6 220	5 539	4 583
6 × 8 BUILT-UP	7 359	6 306	5 511	4 908	4 062
6 × 10 SOLID	11 357	10 804	9 980	8 887	7 997
6 × 10 BUILT-UP	10 068	9 576	8 844	7 878	7 086
8 × 8 SOLID	11 326	9 706	8 482	7 553	6 250
8 × 8 BUILT-UP	9 812	8 408	7 348	6 544	5 416
8 × 10 SOLID	15 487	14 732	13 608	12 116	10 902
8 × 10 BUILT-UP	13 424	12 768	11 792	10 504	9 448

STEEL BEAMS

The method for determining the size of steel beams is the same as for determining the size of wood beams. As wood beams vary in width for a given depth, steel beams vary in weight, depth, and thickness of webs and flanges. Classifications vary accordingly. Table 53-3 shows the relationship of the span, the load, the depth, and the weight of standard I beams and channels. A steel beam may be selected by referring to the desirable span and load and then choosing the most appropriate size (depth and weight) for the I beam. For example, a 5″ × 12.25-pound I beam will support 6.5 kips per given span of 10 feet. A kip is equal to 1000 pounds. Figure 53-13 shows a steel beam supporting wood joists, and Fig. 53-14 shows a steel beam supporting steel joists.

COLUMNS

When girders or beams do not completely span the distance between foundation walls, then wood posts, steel-pipe columns, masonry

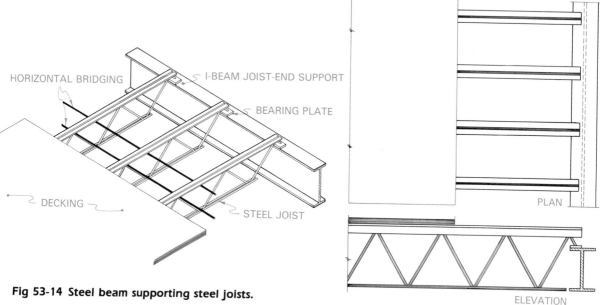

Fig 53-14 Steel beam supporting steel joists.

Table 53-3 SAFE LOADS FOR I BEAMS, SHOWING NUMBER OF KIPS (1000 POUNDS) A BEAM WILL SUPPORT AT A GIVEN SPAN

Weight per foot	4 inches deep by—				5 inches deep by—			6 inches deep by—			7 inches deep by—		
SPAN IN FEET	7.7	8.5	9.5	10.5	10.0	12.25	14.75	12.5	14.75	17.25	15.3	17.5	20.0
4	9.0	9.5	10.1	10.7	14.5	16.2	18.0	21.8	23.8	26.0	31.0	33.4	36.0
5	7.2	7.6	8.0	8.5	11.6	13.0	14.4	17.4	19.0	20.8	24.8	26.7	28.7
6	6.0	6.3	6.7	7.1	9.7	10.8	12.0	14.5	15.9	17.3	20.7	22.2	24.0
7	5.1	5.4	5.7	6.1	8.3	9.3	10.3	12.5	13.6	14.9	17.7	19.1	20.5
8	4.5	4.7	5.0	5.3	7.3	8.1	9.0	10.9	11.9	13.0	15.5	16.7	18.0
9	4.0	4.2	4.5	4.7	6.5	7.2	8.0	9.7	10.6	11.6	13.8	14.8	16.0
10	3.6	3.8	4.0	4.3	5.8	6.5	7.2	8.7	9.5	10.4	12.4	13.3	14.4
11	—	—	—	—	5.3	5.9	6.5	7.9	8.7	9.5	11.3	12.1	13.1
12	—	—	—	—	—	—	—	7.3	7.9	8.7	10.3	11.1	12.0
13	—	—	—	—	—	—	—	6.7	7.3	8.0	9.5	10.3	11.1
14	—	—	—	—	—	—	—	6.2	6.8	7.4	8.9	9.5	10.3
15	—	—	—	—	—	—	—	—	—	—	8.3	8.9	9.6
16	—	—	—	—	—	—	—	—	—	—	7.7	8.3	9.0
17	—	—	—	—	—	—	—	—	—	—	—	—	—
18	—	—	—	—	—	—	—	—	—	—	—	—	—
19	—	—	—	—	—	—	—	—	—	—	—	—	—
20	—	—	—	—	—	—	—	—	—	—	—	—	—

Weight per foot	8 inches deep by—				9 inches deep by—				10 inches deep by—			
SPAN IN FEET	18.4	20.5	23.0	25.5	21.8	25.0	30.0	35.0	25.4	30.0	35.0	40.0
4	42.7	45.2	48.2	51.1	56.6	60.9	67.6	74.2	73.3	80.1	87.5	94.8
5	34.1	36.1	38.5	40.9	45.3	48.7	54.1	59.4	58.6	64.1	70.0	75.8
6	28.5	30.1	32.1	34.1	37.7	40.6	45.1	49.5	48.8	53.4	58.3	63.2
7	24.4	25.8	27.5	29.2	32.3	34.8	38.6	42.4	41.9	45.8	50.0	54.2
8	21.3	22.6	24.1	25.5	28.3	30.5	33.8	37.1	36.6	40.1	43.7	47.4
9	19.0	20.1	21.4	22.7	25.2	27.1	30.0	33.0	32.0	35.6	38.9	42.1
10	17.1	18.1	19.3	20.4	22.6	24.4	27.0	29.7	29.3	32.0	35.0	37.9
11	15.5	16.4	17.5	18.6	20.6	22.2	24.6	27.0	26.6	29.1	31.8	34.5
12	14.2	15.1	16.1	17.0	18.9	20.3	22.5	24.7	24.4	26.7	29.2	31.6
13	13.1	13.9	14.8	15.7	17.4	18.7	20.8	22.8	22.5	24.6	26.9	29.2
14	12.2	12.9	13.8	14.6	16.2	17.4	19.3	21.2	20.9	22.9	25.0	27.1
15	11.4	12.0	12.8	13.6	15.1	16.2	18.0	19.8	19.5	21.4	23.3	25.3
16	10.7	11.3	12.0	12.8	14.2	15.2	16.9	18.6	18.3	20.0	21.9	23.7
17	10.0	10.6	11.3	12.0	13.3	14.3	15.9	17.3	17.2	18.8	20.6	22.3
18	9.5	10.0	10.7	11.4	12.6	13.3	15.0	16.5	16.3	17.8	19.4	21.1
19	9.0	9.5	10.1	10.8	11.9	12.8	14.2	15.6	15.4	16.9	18.4	20.0
20	8.5	9.0	9.6	10.2	11.3	12.2	13.5	14.8	14.7	16.0	17.5	19.0

columns, or steel-beam columns must be used for intervening support. To determine the most appropriate size and classification of posts or columns to support the girders or beams, follow these steps:

1 Determine the total load in pounds per square foot for the entire floor area. Calculate this amount by multiplying the total load by the number of square feet of floor space.

2 Determine the spacing of posts necessary to support the ends of each girder. Great distances between posts should be avoided because great weight would concentrate on one footing. Long spans also require extremely large girders. For example, it is possible to span a distance of 30', but to do so, a 15" I beam would be needed. The extreme weight and cost of this beam would be prohibitive. On the other hand, if only a 6' span were used, the close spacing might greatly restrict the flexibility of the internal design. As a rule, use the shortest span that will not interfere with the design function of the area.

3 Find the number of square feet supported by each post. A post will carry the load on a girder to the midpoint of the span on both sides. For example, post A in Fig. 53-12 carries half the load of girder X and girder Y in the direction of the joist. The post also carries half the load to the near-

est support wall on either side of the post. The number of square feet supported by post A in Fig. 53-12 is therefore 120 square feet (10' × 12').

4 Find the load supported by the post support area. Multiply the number of square feet by the load per square foot (120 × 50).

5 Determine the height of a post. The height of the post is related to the span of a beam. The 4 × 4 post shown in Fig. 53-15 may be more than adequate to support a given weight if the height of the post is 6'. However, this same 4 × 4 post may be totally inadequate to support the same weight when the length is increased to 20'.

6 Determine the type of column needed to support the load at the anticipated height.

7 Select the thickness and width of the post needed to support the load at the given height.

Use Table 53-4 for lumber posts. Use Table 53-5 for I-beam columns. Use Table 53-6 to determine the correct diameter of steel-pipe column supports.

PLANS

The more complete the architectural plan, the better the chances are that the building will be constructed exactly as designed. If a floor framing plan is not prepared to accompany the basic architectural plans, then the framing of the floor system is left entirely to the desires of the builder. Some architectural plans do not include a floor framing plan. Only the direction of joists and the possible location of beams or girders are shown on the floor plan. Figure 53-16A shows a floor plan. Figures 53-16C and D show methods of drawing floor framing plans. All are related to the basic floor plan shown in Fig. 53-16A.

The most complete and most acceptable method of drawing floor framing plans is shown in Fig. 53-16B. Each structural mem-

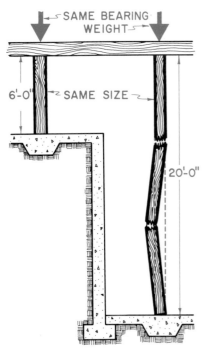

Fig 53-15 A heavier post is needed to support the same load when the height is increased.

Table 53-4 MAXIMUM LOADS FOR LUMBER POSTS

Nominal size, inches	3 × 4	4 × 4	4 × 6	6 × 6	6 × 8	8 × 8
Actual size, inches	2½ × 3½	3½ × 3½	3½ × 5½	5½ × 5½	5½ × 7¼	7¼ × 7¼
Area in square inches	9.51	13.14	20.39	30.25	41.25	56.25
HEIGHT OF COLUMN:						
4 FEET	8 720	12 920	19 850	30 250	41 250	56 250
5 FEET	7 430	12 400	19 200	30 050	41 000	56 250
6 FEET	5 630	11 600	17 950	29 500	40 260	56 250
6 FEET 6 INCHES	4 750	10 880	16 850	29 300	39 950	56 000
7 FEET	4 130	10 040	15 550	29 000	39 600	55 650
7 FEET 6 INCHES	—	9 300	14 400	28 800	39 000	55 300
8 FEET	—	8 350	12 950	28 150	38 300	55 000
9 FEET	—	6 500	10 100	26 850	36 600	54 340
10 FEET	—	—	—	24 670	33 600	53 400
11 FEET	—	—	—	22 280	30 380	52 100
12 FEET	—	—	—	19 630	26 800	50 400

Table 53-5 SAFE LOADS FOR I-BEAM COLUMNS IN KIPS (1000 POUNDS)

Depth in inches	10	9	8	7	6	5	4	3
Weight per pound per foot	25.4	21.8	18.4	15.3	12.5	10.0	7.7	5.7
EFFECTIVE LENGTH:								
3 FEET	110.7	94.8	80.1	66.5	54.2	43.1	33.0	23.5
4 FEET	110.7	94.8	80.1	65.9	52.1	39.7	29.1	20.3
5 FEET	109.5	91.2	74.9	60.0	46.9	35.1	25.3	17.2
6 FEET	101.7	83.9	68.3	54.1	41.8	30.7	21.8	14.6
7 FEET	93.8	76.7	61.8	48.5	37.0	26.8	18.7	12.3
8 FEET	86.0	69.7	55.7	43.3	32.7	23.4	16.1	10.5
9 FEET	78.7	63.2	50.1	38.6	28.9	20.4	13.9	—
10 FEET	71.8	57.2	45.0	34.5	25.5	17.9	—	—
11 FEET	65.5	51.8	40.5	30.8	22.6	—	—	—
12 FEET	59.7	47.0	36.5	27.6	20.2	—	—	—
AREA IN SQUARE INCHES	7.38	6.32	5.34	4.43	3.61	2.87	2.21	1.64

ber is represented by a double line that shows its exact thickness.

The more abbreviated plan shown in Fig. 53-16C is a short-cut method of drawing floor framing plans. A single line is used to designate each member. Chimney and stair openings are shown by diagonals. Only the outline of the foundation and post locations is shown. The abbreviated floor framing plan given in Fig. 53-16D uses a technique similar to the one used in floor plans to show the entire area where uniformly distributed joists are placed. The direction of joists is shown by an arrow.

The size and spacing of joists are shown by notes placed on the arrow. This type of framing plan is usually accompanied by numerous detail drawings such as the ones shown in Figs. 53-3 and 53-5.

The method of cutting and fitting subfloor and finished floor panels is usually determined by the builder. However, where off-site or mass-produced floor systems are built, a plan similar to the one shown in Fig. 53-17 is often prepared to ensure a maximum utilization of materials with a minimal amount of waste.

Table 53-6 SAFE LOADS FOR STEEL-PIPE COLUMNS IN KIPS (1000 POUNDS)

Nominal size, inches	6	5	4½	4	3½	3	2½	2	1½
External diameter, inches	6.625	5.563	5.000	4.500	4.000	3.500	2.875	2.375	1.900
Thickness, inches	.280	.258	.247	.237	.226	.216	.203	.154	.145
EFFECTIVE LENGTH:									
5 FEET	72.5	55.9	48.0	41.2	34.8	29.0	21.6	12.2	7.5
6 FEET	72.5	55.9	48.0	41.2	34.8	28.6	19.4	10.6	6.0
7 FEET	72.5	55.9	48.0	41.2	34.1	26.3	17.3	9.0	5.0
8 FEET	72.5	55.9	48.0	40.1	31.7	24.0	15.1	7.4	4.2
9 FEET	72.5	55.9	46.4	37.6	29.3	21.7	12.9	6.6	3.5
10 FEET	72.5	54.2	43.8	35.1	26.9	19.4	11.4	5.8	2.7
11 FEET	72.5	51.5	41.2	32.6	24.5	17.1	10.3	5.0	—
12 FEET	70.2	48.7	38.5	30.0	22.1	15.2	9.2	4.1	—
AREA IN SQUARE INCHES	5.58	4.30	3.69	3.17	2.68	2.23	1.70	1.08	0.80
WEIGHT PER POUND PER FOOT	18.97	14.62	12.54	10.79	9.11	7.58	5.79	3.65	2.72

DETAILS

Although many floor framing plans are easily interpreted by the experienced builder, others may require that the detail of some segment of the plan be prepared separately to explain more clearly the construction methods recommended. The detail is drawn to

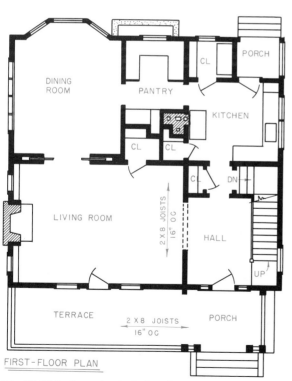

Fig 53-16A A method of showing joist direction on floor plan.

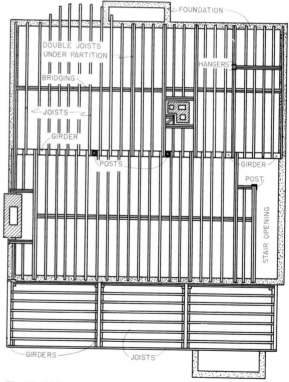

Fig 53-16B A floor-framing plan showing material thickness.

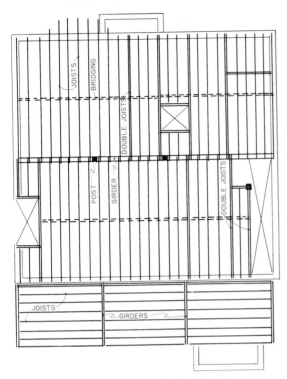

Fig 53-16C A simplified method of drawing floor-framing plans.

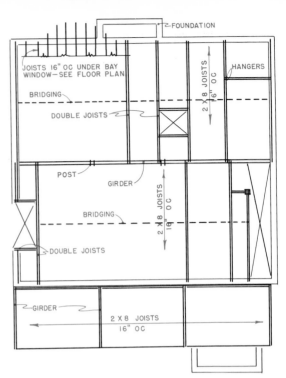

Fig 53-16D An abbreviated method of drawing floor-framing plans.

ALL SUBFLOOR PANELS
4'-0" × 8'-0"

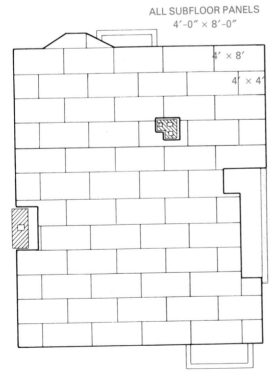

Fig 53-17 Floor panel layout.

eliminate the possibility of error in interpretation or to explain more thoroughly some unique condition of the plan. Details may be merely enlargements of what is already on the floor framing plan. They may be prepared for dimensioning purposes, or they may show a view from a different angle to reveal the underside or elevation view for better interpretation.

Figure 53-18 shows a floor framing plan and several details that have been removed for clarity. Detail 1 shows the position of cross-bridging. Detail 2 shows the relationship of the built-up beam, the double joist under the partition, and the solid bridging. Detail 3 shows the sill construction in relation to the floor joist and rough flooring, and to the foundation. Detail 4 shows the method of supporting the built-up beam by the *lally* (steel) *column* and the joist position on the beam. Detail 5 shows several alternative methods of supporting the joist over a built-up beam or an I beam; thus the builder is given an option. Detail 6 shows the attachment of the typical

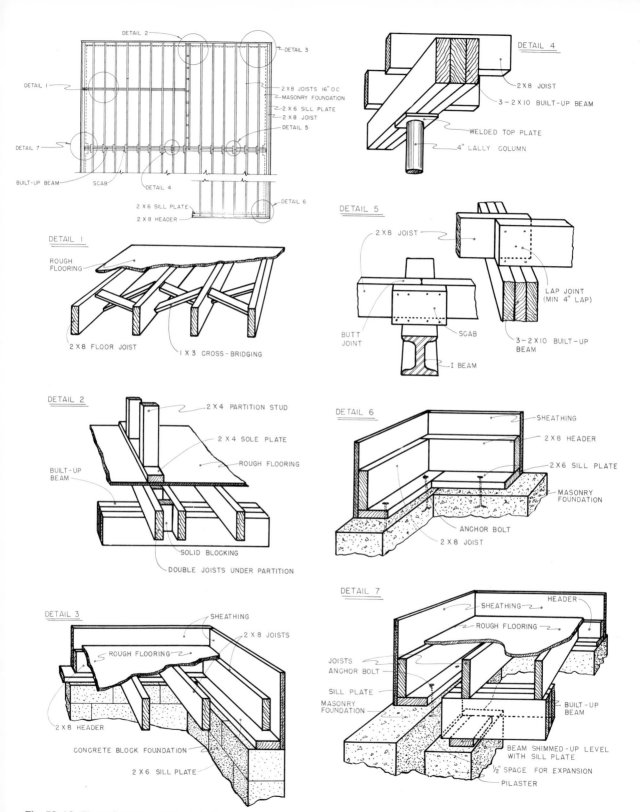

Fig 53-18 Floor-framing plan details.

box sill to the masonry foundation. Detail 7 shows the method of supporting the built-up beam with a pilaster, and the tie-in with the box sill and joist.

SILL SUPPORT DETAILS

Detail drawings showing sill construction details reveal not only the construction of the sill but also the method of attaching the sill to the foundation. Since the *sill* is the transition between the foundation and the exterior walls of a structure, a sill detail is usually included in most sets of architectural plans.

Some sill details are shown in pictorial form, as in Figs. 53-19 and 53-20. However, if pictorial drawings are used, two drawings must be used to show the exterior and interior view. Figure 53-19 shows an exterior pictorial view of a sill corner, and Fig. 53-20 shows an interior pictorial view of a sill corner. Pictorial drawings are easy to interpret but are more difficult and time-consuming to draw and dimension, therefore, most sill details are prepared in sectional form as shown in Fig. 53-21.

The floor area in a sill detail sectional drawing usually shows at least one joist. This

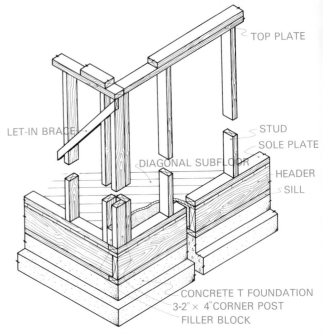

Fig 53-19 Sill details.

is done to show the direction of the joist and its size and placement in relationship to the placement of the subfloor and finished floor. This information is also sometimes shown on a floor framing plan. However, the floor fram-

Fig 53-20 Sill details.

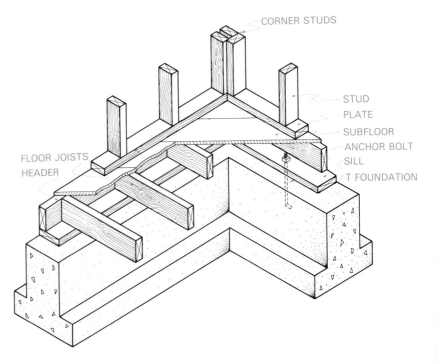

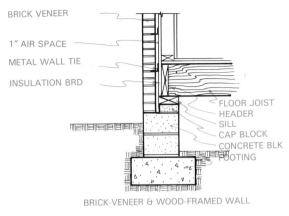

BRICK VENEER

1" AIR SPACE

METAL WALL TIE

INSULATION BRD

FLOOR JOIST
HEADER
SILL
CAP BLOCK
CONCRETE BLK
FOOTING

BRICK-VENEER & WOOD-FRAMED WALL

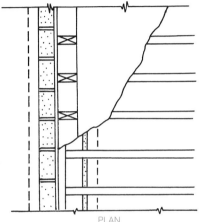

PLAN

Fig 53-21 Sill section detail.

ing plan shows neither the attachment of the floor system and sill to the foundation, nor the intersection of the exterior walls with the floor and sill. Figure 53-22 shows pictorial sill details and floor framing sections related to a balloon framing sill. The floor framing plan in this illustration can show the spacing of girders, blocking, and piers more clearly. However, the elevation section shows the intersections between the floor-system foundation sill and exterior wall more clearly. For this reason, sometimes both drawings are used to describe fully the type of construction required.

Sill details of this type are also required to show the relationship and joining of materials, such as masonry, wood, precast concrete, and structural steel. Figure 53-23 shows a typical masonry sill detail. This section is necessary to show the fire-cut portion of the

joist on the foundation because the fire-cut detail does not show on the floor framing plan.

Precast-concrete and structural-steel construction also require sill and floor details to show the size and spacing of structural members. These details are included in sets of drawings to show the size and spacing of members and the fastening methods and devices used to anchor concrete and masonry to wood, structural concrete, or steel members.

INTERMEDIATE SUPPORT DETAILS

These show the position and method of attachment of *intermediate support members,* such as girders and beams. These details are often shown by either a pictorial drawing, a floor framing plan detail, or an elevation section, as shown in Fig. 53-24A, B, and C. In these three illustrations, notice how the elevation section through the sill and floor-plan detail is used to show the difference between construction methods used with a standard girder. Figure 53-24B shows a girder supported with a box sill. Figure 53-24C shows a fire-cut girder and Fig. 53-24A shows a girder supported in a pocket in a masonry foundation wall.

Since there are so many different methods of attaching intermediate supports to foundation walls, a support detail is always necessary to complete a full set of plans. Figure 53-25 shows several alternative methods of attaching steel joists to masonry walls.

If a beam or girder cannot span the distance between foundation walls, an intermediate vertical support, such as a wood or steel column, is used. Figure 53-26 also shows methods of attaching the column to a girder or beam.

Figure 53-27 shows several methods of connecting intersecting horizontal members. Other intersections between perpendicular beams and floor joists are shown in Fig. 53-28. The joists in the left column rests directly on the beam or girder, while the joists in the right column intersects the girder, thus allowing the top of the girder and the top of the joist to be at or near the same level.

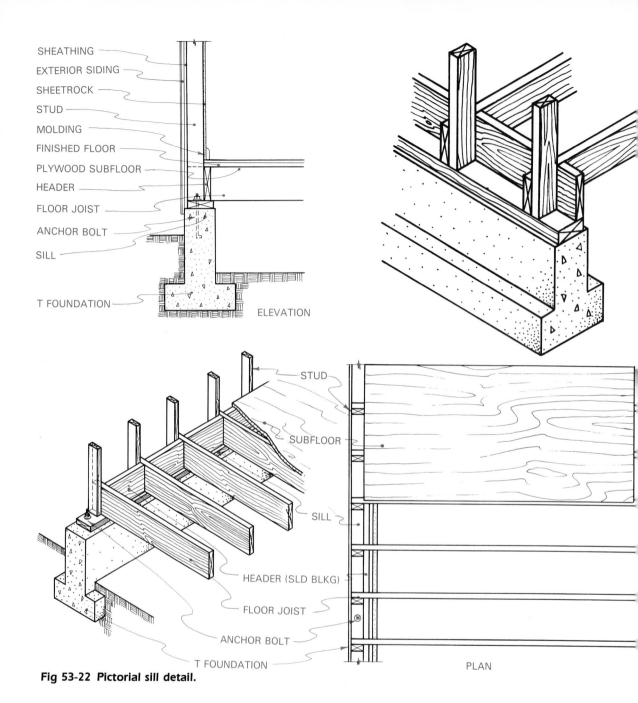

SHEATHING
EXTERIOR SIDING
SHEETROCK
STUD
MOLDING
FINISHED FLOOR
PLYWOOD SUBFLOOR
HEADER
FLOOR JOIST
ANCHOR BOLT
SILL
T FOUNDATION
ELEVATION

STUD
SUBFLOOR
SILL
HEADER (SLD BLKG)
FLOOR JOIST
ANCHOR BOLT
T FOUNDATION

PLAN

Fig 53-22 Pictorial sill detail.

Recommended methods of splicing lumber when necessary should also be detailed. Spliced members should be as strong as single members to eliminate building failures. The splices shown in Fig. 53-29 will resist compression, tension, and bending.

STAIRWELL FRAMING

The stairwell opening as drawn on the floor framing plan shows the relative position of the double joists and headers. Frequently, more information is needed concerning the

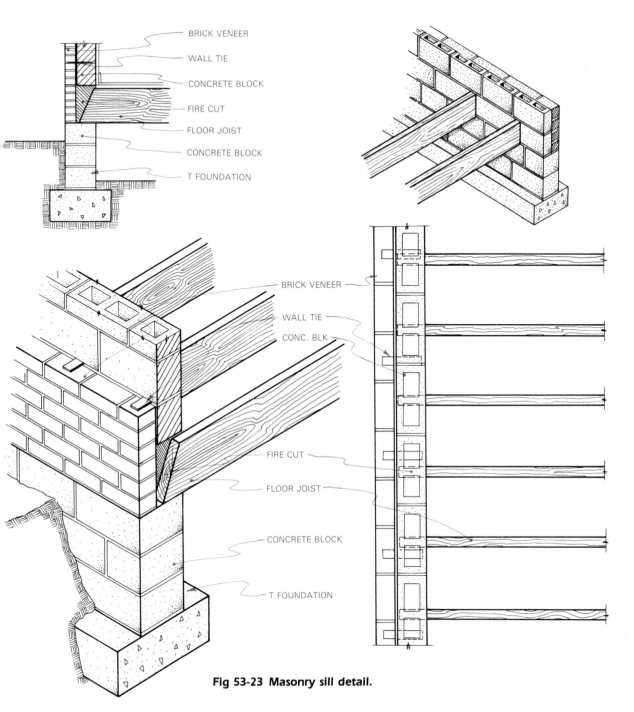

Fig 53-23 Masonry sill detail.

Within the figure the following labels appear:

BRICK VENEER
WALL TIE
CONCRETE BLOCK
FIRE CUT
FLOOR JOIST
CONCRETE BLOCK
T FOUNDATION

BRICK VENEER
WALL TIE
CONC. BLK
FIRE CUT
FLOOR JOIST
CONCRETE BLOCK
T FOUNDATION

relationship of the other parts of the stair assembly to the stairwell opening shown in Fig. 53-30. Information concerning the size and position of the various parts of the stair assembly is shown in Fig. 53-31. Such information is often shown in a separate detail.

Since the stairwell opening must be precisely shown on the floor framing plan, a complete design of the stair system should precede the preparation of the floor framing plan. The steps outlined in Figs. 53-32A through G show the sequences necessary for determining

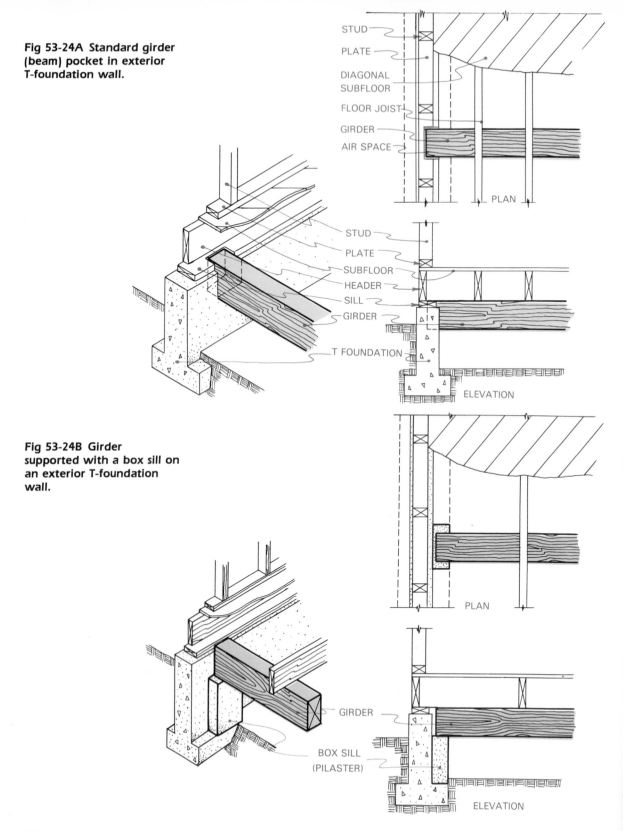

Fig 53-24A Standard girder (beam) pocket in exterior T-foundation wall.

STUD
PLATE
DIAGONAL SUBFLOOR
FLOOR JOIST
GIRDER
AIR SPACE

PLAN

STUD
PLATE
SUBFLOOR
HEADER
SILL
GIRDER
T FOUNDATION

ELEVATION

Fig 53-24B Girder supported with a box sill on an exterior T-foundation wall.

PLAN

GIRDER

BOX SILL (PILASTER)

ELEVATION

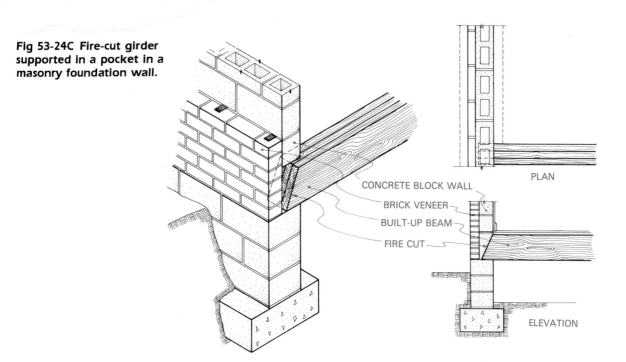

Fig 53-24C Fire-cut girder supported in a pocket in a masonry foundation wall.

CONCRETE BLOCK WALL

BRICK VENEER

BUILT-UP BEAM

FIRE CUT

PLAN

ELEVATION

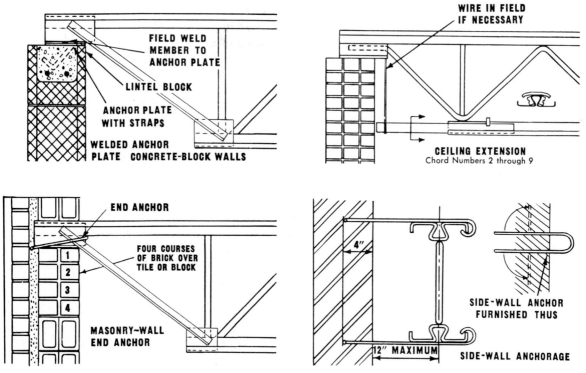

FIELD WELD MEMBER TO ANCHOR PLATE

LINTEL BLOCK

ANCHOR PLATE WITH STRAPS

WELDED ANCHOR PLATE   CONCRETE-BLOCK WALLS

WIRE IN FIELD IF NECESSARY

CEILING EXTENSION
Chord Numbers 2 through 9

END ANCHOR

FOUR COURSES OF BRICK OVER TILE OR BLOCK

MASONRY-WALL END ANCHOR

4"

12" MAXIMUM

SIDE-WALL ANCHOR FURNISHED THUS

SIDE-WALL ANCHORAGE

Fig 53-25 Alternate methods of attaching steel joists to masonry walls.

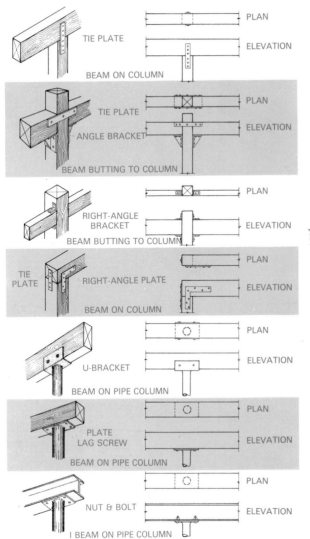

Fig 53-26 Methods of connecting girders or beams to columns.

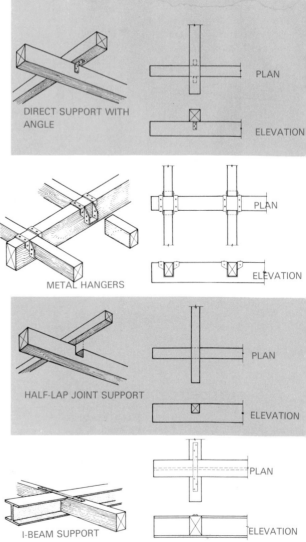

Fig 53-27 Method of connecting intersecting girders and beams to a vertical post.

the exact dimensions of the entire stair structure.

1 Lay out the distance from the first-floor level to the second-floor level exactly to scale (Fig. 53-32A). Convert this distance to inches and add the position of the ceiling line. If working in the metric system, no conversion is necessary.

2 Determine the most desirable riser heights (7½″, or 190 mm, is normal). Divide the number of inches (millimeters) between floor levels by the desired riser height to find the number of risers needed (Fig. 53-32B). Divide the area between the floors into spaces equaling the number of risers needed. This work can be done by inclining the scale.

3 Extend the riser-division lines lightly for about an inch, or 25 mm.

4 Determine the total length of the run (Fig. 53-32C). Lay out this distance from a starting point near the top riser line and measure the total run horizontally. Ex-

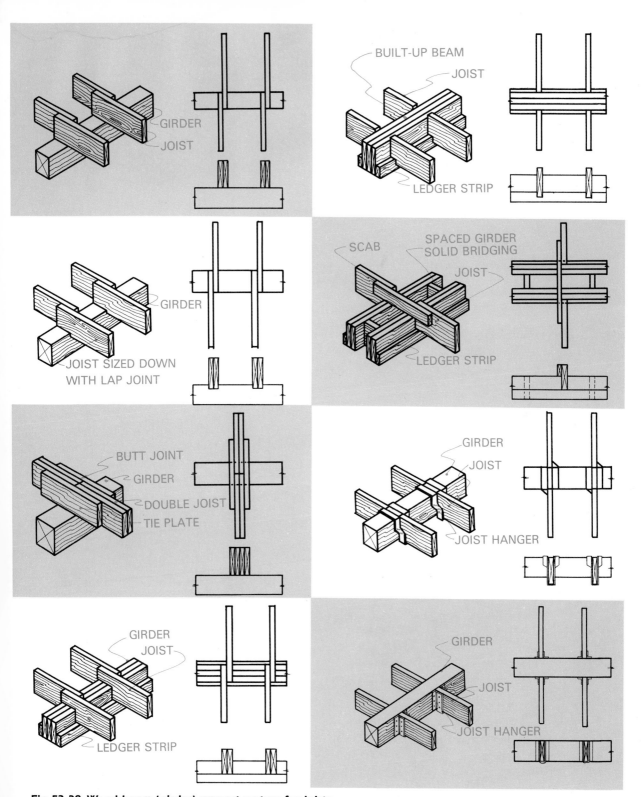

Fig 53-28 Wood beam (girder) support system for joists.

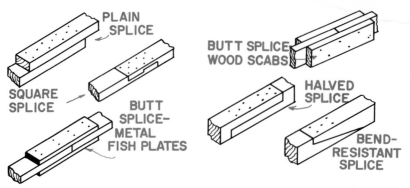

Fig 53-29 Splices that resist compression, tension, and bending.

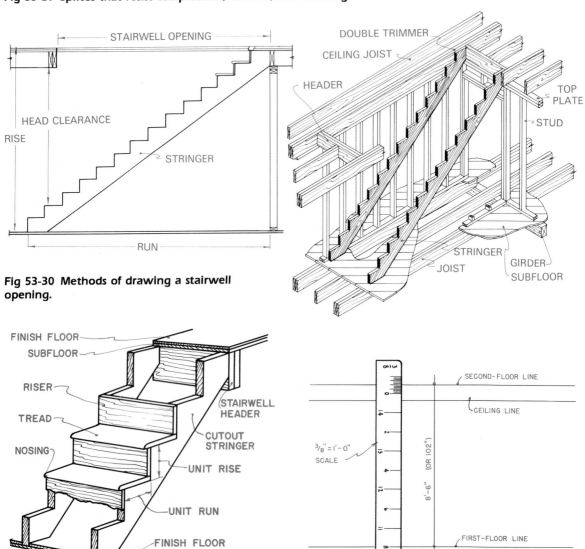

Fig 53-30 Methods of drawing a stairwell opening.

Fig 53-31 Parts of the stair assembly.

Fig 53-32A Lay out the distance from the first-floor level to the second-floor level.

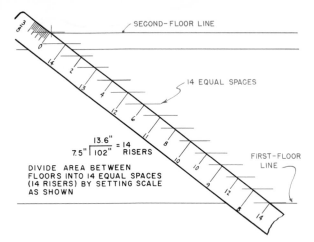

$$\frac{13.6"}{7.5"|\ 102"} = 14 \text{ RISERS}$$

DIVIDE AREA BETWEEN
FLOORS INTO 14 EQUAL SPACES
(14 RISERS) BY SETTING SCALE
AS SHOWN

Fig 53-32B Determine the number of risers and extend the riser lines.

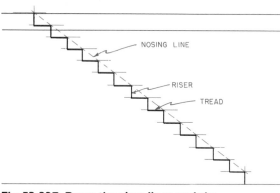

Fig 53-32E Draw the riser lines and the tread lines.

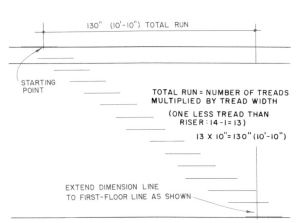

TOTAL RUN = NUMBER OF TREADS
MULTIPLIED BY TREAD WIDTH

(ONE LESS TREAD THAN
RISER: 14-1=13)

13 X 10"=130"(10'-10")

Fig 53-32C Lay out the total run.

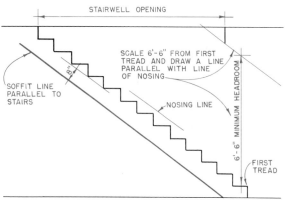

Fig 53-32F Establish the headroom clearance, stairwell opening, and soffit line.

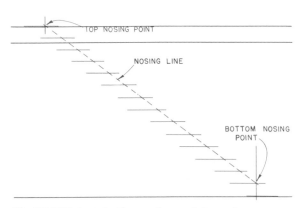

Fig 53-32D Locate the nosing points and draw the nosing line.

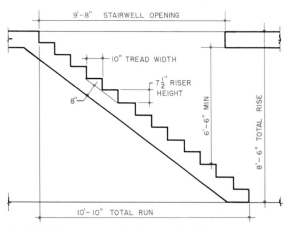

Fig 53-32G Erase guidelines and add dimensions.

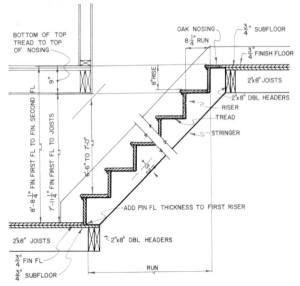

Fig 53-33 Sectional drawing of a stair assembly.

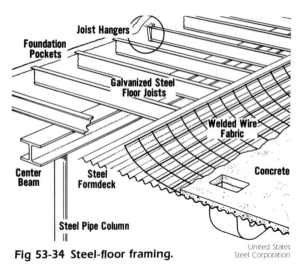

Fig 53-34 Steel-floor framing.

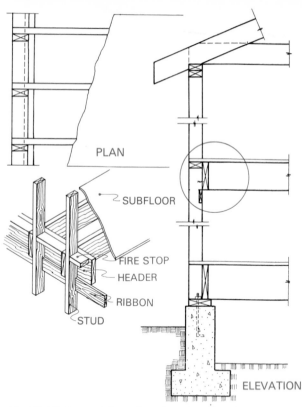

Fig 53-35 Second-floor framing details with balloon framing.

tend this line vertically to the first-floor line. The total run is the number of treads multiplied by the width of each tread. There is always one less tread than riser.

5 Locate the top and bottom nosing points (Fig. 53-32D). Mark the intersection between the starting point of the total run and the intersection between the end of the total run and the first riser line.

6 Draw the nosing line by connecting the bottom nosing point with the top nosing point.

7 Draw riser lines intersecting the nosing points and the light riser lines (Fig. 53-32E).

8 Make the tread lines and the riser lines heavy.

9 Draw the soffit line the same as the thickness of the stringer. Establish headroom clearances. Draw a parallel line 6'—6" (1.980 m) above the nosing line (Fig. 53-32F). Establish the stairwell opening by cutting the joists where the headroom clearance line intersects the bottom of the joist.

10 Show the outline of the carriage or stringer assembly.

11 Erase all layout lines and make all object lines heavier (Fig. 53-32G).

12 Add dimensions to describe the length of the stairwell opening, the size of the tread widths, the riser height, the minimum headroom, the total rise, and the total run.

Fig 53-36 Second floor with western framing.

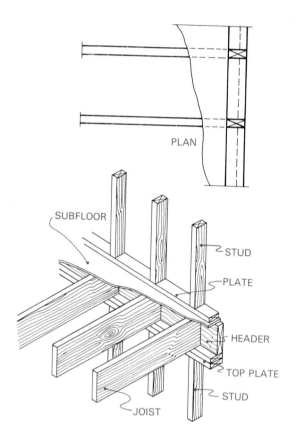

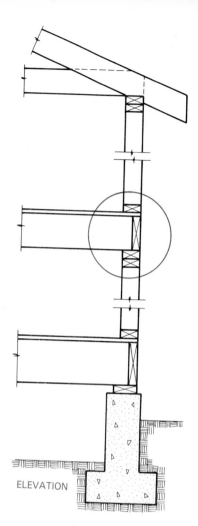

PLAN

SUBFLOOR

STUD

PLATE

HEADER

TOP PLATE

STUD

JOIST

ELEVATION

When the basic information pertaining to the overall dimensions and relationships of the stair assembly is established, a complete sectional drawing showing thicknesses and floor framing tie-ins can be prepared, as shown in Fig. 53-33. In this sectional drawing, the headers and the position of the bearing walls are shown.

STEEL

Floor framing plans for steel construction (Fig. 53-34) are prepared like other floor framing plans. The exact positions of columns, beams, and *purlins* (horizontal members) are dimensioned and the classification of each member indicated on the plan. Details should accompany steel-framing drawings to indi-cate the method of attaching steel members to each other. Lightweight concrete can be poured over steel or wood subfloors.

SECOND-FLOOR PLANS

Second-floor framing details are usually shown with a full section through the exterior wall (Fig. 53-35). Figure 53-35 shows the intersection of the second-floor joists in *balloon* (*eastern*) *framing*. In this style of framing, the studs are continuous from the foundation to the eave. The second-story joists are supported by a ribbon board nailed directly to the studs.

Figure 53-36 shows second-floor construction for *western* (*platform*) *framing*. In this style of framing, the second-floor joists rest

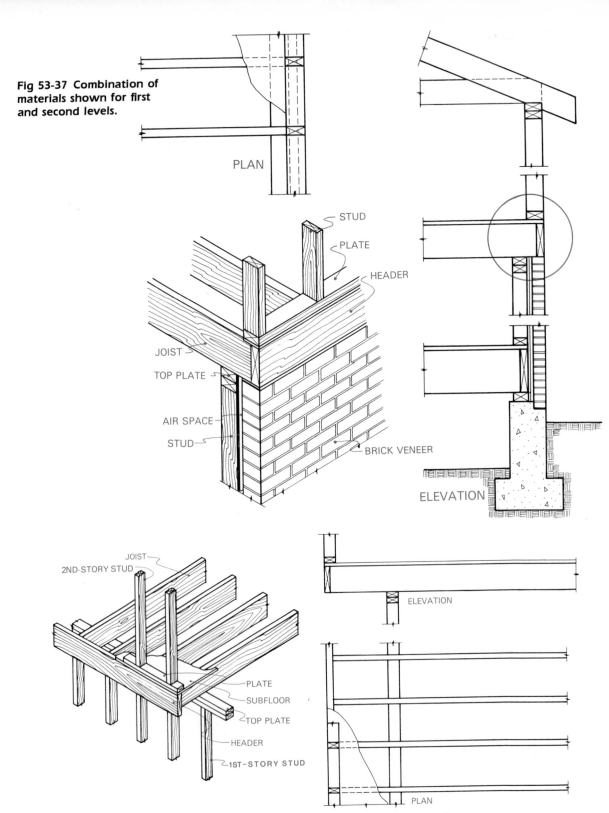

Fig 53-37 Combination of materials shown for first and second levels.

PLAN

PLAN

ELEVATION

STUD

PLATE

HEADER

JOIST

TOP PLATE

AIR SPACE

STUD

BRICK VENEER

JOIST

2ND-STORY STUD

ELEVATION

PLATE

SUBFLOOR

TOP PLATE

HEADER

1ST-STORY STUD

Fig 53-38 Cantilevered second floor with joist perpendicular to exterior wall.

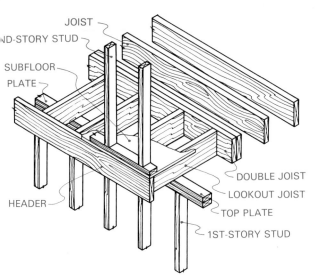

Fig 53-39 **Use of lookout for cantilevered second floor with joists parallel to exterior wall.**

directly on a top plate that rests directly on first-floor studs.

When a combination of exterior covering materials is used, the relationship between the floor system and the exterior wall is shown on the elevation. In Fig. 53-37, a brick veneer covers the first story. The second-floor header and joists rest directly on top of the brick veneer.

If the upper story is cantilevered over the first floor, the second-floor joists will run either parallel or perpendicular to the first-floor top plate that supports the second floor. When the joists are perpendicular, the construction is simple, as shown in Fig. 53-38. When the joists run parallel, a short lookout joist must be used to support the second floor, as shown in Fig. 53-39.

PROBLEMS

1 Identify the floor framing terms illustrated in Fig. 53-40.

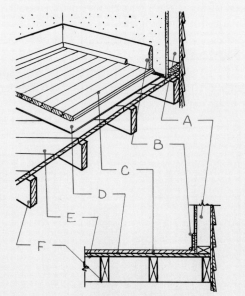

Fig 53-40 **Identify these floor-framing members.**

2 Develop a floor framing plan for as many floors as you are designing in your house plans.

3 Determine the size of joists for the floor framing plan shown in Fig. 53-41. Base your calculations on a combined load of 80 pounds per square foot.

4 Determine the size of the wood girder needed to support 80 pounds per square foot in the plan shown in Fig. 53-41. What size of steel beam would be needed to carry the same load?

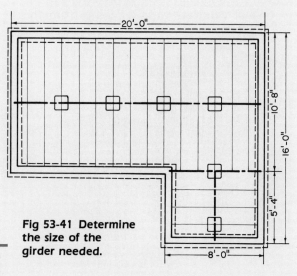

Fig 53-41 **Determine the size of the girder needed.**

5 Define the following architectural terms: *panel framing deflection, load, spacing, modulus of elasticity, fiber stress, maximum span, blocking, bridging, girder pocket, girder, built-up girder, pier, post, column, beam, header, double header, double joists, girder load area, post-load area,* *lally column, I beam, channel, joist hanger, scab, ledger strip, butt joint, square splice, butt splice, halved splice, bent splice, stairwell opening, tread, riser, nosing, unit run, unit rise, stringer, top nosing point, bottom nosing point, nosing line.*

UNIT 54

EXTERIOR-WALL FRAMING PLANS

Exterior walls for most residential buildings are of either conventional or post-and-beam construction. The typical method of erecting walls for most conventional buildings follows the braced-frame system. Prefabrication methods have led to variations in the erection of exterior walls, ranging from the panelization of just a basic frame to the complete panelized exterior wall, including plumbing, electrical work, doors, and windows, as shown in Fig. 54-1.

Large commercial structures usually use the curtain wall for their exterior wall. In this type of construction, nonstructural wall panels cover a steel framework. Figure 54-2 shows types of steel-framework structures and their relationship to height.

Regardless of the method of construction or fabrication, the preparation of exterior-panel drawings is relatively the same, whether they are prepared for factory use or for field use.

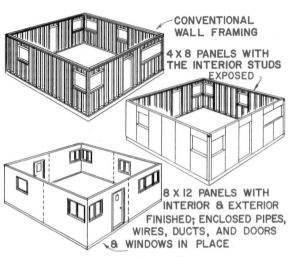

Fig 54-1 Methods of wall paneling.

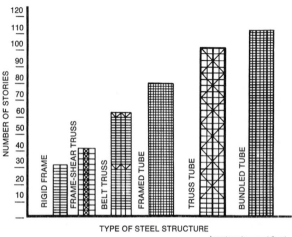

Fig 54-2 Types of steel framework compared to height.

American Iron and Steel Institute

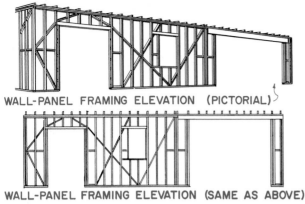

WALL-PANEL FRAMING ELEVATION (PICTORIAL)

WALL-PANEL FRAMING ELEVATION (SAME AS ABOVE)

Fig 54-3 Wall-framing elevation.

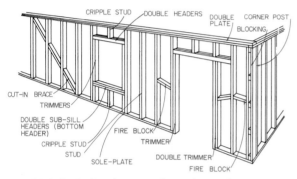

CRIPPLE STUD — DOUBLE HEADERS — DOUBLE PLATE — CORNER POST — BLOCKING

CUT-IN BRACE
TRIMMERS
DOUBLE SUB-SILL HEADERS (BOTTOM HEADER)
CRIPPLE STUD
STUD
SOLE-PLATE
FIRE BLOCK
TRIMMER
DOUBLE TRIMMER
FIRE BLOCK

Fig 54-4 Basic framing members shown in framing elevations.

FRAMING ELEVATIONS

Exterior-wall framing panels are best constructed by using a framing elevation drawing as a guide. The wall-framing elevation drawing is the same as the north, south, east, or west elevation of the building, with all the building materials removed except the basic framing. Figure 54-3 shows a wall-framing elevation compared with a pictorial drawing of the same wall. Notice that the framing elevation is an orthographic projection and does not reveal a second dimension or angle of projection. Figure 54-4 shows some of the basic framing members included in framing elevations.

The framing elevation is projected from the floor plan and elevation, as shown in Fig. 54-5. Since floor-plan wall thicknesses normally include the thickness of siding materials, care should be taken to project the outside of the framing line to the framing drawing and not the outside of the siding line. When drawing door and window framing openings, the sizes as given on the manufacturing specifications or on the door or window schedules should be rechecked as you project the openings from the floor plan and elevation.

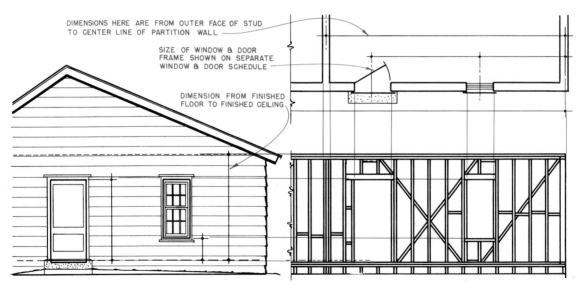

DIMENSIONS HERE ARE FROM OUTER FACE OF STUD TO CENTER LINE OF PARTITION WALL

SIZE OF WINDOW & DOOR FRAME SHOWN ON SEPARATE WINDOW & DOOR SCHEDULE

DIMENSION FROM FINISHED FLOOR TO FINISHED CEILING

Fig 54-5 Projection of an exterior-framing elevation from the floor-plan and elevation drawing.

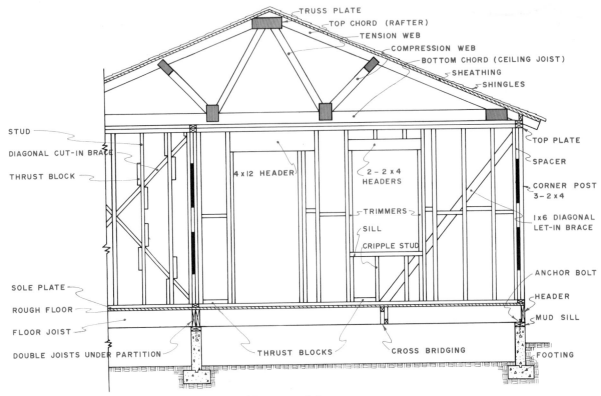

Fig 54-6 A framing elevation incorporated in a complete section of the building.

When aligned correctly, the elevation will supply all the projection points for the horizontal framing members, and the floor plan will provide all the points of projection for the location of vertical members.

COMPLETE SECTIONS

Another method of illustrating the framing methods used in wall construction is shown in Fig. 54-6. In this drawing, the elevation-framing information is incorporated in a complete sectional drawing of the entire structure. The advantage of this drawing is that it shows the relationship of the elevation-panel framing to the foundation-floor system and roof construction. Since this is a sectional drawing, blocking, joists, or any other member that is intersected by the cutting-plane line is shown by crossed diagonals.

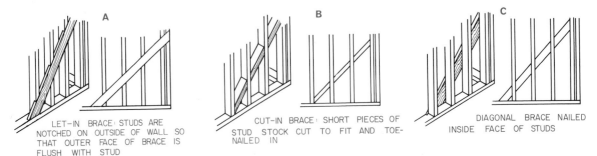

A

LET-IN BRACE: STUDS ARE NOTCHED ON OUTSIDE OF WALL SO THAT OUTER FACE OF BRACE IS FLUSH WITH STUD

B

CUT-IN BRACE: SHORT PIECES OF STUD STOCK CUT TO FIT AND TOE-NAILED IN

C

DIAGONAL BRACE NAILED INSIDE FACE OF STUDS

Fig 54-7 Methods of illustrating braces.

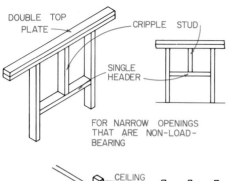

DOUBLE TOP PLATE
CRIPPLE STUD
SINGLE HEADER

FOR NARROW OPENINGS THAT ARE NON-LOAD-BEARING

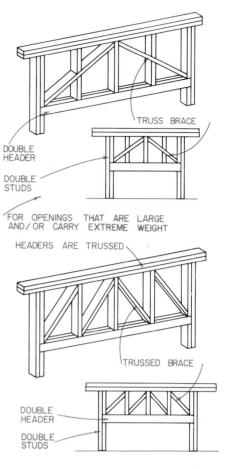

TRUSS BRACE
DOUBLE HEADER
DOUBLE STUDS

FOR OPENINGS THAT ARE LARGE AND/OR CARRY EXTREME WEIGHT

HEADERS ARE TRUSSED

TRUSSED BRACE

DOUBLE HEADER
DOUBLE STUDS

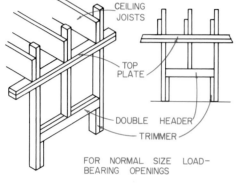

CEILING JOISTS
TOP PLATE
DOUBLE HEADER
TRIMMER

FOR NORMAL SIZE LOAD-BEARING OPENINGS

BRACING

One of the problems in preparing and interpreting framing-elevation drawings is to determine whether bracing is placed on the inside of the wall, on the outside of the wall, or between the studs. Figure 54-7 at A shows the method of illustrating *let-in braces* that are notched on the outside of the wall so that the outer face of the brace is flush with the stud. Figure 54-7 at B shows the method of illustrating *cut-in braces* that are nailed between the studs; Fig. 54-7 at C shows the method of illustrating *diagonal braces* that are nailed on the inside faces of the studs that form the wall.

Similar difficulties often occur in interpreting the true position of headers, cripple studs, plates, and trimmers. Figure 54-8 shows the method of illustrating the position of these members on the framing-elevation drawing to eliminate confusion and to simplify the proper interpretation.

PANEL ELEVATIONS

Panel elevations show the attachment of sheathing to the framing. It is often necessary to show the relationship between the *panel layout* and the *framing layout* of an elevation when the panel drawing and the framing drawing are combined in one drawing. The diagonals that indicate the position of the panels are drawn with dotted lines, as shown in Fig. 54-9. When only the panel layouts are shown, the outline of the panels and diagonals are drawn solid, as shown in Fig. 54-9. In this case, a separate framing plan must also be prepared and correlated with the panel elevation.

389

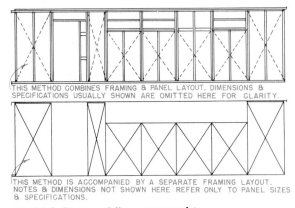

THIS METHOD COMBINES FRAMING & PANEL LAYOUT. DIMENSIONS & SPECIFICATIONS USUALLY SHOWN ARE OMITTED HERE FOR CLARITY.

THIS METHOD IS ACCOMPANIED BY A SEPARATE FRAMING LAYOUT. NOTES & DIMENSIONS NOT SHOWN HERE REFER ONLY TO PANEL SIZES & SPECIFICATIONS.

Fig 54-9 Diagonal lines are used to show the positions of panels.

Fig 54-10 Methods of dimensioning panel and framing elevations.

Fig 54-11 Control dimensions for horizontal member heights.

DIMENSIONS

The method of dimensioning panel and framing-elevation drawings is shown in Fig. 54-10. Overall widths, heights, and spacing of studs should be given. Control dimensions for the heights of horizontal members and *rough openings* (framing openings) for windows should also be included (Fig. 54-11). If the spacing of studs does not automatically provide the rough opening necessary for the window, the rough-opening width of the window should also be dimensioned.

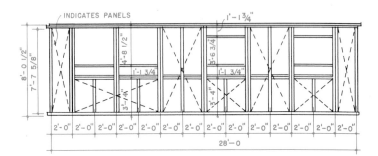

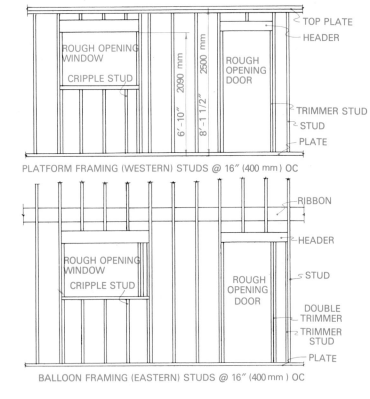

PLATFORM FRAMING (WESTERN) STUDS @ 16″ (400 mm) OC

BALLOON FRAMING (EASTERN) STUDS @ 16″ (400 mm) OC

DETAILS

Not all the information needed to frame an exterior wall can be shown on the elevation drawing. One of the most effective means of showing information at right angles to the elevation drawing is by *removed sections*.

REMOVED SECTIONS

Removed sections may be indexed to the floor plan or elevation, as indicated in Section 11. They may be removed sections from a pictorial drawing, as shown in Fig. 54-12. In this example, Section A describes the framing method employed on the wall and roof intersections, using break lines to expose the framing. Section B shows a wall section at the sill, revealing the intersection between the foundation-floor system and the exterior wall. These sections also show the inside wall treatment, insulation, sheathing, and exterior siding. Removed sections are effective in showing enlarged details.

SECTIONAL BREAKS

A larger scale is used on wall sections if the use of break lines is employed. Figure 54-13 shows the sequence of steps used to lay out and draw a typical external wall section.

1. Determine the width of the walls, foundation, and footer.
2. Lay out the angle of the roof and point of intersection of the roof and top plate. Lay out the width of the joist and sill.
3. Block in the position of roof rafters, top plates, sole plate, and roof floor lines.
4. Draw vertical lines to indicate the width of stud, insulation, air space, and brick.
5. Add details of the outlines of roof boards and shingles. Show outline of cornice construction.
6. Draw horizontal lines representing break lines. Add section-lining symbols.

Rendering by George A. Parenti for Masonite Corporation

Fig 54-12 Removed sections may be indexed to a floor plan and to elevation or pictorial drawings.

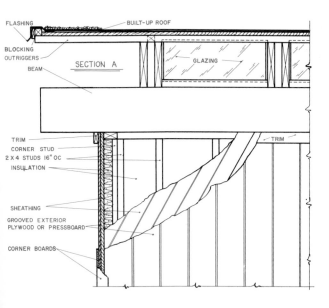

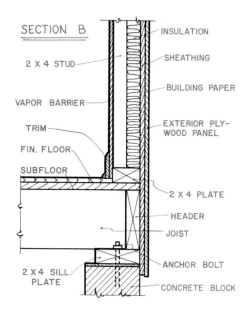

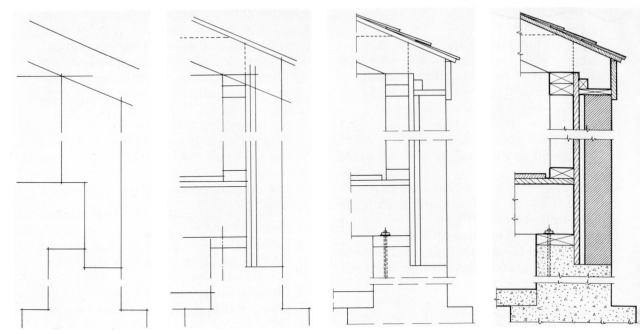

Fig 54-13 The sequence of laying out a typical external wall section.

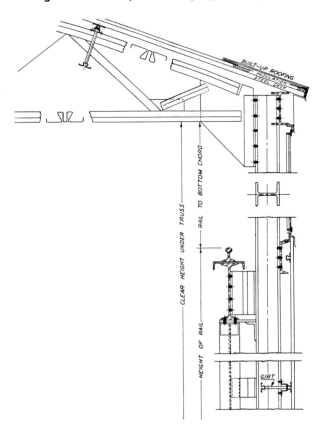

Fig 54-14 Revolved sections.

Sectional breaks can also be used to show a rotated section of the building material in the break area, as shown in Fig. 54-14.

PICTORIAL DETAILS

A *pictorial detail* or horizontal section of a wall is often used to clarify the relationship of framing members. This method is especially helpful in describing the layout of corner posts, as shown in Fig. 54-15. The horizontal section is more accurate in showing exact size and position of studs, but the pictorial drawing is more effective in showing the total relationship between sole plate, corner-post studs, and box-sill construction. See Fig. 53-35 for the use of a pictorial detail to clarify the section of a balloon framing elevation; Fig. 53-36 shows the same detail relating to a platform-system drawing. Pictorial drawings are also often used to expand a detail for clarification, as shown in Fig. 54-16.

EXPLODED VIEWS

Exploded views are most effective in showing internal construction that is hidden when the total assembly is drawn in its completed

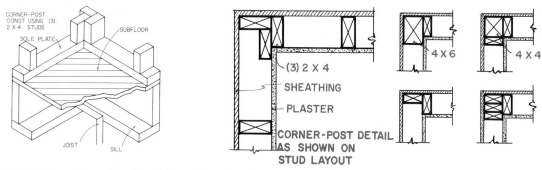

Fig 54-15 Pictorial and horizontal sections showing corner-post construction.

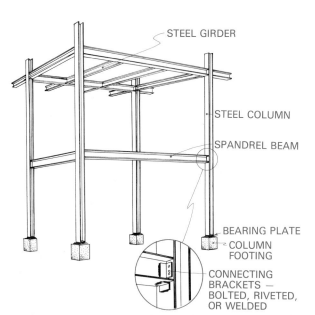

Fig 54-16 Pictorial detail extension.

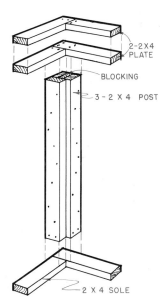

Fig 54-17 An exploded view of corner-post construction.

form. Figure 54-17 is an exploded view of a corner post that shows its construction on the sole plate and the position of the top plate. This method of detailing is also extensively used in cabinet work. Figure 54-18 shows steel-wall framing methods in an exploded view.

SIDING DETAILS

New siding materials are constantly being developed, and new applications found for existing materials. Aluminum is a good example. Today, the residential use of aluminum is most common for door and window frames, gutters and downspouts, and siding.

One method of showing the relationship between the basic framing and siding materials is the *breakaway* pictorial drawing, as shown in Fig. 54-19. This kind of drawing can be most effectively interpreted by the layman. However, it is most difficult to dimension for construction purposes. A more effective means of showing the exact position of siding materials is the vertical or horizontal section. Figures 54-20A through E show the sectional method of representing typical external walls. Figure 54-20A shows brick veneer on frame backing; Fig. 54-20B, solid brick wall; Fig.

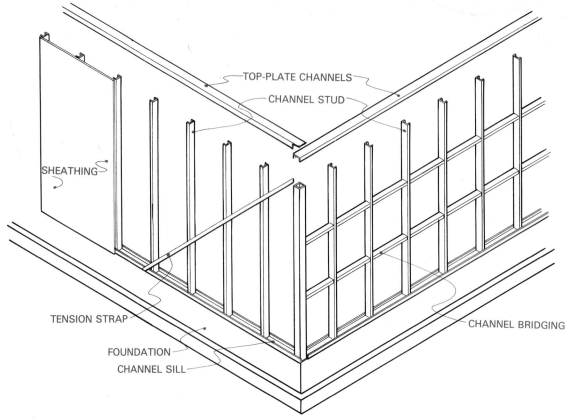

Fig 54-18 Steelwall exploded view.

TOP-PLATE CHANNELS

CHANNEL STUD

SHEATHING

TENSION STRAP

FOUNDATION

CHANNEL SILL

CHANNEL BRIDGING

54-20C, stucco; Fig. 54-20D, horizontal wood siding; and Fig. 54-20E, board-and-batten construction. Compare the plan section and the elevation section with the related pictorial drawing. Follow the relationship of each material as it exists in each drawing. You should be able to visualize the pictorial drawing by studying the sectional drawings of the plan and elevation for these and other similar siding materials.

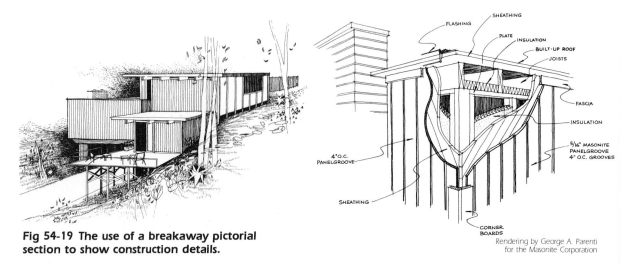

Fig 54-19 The use of a breakaway pictorial section to show construction details.

FLASHING

SHEATHING

PLATE

INSULATION

BUILT-UP ROOF

JOISTS

FASCIA

INSULATION

5/16" MASONITE PANELGROOVE 4" O.C. GROOVES

4" O.C. PANELGROOVE

SHEATHING

CORNER BOARDS

Rendering by George A. Parenti
for the Masonite Corporation

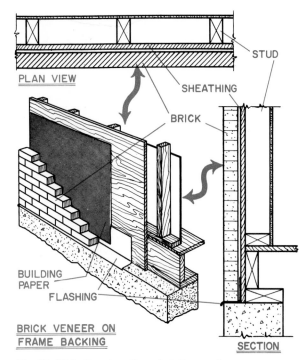

PLAN VIEW

STUD

SHEATHING

BRICK

BUILDING PAPER

FLASHING

SECTION

BRICK VENEER ON FRAME BACKING

Fig 54-20A Construction details can be shown on a plan section or on an elevation section.

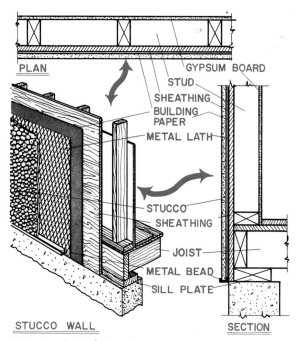

PLAN

GYPSUM BOARD

STUD

SHEATHING

BUILDING PAPER

METAL LATH

STUCCO

SHEATHING

JOIST

METAL BEAD

SILL PLATE

STUCCO WALL

SECTION

Fig 54-20C The relationship between a plan and an elevation section of a stucco wall.

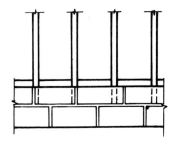

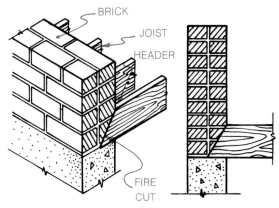

BRICK

JOIST

HEADER

FIRE CUT

Fig 54-20B Solid brick wall shown in plan, elevation, and pictorial views.

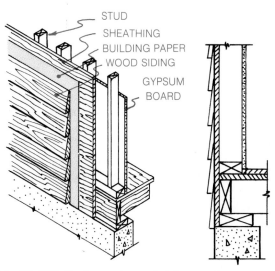

STUD

SHEATHING

BUILDING PAPER

WOOD SIDING

GYPSUM BOARD

Fig 54-20D Horizontal wood siding wall shown in plan, elevation, and pictorial views.

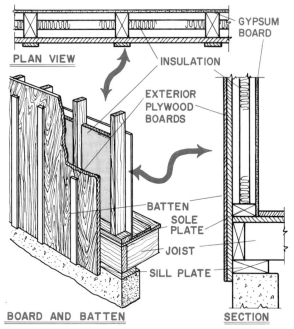

PLAN VIEW

GYPSUM BOARD

INSULATION

EXTERIOR PLYWOOD BOARDS

BATTEN

SOLE PLATE

JOIST

SILL PLATE

BOARD AND BATTEN

SECTION

Fig 54-20E The relationship between a plan and an elevation section of a board-and-batten wall.

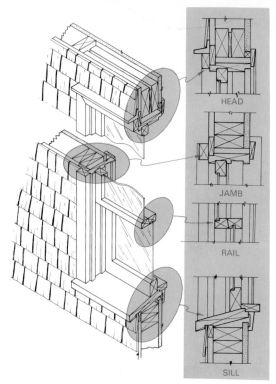

HEAD

JAMB

RAIL

SILL

Fig 54-21 Head, jamb, and sill sections are most commonly used to show window-framing details.

WINDOW-FRAMING DRAWINGS

One of the most effective methods of showing window-framing details is through head, jamb, and sill sections, as described in Section 11 (Fig. 54-21). Most windows are factory-made components ready for installation. Therefore, the most critical framing dimensions are those that describe the exact size of the framing opening. Window-framing drawings should include the sash-opening dimensions in addition to the dimensions of the framing opening (Fig. 54-22).

Figure 54-23 shows rough stud openings and sash openings for some of the more common sizes of windows.

When fixed windows or unusual window treatments are constructed in the field or even at the factory for a specific building, complete framing details must be drawn similar to the detailed drawing shown in Fig. 54-24. The more unusual the use of nonstandard sizes and components, the more complete must be

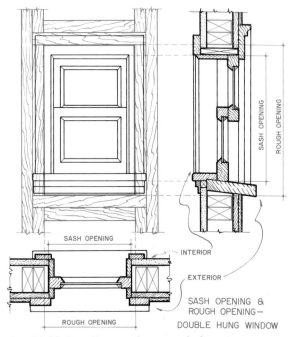

SASH OPENING

ROUGH OPENING

SASH OPENING

ROUGH OPENING

INTERIOR

EXTERIOR

SASH OPENING & ROUGH OPENING— DOUBLE HUNG WINDOW

Fig 54-22 Details are often needed to show the rough openings for doors and windows.

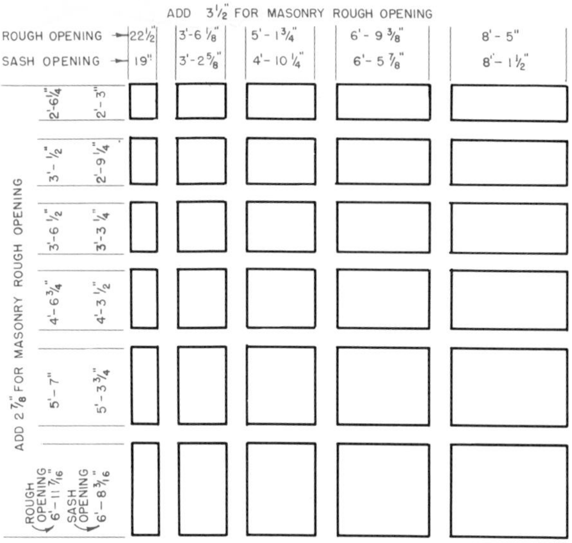
ADD 3½" FOR MASONRY ROUGH OPENING
ROUGH OPENING
SASH OPENING
22½"
19"
3'-6 ⅛"
3'-2⅝"
5'-1¾"
4'-10¼"
6'-9⅜"
6'-5⅞"
8'-5"
8'-1½"
ADD 2⅞" FOR MASONRY ROUGH OPENING
2'-6¼"
2'-3"
3'-½"
2'-9¼"
3'-6½"
3'-3¼"
4'-6¾"
4'-3½"
5'-7"
5'-3¾"
ROUGH OPENING 6'-11 7/16
SASH OPENING 6'-8 3/16

Fig 54-23 Rough-opening dimensions for common sizes of windows.

the detail framing drawings that accompany the design.

DOOR-FRAMING PLANS

The upper part of Fig. 54-25 shows the door and wall relationships for conventional door framing, which are described in wall-

Fig 54-24 Details are always needed for fixed-window construction.

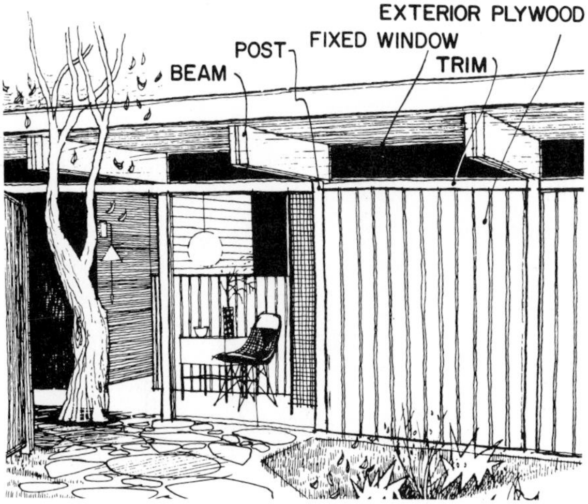
EXTERIOR PLYWOOD
FIXED WINDOW
POST
BEAM
TRIM

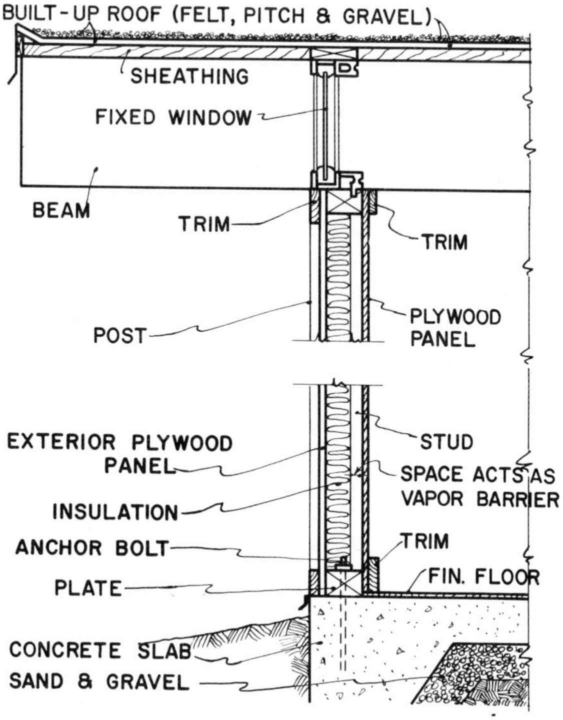
BUILT-UP ROOF (FELT, PITCH & GRAVEL)
SHEATHING
FIXED WINDOW
BEAM
TRIM
TRIM
POST
PLYWOOD PANEL
STUD
EXTERIOR PLYWOOD PANEL
SPACE ACTS AS VAPOR BARRIER
INSULATION
TRIM
ANCHOR BOLT
FIN. FLOOR
PLATE
CONCRETE SLAB
SAND & GRAVEL

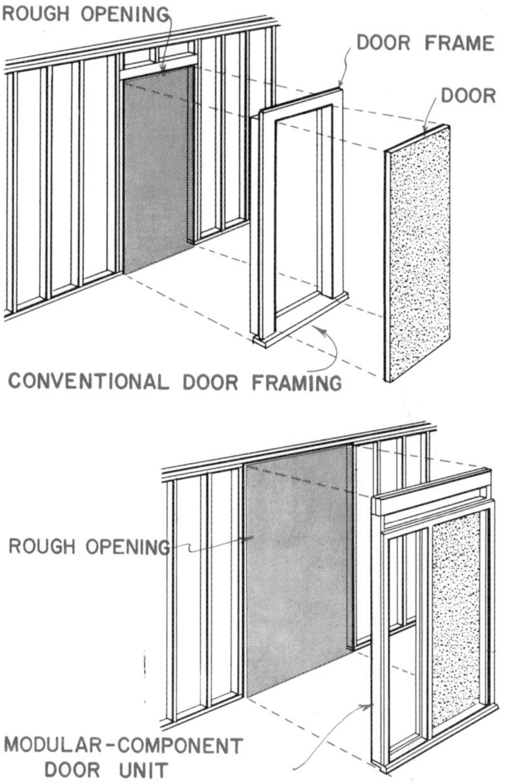
ROUGH OPENING
DOOR FRAME
DOOR
CONVENTIONAL DOOR FRAMING
ROUGH OPENING
MODULAR-COMPONENT DOOR UNIT

Fig 54-25 Modular-component door assembly.

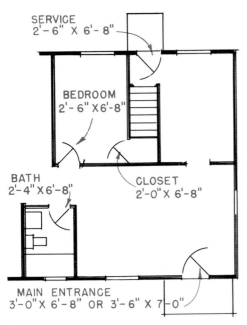

SERVICE
2'-6" X 6'-8"

BEDROOM
2'-6" X 6'-8"

BATH
2'-4" X 6'-8"

CLOSET
2'-0" X 6'-8"

MAIN ENTRANCE
3'-0" X 6'-8" OR 3'-6" X 7'-0"

Fig 54-26 Rough-opening dimensions for standard-sized doors.

framing details. The use of modular-component door units, as shown in the lower part of Fig. 54-25, is increasing throughout the home-building industry. Maintaining accurate rough-opening dimensions for these units is most critical to their installation. Whether the door framing is conventional or of a component design, the exact position of the opening and the dimensions of the rough opening must be clearly illustrated and labeled on the framing drawing. Figure 54-26 shows some rough-opening dimensions for standard-sized doors that are used in various locations through a residence.

Head, sill, and jamb sections, as shown in Section 11, are as effective in describing the door-framing construction as they are in showing window-framing details. Since the door extends to the floor, the relationship of the floor-framing system to the position of the door is critical. The method of intersecting the

Fig 54-27 The relationship between the door assembly and the wall-framing method.

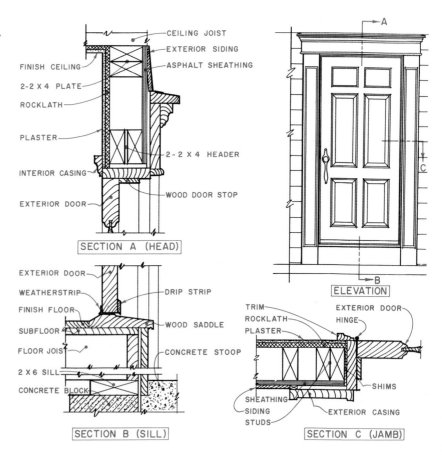

SECTION A (HEAD)

CEILING JOIST
EXTERIOR SIDING
ASPHALT SHEATHING
FINISH CEILING
2-2 X 4 PLATE
ROCKLATH
PLASTER
2-2 X 4 HEADER
INTERIOR CASING
WOOD DOOR STOP
EXTERIOR DOOR

SECTION B (SILL)

EXTERIOR DOOR
WEATHERSTRIP
FINISH FLOOR
SUBFLOOR
FLOOR JOIST
2 X 6 SILL
CONCRETE BLOCK
DRIP STRIP
WOOD SADDLE
CONCRETE STOOP

ELEVATION

SECTION C (JAMB)

TRIM
ROCKLATH
PLASTER
EXTERIOR DOOR
HINGE
SHIMS
SHEATHING
SIDING
STUDS
EXTERIOR CASING

398

door and hinge with the wall framing, as shown in Fig. 54-27, is also important. Section A (head) shows the intersection of the door and the header framing. Section B (sill) shows how the door relates to the floor framing. Section C (jamb) shows how the hinged side is constructed.

PROBLEMS

1 Draw a plan section view of the walls shown in Fig. 54-24.
2 Identify the framing members shown in Fig. 54-28.

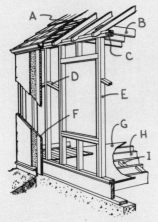

Fig 54-28 Identify these framing members.

3 Draw a wall section, using Fig. 54-29 as a guide. Plan to use stone veneer.

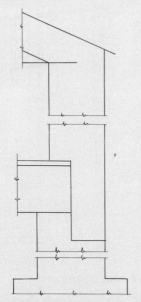

Fig 54-29 Complete a sectional drawing of this wall, using stone veneer.

4 Draw an elevation section of the details shown in Fig. 54-30.

5 Prepare an exterior panel-framing plan for a home of your own design.

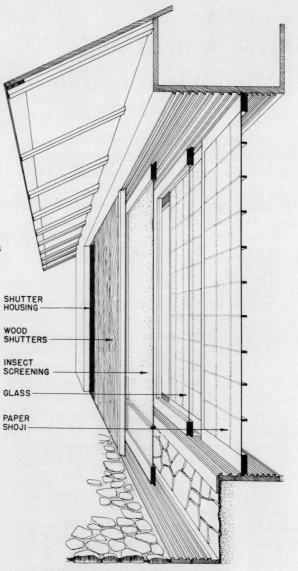

SHUTTER HOUSING

WOOD SHUTTERS

INSECT SCREENING

GLASS

PAPER SHOJI

Fig 54-30 Prepare an elevation section of this wall.

6 Prepare an exterior panel-framing plan for your own home.
7 Prepare an elevation section of the wall shown in Fig. 54-30.
8 Define the following terms: *framing elevation, bracing, let-in, panel elevation, removed sections, exploded view, rough opening, sash opening, sectional breaks.*

UNIT 55
INTERIOR-WALL FRAMING PLANS

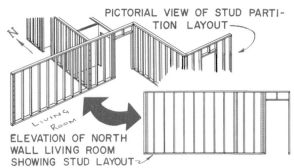

Fig 55-1 Panel elevation of an interior wall.

Interior-framing drawings include plan, elevation, and pictorial drawings of partitions and wall coverings. Detail drawings of interior partitions are also prepared to show intersections between walls and ceilings, floors, windows, and doors.

PARTITION-FRAMING PLANS

Interior partition-framing elevations are most effective in showing the construction of interior partitions. Interior partitions are projected from the partition on the floor plan in a manner similar to the projection of exterior partitions. To ensure the correct interpretation of the partition elevation, each interior-elevation drawing should include a label indicating the room and compass direction of the wall. For example, the elevation shown in Fig. 55-1 should be labeled *North Wall Living Room.* If either the room name or the compass direction is omitted, the elevation may be misinterpreted and confused with a similar wall in another room. The elevation drawing is always projected from the room it represents.

A complete study of the floor plan, elevation, plumbing diagrams, and electrical plans

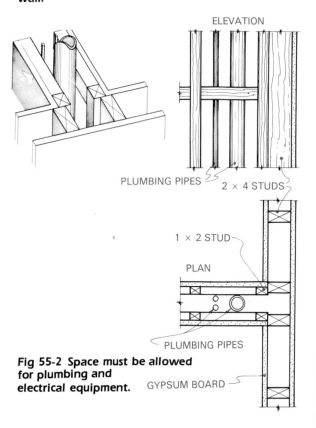

Fig 55-2 Space must be allowed for plumbing and electrical equipment.

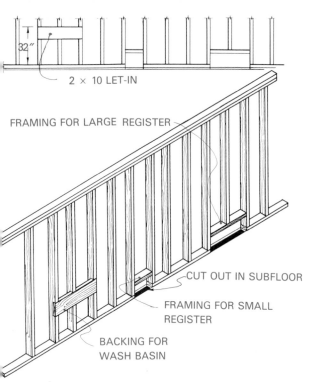

Fig 55-3 Wall-framing plan showing special framing needs.

32″
2 × 10 LET-IN
FRAMING FOR LARGE REGISTER
CUT OUT IN SUBFLOOR
FRAMING FOR SMALL REGISTER
BACKING FOR WASH BASIN

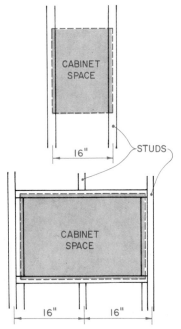

Fig 55-4 Framing-elevation details showing provisions for built-in items.

CABINET SPACE
16″
STUDS
CABINET SPACE
16″   16″

should be made prior to the preparation of the interior wall-framing drawings. Provision must be made in the framing drawings for soil stacks and other large plumbing facilities and for special electrical equipment (Fig. 55-2).

When a stud must be broken to accommodate various items, the framing drawing must show the recommended construction (Figs. 55-3 and 55-4).

WALL-COVERING DETAILS

Basic types of wall-covering materials used for finished interior walls include plaster, dry-wall construction, paneling, tile, and masonry.

PLASTER

Plaster is applied to interior walls by using wire lath or gypsum sheet lath, as shown in Fig. 55-5. Plaster walls are very strong and sound-absorbing. Plaster is also decay-proof and termite-proof. However, plaster walls crack easily and take months to dry. Also, installation costs are rather high.

DRY-WALL CONSTRUCTION

Materials applicable to dry-wall construction include fiber boards, gypsum wallboards, plywood, and asbestos wallboard. The most popular dry-wall construction is gypsum wallboards nailed directly to the studs, as shown in Fig. 55-6. When this construction is used, furring strips may be placed over the joints and nail holes. However, the more com-

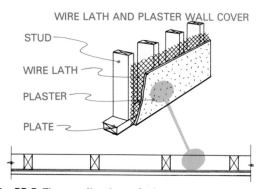

WIRE LATH AND PLASTER WALL COVER
STUD
WIRE LATH
PLASTER
PLATE

Fig 55-5 The application of plaster to interior walls.

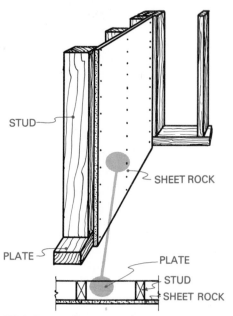

4′ × 8′ GYPSUM BOARD (SHEET ROCK) PANELS NAILED TO 2 × 4 STUDS

STUD

SHEET ROCK

PLATE

PLATE

STUD

SHEET ROCK

Fig 55-6 Dry-wall construction.

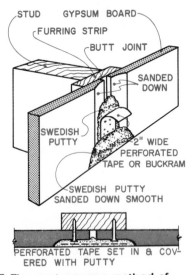

STUD   GYPSUM BOARD

FURRING STRIP

BUTT JOINT

SANDED DOWN

SWEDISH PUTTY

2″ WIDE PERFORATED TAPE OR BUCKRAM

SWEDISH PUTTY SANDED DOWN SMOOTH

PERFORATED TAPE SET IN & COVERED WITH PUTTY

Fig 55-7 The most common method of concealing dry-wall joints.

mon practice is to camouflage the joints by sanding a depression in the wallboard and applying a perforated tape covered with Swedish putty and sanded smooth, as shown in Fig. 55-7.

PANELING

When paneling is used as an interior finish, horizontal furring strips should be placed on the studs to provide a nailing or gluing surface for the paneling (Fig. 55-8). Determining the type of joint that should be used between panels is a design problem that should be solved through the use of a separate detail, as shown in Fig. 55-9. The joint may be exposed by use of the butt joint or cross-lap joint. A series of furring strips can be used between the joints or on the outside of them.

The method of intersecting the outside corners of paneling must also be detailed. Outside corners can be intersected by mitering or overlapping and exposing the paneling. Corner boards, metal strips, or molding may be used on the intersection (Fig. 55-10).

Inside-corner intersections can be drawn as shown in Fig. 55-11.

BASE INTERSECTIONS

The method of intersecting the finished wall materials and the floor should be detailed. The details may be a section or a pictorial drawing, as shown in Fig. 55-12. The position of the sole plate, wallboard or lath and plaster, baseboard, and molding should be shown.

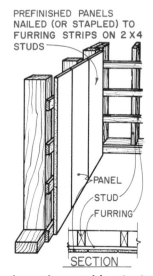

PREFINISHED PANELS NAILED (OR STAPLED) TO FURRING STRIPS ON 2 X 4 STUDS

PANEL

STUD

FURRING

SECTION

Fig 55-8 Furring strips provide a horizontal surface for attaching paneling.

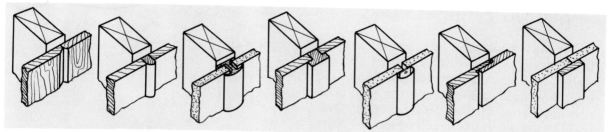

Fig 55-9 Panel-joint details.

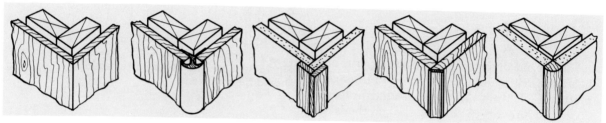

Fig 55-10 Outside-corner panel joints.

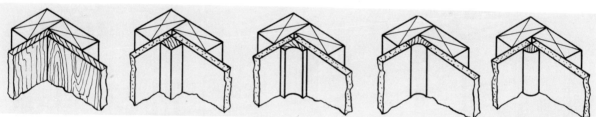

Fig 55-11 Inside-corner panel joints.

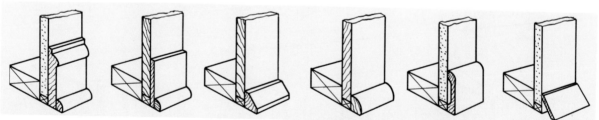

Fig 55-12 A method of intersecting the panel wall with the floor.

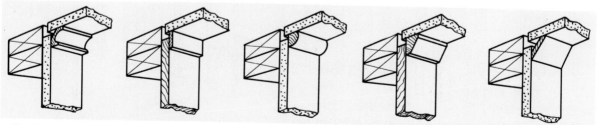

Fig 55-13 A method of intersecting the panel wall with the ceiling.

CEILING INTERSECTIONS

Details should also be prepared to show the intersection between the ceiling and the wall. Details should show the position of the top plate, wallboard-ceiling finish, and position of molding used at the intersection (Fig. 55-13). Care should be taken when designing the base treatment and ceiling-intersection treatment to ensure that the intersections are consistent in style, as shown in Fig. 55-14.

INTERIOR-DOOR DETAILS

Pictorial or orthographic jamb, sill, and head sections should be prepared to illustrate methods of framing used around interior doors. Figure 55-15 shows the methods of

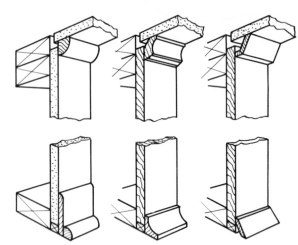

Fig 55-14 Base and ceiling intersections should be consistent.

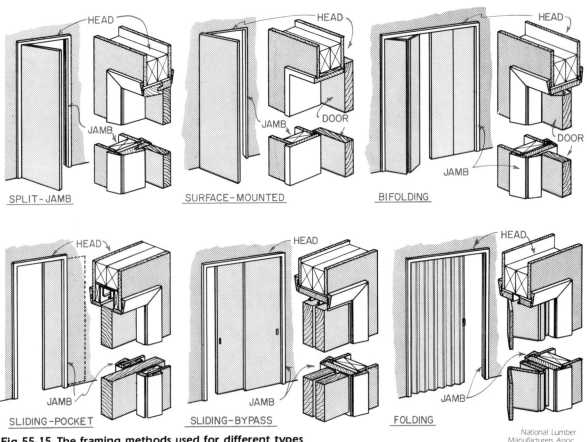

SPLIT-JAMB

SURFACE-MOUNTED

BIFOLDING

SLIDING-POCKET

SLIDING-BYPASS

FOLDING

National Lumber
Manufacturers Assoc.

Fig 55-15 The framing methods used for different types of interior doors.

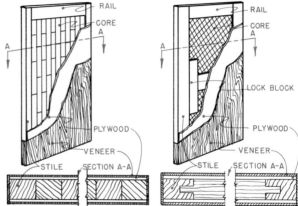

Fig 55-17 Door construction.

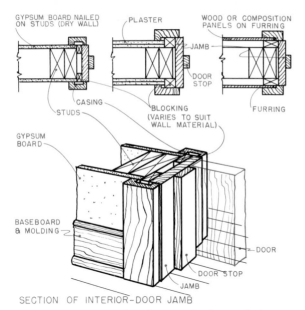

Fig 55-16 The door-framing methods needed for different types of construction.

framing split-jamb, surface-mounted, bifolding, sliding-pocket, sliding-bypass, and folding doors. A detailed drawing need not be prepared for each door but should be prepared for each type of door used in the house and should be keyed to the door schedule for identification. Figure 55-16 shows the relationship between a pictorial section of an interior-door jamb and the variations of this section necessary for plaster, gypsum-board, or paneled wall coverings. Details are not usually necessary for the actual construction of a door, for this is an item that is normally outlined in the specifications. However, it is important to select a proper door from manufacturers' specifications or to prepare a detailed drawing to ensure compliance with minimum standards. Figure 55-17 shows the cutaway drawing and section of two types of solid doors. Hollow-core doors are generally used on interior partitions.

PROBLEMS

1 Project a panel-framing elevation drawing of the plumbing wall of bathroom #1, as shown in Fig. 37-14.

2 Draw a vertical section of the wall shown in Fig. 55-8.

3 Draw plan and elevation sections of one of the joints shown in Fig. 55-9.

4 Draw plan sections for one of the intersections shown in Fig. 55-10 and Fig. 55-11.

5 Draw a typical interior-wall framing plan for a kitchen, bath, and living-area wall of the house you are designing. Use as many detail drawings as you think necessary to support the framing plans.

6 Draw a complete horizontal wall section of the rear living-room wall shown in Fig. 7-5. As part of the fireplace treatment, plan to make the entire wall brick from the fireplace to the door opening.

7 Prepare a plan section similar to the plan shown in Fig. 55-16. Show the position of brick, blocking, casing, and jamb.

8 Define the following terms: *dry wall, plaster, paneling, base detail, interior partition.*

UNIT 56
STUD LAYOUTS

A *stud layout* is a plan similar to a floor plan, showing the position of each wall-framing member. The stud layout is a section through each interior elevation drawing, as shown in Fig. 56-1. The cutting-plane line for purposes of projecting the stud layout is placed approximately at the midpoint of the panel elevation. Figure 56-2 shows a stud layout that represents the framing plan of the panel.

STUD DETAILS

Stud layouts are of two types: the *complete plan*, which shows the position of all framing members on the floor plan, and the *stud detail*, which shows only the position and relationship of several studs or framing intersections.

CORNER POST

The position of each stud in a corner-post layout is frequently shown in a plan view, as illustrated in Fig. 56-3. Occasionally, siding and inside-wall covering materials are shown on this plan. Preparing this type of detail without covering materials is the quickest way to show corner-post construction.

PARTITION INTERSECTIONS

Details of the exact position of each stud and blocking of intersecting walls are shown by a plan section (Fig. 56-4). If wall coverings are shown on the detail, the complete wall structure can be drawn (Fig. 56-5). In prepar-

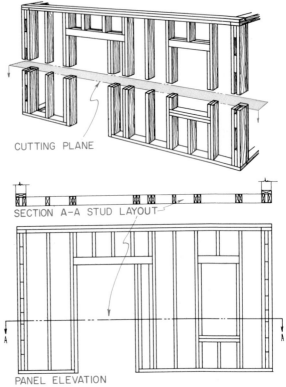

Fig 56-1 The stud layout is a plan section taken through the panel elevation.

ing the plan section, care should be taken to show the exact position of blocking or short pieces of stud stock that may not pass through the cutting-plane line. Blocking should be labeled to prevent the possibility of identifying

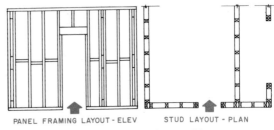

Fig 56-2 The relationship of a stud layout to a panel elevation.

406

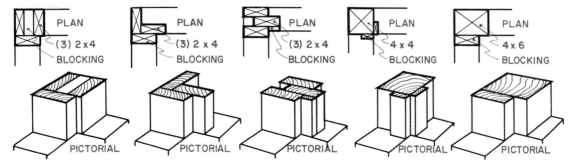

Fig 56-3 Stud details of several corner-post layouts.

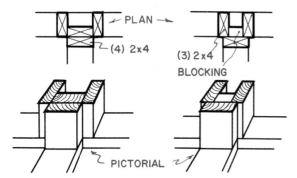

Fig 56-4 Position of studs in a partition intersection.

the blocking as a full-length stud. When laying out the position of all studs, remember that the finished dimensions of a 2×4 are actually $1\frac{1}{2} \times 3\frac{1}{2}$. The exact dressed sizes of other rough stock are as follows:

Rough	Dressed
2×3	$1\frac{1}{2} \times 2\frac{1}{2}$
2×4	$1\frac{1}{2} \times 3\frac{1}{2}$
2×6	$1\frac{1}{2} \times 5\frac{1}{2}$
2×8	$1\frac{1}{2} \times 7\frac{1}{4}$
2×10	$1\frac{1}{2} \times 9\frac{1}{4}$
2×12	$1\frac{1}{2} \times 11\frac{1}{4}$
1×6	$\frac{3}{4} \times 5\frac{1}{2}$
1×8	$\frac{3}{4} \times 7\frac{1}{4}$

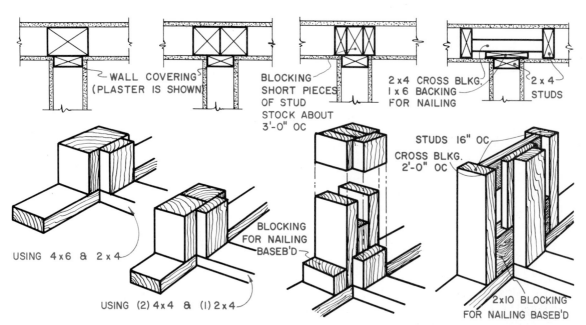

Fig 56-5 Wall covering and blocking can be shown on intersection details.

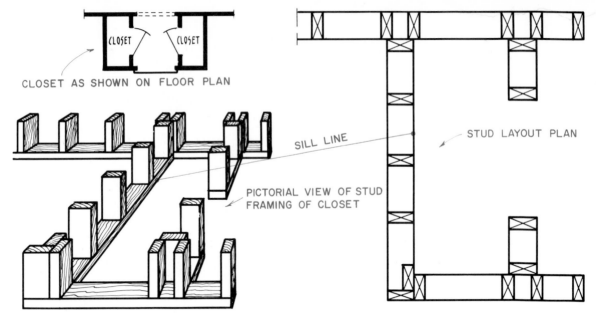

CLOSET AS SHOWN ON FLOOR PLAN

SILL LINE

STUD LAYOUT PLAN

PICTORIAL VIEW OF STUD FRAMING OF CLOSET

Fig 56-6 The outline of the sill is shown in a stud layout.

COMPLETE PLAN

The main purpose of a stud layout is to show how interior partitions fit together and how studs are spaced on the plan. Figure 56-6 shows part of a stud layout. The outline of the plate and the exact position of each stud that falls on an established center (16″, 20″, 24″, or 400 mm) are normally identified by diagonal lines. Studs other than those that are on regular centers are shown by different symbols. Studs that are short, blocking, or different in size are identified by a different key (Fig. 56-7). Using a coding system of this type eliminates the need for dimensioning the position of each stud if it is part of the regular partitioned pattern. The practice of coding studs and other members shown on the stud plan also eliminates the need for showing detailed dimensions of each stud.

Detailed dimensions are normally shown on the key or on a separate enlarged detail.

Distances that are dimensioned on a stud layout include the following:

1 Inside framing dimensions of each room
2 Framing width of the halls
3 Rough openings for doors and arches

4 Length of each partition
5 Width of partition where dimension lines pass through from room to room. (This provides a double check to ensure that the room dimensions plus the partitioned dimensions add up to the overall dimension.) When a stud layout is available, it is used on the job to establish partition positions.

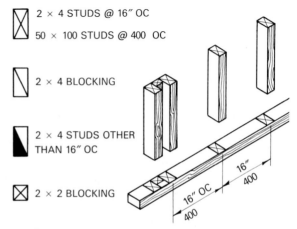

2 × 4 STUDS @ 16″ OC
50 × 100 STUDS @ 400 OC

2 × 4 BLOCKING

2 × 4 STUDS OTHER THAN 16″ OC

2 × 2 BLOCKING

Fig 56-7 Stud-layout symbols.

408

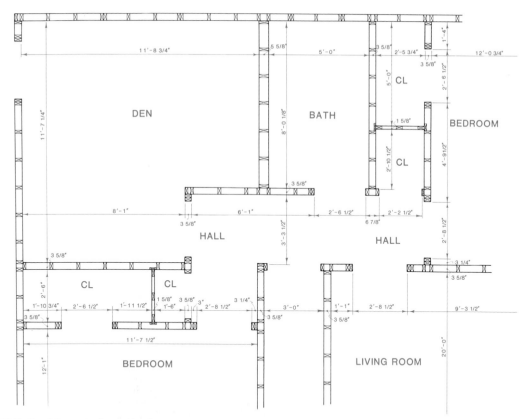

Fig 56-8 Stud-layout dimensioning.

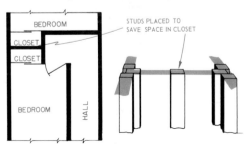

Fig 56-9 Studs are placed flat to conserve space.

Figure 56-8 shows the application of these dimensional practices to a typical stud layout plan.

To conserve space where full partition width is not important, as between closets, studs are sometimes turned so that they are flat. This rotation should be reflected in the stud layout (Fig. 56-9).

PROBLEMS

1. Prepare a stud layout of the floor plan shown in Fig. 33-12.
2. Prepare a corner-post detail for the corner posts shown in Fig. 34-6.
3. Prepare a stud layout for the home in which you now reside.
4. Prepare a stud layout ($\frac{1}{4}'' = 1'-0''$) for a home of your own design.
5. Draw a stud layout of the east living-room partition shown in Fig. 33-12.
6. Define the following terms: *stud layout, stud detail, corner post, rough lumber, dressed lumber, blocking, inside framing dimensions.*

UNIT 57
ROOF FRAMING PLANS

The first structure made for shelter was probably a lean-to roof supported by posts. As structures became larger and more complex, the composition and shape of the roof also changed.

The main function of a roof is to provide protection from rain, snow, sun, and very hot or cold temperatures. The roof of a northern building is designed to withstand heavy snow loads. The thatched roof of a tropical native hut provides protection only from sun and rain.

As roof styles developed through the centuries, *pitches* (angles) were changed, gutters and downspouts were added for better drainage, and overhangs were extended to provide more protection from the sun. As the size of roofs changed, the size and types of material changed accordingly. In any modern residence, the roof is an integral part of the design of the whole house.

STRUCTURAL DESIGN

The walls of the structure are given stability by their attachment to the ground and to the roof. Most buildings are not structurally sound without roofs. Walls cannot resist outside or inside forces unless some horizontal support (roof) is given to the upper part of the wall. This principle is shown in Fig. 57-1.

SUPPORT

The weight of the roof is normally supported by the exterior walls of the structure

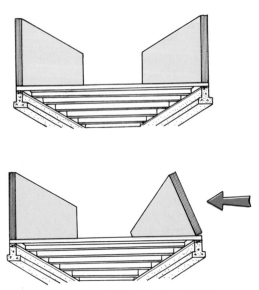
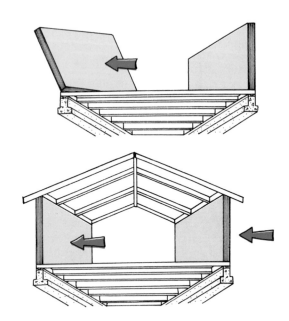

Fig 57-1 A roof adds stability to a structure.

410

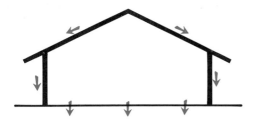

Fig 57-2 The weight of the roof is transmitted to the outside walls.

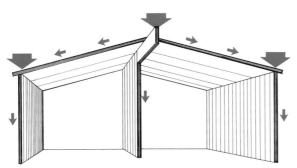

Fig 57-3 Interior load-bearing partitions help support roofs.

Fig 57-4 A roof can be connected directly to the foundation.

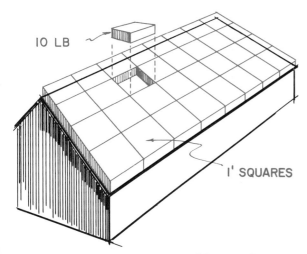

Fig 57-5 Roof loads are measured in pounds per square foot.

(Fig. 57-2). Roofs may be supported by a combination of the exterior walls plus the load-bearing partitions or beams (Fig. 57-3). In a frame or continuous-arch design, the roof is supported by direct connection with the foundation (Fig. 57-4).

LOADS

The structural members of a roof must be sufficiently strong to withstand the loads that bear upon it.

DEAD LOADS
Dead loads that bear upon most roofs include the weight of shingles, sheathing, and rafters.

All loads are computed on the basis of pounds per square foot, or kilograms per square meter if using metric measurements. The typical asphalt-shingle roof weighs approximately 10 pounds per square foot (Fig. 57-5), and a typical asbestos roof weighs approximately 12 pounds per square foot. A Spanish tile roof weighs 17 pounds per square foot. Thus a 40′ × 20′ (800 square feet) asphalt-shingle roof would be designed to carry an 8000 pound load (800 square feet × 10 pounds per square foot).

LIVE LOADS
Live loads that act on the roof include wind loads and snow loads, which vary greatly from one geographical area to another. For example, the combined wind and snow loads in the South Pacific are approximately 20 pounds per square foot. In the central and western parts of the United States, these loads are 30 pounds per square foot, and in the northeastern and northwestern parts of the United States, they are 40 pounds per square foot (Fig. 57-6).

Snow and wind loads vary greatly as the pitch of the roof is changed. Snow loads are exerted in a vertical direction; wind loads are exerted in a horizontal direction. A high-pitch roof will withstand snow loads better than a low-pitch roof (Fig. 57-7). The reverse is true

411

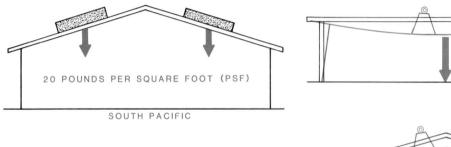

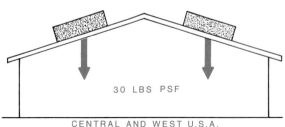

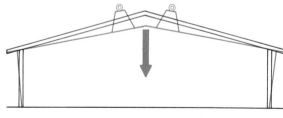

20 POUNDS PER SQUARE FOOT (PSF)

SOUTH PACIFIC

30 LBS PSF

CENTRAL AND WEST U.S.A.

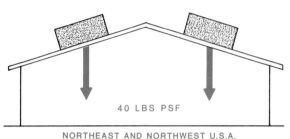

40 LBS PSF

NORTHEAST AND NORTHWEST U.S.A.

Fig 57-6 Live roof loads vary from region to region.

Fig 57-7 Low-pitch roofs need heavier support or shorter spans to withstand snow and wind loads.

of wind loads. There is virtually no wind load exerted on a flat roof, and moderate wind loads (15 pounds per square foot) are exerted on a low-pitch roof. Approximately 35 pounds per square foot is exerted on a high-pitch roof. An excessively resistant wind load is exerted on a completely vertical wall, approximately 40 pounds per square foot, which is equivalent to hurricane force, as shown in Fig. 57-8. For all practical purposes, snow and wind loads are combined in one total live load. Live loads and dead loads are then combined in the total load acting on the roof.

SIZE OF MEMBERS

The size of all structural members used for roof framing depends on the combined loads bearing on the member and the spacing of each member. If the load is increased, either the spacing must be decreased or the size of the member increased to compensate for the increased load. Consequently, if the size of a member is decreased, the members must be spaced more closely or the span must be decreased. If the length of the span is increased, the size of the members must be increased or the spacing made closer.

To compute the most appropriate size of roof rafter for a given load, spacing, and span, follow these steps:

1 To determine the total load per square foot of the roof space, add the live load and the dead load (Fig. 57-9).

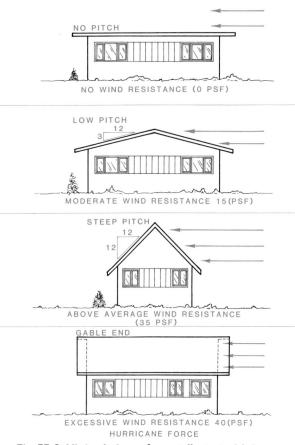

Fig 57-8 High-pitch roofs contribute to high wind loads.

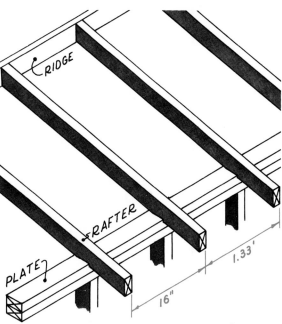

TOTAL LOAD X RAFTER SPACING (FT) = LOAD/LINEAL FT
40 PSF X 1.33 = 53 LBS / LINEAL FT

Fig 57-10 Determining the load per lineal foot on each rafter.

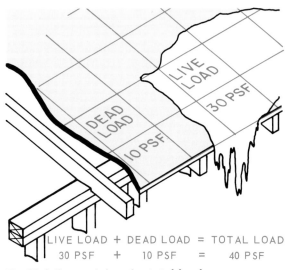

Fig 57-9 Determining the total load per square foot.

LIVE LOAD + DEAD LOAD = TOTAL LOAD
30 PSF + 10 PSF = 40 PSF

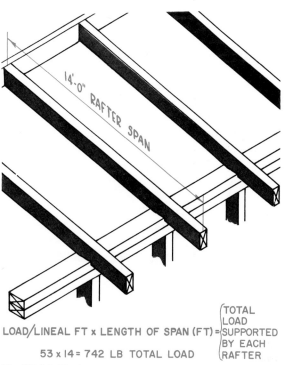

LOAD/LINEAL FT x LENGTH OF SPAN (FT) = {TOTAL LOAD SUPPORTED BY EACH RAFTER

53 x 14 = 742 LB TOTAL LOAD

Fig 57-11 Finding the total load each rafter must support.

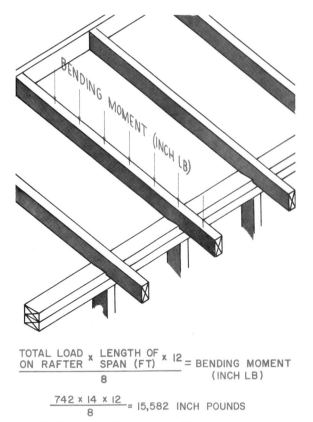

$$\frac{\text{TOTAL LOAD} \times \text{LENGTH OF} \times 12}{8} = \text{BENDING MOMENT}$$
$$\text{(INCH LB)}$$

$$\frac{742 \times 14 \times 12}{8} = 15,582 \text{ INCH POUNDS}$$

Fig 57-12 Computing the bending moment.

2 To determine the load per lineal foot on each rafter, multiply the load per square foot by the spacing of the rafters (Fig. 57-10). If rafters are spaced at 12″ intervals, then the load per square foot and the load per lineal foot will be the same. However,

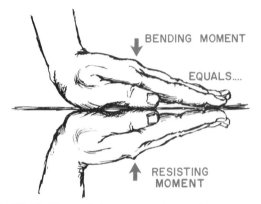

BENDING MOMENT

EQUALS....

RESISTING MOMENT

Fig 57-13 The resisting moment must be equal to or greater than the bending moment.

if the rafters are spaced at 16″ intervals, then each lineal foot of rafter must support $1\frac{1}{3}$ of the load per square foot.

3 To find the total load each rafter must support, multiply the load per lineal foot by the length of the span in feet (Fig. 57-11).

4 To compute the bending moment in inch-pounds, multiply total load supported by product of length of span times 12. Divide this figure by 8. The *bending moment* is the force needed to bend or break the rafter. When the length of the span in pounds is multiplied by the length of the span in feet, the result is expressed in foot-pounds. The span must be multiplied by 12 to convert the bending moment into inch-pounds (Fig. 57-12).

5 Set up the equation to determine the resisting moment. The *resisting moment* is the strength or resistance the rafter must possess to withstand the force of the bending moment. The resisting moment must therefore be equal to or greater than the bending moment of the rafter (Fig. 57-13). The resisting moment is determined by multiplying the fiber stress by the rafter width by the rafter depth squared. This figure is divided by 6. Rafter widths should be expressed in the exact dimensions of the finished lumber (Fig. 57-14). The *fiber stress* is the tendency of the fibers of the wood to bend and become stressed as the member is loaded. Fiber stresses range from 1750 pounds per square inch for Southern dense pine select to 600 pounds per square inch for red spruce. Dense Douglas fir and Southern pine possess average fiber stresses of 1200 pounds per square inch. The rafter depth is squared, since the strength of the member increases by squares. For example, a rafter 12″ deep is not three times as strong as a rafter 4″ deep. It is nine times as strong.

6 Since the bending moment equals the resistance moment, the formulas can be combined, as shown in Fig. 57-15. The formula can then be followed for any of the

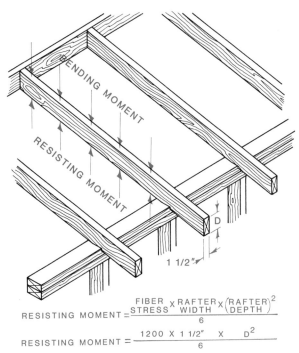

$$\text{RESISTING MOMENT} = \frac{\overset{\text{FIBER}}{\text{STRESS}} \times \overset{\text{RAFTER}}{\text{WIDTH}} \times \left(\overset{\text{RAFTER}}{\text{DEPTH}}\right)^2}{6}$$

$$\text{RESISTING MOMENT} = \frac{1200 \times 1\,1/2'' \times D^2}{6}$$

Fig 57-14 Determining the resistance moment.

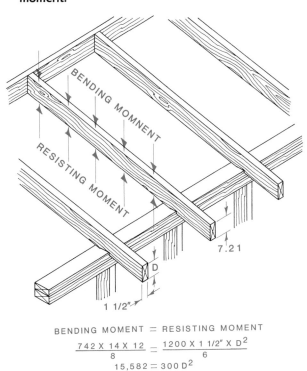

$$\text{BENDING MOMENT} = \text{RESISTING MOMENT}$$

$$\frac{742 \times 14 \times 12}{8} = \frac{1200 \times 1\,1/2'' \times D^2}{6}$$

$$15,582 = 300\,D^2$$

$$7.21 = D$$

Fig 57-15 Combining the bending-moment and resistance-moment formulas.

Lumber size	Spacing, in Inches	Fiber stress, 1200 pounds, for douglas fir and southern yellow pine
2 × 4	24	6'—6"
	20	7'—3"
	16	8'—1"
	12	9'—4"
2 × 6	24	10'—4"
	20	11'—4"
	16	12'—6"
	12	14'—2"
2 × 8	24	13'—8"
	20	15'—2"
	16	16'—6"
	12	18'—4"

Table 57-1 MAXIMUM RAFTER SPANS FOR 5/12 PITCH, 40 PSF LOAD

PITCH: 5/12   LOAD: 40 PSF

variables, preferably the depth of the rafter, since varying the depth will alter the resisting moment more than any other single factor.

Care should be taken in establishing all sizes to ensure that the sizes of materials conform to manufacturers' standards and building-code allowances. Table 57-1 shows a typical space-span chart based on common lumber sizes and spacing. Table 57-2 shows common truss specifications based on normal loading for residential work.

ROOF FRAMING TYPES

The conventional method of roof framing consists of roof rafters or trusses spaced at small intervals such as 16" (406 mm) on center. These roof rafters run perpendicular to the ridge board and align with the partition studs placed on the same centers (Fig. 57-16). The second method is the post-and-beam or

Table 57-2 COMMON TRUSS SPECIFICATIONS

SPAN			26'			28'			30'			32'		
			0"	4"	8"	0"	4"	8"	0"	4"	8"	0"	4"	8"
TOP CHORDS	OVER-HANG A	2/12	33½"	31½"	29½"	45½"	43½"	41½"	33½"	31½"	29½"	45½"	43½"	41½"
		3/12	30¼"	28¼"	26¼"	42¼"	40¼"	38¼"	30¼"	28¼"	26¼"	42¼"	40¼"	38¼"
		4/12	26⅛"	24⅛"	22⅛"	36⅞"	34⅞"	32⅞"	24⅞"	22⅞"	20⅞"	34¾"	32¾"	30¾"
BOTTOM CHORD	B		13'-0"	12'-8"	14'-0"	14'-0"	14'-4"	14'-8"	14'-0"	14'-4"	14'-8"	16'-0"	16'-4"	16'-8"

plank-and-beam (Fig. 57-17). The plank-and-beam roof consists of posts supporting beams that run parallel with the ridge board, or beam. A *ridge beam* is the center of a gable roof. Planks are then placed across the beams. Roof planking can then be used as a ceiling and a base for roofing that will shed water. Exposed plank-and-beam ceilings achieve a distinctive and pleasing architectural effect. When planks are selected for appearance, the only ceiling treatment needed is a desired finish on the planks and beams. Longitudinal beam sizes vary with the span and spacing of the beams. Design variations of end walls are achieved by an extensive use of glass and protecting roof overhangs.

The use of larger members in post-and-beam construction allows the designer to plan larger open areas unobstructed by bearing partitions (Fig. 57-18).

GABLE ROOF

Gable roofs are constructed with conventional rafters and ceiling joists. These are usually spaced 16" on center and covered with sheathing, felt, and shingles (Fig. 57-19). An adaptation of this conventional method of constructing roofs is the use of roof trusses to replace the conventional rafters and ceiling joists (Fig. 57-20). Trusses provide a much more rigid roof but eliminate the use of a space between the joists and rafters for an attic or crawl-space storage. An increasingly

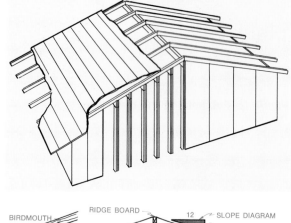

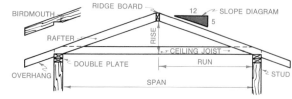

Fig 57-16 Conventional roof framing.

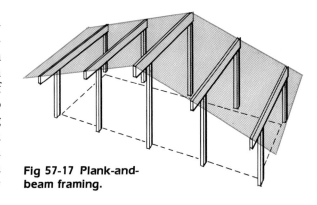

Fig 57-17 Plank-and-beam framing.

Fig 57-18 Post-and-beam framing allows for larger open areas.

Scholz Homes

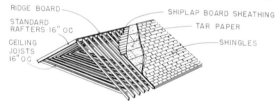

Fig 57-19 A conventionally framed gable roof.

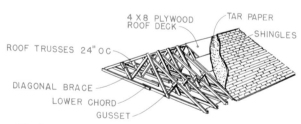

Fig 57-20 A trussed gable roof.

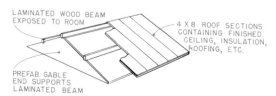

Fig 57-21 A prefabricated post-and-beam gable roof.

popular gable construction is a prefabricated gable end. Beams and roof sections with insulation and finishing are attached to the gable ends (Fig. 57-21). This is one variation of the post-and-beam method of roof construction.

PITCH

A gable roof has pitch on two sides but no pitch on the gable ends. The *pitch* is the angle between the top plate and the ridge board. *Rise* is the vertical distance from the top plate to the ridge. *Run* is the horizontal distance from the top plate to the ridge. The *pitch* is referred to as the *rise over the run*. In a gable roof with the ridge board in the exact center of the building, the run is one-half the span (Fig. 57-22). The run is always expressed in units of 12. Therefore, the rise is the number of inches the roof rises as it moves 12″ horizontally. A $\frac{6}{12}$ pitch means that the roof rises 6″ for every 12″ of horizontal distance (run). Pitch can also be expressed as a fraction indicating the total vertical distance to the total horizontal distance. To easily compute this fraction, use the rise over the span. For example, in Fig. 57-22, the $\frac{6}{12}$ pitch is the fraction $\frac{6}{24}$, or $\frac{1}{4}$.

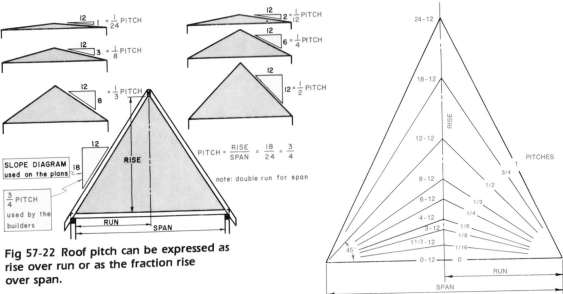

Fig 57-22 Roof pitch can be expressed as rise over run or as the fraction rise over span.

PITCH = $\frac{\text{RISE}}{\text{SPAN}}$ = $\frac{18}{24}$ = $\frac{3}{4}$

note: double run for span

Fig 57-23 Typical roof spans.

Gable-roof pitches vary greatly. The $\frac{1}{12}$ pitch shown in Fig. 57-23 is almost a flat roof. The $\frac{8}{12}$ pitch, however, is a moderately steep roof. The angle of a roof with a $\frac{12}{12}$ pitch is 45°. Metric pitch sizes are not yet established.

RIDGE BEAMS

The ridge board or ridge beam as shown in Fig. 57-24 is the top member in the roof assembly. Rafters are fixed in their exact position by being secured to the ridge board. The ridge beam in a cathedral ceiling of post-and-beam construction may be part of the top plate assembly. Figure 57-25 shows various methods of intersecting rafters with the ridge beam.

GABLE END

The gable end is the side of the house that rises to meet the ridge (Fig. 57-26). In some cases, especially on low-pitch roofs, the entire gable-end wall from the floor to the ridge can be panelized with varying lengths of studs. However, it is more common to prepare a rectangular wall panel and erect separate studs that project from the top plate of the panel to the rafter. Sheathing and siding are then added to the entire gable end of the house. With post-and-beam construction, clerestory windows in the gable end can be used. This is

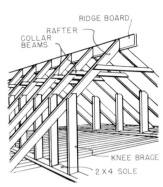

Fig 57-24 The ridge board is the top member in the roof assembly.

because studs are unnecessary on the gable end.

An increased use of windows in gable ends has necessitated the use of larger overhangs on the gable end. Gable-end lookouts can be framed from the first or second rafters on the gable plate, as shown in Fig. 57-27.

OVERHANGS

Post-and-beam construction allows for larger overhangs since larger members are used and rafters can quite often be exposed.

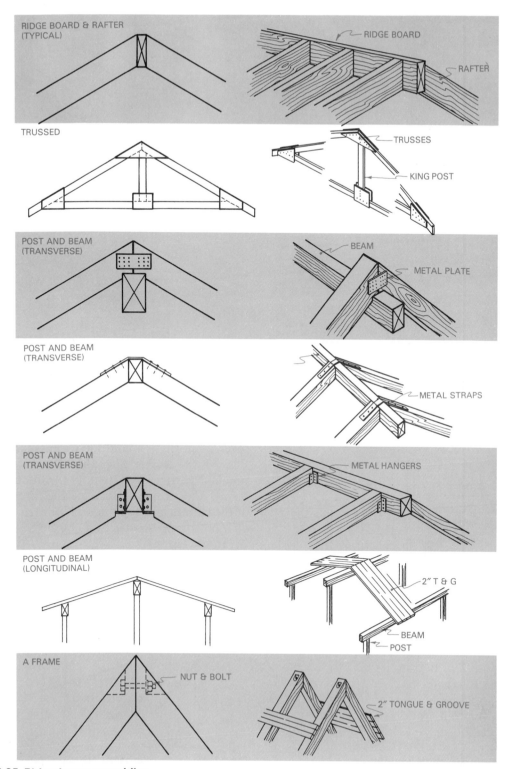

RIDGE BOARD & RAFTER (TYPICAL)

RIDGE BOARD

RAFTER

TRUSSED

TRUSSES

KING POST

POST AND BEAM (TRANSVERSE)

BEAM

METAL PLATE

POST AND BEAM (TRANSVERSE)

METAL STRAPS

POST AND BEAM (TRANSVERSE)

METAL HANGERS

POST AND BEAM (LONGITUDINAL)

2" T & G

BEAM

POST

A FRAME

NUT & BOLT

2" TONGUE & GROOVE

Fig 57-25 Ridge-beam assemblies.

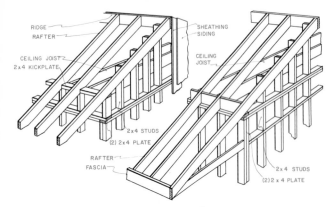

Fig 57-26 Gable-end construction.

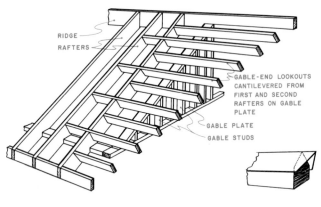

PLAN

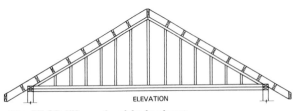

ELEVATION

Fig 57-27 Winged-gable lookout construction.

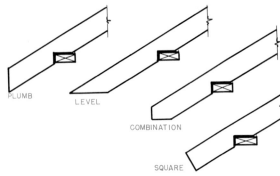

Fig 57-28 Types of rafter tail cuts and plate cuts.

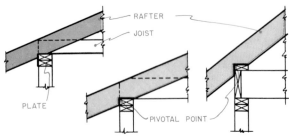

Fig 57-29 Method of intersecting rafters and top plates.

Several variations of cuts are used to finish the rafter end. A comparison of the plumb, level, combination, and square cuts is given in Fig. 57-28. Notice also that the rafters are notched with a *plate* (seat or birdmouth) *cut*, to provide a level surface for the intersection of the rafters and top plates. The area bearing on the plate should not be less than 3″ (75 mm) (Fig. 57-29).

Overhangs are normally larger on the side walls than on gable ends. Overhangs should be designed to provide maximum protection from sun and rain without restricting the light and view. Figure 57-30 shows some

Fig 57-30 Large overhangs are desirable only if designed correctly.

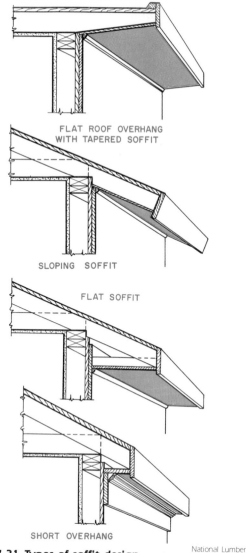

FLAT ROOF OVERHANG
WITH TAPERED SOFFIT

SLOPING SOFFIT

FLAT SOFFIT

SHORT OVERHANG

Fig 57-31 Types of soffit design.

National Lumber
Manufacturers Association

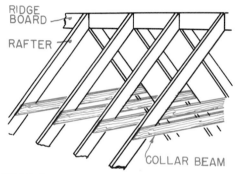

Fig 57-32 Collar beams reduce rafter stress.

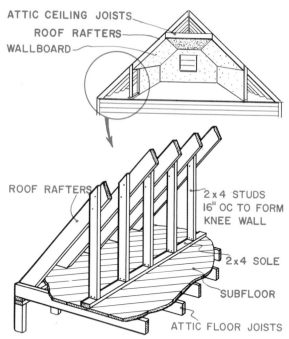

Fig 57-33 Knee walls add rigidity to the rafters.

of the difficulties in designing large overhangs. On a low-pitch roof, the problem is not acute since the rise is relatively small compared with the run. But on a steep-pitch roof, where the rise is large, the light might be completely shut off if the same amount of overhang were used. Furthermore, when the end of the overhang extends below the level of the window, there is no possibility of using a flat soffit. Figure 57-31 shows several alternative soffits.

COLLAR BEAMS

Collar beams provide a tie between rafters. They may be placed on every rafter or only on every other rafter. Collar beams are used to reduce the rafter stress that occurs between the top plate and the rafter cut. They also act as ceiling joists for finished attics (Fig. 57-32).

KNEE WALLS

Knee walls are vertical studs that project from an attic floor to the roof rafters, as shown in Fig. 57-33. Knee walls add rigidity

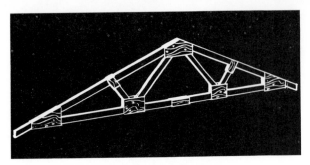

Fig 57-34 Lightweight wood trusses.

to the rafters and also provide wall framing for finished attics.

TRUSSES

Lightweight wood trusses have become increasingly popular for homes and small buildings (Fig. 57-34). Roof trusses allow complete flexibility for interior spacing. They save

approximately 30 to 35 percent on materials, compared with conventional framing methods. Trusses can be fabricated and erected in one-third of the time required for rafter and ceiling-joist construction. Truss construction helps to put the building under cover almost immediately. The use of trusses saves material and erection time and eliminates normal interior load-bearing partitions. Trusses save construction foundations and footings required for load-bearing partitions. Standard types of trusses are shown in Fig. 57-35. Truss construction methods are as applicable to

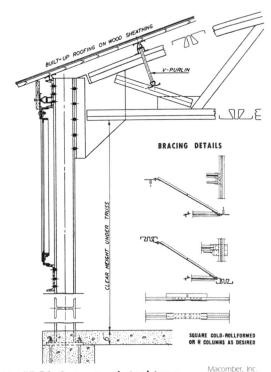

Fig 57-36 A structural-steel truss.

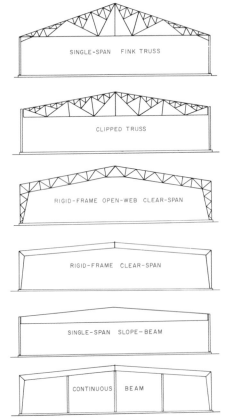

Fig 57-35 Standard types of trusses.

Fig 57-37 A wood-frame truss.

large steel-framed buildings (Fig. 57-36) as to small wood-framed buildings (Fig. 57-37).

HIP ROOF

Hip-roof framing is similar to gable-roof framing except that the roof slopes in two directions instead of intersecting a gable-end wall. The hip roof may be pyramid-shaped on square buildings.

Where two adjacent slopes meet, a *hip* is formed on the external angle. A *hip rafter* extends from the ridge board over the top plate to the edge of the overhang. The hip rafter does the same job as the ridge board.

The internal angle formed by the intersection of two slopes of the roof is known as the *valley*. A *valley rafter* is used on the internal angle as a hip rafter is used on the external angle. Hip rafters and valley rafters are normally 2″ (50 mm) deeper or 1″ (25 mm) wider than the regular rafters, for spans up to 12′ (3.658 m). For spans of over 12′ (3.658 m), the rafter should be doubled in width.

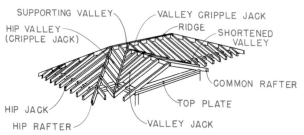

Fig 57-38 Hip-and-gable roof construction.

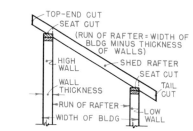

Fig 57-39 Shed-roof framing.

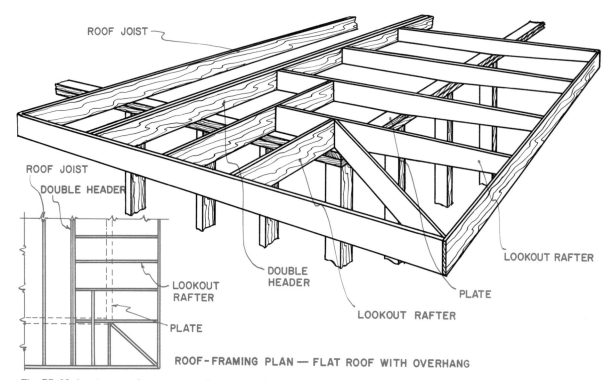

ROOF-FRAMING PLAN — FLAT ROOF WITH OVERHANG

Fig 57-40 Lookout rafters are used to extend the overhang perpendicular to the common rafters.

Jack rafters are rafters that extend from the wall plate to the hip or valley rafter. They are always shorter than *common rafters*. Figure 57-38 illustrates the use of these various framing members in hip-roof construction.

SHED ROOF

A *shed roof* is a roof that slants in only one direction (a gable roof is actually two shed roofs, sloping in opposite directions). Shed-roof rafter design is the same as rafter design for gable roofs, except that the run of the rafter is the same as the span. The shed rafter differs from the common rafter in the gable roof in that the shed rafter has two plate, or seat, cuts, a tail cut, and a top-end cut (Fig. 57-39).

FLAT ROOF

A *flat roof* has no slope. Therefore, the roof rafters must span directly from wall to wall or from wall to bearing partition. When rafters also serve as ceiling joists, the size of the rafter must be computed on the basis of both the roof load and the ceiling load.

OVERHANG

Large overhangs are possible on flat roofs. The roof joists can be extended past the top plate far enough to provide sun protection and, yet, not block the view. This extension is possible because there is no slope. When overhangs are desired on all sides, lookout rafters, as shown in Fig. 57-40, are used to extend the overhang on the side of the building perpendicular to the rafter direction. Figure 57-41 shows a flat roof cornice, or eave, section.

DRAINAGE

Since there is no slope to a flat roof, drainage must be provided by downspouts extending through the overhang. Flat roofs must be designed for a maximum snow load, since snow will not slide off the roof but must completely melt and drain away. A built-up roof consisting of sheathing, roofing paper,

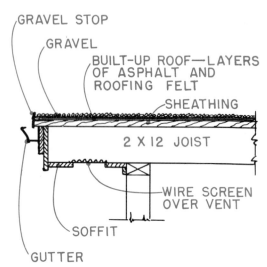

Fig 57-41 Flat-roof cornice section.

and crushed gravel can be used (Fig. 57-42). If a flat roof is so designed, a gravel stop and cant strip can be made high enough to hold water at a specific level. Water could then lie on the roof at all times and provide additional insulation.

STEEL

Steel-construction methods are especially applicable to flat roofs. The simplicity of erecting a steel roof results from the great strength of steel joints. The cross-bracing between widths of a steel *purlin* (horizontal member), as shown in Fig. 57-43, provides the purlin with a strength comparable to that of a

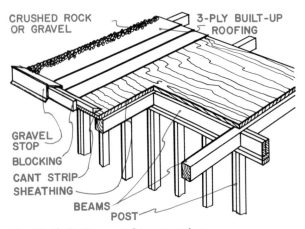

Fig 57-42 Built-up roof construction.

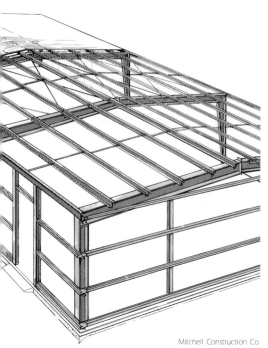

Fig 57-43 Typical steel-roof construction.

Mitchell Construction Co.

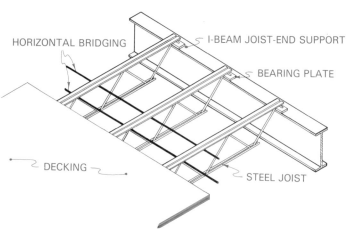

HORIZONTAL BRIDGING | I-BEAM JOIST-END SUPPORT

BEARING PLATE

DECKING

STEEL JOIST

Fig 57-44 A lightweight steel truss.

Macomber, Inc.

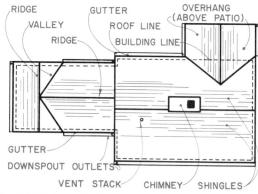

RIDGE   GUTTER   OVERHANG (ABOVE PATIO)
VALLEY   ROOF LINE
RIDGE   BUILDING LINE

GUTTER
DOWNSPOUT OUTLETS
VENT STACK   CHIMNEY   SHINGLES

Fig 57-45 A roof plan.

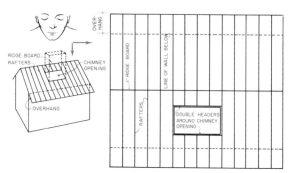

OVER-HANG
RIDGE BOARD
RAFTERS
CHIMNEY OPENING
RIDGE BOARD
LINE OF WALL BELOW
RAFTERS
DOUBLE HEADERS AROUND CHIMNEY OPENING
OVERHANG

Fig 57-46 A roof-framing plan.

truss. Lightweight steel trusses used on a flat roof are shown in Fig. 57-44.

PLAN DEVELOPMENT

A *roof plan* (Fig. 57-45) is one showing the outline of the roof and the major object lines indicating ridges, valleys, hips, and openings. The roof plan is not a framing plan, but a plan view of the roof. To develop a roof framing plan, a roof must be stripped of its covering to expose the position of each structural member and each header (Fig. 57-46). The roof plan can be used as the basic outline for the roof framing plan. The roof framing plan must show the exact position and spacing of each member. Figure 57-47 shows a comparison of a roof plan and a roof framing plan of the same roof.

SINGLE-LINE PLANS

In the roof framing plan shown in Fig. 57-47, each member is represented by a single line. This method of preparing roof framing plans is acceptable when only the general relationship and center spacing are desired.

STEEL CONSTRUCTION

Roof framing plans for steel construction are prepared like those for wood construction. However, in plans for structural steel, single-line drawings are almost universally used. A complete classification of each steel member

425

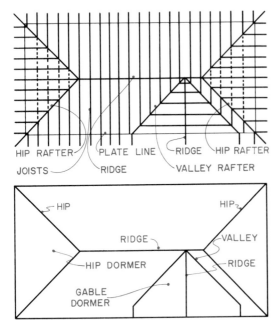

Fig 57-47 Comparison of a roof plan (bottom) and a roof-framing plan (top).

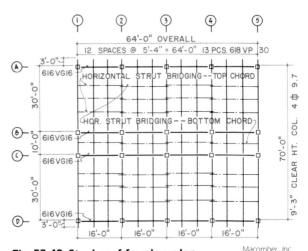

Fig 57-48 Steel roof-framing plan areas are often identified by numbers and letters.

Macomber, Inc.

is shown on the drawing. This includes the size, type, and weight of the beams and columns. Each different type of member is shown by a different line weight, which relates to the size of the member. Structural-steel roof framing plans frequently show *bay areas* (areas between columns) indicating the number of spaces and the spacing of each purlin between columns. Bays are frequently shown in circles: numerically in one direction and alphabetically in the other direction (Fig. 57-48).

COMPLETE PLAN

When more details concerning the exact construction of intersections and joints are needed, a plan showing the thickness of each member, as shown in Fig. 57-49, should be prepared. This type of plan is necessary to show the relative height of one member compared with another; that is, to determine whether one member passes over or under another. In this plan, the width of ridge boards, rafters, headers, and plates should be shown to the exact scale.

When a complete roof framing plan of this type cannot fully describe construction

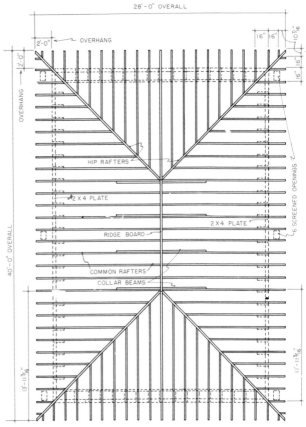

Fig 57-49 A roof-framing plan showing the thickness of each member.

426

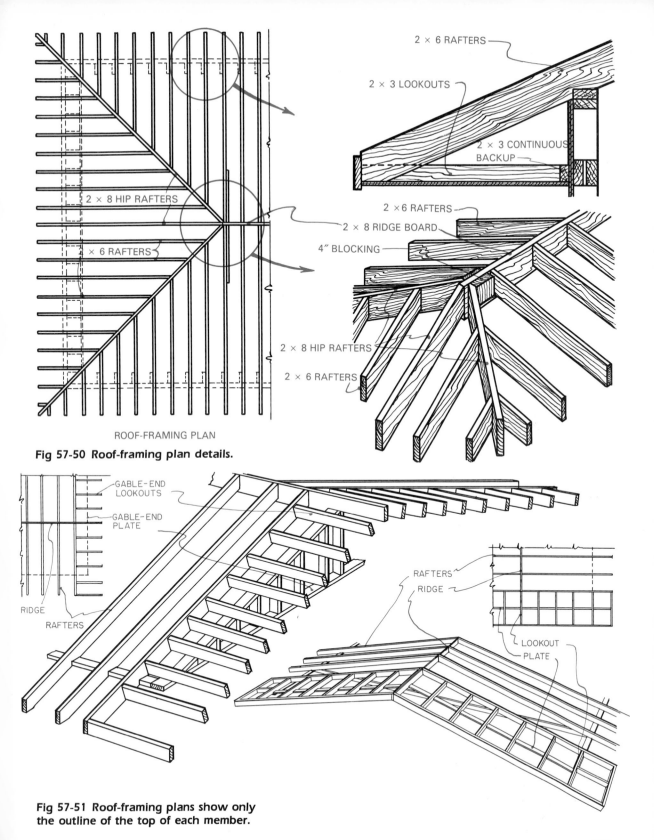

2 × 6 RAFTERS

2 × 3 LOOKOUTS

2 × 3 CONTINUOUS
BACKUP

2 × 8 HIP RAFTERS

× 6 RAFTERS

2 × 6 RAFTERS

2 × 8 RIDGE BOARD

4″ BLOCKING

2 × 8 HIP RAFTERS

2 × 6 RAFTERS

ROOF-FRAMING PLAN

Fig 57-50 Roof-framing plan details.

GABLE-END
LOOKOUTS

GABLE-END
PLATE

RAFTERS

RIDGE

RIDGE

RAFTERS

LOOKOUT
PLATE

**Fig 57-51 Roof-framing plans show only
the outline of the top of each member.**

427

framing details, then additional removed pictorial or elevation drawings should be prepared, as shown in Fig. 57-50. A similar technique of removing details can also be used to increase the size of a particular area in detail for dimensioning purposes.

On roof framing plans, only the outline of the top of the rafters is shown. All areas underneath, including the gable-end plate, are shown by dotted lines. When a gable-end lookout slopes, a true orthographic projection of the plan would indicate three lines—two lines for the top of the rafter and one line for the bottom. However, roof framing plans are normally simplified to show only the outline of the top of each member (Fig. 57-51). The angle or vertical position of any roof framing member should be shown on a roof framing elevation.

ROOF FRAMING ELEVATIONS

Roof framing plans show horizontal relationships of members such as width, length, and horizontal spacing. In a top view (plan), you cannot show vertical dimensions such as pitch, ridge height, and plate height. Transverse sections supply this information through one part of the structure. However, if a comparison of different heights and pitches is desired, a composite framing-elevation drawing should be prepared. This elevation can be projected from the floor framing plan and corresponding lines on the elevation drawings, as shown in Fig. 57-52.

DORMERS

Parts of the roof framing plan that extend above the normal plane of projection, such as dormer rafters, are drawn with dotted lines. This device indicates that the parts do not directly intersect with the other framing members shown on the plan. It is quite common to show the position of dormer rafters or ridge as illustrated in Fig. 57-53. The details of intersecting the dormer-roof framing with dormer

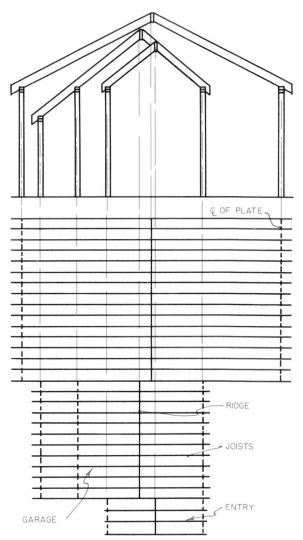

Fig 57-52 A method of projecting roof-framing elevations.

walls should be shown on dormer-roof framing plans or other details (Fig. 57-54).

Dormer rafters and walls do not lie in the same plane as the remainder of the roof rafters. A framing-elevation drawing is needed to show the exact position of the dormer members and their tie-in with the common roof rafters. Figure 57-55 illustrates a side framing elevation of an individual dormer and shows how it is structurally related to other roof framing members. Figure 57-56 shows the side-wall framing of a shed dormer, in which

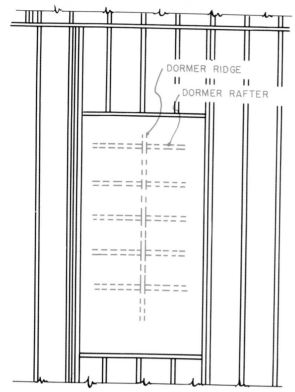

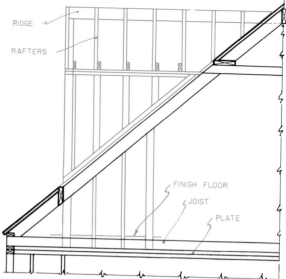

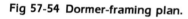
DORMER RIDGE
DORMER RAFTER

Fig 57-53 A method of drawing dormer rafters.

RIDGE
RAFTERS
FINISH FLOOR
JOIST
PLATE

Fig 57-55 A frame elevation of an individual dormer.

the position of the dormer studs is revealed by the elevation drawing.

Parts of roof framing elevations are actually parts of transverse sections. They are used to show the basic relationship between major framing members and the roof covering

Fig 57-54 Dormer-framing plan.

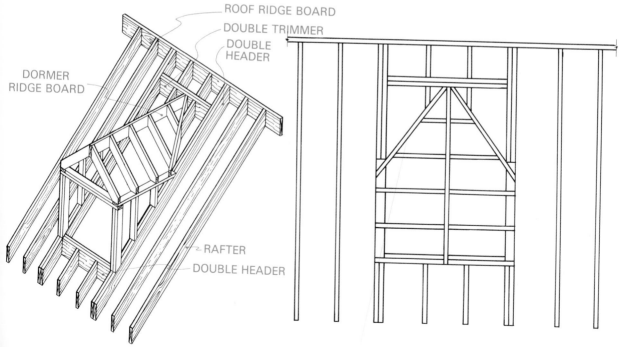

ROOF RIDGE BOARD
DOUBLE TRIMMER
DOUBLE HEADER
DORMER RIDGE BOARD
RAFTER
DOUBLE HEADER

429

Fig 57-56 A framing elevation of a shed dormer.

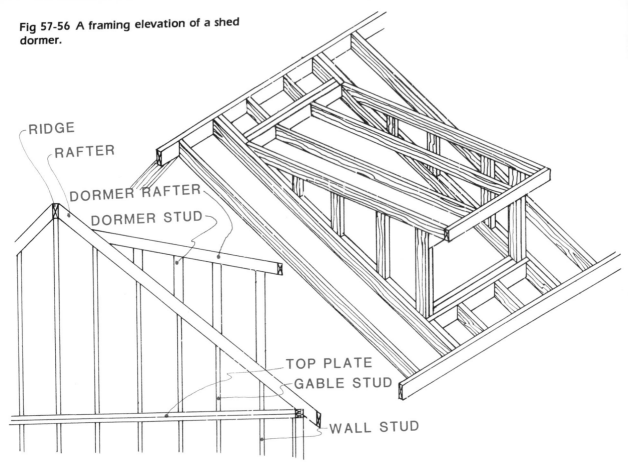

RIDGE

RAFTER

DORMER RAFTER

DORMER STUD

TOP PLATE

GABLE STUD

WALL STUD

and trim details. Figure 57-57 shows the steps in laying out one of the most widely used drawings of this type, a cornice detail. Other cornice details that show the relationship between roof framing members and trim materials are illustrated in Fig. 57-58.

CHIMNEY DETAILS

Chimney roof framing construction details are normally shown on detail drawings. Figure 57-59 shows ceiling joists framed around a chimney. Figure 57-60 shows the framing necessary for the intersection of the chimney and the roof rafters.

BEAMS

The *beams* are the major support of the roof. Many beams have been developed that

are lighter in weight or stronger than a solid beam (Fig. 57-61). The *laminated beam*, or the *built-up beam*, has great strength and can be formed into graceful arches or other shapes (Fig. 57-62).

The *box beam* offers lightness, low cost, and good supporting strength.

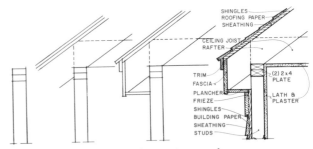

SHINGLES
ROOFING PAPER
SHEATHING
CEILING JOIST
RAFTER
(2) 2 x 4
PLATE
TRIM
FASCIA
PLANCHER
FRIEZE
LATH &
PLASTER
SHINGLES
BUILDING PAPER
SHEATHING
STUDS

Fig 57-57 Steps in laying out a cornice detail.

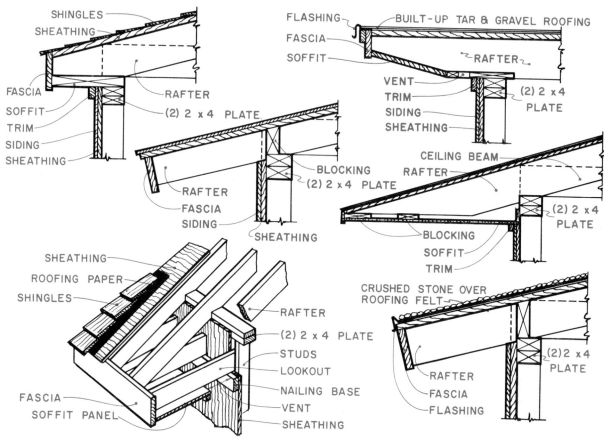

Fig 57-58 Cornice-framing details.

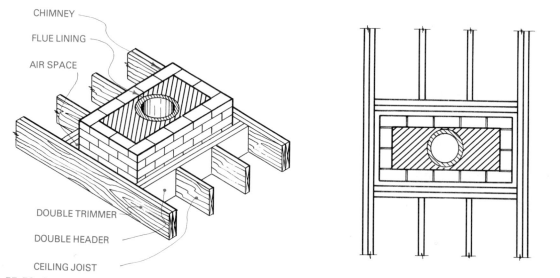

Fig 57-59 Chimney-framing details.

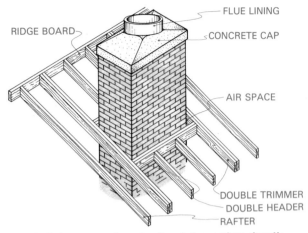

Fig 57-60 Chimney and roof rafter intersection details.

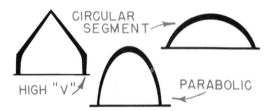

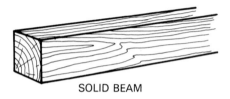

SOLID BEAM

VERTICAL LAMINATED BEAM

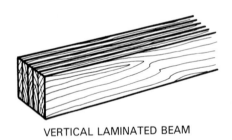

Fig 57-62 Various shapes of laminated beams and arches.

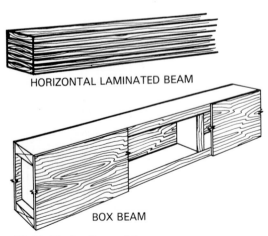

HORIZONTAL LAMINATED BEAM

BOX BEAM

Fig 57-61 Kinds of wood beams.

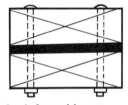

Fig 57-63 Steel-reinforced beam.

The strongest of the built-up beams is the *steel-reinforced beam* (Fig. 57-63). It can support heavy weights and span long distances because of the steel plate bolted between the wood members.

ROOF PANELS

Many forms of lightweight, prefabricated roof units have been developed. Some of the more commonly used units are described.

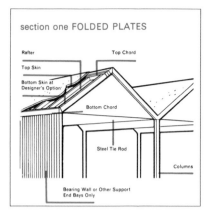

section one FOLDED PLATES

Rafter
Top Chord
Top Skin
Bottom Skin at Designer's Option
Bottom Chord
Steel Tie Rod
Columns
Bearing Wall or Other Support End Bays Only

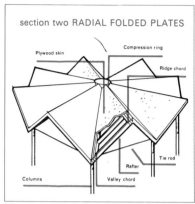

section two RADIAL FOLDED PLATES

Compression ring
Plywood skin
Ridge chord
Rafter
Tie rod
Columns
Valley chord

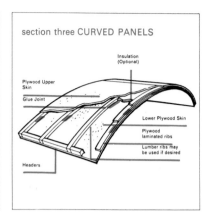

section three CURVED PANELS

Insulation (Optional)
Plywood Upper Skin
Glue Joint
Lower Plywood Skin
Plywood laminated ribs
Lumber ribs may be used if desired
Headers

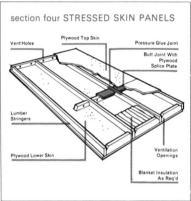

section four STRESSED SKIN PANELS

Vent Holes
Plywood Top Skin
Pressure Glue Joint
Butt Joint With Plywood Splice Plate
Lumber Stringers
Ventilation Openings
Plywood Lower Skin
Blanket Insulation As Req'd

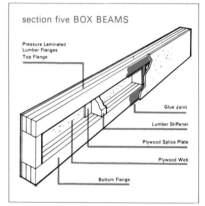

section five BOX BEAMS

Pressure Laminated Lumber Flanges Top Flange
Glue Joint
Lumber Stiffener
Plywood Splice Plate
Plywood Web
Bottom Flange

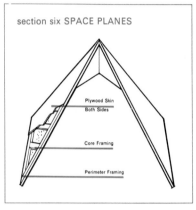

section six SPACE PLANES

Plywood Skin Both Sides
Core Framing
Perimeter Framing

Fig 57-64 Use and construction of laminated wood members.

STRESSED SKIN PANELS

Stressed skin panels are constructed of plywood and seasoned lumber. The simple framing and the plywood skin act as a unit to resist loads. Glued joints transmit the shear stresses, making it possible for the structure to act as one piece. Stressed skin panels (Fig. 57-64) are used in floors and walls, as well as in roofs.

CURVED PANELS

Curved panels are constructed in three types: the *sandwich,* or *honeycomb papercore,* panel; the *hollow-stressed* end panel; and the *solid-core* panel. The arching action of these panels (Fig. 57-64) permits spanning great distances with a relatively thin cross section.

FOLDED PLATE ROOFS

Folded plate roofs are thin skins of plywood reinforced by purlins to form shell structures that can utilize the strength of plywood. The use of folded plate roofs eliminates trusses and other roof members. The tilted plates lean against one another, acting as giant V-shaped beams supported by walls or columns (Fig. 57-64).

CONCRETE

Pouring concrete into forms is certainly not new to the building industry. But the preparation of concrete building components away from the site is relatively new. The use of reinforced and prestressed concrete for floors, roofs, and walls, and the fabrication of concrete into shells account for an increase in the use of concrete as a building medium.

PRESTRESSED CONCRETE

When a beam carries a load, it bends, and its center sags lower than the ends. The bot-

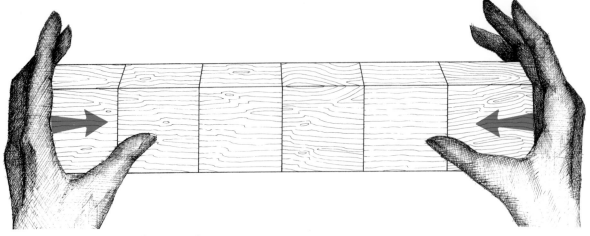

Fig 57-65 The principle of prestressing concrete.

tom fibers are stretched and the top fibers are compressed. Concrete can be *prestressed* to eliminate sag. A prestressed beam is made by first stretching wires longer than the beam between two anchors. Concrete is poured around these wires and allowed to cure, and then the stretched wires are released. The wires want to return to their original shape, and so create a force on the concrete. The wires inside are held under stress.

Prestressing can be compared to holding a row of blocks or books between your hands. As long as sufficient pressure can be exerted, as shown in Fig. 57-65, no sag can occur. The use of prestressed concrete prevents cracks because this concrete is always in compression. Prestressing permits less depth of beams as related to the span. Prestressed concrete has remarkable elastic properties and develops considerable resistance to shear stresses.

PRECAST CONCRETE
Precast concrete is concrete that has been poured into molds prior to its use in construction. When high stresses will not be incurred, precasting without prestressing will suffice.

REINFORCED CONCRETE
Reinforced concrete is precast or poured-on-site concrete with steel reinforcing rods inserted for stability and rigidity. The rods are not placed under stress as are the wires

in prestressed concrete. Reinforced concrete slabs are used extensively for floor systems where short spans make prestressing unnecessary.

CONCRETE SHELLS
Concrete shells are curved, thin sheets of concrete usually poured or sprayed on some material that provides temporary rigidity until the concrete hardens. One method is the use of reinforcing mats that are first laid flat on the ground and then lifted into the desired position. The mats are then sprayed with a coating of concrete that holds the steel rods in place after the concrete solidifies. Concrete-shell construction is becoming increasingly popular in the design of air terminals, auditoriums, and gymnasiums.

ROOF FRAMING DIMENSIONS

In dimensioning roof framing plans, the size and spacing of framing members and major distances between framing components must be shown. Figure 57-66 shows a typical framing plan dimensioned with overall dimensions and subdimensions, and with sizes of all framing materials labeled. Regular interval spacings of structural members, such as roof rafters, floor joists, and wall studs, are not dimensioned if they fall on modular incre-

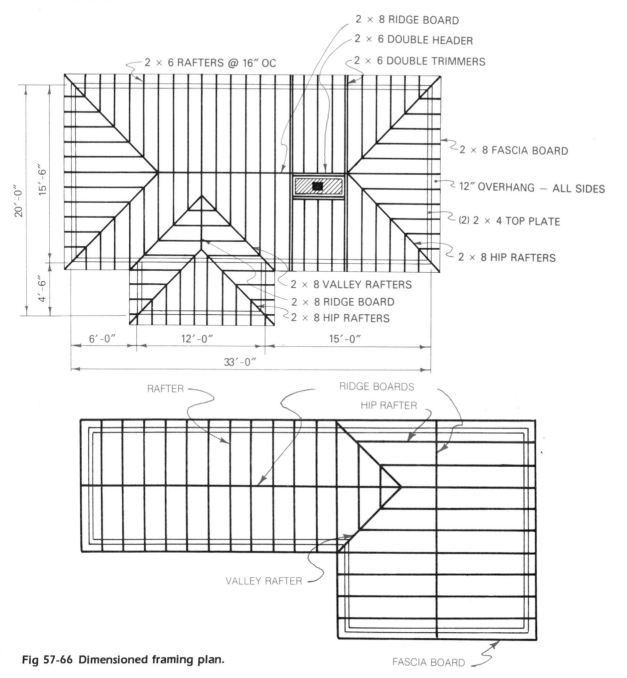

2 × 8 RIDGE BOARD

2 × 6 DOUBLE HEADER

2 × 6 DOUBLE TRIMMERS

2 × 6 RAFTERS @ 16" OC

2 × 8 FASCIA BOARD

12" OVERHANG — ALL SIDES

(2) 2 × 4 TOP PLATE

2 × 8 HIP RAFTERS

2 × 8 VALLEY RAFTERS

2 × 8 RIDGE BOARD

2 × 8 HIP RAFTERS

20'-0"

15'-6"

4'-6"

6'-0"

12'-0"

15'-0"

33'-0"

RAFTER

RIDGE BOARDS

HIP RAFTER

VALLEY RAFTER

FASCIA BOARD

Fig 57-66 Dimensioned framing plan.

ments. Notes are used on framing drawings to show all spacing of members. On detail drawings, overall dimensions are not given; only key distances between structural levels or horizontal distances are shown. If material sizes are not given on the framing drawing, refer to the specifications list for materials description, which includes sizes.

On modular framing drawings, dimensions are sometimes omitted in lieu of using a modular grid. Framing members that fall on the center lines of the grid are modular and can be determined by counting the number of blocks from one member to another. However, framing members that do not fall on the modular grid are dimensioned separately.

PROBLEMS

1 Identify the roof framing members shown in Fig. 57-67.

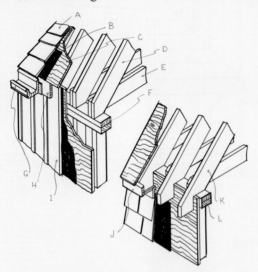

Fig 57-67 Identify these roof-framing members.

2 Draw a roof framing plan for the dormer shown in the roof framing elevation in Fig. 57-68. Use the dormer shown in Fig. 57-56 as a guide.

DORMER RAFTERS

Fig 57-68 Draw a roof-framing plan of this dormer.

3 Identify the roof framing members shown in Fig. 57-69.

Fig 57-69 Identify these members.

4 Identify the roof framing members shown in Fig. 57-70.

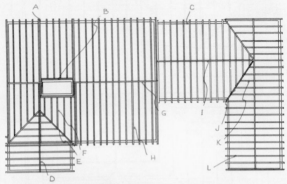

Fig 57-70 Identify these roof-framing members.

5 Prepare a roof framing plan for the house shown in Fig. 33-2. First prepare a roof plan for a gable roof or a hip roof and project the roof framing plan from this.

6 Prepare a roof framing plan for a house of your own design.

7 Draw a roof framing plan for the house shown in Fig. 67-7.

8 Prepare a roof framing plan for your own house.

9 Define the following terms: *wind load, snow load, bending moment, resisting moment, fiber stress, truss, transverse beam, gable end, rise, run, plate cut, collar beam, knee wall, valley, hip, cornice, jack, downspout, roof plan, roof framing plan, dormer, bay.*

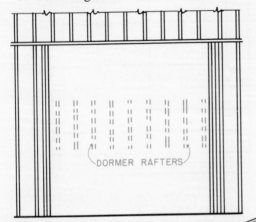

UNIT 58
ROOF COVERING MATERIALS

Roof covering protects the building from rain, snow, wind, heat, and cold. Materials used to cover pitched roofs include wood shingles, asphalt shingles, and asbestos shingles. On heavier roofs, tile or slate may also be used. Roll roofing or other sheet material, such as galvanized iron, aluminum, copper, and tin, may also be used for flat or low-pitched roofs. A built-up roof consisting of layers of roofing felt covered with gravel topping may also be used on low-pitched or flat roofs. If a built-up roof is used on high-pitched roofs, the gravel will weather off.

SHEATHING

Roof *sheathing* consists of 1 × 6 lumber or plywood sheets nailed directly to the roof rafters. Sheathing adds rigidity to the roof and provides a surface for the attachment of waterproofing materials. In humid parts of the country, sheathing boards are sometimes spaced slightly apart to provide ventilation and to prevent shingle rot.

ROLL ROOFING

Roll roofing may be used as an *underlayment* for shingles or as a finished roofing material (Fig. 58-1). Roll roofing used as an underlayment includes asphalt and saturated felt. The underlayment serves as a barrier against moisture and wind. Mineral surface and selvage roll-roofing can be used as the final roofing surface.

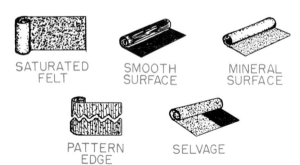

SATURATED FELT   SMOOTH SURFACE   MINERAL SURFACE   PATTERN EDGE   SELVAGE

Fig 58-1 Kinds of roll roofing.

WEIGHT

The weight of roofing materials is important in computing dead loads. A heavier roofing surface makes the roof more permanent than does a lighter surface. Generally, heavier roofing materials last longer than lighter materials. Therefore, heavy roofing, such as strip

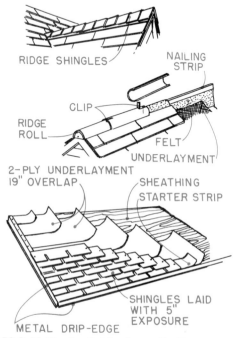

RIDGE SHINGLES   NAILING STRIP   CLIP   RIDGE ROLL   FELT UNDERLAYMENT   2-PLY UNDERLAYMENT 19" OVERLAP   SHEATHING   STARTER STRIP   SHINGLES LAID WITH 5" EXPOSURE   METAL DRIP-EDGE

Fig 58-2 Methods of shingle application.

or individual shingles, is superior. Roof covering materials are classified by their weight per 100 square feet (100 square feet equals 1 *square*). Thus 30-pound roofing felt weighs 30 pounds per 100 square feet. Although metric identification has not become standard, it would be easy to convert the classification to kilograms per square meter.

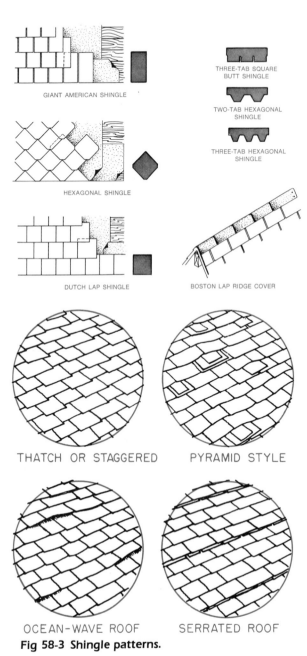

GIANT AMERICAN SHINGLE

THREE-TAB SQUARE
BUTT SHINGLE

TWO-TAB HEXAGONAL
SHINGLE

THREE-TAB HEXAGONAL
SHINGLE

HEXAGONAL SHINGLE

DUTCH LAP SHINGLE

BOSTON LAP RIDGE COVER

THATCH OR STAGGERED

PYRAMID STYLE

OCEAN-WAVE ROOF

SERRATED ROOF

Fig 58-3 Shingle patterns.

SHINGLES

Shingles are commonly made from asphalt, wood, tile, and slate and are available in a variety of patterns and shapes. Shingles and underlayment are overlapped when applied, as shown in Fig. 58-2. Shingles are best for pitches steeper than $\frac{4}{12}$. For pitches less than $\frac{4}{12}$, roll roofing is better. Shingles may be laid flat or, if extra shingles are added, patterns may be produced (Fig. 58-3).

BUILT-UP ROOFS

Built-up roof coverings are used on flat or extremely low-pitched roofs. Because rain or snow may not be immediately expelled from these roofs, complete waterproofing is essential. Built-up roofs may have three, four, or five layers of roofing felt, sealed with tar or asphalt, between each two coatings. The final layer of tar or asphalt is then covered with roofing gravel or a top sheet of roll roofing (Fig. 58-4).

FLASHING

Joints where roof covering materials intersect at the ridge, hip, valley, chimney, and parapet joints must be flashed. *Flashing* is additional covering used on a joint to provide complete waterproofing. Roll-roofing, shingles, or sheet metal is used as the flashing material. For flashing hip and valley joints, shingle flashing is best; it can be attached by nails to wood strips applied over asphalt cement and felt underlayment (Fig. 58-5).

When sheet-metal flashing is used, watertight sheet-metal joints should be used, as shown in Fig. 58-6. Chimney flashing is frequently bonded into the mortar joint and under shingles and is caulked to provide completely waterproof joints.

GUTTERS

Gutters are troughs designed to carry water to the downspouts, where it can be

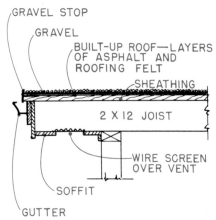

Fig 58-4 Built-up roof construction.

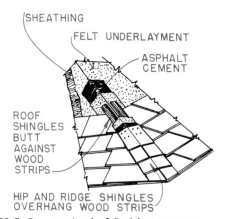

Fig 58-5 One method of flashing corners.

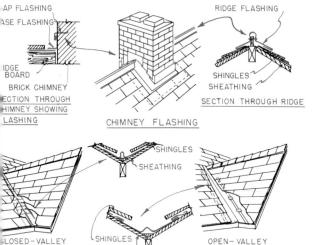

Fig 58-6 Application of sheet-metal flashing.

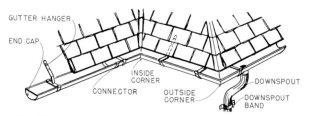

Fig 58-7 Gutter-assembly terminology.

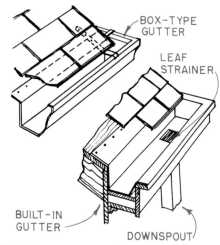

Fig 58-8 Common types of gutters.

emptied into the sewer system (Fig. 58-7). The two materials used most commonly for gutters are sheet metal and wood such as red cedar and redwood (Fig. 58-8). Plastic gutters and downspouts are growing in use. Gutters may be built into the roof structure, as shown in the fascia-board gutter and the pole gutter in Fig. 58-9. Gutters may be made of additional sheet metal or wood attached or hung from the fascia board. All gutters should be pitched sufficiently to provide for drainage to the downspout. In selecting gutters and downspouts, care must be taken to ensure that their size is adequate for the local rainfall.

SUN SCREENS

The design of the roof overhang must be sufficient to provide complete protection from the direct rays of the sun. Such protection is especially important in large areas such as patios and porches. The basic problem is to

439

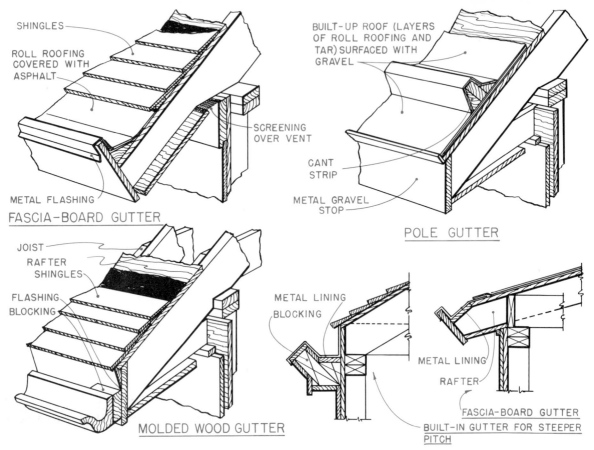

SHINGLES

ROLL ROOFING
COVERED WITH
ASPHALT

SCREENING
OVER VENT

METAL FLASHING

FASCIA-BOARD GUTTER

BUILT-UP ROOF (LAYERS
OF ROLL ROOFING AND
TAR) SURFACED WITH
GRAVEL

CANT
STRIP

METAL GRAVEL
STOP

POLE GUTTER

JOIST
RAFTER
SHINGLES

FLASHING
BLOCKING

MOLDED WOOD GUTTER

METAL LINING

BLOCKING

METAL LINING

RAFTER

FASCIA-BOARD GUTTER

BUILT-IN GUTTER FOR STEEPER
PITCH

Fig 58-9 Built-in gutters.

block the direct rays of the sun without impairing the illumination. Often, a completely solid covering would produce an area so dark that the advantages of outdoor living would be eliminated. The sunshade shown on the building in Fig. 58-10 does not completely block illumination from the window or obstruct the view. It does block the direct rays of the sun from reaching the window.

On many patios, it is desirable to admit the rays of the sun when it is high and block the rays of the sun when it is lower in the sky. To accomplish this, the angle of the sun should be measured at several times during the day. The spacing and angle of louvers are then set to block the rays at the appropriate time (Fig. 58-11). There are many methods that can be used to construct sun shields of this type (Fig. 58-12). Louvers placed only in

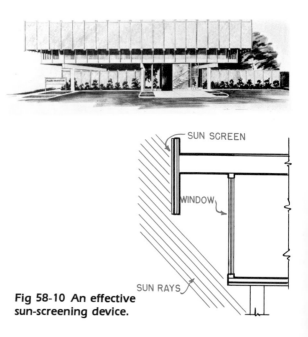

SUN SCREEN

WINDOW

SUN RAYS

Fig 58-10 An effective sun-screening device.

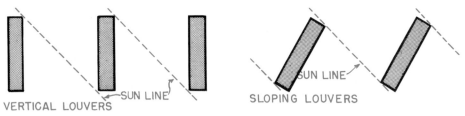

VERTICAL LOUVERS — SUN LINE — SLOPING LOUVERS — SUN LINE

Fig 58-11 The angle and spacing of louvers is important in sun screening.

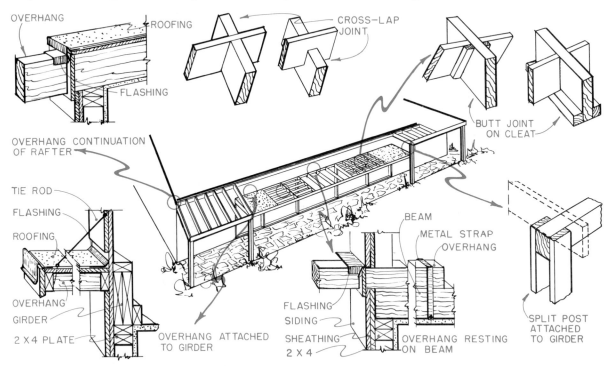

Fig 58-12 There are many methods of screening out the sun's rays.

one direction will block the rays of the sun from the side perpendicular to the louvers.

Louvers placed in egg-crate patterns will block the rays of the sun at all angles.

PROBLEMS

1 Name two types of roll roofing suitable for finished roof covering.

2 Name two types of roll roofing suitable for underlayment.

3 Specify the type of roofing to be used in the house of your design.

4 Draw a cornice section of the house of your design, showing the gutters you have chosen.

5 Define these terms: *roof sheathing, roll roofing, slate, shingles, underlayment, square, roofing felt, flashing, pole gutter, fascia board, louvers.*

ELECTRICAL PLANS

Electricity is the major source of energy for the home. Electricity cooks, washes, cleans, heats, air-conditions, lights, preserves, and entertains. But the finest home is not practical if the wiring is not ade-quate to bring power to the appliances and lighting fixtures. The most important problem in planning the electrical wiring system is to keep up with all the requirements for energy.

UNIT 59
LIGHTING

Planning for adequate lighting involves the eyes, the object, and the light (Fig. 59-1). Planning to light any area involves three questions: How much light is needed? What is the best quality of light? How should this light be distributed? Whether planning lighting for a large commercial building or for a residence, the same design factors must be considered.

TYPES OF LIGHT

Candles and oil and natural-gas lamps were once the major sources of light. Today's major source of light in the home comes from the incandescent lamp and the fluorescent lamp.

INCANDESCENT LIGHTING

Incandescent lamps use a filament inside the bulb to provide a small, concentrated glow of light when an electric current heats the filament to the glowing point. Following

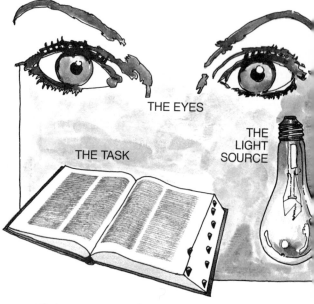

THE EYES

THE TASK

THE LIGHT SOURCE

Fig 59-1 Lighting needs vary according to three factors.

are some of the many types of incandescent bulbs:

> *Inside-frosted bulbs,* used to disperse light evenly
> *White bulbs* for soft light when bulbs are exposed
> *Silver-bowl bulbs* that direct light upward

Outdoor projector bulbs, used as a spot-
  light or floodlight
Colored bulbs for decorative effects
Sun-lamp bulbs for sun-tanning
Infrared bulbs for instant heat
Outdoor yellow bulbs that do not attract
  insects
Night-light bulbs

FLUORESCENT LIGHTING

Fluorescent lamps give a uniform glareless
light that is ideal for large working areas. Fluorescent lamps give more light per watt than
incandescent lamps and last as much as seven
times longer.

In the fluorescent lamp, current flows
through mercury vapor and activates the
light-giving properties of the coating inside
the tube.

LIGHT MEASUREMENTS

You can read in bright sunlight or in a
dimly lit room because your eyes are adaptable to varying intensities of light (Fig. 59-2).
However, you must be given enough time to
adjust slowly to different light levels. Sudden
extreme changes of light cause great discom-
fort.

Light is measured in customary units
called *footcandles.* A footcandle is equal to the
amount of light a candle throws on an object
1' away (Fig. 59-3). Ten footcandles equal the
amount of light that 10 candles throw on a
surface 1' away. A 75-watt bulb provides 30
footcandles of light at a distance of 3'. It provides 20 footcandles at a distance of 6'.

In the metric system the standard unit of
illumination is the *lux* (lx). One lux is equal to
0.093 footcandles. To convert footcandles to
lux, multiply by 10.764.

On a clear summer day, the sun delivers
10,000 footcandles (107 640 lx) of light to the
Earth (Fig. 59-4). This is found at the beaches
and in open fields. In the shade of a tree, there
will be 1000 footcandles (10 764 lx). In the
shade on an open porch, there will be 500 footcandles (5382 lx). Inside the house, a few feet
from the window, there will be 200 footcan-

Fig 59-2 Eyes will adjust to extreme intensities of light.

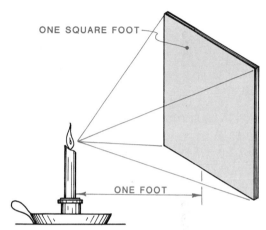

Fig 59-3 One footcandle of light (candela) is equal to the amount of light thrown on a surface 1 foot away.

dles, (2153 lx); and in the center of the house,
10 footcandles (108 lx).

Accepted light levels for various living
activities are as follows:

10 to 20 footcandles (108 to 215 lx): casual
  visual tasks, card playing, conversation, television, listening to music
20 to 30 footcandles (215 to 320 lx):
  easy reading, sewing, knitting, house
  cleaning
30 to 50 footcandles (320 to 540 lx): reading newspapers, doing kitchen and
  laundry work, typing
50 to 70 footcandles (540 to 750 lx): prolonged reading, machine sewing, hobbies, homework
70 to 200 footcandles (750 to 2150 lx):
  prolonged detailed tasks such as fine
  sewing, reading fine print, drafting

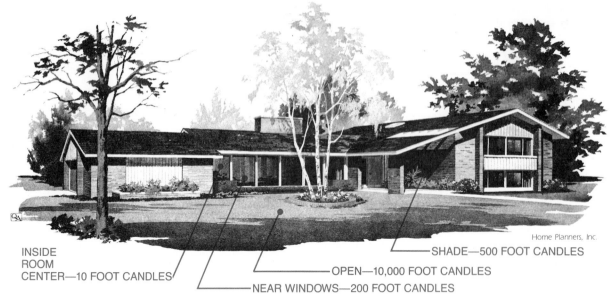

INSIDE
ROOM
CENTER—10 FOOT CANDLES

NEAR WINDOWS—200 FOOT CANDLES

OPEN—10,000 FOOT CANDLES

SHADE—500 FOOT CANDLES

Home Planners, Inc.

Fig 59-4 Light distribution on a sunny day.

DISPERSAL OF LIGHT

After the necessary amount of light is known, the method of spreading, or *dispersing*, the light through the rooms must be determined.

TYPES OF LIGHTING

There are five types of lighting dispersement (Fig. 59-5): direct, indirect, semidirect, semi-indirect, and diffused. *Direct* light shines directly on an object from the light source. *Indirect* light is reflected from large surfaces. *Semidirect* light shines mainly down as direct light, but a small portion of it is directed upward as indirect light. *Semi-indirect* light is mostly reflected but some shines directly. *Diffused* light is spread evenly in all directions.

REFLECTANCE

All objects absorb and reflect light. Some white surfaces reflect 94 percent of the light that strikes them. Some black surfaces reflect only 2 percent. The rest of the light is absorbed. The proper amount of reflectance is determined by the color and type of finish.

The amounts of reflectance that are recommended for a room are from 60 percent to 90 percent for the ceiling, from 35 to 60 percent for the walls, and from 15 to 35 percent for the floor.

All surfaces in a room will act as a secondary source of light when the light is reflected. Glare can be eliminated from this secondary source of light by having a dull, or matte, finish on surfaces and by avoiding strong beams of light and strong contrasts of light. Eliminating excessive glare is essential in designing adequate lighting.

LIGHTING METHODS

Good lighting in a home depends upon three methods. *General lighting* spreads an even, low-level light throughout a room. *Specific (local) lighting* directs light to an area used for a specific visual task. *Decorative lighting* makes use of lights to develop different moods and to accent objects for interest.

GENERAL LIGHTING

General lighting is achieved by direct or indirect methods of light dispersement. Gen-

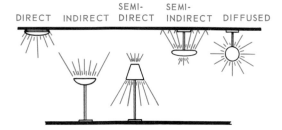

SEMI- SEMI-
DIRECT INDIRECT DIRECT INDIRECT DIFFUSED

Fig 59-5 Methods of light dispersement.

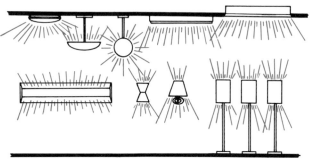

Fig 59-6 Types of general lighting.

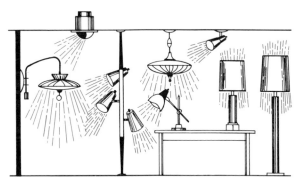

Fig 59-7 Types of specific lighting.

eral light can also be produced by many portable lamps, ceiling fixtures, or long lengths of light on the walls (Fig. 59-6). In the living and sleeping areas, the intensity of general lighting should be between 5 and 10 footcandles (54 to 108 lx). A higher level of general lighting should be used in the service area and bathrooms. In addition to artificial general light sources, skylights can be used to admit light during the day. If the skylight is covered with translucent panels, it can contain an artificial light source for nighttime use.

SPECIFIC LIGHTING

Specific (local) lighting (Fig. 59-7) for a particular visual task is directed into the area in which the task will be done. The specific light in a room will also add to the general lighting level.

DECORATIVE LIGHTING

Decorative lighting (Fig. 59-8) is used for atmosphere and interest when activities do not require much light. Bright lights are stimulating; low levels of lighting are quieting. Decorative lighting strives for unusual effects. Some of these can be obtained with candlelight, lights behind draperies, lights under planters, lights in the bottoms of ponds, lights controlled with a dimmer switch, and different types of cover materials over floor lights and spotlights.

ELECTRICAL FIXTURES

The average two-bedroom home should have between 24 and 35 light fixtures. It should also have from 16 to 20 floor, table, or wall lamps.

Light fixtures fall into three groups: ceiling fixtures (Fig. 59-9), wall fixtures (Fig. 59-10), and portable plug-ins (Fig. 59-11).

Fig 59-8 Decorative lighting.

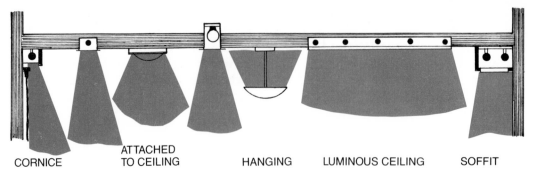

CORNICE ATTACHED TO CEILING HANGING LUMINOUS CEILING SOFFIT

RECESSED IN CEILING RECESSED IN CEILING

Fig 59-9 Examples of ceiling fixtures.

A *valance* is a covering over a long source of light over a window. Its light illuminates the wall and draperies for the spacious effect that daylight gives a room.

A *wall bracket* balances the light of a valance. It gives an upward and downward wash of light difficult to obtain on an inner wall.

A *cornice* is attached to the wall and can be used with or without drapes. All light from this fixture is directed downward, to give an impression of height to the room.

Lamps provide light needed for a seeing task. The bottom of the shade must be below the level of the eyes doing the visual task. The source of light for a lamp should be a short distance at one side of the work area.

ILLUMINATION PLANNING

Following are general rules to observe when planning the lighting of each room.

The kitchen requires a high level of general lighting from ceiling fixtures. Specific lighting for all work areas—range, sink, tables, and counters—is also recommended.

The bathroom requires a high level of general lighting from ceiling fixtures. The shower and water closet, if compartmented, should have a recessed, vaporproof light. The mirror should have lights on two sides.

The living room requires a low level of general lighting but should have specific lighting for areas for reading and other visual tasks. Decorative lighting should be used.

The bedroom requires a low level of general lighting but should have specific lighting for reading in bed and on both sides of the dressing-table mirror. The dressing area requires a high level of general lighting. Chil-

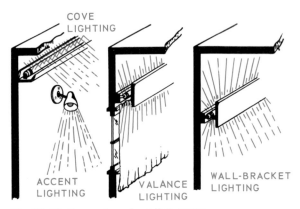

COVE LIGHTING

ACCENT LIGHTING VALANCE LIGHTING WALL-BRACKET LIGHTING

Fig 59-10 Examples of wall fixtures.

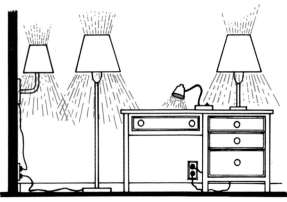

Fig 59-11 Examples of portable plug-in lamps.

dren's bedrooms require a high level of general lighting. Closets should have a fixture placed high at the front.

The dining area requires a low level of general lighting, with local lighting over the dining table.

The entrance and foyer require a high level of general and decorative lighting.

Traffic areas require a high level of general lighting for safety.

Reading and desk areas require a high level of general light and specific light that is diffused and glareless. There should be no shadows.

Television viewing requires a very low level of general lighting. Television should not be viewed in the dark because the strong contrast of dark room and bright screen is tiring to the eyes.

Outdoor lighting is accomplished by waterproof floodlights and spotlights. Extensive outdoor lighting will provide convenience, beauty, and safety. Areas that could be illuminated are the landscaping, game areas, barbecue area, patio, garden, front of picture window, pools, and driveways.

Outdoor lights should not shine directly on windows. Lights near the windows should be placed above the windows to eliminate glare. Ground lights should be shielded by bushes to keep them from shining into windows.

PROBLEMS

1 List several sources of general lighting.
2 List several sources for specific lighting.
3 List several methods for decorative lighting.

4 Plan the lighting needs of the house you are designing.
5 On a floor plan of your home, show the lighting as it now exists.

6 On a floor plan of your home, show how you would plan the lighting.
7 Plan the lighting for the floor plan in Fig. 33-16.
8 Plan the lighting for the floor plan in Fig. 70-1.
9 Define these terms: *incandescent bulb, fluorescent tube, filament, direct light, indirect light, semidirect light, diffused light, reflectance, valance lighting, wall-bracket lighting, cornice lighting.*

UNIT 60
ELECTRICAL PRINCIPLES

In this age of technological innovation and vanishing supplies of inexpensive oil, electrical systems must be designed to serve today's needs and also be adaptable to future requirements. Sources of electrical energy, methods of distribution, and devices that consume energy are all important concerns in the design of modern buildings.

POWER DISTRIBUTION

One of Thomas Edison's greatest inventions was the system of distributing electrical energy. Electrical utility companies and agencies that have grown from his scheme now serve most of the United States and Canada with vast, interconnected, electrical power grids, or networks.

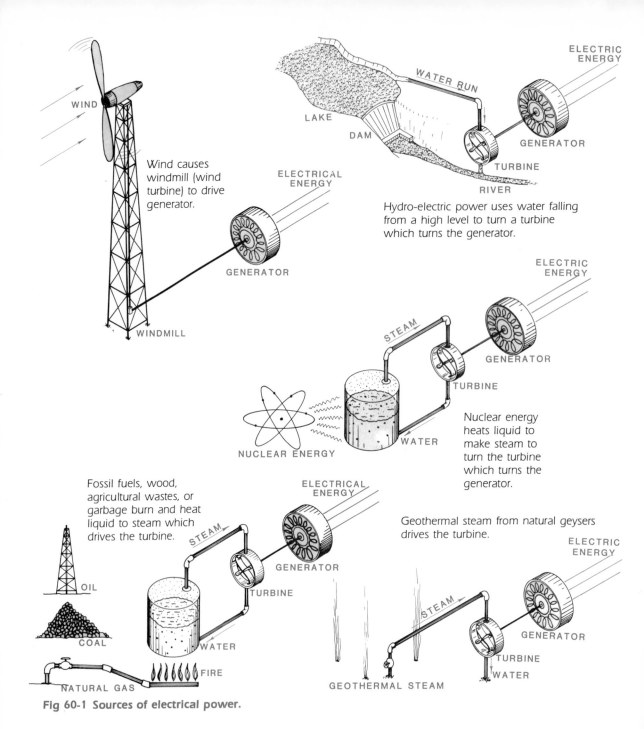

Wind causes windmill (wind turbine) to drive generator.

WIND

WINDMILL

GENERATOR

ELECTRICAL ENERGY

ELECTRIC ENERGY

WATER RUN

LAKE

DAM

RIVER

GENERATOR

TURBINE

Hydro-electric power uses water falling from a high level to turn a turbine which turns the generator.

ELECTRIC ENERGY

STEAM

GENERATOR

TURBINE

NUCLEAR ENERGY

WATER

Nuclear energy heats liquid to make steam to turn the turbine which turns the generator.

Fossil fuels, wood, agricultural wastes, or garbage burn and heat liquid to steam which drives the turbine.

ELECTRICAL ENERGY

STEAM

GENERATOR

TURBINE

WATER

FIRE

OIL

COAL

NATURAL GAS

Geothermal steam from natural geysers drives the turbine.

ELECTRIC ENERGY

STEAM

GENERATOR

TURBINE

WATER

GEOTHERMAL STEAM

Fig 60-1 Sources of electrical power.

Electrical power is generated from a few basic sources of energy: wind, water, nuclear, fossil fuel, and geothermal. In practically every case, the energy source is harnessed to produce a rotary mechanical motion that drives huge generators (Figs. 60-1A through 60-1E).

Electrical power is stepped up to very high voltages (hundreds of thousands of volts) for transmission by wires over long distances.

448

High voltage transmission greatly reduces the loss of power caused by electrical heating of the wires. Wherever the transmission lines enter an industrial or residential community for local power distribution, large transformers are used to step down the voltage to a few thousand volts. Smaller transformers are then used on poles or in underground vaults for final distribution to small groups of houses or individual factories. Examples of voltages used in residences are 240, 230, 220, 120, 115, and 110 volts. Examples of voltages used in small factories and commercial buildings are 480, 277, 240, 208, and 120 volts.

WIRING TERMS

Terms used in describing electrical systems include the units of measure and names of tools, hardware, and supply items.

Fortunately, there is only one system of units used for common electrical measurements. Both metric and customary systems use volts, amperes (amps), and watts as the basic units of measurement.

The *volt* is the unit of electrical pressure or potential. It is this pressure that makes electricity flow through a wire. For a particular electrical load, the higher the voltage, the greater will be the amount of electricity that will flow. The technical term for flow of electricity is *current*.

The *ampere* is the unit used to measure the magnitude of an electric current. An ampere is defined as the specific quantity of electrons passing a point in 1 second. The amount of current in amps in a circuit is used to determine wire sizes and the current rating of circuit breakers and fuses.

The amount of power required to light lamps, heat water, turn motors, and do all types of work is measured in *watts*. Power depends on both potential (volts) and current (amps). Current in amps multiplied by potential in volts equals power in watts (Amps × Volts = Watts).

The actual work done, or energy used, is the basis of our electric bills. The unit used to measure the consumption of electrical energy is the *kilowatt-hour*. A kilowatt is 1000 watts.

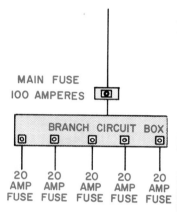

MAIN FUSE
100 AMPERES

BRANCH CIRCUIT BOX

20 AMP FUSE 20 AMP FUSE 20 AMP FUSE 20 AMP FUSE 20 AMP FUSE

Fig 60-2 Branch circuits distribute electricity throughout a structure.

Time is usually measured in hours. Thus, a 1000-watt electric hand iron operating for 1 hour will consume 1 kilowatt-hour (1 kWh). The device used to measure what is consumed is the *watt-hour meter*.

WIRING

Electrical systems in buildings are usually divided into two parts: service and branch circuits. The *service* part consists of all wiring and apparatus needed to bring electricity into the building. *Branch* circuits (Fig. 60-2) distribute the electricity throughout the structure.

Wire used in both service and branch circuits is made of one or more strands of metal, either copper or aluminum, and covered with a flexible plastic insulation. Copper is a better conductor of electricity, more resistant to oxidation and more flexible with age than aluminum. Aluminum is lighter and usually less expensive than copper. Electrical codes usually apply stricter rules on the use of aluminum wire in residences.

The size of the wire used in an electric circuit depends on the current to be carried by the circuit. Wire sizes and diameters are shown in Table 60-1. The current ratings shown are taken from the National Electric

Table 60-1 WIRE SIZE CHART

Branch circuits

Size	Diameter (inches)	Current rating (amperes) Copper	Current rating (amperes) Aluminum
14	0.064	15	—
12	0.081	20	15
10	0.102	30	25
8	0.129	40	30
6	0.162	55	40
4	0.204	70	55
3	0.229	80	65
2	0.258	95	75
1	0.289	110	85
0	0.325	125	100
00 (2/0)	0.365	145	115
000 (3/0)	0.410	165	130
0000 (4/0)	0.460	195	155

Service entrance

3-wire service size (each wire)	Service rating current (amperes) Copper	Service rating current (amperes) Aluminum
4	100	—
3	110	—
2	125	100
1	150	110
0	175	125
00 (2/0)	200	150
000 (3/0)	—	175
0000 (4/0)	—	200

Code ® (NEC) and apply to certain types of rubber- or plastic-covered wire run in metal conduit under specific conditions. The number of strands in various wire sizes is shown in Fig. 60-3.

For safety, convenience, and legal purposes, individual bare wires are not placed within the walls of a building. Wires are covered with insulating materials. Groups of wires may be further covered with plastic or metal jackets. Such groups of wires are called *cables.* Individual wires may be run in pipes or conduits made of steel, aluminum, or plastic. Rigid steel conduit is usually used underground. The steel is heavy-gauge and threaded at both ends. A thinner-gauge con-

duit called *electric metallic tubing* is often used when the conduit is left exposed—on concrete block walls, for example. Electric metallic tubing is too thin to accept threads, so that force fittings must be used on its ends. Flexible steel or aluminum conduit is commonly used for branch circuits located between walls, in ceilings, or under floors (but not in concrete).

Plastic-jacketed multiwire cable is extremely popular for branch circuits because of its low material and installation costs. Its major disadvantage is that it cannot be changed or expanded easily once it is in place in the walls of a structure. However, its lower cost and ease of initial installation usually offset that disadvantage.

SERVICE

Power is supplied to a building via the *service drop.* Three heavy wires, together called the *drop,* extend from a utility pole or an underground source to the structure. These wires are often twisted into an unobtrusive cable. At the building intersection, the overhead wires are fastened to the structure and spliced to service-entrance wires that enter a conduit through a service weather head. If the service is supplied underground, three wires are run in a rigid conduit. An underground service conduit is either brought directly to the meter socket or to a pulling gutter, depending upon local codes and utility-company requirements. The pulling gutter is used so that the heavy service wires can be grasped easily and pulled with sufficient force, without scraping them on the meter-socket housing.

Modern service-entrance equipment is usually built so that the pulling gutter (if re-

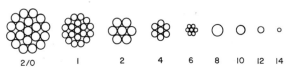

Fig 60-3 Wire strands in various wire sizes.

2/0   1   2   4   6   8   10   12   14

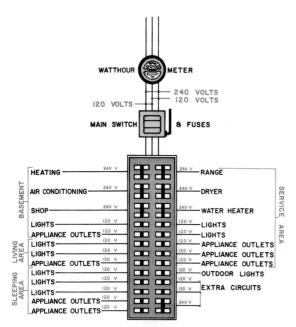

Fig 60-4 Distribution panel.

quired), the meter socket, the main breaker (or switch and fuses), and a bank of branch circuit breakers are mounted in one steel enclosure.

Branch circuits are distributed throughout the home from a distribution panel (Figure 60-4). Each circuit is protected with its own circuit breaker. Some circuits require a

two-pole circuit breaker for protection. *Circuit breakers* are used to protect wiring against overheating and possible fire due to overloading. If the current (amps) in a branch circuit exceeds the rating of its circuit breaker, the breaker will disconnect (*trip*). When the breaker trips, power to the branch circuit is disconnected. If the sum of the current drawn by the individual branch circuits exceeds the rating of the main circuit breaker, the main breaker will trip. This protects the service-entrance wires and equipment from overheating.

PERSONAL SAFETY

In addition to protecting wiring and equipment from overloading, it is important to protect people from shock and electrocution. Two types of protection are incorporated into modern electrical systems. The first is provided by *grounding receptacles* for appliances, and the second by *ground-fault circuit interrupters* (GFCI). To understand what each does requires an explanation of branch-circuit wiring.

Figure 60-5 shows a simplified residential electrical system with a main circuit breaker and eight branch circuits. A receptacle is shown connected to circuit #7. The black

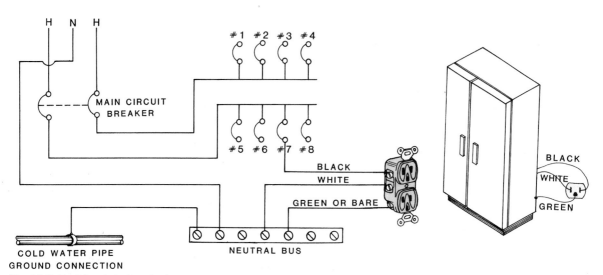

Fig 60-5 Residential electrical system.

wire connected to the circuit breaker is not grounded. It is called a *hot lead* since there is a voltage between it and the ground or neutral. The white wire is the branch-circuit neutral wire. The branch-circuit grounding system (green or bare wires or the conduit in an all-metallic system) is also connected to the neutral bus. A bus is a copper bar used to connect the neutral and ground wires from all circuits. The neutral bus in turn is connected to a ground stake (or stakes) driven into the ground outside the building, usually near the service entrance. The unmetered sides of incoming water lines were commonly used as the earth ground; however, they are no longer considered adequate grounds.

The black and white leads connected to the same receptacle carry the same current.

The refrigerator freezer shown in Fig. 60-5 is connected to the branch circuit by a three-wire cord with a grounding plug. The center prong of the plug is connected directly to the metal frame or cabinet of the appliance. If an uninsulated black (hot) wire should touch the cabinet, excess current would flow in the black wire, and the circuit breaker would trip. If the appliance cabinet was not grounded (that is, if there was no green wire), no excess current would flow, and the appliance would continue to operate. With the hot wire touching the cabinet, any person touching ground (a water pipe, a faucet, a radiator, for example) and the refrigerator would receive a painful shock, possible injury, or electrocution.

Large appliances, including refrigerators, freezers, washers, dryers, and the like, are required to have grounding cords and plugs. Some small appliances and power tools also use the three-wire grounding plug or double insulation for shock protection.

In any properly functioning branch circuit, the current in the black (hot) lead is the same as the current in the white (neutral) lead. In a device such as an electric shaver, there is no grounding (green) wire. If the black wire touches an exposed metal part of the shaver, a path to ground could exist. The current path would be from the black wire to the metal part on the shaver, to the skin of the person touching the metal part, and through the water faucet touched by the person to the ground. This potentially dangerous situation can be avoided by using a ground-fault circuit interrupter (GFCI).

The GFCI operates by sensing the current flowing in the black and white leads. These currents must be equal in magnitude and opposite in direction. If they are not—suppose that the black wire accidentally touches an alternate return path—the GFCI opens the circuit. What makes the GFCI important is that it can detect very low currents that would not trip the branch circuit breaker. These low currents (sometimes called *leakage current*) do not need solid metal paths but can travel along damp surfaces. Though low, they can cause injury and even death.

GFCIs are required by the NEC in new residential construction in bathroom, garage, and outdoor receptacles. A receptacle located not less than 10 or more than 15 feet from the inside wall of a permanently installed swimming pool must also be wired through a GFCI. GFCIs are also recommended for receptacles along kitchen counters and in laundry rooms.

GFCIs are available in two basic forms. Both can be used to protect more than one receptacle. One form of GFCI incorporates a circuit breaker and mounts in the distribution panel. All outlets on the branch circuit connected to this GFCI circuit breaker are protected. The other form of GFCI is part of a receptacle occupying the same space as a duplex receptacle. It has no circuit breaker. It can be used alone or at the beginning of a branch circuit to protect all the outlets that follow. All GFCIs contain a built-in self-testing feature. Regularly, usually monthly, the test button should be pressed to see if the GFCI is functioning properly. GFCIs are available for 15- and 20-amp circuits.

SERVICE AND BRANCH REQUIREMENTS

The National Electric Code (NEC) provides the basis for calculating the requireients for a minimum electrical service. For this example, consider a typical 1500-square-foot single-family house. This house has two bedrooms, two bathrooms, a kitchen, a laundry room/service porch, a dining room, and a living/family room. The house has an unimproved attic and an attached garage. It has no basement. Natural gas is used for cooking and heating. Water is heated by solar energy augmented by a natural-gas hot-water heater. No air conditioning is provided.

The calculations start with the individual branch circuits.

GENERAL LIGHTING LOADS

The NEC requires a minimum general lighting load of 3 watts per square foot. This house requires 4500 watts:

3 watts/sq. ft. × 1500 sq. ft. = 4500 watts

Assuming the line voltage is 120 volts, each 20-amp branch circuit can supply 2400 watts:

20 amps × 120 volts = 2400 watts.

The house should have a minimum of two circuits for the general lighting load. Note that the general lighting load includes general-purpose receptacles.

The total load is distributed between the two hot legs to equalize the load and to pre-vent a total blackout in any one room, where practical. Since two circuits feed each bedroom and the living room, a failure on one circuit will not darken all lights in each room. A three-wire arrangement with a common neutral is employed.

SMALL-APPLIANCE CIRCUITS

A minimum of two branch circuits for small appliances is required by the NEC. These circuits feed only the kitchen, the dining room, and the family room. The two circuits required in the kitchen may be wired alternately to adjacent receptacles or by using split-link receptacles; that is, each half of a duplex receptacle may be on a different circuit. GFCI outlets or circuit breakers offer life-saving protection at kitchen counter receptacles, especially those near sinks. An arrangement using GFCI circuit breakers is shown in Fig. 60-6.

LAUNDRY CIRCUIT

A separate 20-amp circuit is required in a laundry area or room. Its purpose is to feed the washing machine and the motor and controls of the gas dryer. Again, GFCI is not required by many electrical codes, but because of the danger of leakage currents, one is recommended.

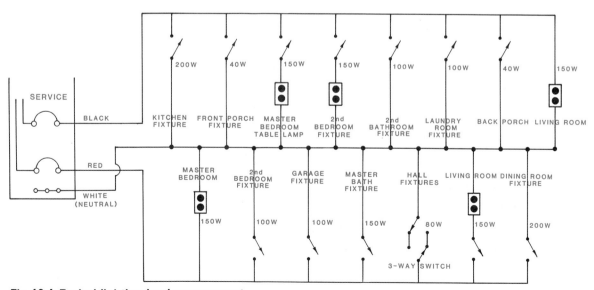

Fig 60-6 Typical lighting load arrangement.

Table 60-2 LOAD REQUIREMENTS FOR ELECTRICAL APPLIANCES

	Typical connected watts	Volts	Wires	Circuit breaker or fuse	Outlets on circuit	Outlet type	Notes
KITCHEN							
RANGE	12,500	120/240	3 #6 + GND	50A	1	14-50R	
OVEN (BUILT-IN)	4,500	120/240	3 #10 + GND	30A	1	14-30R	#1
RANGE TOP	6,000	120/240	3 #10 + GND	30A	1	14-30R	#1
DISHWASHER	1,500	120	2 #12 + GND	20A	1	5-15R	#2
WASTE DISPOSER	800	120	2 #12 + GND	20A	1	5-15R	#2
TRASH COMPACTOR	1,200	120	2 #12 + GND	20A	1	5-15R	#2
MICROWAVE OVEN	1,450	120	2 #12 + GND	20A	1 or more	5-15R	
BROILER	1,500	120	2 #12 + GND	20A	1 or more	5-15R	#3
FRYER	1,300	120	2 #12 + GND	20A	1 or more	5-15R	#3
COFFEEMAKER	1,000	120	2 #12 + GND	20A	1 or more	5-15R	#3
REFRIGERATOR/ FREEZER 16-25 cubic feet	800	120	2 #12 + GND	20A	1 or more	5-15R	#4
FREEZER chest or upright 14-25 cubic feet	600	120	2 #12 + GND	20A	1 or more	5-15R	#4
LAUNDRY							
WASHING MACHINE	1,200	120	2 #12 + GND	20A	1 or more	5-15R	#5
DRYER all-electric	5,200	120/240	3 #10 + GND	30A	1	14-30R	#1
DRYER gas/electric	500	120	2 #12 + GND	20A	1 or more	5-15R	#5
IRONER	1,650	120	2 #12 + GND	20A	1 or more	5-15R	
HAND IRON	1,000	120	2 #12 + GND	20A	1 or more	5-15R	
WATER HEATER	3,000-6,000					DIRECT	#6

Table 60-2 LOAD REQUIREMENTS FOR ELECTRICAL APPLIANCES (continued)

	Typical connected watts	Volts	Wires	Circuit breaker or fuse	Outlets on circuit	Outlet type	Notes
LIVING AREAS							
WORKSHOP	1,500	120	2 #12 + GND	20A	1 or more	5-15R	#7
PORTABLE HEATER	1,300	120	2 #12 + GND	20A	1	5-15R	#3
TELEVISION	300	120	2 #12 + GND	20A	1 or more	5-15R	#8
PORTABLE LIGHTING	1,200	120	2 #12 + GND	20A	1 or more	5-15R	#9
FIXED UTILITIES							
FIXED LIGHTING	1,200	120	2 #12	20A			#10
WINDOW AIR CONDITIONER							
14 000 BTU	1,400	120	2 #12 + GND	20A	1	5-15R	#11
25 000	3,600	240	2 #12 + GND	20A	1	6-20R	#11
29 000	4,300	240	2 #10 + GND	30A	1	6-30R	#11
CENTRAL AIR CONDITIONER							
23 000 BTU	2,200	240					#6
57 000 BTU	5,800	240					#6
HEAT PUMP	14,000	240					#6
SUMP PUMP	300	120	2 #12	20A	1 or more	5-15R	#1
HEATING PLANT oil or gas	600	120	2 #12	20A			#6
FIXED BATHROOM HEATER	1,500	120	2 #12	20A			#6
ATTIC FAN	300	120	2 #12	20A	1	5-15R	

NOTES

#1 May be direct-connected.

#2 May be direct-connected on a single circuit; otherwise, grounded receptacles required.

#3 Heavy-duty appliances regularly used at one location should have a separated circuit. Only one such unit should be attached to a single circuit at a time.

#4 Separate circuit serving only refrigerator and freezer is recommended.

#5 Grounding-type receptacle required. Separate circuit is recommended.

#6 Consult manufacturer for recommended connections.

#7 Separate circuit recommended.

#8 Should not be connected to appliance circuits.

#9 Provide one circuit for each 500 sq. ft (46 m²). Divided receptacle may be switched.

#10 Provide at least one circuit for each 1200 watts of fixed lighting.

#11 Consider 20-amp, 3-wire circuits to all window-type air conditioners. Outlets may then be adapted to individual 120- or 240-volt units. This scheme will work for all but the very largest units.

REQUIRED GFCI CIRCUITS

A minimum of four more receptacles is required by the NEC. They may be on one circuit protected by a single 20-amp GFCI circuit breaker, or they may use individual GFCI receptacles. A receptacle must be located near each sink in each bathroom, in the garage, and on the outside wall of the house. Since outside receptacles are used for such devices as electric garden tools, auto polishers, and barbecue starters and rotisseries, they should be located for maximum convenience.

SERVICE SIZE REQUIREMENTS

Since all lights and all appliances are probably not going to be used at the same time, it is not economical to provide a service capable of supplying the full load. The NEC permits each small-appliance circuit and each laundry circuit to be computed as a 1500 watt load.

The minimum service would include:

—3 watts/sq. ft. for general
   lighting load .... 4500 watts
—1500 watts for each small-
   appliance circuit .... 3000 watts
—1500 watts for laundry
   circuit .... 1500 watts
                             9000 watts

If this house has six or more two-wire branch circuits, the NEC requires a minimum of 100-amp conductors. That is, the wire size must be capable of carrying 100 amperes in a three-wire service (two hot legs and a neutral) leg. Complete procedures for loads of various types are outlined in the National Electrical Code.

LARGE APPLIANCES AND WINDOW AIR CONDITIONERS

Branch circuits for large appliances must be matched to the appliance. The common 120-volt, 15-amp circuit is often inadequate for certain motor loads, for example. Large appliances sometimes require individual circuits and operate on 240 volts. The 240-volt potential is obtained by connecting the two hot legs to the load through circuit breakers in each leg. Table 60-2 shows acceptable electrical loads and circuits for residential wiring systems.

PROBLEMS

1 Figure 60-7 represents a four-circuit system for a one-bedroom apartment. Draw the floor plan to ¼″ scale. List the rooms on each circuit; draw all lighting outlets; draw all circuits; and label the wire size, the line voltage, the maximum watts on each circuit, and the fuse size.

2 Draw Fig. 20-13 and complete the electrical plan. Show all the circuits and label each type. Label the voltage, wattage, wire size, and fuse size for each circuit.

3 List the rooms on each circuit for the house you are designing. Draw each circuit. Locate the position of the service drop and distribution panel.

Fig 60-8 Design and draw circuits for this plan.

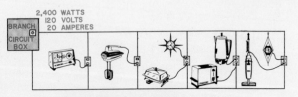

Fig 60-7 Small appliance circuit.

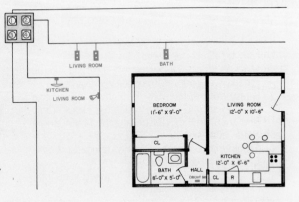

4 Define these terms: *wiring system, generator, transformer, voltage, ampere, watt, circuit, electric current, overloading, conductor, insulator, kilowatt, kilowatt-hour, cables, conduit, electric metallic tubing,* *service drop, service entrance, distribution panel, service circuit, branch circuits, fuse, circuit breaker, outlet, lighting circuit, small-appliance circuit, grounding receptacles, ground-fault circuit interrupter.*

UNIT 61
PLANNING WITH ELECTRICITY

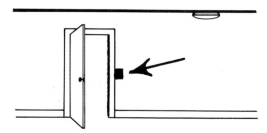
Fig 61-1 The light switch should be conveniently located near a door.

Wiring methods are controlled by building codes. The job of wiring is performed by licensed electricians. However, the wiring plans for a building are prepared by the architect. For large structures, a consulting electrical contractor may aid in the preparation of the final plans. Electrical plans must include information concerning the type and location of all switches, fixtures, and controls.

PLANNING RULES

Basic rules to follow when planning the electrical system are listed below:

1 The main source of light in a room should be controlled by a wall switch located on the latch side of the room's entrance. It should not be necessary to walk into a dark room to find the light switch (Fig. 61-1).

2 Electrical outlets (except in the kitchen) should average one for every 6' (1.8 m) of wall space.

3 Electrical outlets in the kitchen should average one for every 4' (1.2 m) of wall space.

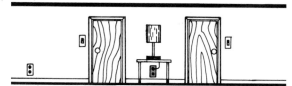
Fig 61-2 Wall spaces between doors should have a convenience outlet.

4 Walls between doors should have an outlet, regardless of the size of the wall space (Fig. 61-2).

5 Each room should have a light outlet in the ceiling or wall that will be a major source of light for the whole room (Fig. 61-3).

6 Each room should have adequate lighting for all visual tasks.

7 Each room should have at least one easy-to-reach outlet for the vacuum cleaner or other appliances that are often used.

8 Not all the lights in one room should be on the same circuit.

9 The height of all outlets in the house should be listed on the plans (Fig. 61-4).

10 GFCI receptacles should be provided as outlined in Unit 60.

SWITCH LOCATION

Switches should be located according to the following guides:

1 Plan the switches needed for all lights and electrical equipment. Toggle switches are available in several different types: single-pole, double-pole, three-way, and four-way (Fig. 61-5).

2 Show location and height of switches.

3 Select the type of switches, type of switch-plate cover, and type of finish.

4 If there are only lamps in a room, the entry switch should control the outlet into which at least one lamp is plugged.

5 Lights for stairways and halls must be controlled from both ends (Fig. 61-6).

6 Bedroom lights should be controlled from bedside and entrance with a three-way switch.

7 Outside lights must be controlled with a three-way switch from the garage and from the exit of the house.

8 Basement lights should be controlled by a switch and a pilot light in the house at the head of the basement stairs (Fig. 61-7).

9 Install wall switches in preference to pull-string switches in closets.

10 Describe all special controls to be used.

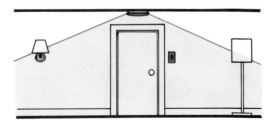

Fig 61-3 A switch by a door should control the main source of light.

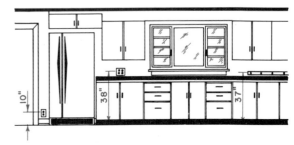

Fig 61-4 The height of all outlets should be noted on wall elevations or in the specifications.

SPECIAL CONTROLS

Special controls make appliances and lighting systems more efficient. Some special controls for electrical equipment include:

Mercury switches are silent, shockproof, long-lasting, and easy to install.
Automatic cycle controls, as on washers, can be installed on appliances to make

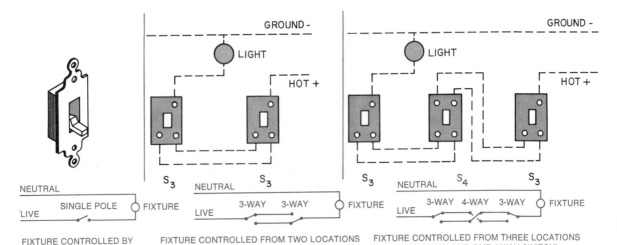

FIXTURE CONTROLLED BY ONE SWITCH

FIXTURE CONTROLLED FROM TWO LOCATIONS (TWO 3-WAY SWITCHES)

FIXTURE CONTROLLED FROM THREE LOCATIONS (TWO 3-WAY AND ONE 4-WAY SWITCH)

Fig 61-5 Types of switching controls.

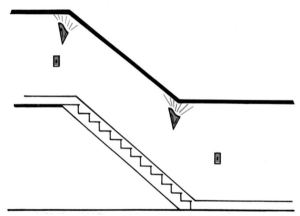

Fig 61-6 Three-way switches should be used on stairway lights.

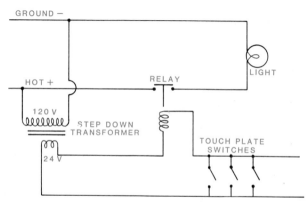

Fig 61-8 A low-voltage control system.

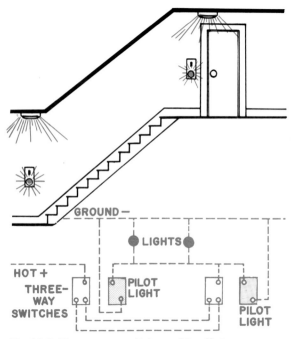

Fig 61-7 Three-way switches with pilot lights should be used on basement stairs.

them perform their functions on a time cycle.

Automatic controls adjust heating and cooling systems.

Clock thermostats adjust heating or cooling units for day and night.

Aquastats keep water heated to selected temperatures.

Dimmers control intensity of light.

Time switches control lights or watering systems.

Safety-alarm systems activate a bell when a circuit on a door or window is broken.

Master switches control switching throughout the home from one location.

Low-voltage switching systems (Fig. 61-8) provide economical long runs.

The low-voltage method of switching offers convenience and flexibility. A *relay* isolates all switches from the 120-volt system. The voltage from the switch to the appliance is only 24 volts. At the appliance, a *magnetic-controlled switch* opens the full 120 volts to the appliance. The magnetic-controlled switch is more commonly called a *touch switch*. The low, 24-volt system permits long runs of inexpensive wiring that is easy to install and safe to use. This makes it ideal for master-control switching from one location in the house.

ELECTRICAL OUTLETS

There are several types of electrical outlets. The *convenience outlet* is used for small-appliance and lamp plugs. It is available in single, double, triple, or strip outlets.

Lighting outlets are for the connection of lampholders, surface-mounted fixtures, flush or recessed fixtures, and all other types of lighting fixtures.

The *special-purpose outlet* is the connection point of a circuit for one special piece of equipment.

The wires that hook up the whole electric system are installed during the construction of the building, in the walls, floors, and ceilings. In a finished house, the entire system is hidden. The conventional wiring system used for outlets, lights, and small appliances consists of a black wire (the hot wire) and a white wire (the neutral or common wire). A third, green, wire is a grounding wire. For large appliances, the wiring consists of a black wire and a red wire both of which are hot wires, and a white wire. All three wires connect through a switch to the appliance.

If the wire is too long or too small, there will be a voltage drop because of the wire's resistance. Another cause of voltage drop is the drawing of too much current from the branch circuit. This will cause heating appliances such as toasters, irons, and electric heaters to work inefficiently. Motor-driven appliances will overwork and possibly burn out. Sufficient circuits with large enough wire must be provided for all appliances.

ELECTRICAL WORKING DRAWINGS

Complete electrical plans will ensure the installation of electrical equipment and wiring exactly as planned. If electrical plans are incomplete and sketchy, the completeness of the installation is largely dependent upon the

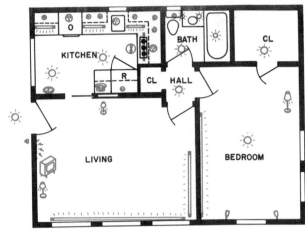

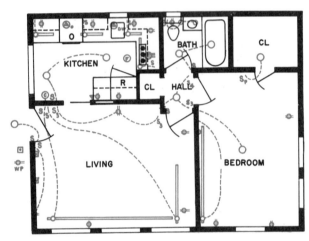

Fig 61-9 Planning home wiring to anticipated needs.

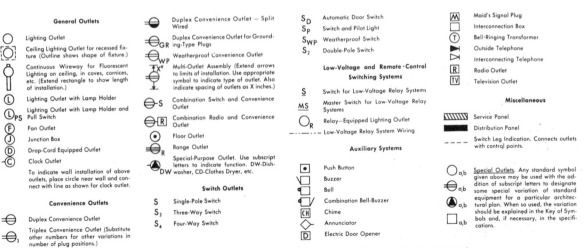

Fig 61-10 Graphic symbols for electrical and layout diagrams used in architecture and building construction.

460

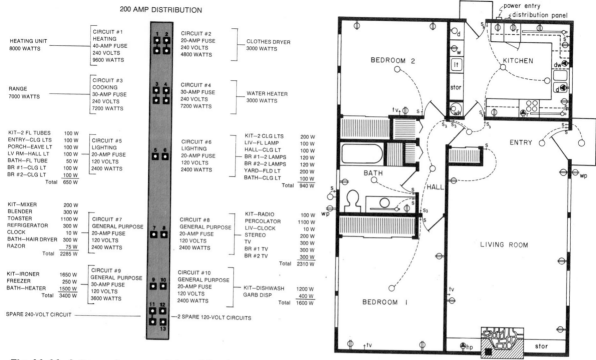

Fig 61-11 A floor plan complete with electrical symbols and the circuits for this plan.

judgment of the electrician. The designer should not rely upon the electrician to design the electrical system, but only to install it.

PREPARING THE ELECTRICAL PLAN

After the basic floor plan is drawn, the designer should determine the exact position of all appliances and lighting fixtures on the plan, as shown in Fig. 61-9. The exact position of switches and outlets to accommodate appliances and fixtures should be determined. Next, the electrical symbols representing the switches, outlets, and electrical devices should be drawn on the floor plan. A line is then drawn from each switch to the connecting fixture. Figure 61-10 shows electrical symbols used for residential wiring plans. The exact position of each wire is determined by the electrician. The designer indicates only the position of the fixture and the switch and the connecting line.

Figure 61-11 shows a typical electrical plan of a residence. The circuits for this plan are also shown. The architectural method as shown in Fig. 61-12 is used on this plan be-

cause of its simplicity. Compare the architectural method with the true wiring diagram and you will see that it would be virtually impossible to complete a true wiring diagram for the entire structure.

ROOM WIRING DIAGRAMS

Figure 61-13 through 61-20 shows some typical wiring diagrams of various rooms in

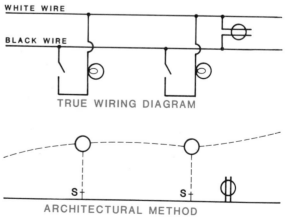

Fig 61-12 Architectural wiring plans do not show the position of each separate wire.

461

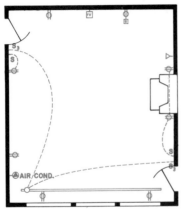

Fig 61-13 The wiring plan for a living room.

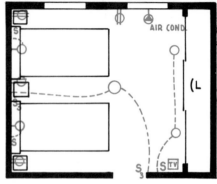

Fig 61-16 The wiring plan for a bedroom.

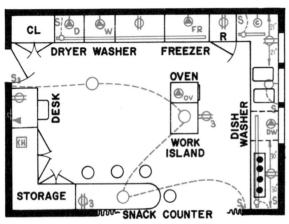

Fig 61-14 The wiring plan for a kitchen.

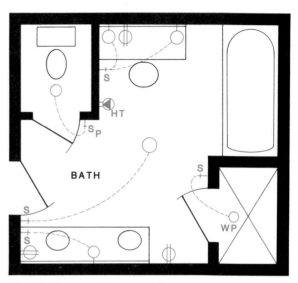

Fig 61-17 The wiring plan for a bathroom.

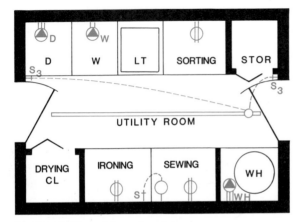

Fig 61-15 The wiring plan for a utility room.

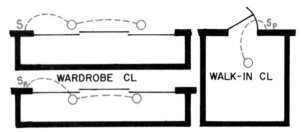

Fig 61-18 A wiring plan for closets.

the home. Refer to the symbols shown in Fig. 61-10 to identify the various symbols. You will notice you can trace the control of each fixture to a switch. You will notice how much more

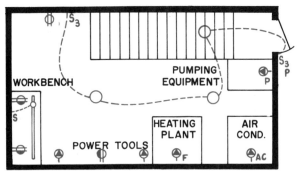

Fig 61-19 The wiring plan for a basement.

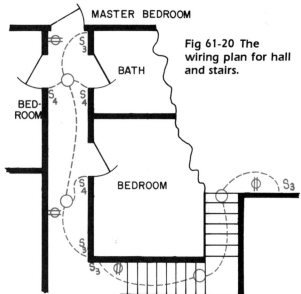

Fig 61-20 The wiring plan for hall and stairs.

involved the electrical appliances for the kitchen and laundry are than those in the other rooms in the house. Notice also the use of three-way and four-way switches in halls and other traffic areas to provide flexibility and control.

PROBLEMS

1 Make a complete electrical drawing of your classroom.

2 Using symbols, draw an electrical plan of your home.

3 Draw the complete electrical plan for the house you are designing. Show all circuits and label the capacity of each. Identify the circuits protected by a GFCI device.

4 Complete the electrical plan for Fig. 61-21.

5 Complete the electrical plan for Fig. 61-22.

6 Go to a store and compile a list of new lighting fixtures, and fixtures and parts of the wiring system.

7 Define these terms: *switch, outlet, toggle switch, single-pole switch, double-pole switch, three-way switch, four-way switch, switch plate, switch and pilot light, mercury switch, automatic-cycle control, photoelectric cells, clock thermostats, aquastats, dimmers, time switch, master-control switch, low-voltage switching system, hot wire, black wire, red wire, white wire, strip outlets, special-purpose outlets, convenience outlets, lighting outlets.*

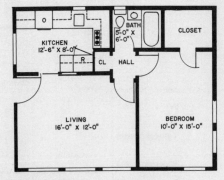

Fig 61-21 Complete a wiring plan for this floor plan.

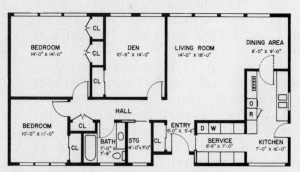

Fig 61-22 Add electrical symbols to this floor plan.

SECTION 15

CLIMATE-CONTROL PLANS

Comfort requires more than just providing warmth in winter and coolness in summer. True comfort means a correct temperature, correct humidity, or amount of moisture in the air, and clean, fresh, odorless air. The achievement of this ideal comfort, or air conditioning, is achieved through the use of a heating system, a cooling system, air filters, and humidifiers. Climate-control plans show systems of maintaining specific degrees of temperature, amounts of moisture, and the exchange of odorless air.

UNIT 62

CLIMATE-CONTROL SYMBOLS

Heating and ventilating equipment is drawn on floor plans using symbols (Fig. 62-1). They show the location and type of equipment, and also the movement of hot and cold air.

The location of horizontal ducts on a heating and ventilating duct plan is shown by outlining the position of the ducts. Since vertical ducts pass through the plane of projection, diagonal lines are used to indicate the position of vertical ducts. The flow of air through the ducts can be easily traced because the direction of air flow is shown by an arrow (Fig. 62-2).

NAME	ABBREV	SYMBOL	NAME	ABBRV	SYMBOL
DUCT SIZE & FLOW DIRECTION	DCT/FD		HEAT REGISTER	R	R
DUCT SIZE CHANGE	DCT/SC		THERMOSTAT	T	T
DUCT LOWERING	DCT/LW	D D	RADIATOR	RAD	RAD
DUCT RISING	DCT/RS	R R	CONVECTOR	CONV	CONV
DUCT RETURN	DCT/RT		ROOM AIR CONDITIONER	RAC	RAC
DUCT SUPPLY	DCT SUP	S	HEATING PLANT FURNACE	HT PLT FUR	
CEILING-DUCT OUTLET	CLG DCT OUT		FUEL-OIL TANK	FOT	OIL
WARM-AIR SUPPLY	WA SUP	WA	HUMIDSTAT	H	H
SECOND-FLOOR SUPPLY	2nd FL SUP		HEAT PUMP	HP	HP
COLD-AIR RETURN	CA RET	CA	THERMOMETER	T	T
SECOND-FLOOR RETURN	2 FL RET		PUMP	P	
GAS OUTLET	G OUT	G	GAGE	GA	
HEAT OUTLET	HT OUT		FORCED CONVECTION	FRC CONV	

Fig 62-1 Climate-control symbols.

Air flow coming from the heating-cooling unit is shown by an arrow pointing out from the diffusers. Return air is indicated by an arrow pointing into the duct.

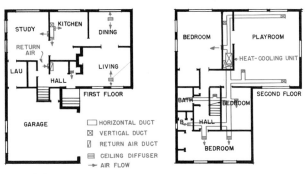

Fig 62-2 Arrows indicate air-flow direction.

PROBLEMS

1 Match the symbols with the terms shown in Fig. 62-3.
2 Define the following terms: *duct, air flow, return air.*

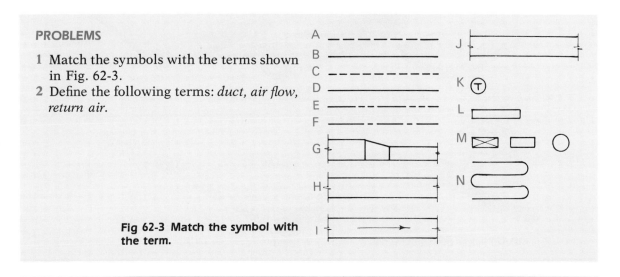

Fig 62-3 Match the symbol with the term.

UNIT 63
CLIMATE-CONTROL METHODS

Many different systems can be used to heat and cool a building. The effective use of insulation, ventilation, roof overhang, caulking, weather stripping, and solar orientation helps to increase the efficiency of any climate-control system.

HEAT TRANSFER

Heat is transferred from a warm to a cool surface by one of three processes: radiation, convection, or conduction (Fig. 63-1).

In *radiation*, heat flows to a cooler surface through space in the same way light travels. The air is not warm but the cooler object it strikes becomes warm. The object, in turn, warms the air that surrounds it.

In *convection*, a warm surface heats the

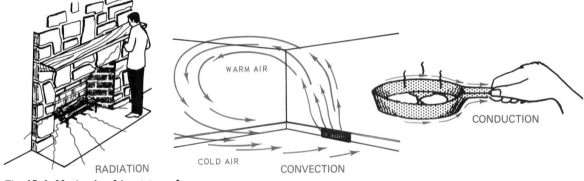

WARM AIR

COLD AIR

RADIATION

CONVECTION

CONDUCTION

Fig 63-1 Methods of heat transfer.

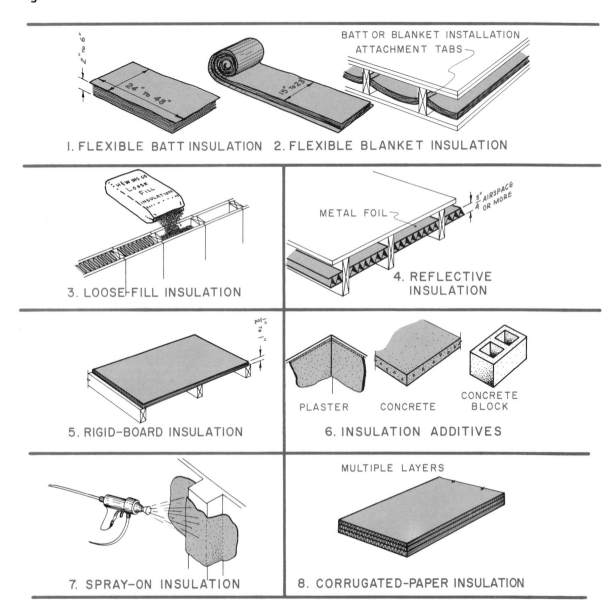

2" to 6"

24" to 48"

15" to 23"

BATT OR BLANKET INSTALLATION
ATTACHMENT TABS

1. FLEXIBLE BATT INSULATION   2. FLEXIBLE BLANKET INSULATION

3. LOOSE-FILL INSULATION

METAL FOIL

3/4" AIRSPACE OR MORE

4. REFLECTIVE INSULATION

1/2" to 1"

5. RIGID-BOARD INSULATION

PLASTER   CONCRETE   CONCRETE BLOCK

6. INSULATION ADDITIVES

7. SPRAY-ON INSULATION

MULTIPLE LAYERS

8. CORRUGATED-PAPER INSULATION

Fig 63-2 Types of insulation.

air about it. The warmed air rises, and cool air moves in to take its place, causing a convection current.

In *conduction*, heat moves through a solid material. The denser the material, the better it will conduct heat. For example, iron conducts heat better than wood.

INSULATION

Insulation is a material used to stop the transfer of heat. It helps keep heat inside in the winter and outside in the summer.

Without insulation, a heating or cooling system must work harder to overcome the loss of warm air or cool air through the walls, floors, and ceilings. Full insulation—6" (150 mm) in the roof, 3" (75 mm) in the walls, and 2" (50 mm) in the floors—can save 40 percent of heating and cooling costs. Properly insulating walls and floors alone can reduce 25 percent of the heat transfer. Because most roofs cannot be sheltered from the sun, 40 percent of all heat transfer is through the roof. Six-inch insulation, with an area for ventilation above the insulation, is most effective. The use of light-colored roofs also helps in reflecting the heat and preventing the absorption of excessive heat.

Windows alone can allow 25 percent of the heat within a house to transfer to the outside. Some deterrents to this transfer are the use of large roof overhangs, trees and shrubbery, drapes and window blinds, and double-paned glass.

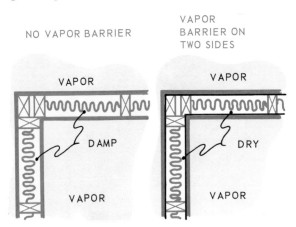

Fig 63-3 Insulation blocks moisture.

In an imperfectly constructed house, cracks around doors, windows, and fireplaces can combine to make the equivalent of a hole of sufficient size to lose all internal heat in less than an hour. Weather stripping and caulking can prevent this heat loss.

Insulation is available in different forms (Fig. 63-2). Insulation is made from a wide variety of vegetable, mineral, plastic, and metal materials. Their purpose is to stop heat transfer, block moisture (Fig. 63-3), stop sound, resist fire, and resist insects.

The different types of insulation (see Fig. 63-2) are:

1 Flexible batt: paper-covered insulating materials that are attached between structural members. The batts are 2" to 6" (50 to 150 mm) thick.
2 Flexible blanket: paper-covered insulating materials that are attached between structural members. The blankets are long sheets, 1" to 3" (25 to 75 mm) thick.
3 Loose fill: materials poured or blown into walls or attic floors.
4 Reflective: multiple spaces of reflecting metal attached between construction members. Reflective material is often mounted on other types of insulation. It is excellent for reflecting heat and for retarding fire, decay, and insects.
5 Rigid board: thin insulating sheathing cover that is manufactured in varying sizes.
6 Additives: lightweight aggregates that are mixed with construction materials to increase their insulating properties.
7 Spray on: insulating materials mixed with an adhesive and sprayed on.
8 Corrugated paper: multiple layers of corrugated paper that are easy to cut and install.

CONVENTIONAL HEATING SYSTEMS

The two most flexible types of heating systems are perimeter heating and radiant heating (Fig. 63-4). In *perimeter heating*, the heat outlets are located on the outside walls of the rooms. The heat rises and covers the coldest areas in the house. In this system, the main loss of heat is through the windows and outside walls. Warm air rises, passes across the ceiling, and returns while still warm. Baseboards, convectors, and radiators can be used to project the heat in the perimeter system.

Radiant heating functions by heating an area of the wall, ceiling, or floor. These warm surfaces in turn radiate heat to cooler objects. The heating surfaces may be lined with pipes containing hot water or hot air, or with electric resistance wires covered with plaster.

HEATING DEVICES

Devices that produce the heat used in the various heating systems include the following: warm-air units, hot-water units, steam units, electrical units, and solar systems.

WARM-AIR UNITS

In a *warm-air unit,* the air is heated in a furnace (Fig. 63-5). Air ducts distribute the heated air to outlets throughout the house (Fig. 63-6). The air supply can be taken from the outside, from the furnace room, or from return-air ducts in heated rooms (Fig. 63-7).

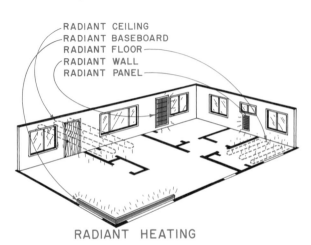

HEAT OUTLETS
DUCTS
HEAT SOURCE

PERIMETER HEATING

RADIANT CEILING
RADIANT BASEBOARD
RADIANT FLOOR
RADIANT WALL
RADIANT PANEL

RADIANT HEATING

Fig 63-4 Two types of heating systems.

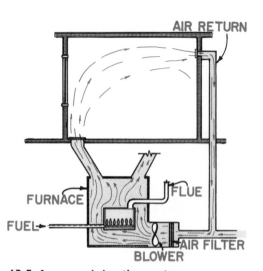

AIR RETURN

FURNACE
FLUE
FUEL
AIR FILTER
BLOWER

Fig 63-5 A warm-air heating system.

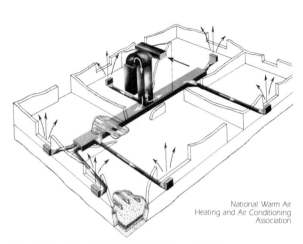

National Warm Air Heating and Air Conditioning Association

Fig 63-6 Air ducts distribute heated air.

Warm-air units can operate either by gravity or by forced air, and they provide almost instant heat. Air filters and humidity control can be combined with the heating unit. The cooling system can use the same ducts as the heating system if the ducts are rustproof.

In *forced-air systems*, the air is blown through ducts by use of a fan in the furnace. *Gravity systems* rely on allowing the warm air to rise naturally to higher levels without the use of a fan. Therefore, the furnace in a gravity system must be located on a level lower than the air to be heated. Warm-air system plans

include the location of each heating outlet and the location of all duct work from the furnace to the outlet, as shown in Fig. 63-8.

Warm-air systems fall into several categories, with respect to duct work: *individual duct* systems, as shown in Fig. 63-8; *extended plenum* systems, as shown in Fig. 63-9; *perimeter loop* systems, such as the one shown in Fig. 63-10; and *perimeter radial* systems, as shown in Fig. 63-11.

When an abbreviated heating and air-conditioning plan is prepared, only the locations of warm-air outlets (Fig. 63-12) are shown on the plan. Figure 63-13 is an abbreviated heating and air-conditioning plan showing only the position of outlets. When this kind of plan is provided, the builder must determine the type, size, and location of all duct work connecting the furnace with the room outlets.

HOT-WATER UNITS

A *hot-water unit* uses a boiler to heat water and a water pump to send the heated water to radiators, finned tubes, convectors, or baseboard outlets (Fig. 63-14). Forcing the water through the pipes with a pump is faster than allowing gravity to make it flow. Hot-water heating provides even heat and keeps

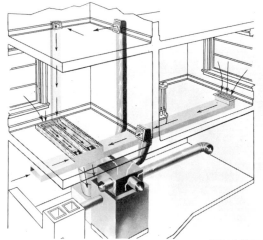

Fig 63-7 Circulation of the air supply.

National Warm Air Heating and Air Conditioning Association

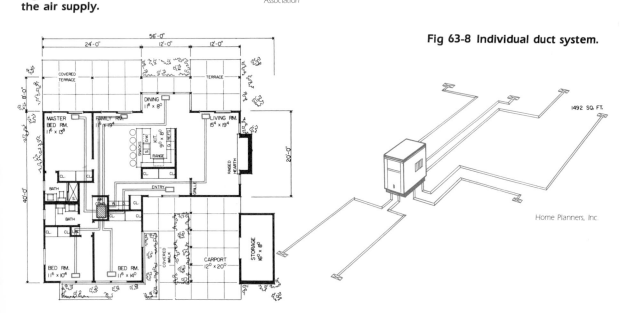

Fig 63-8 Individual duct system.

1492 SQ. FT.

Home Planners, Inc.

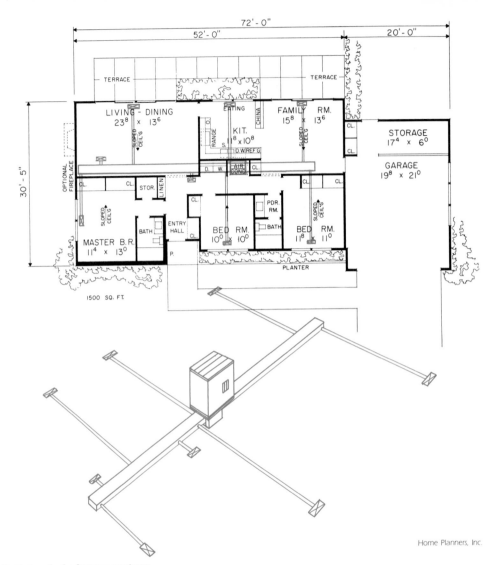

Fig 63-9 Extended plenum system.

heat in the outlets longer than warm-air units. The hot-water boiler is smaller than the warm-air furnace. The hot-water pipe is smaller and easier to install than warm-air ducts. The balance of hot-water and cold-water lines in a hot-water unit is shown in Fig. 63-15. Hot-water units, however, are incompatible with air-conditioning systems, which require the installation of air ducts.

There are several types of hot-water systems used to supply heat from the boiler to heating units: the series-loop system, the one-pipe system, the two-pipe system, and the radiant system.

The *series-loop* system, as shown in Fig. 63-15, is a continual loop of pipes containing hot water that passes through baseboard units. Hot water flows continually from the boiler through the baseboard units and back again to the boiler for reheating. The heat in a series-loop system cannot be controlled except at the source of the loop. Thus, it is effec-

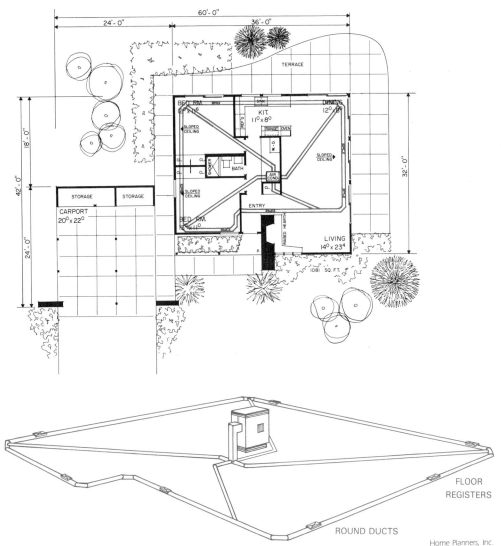

Fig 63-10 Perimeter loop system.

Home Planners, Inc.

tive for only small areas where radiators or convectors produce heat at the same temperature throughout the system. The only way to vary temperature in this type of system is to increase the number of loops in a building. The temperature for each loop can then be varied at each individual loop boiler.

In *one-pipe* systems, heated water is circulated through pipes that are connected to radiators or convectors by means of bypass pipes. This allows each radiator to be individually controlled by valves. Water flows from one side of each radiator to the main line and returns to the boiler for reheating.

In a *two-pipe* system, as shown in Fig. 63-16, there are two parallel pipes: one for the supply of hot water from the boiler to each radiator, and the other for the return of cooled water from each radiator to the boiler. The heated water is directed from the boiler to each radiator but returns from each radiator through the second pipe to the boiler for reheating. In this system, all radiators receive water at nearly the same temperature.

Hot-water heating plans are sometimes shown without piping details. I only the

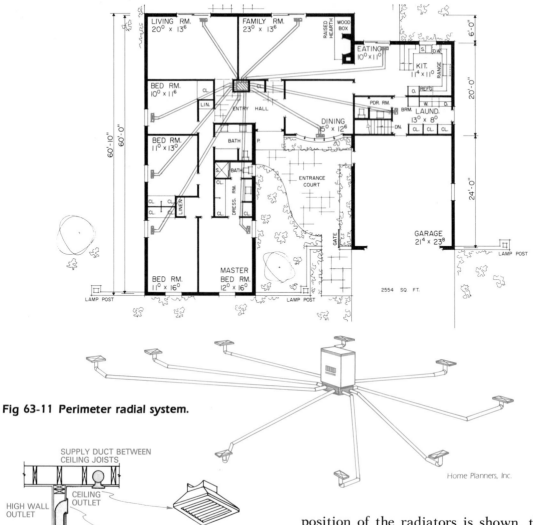

Fig 63-11 Perimeter radial system.

Home Planners, Inc.

SUPPLY DUCT BETWEEN
CEILING JOISTS

HIGH WALL
OUTLET

CEILING
OUTLET

CEILING
REGISTER

WALL
REGISTER

LOW WALL
OUTLET

FLOOR OUTLET

SUPPLY DUCT BETWEEN
FLOOR JOISTS

FLOOR REGISTER

SLAB OUTLET

Fig 63-12 Warm-air system outlets.

position of the radiators is shown, then the plumbing contractor must determine the exact position of piping and also ensure that the radiators or convectors are located as determined on the piping plan.

The *radiant* hot-water heating system distributes hot water through a series of pipes in floors or ceilings. The warm surfaces of the floor or ceiling radiate heat to cooler objects. Ceilings are often used for radiant hot-water heating since furniture and rugs restrict the distribution of heat in floors and walls. Figure 63-17 shows a radiant heating system.

STEAM UNITS

The *steam-heating unit* operates by a boiler used to make steam. The steam is then

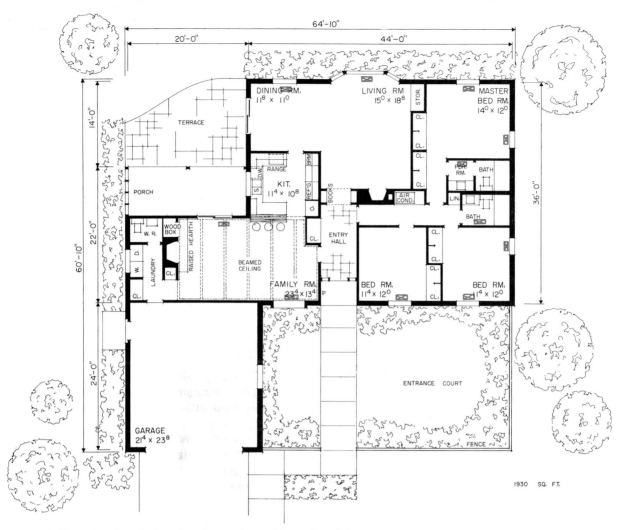

Fig 63-13 Abbreviated plan showing only position of outlets.

transported by pipes to radiators or convectors and baseboards that give off the heat. The steam condenses to water, which returns to the boiler to be reheated to steam. The boiler must always be located below the level of the rooms being heated. Although steam-heating systems function on water vapor rather than hot water, drawings for steam systems are identical with those prepared for hot-water systems.

Steam systems are easy to install and maintain, but they are not suitable for use with most convector radiators. They are most popular for large apartments, commercial buildings, and industrial complexes where separate steam generation facilities are provided. Steam heat is delivered through either perimeter or radial systems.

ELECTRIC HEAT

Electric heat is produced when electricity passes through resistance wires. This heat is usually radiated although it could be fan-blown (convection). Resistance wires can be placed in panel heaters built into the wall or ceiling, or placed in baseboards, or set in plaster to heat the walls, ceilings, or floors. Electric heaters use very little space and require

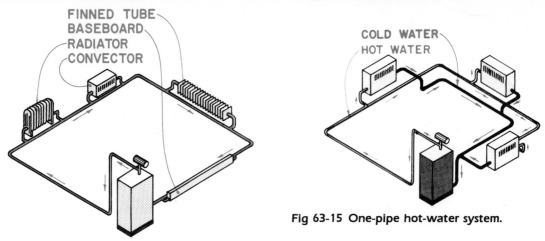

FINNED TUBE
BASEBOARD
RADIATOR
CONVECTOR

Fig 63-14 Hot-water system.

COLD WATER
HOT WATER

Fig 63-15 One-pipe hot-water system.

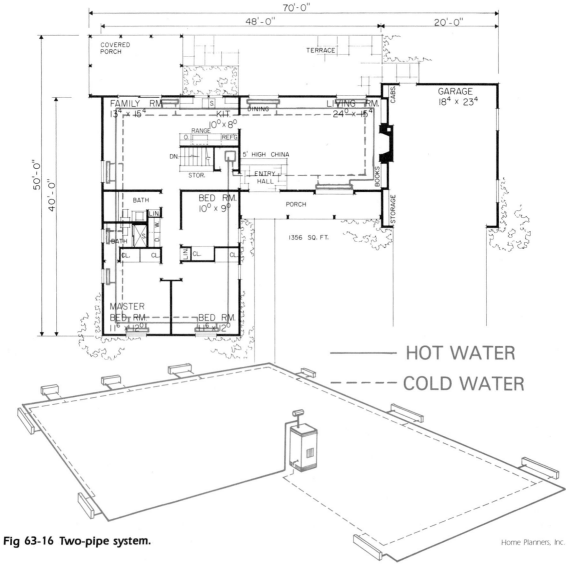

70'-0"
48'-0"
20'-0"

COVERED
PORCH

TERRACE

GARAGE
18⁴ x 23⁴

FAMILY RM.
13⁴ x 15⁴

S

KIT.
10⁰ x 8⁰

DINING

LIVING RM.
24⁰ x 15⁴

CABS.

RANGE

REFG.

DN.

5' HIGH CHINA

STOR.

ENTRY
HALL

BOOKS

BATH

BED RM.
10⁰ x 9⁰

PORCH

STORAGE

50'-0"
40'-0"

LIN.

D. W.

BATH

S

1356 SQ. FT.

CL.

CL.

LIN.

CL.

CL.

MASTER
BED RM.
11⁶ x 12⁰

BED RM.
11 x 12⁰

———— HOT WATER
– – – – COLD WATER

Fig 63-16 Two-pipe system.

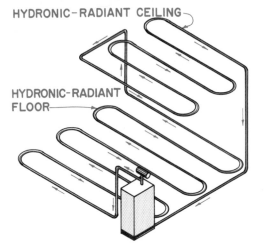

HYDRONIC-RADIANT CEILING

HYDRONIC-RADIANT FLOOR

Fig 63-17 A radiant heating system.

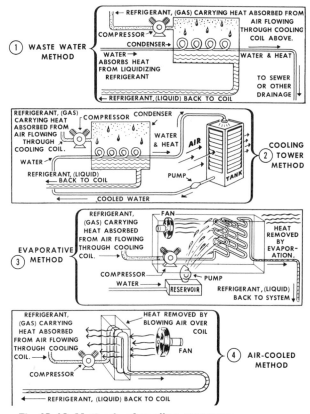

① WASTE WATER METHOD

REFRIGERANT, (GAS) CARRYING HEAT ABSORBED FROM AIR FLOWING THROUGH COOLING COIL ABOVE.

COMPRESSOR
CONDENSER→

WATER ABSORBS HEAT FROM LIQUIDIZING REFRIGERANT

WATER & HEAT

TO SEWER OR OTHER DRAINAGE

←REFRIGERANT, (LIQUID) BACK TO COIL

REFRIGERANT, (GAS) CARRYING HEAT ABSORBED FROM AIR FLOWING THROUGH COOLING COIL.

COMPRESSOR CONDENSER

WATER & HEAT

AIR

② COOLING TOWER METHOD

WATER

REFRIGERANT, (LIQUID) BACK TO COIL

PUMP

TANK

COOLED WATER

EVAPORATIVE ③ METHOD

REFRIGERANT, (GAS) CARRYING HEAT ABSORBED FROM AIR FLOWING THROUGH COOLING COIL.

FAN

HEAT REMOVED BY EVAPORATION.

COMPRESSOR
WATER → RESERVOIR

PUMP

REFRIGERANT, (LIQUID) BACK TO SYSTEM

REFRIGERANT, (GAS) CARRYING HEAT ABSORBED FROM AIR FLOWING THROUGH COOLING COIL. →

HEAT REMOVED BY BLOWING AIR OVER COIL

FAN

④ AIR-COOLED METHOD

COMPRESSOR

←REFRIGERANT, (LIQUID) BACK TO COIL

Fig 63-18 Methods of cooling structures.

no air for combustion. Electric heat is very clean. It requires no storage or fuel and no duct work. Complete ventilation and humidity control must accompany electric heat, since it provides no air circulation and tends to be very dry.

No plans are drawn specifically for electric heat, but notations are made on the floor plans concerning the location of either resistance wires or electric panels. On electrical plans, the location of facilities for power supply and thermostating is shown.

Another use of electricity for air conditioning is to operate the *heat pump*. The heat pump is a year-round air-conditioner. In winter it takes heat from the outside air and pumps it into the house. There is always some heat in the air regardless to the temperature. In summer the pump is reversed and the heat in the house is pumped outside. Thus the pump works like a reversible refrigerator. Drawings for heat-pump duct-work layouts are identical with those used for forced warm-air systems.

The fifth heating device, employing *solar systems*, is discussed in detail later in this unit.

CONVENTIONAL COOLING SYSTEMS

A building is air-conditioned by removing heat. Heat can be transferred in one direction only, from the warmer object to the cooler object. Therefore, to cool a building comfortably, a central air-conditioning system absorbs heat from the house and transfers it to a liquid refrigerant, usually freon. Warm air is carried away from rooms through ducts to the air-conditioning unit where a filter removes dust and other impurities. A cooling coil containing refrigerant then absorbs heat from the air passing through it. Then the blower that pulled the heat-laden air from the rooms pushes heat-free, or cool, air back to the rooms.

There are four main methods of cooling structures: waste-water, cooling-tower, evaporation, and air-cool, as shown in Fig. 63-18.

COOLING UNITS

The cooling unit can be part of the heating unit using the same blower, vent, and perimeter ducts (Fig. 63-19). In this kind of sys-

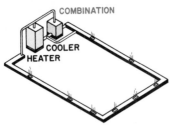

Fig 63-19 A cooling unit can be part of the heating unit.

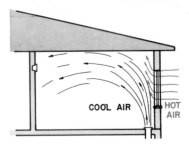

Fig 63-20 Circulation of cool air.

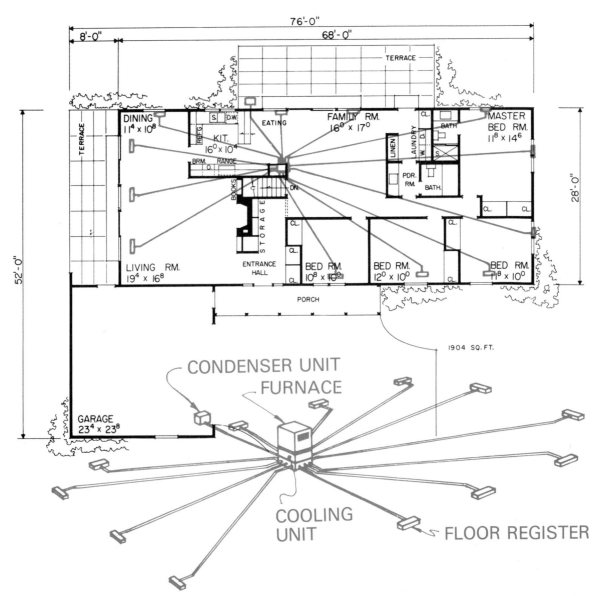

Fig 63-21 A heating and ventilating duct plan.

tem, the cool air rises against the warm walls in the summer and cools the house, as shown in Fig. 63-20. The cooling system can also be separate from the heating system.

When cooling systems are combined with heating systems, a combined heating-and-cooling-system plan is usually prepared, as shown in Fig. 63-21. This plan is read exactly the same as a warm-air heating-duct plan except for the addition of the cooling unit.

The size of air-conditioning equipment is usually rated in *British thermal units* (BTU). Although metric standards for air-conditioning units have yet to be established, British thermal units can be converted to joules (J). Multiply BTU by 1055 to obtain J approximately.

The average small house can be comfortably cooled with central air-conditioning units of 24,000 to 36,000 BTU. Larger homes require a 60,000 BTU unit.

HUMIDITY CONTROL

The proper amount of moisture in the air is important for good air conditioning. Excessive moisture in the home comes from many sources, such as cooking, cleaning, and washing, and from the outside air (Fig. 63-22). To remove excessive moisture from the air, adequate ventilation and a humidification system are necessary. A *humidification system* takes the moisture from the damp air and passes it over cold coils. When the moisture-laden air passes over these coils, it deposits excess moisture on the coils by condensation. Conversely, if the air is too dry, the humidification system adds moisture to the air. A device used only to remove the humidity from the air is known as a *dehumidifier*. A device used only to add humidity to the air is a *humidifier*.

VENTILATION

Ventilation is necessary to keep fresh air circulating. Effective ventilation also controls moisture and keeps air relatively dry (Fig. 63-23). The simplest type of ventilation system is

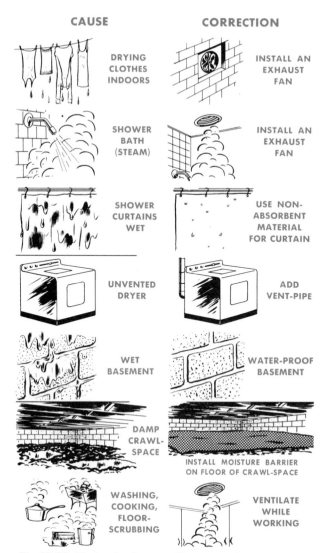

Fig 63-22 Methods of controlling excessive moisture in the home.

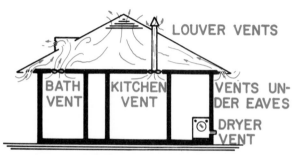

Fig 63-23 Effective ventilation helps control moisture.

cross-ventilation through open windows. However, exhaust fans should be provided in the kitchen, bathroom, and attic to remove moisture, fumes, and warm air. Since large appliances tend to raise the heat of the house by 15 percent, vents for them should be provided.

CONTROL DEVICES

Thermostatic controls keep buildings at a constant temperature by turning climate-control systems on or off when the temperature is beyond a certain setting. Thermostatic controls may be used with any heating or cooling system. The automatic thermostat control should be located on an interior wall away from any sources of heat or cold such as fireplaces or windows. Larger homes may need two or more separate heating or cooling zones that work on separate thermostats (Fig.

63-24). One advantage of electrical heating is that each room may be thermostatically controlled. This is especially important in regulating the temperature of children's rooms.

ACTIVE SOLAR SYSTEMS

Solar heating and/or cooling involves the sun to the fullest extent possible. There are

Fig 63-24 Large homes may require thermostats to control different zones.

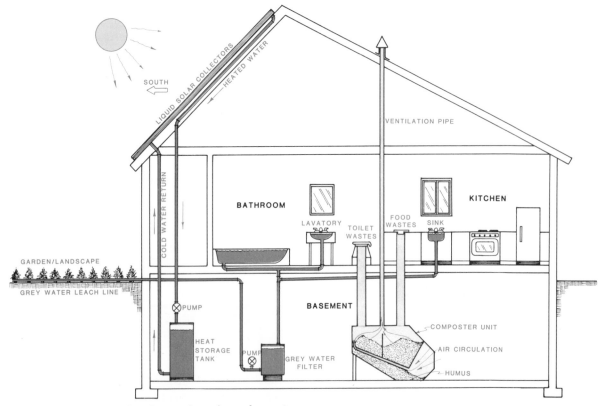

Fig 63-25 Integrated active and passive solar system.

478

two general classifications of solar systems, active and passive.

Passive systems, sometimes called *direct* systems, were covered in Unit 3 and include the total design of the structure and its surroundings. Passive solar design involves orientation, placement and shading of windows, design of roof overhangs, and carefully designed landscaping. In passive systems, heat from the sun is absorbed *directly* and stored in components of the building such as walls and floors. Passive systems are integrated with, and relatively indistinguishable from, the basic design of the structure. Passive systems operate without the use of special mechanical or electronic devices to heat or cool a structure.

Active (*indirect*) systems, however, do use special solar collectors, storage and distribution devices, and other apparatus. A totally effective solar system utilizes both active and passive systems. Figure 63-25 shows an integrated active and passive system.

There are three basic types of active solar systems: the solar furnace, electrical conversion, and individual air or liquid collector systems.

SOLAR FURNACE

The *solar furnace* is a collection of mirrors that focuses the sun's heat on a concentrated area. Temperature as high as 3500 degrees Fahrenheit (1926 degrees Celsius) can be attained and the energy used to heat or cool large structures or clusters of buildings. Solar-furnace collectors must move with the sun.

ELECTRICAL CONVERSION

This type of solar system uses the sun's heat for heating and cooling, and for converting sunlight into electricity to run home appliances. These tasks are accomplished by two large panels or collectors that consist of a number of solar cells. These solar cells are made of sandwiches of cadmium sulfide and copper sulfide between thin layers of glass.

They produce electrical current upon exposure to sunlight. Part of the current produced in this manner is fed immediately into the home's electrical system, to operate lights and appliances. The remainder is used to charge a series of batteries that provide energy when the sun is not shining on the panels.

INDIVIDUAL AIR OR LIQUID COLLECTOR SYSTEMS

These systems, which are most popular for residences, use solar collectors to collect and trap the heat of the sun with antifreeze, oil, water, or air. The heated air or liquid is then pumped or blown to an insulated storage container and then, on demand, pumped or blown to appropriate parts of the structure. These solar systems are divided into three parts: collection, storage, and distribution.

In designing or choosing an individual active solar-heating system, the fluid used to transport the heat must first be determined. Air, water, antifreeze solutions, or oils may be used. If air is used, heat can be stored in rocks, gravel, or small containers of water, and can be distributed through convection or radiant panels.

If liquid is used, the heated liquid is stored in large tanks and distributed through radiators, radiant panels, or liquid to air-heat exchangers as shown in Fig. 63-26.

LIQUID SYSTEMS

Active liquid systems use collectors that consist of an *absorber* placed under a sheet of glass or plastic used as a *cover plate*. Under the absorber is a layer of *insulation* to help prevent heat loss. Collectors may be attached directly to a roof or installed in close proximity to the structure.

Liquid system absorbers are either flat metal or plastic sheets over which a liquid flows, or a network of pipes containing the liquid. Heat from the sun strikes the absorber and heats the liquid. The hot liquid flows to an insulated storage container to be held until needed.

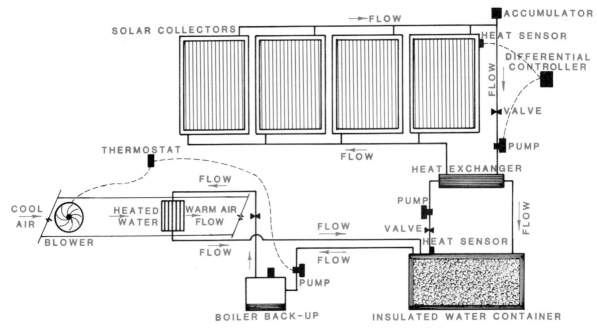

Fig 63-26 Active solar liquid system.

Absorber plates are constructed of steel, copper, aluminum, or plastic, because of their heat conductivity. Absorbers are designed to retain a maximum amount of heat with low emittance. The amount of heat retained is called *absorptance*, and the amount of reflected heat is called *emittance*. Thus an efficient absorber should have high absorptance and low emittance.

Transparent glass or plastic absorber cover plates allow heat to penetrate the absorber while helping to hold the heat in. Insulation behind the absorber retards heat loss from the back side of the absorber.

COLLECTOR ORIENTATION

Ideally, heating collectors should face directly into the sun (at right angles) for the maximum number of hours each day. Unless rotating collectors are used, this ideal position is possible for only a short time each day. Therefore, fixed collectors are usually positioned to face the mid-afternoon sun, since air temperatures are usually higher at that hour. In most North American areas, this means the collector will face slightly west of south.

In addition to the horizontal orientation of the collectors, the vertical tilt must be considered. The tilt angle should be the same as the local latitude for maximum year-round effect; however, a tilt angle of 15° greater than the local latitude is best for winter heating.

HEAT STORAGE

Because heat is needed when the sun is not shining, storage of the absorbed heat is necessary. Stored heat is limited to the capacity of the storage unit. The larger the storage unit, the longer the solar system will operate without the use of auxiliary devices. From 1 to 10 gallons (4.6 to 45 liters) of liquid storage are needed for each square foot of collector surface with liquid systems.

HEAT DISTRIBUTION

Once the solar-heated water is delivered to the storage facility, it remains there until thermostats call for it to be moved to various parts of the structure. When that occurs, the heated liquid is pumped through a series of pipes to radiant heat panels or liquid-air heat

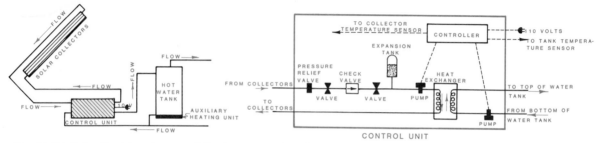

Fig 63-27 Solar liquid system used for hot-water heating.

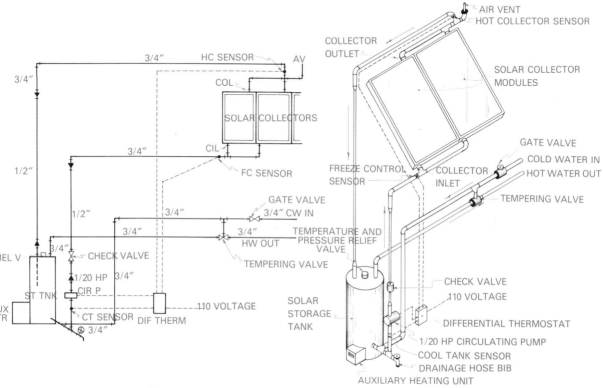

Fig 63-28 Integrated auxiliary system.

exchangers that feed warm-air systems.

In preparing heating and ventilating duct plans for multiple-story buildings, the position of second-story ducts can be determined by placing the second-floor plan on top of the first-floor plan.

LIMITED SOLAR HEATING

Active liquid systems can be used with small collector and storage units to provide

hot water and to heat water for boilers and/or swimming pools, thus reducing the cost of conventional heating. Figure 63-27 shows a typical active liquid solar system used for heating hot water.

AIR SYSTEMS

Active solar systems using air as the heating element are more simple to construct and operate than liquid systems. They are effective for space heating; however, their inability

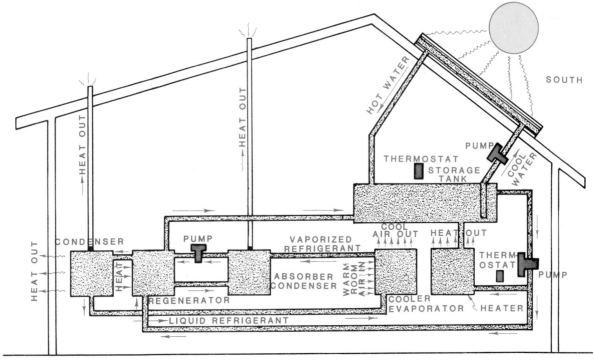

Fig 63-29 Solar heating and cooling system.

to provide hot water is a serious drawback.

Air-systems collectors use sheet-metal absorber plates to heat air trapped between a cover plate and the absorber. This heated air is then blown to the storage facility. From the storage area, the heated air can then be blown directly through a duct system to appropriate rooms in a conventional warm-air system. Because air systems have low heat capacity, large ducts (up to 6″) must be used in this collector.

With air systems, 80 to 400 pounds (36 to 181 kg) of rock are required for each square foot of collector for heat storage. Rock storage requires 2½ times as much volume as water to store the same amount of heat over the same temperature rise.

AUXILIARY HEATING SYSTEMS

Except in very mild climates, most solar-heat storage facilities cannot keep constant pace with peak demand. For this reason, an auxiliary heating system is usually recom-

mended, especially for hot-water production. Figure 63-28 shows a typical active solar-heating unit with an integrated auxiliary heating unit. In the United States, between 50 and 90 percent of residential heating needs can be supplied through solar systems, depending upon location.

SOLAR COOLING

Passive solar cooling is effective, but active cooling systems are somewhat inefficient. Solar cooling is possible through the same absorption-cooling method used in gas refrigerators. However, present equipment is very expensive. Figure 63-29 shows an active solar-heating and cooling system.

Collectors can be used minimally to help cool buildings by exposing them to cooler night air and closing them to daytime exposure. The cooler night air cools the liquid or air that returns to the storage area and is then released the next day to augment passive or conventional cooling systems.

PROBLEMS

1 Sketch the floor plan shown in Fig. 63-30. Sketch a warm-air heating unit in the most appropriate location and locate the outlets for this system.

Fig 63-30 Locate the position of a heating unit and heating outlets on this plan.

Fig 63-31 Locate the positions of all duct work for a forced-air perimeter system on this plan.

2 Sketch the floor plan shown in Fig. 63-31. Indicate the thermostatic zones for this house by using different colored pencils to shade the areas.

3 Sketch the house shown in Fig. 63-31. Locate the position of all duct work for a forced warm-air perimeter system.

4 Draw a plan of the climate-control system appropriate for the house of your design.

5 Answer the following questions related to Fig. 63-32.
   a. What does the abbreviation F.A.U. represent?
   b. How many supply registers are specified?
   c. How many air-return registers are specified?
   d. How is the bathroom heated?
   e. What heating system places supply registers under windows?

6 Define these terms: *air conditioning, humidity, air filter, humidifier, humidification, radiation, convection, conduction, insulation, perimeter, radiant heating, warm air, hot water, steam, electric heating, thermostat, solar heating.*

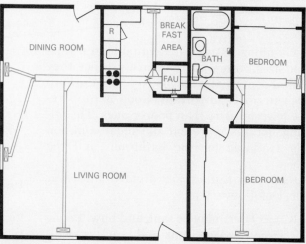

Fig 63-32 Answer questions in problem 5 relating to this plan.

PLUMBING DIAGRAMS

Plumbing refers to the water supply and drainage of waste water and sewage. A plumbing system consists in part of supply pipes that carry fresh water under pressure from a public water supply or individual wells to fixtures. The water is then disposed of through pipes that carry waste to the disposal system by gravity drainage.

UNIT 64
PLUMBING SYMBOLS AND FIXTURES

Plumbing fixtures are available in a variety of sizes, colors, and materials. Since they are used continually for many years, durability is extremely important. Good fixtures require fewer repairs than poorer ones. The following fixtures represent the most common kinds available for the bathroom and the kitchen.

Bathroom fixtures are divided into four kinds, as follows:

Water closets may be tank and bowl in one piece, separate tank and bowl, or wall-hung tank and bowl.

Showers are prefabricated, built on the job, or placed over the bathtub.

Bathtubs are recessed, square, freestanding, or sunken.

Lavatories may be wall-hung, cabinet-mounted, built-in counter-top, or corner.

Kitchen fixtures are divided into five kinds, as follows:

Sinks are available as a sink and drainboard unit, single sink, or double sink.

Laundry tubs may be single, double, or triple.

Dishwashers are either built-in or free-standing.

Hot-water heaters are electric or gas.

Washing machines are mostly top-loading but may be front-loading or wringer models.

For details relating to these fixtures, see Unit 16, Kitchens, and Unit 22, Baths.

Plumbing symbols not only show fixture location and type, but show the different types of plumbing lines, joints, valves, and other related devices. Figures 64-1 through 64-5 show plumbing symbols in plan elevation and pictorial form.

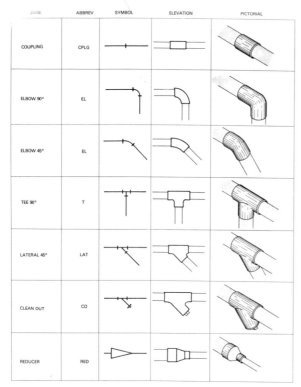

Fig 64-1 Plumbing symbols.

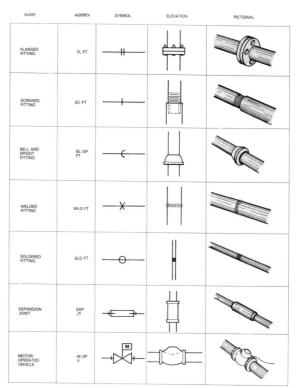

Fig 64-3 Plumbing symbols.

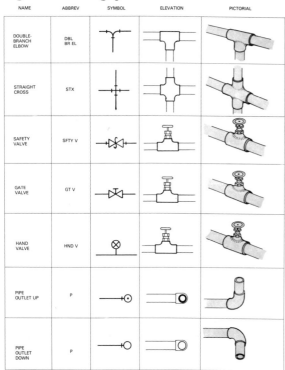

Fig 64-2 Plumbing symbols.

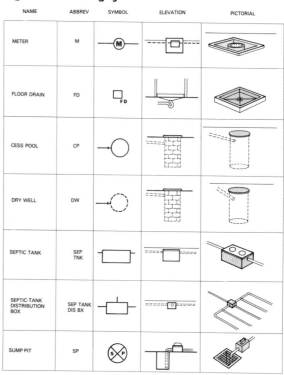

Fig 64-4 Plumbing symbols.

485

NAME	ABBREV	SYMBOL	NAME	ABBRV	SYMBOL
COLD-WATER LINE	CW		AIR-PRESSURE RETURN LINE	APR	
HOT-WATER LINE	HW		ICE-WATER LINE	IW	IW
GAS LINE	G	—G—G—	DRAIN LINE	D	—D——D—
VENT	V		FUEL-OIL FLOW LINE	FOF	—FOF—
SOIL STACK PLAN VIEW	SS		FUEL-OIL RETURN LINE	FOR	——FOR——
SOIL LINE ABOVE GRADE	SL		REFRIGERANT LINE	R	
SOIL LINE BELOW GRADE	SL		STEAM LINE MEDIUM PRESSURE	SL	

NAME	ABBREV	SYMBOL	NAME	ABBRV	SYMBOL
CAST-IRON SEWER	S-CI	S-CI	STEAM RETURN LINE—MEDIUM PRESSURE	SRL	
CLAY-TILE SEWER	S-CT	S-CT	PNEUMATIC TUBE	PT	
LEACH LINE	LEA		INDUSTRIAL SEWAGE	IS	
SPRINKLER LINE	SPR	—S——S—	CHEMICAL WASTE LINE	CW	
VACUUM LINE	VAC	—V——V—	FIRE LINE	F	—F——F—
COMPRESSED AIR LINE	COMP	—A——A—	ACID WASTE LINE	AC WST	ACID
AIR-PRESSURE LINE FLOW	APF		HUMIDIFICATION LINE	HUM	——H——

Fig 64-5 Plumbing symbols.

PROBLEMS

1 Make a sketch to show the positions of the plumbing fixtures on the plan shown in Fig. 64-6 (water closet, shower, bathtub, lavatories, sinks, laundry tub, dishwasher, water heater, and washing machine).

2 Add the plumbing fixtures to the plan shown in Fig. 64-6.

Fig 64-6 Show position of plumbing fixtures on this plan.

3 Match the symbols with the terms in Fig. 64-7.

4 Define these terms: *plumbing fixture, water closet, wall-hung water closet, drainboard.*

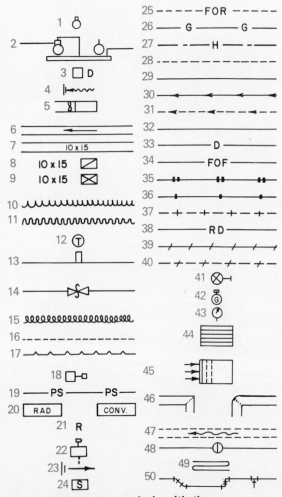

Fig 64-7 Match the symbols with the correct terms.

UNIT 65
SCHEMATIC PLUMBING DRAWINGS

Plumbing diagrams are drawings that describe piping systems that supply water to, and drainage of waste material from, buildings. A plumbing system (Fig. 65-1) consists of supply pipes that carry fresh water under pressure from a public water supply or individual well to building fixtures and pipes, which, in turn, carry wastes to a disposal system by gravity drainage (Fig. 65-2). Plumbing diagrams are shown in both plan and elevation form.

SCHEMATIC PLUMBING PLANS

Plumbing symbols are indicated by one of two methods. They are added to an existing floor plan, or a separate plumbing plan is prepared as shown in Fig. 65-3. Sometimes

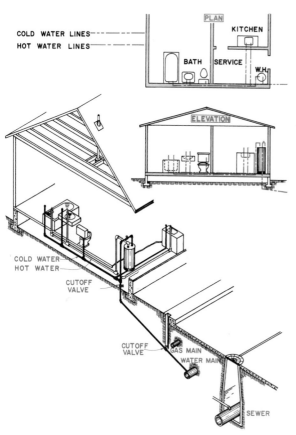

Fig 65-1 A plumbing system.

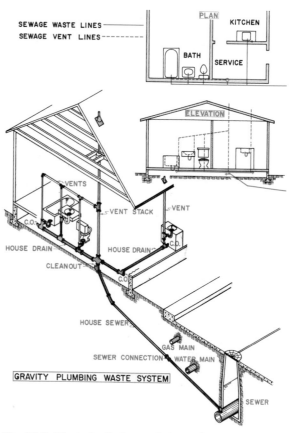

Fig 65-2 Waste is discharged through gravity drainage.

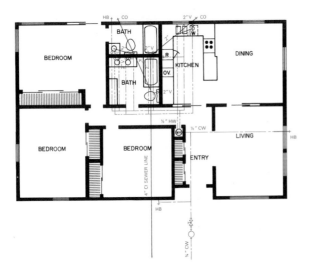

Fig 65-3 Plumbing plan.

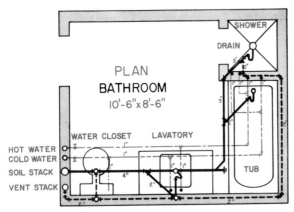

Fig 65-4 A schematic plan of bathroom plumbing lines.

WATER-SUPPLY SYSTEMS

Fresh water is brought to all plumbing fixtures under pressure. This water is supplied either from a public water supply or from private wells. Because this water is under pressure, the pipes may run in any convenient direction after leaving the main control pipe, as shown in Fig. 65-7. Water lines require shutoff valves at the property line and at the entrance of the building. A water meter is located at the shutoff valve near the building.

Hot water is obtained by routing water through a hot-water heater. The hot water is

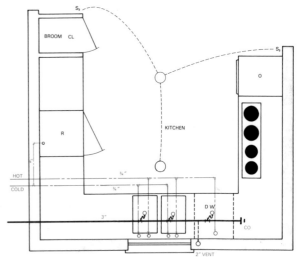

Fig 65-5 A schematic plan of kitchen plumbing lines.

plumbing symbols, electrical symbols, and heating and air-conditioning symbols are all combined in one plan. When that is done, dimensions and other construction notes are eliminated to facilitate reading the symbols without interference. Such procedure is possible because the plumbing contractor is concerned solely with the placement of plumbing fixtures and with the length of piping runs, and not with other construction details.

Since most plumbing fixtures are concentrated in the bathroom, the laundry, and kitchen areas, a detailed schematic plumbing plan is sometimes prepared for those rooms as shown in Figs. 65-4, 65-5, and 65-6.

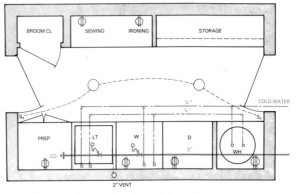

Fig 65-6 A schematic plan of laundry plumbing lines.

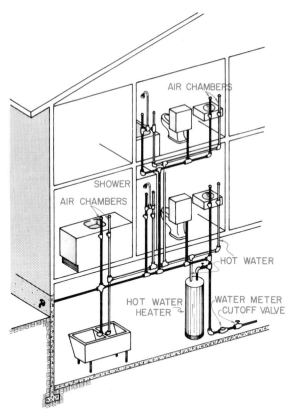

Fig 65-7 A pressure plumbing supply system.

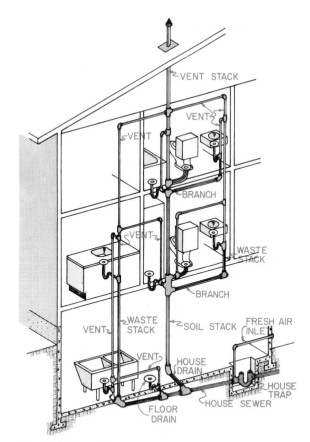

Fig 65-8 Waste lines must be larger than water-supply lines.

then directed, under pressure, to appropriate fixtures. The hot-water valve is always on the left of each fixture as you face it. Placing insulation around hot-water lines conserves hot water and reduces the total cost of fuel for heating water. This is usually included in a note on the plumbing diagram, which specifies the type and thickness of the insulation material.

The size of all water-supply lines for a house ranges from ¾″ to 1″ (19 to 25 mm). Each fixture should have a shutoff valve on the pipe to allow repairs.

All fixtures have a free-flowing supply of water if the lines are the correct size. Lines that are too small cause a whistling as the water flows through at high speeds. Air-cushion chambers stop hammering noises caused by closing valves. Too many changes of direction of pipe cause friction that reduces the water pressure.

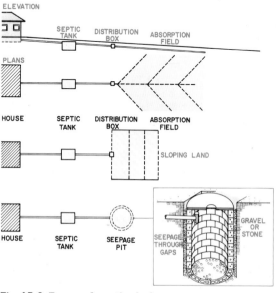

Fig 65-9 Types of septic drainage systems.

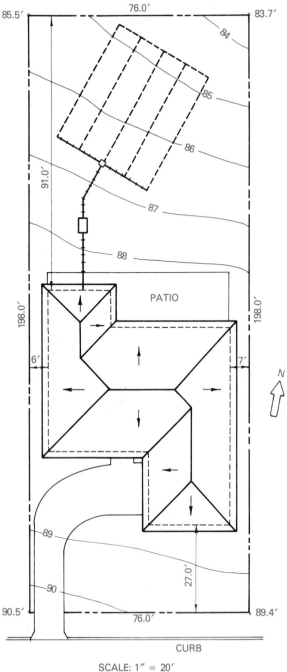

Fig 65-10 A typical septic system drawing.

SCALE: 1" = 20'

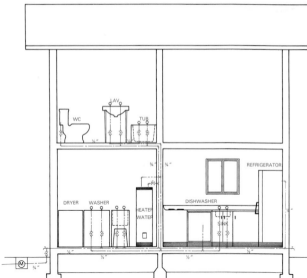

Fig 65-11 Schematic plumbing elevation.

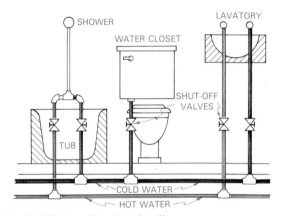

Fig 65-12 Shutoff valve detail.

WASTE-DISCHARGE SYSTEMS

Waste water is discharged through the disposal system by gravity drainage, as shown in Fig. 65-2. All pipes in this system must slant in a downward direction so that the weight of the waste will cause it to move down toward the main disposal system and away from the structure. Because of this gravity flow, waste lines that connect to sewage systems are much larger than the water-supply lines, in which the water is under pressure, as shown

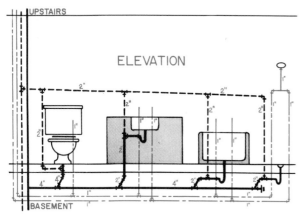

Fig 65-13 Schematic bathroom plumbing elevation.

Fig 65-14 Sewage disposal system in elevation.

in Fig. 65-8. Waste lines are concealed in walls and under floors. The vertical lines are called *stacks,* and the horizontal lines are called *branches.* There are also vents that provide for the circulation of air, permit sewer gases to escape through the roof to the outside, and equalize the air pressure in the drainage system. *Fixture traps* stop gases from entering the building. Each fixture has a separate trap (seal) to prevent backflow of sewer gas. Fixture traps are exposed for easy maintenance; however, water-closet traps are built into the fixture.

The flow of waste water starts at the fixture trap. It flows through the fixture branches to the soil stack. It then continues through the building drain to the sewer drain, and finally reaches the main sewer line.

Waste stacks carry only waste water. The lines that carry solid waste are called *soil lines.* Soil lines are the largest in the system and are flushed with water after each use.

Fresh-water-supply pipes are full of water (*wet pipes*) and under pressure all the time. The waste and soil pipes are wet pipes that have water in them only when waste water is flushed through them. The vent-pipe system is composed of dry pipes that never contain water.

OUTSIDE WASTE SYSTEMS

When municipal sewer-disposal facilities are available, connection of waste pipes to the public system are shown on the plot plan. However, when public systems are not available, a septic-tank system is used, and either a separate drawing is provided or the location of the system is indicated on the plot plan. This location drawing is usually required by the building code and supervised by the local board of health.

A *septic-tank system* converts waste solids into liquid by bacterial action. The building wastes flow into a septic tank buried some distance from the building. The lighter part of the liquid flows out of the septic tank into drainage fields through porous pipes spread over an area to allow wide distribution of liquids.

The size and type of the septic system varies according to the number of occupants of a building, the contour of the terrain, and soil type. Figure 65-9 shows several types of drainage systems. The size of the lines and the distance of the septic tank and drainage fields from the building depend on the building codes of the community. Figure 65-10 shows the type of septic-system drawing required by most boards of health.

SCHEMATIC PLUMBING ELEVATIONS

Schematic plans show only the horizontal positioning of pipes. As a result, the amount of rise above floor level and the flow of fresh water and wastes between levels are difficult to read. Elevation drawings such as the water-distribution-system elevation, shown in Fig. 65-11, provide this vertical orientation. Elevation drawings are also used for some details such as the positioning of shutoff valves (Fig. 65-12).

Since most plumbing work is concentrated in the kitchen, the bathroom, and the utility room, separate schematic elevations are sometimes prepared for only those rooms, as shown in Fig. 65-13.

Unlike plumbing plans, which combine both the water-supply and sewage-disposal systems on one drawing, plumbing elevations usually include only one system on each drawing. Figure 65-14 shows only the sewage-disposal system in elevation form from the second floor to the public sewer drain.

Prefabricated plumbing walls, installed at the factory, save the builder installation time because part of the labor is done on an assembly line. If fixtures are placed close together, many feet of pipe lines can be saved. The kitchen and bathrooms can also be back-to-back or over each other in a two-story house to eliminate long runs of pipe. However, it is important to put the kitchen and bathrooms where they are most convenient, even if they are at opposite ends of the house.

PROBLEMS

1 Make a sketch of Fig. 65-15 and add the water-supply system, using the proper plumbing symbols.

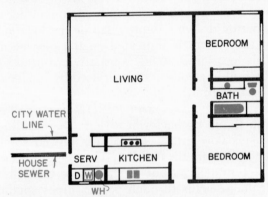

Fig 65-15 Add water-supply lines to this plan.

2 Make a sketch of Fig. 65-16 and indicate a water-supply system, using the proper plumbing symbols.

3 Add the waste lines to the sketch you made for problem 2.

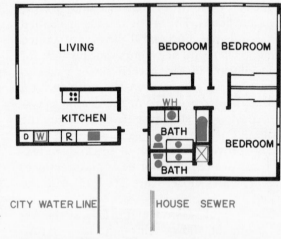

Fig 65-16 Add plumbing symbols to this plan.

4 Prepare a plumbing plan for the house you are designing.

5 Define these terms: *gravity drainage, stack, branch, vent, fixture trap, soil stack, house drain, house sewer, waste stack, septic system, septic tank, drainage field, shutoff valve, air chambers, waste lines.*

MODULAR COMPONENT PLANS

Industrial automation methods have enabled manufacturers to produce high-quality and low-priced products more quickly than ever before. However, the home-building industry, which has constructed over 33 million homes for American families, has not industrialized or standardized its production methods to any great degree. Construction methods in the home-building industry continue to contribute to excessive waste of materials and time.

However, to standardize and automate more fully the home-building industry, lumber manufacturers have developed a program of coordinating dimensional standards and components on standard structural parts such as windows, doors, and trusses. This standardization enables the part to fit into the plan for any home designed according to a standard modular component.

Using a coordinated system of dimensioning for these components results in the most efficient use of materials and time.

UNIT 66
MODULAR SYSTEM OF DESIGNING

The Unicom method of designing includes the use of modular components and the preparation of plans to a modular dimensional standard. *Unicom* means uniform manufacture of components. This modular system was developed by the National Lumber Manufacturers Association. Using this method, the designer must think of the home as a series of component parts. These component parts may be standard factory-made components or built on the job site. In either case, plans are prepared to be consistent with the size of these components. Plans must also be interchangeable and consistent with the Unicom method of dimensioning. Without this dimensional standard, the use of modular component parts is of no value.

ADVANTAGES

The Unicom method is applicable to on-site or shop fabrication and is based on standard lumber sizes. Thus, it may be used effectively by large builders or by the custom builder who erects only a few homes each year.

Homes may be erected completely with factory-made parts, or may be framed conventionally, or a combination method may be used. Faster planning and erection of the house benefit both builder and home buyer. This system makes possible the more efficient

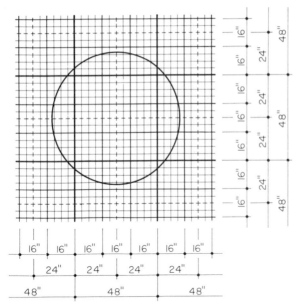

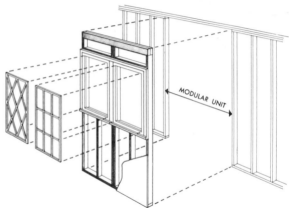

Fig 66-2 Modular-component door and windows.

National Lumber
Manufacturers Assoc.

Fig 66-1 Modular-component grid.

National Lumber
Manufacturers Assoc.

use of materials, thus reducing waste in conventional home construction.

Building inventory costs are cut because of the number of elements needed for maximum design flexibility is small. Perhaps the most important advantage of the Unicom system is that it makes possible the use of modern mass-production techniques. These techniques provide great accuracy in the construction of components and superior quality control in their fabrication.

DESIGNING WITH MODULAR GRIDS

The coordination of modular components with the system of modular dimensions utilizes all three dimensions—length, width, and height. The overall width and length dimensions are most critical in the planning process. The *modular planning grid* is a horizontal plane divided into equal spaces in length and width. It provides the basic control for the modular coordination system. The entire grid, shown in Fig. 66-1, is divided into equal spaces of 4", 16", 24", and 48". The Unicom system is not yet designed to metric standards. Composite dimensions are therefore all multi-

ples of 4". The 16" unit is used in multiples for wall, window, and door panels to provide an increment small enough for flexible planning and optimum inventory of these components.

Increments of 24" and 48" are used for overall dimensions of the house. The 24" module is called the *minor module*. The 48" module is called the *major module*. Figure 66-2 shows the use of the 16" module in design locations for window component panels. Figure 66-3 shows the use of the major and minor modules in establishing basic modular house length and width.

Since the Unicom method does not require the wall, floor, and roof elements to be tied to a large fixed panel size, there is no need for the designer to adhere to a fixed 4' or larger increment in planning.

PREPARING THE MODULAR PLAN

When the basic floor-plan design is completed, the plan should be sketched or drawn on the Unicom modular grid and all non-modular dimensions converted to the nearest modular size. Each square on the grid represents the basic 4" module. Standard 16" modules are represented by the intermediate heavy lines. Major 48" module lines are indicated by the heaviest lines. Minor 24" modules are represented by dotted lines. By employing

494

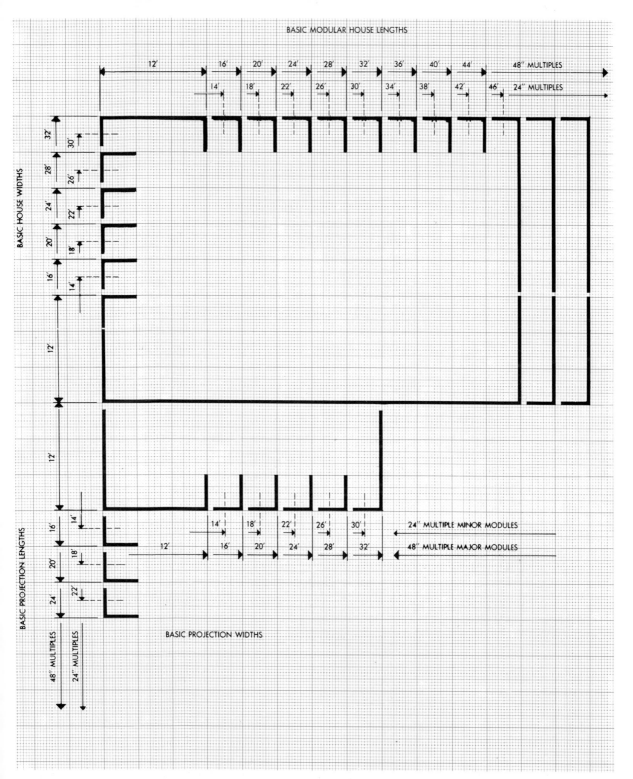

Fig 66-3 Use of major and minor modular width and length increments.

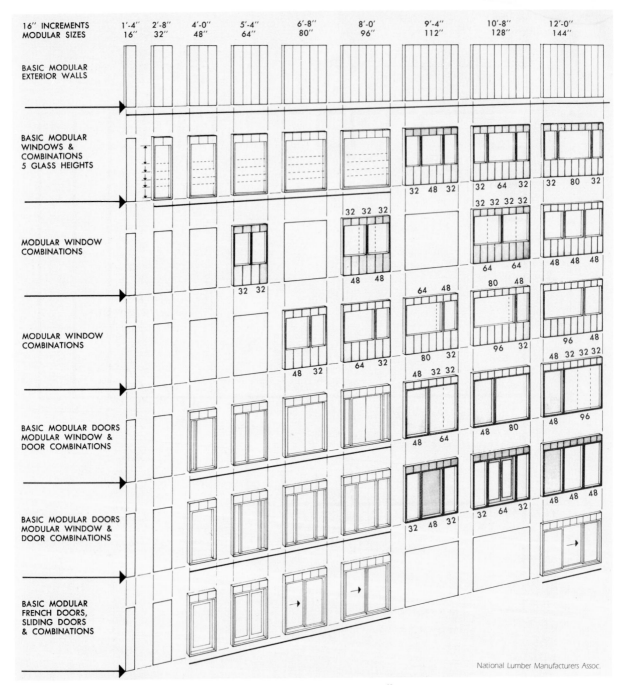

Fig 66-4 Doors, windows, and panels should be located on the 16" module.

modular dimensions in multiples of 2' or 4' for house exteriors, fractional spans for floor and roof framing are eliminated.

Variations in the thickness of exterior and partition walls interfere with true modular dimensioning; therefore the total thicknesses of all of these walls must be subtracted from the overall modular dimension to obtain the net inside dimension. In addition, non-modular dimensions created by existing build-

Table 66-1 ABBREVIATIONS USED TO IDENTIFY COMPONENTS

X	Exterior-wall panels	WP	Fixed picture-window panels
XC	Full-corner exterior-wall panels	WPP	Full-height, fixed, picture-window panels
XCBM	Cantilever-beam exterior-wall corner panels	GG	Glass gable panels
XCA	Cut-back corner exterior-wall panels	D	Door panels with one door
		2D	Door panels with two doors
RP	Roof panels	DS	Door panels with one side light
FP	Floor panels	2DS2	Door panels with two doors and two side lights
P	Interior partition panel		
WC	Casement window panels	DS2	Door panels with two side lights
WD	Double-hung window panels	DSL	Sliding door panels
WS	Sliding window panels	DA	Garage door panels
WAF	Fixed-awning window panels		

ing laws or built-in equipment must be incorporated in the modular coordination system. This end is accomplished by dimensioning conventionally the nonmodular distances where they exist.

After the overall dimensions are established and nonmodular dimensions incorporated in the plan, the panels for exterior doors and windows and for exterior walls should be established on the 16″ module, as

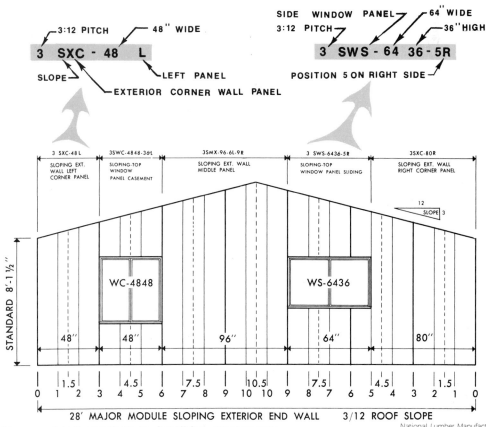

Fig 66-5 The use of code numbers in describing components.

National Lumber Manufacturers Assoc.

497

shown in Fig. 66-4. The precise location of wall openings on the 16″ module also eliminates the extra wall framing commonly encountered in nonmodular home planning; and the 16″ spacing of structural members increases design flexibility by one-third, compared with spacing at the 24″ minor module.

Conventionally framed platform-floor systems provide the most flexible method of floor framing for the variety of design conditions encountered with the Unicom system. Modular sizes of floor-sheathing materials are economically applied to the modular spacing of floor joists.

As previously stated, the Unicom method is based on modular coordination of all three dimensions—width, length, and height. Although width and length are the most critical dimensions, standard heights are necessary to eliminate much waste and to ensure the proper fitting of components. A standard height of 8′—1½″ for exterior-wall components allows for floor- and ceiling-finish appli-

cations with a combined thickness of 1½″. The result is a standard 8′ finished ceiling height.

IDENTIFICATION SYSTEM

A complete system of short-form identification for separate pieces and fabricated components simplifies the practical use of the modular coordination system of building. Table 66-1 shows some of the abbreviations used to identify components. In most cases, the basic identifying letter or combination is directly associated with the element. For example, J stands for joist and R stands for rafter.

The shorthand has been extended to include complete descriptions of wall panels, including information pertaining to the slope, window style, and position, as shown in Fig. 66-5.

Modular construction in industry is important because it eliminates individual constructed items, thereby reducing costs.

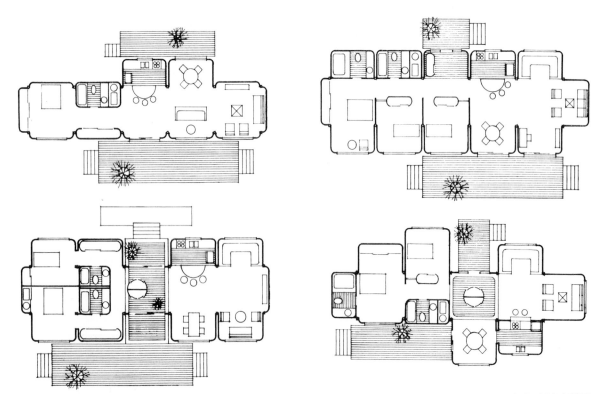

Fig. 66-6 Floor-plan possibilities using portable modular units.

Joe Lombardo, Architect

Portable modular units have been designed that can be transported to the site and assembled with many different floor-plan arrangements (Fig. 66-6).

All structures are built as modules to some extent. That is, not all the materials or components are manufactured or put together on the site. Some structures are simply *precut*. This means that all the materials are cut to modular specification at the factory and then assembled on the site by conventional methods.

With the most common factory-built (prefabricated) homes, the major modular components, such as the walls, trusses, decks, and partitions, are assembled at the factory. The utility work, such as installation of electrical, plumbing, and heating systems, is completed on site. The final finishing work, such as installation of floors, roof coverings, and walls, is also done on site.

There are some factory-built homes, however, that are constructed in complete modules at the factory and require only final electrical-outlet, roof-overhang, and assembly-fastening work on site to complete the job. The time factor is a major advantage of this type of construction. However, the size of the modules is limited to only 12' widths. Twelve feet is the maximum width for a truck load on public roads.

PROBLEMS

1 Resketch the plan shown in Fig. 66-7 on modular grid paper and convert all nonmodular dimensions to the nearest modular size.

2 Define the following terms: *Unicom, modular components, modular planning grid, minor module, major module, nonmodular dimensions, modular dimensions, 16" module.*

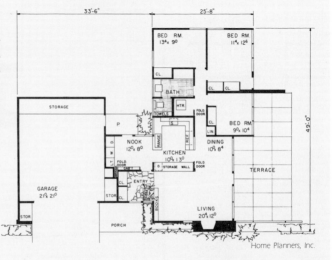

Fig 66-7 Convert this plan to a modular drawing.

Home Planners, Inc.

UNIT 67
DRAWING MODULAR PLANS

The floor plan shown in Fig. 67-1 has been fitted on the modular grid, and the designer has thus properly established the modular relationship of the foundation, floors, walls, windows, doors, partitions, and roof. Establishing the dimensions and components precisely on the 16", 24", and 48" spaces of the modular grid assures accurate and less troublesome fitting of the components of the house at the time of its construction.

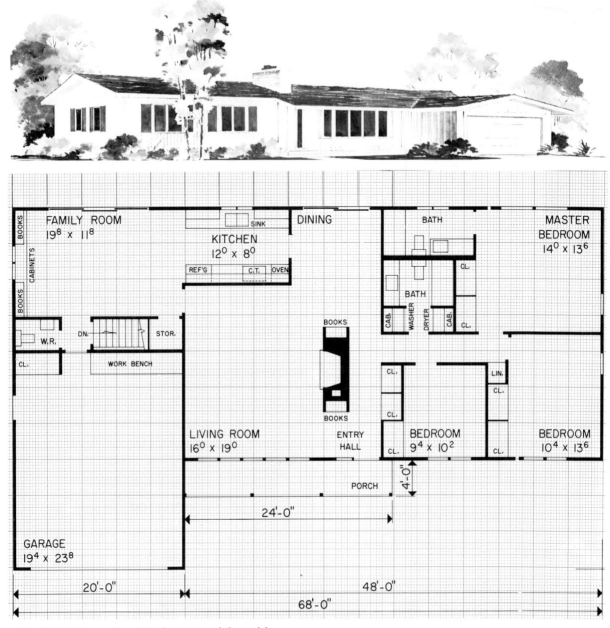

Fig 67-1 A floor plan fitted on a modular grid.

COMPONENT FLOOR PLANS

After completing the basic floor plan, a detailed component plan for fabrication and erection is prepared. Standard symbols are used to identify wall, window, door, and partition components by type and size (Fig. 67-2).

The erection sequence for site assembly is also designated on the plan by ER 1, ER 2, and so on. This basic component floor plan for erection contains all basic dimensions necessary for layout work on the floor platform. Interior partitions may then be erected in varying sequences.

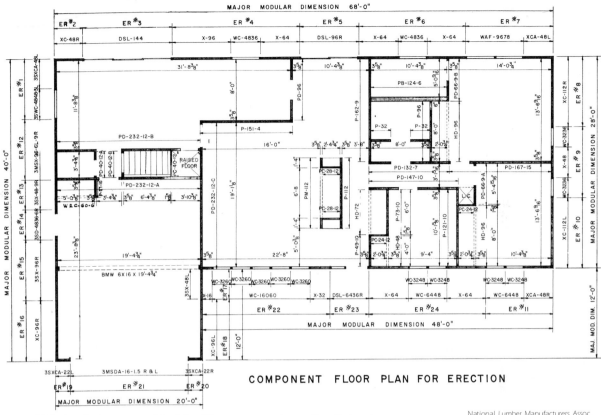

Fig 67-2 Symbols are used to identify components on the floor plan.

National Lumber Manufacturers Assoc.

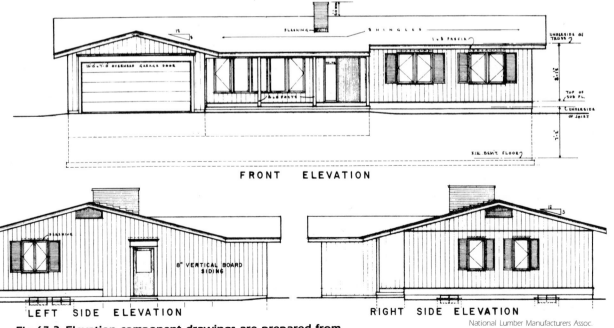

FRONT ELEVATION

LEFT SIDE ELEVATION

RIGHT SIDE ELEVATION

Fig 67-3 Elevation component drawings are prepared from conventional elevations.

National Lumber Manufacturers Assoc.

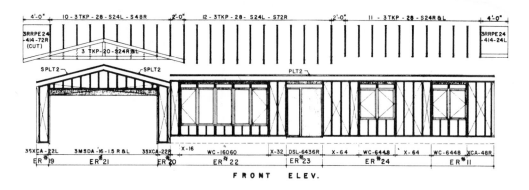

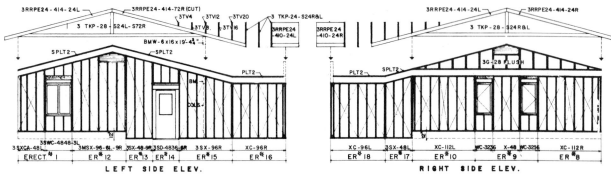

Fig 67-4 An elevation component framing drawing.

National Lumber Manufacturers Assoc.

ELEVATION COMPONENT DRAWINGS

Just as the component floor plan for erection is prepared from the floor plan shown in Fig. 67-1, the elevation component drawings are prepared from standard elevations projected from the floor plan, as shown in Fig. 67-3. Elevation component drawings closely resemble conventional panel-framing elevations, except that wall, window, door, and roof components are identified and shown in their proper relationship, complete with standard Unicom nomenclature and erection sequences. Figure 67-4 shows the component elevation drawings prepared from standard elevations shown in Fig. 67-3.

FRAMING PLANS

From the basic floor plan, a floor framing plan and stud layout, as shown in Fig. 67-5, are projected and dimensioned according to

Unicom standards. Notice the precise rhythm of the 16″, on-center floor joists and the 48″ modular dimensions of the house perimeter. The advantage of designing to these standards is the reduction of wasted material. Waste occurs only in cutting at the stairwell and fireplace openings or other areas that are different from modular dimensions. Modular dimensions and panel code numbers are indicated on all plans.

INTERIOR PARTITION COMPONENTS

Partitions function as interior space separators for room privacy, traffic control, and storage. Their aesthetic value depends on decorative surface materials, doors, and trim designs. Partitions are a maze of intersecting planes that may carry the roof and ceiling loads, depending on the roof design. Partitions must fit between the basic exterior modular increments with allowance for exterior

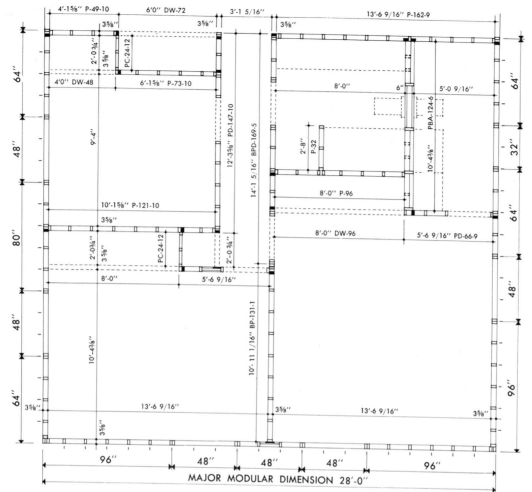

Fig 67-5 An example of a modular study layout.

National Lumber Manufacturers Assoc.

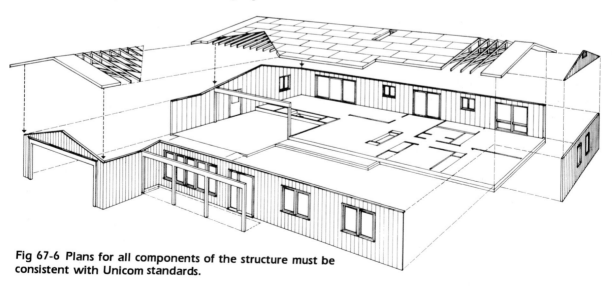

Fig 67-6 Plans for all components of the structure must be consistent with Unicom standards.

wall thicknesses. Space must be provided for intersecting partitions with backup members, proper door placement, vertical and horizontal plumbing runs, medicine cabinets, closets, fireplaces, and flexible room arrangements with varying designs.

Many more modular drawings are needed to describe completely a Unicom plan in every detail. Just as in structures of conventional design, the more detailed the drawings are, the better the chance of achieving the desired outcome. Other plans that may become part of the complete Unicom design include transverse sections, truss and gable component drawings, roof-overhang details, and detailed drawings of many nonstandard components. Figure 67-6 shows the relationship of basic components in a house designed by the modular system. With the Unicom method, all other basic house types may be designed and engineered in the same manner.

PROBLEMS

1 Prepare a component floor plan for the floor plan shown in Fig. 67-7.

2 Prepare an elevation component drawing for the front elevation of the house shown in Fig 67-7.

3 Prepare a floor framing plan for the house shown in Fig. 67-7 and dimension it according to Unicom standards.

4 Prepare a roof framing plan of the floor plan shown in Fig. 67-7 and dimension it to modular standards.

5 Prepare a component floor plan for the house you are designing.

6 Define the following terms: *component floor plan, elevation component drawing, modular increment.*

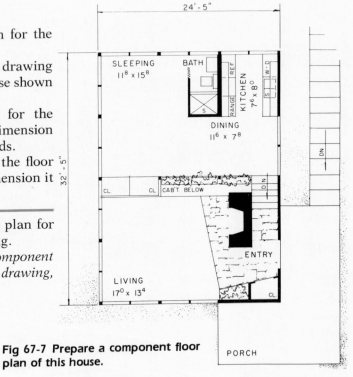

Fig 67-7 Prepare a component floor plan of this house.

504

ARCHITECTURAL PLAN SETS

Previous sections have covered the principles and practices involved in the preparation of each type of architectural drawing. In this unit, the basic guidelines used in the preparation of a complete set of plans are developed. Special emphasis is placed on the relationship and consistency among plan features and dimensions.

UNIT 68
SETS OF PLANS

Drawings used for construction vary from simple floor plans to comprehensive sets of plans complete with details, schedules, and specifications. The number of plans needed to construct a building depends on the complexity of the structure and on the degree to which the designer needs or wants to control the various methods and details of construction. For example, if only a floor plan is prepared, the builder must create the elevation designs. If only the floor plan and elevation drawings are prepared, but no details or specifications are provided, the builder assumes responsibility for many construction details, including selection of framing type, materials used, and many aspects of the interior design. Therefore, the more plans, details, and specifications developed for a structure, the closer the finished building will be to that conceived by the designer.

SET SIZE

Table 68-1 shows the types of construction drawings included in a minimum, average, and maximum set of plans. The preparation of only floor plans, elevations, surveys, and a section, as indicated in the minimum set of plans, provides the builder with great latitude in selection of materials and processes. The maximum set of plans will assure, to the greatest degree possible, agreement between the wishes of the designer and the final constructed building.

INDEXING SYSTEMS

The actual selection of drawings depends on the degree to which the designer wants to control various features of the building. Large sets of plans that include many different details require an indexing system. For large projects involving many buildings with many components, a much more detailed indexing system is needed to locate specific details on any building in a short period of time. In these cases, a master index is prepared that shows the sheet number where each drawing for each building is found. Figure 68-1 shows a title block with a simple indexing system. It includes a design number, sheet number, and the total number of drawings in the set.

The American Institute of Architects (AIA) recommends a numbering system that gives access to the information in a set of drawings. In this system, drawings are identified by letters and numbers for ease of referencing.

For example, the following alphabetical designation is used to identify the work phases of the project:

SK Sketches (used through all phases)
PR Programming
MP Master planning
SC Schematics
DD Design development

A readily identifiable alphabetical prefix is used to denote the specific discipline of work covered by a group of working drawings:

A   Architectural
C   Civil
D   Interior design (color schemes, furniture, furnishings)
E   Electrical
F   Fire protection (sprinkler, standpipes, CO_2, and so forth)
G   Graphics
K   Dietary (food service)
L   Landscape
M   Mechanical (heating, ventilating, air conditioning)
P   Plumbing
S   Structural
T   Transportation/conveying systems

In this system, architectural drawings are divided into 10 specific groups, A0 through A9. The group number will always remain the same, no matter how large the project. Additional drawings may be added within groups without interrupting the alphanumerical order. Figure 68-2 explains the coding system as it would appear in use on a drawing. Figure 68-3 shows a listing of these groups and their symbols.

COMBINATION PLANS

Sometimes, several plans in a complete set of plans are combined. For example, there

Table 68-1 DRAWINGS NECESSARY FOR SETS OF PLANS

Drawings	Size of set of plans		
	Min.	Aver.	Max.
FLOOR PLANS	X	X	X
FRONT ELEVATION	X	X	X
REAR ELEVATION		X	X
RIGHT ELEVATION	X	X	X
LEFT ELEVATION		X	X
AUXILIARY ELEVATIONS			X
INTERIOR ELEVATIONS		X	X
EXTERIOR PICTORIAL RENDERINGS		X	X
INTERIOR RENDERINGS			X
PLOT PLAN		X	X
LANDSCAPE PLAN			X
SURVEY PLAN	X	X	X
FULL SECTION	X	X	X
DETAIL SECTIONS		X	X
FLOOR-FRAMING PLANS			X
EXTERIOR-WALL FRAMING PLANS			X
INTERIOR-WALL FRAMING PLANS			X
STUD LAYOUTS			X
ROOF-FRAMING PLAN			X
ELECTRICAL PLAN		X	X
AIR-CONDITIONING PLAN			X
PLUMBING DIAGRAM			X
SCHEDULES			X
SPECIFICATIONS			X
COST ANALYSIS			X
SCALE MODEL			X

Fig 68-1 A title block with a simple indexing system.

SYSTEM CODE:

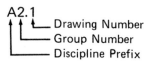

Fig 68-2 An explanation of the use of the system code on drawings.

may be no specific electrical, plumbing, or air-conditioning plan, but these symbols may be added to the basic floor plan. There may be no specific landscape plan, but the landscape features may be added to a survey plan. Details and sections are also quite often combined into one plan. Combined plans are more difficult to read than separate specialized plans. For that reason, separate plans have been presented throughout this text for instructional purposes. Figure 68-4 shows a combination floor plan that includes not only information normally found on a floor plan, but also includes electrical, air-conditioning, plumbing, some landscape, survey, and plot plan symbols.

In studying this kind of plan, the specialized elements must be separated out of the plan through imagination to eliminate confusion. Study only one element at a time. If you are studying the electrical part, refer only to as much of the remainder of the plan as necessary to orient the position of switches, outlets, and so forth. Imagine that the plan is only an electrical plan and that all other features do not exist.

Rooms, doors, windows, and sections are coded and cross-referenced among drawings, as shown in Fig. 68-5. Where sections are shown on the same sheet as the referenced

ARCHITECTURAL DRAWINGS

A0.1,2,3 — General (Index, Symbols, Abbrev. notes, references)
A1.1,2,3 — Demolition, Site Plan, Temporary Work
A2.1,2,3 — Plans, Room Material Schedule, Door Schedule, Key Drawings
A3.1,2,3 — Sections, Exterior Elevations
A4.1,2,3 — Detailed Floor Plans
A5.1,2,3 — Interior Elevations
A6.1,2,3 — Reflected Ceiling Plans
A7.1,2,3 — Vertical Circulation, Stairs (Elevators, Escalators)
A8.1,2,3 — Exterior Details
A9.1,2,3 — Interior Details

STRUCTURAL DRAWINGS

S0.1,2,3 — General Notes
S1.1,2,3 — Site Work
S2.1,2,3 — Framing Plans
S3.1,2 — Elevations
S4.1,2 — Schedules
S5.1,2 — Concrete
S6.1,2 — Masonry
S7.1,2 — Structural Steel
S8.1,2 — Timber
S9.1,2 — Special Design

MECHANICAL DRAWINGS

M0.1,2 — General Notes
M1.1,2 — Site/Roof Plans
M2.1,2 — Floor Plans
M3.1,2 — Riser Diagrams
M4.1,2 — Piping Flow Diagram
M5.1,2 — Control Diagrams
M6.1,2 — Details

PLUMBING DRAWINGS

P0.1,2 — General Notes
P1.1,2 — Site Plan
P2.1,2 — Floor Plans
P3.1,2 — Riser Diagram
P4.1,2 — Piping Flow Diagram
P5.1,2 — Details

ELECTRICAL DRAWINGS

E0.1,2 — General Notes
E1.1,2 — Site Plan
E2.1,2 — Floor Plans, Lighting
E3.1,2 — Floor Plans, Power
E4.1,2 — Electrical Rooms
E5.1,2 — Riser Diagrams
E6.1,2 — Fixture/Panel Schedules
E7.1,2 — Details

Northern California Chapter AIA

Fig 68-3 A coding system for drawings.

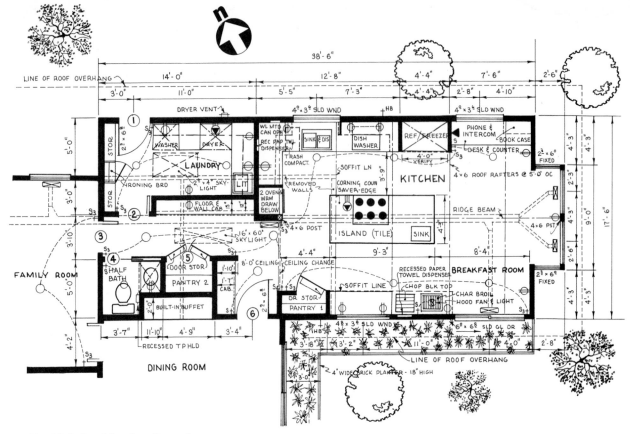

Fig 68-4 Combination floor plan.

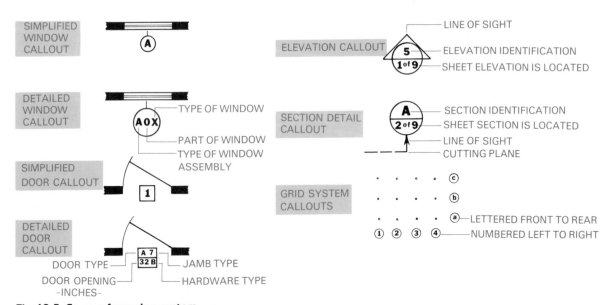

Fig 68-5 Cross-referencing system.

drawing, only alphabetical (A, B, or C) designations are shown. But details that are extensive and fall on several different sheets are located with a system showing the detail, title, and the sheet number where the detail is located. When rooms have the same title, such as bedrooms, classrooms, labs, closets, and so forth, numbers are attached to each room so that schedules, plans, and specifications for that room are consistent and distinctive.

PROBLEMS

1 Prepare an index for the set of plans you have developed.

2 List the minimum number of and the kind of drawings necessary to build the home shown in Fig 33-1.
3 Identify these terms: *plan set, index, title block, master index.*

UNIT 69
RELATIONSHIP OF PLANS

In previous units, samples of architectural (construction) drawings were shown to illustrate various principles and practices related to the reading and interpretation of each specific type of drawing. However, these drawings did not necessarily relate to the same structure. Thus, there was no interrelationship between an electrical plan, plumbing plan, and a survey plan. Drawings in this unit, however, are of the same building; therefore, the interpretation and agreement among plans can be studied more easily.

SEQUENCE

The floor plan that is prepared first relates to most other drawings. The second and successive floor plans are prepared by tracing the first floor-plan outline. Bearing partitions, plumbing wall, stairwells, fireplace and chimney openings, and other components can then be aligned vertically. The basement, floor, and roof framing plans are prepared in the

same way. Stud layouts and the length of interior partition panel layouts are also derived from the floor plan. Horizontal distances on elevation drawings are also projected from the four sides of the floor plan. Because the floor plan functions as a base for so many other drawings, errors on the floor plan can easily be transferred to other drawings. For that reason, the floor plan must be carefully checked for accuracy before other drawings in the set are prepared. The usual sequence in preparing architectural drawings is as follows:

1 Floor plan
2 Foundation plans
3 Front elevation
4 Rear elevation
5 Right elevation
6 Left elevation
7 Auxiliary elevation
8 Plot plans
9 Landscape plans
10 Survey plans
11 Full sections
12 Detail sections
13 Electrical plans
14 Air-conditioning plans
15 Plumbing diagrams
16 Exterior pictorial rendering
17 Interior pictorial rendering

AGREEMENT AMONG DRAWINGS

Selected areas of each plan in this unit have been marked with geometric figures such as circles, rectangles, hexagons, crosses, squares, triangles, and diamonds. Each symbol identifies the identical area shown on each plan. By studying the position of these symbols on each drawing, you can observe how a specific area appears on each drawing in the set. For example, the position of the colored circle on the main-level floor plan represents the area covered with the same colored circle on the right elevation, lower-level plan, rear view, pictorial drawing, or any other plan so marked with a colored circle. The relationship between sectional views and basic drawings can be followed by tracing these geometric

symbols and by locating the position of the appropriate cutting-plane line on the basic plans. Figures 69-1 through 69-11 show a related set of residential plans marked with geometric figures. Study the plans in the sequence listed above and trace the location of each of the geometric figures throughout the set of plans.

Commercial buildings normally have more floors, cover wider areas, use heavier construction members, and may be more interrelated with other buildings. Nevertheless, the sequence of studying and understanding the relationship between drawings is identical.

DIMENSIONS

If a building is to be constructed as designed, it is extremely critical that dimensions describing the size of each component of a building agree on each drawing. If the dimensions of a basement plan do not match related dimensions on the floor plan, prefabricated wall panels may not fit, or the position of stairwell openings and fireplace footers may not align. Whether a dimension describes the overall length or width of a structure or only indicates the size of a subdimension of a detail, like dimensions must agree on each drawing in a set. For this reason, dimensional accuracy is verified by locating one dimension at a time throughout the entire set until each has been checked and agreement is determined.

PROBLEMS

1 List the order in which you would prepare each of the following drawings: stud layout, foundation plan, specifications, floor plan, front elevation, left elevation, exterior rendering, basement plan, second-floor plan.
2 Pick an area on the floor plan shown in Fig. 69-1 not covered by a circle or square. Locate that same area on the other drawings in this unit.
3 Pick a dimension not circled on the floor plan shown in Fig. 69-1. Find that dimension on other drawings in this unit.

4 Refer to Figs. 69-1 through 69-10 and identify the following:
  1. Dimensions of the chimney at the upper level
  2. Type of outside door used in activities room
  3. Plate height of gathering room
  4. Ceiling height of lower-level bath
  5. Width of lower-level east wall
  6. Type of construction used on lower-level west wall
  7. Terrace vertical support members
  8. Right-side siding materials
  9. Roof pitch
  10. Height of balcony handrails

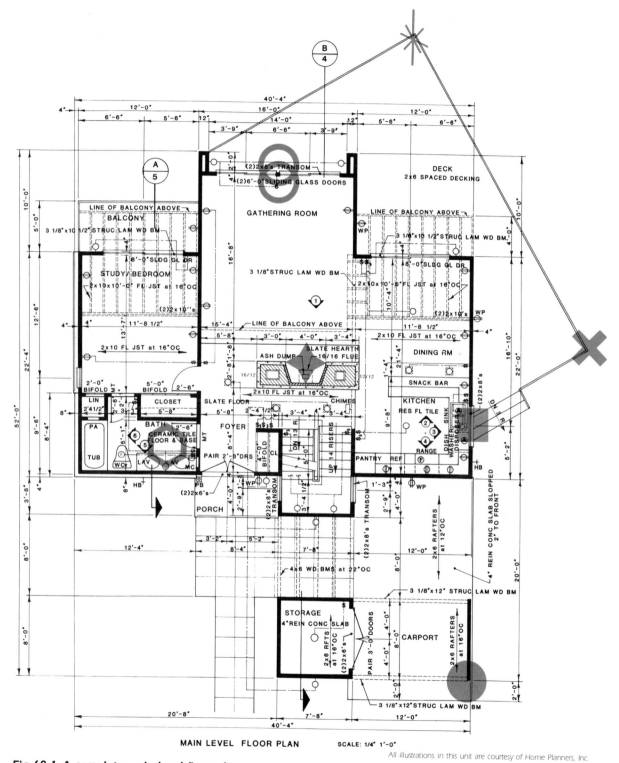

MAIN LEVEL FLOOR PLAN   SCALE: 1/4" 1'-0"

Fig 69-1 A complete main-level floor plan.

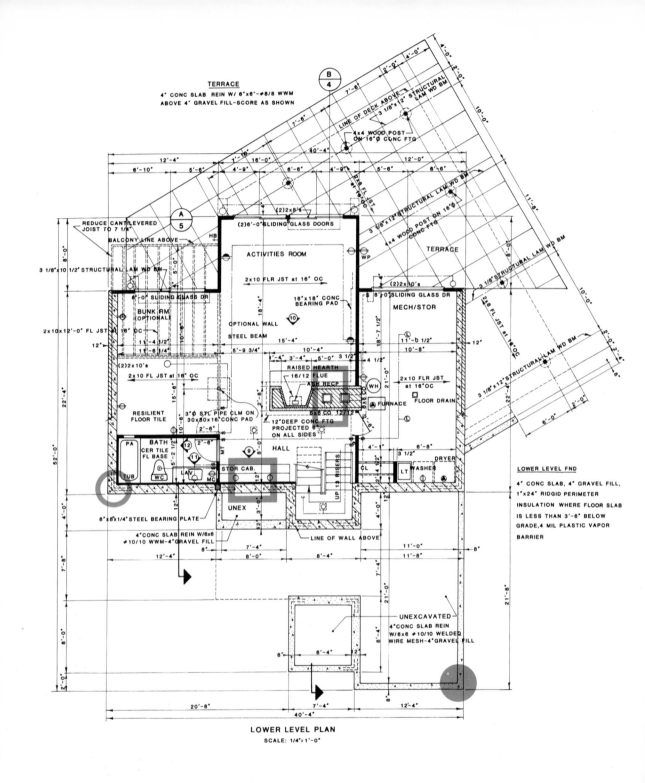

Fig 69-2 A complete lower-level (basement) floor plan.

512

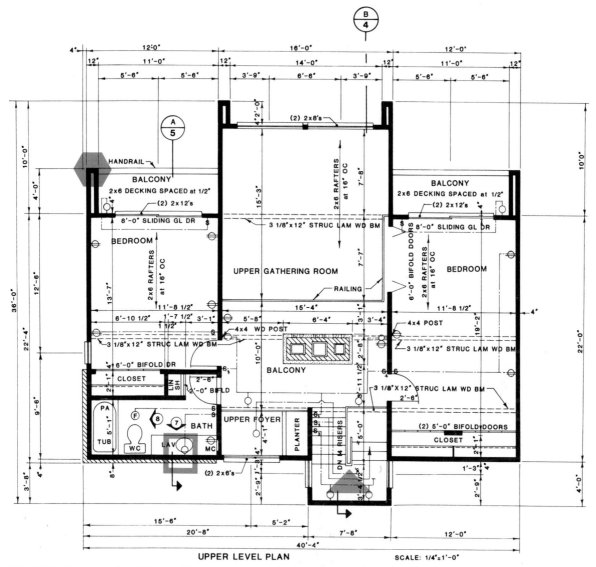

Fig 69-3 An upper-level floor plan.

513

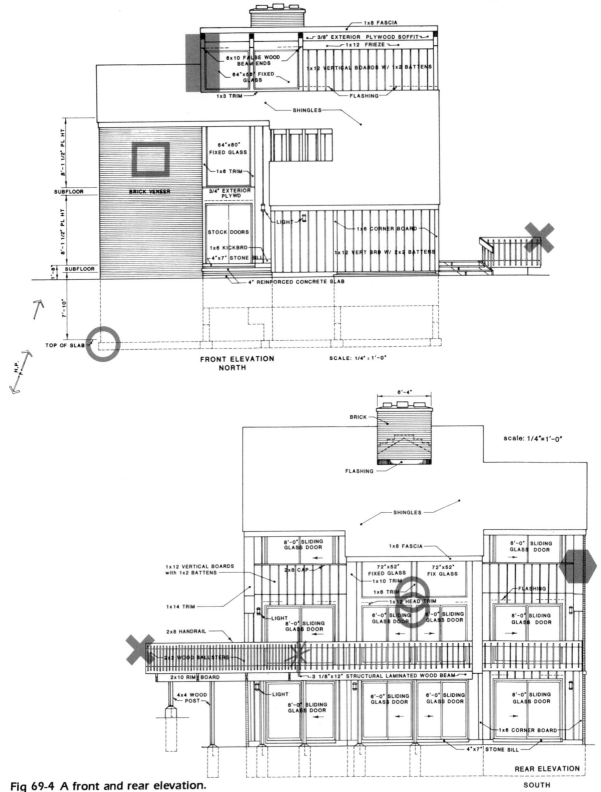

Fig 69-4 A front and rear elevation.

514

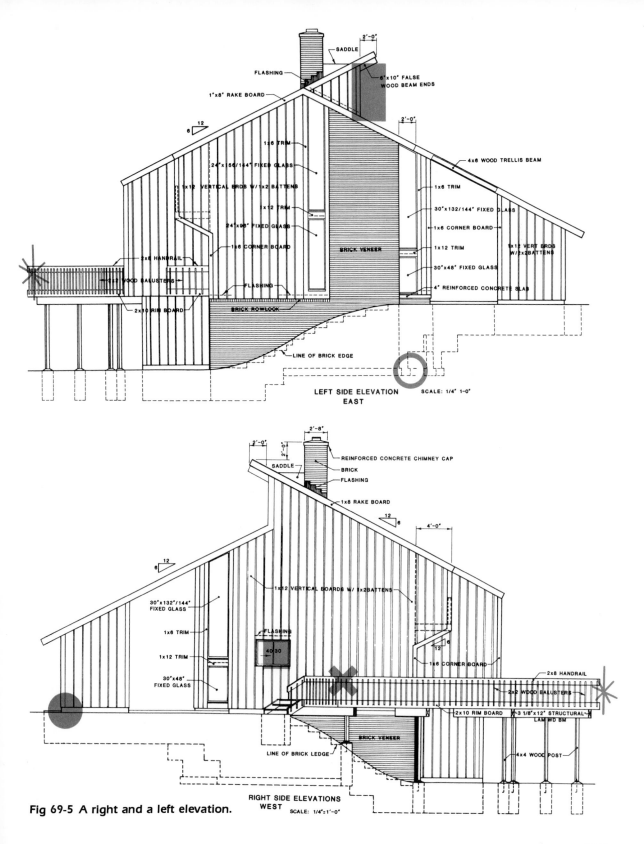

SADDLE

2'-0"

6"x10" FALSE
WOOD BEAM ENDS

FLASHING

1"x8" RAKE BOARD

12
6

2'-0"

1x6 TRIM

4x6 WOOD TRELLIS BEAM

24"x156/144" FIXED GLASS

1x6 TRIM

1x12 VERTICAL BRDS W/1x2 BATTENS

30"x132/144" FIXED GLASS

1x12 TRIM

1x6 CORNER BOARD

24"x96" FIXED GLASS

1x6 CORNER BOARD

1x12 TRIM

1x12 VERT BRDS
W/2x2 BATTENS

BRICK VENEER

2x6 HANDRAIL

30"x48" FIXED GLASS

4" REINFORCED CONCRETE SLAB

2x2 WOOD BALUSTERS

FLASHING

2x10 RIM BOARD

BRICK ROWLOOK

LINE OF BRICK EDGE

LEFT SIDE ELEVATION
EAST

SCALE: 1/4" 1'-0"

2'-8"

2'-0"

REINFORCED CONCRETE CHIMNEY CAP

2'-0"

BRICK

SADDLE

FLASHING

1x8 RAKE BOARD

12
6

4'-0"

12
6

1x12 VERTICAL BOARDS W/ 1x2 BATTENS

30"x132"/144"
FIXED GLASS

1x6 TRIM

1x12 TRIM

FLASHING

40 30

30"x48"
FIXED GLASS

1x6 CORNER BOARD

2x8 HANDRAIL

2x2 WOOD BALUSTERS

2x10 RIM BOARD

3 1/8"x12" STRUCTURAL
LAM WD BM

BRICK VENEER

LINE OF BRICK LEDGE

4x4 WOOD POST

RIGHT SIDE ELEVATIONS
WEST

SCALE: 1/4"=1'-0"

Fig 69-5 A right and a left elevation.

515

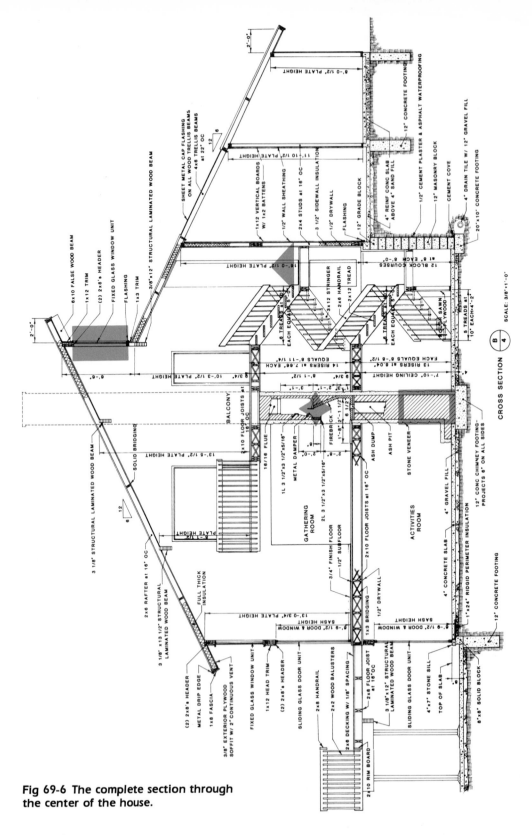

Fig 69-6 The complete section through the center of the house.

516

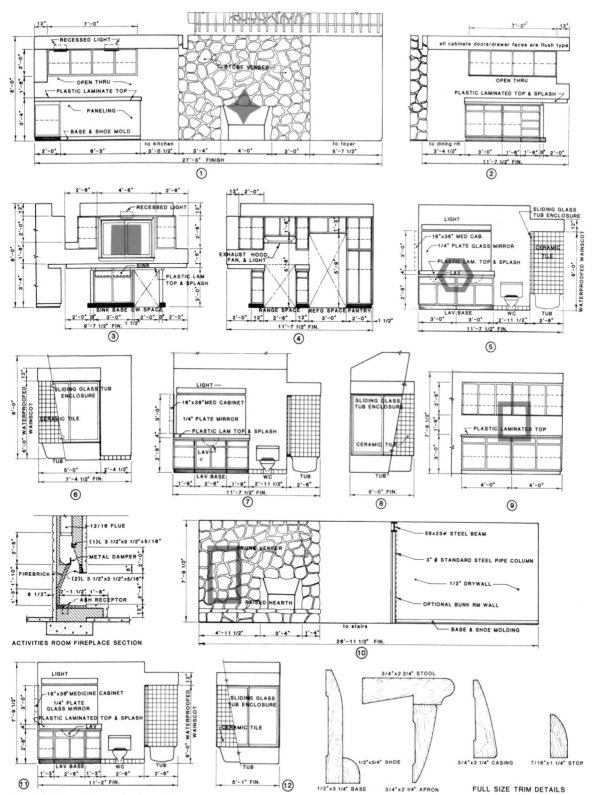

Fig 69-7 Interior wall elevations.

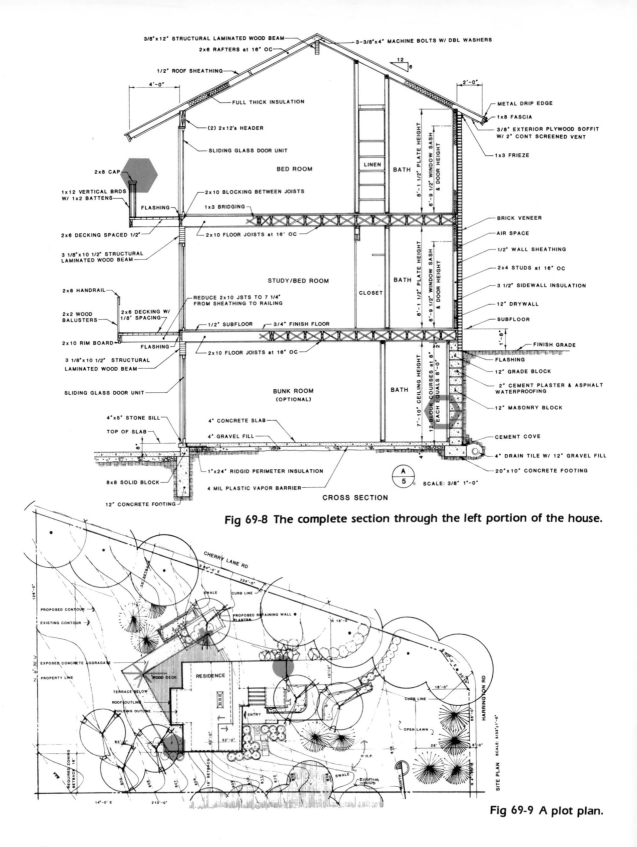

3/8"x12" STRUCTURAL LAMINATED WOOD BEAM

2x6 RAFTERS at 16" OC

— 3-3/8"x4" MACHINE BOLTS W/ DBL WASHERS

1/2" ROOF SHEATHING

12
6

4'-0"

2'-0"

FULL THICK INSULATION

METAL DRIP EDGE

1x8 FASCIA

3/8" EXTERIOR PLYWOOD SOFFIT W/ 2" CONT SCREENED VENT

(2) 2x12's HEADER

SLIDING GLASS DOOR UNIT

1x3 FRIEZE

2x8 CAP

BED ROOM

LINEN

BATH

1x12 VERTICAL BRDS W/ 1x2 BATTENS

2x10 BLOCKING BETWEEN JOISTS

FLASHING

1x3 BRIDGING

8'-1 1/2" PLATE HEIGHT

6'-9 1/2" WINDOW SASH & DOOR HEIGHT

BRICK VENEER

2x6 DECKING SPACED 1/2"

2x10 FLOOR JOISTS at 16" OC

AIR SPACE

3 1/8"x10 1/2" STRUCTURAL LAMINATED WOOD BEAM

1/2" WALL SHEATHING

2x4 STUDS at 16" OC

STUDY/BED ROOM

BATH

3 1/2" SIDEWALL INSULATION

2x8 HANDRAIL

CLOSET

1/2" DRYWALL

2x2 WOOD BALUSTERS

REDUCE 2x10 JSTS TO 7 1/4" FROM SHEATHING TO RAILING

2x6 DECKING W/ 1/8" SPACING

8'-1 1/2" PLATE HEIGHT

6'-9 1/2" WINDOW SASH & DOOR HEIGHT

SUBFLOOR

1/2" SUBFLOOR

3/4" FINISH FLOOR

1'-8"

2x10 RIM BOARD

FLASHING

FINISH GRADE

3 1/8"x10 1/2" STRUCTURAL LAMINATED WOOD BEAM

2x10 FLOOR JOISTS at 16" OC

FLASHING

12" GRADE BLOCK

SLIDING GLASS DOOR UNIT

2" CEMENT PLASTER & ASPHALT WATERPROOFING

BUNK ROOM
(OPTIONAL)

BATH

12" MASONRY BLOCK

4"x5" STONE SILL

7'-10" CEILING HEIGHT

12 BLOCK COURSES at 8" EACH EQUALS 8'-0"

TOP OF SLAB

4" CONCRETE SLAB

CEMENT COVE

4" GRAVEL FILL

4" DRAIN TILE W/ 12" GRAVEL FILL

1"x24" RIGID PERIMETER INSULATION

20"x10" CONCRETE FOOTING

8x8 SOLID BLOCK

A
5

SCALE: 3/8" 1'-0"

12" CONCRETE FOOTING

4 MIL PLASTIC VAPOR BARRIER

CROSS SECTION

Fig 69-8 The complete section through the left portion of the house.

CHERRY LANE RD

SWALE

CURB LINE

PROPOSED CONTOUR

PROPOSED RETAINING WALL

PLANTER

EXISTING CONTOUR

EXPOSED CONCRETE AGGREGATE

PROPERTY LINE

RESIDENCE

TERRACE BELOW

WOOD DECK

CURB LINE

HARRINGTON RD

ROOF OUTLINE

BUILDING OUTLINE

ENTRY

OPEN LAWN

REQUIRED ZONING

SETBACK

SWALE

EXISTING WOODS

SITE PLAN SCALE 3/32"1'-0"

Fig 69-9 A plot plan.

Fig 69-10 Exterior pictorial renderings.

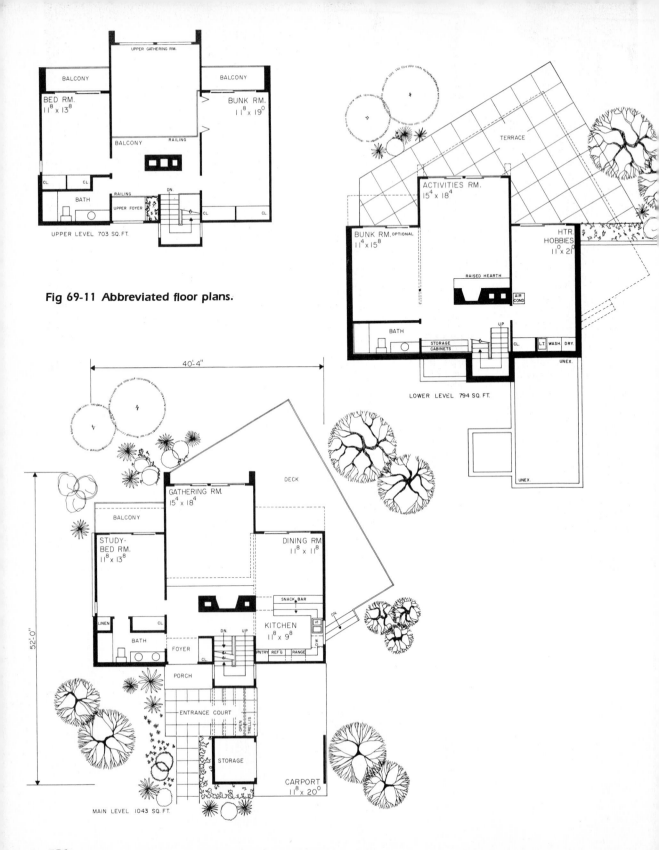

UPPER GATHERING RM.

BALCONY

BALCONY

BED RM.
11^8 x 13^8

BUNK RM.
11^8 x 19^0

BALCONY

RAILING

CL.

CL.

BATH

RAILING

DN.

CL.

CL.

UPPER FOYER

UPPER LEVEL 703 SQ. FT.

Fig 69-11 Abbreviated floor plans.

TERRACE

ACTIVITIES RM.
15^4 x 18^4

BUNK RM. OPTIONAL
11^4 x 15^8

HTR.
HOBBIES
11^0 x 21^0

RAISED HEARTH

AIR
COND.

BATH

STORAGE
CABINETS

UP

CL.

L.T. WASH DRY.

UNEX.

LOWER LEVEL 794 SQ. FT.

UNEX.

40'-4"

DECK

GATHERING RM.
15^4 x 18^4

BALCONY

STUDY-
BED RM.
11^8 x 13^8

DINING RM.
11^8 x 11^8

SNACK BAR

LINEN

CL.

KITCHEN
11^8 x 9^8

52'-0"

BATH

FOYER

DN. UP

D.W.

CL.

PNTRY REF'G RANGE

PORCH

ENTRANCE COURT

OPEN TRELLIS

STORAGE

CARPORT
11^8 x 20^0

MAIN LEVEL 1043 SQ. FT.

PART FIVE

ARCHITECTURAL SUPPORT SERVICES

The development of a total architectural design does not stop with the completion of a set of drawings. There is additional information needed by contractors, financial institutions, and governmental agencies that is not found on architectural drawings. The preparation and use of this information is presented in this part.

SCHEDULES AND SPECIFICATIONS

The plans and drawings of a building are documents prepared to ensure that the building will be constructed as planned. It is sometimes difficult or impossible to show on the drawings all details pertaining to the construction of a building. All features not shown on a drawing should be listed in a schedule or in the specifications.

A schedule is a chart of materials and products. Most plans include a window, door, and interior-finish schedule. Schedules are also prepared for exterior finishes, electrical fixtures, and plumbing fixtures. Schedules can also be prepared for equipment and furnishings specified for the building.

Specifications are lists of details and products to be included in the building. Specifications may be rather brief descriptions of the materials needed, or they may be complete specifications that list the size, manufacturer, grade, color, style, and price of each item of material to be ordered.

UNIT 70
DOOR AND WINDOW SCHEDULES

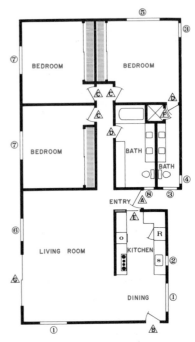

Fig 70-1 Key numbers.

Door and window schedules conserve time and space on a drawing. Rather than include all the information about a door or window on the drawing, attach a key number or letter to each door and window (Fig. 70-1). This symbol is then keyed to the door and window schedule, which includes the width, height, material, type, quantity, and other general information about each window or door (Table 70-1). Window schedules eliminate space-consuming notes on drawings.

Table 70-1 THE KEY SYMBOL IS INDEXED TO A DOOR AND WINDOW SCHEDULE

Door schedule

Symbol	Width	Height	Thickness	Material	Type	Screen	Quantity	Threshold	Remarks	Manufacturer
A	3'-0"	7'-0"	1¾"	Wood—Ash	Slab core	No	1	Oak	Outdoor varnish	A. D. & D. Door, Inc.
B	2'-6"	7'-0"	1¾"	Wood—Ash	Slab core	Yes	1	Oak	Oil stain	A. D. & D. Door, Inc.
C	2'-3"	6'-8"	1⅜"	Wood—Oak	Hollow core	No	3	None	Oil stain	A. D. & D. Door, Inc.
D	2'-0"	6'-8"	1⅜"	Wood—Ash	Hollow core	No	2	None	Oil stain	A. D. & D. Door, Inc.
E	2'-3"	6'-8"	1¼"	Wood—Fir	Plywood	No	1	None	Sliding door	A. D. & D. Door, Inc.
F	1'-9"	5'-6"	½"	Glass & metal	Shower door	No	1	None	Frosted glass	A. D. & D. Door, Inc.
G	4'-6"	6'-6"	½"	Glass & metal	Sliding	Yes	2	Metal	1 sliding screen	A. D. & D. Door, Inc.

Window schedule

Symbol	Width	Height	Material	Type	Screen	Quantity	Remarks	Manufacturer	Catalog number
1	5'-0"	4'-0"	Aluminum	Stationary	No	2		A & B Glass Co.	18BW
2	2'-9"	3'-0"	Aluminum	Louver	Yes	1		A & B Glass Co.	23JW
3	2'-6"	3'-0"	Wood	Double Hung	Yes	2	4 Lites—2 High	A & B Glass Co.	141PW
4	1'-6"	1'-6"	Aluminum	Louver	Yes	1		Hampton Glass Co.	972BW
5	6'-0"	3'-6"	Aluminum	Louvered Sides	Yes	1		Hampton Glass Co.	417CW
6	4'-0"	6'-6"	Aluminum	Stationary	No	1		H & W Window Co.	57DH
7	5'-0"	3'-6"	Aluminum	Sliding	Yes	2	Frosted Glass	H & W Window Co.	22DH
8	1'-9"	3'-0"	Aluminum	Awning	Yes	1		H & W Window Co.	1711JB

Figure 70-2 shows some of the basic information included in a door schedule. Information is shown in chart form on the door and window schedule, but in addition, the door or window design is often drawn separately and indexed to the schedule. Figure 70-3 shows exterior door designs, which may be drawn separately, thus eliminating the need for this detail on the elevation. Unless an interior wall elevation is prepared for every wall in the

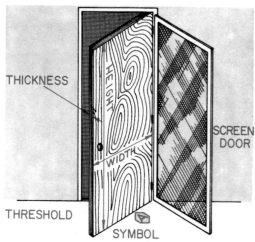

Fig 70-2 Basic information included on a door schedule.

Fig 70-3 Exterior door designs.

FLUSH   PANEL

BLIND OR SUMMER   FRENCH OR CASEMENT

house, it is impossible to determine the style of interior doors from the floor-plan drawing. Figure 70-4 shows drawings of interior door styles that may be indexed to the door schedule.

Window styles are normally depicted on the elevation drawing and complete information included in the window schedule. However, to conserve time, many architectural drafters draw a separate window detail and show only the window outline and the schedule key for that window on the elevation drawing.

Fig 70-4 Interior door designs.

PROBLEMS

1 Prepare a door schedule for the plan shown in Fig. 70-5.

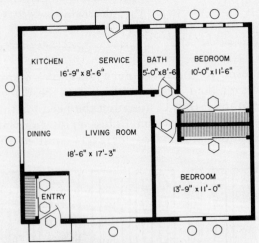

Fig 70-5 Prepare a door and window schedule for this plan.

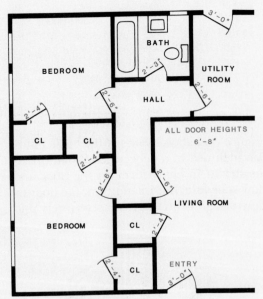

Fig 70-6 Prepare a door schedule for this plan.

2 Prepare a separate drawing showing the several styles of doors you would recommend for the exterior doors shown in Fig. 70-5.

3 Draw the designs you would recommend for the interior doors shown in Fig. 70-6.

4 Prepare a window schedule for the windows shown in Fig. 70-5.

5 Prepare a drawing of each of the window styles you would recommend for the windows shown in Fig. 70-5. Give the manufacturer's name and catalog number for each door and window in your schedule.

6 Prepare a door and window schedule for the windows and doors of the house you are designing.

7 Prepare a door and window schedule for the doors and windows in your home.
8 Define these architectural terms: *schedule, specifications, sliding window, awning window, double-hung window, panel door, flush door, French door, Dutch door.*

UNIT 71
FINISH SCHEDULES

Many types of finishes are used on the interior and the exterior of a building.

PAINT SCHEDULE

To describe the type of finish enamel, paint, and stain, and the amount of gloss and color of each finish for each room would require an exhaustive list with many duplications. A *finishing schedule* is a chart that enables the designer to condense all this information. The interior-finish schedule shown in Table 71-1 includes, in the horizontal column, the parts of each room and the type of finish to be applied. In the vertical column is information pertaining to the application of the finish and the room to which it is to be applied. The exact color classification has been noted in the appropriate intersecting block. The last column, headed "Remarks," is used for making notes about the finish application.

MATERIALS SCHEDULE

To ensure that all floor, wall, and ceiling coverings blend with the overall decor in each room, an interior-finish schedule can be prepared. All the possible materials for each part of the room should be listed in the horizontal column. The rooms are listed in the vertical column. The appropriate block can be checked for the suitable material for the ceiling, wall, wainscoting, base, and floor of each room (Table 71-2). When a schedule is prepared in this manner, it is easy to read and facilitates checking the color scheme of each room and of the overall decor. This kind of schedule condenses pages of unrelated material lists for each room into one chart, thus enabling the designer to see at a glance all the material that should be ordered for each room.

SPECIAL SCHEDULES

To ensure that appliances and fixtures will blend with the decor of each room, a separate schedule can be prepared for them (Table 71-3). Similar schedules are sometimes prepared for furniture and built-in components (Fig. 71-1 and Table 71-4). By preparing schedules of these kinds, the designer can control every aspect of the overall design, including colors, materials, and styles.

USES OF SCHEDULES

Schedules not only are useful in designing and ensuring that the finishing is completed as planned, but also are valuable as aids in ordering manufactured items, such as appliances and fixtures.

Table 71-1 INTERIOR FINISH SCHEDULE

Rooms	Floor			Ceiling					Wall					Base					Trim					Remarks
	FLOOR VARNISH	UNFINISHED	WAXED	ENAMEL GLOSS	ENAMEL SEMI-GLOSS	ENAMEL FLAT	FLAT LATEX	STAIN	ENAMEL GLOSS	ENAMEL SEMI-GLOSS	ENAMEL FLAT	FLAT LATEX	STAIN	ENAMEL GLOSS	ENAMEL SEMI-GLOSS	ENAMEL FLAT	FLAT LATEX	STAIN	ENAMEL GLOSS	ENAMEL SEMI-GLOSS	FLAT LATEX	ENAMEL FLAT	STAIN	
ENTRY			x				Off Wht				Off Wht				Off Wht					Off Wht				Two coats
HALL			x					Lt Brn		Tan					Drk Brn					Drk Brn				Two coats
BEDROOM 1	x						Off Wht					Off Wht				Grey				Grey				One coat primer & sealer —painted surface
BEDROOM 2	x						Off Wht				Lt Yel					Yel						Yel		One coat primer & sealer —painted surface
BEDROOM 3			x				Off Wht						Lt Brn					Drk Brn					Tan	One coat primer & sealer —painted surface
BATH 1				Wht					Wht					Lt Blue					Lt Blue					Water-resistant finishes
BATH 2				Wht					Wht					Lt Blue					Lt Blue					Water-resistant finishes
CLOSETS	x						Brn					Brn					Brn					Brn		
KITCHEN			x		Wht				Yel					Yel						Yel				
DINING			x					Tan		Yel						Yel				Yel				Oil stain
LIVING			x					Tan				Lt Brn					Lt Brn					Lt Brn		Oil stain

526

Table 71-2 MATERIALS SCHEDULE

Rooms	Floor										Ceiling				Wall			Wainscot					Base					Remarks
	ASPHALT TILE	CERAMIC TILE	CORK TILE	LINOLEUM TILE	WOOD STRIP—OAK	WOOD SQS.—OAK	PLYWOOD PANEL	CARPETING	SLATE	TERAZZO	PLASTER	WOOD PANEL	ACOUSTICAL TILE	EXPOSED BEAM	PLASTER	WOOD PANEL	WALL PAPER	WOOD	CERAMIC TILE	PAPER	ASPHALT TILE	STONE VENEER	LINOLEUM	WOOD	RUBBER	TILE—CERAMIC	ASPHALT	
ENTRY									x	x		x			x									x				Terazzo step covering
HALL		x									x				x					x				x				
BEDROOM 1				x									x		x			x									x	Mahogany wainscot
BEDROOM 2				x									x		x		x	x									x	Mahogany wainscot
BEDROOM 3							x	x					x		x										x			See owner for grade carpet
BATH 1		x									x				x				x							x		Water seal tile edges
BATH 2	x										x				x				x							x		Water seal tile edges
KITCHEN			x										x		x						x		x					
DINING			x											x	x	x					x		x					
LIVING					x	x								x		x						x		x				See owner for grade carpet

Table 71-3 FIXTURE AND APPLIANCE SCHEDULES

Appliance schedule

Room	Appliance	Type	Size	Color	Manufacturer	Model no.
KITCHEN	Electric stove	Cook top	4 burner	Yellow	Ideale Appliances	341 MG
KITCHEN	Electric oven	Built-in	30" × 24" × 24"	Yellow	Zeidler Oven Mfg.	27 Mg
SERVICE	Hot-water heater	Gas	50 gal	White	Oratz Water Htr.	249 KG

Fixture schedule

Room	Fixture	Type	Material	Manufacturer	Model number
LIVING	2 electric lights	Hanging	Brass reflectors	Hot Spark Ltd.	1037 IG
BEDROOM 1	2 spotlights	Wall bracket	Flexible neck—aluminum	Gurian & Barris Inc.	1426 SG
BATHS 1 & 2	2 electric lights	Wall bracket	Aluminum—water resistant	Marks Electrical Co.	2432 DG

Table 71-4 FURNITURE/ACCESSORY SCHEDULE

Sym.	Item	Room	Len.	Wid.	Ht.	Material	Color	Quan.
1	Drapes	Bedroom	11'	—	7'	Cotton blend	Brown	1 Set
2	Drapes	Mbr.	12'	—	7'	Cotton blend	Yellow	1 Set
3	Drapes	Den	7'	—	7'	Cotton blend	Yellow	1 Set
4	Drapes	Living/dining	24'	—	7'	Acrylic	Brown pat.	1 Set
5	Chair	Mbr./den	18"	18"	18"	Plastic	Brown	4
6	Chair	Din./kit.	18"	18"	18"	Oak	Natural	9
7	China cab.	Dining	6'	18"	5'-6"	Oak	Natural	1
8	Piano bench	Living	33"	10"	18"	Mahogany	Brn. stain	1
9	Piano	Living	5'-6"	2'-0"	5'-6"	Mahogany	Brn. stain	1
10	Up. wing ch.	Living	33"	30"	20"	Leather	Natural	1
11	Fl. lamp	Living	14" Dia.	—	4'-6"	Metal/cloth	Tan	1
12	Stereo	Living	30"	11"	5'-0"	Teak	Brown	1
13	Sofa/sec.	Living	14'	30"	18"	Velveteen	Red	3 Pcs.
14	Coffee tbl.	Living	30" Dia.	—	15"	Teak	Natural	1
15	Television	Den	21"	18"	30"	21" Color	Brown	1
16	Coffee tbl.	Den	48"	15"	15"	Oak	Natural	1
17	Sofa	Den	6'-6"	30"	18"	Cotton blend	Tan	1
18	Fl. lamp	Mbr./br./den	15" Dia.	—	5'-0"	Wood/cloth	Brown	3
19	Fl. lamp	Den	12" Dia.	—	4'-6"	Wood/plastic	Yellow	1
20	Desk	Mbr./den	39"	18"	29"	Oak	Natural	2
21	Nightstand	Mbr./br.	18"	15"	24"	Oak	Natural	3
22	Tbl. lamp	Mbr.	9" Dia.	—	30"	Wood/plastic	Brown	2
23	Full bed	Mbr.	6'-9"	46"	20"	Standard	—	1
24	Dresser	Mbr.	39"	20"	48"	Oak	Natural	1
25	Dresser	Br.	48"	20"	52"	Oak	Natural	1
26	Twin bed	Br.	6'-9"	42"	20"	Standard	—	1
27	Planter	Mbr./liv./den/por.	10" Dia.	—	12"	Terra cotta	Brown	4
28	Table	Kitchen	36"	22"	30"	Teak	Natural	1
29	Table	Dining	5'-0"	3'-3"	30"	Teak	Natural	1

Manufac.	Cat. #	Cost	Remarks
Sears	CD101	$75	Lined
Sears	CD107	$85	Lined
Sears	CD106	$65	Lined
Sears	CD203	$150	Lined
ID Furn. Co.	X117	$45 ea.	
ID Furn. Co.	L217	$65 ea.	Oil finish
Danish Furn.	13712	$650	Oil finish
Music Co. Inc.	23L19	$50	Piano finish
Music Co. Inc.	P17731	$1750	Piano finish
Danish Furn. Co.	18979	$575	
Danish Furn. Co.	37111	$85	
Danish Furn. Co.	60701	$450	
Danish Furn. Co.	42107	$1200	
Danish Furn. Co.	77310	$110	Natural oil finish
Sony	XL19	$675	
Danish Furn. Co.	78325	$80	Natural oil finish
Danish Furn. Co.	59781	$800	
Danish Furn. Co.	66362	$75 ea.	
Danish Furn. Co.	65731	$50	
Danish Furn. Co.	47772	$225 ea.	Natural oil finish
Danish Furn. Co.	64991	$45 ea.	Natural oil finish
Danish Furn. Co.	65820	$35 ea.	
Acme Bed Co.	AC12	$235	Box spring/mat./frame
Danish Furn. Co.	37452	$125	Dbl. dresser
Danish Furn. Co.	37471	$200	Triple dresser
Acme Bed Co.	Ac08	$190	Box spring/mat./frame
Flowers Inc.	23FP	$10 ea.	
Danish Furn. Co.	17832	$110	Natural oil finish
Danish Furn. Co.	17876	$235	Natural oil finish

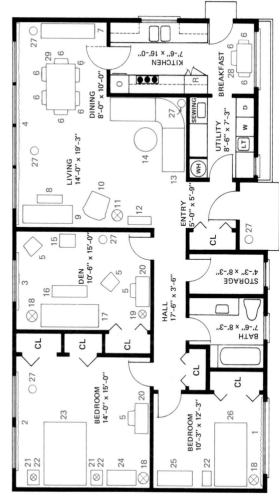

Fig 71-1 Furniture schedule.

PROBLEMS

1 Make a finish schedule for Fig. 13-3.
2 Make a finish schedule for Fig. 70-5.

3 Complete all the schedules for the home of your design. Include as much manufacturing information as you can obtain.

4 Make an appliance schedule for Fig. 11-1A.

5 Make a fixture schedule for Fig. 70-5.

6 Complete all the schedules for your own home. List the types of fixtures, finishes, and doors that you prefer.

7 Know these architectural terms: *finish schedule, trim, base, wainscot, fixture schedule, appliance schedule, flat latex, enamel, primer, sealer, asphalt tile, slate, terazzo, acoustical tile, veneer, ceramic tile.*

UNIT 72
SPECIFICATIONS

Specifications are written instructions describing the basic requirements for constructing a building. Specifications describe sizes, kinds, and quality of building materials. The methods of construction, fabrication, or installation are also spelled out explicitly. Specifically, they tell the contractor, "These are the materials you must use, and this is how you must use them, and these are the conditions under which you undertake this job." Specifications guarantee the purchaser

LINE NO.	ITEM COLUMN NO. 1	QUANTITY & UNIT MEAS.	MATERIAL (TYPE and/or SIZE)	UNIT COST	TOTAL COST
1	DESIGN NO. H.P.2511				
2	MASONRY				
3	Footings				
4		21 Lin.Ft.	16 x 8"		
5		84 " "	20 x 10"		
6		63 " "	8 x 42"		
7		100 " "	12 x 42"		
8		1 Pad	30 x 30 x 16"		
9		1 "	3'-8"x11'-4" x 12"		
10		6 Piers	16" Diam. x 42"		
11					
12					
13		27 Cu.Yds.	2500# Concrete		
14		180 Sq.Ft.	1" Fiberglass Perimeter Insulation		
15		100 Pcs.	4" Drain Tile		
16		8 "	4" " Els		
17		5 "	4" " Tees		
18		5 "	4" Vitrified Crock Tile		
19		1 Roll	15# 4" Strip Felt		
20		5 Cu.Yds.	Pea Gravel		
21					
22	Masonry Block Walls				
23		46 Pcs.	12 x 8 x 16" Masonry Grade Blocks		
24		12 "	12 x 8 x 16" " Corner "		
25		10 "	12 x 8 x 8" " " "		
26		24 "	8 x 8 x 16" " " "		
27		10 "	8 x 8 x 8" " " "		
28		784 "	12 x 8 x 16" " Regular "		
29		188 "	8 x 8 x 16" " " "		
30		72 "	4 x 8 x 12" " Solid "		
31		58 "	4 x 8 x 16" " " "		
32		56 "	8 x 8 x 16" " " "		
33		58 "	8 x 8 x 16" " " Ell Blocks		
34		11 Cu.Yds.	50/50 Mason Sand		
35		56 Sacks	Mortar		
36		20 "	Cement		
37		20 Gals.	Asphalt Foundation Coating		
38		7 Pcs.	4" x 12" Flue Linings		
39		2 "	8 x 8" Cleanout Doors		
40			8" Diameter Steel Furnace Thimble		

Fig 72-1 Part of a contractor's materials list.

Fig 72-2 Furniture material specifications.

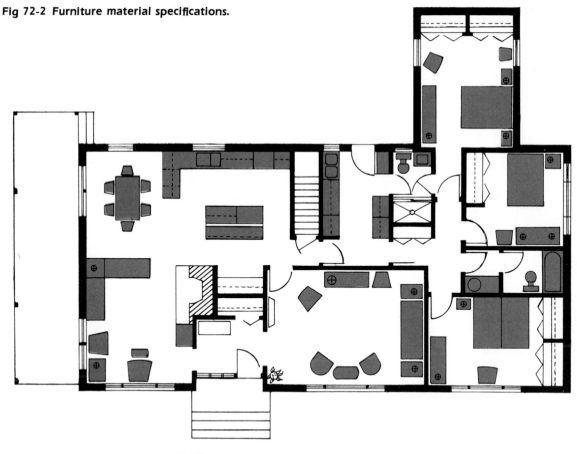

PLANNING ON PAPER

that the contractor will deliver the building when it is finished exactly as specified.

Information that cannot be conveniently included in the drawings, such as the legal responsibilities, methods of purchasing materials, and insurance requirements, is included in the specifications. In order to make an accurate construction estimate, contractors refer to the material lists that are included in the specifications (Fig. 72-1). When descriptions are difficult to write, samples as shown in Fig. 72-2 are used to relate items to materials.

Specifications help ensure that the building will be constructed according to standards that the building laws require. Specifications are used frequently by banks and federal agencies in appraising the market value of a building.

Since many specifications are similar, the use of a fill-in form is often desirable. Fill-in forms include all the major classifications included in most specifications. The designer adds the exact size and kind of material required. Figure 72-3 shows a standard form used by the Federal Housing Administration and Veterans' Administration for describing materials to secure FHA or VA loan approval.

The following specifications outline shows the major divisions and subdivisions of a typical set of specifications. This outline does not include the exact size and kind of material included under each category, as these would vary with each building. You will notice that the sequence of the outline roughly approximates the sequence of actual construction.

For accurate register of carbon copies, form may be separated along above fold. Staple completed sheets together in original order.

Form approved.
Budget Bureau No. 63-R055.11.

☐ Proposed Construction

☐ Under Construction

DESCRIPTION OF MATERIALS

No. _____
(To be inserted by FHA or VA)

Property address _____ City _____ State _____

Mortgagor or Sponsor _____ _____
(Name) (Address)

Contractor or Builder _____ _____
(Name) (Address)

INSTRUCTIONS

1. For additional information on how this form is to be submitted, number of copies, etc., see the instructions applicable to the FHA Application for Mortgage Insurance or VA Request for Determination of Reasonable Value, as the case may be.
2. Describe all materials and equipment to be used, whether or not shown on the drawings, by marking an X in each appropriate check-box and entering the information called for in each space. If space is inadequate, enter "See misc." and describe under item 27 or on an attached sheet.
3. Work not specifically described or shown will not be considered unless

required, then the minimum acceptable will be assumed. Work exceeding minimum requirements cannot be considered unless specifically described.
4. Include no alternates, "or equal" phrases, or contradictory items. (Consideration of a request for acceptance of substitute materials or equipment is not thereby precluded.)
5. Include signatures required at the end of this form.
6. The construction shall be completed in compliance with the related drawings and specifications, as amended during processing. The specifications include this Description of Materials and the applicable Minimum Construction Requirements.

1. EXCAVATION:
Bearing soil, type _____

2. FOUNDATIONS:
Footings: concrete mix _____ ; strength psi _____ Reinforcing _____
Foundation wall: material _____ Reinforcing _____
Interior foundation wall: material _____ Party foundation wall _____
Columns: material and sizes _____ Piers: material and reinforcing _____
Girders: material and sizes _____ Sills: material _____

Basement entrance areaway _____ Window areaways _____
Waterproofing _____ Footing drains _____
Termite protection _____
Basementless space: ground cover _____ ; insulation _____ ; foundation vents _____
Special foundations _____
Additional information: _____

3. CHIMNEYS:
Material _____ Prefabricated (make and size) _____
Flue lining: material _____ Heater flue size _____ Fireplace flue size _____
Vents (material and size): gas or oil heater _____ ; water heater _____
Additional information: _____

4. FIREPLACES:
Type: ☐ solid fuel; ☐ gas-burning; ☐ circulator (make and size) _____ Ash dump and clean-out _____
Fireplace: facing _____ ; lining _____ ; hearth _____ ; mantel _____
Additional information: _____

5. EXTERIOR WALLS:
Wood frame: wood grade, and species _____ ☐ Corner bracing. Building paper or felt _____
Sheathing _____ ; thickness _____ ; width _____ ; ☐ solid; ☐ spaced _____ " o. c.; ☐ diagonal; _____
Siding _____ ; grade _____ ; type _____ ; size _____ ; exposure _____ "; fastening _____
Shingles _____ ; grade _____ ; type _____ ; size _____ ; exposure _____ "; fastening _____
Stucco _____ ; thickness _____ "; Lath _____ ; weight _____ lb.
Masonry veneer _____ Sills _____ Lintels _____ Base flashing _____
Masonry: ☐ solid ☐ faced ☐ stuccoed; total wall thickness _____ "; facing thickness _____ " facing material _____
Backup material _____ ; thickness _____ "; bonding _____
Door sills _____ Window sills _____ Lintels _____ Base flashing _____
Interior surfaces: dampproofing _____ coats of _____ ; furring _____
Additional information: _____
Exterior painting: material _____ ; number of coats _____
Gable wall construction: ☐ same as main walls; ☐ other construction _____

6. FLOOR FRAMING:
Joists: wood, grade, and species _____ ; other _____ ; bridging _____ ; anchors _____
Concrete slab: ☐ basement floor; ☐ first floor; ☐ ground supported; ☐ self-supporting; mix _____ ; thickness _____
reinforcing _____ ; insulation _____ ; membrane _____
Fill under slab: material _____ ; thickness _____ ". Additional information: _____

7. SUBFLOORING: (Describe underflooring for special floors under item 21.)
Material: grade and species _____ ; size _____ ; type _____
Laid: ☐ first floor; ☐ second floor; ☐ attic _____ sq. ft.; ☐ diagonal; ☐ right angles. Additional information: _____

8. FINISH FLOORING: (Wood only. Describe other finish flooring under item 21.)

Location	Rooms	Grade	Species	Thickness	Width	Bldg. Paper	Finish
First floor							
Second floor							
Attic floor _____ sq. ft.							
Additional information:							

Fig 72-3 An FHA and VA description of materials.

9. PARTITION FRAMING:

Studs: wood, grade, and species _____ size and spacing ____ _____ Other _____

Additional information: _____

10. CEILING FRAMING:

Joists: wood, grade, and species _____ Other _____ Bridging _____

Additional information: _____

11. ROOF FRAMING:

Rafters: wood, grade, and species _____ Roof trusses (see detail): grade and species _____

Additional information: _____

12. ROOFING:

Sheathing: wood, grade, and species _____; ☐ solid; ☐ spaced _____" o.c.

Roofing _____; grade _____; size _____; type _____

Underlay _____; weight or thickness _____; size _____; fastening _____

Built-up roofing _____; number of plies _____; surfacing material _____

Flashing: material _____; gage or weight _____; ☐ gravel stops; ☐ snow guards

Additional information: _____

13. GUTTERS AND DOWNSPOUTS:

Gutters: material _____; gage or weight _____; size _____; shape _____

Downspouts: material _____; gage or weight _____; size _____; shape _____; number _____

Downspouts connected to: ☐ Storm sewer; ☐ sanitary sewer; ☐ dry-well. ☐ Splash blocks: material and size _____

Additional information: _____

14. LATH AND PLASTER

Lath ☐ walls, ☐ ceilings: material _____; weight or thickness _____ Plaster: coats _____; finish _____

Dry-wall ☐ walls, ☐ ceilings: material _____; thickness _____; finish _____

Joint treatment _____

15. DECORATING: *(Paint, wallpaper, etc.)*

ROOMS	WALL FINISH MATERIAL AND APPLICATION	CEILING FINISH MATERIAL AND APPLICATION
Kitchen ___		
Bath ___		
Other ___		

Additional information: _____

16. INTERIOR DOORS AND TRIM:

Doors: type _____; material _____; thickness _____

Door trim: type _____; material _____ Base: type _____; material _____; size _____

Finish: doors _____; trim _____

Other trim *(item, type and location)* _____

Additional information: _____

17. WINDOWS:

Windows: type _____; make _____; material _____; sash thickness _____

Glass: grade _____; ☐ sash weights; ☐ balances, type _____; head flashing _____

Trim: type _____; material _____ Paint _____; number coats _____

Weatherstripping: type _____; material _____ Storm sash, number _____

Screens: ☐ full; ☐ half; type _____; number _____; screen cloth material _____

Basement windows: type _____; material _____; screens, number _____; Storm sash, number _____

Special windows _____

Additional information: _____

18. ENTRANCES AND EXTERIOR DETAIL:

Main entrance door: material _____; width _____; thickness _____". Frame: material _____; thickness ____"

Other entrance doors: material _____; width _____; thickness _____". Frame: material _____; thickness ____"

Head flashing _____ Weatherstripping: type _____; saddles _____

Screen doors: thickness _____"; number _____; screen cloth material _____ Storm doors: thickness _____"; number _____

Combination storm and screen doors: thickness _____"; number _____; screen cloth material _____

Shutters: ☐ hinged; ☐ fixed. Railings _____, Attic louvers _____

Exterior millwork: grade and species _____ Paint _____; number coats _____

Additional information: _____

19. CABINETS AND INTERIOR DETAIL:

Kitchen cabinets, wall units: material _____; lineal feet of shelves _____; shelf width _____

Base units: material _____; counter top _____; edging _____

Back and end splash _____ Finish of cabinets _____; number coats _____

Medicine cabinets: make _____; model _____

Other cabinets and built-in furniture _____

Additional information: _____

20. STAIRS:

STAIR	TREADS		RISERS		STRINGS		HANDRAIL		BALUSTERS	
	Material	Thickness	Material	Thickness	Material	Size	Material	Size	Material	Size
Basement ___										
Main ___										
Attic ___										

Disappearing: make and model number _____

Additional information: _____

Fig 72-3 Continued

21. SPECIAL FLOORS AND WAINSCOT:

	LOCATION	MATERIAL, COLOR, BORDER, SIZES, GAGE, ETC.	THRESHOLD MATERIAL	WALL BASE MATERIAL	UNDERFLOOR MATERIAL
FLOORS	Kitchen _____				
	Bath _____				

	LOCATION	MATERIAL, COLOR, BORDER, CAP. SIZES, GAGE, ETC.	HEIGHT	HEIGHT OVER TUB	HEIGHT IN SHOWERS (FROM FLOOR)
WAINSCOT	Bath _____				

Bathroom accessories: ☐ Recessed; material _____; number _____; ☐ Attached; material _____; number _____
Additional information: _____

22. PLUMBING:

FIXTURE	NUMBER	LOCATION	MAKE	MFR'S FIXTURE IDENTIFICATION NO.	SIZE	COLOR
Sink _____						
Lavatory _____						
Water closet _____						
Bathtub _____						
Shower over tub△ _____						
Stall shower△ _____						
Laundry trays _____						

△☐ Curtain rod   △☐ Door   ☐ Shower pan: material _____
Water supply: ☐ public; ☐ community system; ☐ individual (private) system.★
Sewage disposal: ☐ public; ☐ community system; ☐ individual (private) system.★
★*Show and describe individual system in complete detail in separate drawings and specifications according to requirements.*
House drain (inside): ☐ cast iron; ☐ tile; ☐ other _____ House sewer (outside): ☐ cast iron; ☐ tile; ☐ other _____
Water piping: ☐ galvanized steel; ☐ copper tubing; ☐ other _____ Sill cocks, number _____
Domestic water heater: type _____; make and model _____; heating capacity _____
_____ gph. 100° rise. Storage tank: material _____; capacity _____ gallons.
Gas service: ☐ utility company; ☐ liq. pet. gas; ☐ other _____ Gas piping: ☐ cooking; ☐ house heating.
Footing drains connected to: ☐ storm sewer; ☐ sanitary sewer; ☐ dry well. Sump pump; make and model _____
_____; capacity _____; discharges into _____

23. HEATING:
☐ Hot water. ☐ Steam. ☐ Vapor. ☐ One-pipe system. ☐ Two-pipe system.
   ☐ Radiators. ☐ Convectors. ☐ Baseboard radiation. Make and model _____
   Radiant panel: ☐ floor; ☐ wall; ☐ ceiling. Panel coil: material _____
   ☐ Circulator. ☐ Return pump. Make and model _____; capacity _____ gpm.
   Boiler: make and model _____ Output _____ Btuh.; net rating _____ Btuh.
Additional information: _____
Warm air: ☐ Gravity. ☐ Forced. Type of system _____
   Duct material: supply _____; return _____ Insulation _____, thickness _____ ☐ Outside air intake.
   Furnace: make and model _____ Input _____ Btuh.; output _____ Btuh.
   Additional information: _____
☐ Space heater; ☐ floor furnace; ☐ wall heater. Input _____ Btuh.; output _____ Btuh.; number units _____
   Make, model _____ Additional information: _____
Controls: make and types _____
Additional information: _____
Fuel: ☐ Coal; ☐ oil; ☐ gas; ☐ liq. pet. gas; ☐ electric; ☐ other _____; storage capacity _____
   Additional information: _____
Firing equipment furnished separately: ☐ Gas burner, conversion type. ☐ Stoker: hopper feed ☐; bin feed ☐
   Oil burner: ☐ pressure atomizing; ☐ vaporizing _____
   Make and model _____ Control _____
   Additional information: _____
Electric heating system: type _____ Input _____ watts; @ _____ volts; output _____ Btuh.
   Additional information: _____
Ventilating equipment: attic fan, make and model _____; capacity _____ cfm.
   kitchen exhaust fan, make and model _____

Other heating, ventilating, or cooling equipment _____

24. ELECTRIC WIRING:
Service: ☐ overhead; ☐ underground. Panel: ☐ fuse box; ☐ circuit-breaker; make _____ AMP's _____ No. circuits _____
Wiring: ☐ conduit; ☐ armored cable; ☐ nonmetallic cable; ☐ knob and tube; ☐ other _____
Special outlets: ☐ range; ☐ water heater; ☐ other _____
☐ Doorbell. ☐ Chimes. Push-button locations _____ Additional information: _____

25. LIGHTING FIXTURES:
Total number of fixtures _____ Total allowance for fixtures, typical installation, $ _____
Nontypical installation _____
Additional information: _____

3

DESCRIPTION OF MATERIALS

Fig 72-3 Continued

534

26. INSULATION:

LOCATION	THICKNESS	MATERIAL, TYPE, AND METHOD OF INSTALLATION	VAPOR BARRIER
Roof			
Ceiling			
Wall			
Floor			

HARDWARE: (make, material, and finish.) _____

SPECIAL EQUIPMENT: (State material or make, model and quantity. Include only equipment and appliances which are acceptable by local law, custom and applicable FHA standards. Do not include items which, by established custom, are supplied by occupant and removed when he vacates premises or chattles prohibited by law from becoming realty.)_____

27. MISCELLANEOUS: (Describe any main dwelling materials, equipment, or construction items not shown elsewhere; or use to provide additional information where the space provided was inadequate. Always reference by item number to correspond to numbering used on this form.) _____

PORCHES:

TERRACES:

GARAGES:

WALKS AND DRIVEWAYS:
Driveway: width _____ ; base material _____ ; thickness _____ "; surfacing material _____ ; thickness _____ "
Front walk: width _____ ; material _____ ; thickness _____ ". Service walk: width _____ ; material _____ ; thickness _____ "
Steps: material _____ ; treads _____ "; risers _____ ". Cheek walls _____

OTHER ONSITE IMPROVEMENTS:
(Specify all exterior onsite improvements not described elsewhere, including items such as unusual grading, drainage structures, retaining walls, fence, railings, and accessory structures.)

LANDSCAPING, PLANTING, AND FINISH GRADING:
Topsoil _____ " thick: ☐ front yard; ☐ side yards; ☐ rear yard to _____ feet behind main building.
Lawns (seeded, sodded, or sprigged): ☐ front yard _____ ; ☐ side yards _____ ; ☐ rear yard_____
Planting: ☐ as specified and shown on drawings; ☐ as follows:
_____ Shade trees, deciduous, _____ " caliper.   _____ Evergreen trees. _____ ' to _____ ', B & B.
_____ Low flowering trees, deciduous, _____ ' to _____ '   _____ Evergreen shrubs. _____ ' to _____ ', B & B.
_____ High-growing shrubs, deciduous, _____ ' to _____ '   _____ Vines, 2-year _____
_____ Medium-growing shrubs, deciduous, _____ ' to _____ '
_____ Low-growing shrubs, deciduous, _____ ' to _____ '

IDENTIFICATION.—This exhibit shall be identified by the signature of the builder, or sponsor, and/or the proposed mortgagor if the latter is known at the time of application.

Date_____   Signature _____

Signature _____

FHA Form 2005
VA Form 26-1852

4

GPO 1908 o48-16-80081-1 296-152

Fig 72-3 Continued

SPECIFICATIONS OUTLINE

Owner's name and address
Contractor's name and address
Location of new structure

General information

List of all drawings, specifications, legal documents

Allowances of money for special orders, such as wallpaper, carpeting, fixtures

Completion date

Contractor's bid

List of manufactured items bought for the job

Guarantees for all manufactured items

Legal responsibilities—contractor

Good workmanship

Adherence to plans and specifications

Fulfillment of building laws

Purchase of materials

Hiring and paying all workers

Obtaining and paying for all permits

Providing owner certification of passed inspection

Responsibility for correction of errors

Responsibility for complete cleanup

Furnish all tools and equipment

Providing personal supervision

Having a supervisor on the job at all times

Providing a written guarantee of work

Legal responsibilities—homeowner

Carrying fire insurance during construction

Paying utilities during construction

Specifying method of payment

Earthwork

Excavation, backfills, gradings

Irregularities in soil

Location of house on lot

Clearing of lot

Grading for water drainage

Preparation of ground for foundation

Concrete and cement work

Foundation sizes

Concrete and mortar mix

Cement, sand, and gravel

Curing the concrete

Finishing-off concrete flatwork

Vapor seals and locations

Type and size of reinforcing steel and locations

Outside concrete work, sizes and locations

Cleaning of masonry work

Porches, patios, terraces, walks, driveways: sizes and locations

Carpentry, rough

Required types of wood grades

Maximum amount of moisture in wood

List of construction members, sizes, and amount of wood needed

Special woods, millwork

Nail sizes for each job

Floors

Type, size, and finish of floor

Floor coverings

Roofing

Type of coverings

Amount of coverings

Methods to bond coverings

Color of final layer

Sheet metal

List of flashing and sizes

List of galvanized iron and sizes

Protective metal paint and where to use

Size and amount of screens for vents, doors, and windows

Doors and windows

Sizes

Material

Type

Quantity

Manufacturer and model number

Window and door trims

Frames for screens

Amount of window space per room
Types of glass and mirrors
Types of sashes
Window and door frames
Weather stripping and caulking

Lath and plaster

Type, size, and amount of lath needed
Type, size, and amount of wire mesh, felt paper, and nails
Types of interior and exterior plaster
Instructions of manufacturer for mixing and applying
Number of coats
Finishing between coats
Drying time

Dry walls

Sizes, manufacturer's model number

Insulation

List of types, makes, sizes, model number
Instructions for applying

Electrical needs

Electrical outlets and their locations
Electrical switches and their locations
Wall brackets and their locations
Ceiling outlets and their locations
Signed certificate that electrical work has passed the building inspection
Guarantee for all parts
List of all electrical parts with name, type, size, color, model number, and lamp wattage
Locations for television outlet and aerial, telephone outlet, main switches, panel board, circuits, and meter
Size of wire used for wiring
Number of circuits

Plumbing

List of fixtures with make, color, style, manufacturer, and catalog number
List of type and size of plumbing lines— gas, water, and waste
Vent pipes and sizes
Inspection slips on plumbing

Guarantees for plumbing
Instructions for installing and connecting pipe lines

Heating and air conditioning

List of all equipment with make, style, color, manufacturer's name, catalog number
Guarantee for all equipment
Signed equipment-inspection certificate
List and location of all sheet-metal work for ducts
List of fuels, outlets, exhausts, and registers
Types of insulation
Location for heating and air-conditioning units

Stone and brickwork

List and location of all stone and brick-work (fireplace, chimney, retaining walls)
Concrete and mortar mix
Reinforcing steel
Kind, size, and name of manufacturer of any synthetic stone

Built-ins

List of all built-ins to be constructed on the job
Dimensions
Kinds of materials
List of all manufactured objects to be built in
Model number
Make
Color
Catalog number
Manufacturer

Ceramic tile

List of types, sizes, color, manufacturers, catalog numbers
Mortar mix

Painting

List of paints to be used—type, color, manufacturer's name, catalog number

Painting (cont.)

Preparation of painted surface

Number of coats and preparation of each

Instructions for stained surfaces or special finishes (type of finish, color, manufacturer, and catalog number)

Finish hardware

List of hardware—type, make, material, color, manufacturer's name, catalog number

Exterior

List of types of finishes for each exterior wall

Instructions for each type

Color, manufacturer, and catalog number

Miscellaneous

List and location of all blacktop areas

PROBLEMS

1 Make a specifications list for a single garage.

2 Make a specifications list for Fig. 70-5.

3 Obtain a specifications list from a set of plans.

4 Define these terms: *specifications, guarantee, documents, contractor.*

BUILDING CODES

A building code is a collection of laws that maintain minimum standards for a community for safeguarding life and health. These laws help to control design, construction, materials, maintenance, location and use of a structure, and quality and use of materials. To stay within the law, designers and builders must observe the code.

Before anything is built, altered, or repaired, a building permit must be obtained from the building department in a community. This permit ensures the appearance of an inspector to inspect the work. The inspections usually made for a house cover the plans, grading of land, excavations, foundation forms, foundations, carpentry, plumbing, heating, ventilation, and electrical work.

Building laws have lessened the loss of life and property from earthquakes, storms, and fires. The homeowner knows that when the home is finished, it will be a secure and well-constructed dwelling. It will be free from shoddy materials and poor workmanship. In addition, it will have a good resale value, and a mortgage loan will be obtainable for it.

The codes of some communities are better than others because the laws are continually being revised to keep pace with new types of construction and materials. These codes accept any material and method of construction that does the job safely. Using newer methods may save the owner money through efficiency of construction.

Building codes are different in each community because of geographical differences. However, a problem arises concerning such differences. The codes vary in their makeup as well as in their methods of construction, which leads to confusion among builders. A method of construction used in one community is barred in another because of a different interpretation of the law. What is needed is a uniform code that has a simple interpretation of each law. Each community would have this law adjusted to fit the physical conditions of the area. For example, the foundation footings need to be deep in the ground in cold climates. They must be below the frost line where the earth does not freeze. In warm climates, there is no need for such depth. The law concerning foundation footings should be stated and cataloged in the same way in all building codes, except that the specification for distance beneath the ground should vary according to the community. Required sizes, classifications, and kinds of materials are shown in building codes.

UNIT 73
REQUIRED SIZES

Each municipality makes its own building-code requirements. Building codes are necessary to ensure that substandard, unsafe, and unattractive buildings are not built in the area. Building codes also help to regulate the kinds of structures that can be built in a specific area, by zoning. Zones are classified as residential, commercial, and industrial. Size restrictions are a vital part of every code.

Building-code information is presented in printed material, charts, sectional drawings, specifications, and pictorial drawings (Fig.

73-1). Building codes also contain regulations pertaining to building permits, fees, inspection requirements, drawings, property location, zoning, and general legal implications connected with building.

Some of the more common items included in family-dwelling building codes are as follows:

Minimum room sizes
Ceiling heights
Window areas
Foundations (Fig. 73-2)
Retaining walls
Concrete mix
Girders (Fig. 73-3)
Lintels (Fig. 73-4)

Walls and partitions
Joists (Fig. 73-5)
Wood floors
Concrete blocks
Steel reinforcing
Fireplaces
Chimneys
Roof construction (Fig. 73-6)
Stairways
Electrical equipment
Gas piping
Heating
Air conditioning
Plumbing
Sanitation
Garages

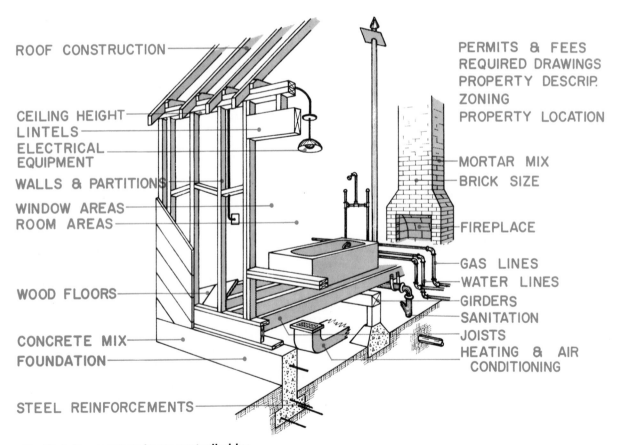

Fig 73-1 The common items controlled by building codes.

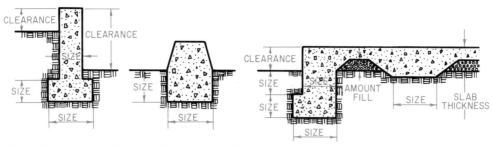

Fig 73-2 Size, clearance, and composition of foundations are determined by building codes.

TYPICAL SPANS FOR WOOD GIRDERS

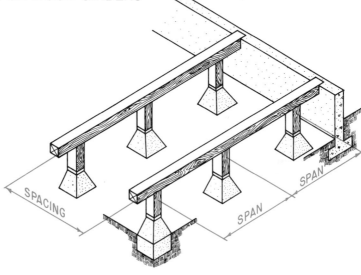

SIZE	1-STORY	2-STORY
4" X 6"	5' — 0"	4' — 0"
6" X 6"	6' — 0"	5' — 0"
4" X 8"	6' — 6"	5' — 6"
6" X 8"	8' — 0"	7' — 0"
4" X 10"	8' — 0"	7' — 0"
6" X 10"	9' — 0"	7' — 0"

Fig 73-3 Girder size and spacing are prescribed by building codes.

LINTEL SPANS

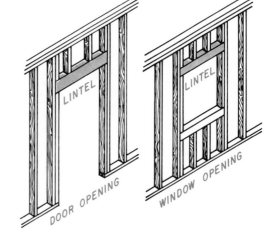

SUPPORTING ROOF & CEILING ONLY		SUPPORTING FLOOR, ROOF & CEILING ONLY	
SIZE	SPAN	SIZE	SPAN
4 x 4	3' – 0"	4 x 4	3' – 6"
4 x 6	4' – 0"	4 x 6	5' – 0"
4 x 8	6' – 0"	4 x 8	5' – 6"
4 x 10	8' – 0"	4 x 10	7' – 0"
4 x 12	9' – 0"	4 x 12	8' – 0"
4 x 14	10' – 0"	4 x 14	9' – 0"
4 x 16	12' – 0"	4 x 16	10' – 0"

Fig 73-4 The size and span of lintels are outlined in building codes.

JOIST SPANS

JOIST SIZE	JOIST SPACING	JOIST SPAN
2 x 4	12" 16" 24"	10'-0" 9'-0" 7'-0"
2 x 6	12" 16" 24"	13'-0" 12'-0" 10'-6"
2 x 10	12" 16" 24"	16'-0" 15'-0" 12'-0"
2 x 12	12" 16" 24"	20'-0" 18'-0" 15'-0"
2 x 14	12" 16" 24"	23'-0" 21'-0" 17'-0"

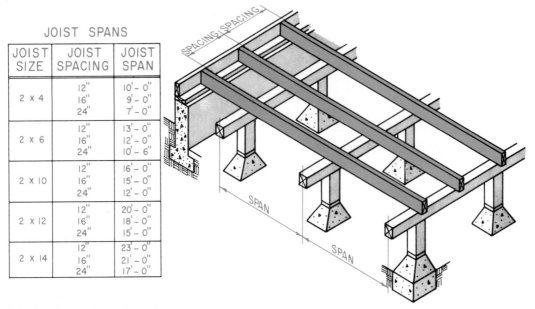

Fig 73-5 The size and spacing of joists are outlined in building codes.

Fig 73-6 Roof types, pitches, size of materials, and spacing of rafters and joists are determined by building codes.

RAFTER SPANS

SIZE	RAFTER SPACING	SPAN·ROOF PITCH LESS THAN 4:12	SPAN·ROOF PITCH MORE THAN 4:12
2 X 4	12" 16" 24" 32"	9'-0" 8'-0" 6'-6" 5'-6"	10'-0" 8'-6" 7'-0" 6'-0"
2 X 6	12" 16" 24" 32"	14'-0" 12'-6" 10'-6" 9'-0"	16'-0" 13'-6" 11'-0" 9'-6"
2 X 8	12" 16" 24" 32"	19'-0" 17'-0" 13'-6" 11'-6"	21'-0" 18'-6" 15'-0" 13'-0"
2 X 10	12" 16" 24" 32'	23'-0" 21'-0" 17'-6" 15'-0"	25'-0" 22'-6" 19'-0" 16'-6"

CEILING JOIST SPANS

SIZE	JOIST SPACING	SPAN
2 x 4	12" 16" 24"	10'-0" 9'-0" 8'-0"
2 x 6	12" 16" 24"	16'-0" 14'-6" 12'-6"
2 x 8	12" 16" 24"	21'-6" 19'-0" 17'-0"

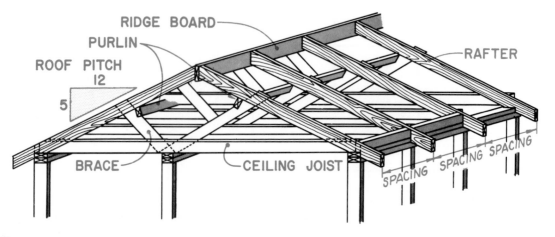

1 Determine the distance between the posts shown in Fig. 73-3, using the building code of your community.
2 Sketch the joists shown in Fig. 73-3. Dimension them according to the building code in your community.
3 Draw Fig. 73-2 and put in the T-foundation members according to the building laws of your community.
4 From study of your building code, what other parts of construction can be added to the list of building requirements in this unit?
5 Does your building code permit the use of prefabricated materials?
6 Define these architectural terms: *building code, building permit, cutaway view, legal description, zoning.*

UNIT 74
BUILDING LOADS

The weight of all the materials used in the construction of a building, including all permanent structures and fixtures, constitutes the *dead load* of a building. All movable items, such as the occupants and furniture, are the *live load.* The total weight of the live load plus that of the dead load is called the *building load.*

MAXIMUM ALLOWANCES

The maximum amount of load permissible for each kind of structure is always listed in the building code. The size of the various structural members to support the various loads is also included in the code.

When material-size regulations are compiled for the building codes, they are computed on the basis of maximum allowable loads. Engineers who are drawing up the code determine the correct size of construction members for carrying a maximum load. A safety factor is then added to size of the materials to eliminate any possibility of building failure.

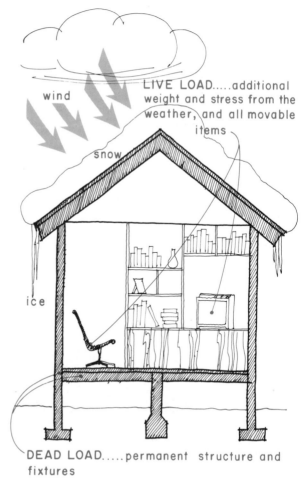

Fig 74-1 Building codes help ensure that the structure will resist and support all loads.

Structural sizes required by building codes not only provide for the support of all weight in a vertical direction but also allow for all possible horizontal loads, such as come from winds and earthquakes (Fig. 74-1).

LIVE LOADS

Live loads include the weight of any movable object on the floors, roofs, or ceilings. Live loads acting on floors include persons and furniture. Live loads acting on roofs include wind and snow loads. Live loads acting on walls are wind loads. Lateral loads from earthquakes may also be considered.

The horizontal load acting on exterior walls is considerably greater than the horizontal load acting on the interior walls, mainly due to wind (Fig. 74-2). Most exterior walls must be designed to withstand a load of 20 pounds per square foot (958 pascals), whereas interior walls need withstand a load of only 15 pounds per square foot (718 Pa). In the metric system, force is measured in pascals (Pa). Multiply pounds per square foot by 47.88 to obtain pascals approximately. The types of exterior-wall sheathing differ greatly in their ability to withstand horizontal loads. Figure 74-3 shows that horizontal sheathing will withstand only 1021 pounds per square foot (49 kPa). Diagonal sheathing will withstand 1907 pounds per square foot (91 kPa), and insulation-board sheathing will withstand up to 2179 pounds per square foot (104 kPa).

DEAD LOADS

A building must be designed to support its own weight (dead load). Building codes specify the size and type of materials that are used in foundations to support maximum live loads. The size and spacing and type of materials used in walls that support the roof load is also specified. Loads become greater as the distance from the footing diminishes. For example, the load on the attic shown in Fig. 74-4 is only 25 pounds per square foot (1197 Pa). The load on the first floor is 45 pounds per

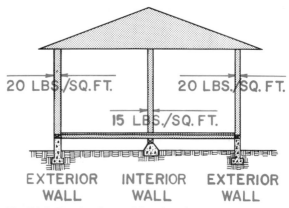

20 LBS./SQ.FT.　　20 LBS./SQ.FT.

15 LBS./SQ.FT.

EXTERIOR WALL　INTERIOR WALL　EXTERIOR WALL

Fig 74-2 The horizontal load acting on exterior walls is greater than the load acting on interior walls.

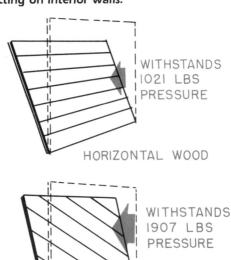

WITHSTANDS 1021 LBS PRESSURE

HORIZONTAL WOOD

WITHSTANDS 1907 LBS PRESSURE

DIAGONAL WOOD

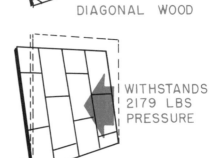

WITHSTANDS 2179 LBS PRESSURE

INSULATING SHEATHING

Fig 74-3 Ability of sheathing to resist horizontal loads in pressure (pounds per square inch).

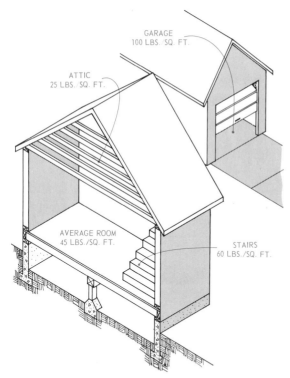

GARAGE
100 LBS. /SQ. FT.

ATTIC
25 LBS. /SQ. FT.

AVERAGE ROOM
45 LBS./SQ. FT.

STAIRS
60 LBS./SQ. FT.

Fig 74-4 Loads increase closer to the foundation.

square foot (2155 Pa). However, the typical floor load for an average room will vary from 30 to 40 pounds per square foot (1436 to 1915 Pa).

Roof loads are comparatively light, but vary according to the pitch of the roof. Flat roofs offer more resistance to loads than do pitch roofs. Low-pitched roofs—those below 3/12 pitch—must often be designed to support wind and snow loads of 20 pounds per square foot (958 Pa). High-pitched roofs—those over 3/12 pitch—need be designed to support only 15 pounds per square foot (718 Pa). Since these loads, especially snow loads, vary greatly from one part of the country to another, local building codes establish the amount of load a roof must be designed to support at any given pitch (Fig. 74-5).

12

3

3:12 PITCH OR UNDER   20 LBS./SQ. FT.

3:12 PITCH OR OVER   15 LBS./SQ. FT.

Fig 74-5 Roofs must be designed to support load limits established by local building codes.

PROBLEMS

1 List 20 items used in the construction of a home that are part of the dead load.
2 List 20 objects that are part of the live load.
3 Why is load specified in pounds per square foot?
4 Why is a low-pitched roof constructed to support more weight per square foot than a roof of steeper pitch?

5 A room has 600 square feet. How much load should it be designed to support?
6 An exterior wall is 8' high and 30' long and is sheathed with diagonal sheathing. How much vertical load will the entire wall support?
7 Define these terms: *maximum allowance, live loads, dead loads, building load, wind load, snow load.*

METHODS OF CHECKING

The appropriateness of the size and layout of a building should be completely checked by the architect, designer, builder, and occupant before a completed architectural plan is used for actual construction purposes. The technical authenticity of the drawing should first be checked by the drafter and/or by a checker. He or she should be certain that all dimensions and symbols are correct and that each detail drawing agrees with the basic plan.

People without technical training often find it difficult to interpret engineering and architectural drawings adequately. For this reason, it is sometimes advisable to construct an architectural model that represents the appearance of the finished building.

Another concept that is sometimes difficult for untrained people to grasp is the relationship of the size of rooms to the furniture and equipment that will actually be placed in these rooms. Checking the adequacy of room size can be done by placing templates of furniture, equipment, and even people on drawings of the rooms.

UNIT 75
ARCHITECTURAL MODELS

The use of an architectural model is the only way to actually see the finished design in three dimensions. A model is also the only representation of a building that can be viewed from any angle.

FUNCTION

Models may be used in planning cities or parts of city redevelopments. Models are often used to check the design of large commercial buildings, as shown in Fig. 75-1. They also

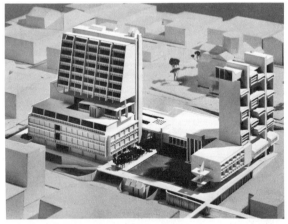

Fig 75-1 Models are often used to check the designs of commercial buildings.

Dap, Inc.

may be used to check the design of a residence (Fig. 75-2).

The appropriateness of size and layout can be seen better on a model than through

Fig 75-2 The use of a model to check the design of a home.

Fig 75-4 The use of a model to check structural qualities.

Steel Products News Bureau

any other device. The relationship to other objects, such as people, cars, trees, and other buildings, becomes more apparent when the structure is viewed in three-dimensional form. For these reasons, it is advisable to include within the overall model as many scale models of furniture, equipment, cars, and people as possible. Figure 75-3 shows a model with cutaway walls, revealing the relationship among furnishings, room size, and layout. It is sometimes advisable to prepare basic outline blocks representing adjacent build-

ings in order to compare their relative size and position with those of the building being designed. The model can also be used to design effectively or to check the color scheme of the entire house or of individual rooms since the entire house can be seen at a glance.

Some models are prepared to check only the structural qualities of the building. An example is the structural model of a convention-center exhibit hall shown in Fig. 75-4. When a structural model of this type is prepared, balsa wood strips are used to represent

Fig 75-3 Cutaway walls help show space relationships.

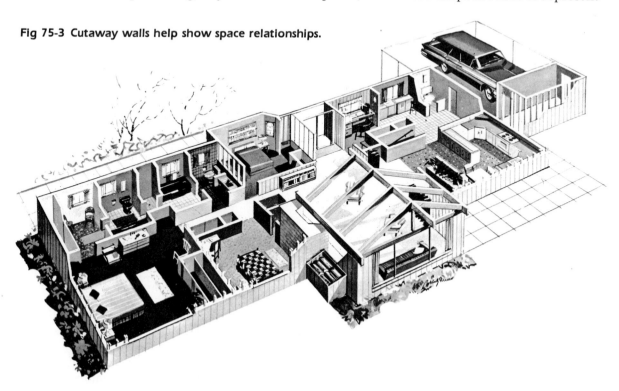

Table 75-1 MATERIALS USED ON ARCHITECTURAL MODELS

Part	Model materials	Methods of construction
WALLS	Soft wood; cardboard	Cut wall to exact dimensions of elevations. Allow for overlapping of joints at corners. Have wall thicknesses to scale.
ROOFS	Thin, stiff cardboard; paint-colored sand; sandpaper; wood pieces	Cut out roof patterns and assembly. For sand or gravel roof, paint with slow-drying enamel the color of roof. Sprinkle on sand. For shingle roof, cut sandpaper or thin wood pieces, and glue on as if laying shingle roof.
BRICK & STONE	Commercially printed paper	Glue paper in place; cut grooves in wood, and paint color of bricks or stones.
WOOD PANELING	Commercially printed paper; 1/32" veneer wood	Glue paper in place; with veneer wood, rule on black lines for strip effect, and glue in place. Mahogany veneer equals redwood.
STUCCO	Plaster of Paris	Mix and dab on with brush.
WINDOWS & DOORS	Preformed plastic; wood strips and clear plastic	Purchase ready-made windows to scale in model store; or frame openings with wood strips and glue in clear plastic for windows or wood panel for door.
FLOORS	Flocked carpet; commercially printed paper; 1/32" veneer wood	Paint area with slow-drying colored enamel, and apply flock, removing excess when dry. With paper, glue in place. With veneer, rule on black lines for strip effect, and glue in place.
FURNITURE	Cardboard, nails, flock, wood, clay	Fashion furniture to scale. Paint and flock to give effect of material.
SITE AREAS	Wood slab, wire screen, papier-mâché	Build up hilly areas with sticks and wire. Place papier-mâché over wire.
GRASS	Green enamel paint and flock	Paint grass area. Apply flock, removing excess when dry.
TREES & BUSHES	Sponge; lichen	Grind up sponges and paint different shades of green. Use small pieces for bushes. Glue small pieces to tree twigs for trees. Lichen may be purchased in model stores and used in the same manner as sponges.
AUTOS & PEOPLE	Toys and miniatures	If time permits, carve from soft wood.

sills, studs, rafters, and beams. These structural members are prepared to the exact scale of the model, and the balsa wood members are attached together with modelmakers' glue or with small pins, to approximate the methods used in nailing the full-sized house. Precut model lumber is often used.

MODEL CONSTRUCTION

Since the materials used in full-size buildings are too large for model construction, they must be simulated by other materials and other products. For example, coarse sandpaper may be used to simulate a built-up

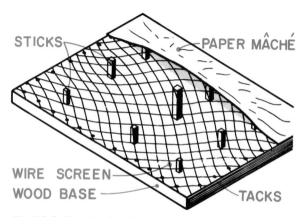

Fig 75-5 Developing the contour of a lot.

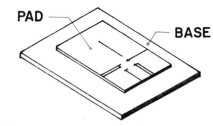

Fig 75-6 A pad attached to a base.

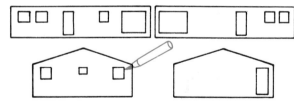

Fig 75-7 Cutouts of exterior walls.

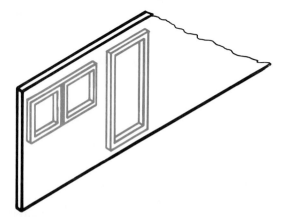

Fig 75-8 Small strips of wood or paper can represent framing and trim around windows and doors.

gravel roof. Sponges may be used to simulate trees, and green flocking may be used for grass. In addition to such substitute materials, a great variety of commercially prepared model materials is now available. Table 75-1 shows some of the special materials used to make various parts of architectural models.

Methods of constructing models vary greatly, just as methods of constructing full-sized structures vary, according to the building materials used. Nevertheless, the following procedures represent the normal sequence of constructing models, even though some of the techniques may vary with the use of different materials.

1 A floor plan and elevation outline should be prepared to the size to which the model will be built. Small structures such as houses can be built conveniently at the scale $\frac{1}{2}'' = 1'—0''$. Larger structures such as commercial office buildings should be built to the scale $\frac{1}{4}'' = 1'—0''$ or even smaller.

2 The contour of the lot should be developed, as shown in Fig. 75-5.

3 Glue or trace the floor-plan outline on a $\frac{1}{4}''$ (6-mm) thick pad, and tack or glue this pad to a base, as shown in Fig. 75-6.

4 Cut exterior walls from balsa wood or heavy cardboard. Carefully cut out the openings for windows and doors with a razor blade, as shown in Fig. 75-7. When cutting side walls, cut them long to allow overlapping of the front and back walls.

5 Glue small strips of wood or paper around the windows to represent framing and trim, as shown in Fig. 75-8. Glue clear plastic inside the window openings to represent window glass and cover the joint with trim. Cut out doors and hang them on the door openings, using transparent tape, as shown in Fig. 75-9. Add siding materials to the exterior of the wall panels to simulate the materials that will be used on the house, as shown in Fig. 75-10.

6 Glue the exterior walls to the pad and to each other at the corners (Fig. 75-11).

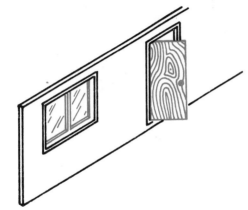

Fig 75-9 Doors can be hung with transparent tape.

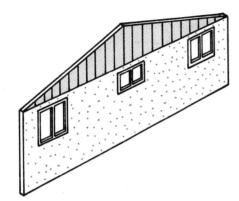

Fig 75-10 Siding materials are added to the exterior panels.

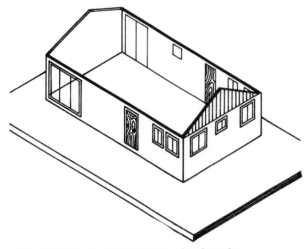

Fig 75-11 Exterior walls are glued to the pad.

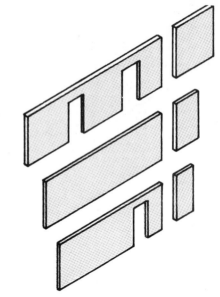

Fig 75-12 Openings in interior walls are cut out.

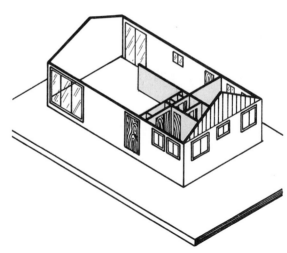

Fig 75-13 Interior walls are glued to exterior walls and to the pad.

7 Cut out openings in interior walls for doors, arches, and fireplaces, as shown in Fig. 75-12.

8 Glue interior walls to the partition lines of the floor plan (Fig. 75-13).

9 Add interior fixtures such as built-in cabinets, kitchen equipment, bathroom fixtures. Paint the interior surfaces to determine the color scheme and add furniture if desired (Fig. 75-14).

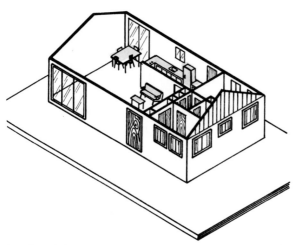

Fig 75-14 Furniture, fixtures, and color schemes are added.

Fig 75-15 Roof sections are joined and braced.

10 Cut out roof parts, join roof parts together, and brace them so that the roof will lift off. Add material to simulate the roof treatment on the exterior of the roof (Fig. 75-15).

11 Add landscaping features such as trees, shrubs, grass, patios, walkways, and outdoor furniture to add to the authentic appearance of the model.

PROBLEMS

1 Construct a model similar to the one shown in Fig. 75-14.
2 Construct a model of your own home. Make any design adjustments you would recommend in the basic plan.
3 Construct a model of the home you have designed.
4 Construct a model of the house shown in Fig. 8-4.
5 Define these terms: *scale model, structural model, balsa wood, flocking.*

UNIT 76
TEMPLATE CHECKING

Room sizes often appear adequate on the floor plan, but when furniture is placed in the rooms, the occupants may find them too small or proportioned incorrectly. After the house is built, it is too late to change the sizes of most rooms. Therefore, extreme care should be taken in the planning stage to ensure that the plan as designed will accommodate the furniture, fixtures, and traffic anticipated for each area.

TEMPLATE PREPARATION

One method of determining the adequacy of room sizes and proportions is to prepare templates of each piece of furniture and equipment that will be placed in the room.

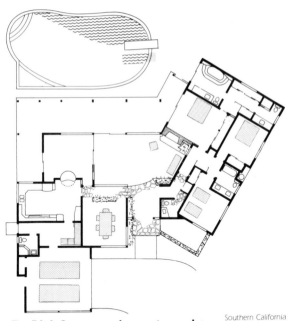

Fig 76-1 Space requirements can be determined by placing furniture templates on the floor plans.

Southern California Gas Co.

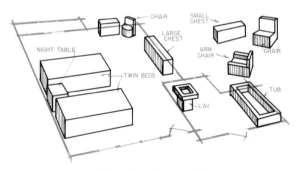

NIGHT TABLE
CHAIR
SMALL CHEST
LARGE CHEST
ARM CHAIR
CHAIR
TWIN BEDS
LAV
TUB

Fig 76-2 Three-dimensional templates.

These templates have the same scale as the floor plan. Placing the templates on the floor plan will show graphically how much floor space is occupied by each piece of furniture. The home planner can determine whether there is sufficient traffic space around the furniture, whether the room must be enlarged, whether the proportions should be changed, or whether, as a last resort, smaller items of furniture should be obtained.

The placement of the templates on the plan in Fig. 76-1 indicates that some rearrangement or adjustment should be made in the furniture placement in bedroom No. 3,

and that the dining room might be inadequate if the table is expanded.

Checking by templates can be significant only if the templates are carefully prepared to the same scale as the floor plan and if the actual furniture dimensions are used in the preparation of the templates. The floor-plan design can be checked much more quickly by the template method than it can by a model. Furthermore, if templates are used while the plan is still in the sketching stage, adjustments can be made easily and rooms rearranged to produce a more desirable plan.

THREE-DIMENSIONAL TEMPLATES

The template method of checking room sizes does not reveal the three-dimensional aspect of space planning as a model does. One compromise between the model method and the template method of checking drawings is the preparation of three-dimensional templates. Three-dimensional templates not only have width and length but also height, as shown in Fig. 76-2. This method of checking is essentially the same as placing furniture on a model, except that the walls do not exist and adjustments can be made much more easily. Figure 76-3 shows the height of typical pieces of furniture for use in preparing three-dimensional templates. These dimensions are typical and may vary slightly with different manufacturers.

TRAFFIC PATTERNS

A well-designed structure must provide for efficient and smooth circulation of traffic. Traffic patterns must be controlled, and yet sufficient space must be allowed for adequate passage and flexibility in the traffic pattern. Rooms should not be used as hallways or access areas to other rooms. Any room should be accessible from the front entrance or the service entrance without the necessity of passing through other rooms. The length of halls should be minimized because halls provide only traffic access and do not contribute livable space.

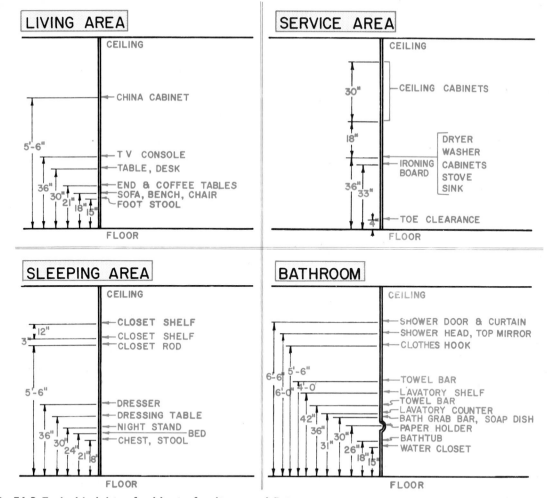

Fig 76-3 Typical heights of cabinets, furniture, and fixtures.

One method of checking the traffic pattern is to use a scale drawing and trace, with a pencil, the movements of your daily routine,

Fig 76-4 Checking traffic patterns.

as shown in Fig. 76-4. If you prepare a template of a person (an overhead view of yourself with arms outstretched), you will be able to determine the effectiveness of the traffic pattern as it relates to the size of each room and the layout of the entire plan. Table 76-1 is a checklist of traffic-pattern adequacies.

TECHNICAL CHECKING

The drafter should always check dimensions, labels, and symbols before the drawing is removed from the board. A more formal check of these factors should be made on a print prepared for checking purposes, called a check print. After the drafter has made this check, another drafter, architect, or checker

Table 76-1 A CHECKLIST FOR TRAFFIC PATTERNS

	Excellent	Fair	Poor	Distance		Excellent	Fair	Poor	Distance
SERVICE CIRCULATION					**GUEST'S CIRCULATION**				
Service door to kitchen	x			5'	Front door to closet	x		.	3'
Service door to living area	x			12'	Front door to living room	x			10'
Service door to bathroom			x	30'	Front door to bathroom	x			16'
Service door to bedrooms			x	36'	Front door to outdoor living			x	33'
Kitchen to bathrooms		x		14'	Living room to bathroom	x			8'
Paths around work triangle			x	24'					

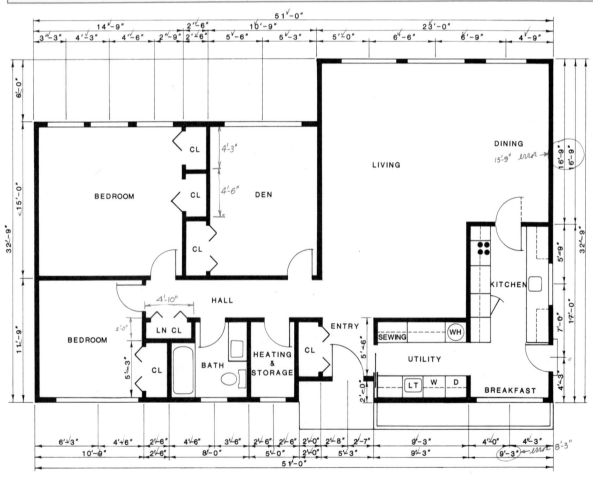

Fig 76-5 Checking architectural drawings by using a colored pencil.

	Excellent	Fair	Poor	Distance
OCCUPANTS' CIRCULATION				
Front door to kitchen	x			6'
Kitchen to bedrooms		x		15' to 35'
Kitchen to children's play area		x		15'
Kitchen to children's sleeping area		x		17'
Bedrooms to bathrooms	x			4' to 10'
Outdoor living area to bathroom			x	25'
Living room to outdoor living area	x			3'

should also scrutinize the drawing for dimensional accuracy, proper labeling, and correctness of symbols.

One of the most effective methods of checking architectural drawings is the use of a colored pencil, as shown in Fig. 76-5. A checker draws a line through each dimension, label, and symbol as it is checked. Otherwise, the result is rechecking the same dimensions and missing many others. Many architectural offices use a color-coding system to indicate the checker's reaction to the drawing. In one system, a yellow pencil is used for checking items that are correct, a red pencil for checking errors, and a blue pencil for marking recommended changes.

Regardless of the checking method used, one of the most important items to check on architectural drawings is the correctness of dimensions. Dimensioning errors cause more difficulty on the construction job than any other single factor related to architectural drawings. Dimensions must be added to ensure that they total the overall dimension. Interior dimensions must be added to ensure that their total agrees with the exterior dimensions.

PLAN AGREEMENT

An important relationship that must be very carefully checked on architectural drawings is the agreement of plans with each other. The design and dimensions of the floor plan must be compared with the design and dimensions of the elevation. The floor plan must also be compared with the foundation to ensure complete alignment on the perimeter, over the beams, and through the chimney. The foundation plan must also be compared with the elevation. Sectional drawings and all detail must be compared with the floor-plan and elevation drawing to which they relate. It is, therefore, mandatory that a complete system of checking be established and carefully followed in the preparation of all architectural plans.

PROBLEMS

1 Prepare a set of furniture templates. Sketch the floor plan of your own home and check its adequacy with these templates.

2 Use the templates you have prepared to check the floor plan of your own design.

3 Check the traffic pattern of the plan shown in Fig. 10-11. What recommendations would you make to improve the traffic pattern?

4 Sketch the plan shown in Fig. 14-5 and determine the adequacy of room sizes by the use of templates.

5 Define these architectural terms: *template, two-dimensional template, three-dimensional template, traffic pattern, checker, check print.*

UNIT 77
ARCHITECTURAL CHECKLISTS

The number and type of architectural drawings prepared for any structure depend on the amount of control the designer demands. The more control the designer wants, the more drawings must be prepared. For example, if a designer prepares only a floor plan, the contractor is allowed to specify and build the exterior of the structure. Thus, the amount and type of drawings determine the degree of control the designer achieves. For maximum control, a complete set of architectural plans should include the following drawings and schedules:

Preliminary sketches
Presentation drawing
Specifications
Plot plan
Landscape plan
Floor plan
Foundation and basement plan
Exterior elevations
Interior elevations
Electrical plan
Plumbing plan
Floor framing plan
Roof framing plan
Heating and air-conditioning plan
Wall details
Stair details
Cabinet details
Window schedule
Door schedule

Architectural drawings are prepared for a variety of purposes. They show dimensions of a lot, types of siding material, sizes and shapes of the floor plan, types and styles of exteriors, and so forth. Because each drawing must agree with all other drawings in a set, the designer must be sure that each drawing includes all the information for which it was intended. Checklists serve this purpose. The following checklists are for the most essential plan. A complete set of checklists will be found in the Teacher's Manual to accompany *Architecture: Drafting and Design*, Fourth Edition.

FLOOR PLAN

Rooms and sizes
Overall dimensions
Location dimensions of all structural members
Closets
Storage
Partition thicknesses
Windows
Doors
Ceiling joists—size, spacing, direction
Lintels
Beams
Fireplace and hearth
Patios
Walks
Landings
Garage
Garage drainage
Stairs—number, size, direction
Major appliances
Major fixtures
Heating and air-conditioning unit
Hose bib
Window and door callout symbols
Arches and openings
Balconies
Decks
Attic
Additional floors
Medicine cabinets
Built-ins

Compass orientation
Square footage
Clipped ceilings
Scuttle
Title block:
    Title of drawings
    Scale
    Owner's name
    Firm's name and address
    Architect's name
    Drafter's name
    House number and street
    Sheet number

EXTERIOR ELEVATIONS

Title block (see floor plan)
Elevation for each side of house
Foundation outline
Overall dimensions
Dimension floor line to ceiling
Dimension floor line to top of windows
    and doors
Dimension finish grade to floor line
Dimension eave to ridge
Dimension ridge to chimney top
Window-opening symbols
Grade line
Vents
Access areas
Finish materials for roof
Finish materials for walls
Stairs
Porches
Balconies
Decks
Drawing callouts
Exterior trim
Exterior lights
Gutters
Downspouts
Fascia
Flashing
Roof pitch
Hose bibs
Chimney

PLOT PLAN

Property lines
Building lines—setback

House and all structures
Overall dimensions
Setback dimensions
Roof overhang
Patios
Walks
Driveway
Fences
Pools
Public utilities—gas, water, sewer, elec-
    tricity, telephone
Curb line
Street center, name, elevation
House elevation
Elevations of walks and driveway
Tree elevations
Contour lines
Property-line compass orientation
North arrow
Land cuts
Landscape
Drainage
Retaining walls
Datum reference
Radius of curves
Outdoor living area

INTERIOR ELEVATIONS

Title block (see floor plan)
Elevations of selected rooms
Overall dimensions
Location dimensions
Elevation callouts
Windows
Doors
Cabinets
Shelves
Drawers
Stairs
Cabinet sections
Furred-out ceilings
Closets—rods and shelves
Built-ins
Mirrors
Major appliances
Fireplace
Finish materials
Lights

COST ANALYSIS

Architects would welcome the opportunity to design a structure free from financial limitations. Such a condition, however, rarely exists. Budgets are the necessary framework within which architects must design most buildings, ranging from the smallest residence to the largest office building.

There is, of course, more flexibility in some budgets than in others, but in every design problem the designer must strive to create a design that will provide optimum facilities and keep within the budget.

UNIT 78
BUILDING COSTS

Approximately 40 percent of the cost of the average home is for materials. Labor costs account for another 40 percent. The remaining 20 percent is taken up by the price of the lot. As labor, material costs, and land values rise, the cost of homes increases proportionately.

TOTAL COST

Many factors influence the total cost of the house. The location of the site is extremely important. An identical house built on an identical lot can vary several thousand dollars in cost, depending on whether it is located in a city, in a suburb, or in the country. Labor costs also vary greatly from one part of the country to another and from urban to rural areas. Normally, labor costs are lower in rural areas. The third important variable contributing to the difference in housing costs is the cost of materials. Material costs vary greatly,

depending upon whether materials native to the region are used for the structure. In some areas, brick is a relatively inexpensive building material. In other parts of the country, a brick home may be one of the most expensive. Climate also has some effect on the cost of building. In moderate climates, many costs can be eliminated by excluding heating plants and frost-deep foundations. In other climates, air conditioning is mandatory.

ESTIMATING COSTS

MAJOR-PROJECT ESTIMATING
Major construction projects are usually subject to a bidding system. Architects and contractors estimate how much they would charge to design or erect a building. That estimate must be based upon estimates of their costs in designing or constructing the building.

The owner of the proposed building may select an architect through referral or design competition or by reputation and/or past experience.

When the time comes for contractors to bid on public construction, they too find out about projects from advertisements in trade journals, or they may subscribe to Dodge Reports. (General contractors for private construction are invited directly to bid on the project.) Dodge Reports inform contractors when the kinds of jobs they are interested in are first conceived, who the owner is, when an architect is selected, who the architect is, who the general contractors bidding on the job are, and where and when the plans will be available. The Dodge Report also tells a contractor what kind of job it will be, where the building will be constructed, and how much it will cost. Each time a project moves to the next construction stage, another Dodge Report (Fig. 78-1) is issued.

A subcontractor must be able to see the plans and specifications of the building in order to estimate the cost of construction. These plans may be available from the architect in the form of blueprints, or the subcontractor may subscribe to the Dodge/SCAN microfilm system. With this system, bidding documents are reproduced on microfilm and mailed to subscribers. The subcontractor receiving the microfilm uses a patented SCAN viewing table (Fig. 78-2) to project the plans back to original size and accurate scale. From the accurate original sizes, contractors can make their estimates for the construction project. The SCAN system saves time and expense of travel and cuts costs of reproducing and distributing the blueprints and other bidding documents on a project.

RESIDENTIAL ESTIMATING

There are two basic methods of determining the cost of a house. One is adding the total cost of all the materials to the hourly rate for labor multiplied by the anticipated number of hours it will take to build the home. The cost of the lot, landscaping, and various architects' and surveyors' fees must also be added to this figure. This process requires much computation and adequate techniques for estimating construction costs.

Two quicker, rule-of-thumb methods for estimating the cost of the house are the square-foot method and the cubic-foot method. These methods are not as accurate as

```
Dodge     MN 592 874 4          0-A              PLAN
Reports                                          2-10-xx,
Dodge     OFFICE BLDG $400,000
Reports   GOSHEN IA (SALMON CO) N ORBACH RD
          SCHEMATIC DWGS BEGINNING-DESIGN DEV TO START
Dodge        1 MO-WKG DWGS BEGIN 3 MOS-COULD ADVANCE FOR
Reports         FIGURING IN 8 MOS
          OWNER-JAYSON REALTY CO RAYMOND WILSON (VP)
Dodge        11 COUNTRY VIEW LANE GOSHEN IA 56841
Reports      (619/923-8111)
          ARCH-THE MAJOR DESIGN GROUP-THE OFFICE GREEN
Dodge        DUCHARME PARK DUBUQUE IA 52001 (619/741-1881)
Reports      BRK EXT-2 STYS-PT BSMT-13,000 SQ FT
Dodge
```

McGraw-Hill Information Systems Co.

Fig 78-1 An example of a Dodge Report.

itemizing the cost of all materials, labor, and other items. However, they do provide a quick estimate for speculative purposes.

SQUARE-FOOT METHOD In general, the cost of the average home ranges from $20 to $30 per square foot of floor space, depending on the geographical location (Fig. 78-3). Each local office of the Federal Housing Administration can supply current estimating information peculiar to the locale.

CUBIC-FOOT METHOD The cubic-foot method of estimating is slightly more accurate than the square-foot method and is more appropriate for multiple-story dwellings (Fig. 78-4).

METRIC MEASUREMENTS If you have been using metric measurements, a cost estimate would be figured using square meters or

Fig 78-2 Using Dodge/SCAN microfilm to estimate building costs.

McGraw-Hill Information Systems Co.

559

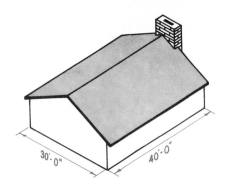

CONSTRUCTION COST: $30 PER SQ FT
SQUARE FOOTAGE: 30' x 40' = 1200 SQ FT
COST: 1200 x $30 = $36 000

Fig 78-3 The square-foot method of determining costs.

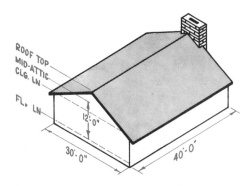

CONSTRUCTION COST: $2.50 PER CU FT
CUBIC VOLUME = FLOOR AREA x HEIGHT
CUBIC VOLUME: 1200 x 12 = 14 400 CU FT
TOTAL COST: CUBIC VOLUME x COST PER CU FT
TOTAL COST: 14 400 x $2.50 = $36 000

Fig 78-4 The cubic-foot method of determining costs.

Table 78-1 A METHOD OF DETERMINING THE COST OF A COMMERCIAL BUILDING BY COMPUTING THE COST OF BUILDING MATERIALS		
Principal items	**Cost**	**Percentage of total cost**
Excavation and site improvements	$ 65,524	4.45%
Foundations	107,101	7.28
Structural frame	140,080	9.52
Cement finish	80,018	5.44
Exterior masonry	96,776	6.58
Interior partitions	71,956	4.89
Carpentry and millwork	71,184	4.84
Sash and glazing	70,213	4.77
Roofing	36,374	2.47
Insulation	33,562	2.28
Waterproofing and dampproofing	1,700	0.12
Metal lath, furring, and plastering	52,424	3.56
Hollow metal work ...	16,730	1.14
Miscellaneous iron and ornamental metal .	27,955	1.90
Tile, terrazzo, and marble	22,068	1.50
Floor covering	15,284	1.04
Painting	25,154	1.71
Finish hardware	22,825	1.55
Acoustical ceiling	53,040	3.60
Plumbing	109,335	7.43
Heating, ventilating, and air conditioning ..	220,585	14.99
Electrical work and light fixtures	131,560	8.94
Total	$1,471,448	100%

Engineering News-Record

cubic meters. The cost for the average home would be between $215 and $322 per square meter. If conversion from square feet to square meters is desired, multiply square feet by 0.0929 for an approximate answer.

Using a cubic-meter method of estimating costs, the average home would cost between $58.66 and $88.34 per cubic meter. If conversion from cubic feet to cubic meters is desired, multiply cubic feet by 0.0283 for an approximate answer.

BUILDING-MATERIALS METHOD The square-foot and cubic-foot methods are at best rough estimates. The final cost of a building will depend upon the quality of building materials used. Table 78-1 shows the percentage of total cost of each material in a typical building. A 2000-square-foot home constructed with inexpensive materials may vary in cost several thousand dollars from a 2000-square-foot home constructed with more expensive materials.

Table 78-2 COST OF LANDSCAPING	
Fine grading . . . . $	.10 per sq. ft.
Site cleanup	20.00 per hour
Medium trees	
15 gal. container	75.00
20″ box container	150.00
Small trees and shrubs	
5 gal. container	25.00
1 gal. container	6.00
1 qt. container	2.00
Redwood header boards	1.20 per lineal ft.
Boulders—24″ to 36″	40.00 each
Crushed rock	.40 per sq. ft.
Ground cover	
Ivy	.20 per sq. ft.
Ice plant	.24 per sq. ft.
Strawberry	.24 per sq. ft.
Lawns	
Top quality	.35 per sq. ft.
Medium	.25 per sq. ft.
Inexpensive	.20 per sq. ft.

LOTS The cost of the lot and landscaping must be added to the total cost of the materials.

Table 78-3 CLOSING COSTS FOR A $55,000 HOME	
Loan charges	$300
(Mortgage service charge) (Loan origination fee) (Points on loan)	
Notary fee	4
Recording deed	10
Title search	200
Title insurance	450
Household insurance	75
Appraisal fee	100
Credit report	60
Federal revenue stamps	40
State revenue stamps	30
Conveyancing fee	50
Lawyer's fee	400
Survey	300
Total	$2,019

The cost of residential lots in the United States varies considerably, as does the cost of landscaping a typical residence (Table 78-2). Other costs in addition to the cost of the home must also be considered. These include service charges, title search, insurance costs, and transfer taxes. These are called *closing costs*. Table 78-3 shows a breakdown of typical closing costs.

The lawyer's, architect's, and surveyor's fees are sometimes included in the closing costs. Lawyers' fees range between $150 and $400, and surveys cost between $100 and $200. Architects usually work on a 7 percent commission basis. If they supervise construction in addition to doing the designing, they get 10 percent.

CUTTING COSTS

Some construction methods and material utilization that may greatly affect the ultimate cost of the home are listed as follows:

1 Square or rectangular homes are less expensive to build than irregular-shaped homes.
2 It is less expensive to build on a flat lot than on a sloping or hillside lot.
3 Using locally manufactured or produced materials cuts costs greatly.
4 Using stock materials and stock sizes of components takes advantage of mass-production cost reductions.
5 Using materials that can be quickly installed cuts labor costs. Prefabricating large sections or panels eliminates much time on the site.
6 Using prefinished materials saves labor costs.
7 Using prehung doors cuts considerable time from the finishing process.
8 Designing the home with a minimum amount of hall space increases the usable square footage and provides more living space for the cost.
9 Using prefabricated fireboxes for fireplaces cuts installation costs.
10 Investigating existing building codes be-

fore beginning construction eliminates unnecessary changes as construction proceeds.

11 Refraining from changing the design or any aspect of the plans after construction begins reduces costs.

12 Minimizing special jobs or custom-built items keeps costs from increasing.

13 Designing the house for short plumbing lines saves on materials.

14 Proper insulation saves heating and cooling costs.

UNIT 79
FINANCIAL PLANNING

Few people can accumulate sufficient funds to pay for the entire cost of the home at one time. Therefore, most home buyers pay a percentage—10, 20, 30 or more percent—at the time of purchase, and arrange a loan (*mortgage*) for the balance.

MORTGAGE

A mortgage is obtained from a mortgage company, bank, savings and loan association, or insurance company. The lending institution pays for the house, and through the mortgage loan agreement collects this amount from the home buyer over a long period of time: 10, 20, or even 30 years.

INTEREST

In addition to paying back the lending institution the exact cost of the house, the homeowner must also pay for the services of the institution. Payment is in the form of a percentage of the total cost of the home and is known as *interest*. Normal interest rates range from 11 to 17 percent. Rates of 13 and 15 percent, however, are most common. The interest payments increase with the length of time needed to pay back the loan. On a long-term loan—for example, 30 years—the monthly payments will be smaller but the overall cost will be much greater because the total interest is higher. A long-term loan can, over the life of the loan, accumulate 200 percent interest.

A comparison of the time factor, amount of payment, and number of payments on a

Table 79-1 PAYMENTS ON A $30,000 MORTGAGE AT 13 PERCENT INTEREST

Time in years	Monthly payments	Number of payments	Total cost
10	$447.94	120	$ 53,752.80
15	379.58	180	68,324.40
20	351.48	240	84,355.20
25	338.36	300	101,508.00
30	331.86	360	119,469.60

Table 79-2 PAYMENTS ON A $50,000 MORTGAGE AT 13 PERCENT INTEREST

Time in years	Monthly payments	Number of payments	Total cost
10	$746.56	120	$ 89,587.20
15	632.63	180	113,873.40
20	585.79	240	140,589.60
25	563.92	300	169,179.00
30	553.10	360	199,116.00

Table 79-3 PAYMENTS ON AN $80,000 MORTGAGE AT 13 PERCENT INTEREST

Time in years	Monthly payments	Number of payments	Total cost
10	$1,194.49	120	$143,338.80
15	1,012.20	180	182,196.00
20	937.27	240	224,944.80
25	902.27	300	270,681.00
30	884.96	360	318,585.60

$30,000 loan at 13 percent interest is shown in Table 79-1. Table 79-2 shows similar information for a $50,000 loan, and Table 79-3 shows the same information for an $80,000 loan.

TAXES

In addition to the *principal* (amount paid back that is credited to the payment for the house) and the interest, the taxes on the house must be added to the total cost of the home. Taxes on residential property vary greatly.

Table 79-4 INSURANCE RATES PER THREE-YEAR PERIOD

Type of insurance	$20,000 home	$50,000 home
MINIMUM COVERAGE		
FIRE	$200	$315
PUBLIC LIABILITY		
AVERAGE COVERAGE		
FIRE		
PUBLIC LIABILITY	$235	$350
PROPERTY DAMAGE		
THEFT		
MAXIMUM COVERAGE		
FIRE		
PUBLIC LIABILITY		
PROPERTY DAMAGE		
THEFT		
MEDICAL		
PERSONAL LIABILITY	$350	$450
LANDSCAPE INSURANCE		
WIND		
FLOOD		
EARTHQUAKE		

Taxes on a $50,000 home in many residential suburban communities range between $1000 and $2000 per year.

INSURANCE

The purchase of a home is a large investment and must be insured for the protection of the home buyer and for the protection of the lending institution. Insurance rates vary greatly, depending on the cost of the home, location, type of construction, and availability of fire-fighting equipment (Table 79-4). The home should be insured against fire, public liability, property damage, vandalism, natural destruction, and accidents to trespassers and workers.

BUDGETS

Since most household budgets are established on a monthly basis, the monthly payments needed to purchase and maintain a res-

Table 79-5 PRINCIPAL, INTEREST, TAXES, AND INSURANCE COSTS FOR A $50,000 LOAN AT 13 PERCENT INTEREST

10-year loan-$50,000 amortization-$746.56

Payment breakdown	First payment	5th-year payment	Last payment
Principal	$204.91	$386.94	$738.61
Interest	541.65	359.62	7.95
Taxes (varies)	200.00	200.00	200.00
Insurance (varies)	50.00	50.00	50.00
Total Monthly Payments	$996.56	$996.56	$996.56

Note: Total interest for 10 years is $39,582.87

20-year loan-$50,000 amortization-$585.79

Payment breakdown	First payment	10th-year payment	Last payment
Principal	$ 44.14	$159.10	$579.71
Interest	541.65	426.69	6.08
Taxes (varies)	200.00	200.00	200.00
Insurance (varies)	50.00	50.00	50.00
Total Monthly Payments	$835.79	$835.79	$835.79

Note: Total interest for 20 years is $90,571.20

30-year loan-$50,000 amortization-$553.10

Payment breakdown	First payment	15th-year payment	Last payment
Principal	$ 11.45	$ 78.78	$547.91
Interest	541.65	474.32	5.19
Taxes (varies)	200.00	200.00	200.00
Insurance (varies)	50.00	50.00	50.00
Total Monthly Payments	$803.10	$803.10	$803.10

Note: Total interest for 30 years is $149,047.31

idence are more significant than the total cost of the home. Monthly payments are broken into four categories: principal, interest, taxes, and insurance (PITI). Table 79-5 shows the amortization for a 10-year, 20-year, and 30-year loan.

The prospective home buyer and builder should consider the following factors before selecting a particular institution for a mortgage. He or she should know the interest rate, the number of years needed to repay, prepayment penalties, total amount of monthly payment, conditions of approval, placement fees, amount of down payment required, service fees, and closing fees. Typical closing costs on a home would include lawyers' fees, transfer taxes, escrow deposit, insurance, and survey fees.

SALARY AND HOME COSTS

If the home buyer considers the purchase or the building of a home as an investment, he or she should take steps to ensure the maximum return on investment. If the home buyer purchases a home that costs considerably less than he or she can afford, the buyer is not investing adequately. On the other hand, if the home buyer attempts to buy a home that is more expensive than he or she can afford, the payments will become a drain on the family budget and undue sacrifices will have to be made to compensate.

Family budgets vary greatly, and a house that may be a burden for one person to purchase may be quite suitable for another, even if the two owners are earning the same relative salary. In general, the cost of the house should not exceed two and one-half times the annual income.

PROBLEMS

1 What is the cost of the home you could afford if you were earning $10,000 a year? $20,000 a year? $30,000 a year?

2 You purchase a home valued at $40,000 and make a 10 percent down payment. Your interest rate is 9 percent. What amount of interest will you pay over the life of a 25-year mortgage?

3 What will be your total monthly payment on an $38,000 home if you have made a 10 percent down payment and are paying an interest rate of 10 percent? Your yearly taxes are $1000, and your insurance is $150.

4 What will your monthly mortgage payment be if you buy the house shown in Fig. 79-1 for $20 per square foot? Your interest is 9 percent for 25 years. You make a down payment of 9 percent of the total price. Your closing costs total $1000.

5 Define these terms: *interest, principal, escrow, mortgage, closing costs, taxes, insurance.*

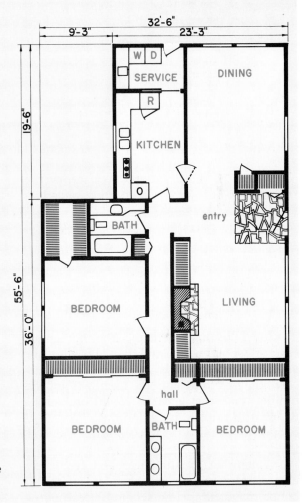

Fig 79-1 Compute the monthly mortgage payments for this house.

LEGAL DOCUMENTS

In Unit 78, "Building Costs," you learned that contractors must bid on construction projects in order to build them. This unit will give you a sample of the legal documents that make up those bids.

DEFINITION

Legal documents define the agreement reached between the architect, builder, and owner of the building. This agreement indicates the fees to be paid the architect and the builder and the general conditions under which the project is undertaken. The legal document usually takes the form of a contract.

A contract includes fees and fee schedules, performance bond, labor and materials bonds, payments, time schedules, estimates, general conditions, and supplementary conditions. Schedules, specifications, and working drawings are also attached to the contracts so that they become legal documents too. Contracts describe the responsibilities for any financial changes that may be affected by time schedules or unavoidable delays caused by such things as acts of God and strikes.

A *performance bond* is offered by the contractor and guarantees that the performance of responsibilities as builder will be in accordance with the conditions of the contract.

Labor and materials bonds posted by the contractor guarantee that invoices for materials, supplies, and services of subcontractors will be paid by the prime contractor according to the terms of the contract.

Payment schedules are an important part of any contract. Payments are directly related to completion of various phases of the work, such as acceptance of the bid, beginning of the work, completion of phases of construction, and approval by the building inspector.

Licensed subcontractors such as electricians and plumbers are specified and required on most construction jobs. Indications of licensing requirements are usually included in the construction contract.

An architect's seal is placed on all sets of plans indicating that they are complete and official.

CONTRACT BIDS

Contractors receive invitations to bid by mail, through newspaper advertisements, or through private resources such as McGraw-Hill Dodge reports. Construction bid forms are very specific in indicating the availability of documents, and when the documents can be examined. They also provide for the resolution of questions, approval for submission of materials, specific dates for bids submission, and the form for preparing bids. The bid form includes specific instructions to the bidders, the price of the bid, substitutions, restrictions, and the involvement of subcontractors.

The bid form is a letter that is sent from the bidder to the owner or architect. The letter covers the following points: verification of receipt of all drawings and documents, specific length of time the bid will be held open, price quotation for the bid, and a listing of substitute materials or components if any item varies from specified requirements. When the bidder signs this bid form, he or she agrees to abide by all conditions of the bid, including the price, time, quality of work, materials as specified in the contract documents, and drawings.

Sample instructions to the bidder, outlined by the Construction Specification Institute, are as follows:

DOCUMENTS Bona fide prime bidders may obtain __3__ sets of drawings and specifications from the architect upon deposit of $__100__ per set. Those who submit prime bids may obtain refund of deposits by returning sets in good condition no more than __10__ days after bids have been opened. Those who do not submit prime bids will forfeit deposits unless sets are returned in good condition at least __2__ days before bids are opened. No partial sets will be issued; no sets will be issued to sub-bidders by the architect. Prime bidders may obtain additional copies upon deposit of $__50__ per set.

EXAMINATION Bidders shall carefully examine the documents and the construction site to obtain firsthand knowledge of existing conditions. Contractors will not be given extra payments for conditions that can be determined by examining the site and documents.

QUESTIONS Submit all questions about the drawings and specifications to the architect, in writing. Replies will be issued to all prime bidders of record as addenda to the drawings and specifications and will become part of the contract. The architect and owner will not be responsible for oral clarification. Questions received less than __4__ hours before the bid opening cannot be answered.

SUBSTITUTIONS To obtain approval to use unspecified products, bidders shall submit written requests at least 10 days before the bid date and hour. Requests received after this time will not be considered. Requests shall clearly describe the product for which approval is asked, including all data necessary to demonstrate acceptability. If the product is acceptable, the architect will approve it in an addendum issued to all prime bidders on record.

BASIS OF BID The bidder must include all unit cost items and all alternatives shown on the bid forms; failure to comply may be cause for rejection. No segregated bids or assignments will be considered.

PREPARATION OF BIDS Bids shall be made on unaltered bid forms furnished by the architect. Fill in all blank spaces and submit two copies. Bids shall be signed with name typed below signature. Where bidder is a corporation, bids must be signed with the legal name of the corporation followed by the name of the state of incorporation and legal signatures of an officer authorized to bind the corporation to a contract.

BID SECURITY Bid security shall be made payable to the __Clark Trust Co.__ , in the amount of __10__ percent of the bid sum. Security shall be either certified check or bid bond issued by surety licensed to conduct business in the State of __Ohio__ . The successful bidder's security will be retained until bidder has signed the contract and furnished the required payment and performance bonds. The owner reserves the right to retain the security of the next __3__ bidders until the lowest bidder enters into contract or until __2__ days after bid opening, whichever is the shorter. All other bid security will be returned as soon as practicable. If any bidder refuses to enter into a contract the owner will retain his bid security as liquidated damages, but not as a penalty. The bid security is to be submitted __2__ day(s) prior to the submission of bids.

PERFORMANCE BOND AND LABOR AND MATERIAL PAYMENT BOND Furnish and pay for bonds covering faithful performance of the contract and payment of all obligations arising thereunder. Furnish bonds in such form as the owner may prescribe and with a surety company acceptable to the owner. The bidder shall deliver said bonds to the owner not later than the date of execution of the contract. Failure or neglecting to deliver said bonds, as specified, shall be considered as having abandoned the contract and the bid security will be retained as liquidated damages.

SUBCONTRACTORS Names of principal subcontractors must be listed and attached to the bid. There shall be only one subcontractor named for each classification listed.

SUBMITTAL Submit bid and subcontractor listing in an opaque, sealed envelope. Identify the envelope with: (1) project name, (2) name of bidder. Submit bids in accord with the invitation to bid.

MODIFICATION AND WITHDRAWAL Bids may not be modified after submittal. Bidders may withdraw bids at any time before bid opening, but may not resubmit them. No bid may be withdrawn or modified after the bid opening except where the award of contract has been delayed for __2__ days.

DISQUALIFICATION The owner reserves the right to disqualify bids, before or after opening, upon evidence of collusion with intent to defraud or other illegal practices upon the part of the bidder.

GOVERNING LAWS AND REGULATIONS: NONDISCRIMINATORY PRACTICES Contracts for work under the bid will obligate the contractor and subcontractors not to discriminate in employment practices. Bidders must submit a compliance report in conformity with the President's Executive Order No. 11246.

U.S. GOVERNMENT REQUIREMENTS This contract is federally assisted. The contractor must comply with the Davis-Bacon Act, the Anti-Kickback Act, and the Contract Work Hours Standards.

STATE EXCISE TAX Bidders should be aware of any state laws as they relate to tax assessments on construction equipment.

OPENING Bids will be opened as announced in the invitation to bid.

AWARD The contract will be awarded on the basis of low bid, including full consideration of unit prices and alternatives.

EXECUTION OF CONTRACT The owner reserves the right to accept any bid, and to reject any and all bids, or to negotiate contract terms with the various bidders, when such is deemed by the owner to be in his best interest.

Each bidder shall be prepared, if so requested by the owner, to present evidence of experience, qualifications, and financial ability to carry out the terms of the contract.

Notwithstanding any delay in the preparation and execution of the formal contract agreement, each bidder shall be prepared, upon written notice of bid acceptance, to commence work within __30__ days following receipt of official written order of the owner to proceed, or on date stipulated in such order.

The accepted bidder shall assist and cooperate with the owner in preparing the formal contract agreement, and within __10__ days following its presentation shall execute same and return it to the owner.

PROBLEMS

1 What is the main purpose of a legal document?
2 What is meant by an "act of God"?
3 What is a performance bond?
4 What is a materials bond?
5 How do architects display their licensing as architects on the sets of plans?

PART SIX

APPENDIX

Information frequently used in the preparation of architectural drawings and documents is repeated in the appendix, consisting of a glossary, architectural synonyms, a matchup of terms and architectural abbreviations. The appendix begins with a section about major careers for which a background in architectural drawing is necessary or helpful and a section of basic mathematical formulas most commonly used in architectural drafting and design.

CAREERS RELATED TO ARCHITECTURE

A career in one of the many architecture-related fields is rewarding, involves hard work, and offers good to excellent financial returns. The greatest satisfaction, whether you become a drafter or a structural engineer, is the reward of seeing your creations and efforts take form in structures that become part of our physical environment. Architecture-related professional and technical careers, including educational requirements, are described in this unit.

RECOMMENDED SUBJECTS

The subjects listed here are recommended for those students who are considering careers in architecture. The following high-school subjects are listed in order of importance: math, physics, English, social studies, chemistry, mechanical drafting, architectural drafting, art, physical education, foreign-language elective, and industrial-arts elective.

The following are courses that architectural students will probably take in the first year of college study: architectural design, analytical geometry, calculus, physics, materials of construction, surveying, English and public speaking, architectural rendering, history of architecture, psychology, and physical education. For further information write to:

American Institute of Architects
1735 New York Avenue, NW
Washington, DC 20006

ARCHITECTURAL-RELATED CAREERS

The *architect* must be an artist, engineer, and executive. Special qualities are required of the architect. He or she must understand people. She or he must have a talent for creative design and have skill in math and science. And the architect must be able to communicate ideas and designs graphically.

The architect is trained in school and then must serve an internship before entering practice. High school preparation is the first step in becoming an architect. All accredited architectural colleges have the same general requirements, although it is a good idea to write to the college of your choice for exact information. If you are planning to attend a junior or community college first, check with your prospective university concerning what courses will be accepted for transfer of credit.

Practical experience is invaluable. Some architects will hire students for summer or

Fig 80-1 Architecture-related careers. Clockwise from upper left: architect, landscape architect, structural engineer, estimator, and architectural drafter.

part-time work if the students are known to be responsible and are interested in becoming architects. Take any job that will enable you to work near practicing architects. The *architectural drafter* is the channel of communication between the architect and the builders. The architectural drafter translates the ideas, sketches, and designs of an architect into sets of drawings from which a structure can be built. The work includes drawing, sketching, tracing, computation, and detailing.

The architectural drafter must be able to get along with people. He or she must be able to take criticism and follow instructions carefully and must be able to work as a member of a team. An architectural drafter may become an architect by gaining architectural drafting and design experience, by obtaining letters of recommendation, by additional education, and by passing a state examination. For further information write to:

American Federation of Technical
   Engineering
1126 16th Street, NW
Suite 28
Washington, DC 20036

The *city planner* studies and plans the development or redevelopment of large areas such as cities, communities, housing projects, commercial projects, and so forth. The planning takes into account the utilities and necessities required for today's living. After designs are completed, the individual buildings may be designed by other architects. The other facets of the planner's overall design are handled and completed by other engineering specialists.

The planner's college degree should be in architecture, planning, engineering, or landscaping, with further training for a master's degree in planning. For further information write to:

American Institute of Planners
917 15th Street, NW
Washington, DC 20005

The *landscape architect* controls the development of the site, which includes earthwork, planting, layout of streets and walks, and the orientation of the structure. She or he should have an understanding of plant life and a background in math, art, architectural drafting, and rendering.

A college degree in landscape architecture is required. For further information write to:

American Society of Landscape
   Architects, Inc.
2000 K Street, NW
Washington, DC 20006

The *structural engineer*, through the use of calculations, designs the structural part of buildings. He or she is usually a civil engineer who specializes in structures. Of all the professional areas in the building trades, this is considered one of the most difficult, because of the high competence it requires in physics and math. For further information write to:

American Society of Civil Engineers
345 East 47th Street
New York, NY 10017

The *civil engineer* does the calculating and designing that are also done by the structural engineer. In addition, he or she may survey, or may conduct large-scale planning of utilities, roads, structures, harbors, airfields, tunnels, bridges, and sewage plants. The field of civil engineering is so broad that a civil engineer has to specialize in one area, such as structures. The civil engineer's college degree is in civil engineering. For further information write to:

American Society of Civil Engineers
345 East 47th Street
New York, NY 10017

Electrical engineers form the largest group of engineers. The need for them is great in the computer sciences and in the fields of aviation. The electrical engineer in the building trades designs the electrical components of structures. The electrical engineer's college degree is in electrical engineering. For further information write to:

Institute of Electrical and Electronic
   Engineers
345 East 47th Street
New York, NY 10017

The *air-conditioning engineer* designs the heating, ventilation, air-conditioning, and refrigeration systems for structures. This person's college degree is in mechanical engineering, and he or she will specialize in air conditioning. For further information write to:

The American Society of Mechanical
   Engineers
United Engineering Center
345 East 47th Street
New York, NY 10017

The *acoustics engineer* is responsible for controlling sound in the structure. However, this work is not confined to buildings; it can also be applied to noise suppression in machines, industrial factories, aircraft, and rockets; anywhere there is loud noise. This field is very technical. The acoustics engineer needs a broad background in math and physics. Her or his college degree is in physics, engineering, architecture, or math. For further information write to:

American Institute of Physics
335 East 45th Street
New York, NY 10017

The *mechanical engineer* is the engineer who does not specialize in one area. He or she works in production, the use of power, and machines which use power. The mechanical engineer who works in the building trades designs for operational parts of a structure. The degree is in mechanical engineering. For further information write to:

The American Society of Mechanical
   Engineers

The *estimator* prepares estimates of the cost of building projects by figuring material requirements and labor costs. Her or his work must be accurate, because mistakes are expensive.

An estimator working in large construction should have a general or specialized college degree and a knowledge of construction and building. His or her math skills must be good. An estimator for small construction, such as that of homes, can come from the ranks of the craftsman. The estimator's skills are largely learned in the office and in the field. For further information write to:

Associated General Contractors of
   America, Inc.
1957 E Street NW
Washington, DC 20006

The *specification writer* prepares specifications (a written description of exact materials, methods of construction, finishes, and tests and performances of everything required for the structure). A knowledge of all types of construction is needed, as is a technical background and experience in building.

His or her college degree can be general or specialized. Specification writers for small construction can come from the ranks of the craftsman. The specification writer's skills are learned in the office and in the field. For further information write to:

Associated General Contractors of
   America, Inc.
1957 E Street, NW
Washington DC 20006

The *surveyor* defines in both words and pictures (usually maps) the specific space, position, and topography of a piece of land. The accuracy of the work is essential for proper foundations and construction. This work is the first step in the construction of roads, airfields, bridges, dams, and other structures. Her or his college degree is in civil engineering. One may become a surveyor's aide with two years of junior college and on-the-job experience. For further information write to:

American Congress on Surveying and
   Mapping
Woodward Building
Washington, DC 20005

The *architectural designer* designs and plans homes and other small buildings. She or he is usually an outstanding architectural drafter but does not have a degree in architecture. The engineering for their structures is done by architects or structural engineers. For further information write to:

American Institute of Building Design
408 Union Bank Plaza
1523 Ventura Boulevard
Sherman Oaks, CA 91403

MATHEMATICS RELATED TO ARCHITECTURE

This unit contains basic rules and formulas commonly used in architectural computations. For more detailed instructional information, refer to a text in descriptive geometry, trigonometry, or algebra.

The square of the hypotenuse of a right triangle is equal to the sum of the squares of the other two sides.

$$C^2 = A^2 + B^2$$

The square of one side of a right triangle equals the squares of the hypotenuse minus the square of the other side.

$$A^2 = C^2 - B^2$$

The area of a triangle is equal to one-half the product of the base and height.

$$A = \frac{1}{2}(B \times H) \quad \text{or} \quad \frac{B \times H}{2}$$

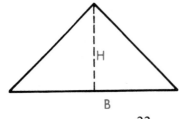

$$\pi = 3.1416 \quad \text{or} \quad \frac{22}{7}$$

The circumference of a circle is equal to π multiplied by the diameter.

$$C = \pi \times D$$

The area of a circle is equal to π multiplied by the radius squared.

$$A = \pi \times R^2$$

The area of a circle is equal to the circumference multiplied by one-half the radius.

$$A = C \times \frac{1}{2}R \quad \text{or} \quad \frac{C \times R}{2}$$

To find the area of a square or rectangle, multiply the length of one side by the length of an adjacent side.

$$A = S_1 \times S_2$$

To find the perimeter of a polygon, add the length of all sides.

$$P = S_1 + S_2 + S_3 + S_4 + S_n \ldots$$

To find the area of a trapezoid, multiply its height by one-half the sum of the parallel sides.

$$A = \frac{1}{2} (L_1 + L_2) \times H \text{ or } A = \frac{(L_1 + L_2) \times H}{2}$$

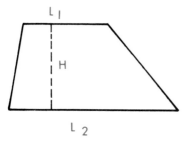

To find the volume of a square or rectangular solid, multiply the length by the height by the width.

$$V = L \times H \times W$$

To find the volume of a sphere, multiply the diameter cubed by π by one-sixth.

$$V = \frac{1}{6} \times \pi \times D^3 \quad \text{or} \quad V = \frac{\pi \times D^3}{6}$$

To find the volume of a cylinder, multiply the area of its base by its height.

$$V = \pi R^2 \times H$$

To find the volume of a pyramid, multiply the height by one-third its base area.

$$V = \frac{1}{3} H \times W \times D$$

To find the volume of a cone, multiply one-third of the product of its base area by the height.

$$V = \frac{1}{3} \pi R^2 \times H$$

The diagonal of a square is equal to the square root of twice the area.

$$D = \sqrt{2A}$$

To find the tread width, divide the run of the stairs by the number of treads. This is always one less tread than riser.

$$\text{Tread width} = \frac{\text{Run of stairs}}{\text{Number of treads}}$$

To find the height of a riser, divide the height of the stairs by the number of risers.

$$\text{Riser height} = \frac{\text{Height of stairs}}{\text{Number of stairs}}$$

To find the number of risers, divide the height of the stairs by the height of each riser.

$$\text{Riser number} = \frac{\text{Height of stairs}}{\text{Height of risers}}$$

To find the number of board feet in a piece of lumber, multiply the length in feet by the width in inches by the thickness in inches, divided by 12.

$$BF = \frac{L \times W \times T}{12}$$

To find the electrical resistance in a circuit, divide the voltage (E) by the amperage (I).

$$R = \frac{E}{I}$$

To find the electric current in amperes (I) in a circuit, divide the voltage (E) by the resistance in ohms (R).

$$I = \frac{E}{R}$$

To find the voltage in an electric circuit, multiply the current in amperes (I) by the resistance in ohms (R).

$$E = I \times R$$

575

ARCHITECTURAL GLOSSARY

Abstract of title A summary of all deeds, wills, and legal actions to show ownership.

Acoustics The science of sound. In housing, acoustical materials used to keep down noise within a room or to prevent it from passing through walls.

Adobe construction Construction using sun-dried units of adobe soil for walls; usually found in the southwestern United States.

Air conditioner An apparatus that can heat, cool, clean, and circulate air.

Air-dried lumber Lumber that is left in the open to dry rather than being dried by a kiln.

Air duct A pipe, usually made of sheet metal, that conducts air to rooms from a central source.

Air trap A U-shaped pipe filled with water and located beneath plumbing fixtures to form a seal against the passage of gases and odors.

Alcove A recessed space connected at the side of a larger room.

Alteration A change in, or addition to, an existing building.

Amortization An installment payment of a loan, usually monthly for a home loan.

Ampere The unit used in the measure of the rate of flow of electricity.

Anchor bolt A threaded rod inserted in masonry construction for anchoring the sill plate to the foundation.

Angle iron A structural piece of rolled steel shaped to form a 90° angle.

Appraisal The estimated price of a house which a buyer would pay and the seller accept for a property. An appraisal is a detailed evaluation of the property.

Apron The finish board immediately below a window sill. Also the part of the driveway that leads directly into the garage.

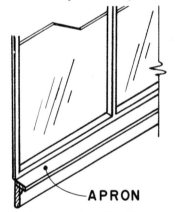

—APRON

Arcade A series of arches supported by a row of columns.

Arch A curved structure that will support itself by mutual pressure and the weight above its curved opening.

Architect A person who plans and designs buildings and oversees their construction.

Area wall A wall surrounding an areaway.

Areaway A recessed area below grade around the foundation to allow light and ventilation into a basement window or doorway.

Ashlar A facing of squared stones.

Ashpit The area below the hearth of a fireplace which collects the ashes.

Asphalt Bituminus sandstones used for paving streets and waterproofing flat roofs.

Asphalt shingles Composition roof shingles made from asphalt-impregnated felt covered with mineral granules.

Assessed value A value set by governmental assessors to determine tax assessments.

Atrium An open court within a building.

Attic The space between the roof and the ceiling.

Awning window An out-swinging window hinged at the top.

Backfill Earth used to fill in areas around exterior foundation walls.

Backhearth The part of the hearth inside the fireplace.

Baffle A partial blocking against a flow of wind or sound.

Balcony A deck projecting from the wall of a building above the ground.

Balloon framing The building-frame construction in which each of the studs is one piece from the foundation to the roof of a two-story house.

Balustrade A series of balusters or posts connected by a rail, generally used for porches and balconies.

Banister A handrail.

Base The finish of a room at the junction of the walls and floor.

Baseboard The finish board covering the interior wall where the wall and floor meet.

Base course The lowest part of masonry construction.

Base line A located line for reference control purposes.

Basement The lowest story of a building, partially or entirely below ground.

Base plate A plate, usually of steel, upon which a column rests.

Base shoe A molding used next to the floor in interior baseboards.

Batt A blanket insulation material usually made of mineral fibers and designed to be installed between framing members.

Batten A narrow strip of board, used to cover cracks between the boards in board-and-batten siding.

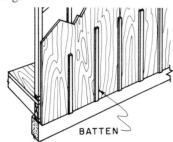

BATTEN

Batter Sloping a masonry or concrete wall upward and backward from the perpendicular.

Batter boards Boards at exact elevations nailed to posts just outside the corners of a proposed building. Strings are stretched across the boards to locate the outline of the foundation.

Bay window A window projecting out from the wall of a building to form a recess in the room.

Beam A horizontal structural member that carries a load.

Beam ceiling A ceiling in which the ceiling beams are exposed to view.

Bearing plate A plate that provides support for a structural member.

Bearing wall or partition A wall supporting any vertical load other than its own weight.

Bench mark A metal or stone marker placed in the ground by a surveyor with the elevation on it. This is the reference point to determine lines, grades, and elevations in the area.

Bending moment A measure of the forces that break a beam by bending.

Bent A frame consisting of two supporting columns and a girder or truss used in vertical position in a structure.

Bevel siding Shingles or other siding board thicker on one edge than the other. The thick edge overlaps the thin edge of the next board.

Bib A threaded faucet allowing a hose to be attached.

Bill of material A parts list of material accompanying a structural drawing.

Blanket insulation Insulation in rolled-sheet form, often backed by treated paper that forms a vapor barrier.

Blocking Small wood framing members that fill in the open space between the floor and ceiling joists to add stiffness to the floors and ceiling.

Blueprint An architectural drawing used by workers to build from. The original drawing is transferred to a sensitized paper that turns blue with white lines when printed. Also, prints of blue lines on white paper.

Board measure A system of lumber measurement having as a unit a board foot. One board foot is the equivalent of 1 foot square by 1 inch thick.

Brace Any stiffening member of a framework.

Braced framing Frame construction with posts and braces used for stiffening. More rigid than balloon framing.

Breezeway A roofed walkway with open sides. It connects the house and garage. If large enough, it can be used as a patio.

Broker An agent in buying and selling property.

BTU Abbreviation for British thermal unit, a standard unit for measuring heat gain or loss.

Buck Frame for a door, usually made of metal, into which the finished door fits.

Building code A collection of legal requirements for buildings designed to protect the safety, health, and general welfare of people who work and live in them.

Building line An imaginary line on a plot beyond which the building cannot extend.

Building paper A heavy, waterproof paper used over sheathing and subfloors to prevent passage of air and water.

Building permit A permit issued by a municipal government authorizing the construction of a building or structure.

Built-up beam A beam constructed of smaller members fastened together.

Built-up roof A roofing material composed of several layers of felt and asphalt.

Butterfly roof A roof with two sides sloping down toward the interior of the house.

Butt joint A joint formed by placing the end of one member against another member.

Buttress A mass of masonry projecting beyond a wall to take thrust or pressure. A projection from a wall to create additional strength and support.

BX cable Armored electric cable wrapped in plastic and protected by a flexible steel covering.

Cabinet work The finish interior woodwork.

Canopy A projection over windows and doors to protect them from the weather.

Cantilever A projecting member supported only at one end.

Cant strip An angular board used to eliminate a sharp right angle on roofs or flashing.

Carport An automobile shelter not fully enclosed.

Carriage The horizontal part of the stringers of a stair that supports the treads.

Casement window A hinged window that opens out, usually made of metal.

Casing A metal or wooden member around door and window openings to give a finished appearance.

Catch basin An underground structure for drainage into which the water from a roof or floor will drain. It is connected with a sewer or drain.

Caulking A waterproof material used to seal cracks.

Cavity wall A hollow wall usually made up of two brick walls built a few inches apart and joined together with brick or metal ties.

Cedar shingles Roofing and siding shingles made from western red cedar.

Cement A masonry adhesive material purchased in the form of pulverized powder. Any substance used in its soft state to join other materials together and which afterward dries and hardens.

Central heating A single source of heat that is distributed by pipes or ducts.

Certificate of title A document given to the home buyer with the deed, stating that the title to the property named in the deed is clearly established.

Cesspool A pit or cistern to hold sewage.

Chalk line A string that is heavily chalked, held tight, then plucked to make a straight guideline against boards or other surfaces.

Chase A vertical space within a building for ducts, pipes, or wires.

Checks Splits or cracks in a board, ordinarily caused by seasoning.

Check valve A valve that permits passage through a pipe in only one direction.

Chimney A vertical flue for passing smoke and gases outside a building.

Chimney stack A group of flues in the same chimney.

Chord The principal members of a roof or bridge truss. The upper members are indicated by the term *upper chord*. The lower members are identified by the term *lower chord*.

Cinder block A building block made of cement and cinder.

Circuit The path of an electric current. The closed loop of wire in which an electric current can flow.

Circuit breaker A device used to open and close an electrical circuit.

Cistern A tank or other reservoir to store rainwater that has run off the roof.

Clapboard A board, thicker on one side than the other, used to overlap an adjacent board to make house siding.

Clearance A clear space to allow passage.

Clerestory A set of high windows often above a roof line.

Clinch To bend over the protruding end of a nail.

Clip A small connecting angle used for fastening various members of a structure.

Collar beam A horizontal member fastening opposing rafters below the ridge in roof framing.

Column In architecture: a perpendicular supporting member, circular in section; in engineering: a vertical structural member supporting loads acting on or near and in the direction of its longitudinal axis.

Common wall A wall that serves two dwelling units.

Compression A force that tends to make a member fail because of crushing.

Concrete A mixture of cement, sand, and gravel with water.

Concrete block Precast hollow or solid blocks of concrete.

Condemn To legally declare unfit for use.

Condensation The formation of frost or drops of water on inside walls when warm vapor inside a room meets a cold wall or window.

Conductor In architecture: a drain pipe leading from the roof; in electricity: anything that permits the passage of an electric current.

Conductor pipe A round, square, or rectangular metal pipe used to lead water from the roof to the sewer.

Conduit A channel built to convey water or other fluids; a drain or sewer. In electrical work, a channel that carries wires for protection and for safety.

Construction loan A mortgage loan to be used to pay for labor and materials going into the house. Money is usually advanced to the builder as construction progresses and is repaid when the house is completed and sold.

Continuous beam A beam that has three or more supports.

Contractor A person offering to build for a specified sum of money.

Convector A heat-transfer surface that uses convection currents to transfer heat.

Coping The top course of a masonry wall that projects to protect the wall from the weather.

COPING

Corbel A projection in a masonry wall made by setting courses beyond the lower ones.

Corner bead A metal molding built into plaster corners to prevent the accidental breaking off of the plaster.

Cornice The part of a roof that projects out from the wall.

Counterflashing A flashing used under the regular flashing.

Course A continuous row of stone or brick of uniform height.

Court An open space surrounded partly or entirely by a building.

Crawl space The shallow space below the floor of a house built above the ground. It is surrounded by the foundation walls.

Cricket A roof device used at intersections to divert water.

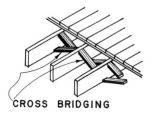
CRICKET

Cripple A structural member that is cut less than full length, such as a studding piece above a window or door.

Cross bracing Boards nailed diagonally across studs or other boards to make framework rigid.

Cross bridging Bracing between floor joists to add stiffness to the floors.

CROSS BRIDGING

Crosshatch Lines drawn closely together at an angle of 45 degrees, to show a section cut.

Cull Building material rejected as below standard grade.

Culvert A passage for water below ground level.

Cupola A small structure built on top of a roof.

Curb A very low wall.

Cure To allow concrete to dry slowly by keeping it moist to allow maximum strength.

Curtain wall An exterior wall that provides no structural support.

Damp course A layer of waterproof material.

Damper A movable plate that regulates the draft of a stove, fireplace, or furnace.

Datum A reference point of starting elevations used in mapping and surveying.

Deadening Construction intended to prevent the passage of sound.

Dead load All the weight in a structure made up of unmovable materials. See also Loads.

Decay The disintegration of wood through the action of fungi.

Dehumidify To reduce the moisture content in the air.

Density The number of people living in a calculated area of land such as a square mile or square kilometer.

Depreciation Loss of value.

Designer A person who designs houses but is not a registered architect.

Detail To provide specific instruction with a drawing, dimensions, notes, or specifications.

Dimension building material Building material that has been precut to specific sizes.

Dimension line A line with arrowheads at either end to show the distance between two points.

Dome A hemispherical roof form.

Doorstop The strips on the doorjambs against which the door closes.

Dormer A structure projecting from a sloping roof to accommodate a window.

Double glazing A pane made of two pieces of glass with air space between and sealed to provide insulation.

Double header Two or more timbers joined for strength.

Double-hung A window having top and bottom sashes each capable of movement up and down.

Downspout A pipe for carrying rainwater from the roof to the ground.

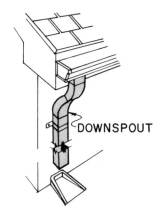
DOWNSPOUT

Drain A pipe for carrying waste water.

Dressed lumber Lumber machined and smoothed at the mill. Usually ½ inch less than nominal (rough) size.

Drip A projecting construction member or groove below the member to prevent rainwater from running down the face of a wall or to protect the bottom of a door or window from leakage.

Dry rot A term applied to many types of decay, especially an advanced stage when the wood can be easily crushed to a dry powder. The term is actually inaccurate because all fungi require considerable moisture for growth.

Dry-wall construction Interior wall covering other than plaster, usually referred to as gypsumboard surfacing.

Dry well A pit located in porous ground and lined with rock that allows water to seep through the pit. Used for the disposal of rainwater or the effluent from a septic tank.

Ducts Sheet-metal conductors for warm- and cold-air distribution.

Easement The right to use land owned by another, such as a utility company's right-of-way.

Eave That part of a roof that projects over a wall.

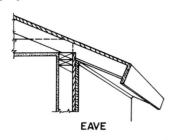

EAVE

Efflorescence Whitish powder that forms on the surface of bricks or stone walls due to evaporation of moisture containing salts.

Effluent The liquid discharge from a septic tank after bacterial treatment.

Elastic limit The limit to which a material can be bent or pulled out of shape and still return to its former shape and dimensions.

Elbow An L-shaped pipe fitting.

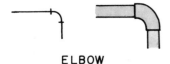

ELBOW

Elevation The drawings of the front, side, or rear face of a building.

Ell An extension or wing of a building at right angles to the main section.

Embellish To add decoration.

Eminent domain The right of the local government to condemn for public use.

Enamel Paint with a considerable amount of varnish. It produces a hard, glossy surface.

Equity The interest in or value of real estate the owner has in excess of the mortgage indebtedness.

Escutcheon The hardware on a door to accommodate the knob and keyhole.

Excavation A cavity or pit produced by digging the earth in preparation for construction.

Fabrication Work done on parts of a structure at the factory before delivery to the building site.

Facade The face or front elevation of a building.

Face brick A brick used on the outside face of a wall.

Facing A finish material used to cover another.

Fascia A vertical board nailed on the ends of the rafters. It is part of the cornice.

Fatigue A weakening of structural members.

Federal Housing Administration (FHA) A government agency that insures loans made by regular lending institutions.

Felt papers Papers, sometimes tar-impregnated, used on roofs and side walls to give protection against dampness and leaks.

Fenestration The arrangement of windows.

Fiberboard A building board made with fibrous material—used as an insulating board.

Filled insulation A loose insulating material poured from bags or blown by machines into walls.

Finish lumber Dressed wood used for building trim.

Firebrick A brick that is especially hard and heat-resistent. Used in fireplaces.

Fireclay A grade of clay that can withstand a large quantity of heat. Used for firebrick.

Fire cut The angular cut at the end of a joist designed to rest on a brick wall.

Fire door A door that will resist fire.

Fire partition A partition designed to restrict the spread of fire.

Fire stop Obstruction across air passages in buildings to prevent the spread of hot gases and flames. A horizontal blocking between wall studs.

Fished A splice strengthened by metal pieces on the sides.

Fixed light A permanently sealed window.

Fixture A piece of electric or plumbing equipment.

Flagging Cut stone, slate, or marble used on floors.

Flagstone Flat stone used for floors, steps, walks, or walls.

Flashing The material used for and the process of making watertight the roof intersections and other exposed places on the outside of the house.

Flat roof A roof with just enough pitch to let water drain.

Flitch beam A built-up beam formed by a metal plate sandwiched between two wood members and bolted together for additional strength.

Floating Spreading plaster, stucco, or cement on walls or floors with use of a tool called a float.

Floor plan The top view of a building at a specified floor level. A floor plan includes all vertical details at or above windowsill levels.

Floor plug An electrical outlet flush with the floor.

Flue The opening in a chimney through which smoke passes.

Flue lining Terra-cotta pipe used for the inner lining of chimneys.

Flush surface A continuous surface without an angle.

Footing An enlargement at the lower end of a wall, pier, or column, to distribute the load into the ground.

Footing form A wooden or steel structure placed around the footing that will hold the concrete to the desired shape and size.

Framing (western) The wood skeleton of a building.

Frieze The flat board of cornice trim that is fastened to the wall.

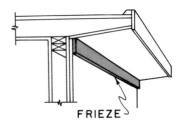

FRIEZE

Frost line The depth of frost penetration into the soil.

Fumigate To destroy harmful insect or animal life with fumes.

Furring Narrow strips of board nailed upon walls and ceilings to form a straight surface for the purpose of attaching wallboards or ceiling tile.

Fuse A strip of soft metal inserted in an electric circuit and designed to melt and open the circuit should the current exceed a predetermined value.

Gable The triangular end of an exterior wall above the eaves.

Gable roof A roof that slopes from two sides only.

Galvanize A lead and zinc bath treatment to prevent rusting.

Gambrel roof A symmetrical roof with two different pitches or slopes on each side.

Garret An attic.

Girder A horizontal beam supporting the floor joists.

GIRDER

Glazing Placing of glass in windows or doors.

Grade The level of the ground around a building.

Gradient The slant of a rod, piping, or the ground, expressed in percent.

Graphic symbols Symbolic representations used in drawing that simplify presentations of complicated items.

Gravel stop A strip of metal with a vertical lip used to retain the gravel around the edge of a built-in roof.

Green lumber Lumber that still contains moisture or sap.

Ground Fault Circuit Interrupter (GFCI) An electrical device that breaks an electric circuit when an excessive leakage current is detected. Intended to eliminate shock hazards to people.

Grout A thin cement mortar used for leveling and filling masonry holes.

Gusset A plywood or metal plate used to strengthen the joints of a truss.

Gutter A trough for carrying off water.

Gypsum board A board made of plaster with a covering of paper.

Half timber A frame construction of heavy timbers in which the spaces are filled in with masonry.

Hanger An iron strap used to support a joist beam or pipe.

Hardpan A compacted layer of soils.

Head The upper frame on a door or window.

Header The horizontal supporting member above openings that serves as a lintel. Also one or more pieces of lumber supporting ends of joists. Used in framing openings of stairs and chimneys.

Headroom The clear space between floor line and ceiling, as in a stairway.

Hearth That part of the floor directly in front of the fireplace, and the floor inside the fireplace on which the fire is built. It is made of fire-resistant masonry.

Heel plate A plate at the ends of a truss.

Hip rafter The diagonal rafter that extends from the plate to the ridge to form the hip.

Hip roof A roof with four sloping sides.

House drain Horizontal sewer piping within a building that receives wastes from the soil stacks.

House sewer The watertight soil pipe extending from the ex-terior of the foundation wall to the public sewer.

Humidifier A mechanical device that controls the amount of water vapor to be added to the atmosphere.

Humidistat An instrument used for measuring and controlling moisture in the air.

I beam A steel beam with an I-shaped cross section.

Indirect lighting Artificial light that is bounced off ceiling and walls for general lighting.

Insulating board Any board suitable for insulating purposes, usually manufactured board made from vegetable fibers, such as fiberboard.

Insulation Materials for obstructing the passage of sound, heat, or cold from one surface to another.

Interior trim General trim for all the finish molding, casing, baseboard, etc.

Jack rafter A short rafter, usually used on hip roofs.

Jalousie A type of window consisting of a number of long, thin, hinged panels.

Jamb The sides of a doorway or window opening.

Jerry-built Poorly constructed.

Joints The meeting of two separate pieces of material for a common bond.

Joist A horizontal structural member that supports the floor system or ceiling system.

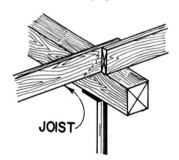

JOIST

Kalamein door A fireproof door with a metal covering.

Keystone The top, wedge-shaped stone of an arch.

Kiln A heating chamber for drying lumber.

King post In a roof truss, the central upright piece.

Knee brace A corner brace, fastened at an angle from wall stud to rafter, stiffening a wood or steel frame to prevent angular movement.

Knee wall Low wall resulting from one-and-one-half-story construction.

Knob and tube Electric wiring through walls where insulated wires are supported with porcelain knobs and tubes when passing through wood construction members.

Lally column A steel column used as a support for girders and beams.

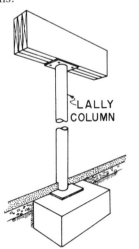

Laminated beam A beam made by bonding together several layers of material.

Landing A platform in a flight of steps.

Landscape architect A professional person who utilizes and adapts land for people's use.

Lap joint A joint produced by lapping two pieces of material.

Lath (metal) Sheet-metal screening used as a base for plastering.

Lath (wood) A wooden strip nailed to studding and joists to which plaster is applied.

Lattice A grille or openwork made by crossing strips of wood or metal.

Lavatory A washbasin or a room equipped with a washbasin.

Leaching bed A system of trenches that carries wastes from sewers. It is constructed in sandy soils or in earth filled with stones or gravel.

Leader A vertical pipe or downspout that carries rainwater from the gutter to the ground.

Lean-to A shed whose rafters lean against another building or other part of the same building.

Ledger A wood strip nailed to the lower side of a girder to provide a bearing surface for joists.

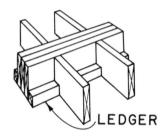

Lessee The tenant who holds a lease.

Lessor The owner of leased property.

Lien A legal claim on a property that may be exercised in default of payment of a debt.

Lineal foot A measurement of 1 foot along a straight line.

Lintel A horizontal piece of wood, stone, or steel across the top of door and window openings to bear the weight of the walls above the opening.

Loads Live load: the total of all moving and variable loads that may be placed upon a building. Dead load: the weight of all permanent, stationary construction included in a building.

Load-bearing walls Walls that support weight from above as well as their own weight.

Loggia A roofed, open passage along the front or side of a building. It is often at an upper level, and it often has a series of columns on either or both sides.

Lookout A horizontal framing member extending from studs out to end of rafters.

Lot line The line forming the legal boundary of a piece of property.

Louver A set of fixed or movable slats adjusted to provide both shelter and ventilation.

Mansard roof A roof with two slopes on each side, with the lower slope much steeper than the upper.

Mantel A shelf over a fireplace.

Market price The amount that property can be sold for at a given time.

Market value The amount that property is worth at a given time.

Masonry Anything built with stone, brick, tiles, or concrete.

Meeting rail The horizontal rails of a double-hung sash that fit together when the window is closed.

Member A single piece in structure that is complete in itself.

Metal tie A strip of metal used to fasten construction members together.

Metal wall ties Strips of corrugated metal used to tie a brick veneer wall to framework.

Mildew A mold on wood caused by fungi.

Millwork The finish woodwork in a building, such as cabinets and trim.

Mineral wool An insulating material made into a fibrous form from mineral slag.

Modular construction Construction in which the size of the building and the building materials are based on a common unit of measure.

Moisture barrier A material such as specially treated paper that retards the passage of vapor or moisture into walls and prevents condensation within the walls.

Monolithic Concrete construction poured and cast in one piece without joints.

Monument A boundary marker set by surveyors to locate property lines.

Mortar A mixture of cement, sand, and water, used as a bonding agent by the mason for binding bricks and stone.

Mortgage A pledging of property, conditional on payment of the debt in full.

Mortgagee The lender of money to the mortgagor.

Mortgagor The owner who mortgages property in return for a loan.

Mosaic Small colored tile, glass, stone, or similar material arranged on an adhesive ground to produce a decorative surface.

Mud room A small room or entranceway where muddy overshoes and wet garments can be removed before entering other rooms.

Mullion A vertical bar in a window that separates the window into sections.

Muntin A small bar separating the glass lights in a window.

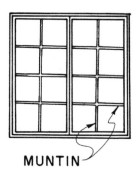

MUNTIN

Newel A post supporting the handrail at the top or bottom of a stairway.

Nominal dimension Dimensions for finished lumber in which the stated dimension is usually larger than the actual dimen-

sion. These dimensions are usually larger by an amount required to smooth a board.

Nonbearing wall A dividing wall that does not support a vertical load other than its own weight.

Nonferrous metal Metal containing no iron, such as copper, brass, or aluminum.

Nosing The rounded edge of a stair tread.

Obscure glass Sheet glass that is made translucent instead of transparent.

On center Measurement from the center of one member to the center of another (noted *oc*).

Open-end mortgage A mortgage that permits the remaining amount of the loan to be increased, as for improvements, by mutual agreement of the lender and borrower, without rewriting the mortgage.

Orientation The positioning of a house on a lot in relation to the sun, wind, view, and noise.

Outlet Any kind of electrical box allowing current to be drawn from the electrical system for lighting or appliances.

Overhang The horizontal distance that a roof projects beyond a wall.

Panelboard The center for controlling electrical circuits.

Parapet A low wall or railing around the edge of a roof.

Parging A thin coat of plaster applied to masonry surfaces for smoothing purposes.

Parquet flooring Flooring, usually of wood, laid in an alternating or inlaid pattern to form various designs.

Partition An interior wall that separates two rooms.

Party wall A wall between two adjoining buildings in which both owners share, such as a

common wall between row houses.

Patio An open court.

Pediment The triangular space forming the gable end of a low-pitched roof. A similar form is often used as a decoration over doors in classic architecture.

Penny A term for the length of a nail, abbreviated *d*.

Periphery The entire outside edge of an object.

Perspective A drawing of an object in a three-dimensional form on a plane surface. An object drawn as it would appear to the eye.

Pier A block of concrete supporting the floor of a building.

Pilaster A portion of a square column, usually set within or against a wall for the purpose of strengthening the wall. Also a decorative column attached to a wall.

Piles Long posts driven into the soil in swampy locations, or whenever it is difficult to secure a firm foundation, upon which the foundation footing is laid.

Pillar A column used for supporting parts of a structure.

Pinnacle Projecting or ornamental cap on the high point of a roof.

Plan A horizontal, graphic representational section of a building, showing the walls, doors, windows, stairs, chimneys, and surrounding objects as walks and landscape.

Planks Material 2 or 3 inches (50 or 75 mm) thick and more than 4 inches (100 mm) wide, such as joists, flooring, and the like.

Plaster A mortarlike composition used for covering walls and ceilings. Usually made of portland cement mixed with sand and water.

Plasterboard A board made of plastering material covered on both sides with heavy paper. It is often used instead of plaster. Also called gypsum board.

Plaster ground A nailer strip included in plaster walls to act as a gage for thickness of plaster and to give a nailing support for finish trim around openings and near the base of the wall.

Plat A map or chart of an area showing boundaries of lots and other pieces of property.

Plate The top horizontal member of a row of studs in a frame wall to carry the trusses of a roof or to carry the rafters directly. Also a shoe or base member, as of a partition or other frame.

Plate cut The cut in a rafter that rests upon the plate. It is also called the *seat cut* or *bird-mouth*.

Plate glass A high-quality sheet of glass used in large windows.

Platform or Western Framing Multistory house framing in which each story is built upon the other.

Plenum system A system of heating or air conditioning in which the air is forced through a chamber connected to distributing ducts.

Plot The land on which a building stands.

Plow To cut a groove running in the same direction as the grain of the wood.

Plumb Said of an object when it is in true vertical position as determined by a plumb bob.

Plywood A piece of wood made of three or more layers of veneer joined with glue and usually laid with the grain of adjoining piles at right angles.

Porch A covered area attached to a house at an entrance.

Portico A roof supported by columns, whether attached to a building or wholly by itself.

Portland cement A hydraulic cement, extremely hard, formed by burning silica, lime, and alumina together and then grinding up the mixture.

Post A perpendicular supporting member.

Post-and-beam construction Wall construction consisting of posts rather than studs.

Precast Concrete shapes made separately before being used in a structure.

Prefabricated houses Houses that are built in sections or component parts in a factory, and then assembled at the site.

Primary coat The first coat of paint.

Principal The original amount of money loaned.

Purlin A structural member spanning from truss to truss and supporting the rafters.

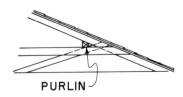

PURLIN

Quad An enclosed court.

Quarry tile A machine-made, unglazed tile.

Quoins Large squared stones set in the corners of a masonry building for appearance.

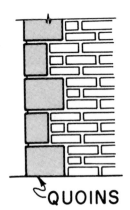

QUOINS

Radiant heating A system using heating elements in the floors, ceilings, or walls to radiate heat into the room.

Rafters Structural members used to frame a roof. Several types are common: hip, jack, valley, and cripple.

Raglin The open joint in masonry to receive flashing.

Realtor A real-estate broker who is a member of a local chapter of the National Association of Real Estate Boards.

Register The open end of a duct in a room for warm or cool air.

Reinforced concrete Concrete in which steel bars or webbing has been embedded for strength.

Rendering The art of shading or coloring a drawing.

Restoration Rebuilding a structure so it will appear in its original form.

Restrictions Limitations on the use of real estate as set by law or contaned in a deed.

Retaining wall A wall to hold back an earth embankment.

Rheostat An instrument for regulating electric current.

Ribbon A support for joists. A board set into studs that are cut to support joists.

Ridge The top edge of the roof where two slopes meet.

Ridge cap A wood or metal cap used over roofing at the ridge.

Riprap Stones placed on a slope to prevent erosion. Also broken stone used for foundation fill.

Rise The vertical height of a roof.

Riser The vertical board in a stairway between two treads.

Rock wool An insulating material that looks like wool but is composed of such substances as granite or silica.

Rodding Stirring freshly poured concrete with a vibrator to remove air pockets.

Roll roofing Roofing material of fiber and asphalt.

Rough floor The subfloor on which the finished floor is laid.

Rough hardware All the hardware used in a house, such as nails and bolts, that cannot be seen in the completed house.

Roughing in Putting up the skeleton of the building.

Rough lumber Lumber as it comes from the saw.

Rough opening Any unfinished opening in the framing of a building.

Run Stonework having irregular-shaped units and no indication of systemic course work. The horizontal distance covered by a flight of stairs. The length of a rafter.

Saddle The ridge covering of a roof designed to carry water from the back of chimneys. Also called a *cricket*. A threshold.

Safety factor The ultimate strength of the material divided by the allowable working load. The element of safety needed to make certain that there will be no structural failures.

Sand finish A final plaster coat; a skim coat.

Sap All the fluids in a tree.

Sash The movable framework in which window panes are set.

Scab A small wood member, used to join other members, which is fastened on the outside face.

SCAB

Scarfing A joint between two pieces of wood that allows them to be spliced lengthwise.

Schedule A list of parts or details.

Scratch coat The first coat of plaster. It is scratched to provide a good bond for the next coat.

Screed A guide for the correct thickness of plaster or concrete being placed on surfaces.

Scuttle A small opening in a ceiling to provide access to an attic or roof.

Seasoning Drying out of green lumber, either in an oven or kiln or by exposing it to air.

Second mortgage A mortgage made by a home buyer to raise money for a down payment required under the first mortgage.

Section The drawing of an object that is cut to show the inte-

rior. Also, a panel construction used in walls, floors, ceilings, or roofs.

Seepage pit A pit or cesspool into which sewage drains from a septic tank, and which is so constructed that the liquid waste seeps through the sides of the pit into the ground.

Septic tank A concrete or steel tank where sewage is reduced partially by bacterial action. About half the sewage solids become gases that escape back through the vent stack in the house. The other solids and liquids flow from the tank into the ground through a tile bed.

Service connection The electric wires to the building from the outside power lines.

SERVICE
CONNECTION

Set The hardening of cement or plaster.

Setback A zoning restriction on the location of the home on a lot.

Settlement Compression of the soil or the members in a structure.

Shakes Thick hand-cut shingles.

Sheathing The structural covering of boards or wallboards, placed over exterior studding or rafters of a structure.

Sheathing paper A paper barrier against wind and moisture applied between sheathing and outer wall covering.

Shed roof A flat roof slanting in one direction.

SHED ROOF

Shim A piece of material used to level or fill in the space between two surfaces.

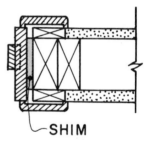

SHIM

Shingles Thin pieces of wood or other materials that overlap each other in covering a roof. The number and kind needed depend on the steepness of the roof slope and other factors. Kinds of shingles include tile, slate shingles, and asphalt shingles.

Shiplap Boards with lapped joints along their edges.

Shoe mold The small mold against the baseboard at the floor.

Shoring Lumber placed in a slanted position to support the structure of a building temporarily.

Siding The outside boards of an exterior wall.

Sill The horizontal exterior member below a window or door opening. Also the wood member placed directly on top of the foundation wall in wood-frame construction.

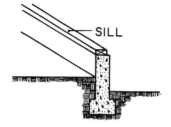

SILL

Skeleton construction Construction where the frame carries all the weight.

Skylight An opening in the roof for admitting light.

Slab foundation A reinforced concrete floor and foundation system.

Sleepers Strips of wood, usually 2 × 2's, laid over a slab floor to which finished wood flooring is nailed.

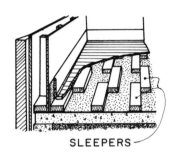

SLEEPERS

Smoke chamber The portion of a chimney flue located directly over the fireplace.

Soffit The undersurface of a projecting structure.

SOFFIT

Softwood Wood from trees having needles rather than broad leaves. The term does not necessarily refer to the softness of the wood.

Soil stack The main vertical pipe that receives waste from all fixtures.

Solar heat Heat from the sun's rays.

Sole The horizontal framing member directly under the studs.

Spacing The distance between structural members.

Spackle To cover wallboard joints with plaster.

Span The distance between structural supports.

Specification The written or printed direction regarding the details of a building or other construction.

Spike A large, heavy nail.

Splice Joining of two similar members in a straight line.

Stack A vertical pipe.

Stakeout Marking the foundation layout with stakes.

Steel framing Skeleton framing with structural steel beams.

Steening Brickwork without mortar.

Stile A vertical member of a door, window, or panel.

Stirrup A metal U-shaped strap used to support framing members.

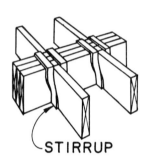

STIRRUP

Stock Common sizes of building materials and equipment available from most commercial industries.

Stool An inside windowsill.

Stop A small strip to hold a door or window sash in place.

Storm door or window An extra door or extra window placed outside an ordinary door or window for added protection against cold.

Storm sewer A sewer that is designed to carry away water from storms, but not sewage.

Stress Any force acting upon a part or member used in construction.

Stress-cover construction Construction consisting of panels or sections with wood frameworks to which plywood or other sheet material is bonded with glue so that the covering carries a large part of the loads.

Stretcher course A row of masonry in a wall with the long side of the units exposed to the exterior.

Stringer One of the sides of a flight of stairs. The supporting member cut to receive the treads and risers.

Stripping Removal of concrete forms from the hardened concrete.

Stucco Any of various plasters used for covering walls, especially an exterior wall covering in which cement is used.

Stud Upright beams in the framework of a building. Usually referred to as 2 × 4's, and spaced at 16 inches from center to center.

Subfloor The rough flooring under the finish floor that rests on the floor joists.

Sump A pit in a basement floor to collect water, into which a sump pump is placed to remove the water through sewer pipes.

Surfaced lumber Lumber that is dressed by running it through a planer.

Surveyor A person skilled in land measurement.

Swale A drainage channel formed where two slopes meet.

Tamp To ram and concentrate soil.

Tar A dark heavy oil used in roofing and roof surfacing.

Tempered Thoroughly mixed cement or mortar.

Tensile strength The greatest stretching stress a structural member can bear without breaking or cracking.

Termite shield Sheet metal used to block the passage of termites.

Thermal conductor A substance capable of transmitting heat.

Thermostat A device for automatically controlling the supply of heat.

Threshold The beveled piece of stone, wood, or metal over which the door swings. It is sometimes called a carpet strip, or a saddle.

Throat A passage directly above the fireplace opening where a damper is set.

Tie A structural member used to bind others together.

Timber Lumber with a cross section larger than 4 by 6 inches (100 by 150 mm), for posts, sills, and girders.

Title insurance An agreement to pay the buyer for losses in title of ownership.

Toe nail To drive nails at an angle.

Tolerance The acceptable variance of dimensions from a standard size.

Tongue A projection on the edge of wood that joins with a similarly shaped groove.

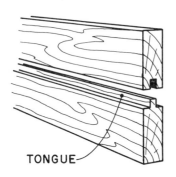

TONGUE

Total run The total of all the tread widths in a stair.

Transom A small window over a door.

Tread The step or horizontal member of a stair.

Trimmers Single or double joists or rafters that run around an opening in framing construction.

Truss A triangular-shaped unit for supporting roof loads over long spans.

Underpinning A foundation replacement or reinforcement for temporary braced supports.

Undressed lumber Lumber that is not squared or finished smooth.

Unit construction Construction that includes two or more preassembled walls, together with floor and ceiling construction, for shipment to the building site.

Valley The internal angle formed by the two slopes of a roof.

Valley jacks Rafters that run from a ridgeboard to a valley rafter.

Valley rafter The diagonal rafter forming the intersection of two sloping roofs.

Valve A device that regulates the flow of material in a pipe.

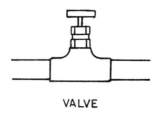

VALVE

Vapor barrier A watertight material used to prevent the passage of moisture or water vapor into and through walls.

Veneer A thin covering of valuable material over a less expensive material.

Vent A screened opening for ventilation.

Ventilation The process of supplying and removing air by natural or mechanical means to or from any space.

Vent pipes Small ventilating pipes extending from each fixture of a plumbing system to the vent stack.

Vent stack The upper portion of a soil or waste stack above the highest fixture.

Vergeboard The board that serves as the eaves finish on the gable end of a building.

Vestibule A small lobby or entrance room.

Vitreous Pertaining to a composition of materials that resemble glass.

Volume The amount of space occupied by an object. Measured in cubic units.

Wainscot Facing for the lower part of an interior wall.

Wallboard Wood pulp, gypsum, or similar materials made into large rigid sheets that may be fastened to the frame of a building to provide a surface finish.

Warp Any change from a true or plane surface. Warping includes bow, crook, cup, and twist.

Warranty deed A guarantee that the property is as promised.

Wash The slant upon a sill, capping, etc., to allow the water to run off.

Waste stack A vertical pipe in a plumbing system that carries the discharge from any fixture.

Waterproof Material or construction that prevents the passage of water.

Water table A projecting mold near the base on the outside of a building to turn the rainwater outward. Also the level of subterranean water.

Watt A unit of electrical energy.

Weathering The mechanical or chemical disintegration and discoloration of the surface of exterior building materials.

Weather strip A strip of metal or fabric fastened along the edges of windows and doors to reduce drafts and heat loss.

Weep hole An opening at the bottom of a wall to allow the drainage of water.

Well opening A floor opening for a stairway.

Zoning Building restrictions as to size, location, and type of structures to be built in specific areas.

SECTION 27

ARCHITECTURAL SYNONYMS

Architectural terms are standard. Nevertheless, architects, drafters, and builders often use different terms for the same object. Geographic location can influence a person's word choice. For instance, what is referred to as a faucet in one area of the country is called a tap in another area. What one person calls an attic, another calls a garret, and still another a loft. Each entry below is followed by a word or words that someone—somewhere—uses to refer to the entry.

Abutment: support
Adobe brick: firebrick, fireclay brick
Aeration: ventilation
Aggregate: cement matrix, concrete, mortar, plaster
Anchorage: footing, footer
Anchor bolt: securing bolt, sill bolt
Apartment: tenement, multiple dwelling, condominium
Arcade: corridor
Armored cable: conduit, tubing, metal casing, BX
Attic: garret, cot loft, half story, loft
Awning: overhang, canopy

Backfill: fill, earth
Back plaster: parget
Baffle: screen
Baked clay: terra-cotta
Balcony: ledge, gallery, platform, veranda
Baseboard: mopboard, finish board, skirting
Basement: cellar, storm cellar, cyclone cellar, substructure
Base mold: shoe mold
Batten: cleat
Bead: thin molding

Beam: rafter, shaft, timber, girder, wood, spar, lumber
Bearing partition: support partition, bearing wall
Bearing plate: sill, load plate
Bearing soil: compact soil
Beveled: mitered, chamfered
Bibs: faucets, taps
Birdmouth: plate cut, seat cut, seat of a rafter
Blind nailing: secret nailing
Board insulation: heat barrier
Border: curb, parapet
Brick: stone, masonry
Bridging: bracing, joining, cross supports, strutting
Buck: doorframe
Building area: setback, building lines
Building board: compo board, insulating board, dry wall, gypsum board, Sheetrock, wallboard, rocklath, plasterboard
Building lines: setback, building area
Building paper: felt, tar paper, sheathing paper, construction paper, roll roofing
Building steel: structural steel
BX: conduit, tubing, metal casing, armored cable

Candela: footcandle
Canopy: awning, overhang
Caps: coping
Carpenter's cloth: wire mesh, screen, wire cloth
Carport: car shed, open garage
Carriage: stringer
Carriage bolt: square bolt, threaded rod
Casement window: hinged window
Casing: window frame
Catch basin: cistern, dry well, reservoir
Caulking: sealer, oakum, pointing, masonry
Cavity wall: hollow wall
Ceiling clearance: headroom
Cellar: basement, storm cellar, cyclone cellar, substructure
Cement matrix: aggregate, concrete, mortar, plaster
Cesspool: sewage basin, seepage pit
Chamfered: beveled, mitered
Chimney pot: flue cap
Cinder: rock, slag
Circuit box: fuse box, power panel, distribution panel
Cistern: catch basin, dry well, reservoir
Cleat: batten

588

Clipped ceiling: hung ceiling, drop ceiling

Closet: cloakroom, storage area

Colonnade: portico

Column: post, pillar, cylinder, pile, spile

Column base: plinth, wall base

Comb board: cricket, saddle

Common wall: party wall

Compact soil: bearing soil

Compo board: insulating board, building board, dry wall, gypsum board, Sheetrock, wallboard, rocklath, plasterboard

Composition board: fiberboard, particle board

Concrete: cement matrix, aggregate, mortar, plaster

Condominium: apartment, tenement, multiple dwelling

Conduit: tubing, metal casing, BX, armored cable

Connectors: splice

Construction paper: building paper, felt, tar paper, sheathing paper, roll roofing

Coping: caps

Corridor: arcade, hallway, passageway, lanai

Cot loft: attic, garret, half story, loft

Cover: escutcheon, shield, plate, hood

Cricket: saddle, threshold, doorsill

Cripple stud: short stud

Cross supports: joining, bracing, bridging

Culvert: gutter, channel, ditch, waste drain

Curb: border, parapet

Curtain wall: filler wall

Cyclone cellar: basement, storm cellar, substructure, cellar

Damper: flue control

Deck: landing, platform

Decking: floor

Decorative: ornamental

Den: library, reading room, quiet room, sitting room

Disposal system: leach lines, sewage line

Distribution panel: power panel, fuse box, circuit box

Ditch: culvert, gutter, channel, waste drain

Domicile: home, house, dwelling, residence

Doorframe: buck

Doorsill: saddle, threshold, cricket

Dormer: gable window, projected window, eyebrow

Double-hung: double-sashed

Double plate: top plate

Downspout: drainage pipe, rain drainage

Drainage hole: weep hole

Drainage pipe: downspout, rain drainage

Drain line: flow line

Drop ceiling: clipped ceiling, hung ceiling

Drop support: hanger, iron strap

Dry wall: gypsum board, Sheetrock, wallboard, building board, rocklath, plasterboard, compo board, insulating board

Dry well: cistern, catch basin, reservoir

Duct: pipeline, vent, raceway, plenum

Dumbwaiter: elevator, hoist, lift

Dwelling: domicile, home, house, residence

Earth: fill, backfill, topsoil

Easement: right-of-way

Eave overhang: roof projection, roof overhang

Elevator: dumbwaiter, hoist, lift

Entrance: lobby, vestibule, stoop, porch, portal

Escalator: motor stairs

Escutcheon: shield, plate, cover

Exterior: facade, proscenium, facing

Exterior brick: face brick

Eyebrow: dormer

Facade: proscenium, facing, exterior

Face brick: exterior brick

Facing: facade, proscenium, exterior

Fan: blower

Faucets: taps, bibs

Felt: building paper, tar paper, sheathing paper, roll roofing, construction paper

Fiberboard: composition board, particle board

Fill: backfill

Fillers: shims

Filler stud: trimmer

Filler wall: curtain wall

Finish board: baseboard, mop board

Finish work: trim, millwork

Firebrick: adobe brick, fireclay brick

Fire door: resistance door

Fireplace: ingle

Flashing: vapor barrier

Flat roof: horizontal roof, shed roof, pent roof

Float valve: flush valve

Floor: decking

Flow line: drain line

Flue cap: chimney pot

Flue control: damper

Flush plate: switch plate

Flush valve: float valve

Footcandle: candela

Footer: anchorage, footing

Footing: anchorage, footer

Foundation sill: mudsill

Framing: rough carpentry, skeleton

Fuse box: power panel

Gable window: dormer, projected window

Gallery: balcony, ledge, platform

Garret: attic, cot loft, half story, loft

Girder: beam, timber

Glazing bar: muntin, pane frames, sash bars

Grade: ground level, ground line, grade line

Grease trap: U trap

Ground line: grade, grade line, ground level

Gutter: culvert, channel, ditch, waste drain

Gypsum: plaster

Gypsum board: dry wall, Sheetrock, wallboard, building board, insulating board, compo board, rocklath

Half story: loft, cot loft, garret, attic

Hallway: corridor, passageway, lanai

Hanger: drop support, iron strap

Hatchway: opening, trapdoor, scuttle
Header: lintel
Headroom: ceiling clearance
Hinged window: casement window
Hoist: lift, elevator, dumbwaiter
Hollow-core door: veneer door
Hollow wall: cavity wall
Hood: cover
Horizontal roof: shed roof, flat roof, pent roof
Hung ceiling: drop ceiling, clipped ceiling

Ingle: fireplace
Insulating board: compo board, building board, dry wall, gypsum board, rocklath, Sheetrock, wallboard
Iron strap: drop support, hanger

Jalousies: louvers
Joining: bridging, bracing, cross supports

Lambert: light unit, lumen
Lanai: passageway, corridor, hallway
Landing: platform, deck
Larder: pantry
Laundry: utility room, service porch
Laundry tray: slop sink, work sink
Lavatory: sink
Leach lines: disposal system, sewage line
Ledge: gallery, platform, balcony
Library: den, reading room, quiet room, sitting room
Lift: dumbwaiter, elevator, hoist
Light unit: lumen, lambert
Lintel: header
Live load: moving load
Load: weight
Load plate: bearing plate, sill
Lobby: vestibule, stoop, porch, portal, entrance
Loft: half story, cot loft, garret, attic
Lot: plot, property, site
Louvers: jalousies
Lumen: light unit, lambert

Mantel: shelf
Masonry: stone, brick, pointing, caulking
Metal casing: tubing, conduit, BX, armored cable
Millwork: trim, finish work
Mitered: beveled, chamfered
Moisture barrier: vapor barrier
Mopboard: baseboard, finish board
Mortar: aggregate, cement matrix, concrete, plaster
Motor stairs: escalator
Mudsill: foundation sill
Mullion: window divider
Multiple dwelling: apartment, tenement, condominium
Muntin: glazing bar, pane frame, sash bar

Opening: trapdoor, scuttle, hatchway
Overhang: awning, canopy

Pane frames: sash bar, glazing bar, muntin
Pantry: larder
Parapet: curb, border
Parget: back plaster
Particle board: composition board, fiberboard
Partition: wall
Party wall: common wall
Passageway: lanai, corridor, hallway
Patio: quad, court, yard, terrace
Pent roof: shed roof, flat roof
Pier: support, abutment
Pilaster: wall column
Pillar: post, column, pile, spile, cylinder
Pipeline: vent, raceway, duct, plenum
Pitch: slant, slope
Plank-and-beam: post-and-beam, post-and-lintel
Plaster: mortar, gypsum, concrete, cement matrix, aggregate
Plasterboard: dry wall, Sheetrock
Plastic membrane: vapor barrier, sisalkraft
Plate: escutcheon, shield, cover, shoe, scantling, sole
Plate cut: birdmouth, seat cut, seat of a rafter

Platform: balcony, ledge, gallery
Platform framing: western framing
Plenum: pipeline, vent, raceway, duct
Plinth: column base, wall base
Pointing: caulking, masonry
Porch: stoop, lobby, entry, ingress, entrance, portal, gallery, lanai, terrace, veranda, vestibule
Portico: colonnade
Post: column, pillar, cylinder, pile, spile
Post-and-lintel: post-and-beam, plank-and-beam
Power and panel: distribution panel, fuse box, circuit box
Proscenium: facade, facing, exterior

Quad: patio, court
Quiet room: sitting room, reading room, library, den
Quoins: stone coping

Raceway: duct, pipeline, plenum, vent
Rafter: beam, shaft, timber
Rain drainage: drainage pipe, downspout
Reading room: quiet room, sitting room, library, den
Reservoir: catch basin, cistern, dry well
Residence: domicile, home, house, dwelling
Resistance door: fire door
Ridge: roof peak, ridge pole, ridge board
Right-of-way: easement
Rock: slab, cinder
Rocklath: compo board, insulating board, building board, dry wall, gypsum board, Sheetrock, wallboard
Roll roofing: construction paper, sheathing paper, tar paper, felt, building paper
Roof overhang: roof projection, eave overhang
Roof peak: ridge, ridge board, ridge pole
Rough carpentry: framing
Rough floor: subfloor
Rough lumber: undressed lumber

Saddle: threshold, doorsill, cricket
Sanitary sewer: storm sewer
Sash bar: pane frames, glazing bar, muntin
Scaffold: staging
Scantling: shoe, sole, plate
Screen: wire mesh, wire cloth, carpenter's cloth, baffle
Scupper: wall drain
Scuttle: hatchway, opening, trapdoor
Sealer: oakum, caulking
Seat of a rafter: seat cut, plate cut, birdmouth
Secret nailing: blind nailing
Securing bolt: anchor bolt, sill bolt
Seepage pit: sewage basin, cesspool
Service porch: laundry, utility room
Setback: building lines, building area
Sewage basin: cesspool, seepage pit
Sewage line: leach lines, disposal system
Shaft: beam, rafter, timber
Sheathing paper: building paper, felt, tar paper, construction paper, roll roofing
Shed roof: flat roof, horizontal roof, pent roof
Sheet insulation: compo board, insulating board, building board, dry wall, gypsum board, wallboard, rocklath, plasterboard
Shelf: mantel
Shield: plate cover, escutcheon
Shims: fillers
Shoe: plate, scantling, sole
Shoe mold: base mold
Shoring: supporting, timber brace
Short stud: cripple stud
Sill: bearing plate, load plate
Sill bolt: securing bolt, anchor bolt
Sink: lavatory
Sisalkraft: vapor barrier, plastic membrane, membrane, sheet
Sitting room: quiet room, reading room, library, den
Skeleton: framing
Skirting: baseboard
Slag: cinder, rock

Slope: slant, pitch
Slop sink: work sink, laundry tray
Sole: shoe, plate, scantling
Spaced bars: grate
Spar: lumber, beam, wood, timber
Spile: pile, column, pillar, post
Splice: connectors
Square bolt: carriage bolt, threaded rod
Staging: scaffold
Steel connector: strap
Step: tread
Stiffener: tie
Stone coping: quoins
Stoop: porch, portal, vestibule, lobby, entrance
Storage area: cloakroom, closet
Storm cellar: basement, cyclone cellar, substructure, cellar
Storm sewer: sanitary sewer
Strap: steel connector
Stringer: carriage
Strip insulation: weather stripping
Structural steel: building steel
Strutting: bridging
Substructure: storm cellar, basement, cyclone cellar, cellar
Support partition: bearing partition
Surface drainage: surface flow
Switch plate: flush plate

Taps: faucets, bibs
Tar paper: building paper, felt, sheathing paper, construction paper, roll roofing
Tenement: apartment, multiple dwelling, condominium
Terra-cotta: baked clay
Thin molding: bead
Threaded rod: square bolt, carriage bolt
Threshold: saddle, doorsill, cricket
Tie: stiffener
Timber: shaft, rafter, beam, girder, lumber, wood
Timber brace: shoring, supporting
Top plate: double plate
Topsoil: earth
Trapdoor: scuttle, hatchway, opening
Tread: step

Trim: finish work, millwork
Trimmer: filler stud
Trough: chute
Trussing: bracing
Tubes: ducts, channels, air pipes
Tubing: BX, conduit, metal casing, armored cable

Underside: soffit
Undressed lumber: rough lumber
Utility room: service porch, laundry
U trap: grease trap

Vapor barrier: flashing, sisalkraft, plastic membrane, moisture barrier
Veneer: plywood
Veneer door: hollow-core door
Vent: duct, opening
Ventilation: aeration
Veranda: passageway, balcony
Vestibule: stoop, porch, portal, lobby, entrance

Wall: partition
Wall base: column base, plinth
Wallboard: compo board, insulating board, building board, dry wall, gypsum board, Sheetrock
Wall column: pilaster
Wall drain: scupper
Waste drain: gutter, culvert, channel, ditch
Water closet: toilet, W.C.
Water table: water level
W.C.: water closet, toilet
Weather stripping: strip insulation
Weep hole: drainage hole
Weight: load
Western framing: platform framing
Winding stairs: spiral stairs, screw stairs
Window divider: mullion
Window frame: casing
Window shade: blind
Wire cloth: screen, wire mesh, carpenter's cloth
Wood: beam, spar, lumber, timber
Work sink: laundry tray, slop sink

ARCHITECTURAL ABBREVIATIONS

Architects and drafters print many words on a drawing. Often they use abbreviations. By using the standard abbreviations listed below, they ensure that their drawings are accurately interpreted.

Here are five points to remember:

1 Most abbreviations are in capitals.

2 A period is used only when the abbreviation may be confused with a whole word.

3 The same abbreviation can be used for both the singular and the plural.

4 Sometimes several terms use the same abbreviation.

5 Many abbreviations are very similar.

Access panel	AP
Acoustic	ACST
Actual	ACT.
Addition	ADD.
Adhesive	ADH
Aggregate	AGGR
Air condition	AIR COND
Alternating current	AC
Aluminum	AL
Ampere	AMP
Anchor bolt	AB
Apartment	APT.
Approved	APPD
Approximate	APPROX
Architectural	ARCH
Area	A
Asbestos	ASB
Asphalt	ASPH
At	@
Automatic	AUTO
Avenue	AVE
Average	AVG
Balcony	BALC
Basement	BSMT
Bathroom	B
Bathtub	BT
Beam	BM
Bearing	BRG

Bedroom	BR
Bench mark	BM
Between	BET.
Blocking	BLKG
Blower	BLO
Blueprint	BP
Board	BD
Boiler	BLR
Both sides	BS
Brick	BRK
British thermal units	BTU
Bronze	BRZ
Broom closet	BC
Building	BLDG
Building line	BL
Cabinet	CAB.
Caulking	CLKG
Cast concrete	C CONC
Cast iron	CI
Catalog	CAT.
Ceiling	CLG
Cement	CEM
Center	CTR
Center line	CL
Center to center	C to C
Ceramic	CER
Circle	CIR
Circuit	CKT
Circuit breaker	CIR BKR

Circumference	CIRC
Cleanout	CO
Clear	CLR
Closet	CL
Coated	CTD
Column	COL
Combination	COMB.
Common	COM
Composition	COMP
Concrete	CONC
Conduit	CND
Construction	CONST
Continue	CONT
Contractor	CONTR
Corrugate	CORR
Courses	C
Cross section	X-SECT
Cubic foot	CU FT
Cubic inch	CU IN.
Cubic yard	CU YD
Damper	DMPR
Dampproofing	DP
Dead load	DL
Degree	(°) DEG
Design	DSGN
Detail	DET
Diagonal	DIAG
Diagram	DIAG
Diameter	DIA

Dimension .... DIM
Dining room .... DR
Dishwasher .... DW
Ditto .... DO.
Division .... DIV
Door .... DR
Double .... DBL
Double-hung .... DH
Down .... DN
Downspout .... DS
Drain .... DR
Drawing .... DWG
Dryer .... D

East .... E
Electric .... ELEC
Elevation .... EL
Enamel .... ENAM
Entrance .... ENT
Equal .... EQ
Equipment .... EQUIP.
Estimate .... EST
Excavate .... EXC
Existing .... EXIST.
Exterior .... EXT

Fabricate .... FAB
Feet .... (′) FT
Feet board measure .... FBM
Finish .... FIN.
Fireproof .... FPRF
Fixture .... FIX.
Flashing .... FL
Floor .... FL
Floor drain .... FD
Flooring .... FLG
Fluorescent .... FLUOR
Foot .... (′) FT
Footcandle .... FC
Footing .... FTG
Foundation .... FDN
Full size .... FS
Furred ceiling .... FC

Galvanize .... GALV
Galvanized iron .... GI
Garage .... GAR
Gas .... G
Gage .... GA
Girder .... G
Glass .... GL
Grade .... GR
Grade line .... GL
Gypsum .... GYP

Hall .... H
Hardware .... HDW
Head .... HD
Heater .... HTR
Height .... HT
Horizontal .... HOR
Hose bib .... HB
Hot water .... HW
House .... HSE
Hundred C

I beam I
Impregnate .... IMPG
Inch .... (″) IN.
Incinerator .... INCIN
Insulate .... INS
Intercommunication ....
                   INTERCOM
Interior .... INT
Iron I

Joint .... JT
Joist .... JST

Kilowatt .... kW
Kilowatt hour .... kWh
Kip (1000 lb.) .... K
Kitchen .... KIT

Laminate .... LAM
Laundry .... LAU
Lavatory .... LAV
Left L
Length .... LG
Length overall .... LOA
Light .... LT
Linear .... LIN
Linen closet .... L CL
Live load LL
Living room .... LR
Long .... LG
Louver LV
Lumber .... LBR

Main .... MN
Manhole .... MH
Manual .... MAN.
Manufacturing .... MFG
Material .... MATL
Maximum .... MAX
Medicine cabinet .... MC
Membrane .... MEMB
Metal .... MET.

Meter .... M
Minimum .... MIN
Minute .... (′) MIN
Miscellaneous .... MISC
Mixture .... MIX.
Model .... MOD
Modular .... MOD
Motor .... MOT
Molding .... MLDG

Natural .... NAT
Nominal .... NOM
North .... N
Not to scale .... NTS
Number .... NO.

Obscure .... OB
On center .... OC
Opening .... OPNG
Opposite .... OPP
Overall .... OA
Overhead .... OVHD

Panel .... PNL
Parallel .... PAR.
Part .... PT
Partition .... PTN
Penny (nails) .... d
Permanent .... PERM
Perpendicular .... PERP
Piece .... PC
Plaster .... PL
Plate .... PL
Plumbing .... PLMG
Pound .... LB
Precast .... PRCST
Prefabricated .... PREFAB
Preferred .... PFD

Quality .... QUAL
Quantity .... QTY

Radiator .... RAD
Radius .... R
Range .... R
Receptacle .... RECP
Reference .... REF
Refrigerate .... REF
Refrigerator .... REF
Register .... REG
Reinforce .... REINF
Reproduce .... REPRO

593

Required	REQD	Street	ST	Urinal	UR
Return	RET	Storage	STG		
Riser	R	Structural	STR		
Roof	RF	Supply	SUP	Valve	V
Room	RM	Surface	SUR	Vaporproof	VAP PRF
Round	RD	Switch	SW	Vent pipe	VP
		Symmetrical	SYM	Ventilate	VENT.
		System	SYS	Vertical	VERT
Safety	SAF			Vitreous	VIT
Sanitary	SAN			Volt	V
Scale	SC			Volume	VOL
Schedule	SCH	Tar and gravel	T & G		
Second	(") SEC	Tangent	TAN.		
Section	SECT	Tarpaulin	TARP		
Select	SEL	Tee	T	Washing machine	WM
Service	SERV	Telephone	TEL	Water closet	WC
Sewer	SEW.	Television	TV	Water heater	WH
Sheet	SH	Temperature	TEMP	Waterproofing	WP
Sheathing	SHTHG	Terra-cotta	TC	Watt	W
Shower	SH	Terrazzo	TER	Weather stripping	WS
Side	S	Thermostat	THERMO	Weatherproof	WP
Siding	SDG	Thick	THK	Weep hole	WH
Similar	SIM	Thousand	M	Weight	WT
Sink	S	Through	THRU	West	W
Soil pipe	SP	Toilet	T	Width	W
South	S	Tongue and groove	T & G	Window	WDW
Specification	SPEC	Total	TOT.	With	W/
Square	SQ	Tread	TR	Without	W/O
Stairs	ST	Tubing	TUB.	Wood	WD
Steam	ST	Typical	TYP	Wrought iron	WI
Standard	STD				
Steel	STL				
Stock	STK	Unfinished	UNFIN	Yard	YD

INDEX